WHERE TO GO WHEN
GREAT BRITAIN & IRELAND

WHERE TO
GO WHEN
GREAT BRITAIN & IRELAND

FOREWORD BY
JULIA BRADBURY

DK

LONDON, NEW YORK, MELBOURNE,
MUNICH AND DELHI

LIST MANAGER Christine Stroyan
PROJECT EDITOR Alexandra Farrell
DESIGN MANAGERS Mabel Chan, Sunita Gahir
JACKET DESIGNER Tessa Bindloss
DTP DESIGNER Jamie McNeill

PICTURE RESEARCHER Ellen Root
CARTOGRAPHER Stuart James
PRODUCTION CONTROLLER Liz Cherry

PUBLISHER Douglas Amrine

Produced for Dorling Kindersley by

cobaltid

The Stables, Wood Farm, Deopham Road,
Attleborough, Norfolk NR17 1AJ
www.cobaltid.co.uk

EDITORS Kati Dye, Louise Abbott,
Robin Sampson, Sarah Tomley, Maddy King,
Neil Mason, Marek Walisiewicz

DESIGNERS Lloyd Tilbury, Paul Reid,
Annika Skoog, Claire Dale, Darren Bland

Printed and bound in Singapore by Star Standard

First American Edition 2010
10 11 12 13 10 9 8 7 6 5 4 3 2 1

Published in the United States by Dorling Kindersley
Publishing, 375 Hudson Street, New York 10014

Every effort has been made to ensure that this book is as up-to-date as
possible at the time of going to press. Some details, however, such as
telephone numbers, opening hours, prices, and travel information are liable
to change. The publishers cannot accept responsibility for any consequences
arising from the use of this book, nor for any material on third-party
websites, and cannot guarantee that any website address in this book will be
a suitable source of travel information. We value the views and suggestions
of our readers very highly. Please write to: Publisher, DK Travel Guides,
Dorling Kindersley, 80 Strand, London, WC2R 0RL, Great Britain.

www.traveldk.com

MAIN COVER IMAGE: Stonehenge, Wiltshire
HALF TITLE PAGE IMAGE: Sphinx rock on Great Gable, Lake District
TITLE PAGE IMAGE: Sunset over Esthwaite Water, Lake District
CONTENTS: View of River Wye from Symonds Yat, Herefordshire
FOREWORD IMAGE: Temple Bar district, Dublin, Ireland

CONTENTS

Local codes are given for all telephone numbers in this book. If you are dialing from abroad, use the appropriate international dialing code.

FOREWORD

There are some places that you don't need an excuse or reason to visit – you simply must. These are places that add essential and memorable experiences to your personal history. Arriving at the summit of Scafell Pike in the Lake District is one of my moments. It was late, and the evening light glistened over the boulder-strewn landscape. When I reached the summit (camera crew in tow), powerful fresh winds blustered all around – gusts strong enough to fall back onto. I was sure I could hear a loose spinnaker fluttering in the wind, but there were no boats up there on that ragged rocky surface. The sky was tinged a perfect shade of misty pink. It was intoxicating.

I am lucky enough to have adventured through quite a few spots on the globe because of my work. I have met and traveled with people who have taught me lots and shown me wonderful places – from the lush, singing forests of Costa Rica to the mammoth Navajo Sandstone Zion Canyon in Utah and the ever-reaching bush veldt of South Africa – but

I can honestly say there is no place like home. My peregrinations abroad have added to my personal history and stretched my imagination, but there is still so much I want to do and see on our islands – so much that I find just as exciting as anything the rest of the world has to offer. Giant's Causeway, for example, is one of the most unusual and spectacular sights you could ever come across – a natural geological phenomenon that looks as if it were dreamed up by a pioneering architect like Zaha Hadid. I was born in Ireland, so I am drawn back to its romantic landscape time and time again, but it is years since I visited Giant's Causeway – and a revisit is long overdue. If you were to follow its tens of thousands of hexagonal rock columns into the sea at the Antrim coast you would emerge in Scotland! Tiptoeing over tiles 60 million years old – now that would be an aquatic adventure to remember...

A man who understands the power of the pilgrimage is the actor Peter Florence, creator of the Hay Festival and still involved today. This now-annual literary love-fest is the perfect meeting of culture and countryside. The two have long been intertwined; writers, poets, and artists have always been inspired by landscape and nature. Anyone who

has heard a chorus sung from a hilltop, or watched *A Midsummer Night's Dream* sitting on a grassy bank, cannot help but be drawn to Hay. Such a simple idea – go to one of the most beautiful parts of the country, sit on a patch of green softness, and read, listen, and chat with people who, like you, care passionately about books, writing, creativity, and the countryside. Bill Clinton called it "the Woodstock of the mind."

If, like me, you can only sit for so long, then combine your literary leanings at Hay with adventure, and explore farther over the Welsh border into the Brecon Beacons. This stunning location is an outdoor paradise. Kayak up the River Wye (why? because you can), pony-trek across the Black Mountains, or hike across the Beacons themselves. Or do you prefer to be beside the seaside? Why not combine Brighton's vibrant annual Arts Festival in May with an exploration of the South Downs? This vast, beautiful swath of chalky uplands and dramatic cliffs is a nature-lover's delight, with butterflies and bluebells, rare wild orchids, swallows and swifts, warblers and linnets.

Do ruins leave you stone cold? Put your imagination in gear, do a little research, and ruins can come alive. There is something about stopping to think about how things used to be not so long ago that makes you appreciate where we are now. Fountains Abbey in North Yorkshire has been described as "England's most sublime architectural ruin" and Tintern Abbey in the Wye Valley inspired Turner to put paint to canvas, and Wordsworth ink to paper. Perhaps you will be equally stimulated.

I hope this book is not just a coffee table companion to impress your friends and family with what you "could" or "may" do, but an inspirational guide as to what you "will" and "can" do over the course of one or more visits to Great Britain and Ireland. Exploration really does stir the imagination. Whether it's a canal cruise along the Cheshire Ring, a walk along mighty Hadrian's Wall, a tour around the city streets of Liverpool or an escape to Broadstairs on the Kent coast (where Charles Dickens penned *David Copperfield*), more than 2,000 special places and marvelous things to do await you in this beautiful book. Each one promises to be an adventure, so remember to keep notes. This is a little bit of personal history you're making.

Julia Bradbury

SPRING

A bluebell wood
in Hertfordshire,
England

SPRING IN GREAT BRITAIN AND IRELAND

I N THE GARDEN COUNTIES OF SOUTHERN ENGLAND and the mellow Atlantic shores of southern Ireland, spring flowers begin to bloom and winter's weakening grip on the land is signaled by the appearance of the first migrant swifts and swallows in the skies. In the countryside, you might hear the distinctive call of a cuckoo. With luck, Easter will be warm and sunny enough for barbecues in backyards and picnics in the country. But spring, more than any other season, highlights the amazingly varied microclimates of Britain and Ireland. In Cornwall or Cork, it may be warm enough for a day at the beach, but in the high wilderness of the Cairngorms, winter sports enthusiasts will be reveling in fresh-fallen snow and the best ski conditions of the year. Farther north, the Orkney and Shetland Isles may still be swathed in freezing fog. A spring journey in Britain and Ireland calls for careful planning.

> Winter's weakening grip on the land is signaled by the appearance of the first migrant swifts.

Even along the south coast of England, winter sometimes clings to the countryside until March. It is not unheard of for Kent – nicknamed the "garden of England" – to be blanketed in snow just a few weeks before Easter. So the sudden appearance of green buds and of cherry, hawthorn, and apple blossom is sometimes as surprising as it is welcome. The first spring sunshine normally bathes the south coast of England, warming resorts such as Margate in Kent, Brighton in Sussex, and Torquay in Devon – where carefully tended palm trees bear witness to one of England's balmiest climates – and the rugged shores of Cornwall that stretch down to the southernmost point of mainland Britain.

In and around London, some of the world's most famous gardens and green spaces are already in bloom. The Royal Botanic Gardens at Kew are carpeted with more than a million crocuses in early spring, and blossoming camellias soon give way to sweet-scented lilacs. The Privy and Pond Gardens at Henry VIII's Hampton Court Palace are at their best in April, when the long lines of pretty spring flowers bring the formal shapes of this historic garden to life.

On the North Sea coast, from East Yorkshire to Scotland, spring brings migrant birds in ones and twos, or in vast, spectacular flocks. At Bempton Cliffs in Yorkshire, more than 200,000 birds gather to breed, including puffins, guillemots, fulmars, and razorbills, building nests on every ledge and in every nook of these high, vertiginous cliffs.

Below (left to right): Apple blossoms in an orchard in Kent; gannets nesting on a cliff at Bass Rock on the Firth of Forth

Farther north, on the Bass Rock in the Firth of Forth, so many gannets gather to nest that they whiten the rocks; these large birds have a 6-ft (2-m) wingspan, and the sight of their flocks at sea is one of Britain's greatest wildlife spectacles.

The woods and waters of the Lake District are famously linked with spring. The first daffodils emerge in March, and within a few weeks there are broad swaths of vivid yellow in gardens, by roadsides, and all along the shores of Ullswater and Grasmere, where the daffodils nod and dance in vivid contrast to the dark woodlands behind them, which are only just beginning to come into leaf.

Yellow is the signature color of spring in Scotland, too: the blossoming broom and gorse runs in bright bands across the wild hills and curlew-haunted moors, dotted with the purple of heather. A sunny mid-April day may tempt you to walk up Arthur's Seat – the main peak of the high hills in the heart of Edinburgh – wearing just shorts and a T-shirt. But there's likely to be a cutting wind at

St. Patrick's Day turns all of Ireland – but especially Dublin – into a great place for the *craic*.

the summit, and the gleam of snow-capped peaks on the northern horizon, so don't be deceived by the April sunshine, even in southern Scotland. Fresh snow can fall on the slopes of the Cairngorms and the northwest Highlands as late as May, and walkers may find unmelted pockets even in June. But there are areas of unexpected warmth even in Scotland's far northwest; at the National Trust for Scotland's gardens at Inverewe, sub-tropical exotics, such as Tasmanian gum trees and Chinese rhododendrons, flourish within sight of snow-tipped summits.

Spring is not just a season of natural splendor. Easter is one of the most important festivals of the Christian year, when Easter services, choral performances, and midnight Masses take place at great English cathedrals such as St. Paul's, Canterbury, Winchester, and York Minster in late March or early April. In Wales, St. David's Day (March 1) is celebrated throughout the country, from the small festivities in towns and villages to the awesome sound of a 1,000-strong male-voice choir in full song in St. David's Hall in Cardiff. St. Patrick's day turns all of Ireland, but especially Dublin, into a great place for the *craic* on March 17, with music, dancing, and a drop of two of Irish whiskey. And in England, St. George's Day, on April 23, is another excuse for public celebration, with concerts and colorful processions in London and other cities. By then, spring is in full swing, and summer is just around the corner.

Below (left to right): Reflections of flowering gorse in Loch Duich, in the Scottish Highlands; tortoiseshell butterfly; Hampton Court Palace Pond Garden

Britain in Bloom

Above: 1893 advert with slogan "Carters' Bouquet of Pretty Cut Flowers, Easily Grown from Seed"
Right: Seed packets from the early 20th century

F rom colorful cottage flowerbeds and lovingly tended inner-city allotments to the serenely landscaped estates of grand English houses and botanical gardens that continue centuries-old traditions of research into the healing powers of plants, Britain's gardens are legendary.

Great Britain and Ireland start to come into bloom as early as February, when the first, aptly named, snowdrops appear in woods and gardens, to be followed soon after by bluebells, daffodils, and early crocuses. Around the same time, the first sunny days bring out bumblebees and tortoiseshell butterflies that have overwintered under cottage eaves and in attics and greenhouses.

Myriad microclimates make it possible for imaginative gardeners to cultivate an array of exotic imports. Some of our grandest and most fascinating gardens date from Britain's colonial heyday, when botanists searched the Himalayan foothills, Alpine meadows, and the jungles of Brazil and Borneo for evermore-exotic decorative, commercially useful, or simply unusual plant species. The grand country estates of Scotland and Ireland are splashed with the pink, white, and purple blooms of azaleas and rhododendrons, originally imported from sub-tropical Asia, and it's hard to imagine south-coast resorts, such as Torquay in Devon, without their decorative palms.

HARLOW CARR

LOST GARDENS OF HELIGAN

THE EDEN PROJECT

SISSINGHURST CASTLE GARDENS

Royal Botanic Garden Edinburgh, Southern Scotland Britain's tallest palm house, giant sequoias, a Highland heath garden, and a world-famous Alpine rock garden can be found here. *www.rbge.org.uk*

Mount Stewart House and Gardens, Northern Ireland Thanks to the mild microclimate of the Ards Peninsula, spring comes early to these glorious gardens. *www.nationaltrust.org.uk*

Blarney Castle and Gardens, Southern Ireland Spring bluebells burst into flower in the beautiful gardens on the estate of this famous castle, where cattle graze in lush lakeside pastures. *www.blarneycastle.ie*

Bodnant Garden, North Wales Azaleas rhododendrons, magnolias, and camellias put on a stunning show in spring in this garden, which has superb views of Mount Snowdon. *www.bodnantgarden.co.uk*

Wordsworth Daffodil Garden, Northwest England In spring, this space between Grasmere's church and the River Rothay is smothered in the daffodils that inspired William Wordsworth (*see pp46–7*).

Harlow Carr, Northeast England Bluebells and mixed primulas flourish in sun-dappled clearings in the woods of this Yorkshire garden, with its streams and rocky outcrops. *www.rhs.org.uk*

Biddulph Grange Garden, West Midlands A Chinese garden, Egyptian courtyard, stumpery, and "upside-down tree" make this one of Britain's quirkiest gardens. *www.nationaltrust.org.uk*

Hidcote Manor Garden, West Midlands Gardens designed as "outdoor rooms" and enclosed by immaculately trimmed hedges are the keynote of this masterpiece of Arts and Crafts design. *www.nationaltrust.org.uk*

Anglesey Abbey and Gardens, Eastern England Outstanding garden created in the 1930s by Lord Fairhaven as an ambitious, Classical landscape of trees, sculptures, and pretty borders. *www.nationaltrust.org.uk*

Royal Botanic Gardens, Kew, London One of the world's most important centers for plant science and conservation, with palm houses, hothouses, landscaped lawns, and shrubberies. *www.kew.org*

Chelsea Physic Garden, London A sanctuary in the heart of London with beds of ferns, herbs, and aromatics. Founded in 1673, it continues research into medicinal plants. *www.chelseaphysicgarden.co.uk*

Wisley, Southeast England The flagship garden of the Royal Horticultural Society is more than a century old and boasts lavishly planted borders, velvety lawns, lush rose gardens, and glasshouses. *www.rhs.org.uk*

Sissinghurst Castle Gardens, Southeast England A charming complex of gardens and courtyards created by the writer Vita Sackville-West and her husband, Harold Nicholson. *www.nationaltrust.org.uk*

The Eden Project, Southwest England In March, the beds are awash with daffodils in every shade of yellow. In April, it's the turn of English wildflowers, such as campions and violets. *www.edenproject.com*

Lost Gardens of Heligan, Southwest England Neglected for almost a century, the gardens of this Cornish estate have been lovingly restored; fruit, bamboo, and banana plants flourish here. *www.heligan.com*

Rosemoor Garden, Southwest England A magnificent 65 acres (260 hectares) of gardens, including bluebell woods, two rose gardens, a formal garden, a French-style potager, and stream. *www.rhs.org.uk*

ROYAL BOTANIC GARDENS, KEW

BODNANT GARDEN

A LITERARY PILGRIMAGE

Fortified in medieval times by English lords against Welsh rebels, the border town of Hay-on-Wye now welcomes a very different type of invasion. Every spring, the Hay Festival (late May/early June) brings some 85,000 literary pilgrims to 10 days of readings, masterclasses, debates, and entertainment centered on a tented village. There are dense daily programs of ticketed events, which often sell out well in advance – but it's free to go in and simply soak up the vibrant atmosphere while you read or people-watch from one of the many deck chairs scattered around the site. Later in the day, festival-goers and star guests spread out informally between the live bands, comedy performances, and town pubs to continue the fun.

THE ESSENTIALS

GETTING THERE AND AROUND
Hay-on-Wye is on the Welsh side of the border with England. Cardiff and Birmingham airports are 70 miles (115 km) and 85 miles (137 km) away respectively. Trains run from London to Hereford, from where there are both festival and regular bus services to Hay-on-Wye.

WEATHER
This area is drier than west Wales, but it can be cold and windy on the hilltops, with an average daytime temperature of 45–55°F (8–12°C) in late spring.

ACCOMMODATIONS
Treat Yourself The Swan at Hay, in Hay-on-Wye, is a Georgian coaching inn with fine dining and beautiful gardens. *www.swanathay.co.uk*

On a Budget Hay Outdoor Training Centre, in Hay-on-Wye, is a quiet campsite, open from March to November, just 5 minutes' walk from the festival site. *www.training-activities.co.uk*

EATING OUT
Treat Yourself The Swan at Hay's elegant restaurant overlooks the hotel's gardens and boasts French-trained chefs who use local produce. *www.swanathay.co.uk*

On a Budget The Blue Boar, in Hay-on-Wye, is a friendly pub with an evocative medieval bar, a bright, cheery atmosphere, and hearty traditional food. Tel: 01497 820884

PRICE FOR TWO PEOPLE
Around $330 a day for food, accommodations, and admission fees.

WEBSITE
www.hay-on-wye.co.uk

The Hay Festival brings some 85,000 literary pilgrims to 10 days of readings, masterclasses, debates, and entertainment centered on a tented village.

Hip young families and cultured book-lovers might rub shoulders with authors, poets, and performers, as well as a horde of TV commentators and journalists – the *Guardian* newspaper is the event's main sponsor. Famous names that have made an appearance include Alan Bennett, Carol Ann Duffy, Sting, and Archbishop Desmond Tutu. Hay Fever, the parallel children's festival, offers younger visitors a hands-on chance to make their own puppets and pottery.

This cosmopolitan festival was started in 1988 by local actor Peter Florence, who still runs the event and is now exporting the concept to new venues such as Segovia, Nairobi, and, famously, Cartagena, Colombia. There's a strong US connection. In the festival's second year, playwright Arthur Miller agreed to be the star guest – after reportedly asking if Hay-on-Wye was some kind of sandwich; in 2001 former President Bill Clinton described it as "the Woodstock of the mind."

For some, the greatest surprise of the festival is its setting. The site is normally pasture: this is hill-farming country, where for most of the year there are more sheep than people. Hay's stone buildings huddle together in typical Welsh small-town fashion, around a market place and a clock tower, with a semi-ruined castle on the skyline and the slopes of the Black Mountains in the distance. The town's famous bookstores and traditional shops have been joined by specialty and fashion shops, putting Hay firmly on the cultural map of Britain.

Main: Book-lovers of all ages delight in the literary atmosphere **Inset:** Typically quirky sight at the Hay Festival
Below: Visitors browse outdoor bookshelves in Hay-on-Wye

The King of Hay
Oxford graduate Richard Booth, convinced Hay could become a base for international book trading, opened a secondhand bookstore there in 1961. By the late 1970s, dozens more had opened, and Booth proclaimed Hay the world's first Book Town. On April Fools' Day 1977, he declared independence for Hay and proclaimed himself King. His joke received so much international publicity that he has kept it going for decades, printing a declaration of independence and conferring his own titles.

FURTHER DETAILS

HAY FESTIVAL
Hay-on-Wye. The festival takes place over 10 days annually, around the late-May Bank Holiday weekend (dates vary); tickets for festival events can be purchased in advance using the online booking service, or through the festival box office (tel: 01497 822 629). *www.hayfestival.com*

WHAT ELSE TO SEE AND DO
Brecon Beacons
You can drive from Hay-on-Wye up the winding Forest Road toward Hay Bluff, park at the viewpoint, and walk uphill on the Offa's Dyke Path to the windswept ridge. Here you can see far across the Welsh border country and the Brecon Beacons National Park *(see pp188–9)*. *www.breconbeacons.org/visit-us/ outdoors-activities/walking*

River Trips
It's possible to rent a canoe or a kayak, take a picnic, and canoe downstream on the tranquil River Wye. Paddles and Pedals, based in Hay-on-Wye, offers a pick-up service that returns you to your starting point. *www.paddlesandpedals.co.uk*

Riding
The Black Mountains and Brecon Beacons, with their springy grass trails, make superb riding country. You can rent a pony for as little as an hour or take a longer trip involving an overnight stay. Tregoyd Mountain Riders in Tregoyd, Powys, offers a range of options for all ages and levels of experience. FreeRein in Clyro, Radnorshire, offers tours with accommodations at farms and country inns, including unescorted trips for experienced riders.
Tregoyd Mountain Riders: *www.tregoydriding.co.uk*
FreeRein Riding Holidays: *www.free-rein.co.uk*

Below (top to bottom): Richard Booth, the King of Hay; Brecon Beacons National Park

THE KEY TO ENGLAND

STEEPED IN HISTORY, and besieged today by little more than fantastic views and wheeling seagulls, the magnificent clifftop medieval bastion of Dover Castle dominates the famous White Cliffs. Strategically located, the battlements that once roared with cannon fire and the shouts of soldiers today welcome far more serene invasions of vacationing families, weekending couples, and camera-toting tourists, but the castle remains a commanding and imposing edifice. April and May – as the days lengthen and fine weather returns – are particularly pleasant months for exploration and photography, with blossoming trees and all the color of spring in this coastal corner of Kent.

Long regarded as the "key to England" – guarding the shortest distance to once-hostile French shores – the castle's lofty keep (the Great Tower) and curtain walls constitute one of southeast England's hallmark fortresses. There was once an Iron Age fort here, and the first

THE ESSENTIALS

GETTING THERE AND AROUND
Dover is at the southeastern tip of Kent. Regular trains link London Victoria and Charing Cross with Dover Priory (reduced service on Sundays). There are regular buses to Deal and Canterbury (reduced service on Sundays), while trains connect Dover Priory with Canterbury East.

WEATHER
The average spring daytime temperature in Dover is around 43–55°F (6–12°C). Be prepared for coastal wind chills and changeable weather conditions.

ACCOMMODATIONS
Treat Yourself Wallett's Court Country House, 4 miles (6.5 km) east of Dover, is a magnificent country house boasting superb rooms set within serene countryside in White Cliffs country.
www.wallettscourthotel.com

On a Budget Hubert House, on Castle Road, is a gem of a B&B with a popular restaurant, good rooms, and friendly owners.
www.huberthouse.co.uk

EATING OUT
Treat Yourself The restaurant at Wallett's Court Country House offers fabulous food in the magnificent rural setting of a 17th-century country estate just outside Dover.
www.wallettscourthotel.com

On a Budget Cullins Yard, on Cambridge Road, is a popular seafood bistro with a nautical theme.
www.cullinsyard.co.uk

PRICE FOR TWO PEOPLE
From $250 a day for food, accommodations, and admission fees.

WEBSITE
www.whitecliffscountry.org.uk

The Secret Wartime Tunnels

A long tunnel complex was hewn into the cliffs here at the end of the 18th century to barrack troops, and was later enlisted during World War II when it served as a bombproof command center with a subterranean hospital. Exploring the (supposedly haunted) tunnels offers a unique insight into the strategic significance of the castle and its continuing role in the defense of Britain. The tunnels played an important part both in the Allied evacuation from Dunkirk in 1940 and in the Battle of Britain.

The battlements that once roared with cannon fire and the shouts of soldiers today welcome far more serene invasions of holidaying families and weekending couples.

castle was erected by William the Conqueror in 1066. The one we see today dates from the reign of Henry II, around 100 years later. Unlike many other castles, Dover has survived largely intact, and the rooms of the Great Tower have been restored to recreate the atmosphere of Henry II's fortress. Climb to the top for far-reaching views over the Strait of Dover all the way to the shores of France – historically England's greatest enemy.

Parts of the site date from the times of those other famous foreign invaders, the Romans – the 80-ft- (24-m-) high, well-preserved *pharos* (lighthouse) is England's tallest surviving Roman relic. Adjacent to the lighthouse stands the ancient Saxon church of St. Mary-in-Castro ("St. Mary-in-the-Castle"), which dates from the 7th century.

There's a lot to do at Dover Castle, so prepare for extensive reconnaissance: after exploring the castle and its grounds, sit down with a picnic and recharge for the next assault – on its secret tunnels. Once you've finally exhausted the castle's possibilities, head down to the town of Dover, home to many museums that chronicle this important settlement's eventful history. Round off your day with a boat tour of the famous White Cliffs themselves.

FURTHER DETAILS

DOVER CASTLE
Dover, Kent; open Apr–Jul: 10am–6pm daily; Aug: 9:30am–6pm daily; Sep: 10am–6pm daily; Oct: 10am–5pm daily; Nov–Jan: 10am–4pm Thu–Mon; Feb–Mar: 10am–4pm daily.
www.english-heritage.org.uk

Dover
The town of Dover is much more than just a ferry port. There's a Roman fort and Napoleonic fortifications to explore, and walks along the seafront and the Prince of Wales Pier. The Dover Museum provides a good account of this strategic town's history over the centuries.
Dover Museum: *www.dovermuseum.co.uk*

White Cliffs Walk
Dover's signature image, the imposing chalk cliffs are ideal for walks and panoramic views out over the Strait of Dover. A hike up to the coastal fortifications of the Western Heights offers views of the European continent on a clear day.

White Cliff Boat Tours
These boats bounce over the waves, giving the best perspective on the white cliffs (and Dover Castle). Vessels leave regularly for the 40-minute cruise.
www.doverwhiteclifftours.com

WHAT ELSE TO SEE AND DO
Deal Castle & Walmer Castle
The two Tudor castles of Deal and Walmer, at picturesque seaside Deal northeast along the coast, provide an opportunity to compare and contrast with Dover Castle. Regular buses from Dover take 30 minutes.
www.aboutdeal.co.uk

Canterbury
The historic cathedral city of Canterbury, 18 miles (29 km) northwest of Dover, is easily reached by train or tour bus from Dover. It has a host of things to see, including the famous Cathedral – site of the murder of St. Thomas Becket, and pilgrimage destination of Chaucer's *Canterbury Tales*. The town is also home to the Museum of Canterbury, a Roman Museum, and the Canterbury Tales attractions – a recreation of 14th-century Canterbury.
www.canterbury.co.uk

Hop Over to France
There are regular crossings to France on the ferry from Dover. It's quite feasible to visit Calais or Boulogne for the day. Don't forget your passport.
www.poferries.com

Main: Aerial view of Dover Castle, overlooking the Strait of Dover

Far left (top to bottom): Historical reenactment at the castle; interior view of the castle's Grand Shaft Staircase

Above: Main entrance gate to Dover Castle

Below: Iconic White Cliffs of Dover

THE ESSENTIALS

GETTING THERE AND AROUND
The Suffolk Heritage Coast is in eastern England, running from south of Lowestoft to Felixstowe. The nearest international airport is London Stansted, which is 45 miles (72 km) west of Felixstowe. The best way to explore the area's country roads is by bicycle or car.

WEATHER
March to May are the driest months on the Suffolk coast. The weather is mild, with average spring daytime temperatures of 45–55°F (7–13°C), but there can be brisk sea breezes.

ACCOMMODATIONS
Treat Yourself The Swan, on Market Square in Southwold, superbly blends old coaching-inn traditions with luxurious modern comforts.
www.adnams.co.uk

On a Budget Field End, in Leiston, offers good-quality 4-star guesthouse accommodations in an Edwardian house just north of Aldeburgh.
www.fieldendbedandbreakfast.co.uk

EATING OUT
Treat Yourself The Butley Orford Oysterage, in Orford, is a characterful café-style restaurant that has cultivated its own oysters since the 1950s.
www.butleyorfordoysterage.co.uk

On a Budget The Randolph Inn, in Reydon near Southwold, is gastronomic heaven with a menu of innovative but affordable dishes.
www.therandolph.co.uk

PRICE FOR TWO PEOPLE
Around $330 a day for accommodations, food, and entry to the reserves.

WEBSITES
www.visiteastofengland.com
www.visit-suffolk.org.uk

The Return of the Bittern

The bittern's return to Britain as a resident rather than as a migrant is a conservation success story. Colloquially known as "bog-hens" or "bog-trotters," bitterns had not bred on these shores since 1886. Some birds would still winter on the Suffolk coast, but would return to Europe to find the reed beds in which they like to breed. A nationwide project, launched in 2002 to make Britain's reed beds more "bittern-friendly," has encouraged bitterns to breed here again, with 55 breeding pairs recorded in 2004.

A BOOMING BUSINESS

THE STRANGE AND UNEARTHLY BOOMING CALL of a bittern is something that, once heard, is never forgotten. It was a sound that was on the wane in Britain until the early 2000s, when conservation programs enabled the bittern population to grow again. The Suffolk Heritage Coast is a favorite haunt of these enigmatic birds; wait patiently at one of the region's wonderful nature reserves, and you might be lucky enough to hear that haunting noise.

Spring also brings migrant birds to these shores in their thousands. They nest all along the coast, but especially in the three RSPB reserves at Minsmere, North Warren, and Havergate Island. The unspoilt landscape, the peace and quiet, and the abundant local seafood are a draw not only for birds but also for visitors to this tranquil corner of England.

The Suffolk Heritage Coast, running between Lowestoft and Felixstowe, is not a dramatic coastline of high cliffs and rugged bays. It is an area of understated beauty, of quiet beaches interspersed with marshes and reed beds that sprawl underneath vast expanses of sky. It is also dotted with sophisticated seaside towns, such as Southwold and Aldeburgh. Creative types may know Aldeburgh for its music and opera festival in the summer, but naturalists visit in spring for the flocks of avocets that arrive at this time of year. The RSPB reserve on Havergate Island, in the River Ore near Aldeburgh, is one of the delights of this quiet coast. You can only reach it by boat, which adds to its otherworldly charm, and in spring you are sure to see the rare and beautiful avocets, sifting through the sands for food with their unusual upturned bills.

Also near Aldeburgh is the North Warren reserve, a place where bitterns gather and where the equally rare and beautiful sound of the nightingale can still be heard. The biggest reserve on the coast, RSPB Minsmere, south of Dunwich, is home to a huge number of birds, including avocets and nightingales. In spring, marsh harriers – birds of prey that have inhabited England since the Iron Age – perform impressive aerobatic displays to impress their mates, wheeling and diving above the marshland where the shy, booming bitterns lurk, hidden among the reeds.

FURTHER DETAILS

RESERVES OF THE SUFFOLK HERITAGE COAST

RSPB Havergate Island Nature Reserve
Havergate Island is only accessible by boat from Orford Quay; open Apr–Aug: first and third weekends of the month and every Thu; Sep–Mar: first Sat of each month only.
www.rspb.org.uk

RSPB Minsmere Nature Reserve
Minsmere is just off the A12 between Yoxford and Blythburgh, signposted with brown tourist signs; open daily during daylight hours.
www.rspb.org.uk

RSPB North Warren Nature Reserve
North Warren is to the north of Aldeburgh, on the Thorpe Road, which leads to Thorpeness; open 24 hours a day.
www.rspb.org.uk

WHAT ELSE TO SEE AND DO

The Suffolk Coast and Heaths Path
This long-distance footpath follows the Suffolk Heritage Coast for 50 miles (80 km) between Lowestoft and Felixstowe, passing close to all three of the RSPB reserves.
www.suffolkcoastandheaths.org

Dunwich
Sandwiched between Southwold and Aldeburgh, Dunwich was once a substantial medieval town and the capital of East Anglia. Since the 14th century, major coastal erosion has reduced it to the size of a village, but it is still an important site of historical interest.
www.visit-dunwich.co.uk

Adnams Brewery
One of the most highly regarded breweries in the country, Adnams, in Southwold, offers guided tours, demonstrations of the beer-making process, and beer-tastings.
www.adnams.co.uk

Below (top to bottom): Minsmere RSPB reserve; coastal town of Southwold

You can only reach Havergate Island by boat, which adds to its otherworldly charm, and in spring you are sure to see the rare and beautiful avocets.

Main: Elusive bittern in its reed-bed habitat **Inset:** Barn swallow at Minsmere RSPB reserve
Below: Avocets wading in the mud

THE ESSENTIALS

GETTING THERE AND AROUND
Liverpool is on the northwest coast of England. It has its own international airport, Liverpool John Lennon Airport, which is about 8 miles (12 km) southeast of the city and is easily reached by rail (2½ hours from London). Many downtown sights are easily reached on foot or by the Merseyrail rail network, which also has a station close to Aintree Racecourse.

WEATHER
Liverpool has a rather wet climate in the spring, with rainfall above the national average. Spring daytime temperatures range from 42 to 54°F (6–12°C).

ACCOMMODATIONS
Treat Yourself The Hard Day's Night Hotel is a 4-star Beatles-themed hotel in a historic building in the center of town. *www.harddaysnighthotel.com*

On a Budget The Cocoon is a "pod" hotel on South Hunter Street providing small but comfortable rooms a short walk from the downtown area. *www.cocoonliverpool.co.uk*

EATING OUT
Treat Yourself The Panoramic, on Brook Street, does indeed offer a panoramic view over the city, and serves equally impressive contemporary food. *www.panoramicliverpool.com*

On a Budget The Side Door, on Hope Street, is not far from the center of town and is a popular pre-theater dining option. *www.thesidedoor.co.uk*

PRICE FOR TWO PEOPLE
Around $370 a day for food, accommodations, local transportation, and admission fees.

WEBSITE
www.visitliverpool.com

The Beatles Trail

Liverpool's biggest cultural claim to fame is as the home of The Beatles. The easiest way to follow in the footsteps of the Fab Four is to join an organized Beatles tour. Mendips and 20 Forthlin Road, the childhood homes of the band's songwriters, John Lennon and Paul McCartney, are owned by the National Trust and are open for guided tours. You can also visit Penny Lane and Strawberry Fields, referenced in Beatles songs, although the Cavern Club, site of their first gigs, has been rebuilt.

Above (top to bottom): Photomontage at the Beatles Story Museum; Walker Art Gallery; Grand National at Aintree Racecourse
Main: Albert Dock and the Port of Liverpool Building

THE MERSEY BEAT

SOME PEOPLE MIGHT HAVE BEEN SURPRISED when Liverpool was named European Capital of Culture for 2008. After all, this historic port on the River Mersey is better known for its distinguished soccer clubs; for the famous Grand National steeplechase that takes place at Aintree Racecourse in April; and as the home of The Beatles. But there's more to Liverpool than meets the eye, and spring is an ideal time to explore this lively city's thriving cultural scene.

During its maritime heyday in the 18th and 19th centuries, Liverpool was the second city of the British Empire and handled 40 percent of the world's trade, but its extensive docks and quays gradually fell into dereliction in the 1970s and 1980s. Now, however, after major regeneration of the area, the rough-and-tumble waterfront has become a UNESCO World Heritage Site and its renovated warehouses hold world-class museums and art galleries.

At Albert Dock on the waterfront, you can find out more about Liverpool's seafaring past. The Merseyside Maritime Museum has displays on the rise and decline of the city's docks and the smuggling of goods, and poignant mementos of the ill-fated *Titanic* and *Lusitania* ocean

FURTHER DETAILS

LIVERPOOL

The Grand National
Aintree Racecourse, Ormskirk Road, Aintree, Liverpool.
The race is run in the first or second week of April.
www.aintree.co.uk

Merseyside Maritime Museum
Albert Dock; open 10am–5pm daily.
www.liverpoolmuseums.org.uk

The Beatles Story
Britannia Vaults, Albert Dock; open 10am–7pm daily.
www.beatlesstory.com

Tate Liverpool
Albert Dock; open Sep–May: 10am–5:50pm Tue–Sun;
Jun–Aug: 10am–5:50pm daily.
www.tate.org.uk/liverpool

Walker Art Gallery
William Brown Street. The Gallery showcases diverse
works of art, from the 13th century to the modern day;
open 10am–5pm daily.
www.liverpoolmuseums.org.uk

World Museum Liverpool
William Brown Street. The Museum houses historic
treasures from across the globe; open 10am–5pm daily.
www.liverpoolmuseums.org.uk

National Conservation Centre
Whitechapel; open 10am–5pm daily.
www.liverpoolmuseums.org.uk

Anglican Cathedral Church of Christ
St. James's Mount; open 8am–6pm daily.
www.liverpoolcathedral.org.uk

Catholic Metropolitan Cathedral of Christ the King
Mount Pleasant; open 8am–6pm daily.
www.liverpoolmetrocathedral.org.uk

Mersey Ferry
Pier Head, Georges Parade. River Explorer ferries run
to Woodside Ferry Terminal in Birkenhead 10am–3pm
Mon–Fri, 10am–6pm Sat–Sun.
www.merseyferries.co.uk

Mendips and 20 Forthlin Road
Allerton and Woolton, Liverpool; open late Feb–Nov:
Wed–Sun; admission by National Trust guided tour only.
www.nationaltrust.org.uk

Liverpool Beatles Tours
Personalized tours to suit visitors' time and level of
interest, from 2 hours to 3 days long, by booking only.
www.beatlestours.co.uk

Below: Liverpool Metropolitan Cathedral, consecrated in 1967

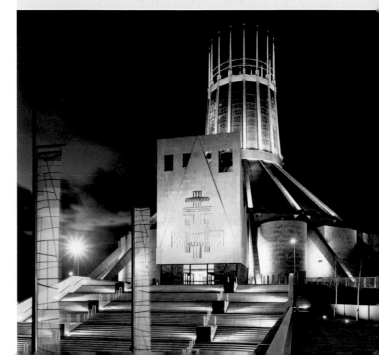

liners. The heart-wrenching International Slavery Museum, in the same building, reveals a darker side of Liverpool's past – at one time the city was the world's biggest slave port.

Liverpool has something to satisfy every cultural taste. If you are interested in pop culture, the Beatles Story museum at Albert Dock traces the rise of the Fab Four, with memorabilia including a real-life yellow submarine. For art-lovers, Tate Liverpool is the northern home of the National Collection of Modern Art and hosts major international exhibitions. The city also boasts the Walker Art Gallery, the World Museum Liverpool, and the National Conservation Centre, which explores how museums preserve artifacts. The city's architecture is particularly impressive. Maritime wealth left a legacy of monumental buildings, and lining the waterfront at Pier Head are the "Three Graces" – the imposing Port of Liverpool Building, the Cunard Building, and the Royal Liver Building, whose "Liver Birds" sculptures on its clock tower are the city's symbol. The Anglican Cathedral is the fifth-largest in the world and is rivaled in the city only by its Catholic counterpart – the Metropolitan Cathedral – with its striking modernist design.

In the 1960s, pop star Gerry Marsden eulogized Liverpool in his song "Ferry 'Cross the Mersey." You can still catch the Mersey ferry from Pier Head to Birkenhead – a perfect way to step back and admire this vibrant city's magnificent and historic waterfront.

THE ESSENTIALS

GETTING THERE AND AROUND
Speyside is in northeast Scotland. The nearest airport and train services are at Inverness, 38 miles (61 km) from Elgin, with flights from several UK airports and trains from Glasgow, Edinburgh, and London. ScotRail (*www.scotrail.com*) runs the overnight Caledonian Sleeper service from London Euston (journey time 12 hours). Buses link the distilleries and villages of Aberlour, Craigellachie, Dufftown, Elgin, Fochabers, Forres, Glenlivet, Grantown on Spey, Keith, Knockando, and Rothes.

WEATHER
Be prepared for any kind of weather in Speyside in spring, with daytime temperatures of 32–50°F (0–10°C). Warm, waterproof clothing and footwear are essential.

ACCOMMODATIONS
Treat Yourself Glenmorangie House in Cadboll is an informal, luxurious country-house hotel.
www.theglenmorangiehouse.com

On a Budget Tannochbrae, in Dufftown, is a quaint little guesthouse with cozy rooms and a decent bar.
www.tannochbrae.co.uk

EATING OUT
Treat Yourself The Glass House, in Grantown on Spey, is a delightful conservatory restaurant serving Scottish classics.
www.theglasshouse-grantown.co.uk

On a Budget Ord Bàn Restaurant Café, in Aviemore, offers delicious, simple, locally sourced food and home baking.
www.ordban.com

PRICE FOR TWO PEOPLE
$250–370 a day for food, accommodations, and admission fees.

WEBSITE
www.greaterspeyside.com

Malt Whiskey

A single malt whiskey is made from a spirit distilled from malted barley, but its flavor is largely determined by the casks in which it matures. Distillers are now creating new flavors of malt by eschewing the traditional sherry casks for wine barrels. Good malt whiskey is aged "in the wood" for at least five years, and top-quality malts for much longer. "Cask strength" malts – almost 100-percent alcohol – are growing in popularity, but most malts are diluted with springwater to around 40-percent alcohol.

ONE SIP AT A TIME

IN THE WORDS OF SCOTLAND'S BARD, Robert Burns, "freedom and whisky gang the gither" (go together), and there's no denying that Scottish whisky is the very essence of the Highlands. For many connoisseurs, Speyside, home of Glenlivet and Glenfiddich and the birthplace of many other world-renowned whiskies, is the heart of Scotland's malt industry.

The Spirit of Speyside Whisky Festival is a wonderful opportunity for aficionados to sample some of the world's best whiskies, while also enjoying a broader range of Scottish delights. The festival takes place each year in May, when Speyside opens its doors for ten days of whiskey sampling, gourmet food, and outdoor activities from hill-walking to golf, ending with a grand finale of fireworks and music on the banks of the River Spey.

Speyside is at its loveliest in late spring, with the fresh greenery of silver birch and rowan trees on the riverbanks, blazing swaths of yellow broom on the slopes above, nodding fields of barley in the fertile farmlands and streams gushing from heathery hillsides to join the lovely River Spey. The pure water of the Spey's many tributaries has always been an essential ingredient of the region's fine whiskeys, along with a ready supply of barley from the farmlands of Moray and Aberdeenshire.

Combine the Whisky Festival with the world's only Malt Whisky Trail for a trip that will satisfy the most demanding connoisseur, linking eight world-famous distilleries, each offering tours, tastings, and insight into *uisghe beatha*: a Gaelic term meaning "water of life." The Trail meanders through lush countryside, wending its way to the waters of the Moray Firth.

Just as each malt whiskey has a unique flavor, each distillery is a unique slice of living history, from the old-fashioned distillery at Dallas Dhu to little Benromach, which reopened in 1998, and Glenlivet, one of Scotland's largest distilleries, producing a world-renowned malt. Speyside's whiskey-makers have a passion for their art, and Speyside's distillers continue to create new and inspiring malt whiskeys. Just take them one sip at a time.

> The pure water of the Spey's many tributaries has always been an essential ingredient of the region's fine whiskeys.

Main: Drams of finest Speyside malt whiskey **Inset:** River Spey near Craigellachie
Below: Glenlivet Whisky Distillery

FURTHER DETAILS

SPEYSIDE WHISKEY
Speyside Whisky Festival
www.spiritofspeyside.com

Malt Whisky Trail
www.maltwhiskytrail.com

The Glenlivet Distillery
Balindalloch; open Apr–Oct: 10am–4pm
Mon–Sat, 12:30–4pm Sun; closed Nov–Mar.
www.theglenlivet.com

Glenfiddich Distillery
Dufftown; open mid-Apr–mid-Oct: 9:30am–4:30pm
Mon–Sat, noon–4:30pm Sun.
www.glenfiddich.com

Dallas Dhu Distillery
Mannachie Road, Forres; open Apr–Sep:
9:30am–5:30pm daily; Oct: 9:30am–4:30pm daily;
Nov–Mar: 9:30am–4:30pm Mon–Wed and Sat–Sun.
Tel: 01309 676 548

Benromach Distillery
Invererne Road, Forres; open May–Sep: 9:30am–5pm
Mon–Sat; Jun–Aug: noon–4pm Sun; Oct–Apr:
10am–4pm Mon–Fri.
www.benromach.com

Cardhu Distillery
Knockando, Aberlour; open Easter–Jun: 10am–5pm
Mon–Fri; Jul–Sep: 10am–5pm Mon–Sat, noon–4pm Sun;
Oct–Easter: 11am–3pm Mon–Fri. Tel: 01479 874635

Glen Grant Distillery
Rothes, Aberlour; open mid-Jan–mid Dec: 9:30am–5pm
Mon–Sat, 12pm–5pm Sun.
www.glengrant.com

Glen Moray Distillery
Bruceland Road, Elgin; open Oct–April: 9am–5pm Mon–Fri; May–Sep: 9am–5pm Mon–Fri, 10am–4:30pm Sat.
www.glenmoray.com

Strathisla Distillery
Seafield Avenue, Keith; open Easter–Oct: 9:30am–4pm
Mon–Sat, noon–4pm Sun.
Tel: 01542 783044

WHAT ELSE TO SEE AND DO
Speyside Cooperage
You can see skilled coopers make wooden casks here.
www.speysidecooperage.co.uk

Below: Stacked whiskey casks, Speyside Cooperage

THE ESSENTIALS

GETTING THERE AND AROUND
Alresford is in Hampshire in southern England, 8 miles (13 km) from Winchester and 11 miles (18 km) from Alton; both have mainline rail connections to London. The nearest international airports are at Heathrow and Gatwick, 51 miles (82 km) and 66 miles (106 km) from Alresford respectively. You can arrive by steam train on the Mid Hants Railway and explore the compact town center on foot, but to visit outlying villages or nearby Winchester, a car is essential as buses are infrequent.

WEATHER
Alresford experiences a typically mild but changeable English spring; be prepared for both sunshine and rain. Daytime temperatures average 45–54°F (7–12°C).

ACCOMMODATIONS
Treat Yourself Lainston House, in nearby Sparsholt, is an award-winning hotel in its own 63-acre (26-hectare) grounds.
www.lainstonhouse.com

On a Budget The Bell, in Alresford, is a centrally located former coaching inn with private bathrooms and a great restaurant.
www.bellalresford.com

EATING OUT
Treat Yourself The Hotel du Vin bistro, in Winchester, offers classic European cuisine with a contemporary twist.
www.hotelduvin.com/winchester

On a Budget The Bush Inn in nearby Ovington boasts good pub food and lovely gardens beside the River Itchen.
Tel: 01962 732764

PRICE FOR A FAMILY OF FOUR
$500 a day for food, accommodations, admission fees, and tickets for the Watercress Line.

WEBSITES
www.alresford.org
www.visitwinchester.co.uk

The Watercress Festival

Watercress has been farmed in Alresford and the surrounding areas for hundreds of years, but it was not widely exported until the railroads arrived in the region in 1865. The town celebrates its agricultural heritage at the very popular annual Watercress Festival, which attracts over 10,000 visitors each year. Local food producers and celebrity chefs provide delicious food to go, live music fills the air, and the fun really starts as the champion watercress-eating contenders start to limber up.

GEORGIAN CHARM

THE QUAINT HAMPSHIRE TOWN OF NEW ALRESFORD (pronounced "Allsford") bustles with life. Its pretty streets are energized by busy residents popping in and out of its many charming independent shops, and by visitors who pour into the area daily to appreciate the town's historic houses and picturesque surroundings. Its bright, color-washed Georgian street frontages offer both a friendly face to the world and an architectural continuity that puts many other towns in Britain to shame. All this is set against glorious rolling fields hiding a necklace of idyllic chalk streams that feed the thriving local watercress industry. This small town is many people's idea of perfection.

The 13th-century Bishops of Winchester were Alresford's original architects, but it is thanks to a devastating fire in 1689 and the quick thinking of an American World War II pilot that New Alresford is the Georgian wonder you see today. After the fire, vulnerable timber was replaced

Set against glorious rolling fields hiding a necklace of idyllic chalk streams… this small town is many people's idea of perfection.

by resilient red brick, and in 1942, Captain Robert Cogswell averted another major disaster by steering his failing bomber plane away from the town, bailing out just before it crashed near old Alresford Pond. Today, a plaque can be seen near the water's edge honoring his bravery.

This thriving town is also a historical time capsule. Antiquated buildings house jolly cafés and heritage trains regularly steam into the town's "olde worlde" station. On the banks of the River Arle, the impossibly pretty Fulling Mill charms passers-by and the Eel House parades its unique past. Children will enjoy learning about the ingenious methods the river-keepers used to catch young eels before they left the Arle for their spawning grounds in the Atlantic Ocean. They will also love the many river walks, which offer a chance to spot swans and otters.

There can be no better reason to visit Alresford in springtime than to catch May's Watercress Festival, when the town center becomes a stage for an entertaining celebration of Alresford's star export. Food, music, dancing, and comedy announce the season's first watercress harvest. Hop aboard an old-fashioned steam train for a nostalgia-filled journey along the Watercress Line, and arrive at this fun-packed festival in style.

FURTHER DETAILS

ALRESFORD

Eel House
The center of the town's eel-catching industry, the Eel House is open on festival days and on selected dates each year.
www.towntrust.org.uk/eel_house.htm

Millennium and Arle River Trails and Old Alresford Pond
These trails use a series of existing paths around the town to provide pleasant and informative walks.
www.alresford.org/millen.php

Watercress Festival
The festival is held on the third Sunday in May, from 10am to 4pm.
www.watercressfestival.org

Mid Hants Railway Watercress Line
The 10-mile- (16-km-) long family-oriented line operates between Alresford and Alton.
www.watercressline.co.uk

WHAT ELSE TO SEE AND DO

Intech
Set in an award-winning 38,000-sq-ft (3,500-sq-m) building near Winchester, Intech is a hands-on science center and planetarium. It has more than 100 fun, interactive exhibits that demonstrate fundamental science principles and ways in which we use them.
www.intech-uk.com

Jane Austen's House
This 17th-century country house at nearby Chawton is where the novelist spent the last eight years of her life, and wrote most of her comedies of middle-class manners in Georgian England, including *Pride and Prejudice*.
www.jane-austens-house-museum.org.uk

Gilbert White's House and Oates Museum
Home to the renowned naturalist, this fascinating museum commemorates important pioneers in the exploration of the natural world. The house is set in the historic village of Selborne and is surrounded by exquisite countryside.
www.gilbertwhiteshouse.org.uk

Marwell Wildlife
You can see over 250 species of exotic and endangered animals at this wildlife park near Eastleigh, including laughing kookaburras, frilled lizards, Siamang gibbons, and snow leopards. The park covers 140 acres (56 hectares) of beautiful landscaped grounds.
www.marwell.org.uk

Main: Fulling Mill on the River Arle

Above: Horse and carriage at the Watercress Festival, on its way to the watercress farms

Left panel (top to bottom): Watercress harvest; steam train on the Watercress Line

Below: Color-washed Georgian buildings in Alresford

THE ESSENTIALS

GETTING THERE AND AROUND
Pendle Hill is in Lancashire in northwestern England, 1 mile (1.6 km) from the village of Barley. The nearest major airport is Manchester International Airport, 48 miles (77 km) south of Barley. There are bus services connecting the villages around Pendle Hill, but a car is best for exploration if you are comfortable with the area's narrow country roads.

WEATHER
The climate around Pendle Hill varies enormously; expect anything from torrential rain to hot sunshine – sometimes on the same day. Average spring daytime temperatures range from 41 to 50°F (5–10°C).

ACCOMMODATIONS
Treat Yourself Northcote Manor, in Langho, offers a Michelin-starred restaurant in a 19th-century manor house, with luxury bedrooms and landscaped gardens. *www.northcote.com*

On a Budget Dam Head Barn, in the "witches' village" of Roughlee, is a converted barn with spacious rooms and private baths. *www.damheadbarn.com*

EATING OUT
Treat Yourself Weezos, in Clitheroe, uses fresh local produce to create tasty modern European cuisine. *www.weezos.co.uk*

On a Budget The Well Springs, in Sabden, on the opposite side of Pendle Hill from Barley, is a popular Spanish/Mexican restaurant. *www.thewellsprings.co.uk*

PRICE FOR TWO PEOPLE
Around $230 a day for food and accommodations.

WEBSITE
www.visitlancashire.com

Phoning Home

Pendle Hill is about 15 miles (24 km) from the exact geographical center of the British Isles, which, according to the Ordnance Survey, is a place called the Whittendale (or Whitendale) Hanging Stones, to the north of the village of Dunsop Bridge. As Dunsop Bridge is the closest settlement to this landmark point, British Telecom placed its 100,000th phone booth there to mark the site's significance, with a sign on it to make people aware of exactly where they are calling from.

Main: Rays of sunlight illuminating Pendle Hill
Right (top to bottom): "Witch graves" in St. Leonard's graveyard; public footpath sign for Pendle Hill circular walks

BEWITCHING VIEWS

THE BROODING FORM OF PENDLE HILL became infamous in the 17th century as the focal point for the most celebrated witch trial in English history. If you approach the isolated 1,827-ft- (557-m-) high Lancashire hill on a misty day, it's not difficult to imagine the uneasy atmosphere here in the early 1600s. At the time, religious fervor and superstition ran riot throughout the country, even among royalty. When King James I came to the throne, he enacted a death penalty for anyone suspected of causing harm through magic. Pendle Hill, long regarded as a wild and lawless part of England, experienced this legislation firsthand when ten women and two men from villages around the hill were accused of witchcraft.

In 1612 a pedlar named John Law suffered a stroke after an altercation with a village woman, Alizon Device. He accused her of witchcraft, and the allegations snowballed with the ensuing investigations. Elderly women who acted as village healers, attempting medical cures using herbs and potions, were also accused. Healing was a common way to make a living in the early 17th century, and it's thought that some Pendle healers made false charges to discredit

FURTHER DETAILS

PENDLE HILL
Walking Routes
There are several paths up to the top of Pendle Hill. The route from the village of Sabden, on the southwest side of the hill, is a 3–4-hour round trip. There is a good car park at Barley – which also has restaurants and hotels – on the southeastern side of the hill, and the round trip from here is just under 4 miles (about 6 km); it should take anyone of average fitness just under 3 hours. It is a very popular walk and likely to be busy on a fine spring day. Check the weather forecast, as the weather can change quickly and mist or rain can descend.

WHAT ELSE TO SEE AND DO
Roughlee
This village is a 5-minute drive east of Barley. It features the pretty stream known as Pendle Water and the picturesque Roughlee Hall, once thought to be the home of the most famous Pendle witch, Alice Nutter.

Blacko
A few minutes' drive east of Roughlee is the village of Blacko. Here the "witch" with the splendid name of Old Mother Demdike – although her real name was the rather more prosaic Elizabeth Southern – lived at Malkin Tower Farm, now converted into vacation cottages.
Malkin Tower Farm: www.malkintowerfarm.co.uk

Newchurch
About half a mile (1 km) south of Barley, Newchurch village is named after St. Mary's Church, which has the "Eye of God" painted on its tower to ward off evil. Alice Nutter is supposed to lie buried in the churchyard, but no grave has yet been found.

Downham
This quaint village is popular with filmmakers – it lies in an estate whose owners forbid the erection of overhead cables and satellite dishes. One of the period dramas filmed here over the years was the 1960s classic *Whistle Down the Wind*.

Below (top to bottom): Village of Downham; hiking up Pendle Hill

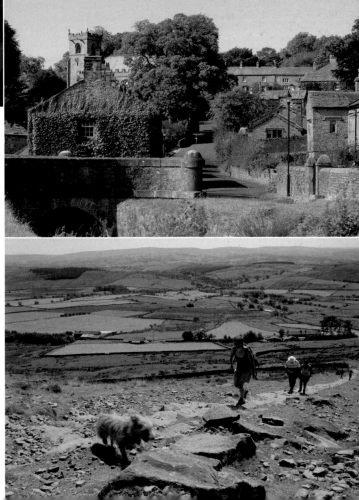

If you climb up the not-too-strenuous slopes of Pendle Hill…
you will be rewarded with bewitching views that stretch
as far as the Lancashire coast.

their rivals. The witch hunt turned deadly, however, and of the 12 accused, only one was acquitted – the rest were hanged and buried in the graveyard of St. Leonard's church in Downham.

Today the locals are happy to exploit their notorious past. Signposts for walking routes show silhouettes of witches on broomsticks, and the villages surrounding the hill – Barley, Downham, Roughlee, and Sabden – do a roaring trade in occult souvenirs. That isn't the only reason to pay a visit, however. The quaint stone houses and narrow streets have changed little over the years, and when the sun shines over these quiet backwaters, they easily rival the more famous Cotswold villages for beauty and charm, giving you the perfect start to a day of hiking. If you climb up the not-too-strenuous slopes of Pendle Hill on one of the well-marked paths, you will be rewarded with bewitching views that stretch as far as the Lancashire coast, 31 miles (50 km) away. You may not encounter a witch, but the scenery is definitely magical.

THE ESSENTIALS

GETTING THERE AND AROUND
Derry is in northwestern Northern Ireland, close to the border with the Republic of Ireland. It has its own small airport, the City of Derry Airport, 7 miles (11 km) southwest of the city. Belfast International Airport is 60 miles (96 km) southeast of Derry, with airport bus connections between the two. Central Derry is easily explored on foot.

WEATHER
Ireland gets a lot of rain, but Derry is at its driest in spring. The average daytime temperature is 46–50ºF (8–10ºC).

ACCOMMODATIONS
Treat Yourself The 4-star City Hotel Derry, on Queens Quay, offers luxury rooms right on the banks of the River Foyle, within walking distance of the downtown. *www.cityhotelderry.com*

On a Budget The Derry City Independent Hostel, on Great James Street, has private rooms as well as dormitories, and offers comfort and good value. *www.derryhostel.com*

EATING OUT
Treat Yourself Mange2, on Strand Road, serves Irish foods cooked in delicious French-bistro style. *www.mange2derry.com*

On a Budget Fitzroy's Bistro, on Bridge Street, is a relaxed restaurant in the center of town serving international cuisine. *www.fitzroysrestaurant.com*

PRICE FOR TWO PEOPLE
Around $250 a day for accommodations, food, and admission fees.

WEBSITE
www.derryvisitor.com

Stroke City

Derry is named after the oak grove (*daire* in old Irish) that once stood here beside the River Foyle, where St. Columb founded his monastery. But during the 1620s Plantation of Ulster, English and Scottish Protestant workers were forcibly settled in Derry by wealthy London trade guilds, giving rise to the new name of "Londonderry." Though this remains the city's official name, most people prefer "Derry." As all maps and signs refer to "Derry/Londonderry," it has gained the nickname "Stroke City."

THE WALLED CITY

D ERRY MAY BE NORTHERN IRELAND'S SECOND CITY, but first-rate music echoes from within its historic walls each spring, when it hosts the City of Derry Jazz and Big Band Festival. The region's biggest and most renowned jazz event, it attracts national and international performers over four days in late April and early May. The range of music is impressive, blending traditional and contemporary jazz and big-band sounds with hip-hop, salsa, reggae, blues, and swing. You can hear free concerts at pubs and hotels around the city, or see headline acts at the Millennium Forum, the newest landmark inside its venerable walls.

Once you've satisfied your musical cravings, take a tour of the city's old town. Its impressive 20-ft- (6-m-) high defensive walls were built between 1613 and 1618 by Protestant settlers from London. Despite three Catholic sieges – including the 105-day Siege of Derry in 1688–89, the longest siege in British history – these well-preserved walls were never breached. You can walk along the top of them, following their 1-mile (1.5-km) circuit around the city, and drop down to visit any of the fascinating historical sites you see en route. If you start your day with a visit to the spectacular Neo-Gothic Guildhall, or the Tower Museum with its high-tech displays that tell the city's story, you'll find yourself very near Shipquay Gate, where there are steps leading to the top of the walls. The ramparts here are dotted with original cannons. Follow the walls counter-clockwise, and you'll soon be tempted down by the Apprentice Boys Memorial Hall and its Siege of Derry exhibition, the small but beautiful St. Augustine's Church, and St. Columb's Cathedral – the first Protestant cathedral in the British Isles, built after the Reformation and dedicated to the Ulster monk who founded the first settlement here. It too contains relics of the great Siege.

From the height of Derry's walls there are thought-provoking views of this once-divided city. To the west lies the Catholic Bogside district, its large, distinctive political murals a reminder of Northern Ireland's troubled history, while to the east, across the River Foyle, Maurice Hannon's profound *Hands Across the Divide* sculpture symbolizes reconciliation.

FURTHER DETAILS

DERRY

The City of Derry Jazz and Big Band Festival
The festival is held over four days in late April/early May.
www.cityofderryjazzfestival.com

Millennium Forum
Newmarket Street. This theater and conference center lies in the heart of the city.
http://gcldvsh.sed2.info

The Guildhall
Guildhall Square; open 9am–5pm Mon–Fri.
www.derrycity.gov.uk

The Tower Museum
Union Hall Place; open 10am–5pm Tue–Sat;
(and Jul–Aug: 10am–5pm Mon and 11am–3pm Sun).
www.derrycity.gov.uk/museums

Apprentice Boys Memorial Hall
Society Street; open Jul–Oct: 10am–5pm Mon–Fri.
www2.apprenticeboys.co.uk

St. Augustine's Church
Palace Street; open daily.
www.btinternet.com/~st.augustine

St. Columb's Cathedral
London Street; open Apr–Oct: 9am–5pm Mon–Sat;
Nov–Mar: 9am–4pm.
www.stcolumbscathedral.org

WHAT ELSE TO SEE AND DO
Harbour Museum
A replica of St. Columb's *currach* – a boat made from animal hide – is on display in this museum, which is dedicated to Derry's maritime history.
www.derrycity.gov.uk/museums

Below (top to bottom): St. Columb's Cathedral; the *Hands Across the Divide* sculpture

> To the west lies the Catholic Bogside district, its large, distinctive political murals a reminder of Northern Ireland's troubled history.

Main: Cannon on the walls of Derry **Inset:** Political mural on the side of a house in the Bogside district
Below: Jazz band playing at the City of Derry Jazz and Big Band Festival

THE ESSENTIALS

GETTING THERE AND AROUND
Bempton Cliffs Reserve is in northeastern England, 67 miles (108 km) east of Leeds. The reserve is 1½ miles (2.5 km) from Bempton village and train station. Several of the cliffside viewpoints within the reserve are wheelchair-accessible.

WEATHER
Be prepared for cold winds and rain off the North Sea, with spring daytime temperatures of 46–54°F (8–12°C).

ACCOMMODATIONS
Treat Yourself The Crown Spa Hotel, in Scarborough, has the distinction of being the only 4-star hotel on the Yorkshire coast.
www.crownspahotel.com

On a Budget An Oasis Guest House, in Bridlington, is a cozy B&B that offers comfortable beds and hearty breakfasts.
www.anoasisbrid.co.uk

EATING OUT
Bempton is a small and relatively remote village, with limited dining options that all offer a mid-priced menu.

Rags Hotel & Restaurant, in Bridlington, is a classy restaurant that specializes in fresh seafood and other local delicacies.
www.ragshotel.co.uk

The White Horse, on Bempton High Street, is a family-friendly pub serving real ales and pub grub, within walking distance of Bempton Cliffs.
Tel: 01262 850266

PRICE FOR TWO PEOPLE
From around $200 a day for accommodations, food, and admission fees for the nature reserve and other attractions.

WEBSITE
www.yorkshire.com

Puffins in Peril

The RSPB has placed the puffin on its "amber list" of species that are under threat. Although the UK is home to around 10 percent of the world's puffins, the majority are found in fewer than 10 sites around the country. This makes them vulnerable to local threats, such as the overfishing by humans of their favored food – sand eels – or increases in the numbers of predators attacking their nests. It doesn't help that puffins are not prolific breeders – the female lays just one egg a year.

Main: Puffin in flight from the cliffs at Bempton
Right (top to bottom): Two black-legged kittiwakes sparring with their beaks; colony of guillemots

BIRD-WATCHERS' PARADISE

COMICAL, CUTE, AND CLUMSY-LOOKING, puffins are the most enchanting of British sea birds. To see them is to love them, and at Bempton Cliffs on the Yorkshire coast you can see them by the hundred in spring and early summer, along with vast flocks of other sea birds.

Bempton's white chalk cliffs rise dramatically out of the waves, offering the perfect nesting place for puffins, which wheel and soar from the shore far out above the gray waters of the North Sea. It's a wildlife spectacle unequaled in Britain, and it has to be seen – and heard – to be believed. From viewing points on the cliffs, you can watch these fat little creatures setting off on fishing expeditions from which they return with flimsy-looking wings beating gallantly and their colorful beaks stuffed with silvery sand eels – dinner for the chick that huddles in their cliffside burrow. Out at sea, the adult birds can be seen afloat in large flocks that suddenly vanish beneath the waves when they detect a shoal of fish below.

The puffins arrive at their breeding colonies in the spring and, after breeding, they leave en masse. Toward the end of the breeding season, Bempton Cliffs throngs with adults feeding

FURTHER DETAILS

RSPB BEMPTON CLIFFS NATURE RESERVE
Near Bempton, East Yorkshire; reserve is open at all times; visitor center open Mar–Oct: 10am–5pm daily; Nov–Feb: 10am–4pm daily.
www.rspb.org.uk

WHAT ELSE TO SEE AND DO
RSPB Blacktoft Sands Nature Reserve
These vast reedbeds are home to bearded tits, bitterns, and marsh harriers; open 9am–9pm daily.
www.rspb.org.uk

RSPB Dearne Valley Old Moor Nature Reserve
This moorland reserve is home to kingfishers and huge flocks of lapwings; visitor center open 9:30am–5pm daily.
www.rspb.org.uk

RSPB Fairburn Ings Nature Reserve
Kingfishers, reed and sedge warblers, little ringed plovers, and garganey ducks are among the species here in spring and early summer; visitor center open 9am–4pm daily.
www.rspb.org.uk

Flamborough Head, Flamborough
This looming headland, with its historic lighthouse, affords breathtaking views out to the North Sea.
www.flamboroughhead.co.uk

The Deep, Hull
This spectacular aquarium offers a puffin's-eye view of the undersea world. You can view sharks and 3,500 other fish of various species from an underwater tunnel.
www.thedeep.co.uk

Scarborough Castle, Scarborough
There are superb views of the North Sea coast from the imposing ramparts of this ruined castle, built during the reign of King Stephen in the 1130s.
www.english-heritage.org.uk/yorkshire

Below: Grass-topped chalk cliffs at Bempton

Bempton's white-chalk cliffs rise dramatically out of the waves, offering the perfect nesting place for puffins, which wheel and soar… far out above the gray waters of the North Sea.

greedy chicks. A few days later, it is bereft of puffins, with adult birds heading back into the wide spaces of the North Sea and their newly fledged offspring struggling to keep up as they set out on their first maritime pilgrimage. These youngsters will spend five or six years at sea, before returning to lay their own eggs on Bempton's chalk ledges.

Puffins are the starring players at Bempton, but there is always a strong supporting cast. Gannets – among the most impressive of British sea birds – patrol the waters close to shore and can be seen plummeting after fish from on high. Dainty little kittiwakes fill the air with their distinctive calls and huddle together on their precarious nesting ledges; razorbills and guillemots crowd rocky ledges and, like the puffins, arrow out to sea in squadrons in search of a fish supper. If you are a nature-lover at heart, you could do much worse than spend a day's blissful bird-watching on this beautiful coastline.

THE ESSENTIALS

GETTING THERE AND AROUND
Stratford-upon-Avon is in the county of
Warwickshire, in the West Midlands; the
nearest airport is Birmingham International.
There are hourly trains from Birmingham
and a twice-hourly service from London
Marylebone (via Warwick). The town is
also served by long-distance bus. Most of
Stratford's tourist sights are within walking
distance of each other.

WEATHER
Warwickshire has a mild climate in spring,
with average daytime temperatures of
around 42–54°F (6–12°C).

ACCOMMODATIONS
Treat Yourself Ettington Park Hotel,
just outside Stratford, is Britain's "most
haunted hotel" – a 4-star neo-Gothic pile
with excellent rooms and attentive staff.
www.handpickedhotels.co.uk

On a Budget Quilt and Croissants, in
Evesham Place, is a popular Victorian B&B
with very welcoming owners, clean rooms,
and good breakfasts.
www.quiltcroissants.co.uk

EATING OUT
Treat Yourself Marlowes, on High Street,
revels in its quaint Elizabethan setting and
theatrical connections; chargrilled steaks
are a specialty.
www.marlowes.biz

On a Budget Edward Moon, on Chapel
Street, is known for its food, service, and
the excellent value of its fixed-price menu.
www.edwardmoon.com

PRICE FOR TWO PEOPLE
From $330 a day for accommodations,
food, admission fees, and theater tickets.

WEBSITE
www.stratford-upon-avon.co.uk

Shakespeare's Birthday

No one has ever been able to establish conclusively
the date of the Bard's birth, but his birthday has
traditionally been cited as April 23, and this is when
it is celebrated in festivities at Stratford-upon-Avon
and worldwide. However, the playwright's exact
birthday is a matter of constant conjecture. He was
baptized on April 26, 1564, so he was probably
born a few days earlier. He certainly died on
April 23 (St. George's Day), and this may explain
the adoption of the same date for his birthday.

THE BARD'S BIRTHDAY

THE MODEST SOUTH WARWICKSHIRE TOWN of Stratford-upon-Avon would be no more than an inconsequential blip on the tourist radar but for the dazzling brilliance of its most famous luminary, William Shakespeare. Literary pilgrims the world over dream of coming to England specifically to visit Stratford-upon-Avon; to such aficionados, exploring the rest of the United Kingdom can be a mere afterthought. With legions of British schoolchildren also visiting Stratford-upon-Avon to learn about the author of *King Lear* and *Hamlet*, the town is guaranteed to offer an uninterrupted tourist bonanza.

Stratford-upon-Avon offers an overflowing cornucopia of sights associated with the playwright and all things Shakespearean. The museum – the half-timbered house where the Bard was born in 1564 – is the first stop on the trail, and almost certainly the most visited house in Britain. Nash's House, on Chapel Street, is an attractive period building that houses

Stratford-upon-Avon
offers an overflowing
cornucopia of sights
associated with the
playwright and
all things
Shakespearean.

the local history museum; next door you can visit the foundations of New Place, where Shakespeare lived when not in London, and where he died in 1616. Two other houses are well worth a visit: Hall's Croft, a snapshot of Elizabethan England, was the home of Shakespeare's eldest daughter, while the half-timbered and thatched Anne Hathaway's Cottage was the home of Shakespeare's wife. The playwright's resting place, Holy Trinity Church, draws a natural conclusion to literary explorations. A late-afternoon trip down the River Avon provides perfect calm in which to muse over his life, and see the town from a different perspective.

Shakespeare's birthday on April 23 has been commemorated in the town for over 200 years. Today it is celebrated with four or five days of cultural events, from street theater to poetry readings, musical performances, folk dancing, processions, and marching bands. The Shakespeare Birthday Parade is held on the Saturday closest to April 23, when a procession forms a pilgrimage from Shakespeare's birthplace to his grave. The Bard's plays are staged everywhere – from the Royal Shakespeare Theatre to the streets and even boats. It's impossible not to become swept up in this piece of Elizabethan fun, celebrating Britain's most famous writer.

FURTHER DETAILS

SHAKESPEARE SITES
Details of places and events can be found at:
www.shakespeare-country.co.uk
www.shakespeare.org.uk

Shakespeare's Birthplace
Henley Street; open summer: 9am–5pm daily; winter: 10am–4pm daily.

Nash's House & New Place
Chapel Street; open summer: 10am–5pm daily; winter: 11am–4pm daily.

Hall's Croft
Old Town; open Apr–May and Sep–Oct: 11am–5pm daily; Nov–Mar: 11am–4pm daily; Jun–Aug: 9:30–5pm Mon–Sat, 10am–5pm Sun.

Anne Hathaway's Cottage
Shottery; open summer: 9am–5pm daily, winter: 10am–4pm daily.

Holy Trinity Church
Shakespeare's burial place, in Trinity Street; open Apr–Sep: 8:30am–6pm Mon–Sat, 12:30–5pm Sun; Mar and Oct: 9am–5pm Mon–Sat, 12:30–5pm Sun; Nov–Feb: 9am–4pm Mon–Sat, 12:30–5pm Sun.

Avon Boating
Rowboat and motorboat rental, plus guided river cruises on quiet, electric-powered boats.
www.avon-boating.co.uk

Royal Shakespeare Company
Britain's most famous repertory theatre company produces plays by Shakespeare and his contemporaries as well as living playwrights at their two Stratford homes: the Royal Shakespeare Theatre and the Courtyard Theatre.
www.rsc.org.uk

WHAT ELSE TO SEE AND DO
Charlecote Park
Shakespeare was apocryphally caught poaching deer on the estate of this beautiful Tudor house, 5 miles (8 km) from Stratford-upon-Avon. The magnificent gardens by the River Avon were designed by Capability Brown.
www.nationaltrust.org.uk

Mary Arden's House
The childhood home of Shakespeare's mother lies just outside Stratford at Wilmcote.
www.nationaltrust.org.uk

Main: Rowboats on the River Avon

Far left (top to bottom): Performance of *Love's Labour's Lost* in Stratford; Shakespeare's birthplace

Above: Shakespeare Birthday Parade in Stratford

Below: Holy Trinity Church in Stratford, Shakespeare's resting place

Below: Ann Hathaway's thatched cottage at Shottery

THE ESSENTIALS

GETTING THERE AND AROUND
Hadrian's Wall Path National Trail
crosses northern England, from Wallsend
near Newcastle-upon-Tyne in the east
to Bowness-on-Solway in the west.
The closest international airport is at
Newcastle. The A69 and B6318 lead to
major sections of the wall. The AD122
bus operates Easter–Oct, running from
Newcastle Central Station to Carlisle with
stops at all the wall's main visitor centers.

WEATHER
Spring weather is variable, and you could
see anything from snow to warm sunshine.
Daytime temperatures average 37–52°F
(3–11°C).

ACCOMMODATIONS
Treat Yourself Jesmond Dene House,
in Newcastle, is a historic 19th-century
building that won the AA Hotel of the Year
award in 2008–9.
www.jesmonddenehouse.co.uk

On a Budget The Centre of Britain Hotel
and Restaurant, in Haltwhistle, is set in a
15th-century building.
www.centre-of-britain.org.uk

EATING OUT
Treat Yourself The Bouchon Bistrot,
in Hexham, close to the Corbridge site,
serves up classy French-style dishes.
www.bouchonbistrot.co.uk

On a Budget The Rat Inn, at Anick,
between Corbridge and Hexham, is an
18th-century inn serving superior pub food
as well as sandwiches and bar snacks.
www.theratinn.com

PRICE FOR TWO PEOPLE
$300–320 a day for food, local
transportation, accommodations,
and admission fees.

WEBSITE
www.hadrians-wall.org

Roman Britain

The Romans' full-scale invasion of Britain began in
AD 43. Within 35 years they controlled everything
up to present-day Scotland. However, they could
not sustain their advance against the Pictish tribes
of Scotland and fell back to the River Tyne. Emperor
Hadrian ordered the building of the wall in AD 122,
as a way of consolidating this border of the Empire
at the time of his succession. It was manned until
AD 410, when the Romans abandoned Britain.

Main: Hadrian's Wall, looking east from Holbank Crags
Right (top to bottom): Housesteads Fort on Hadrian's Wall; hiking beside the wall

BORDER PATROL

I T WAS BUILT BY AN INVADING FORCE as a symbol of control and military might. Yet there's
something romantic about Hadrian's Wall, which curves so majestically through the rolling
hills of northern England. The Romans erected the wall early in the 2nd century, and for
nearly 300 years it marked the northern frontier of their empire. Some sections are no longer
visible, as much of the stone was recycled in churches and other local buildings over the
centuries. Enough remains, however, for its designation as a UNESCO World Heritage Site.

The 84-mile (135-km) Hadrian's Wall Path National Trail follows the historic line of
the wall. Starting in the east at Segedunum Roman Fort in Wallsend, it follows the river
in Tyneside, runs through pretty Tynedale farmland, and snakes up and down the stark,
windswept fells of Northumberland. The wall reaches its highest point of 1,130 ft (345 m) at
Whinshields Crags, before descending gently through the fertile pastures of Cumbria on its
way to the saltmarsh estuary of the Solway Firth. The central sections of the wall within
Northumberland National Park are some of the best-preserved and they cut through dramatic

FURTHER DETAILS

ROMAN SITES ALONG HADRIAN'S WALL

Segedunum Roman Fort
Buddle Street, Wallsend. Interactive computer displays, excavated finds, a reconstructed bathhouse and more paint a picture of Roman life as it played out here at the wall's eastern end. There are splendid views over the ruins from the watchtower; open Apr–Oct: 10am–5pm daily; Nov–Mar: 10am–3pm daily.
www.twmuseums.org.uk/segedunum

Chesters Roman Fort
Chollerford, Humshaugh, Hexham. This cavalry fort, in a lovely riverside setting, was one of the first along the wall. It has well-preserved gateways and foundations, and a military bathhouse. Its museum displays important archaeological discoveries; open Apr–Sep: 10am–6pm daily; Oct–Mar: 10am–4pm daily.
www.english-heritage.org.uk

Vindolanda
Bardon Mill, Hexham. Some of the finest and most unusual Roman artifacts were found at this settlement and are on display in the excellent museum here. They include jewelry, shoes and even letters written on wooden tablets. A temple and other buildings are reconstructed in the garden, and you can watch ongoing excavations; open Apr–Sep: 10am–6pm daily; Oct–mid-Nov and Feb–Mar: 10am–5pm daily (closed mid-Nov–Jan).
www.vindolanda.com

Housesteads Roman Fort and Museum
Bardon Mill, Hexham. Many features have been excavated at Britain's best-preserved Roman fort, including double portal gateways, turrets, a hospital, and even latrines. The museum contains a model of how the site looked in its entirety; open Apr–Sep: 10am–6pm daily; Oct–Mar: 10am–4pm daily.
www.english-heritage.org.uk

Corbridge Roman Site and Museum
Corchester Lane, Corbridge. The remains of this bustling garrison town include barracks, temples, granaries, and a fountain house with an aqueduct. The museum displays the broad range of Roman artifacts found here; open Apr–Sep: 10am–5:30pm daily; Oct–Mar: 10am–4pm daily.
www.english-heritage.org.uk

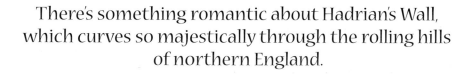

Below: Bathhouse complex at Chesters Roman Fort

There's something romantic about Hadrian's Wall, which curves so majestically through the rolling hills of northern England.

scenery little changed since Roman times. It takes between four and seven days to walk the entire length of this ancient fortification, but there are more than 80 shorter paths and circular routes on either side. There's also a cycle trail that runs the length of the wall.

Whichever route you choose, picture the wall as it was in Roman times: 16 ft (5 m) high, with a deep ditch bordering the south side, and whitewashed to make it stand out against the landscape and intimidate the Scottish tribes. Some 15,000 soldiers were stationed along its length. There was a watchtower roughly every 550 yards (500 meters), a "milecastle" and gate every Roman mile of 1,000 paces (just over 1,600 yards/1.5 km), and a fort every 7 miles (11 km) or so. Archaeological sites such as Chesters Roman Fort, Vindolanda, Housesteads Fort, and the Corbridge Roman Site still remain, giving you a glimpse of life in this distant and most heavily fortified frontier of the Empire.

THE ESSENTIALS

GETTING THERE AND AROUND
Brighton is on England's southeastern coast, 53 miles (85 km) from London. The nearest airport is London Gatwick, 30 miles (48 km) north of Brighton. Fast trains run regularly to Brighton from central London and from Gatwick, with a journey time of less than an hour. Brighton town center is easily navigable by foot.

WEATHER
Brighton enjoys a mild maritime climate, with average daytime temperatures of 45–57°F (7–14°C) in spring.

ACCOMMODATIONS
Treat Yourself Drakes, on Marine Parade, is a very comfortable, 4-star boutique town house on the seafront that describes its ambience as "laid-back glamour."
www.drakesofbrighton.com

On a Budget Gulliver's, on New Steine, is a centrally-located B&B in an elegant and charming Georgian town house close to the sea.
www.gullivershotel.com

EATING OUT
Treat Yourself Pub du Vin, on Ship Street, offers "gastropub" lunches and suppers, all sourced from local ingredients, in a former arts center.
www.hotelduvin.com/pubduvin/brighton

On a Budget Bardsleys, on Baker Street near the train station, serves up perhaps the best fish and chips in town in a restaurant that has been owned by the same family for four generations.
www.bardsleys-fishandchips.co.uk

PRICE FOR TWO PEOPLE
From $250 a day for food, accommodations, and entertainment.

WEBSITES
www.visitbrighton.com
www.realbrighton.com

Brighton Festival and Fringe

Running for the month of May, the Brighton Festival adds an extra layer of fun and *joie de vivre* to a city that already has both in spades. The festival packs in attractions as diverse as sculpture displays in artists' own gardens, a *spiegeltent* (mirrored tent), The Ladyboys of Bangkok, literary debates, and ballet displays. With a wide program of family-friendly activities and performances from big names, too, the festival and its fringe have built up a UK reputation second only to Edinburgh's.

BRIGHTON ROCKS!

CHERRY-PICKING MANY OF THE BEST features of the English capital and relocating them to the beach, the city of Brighton has earned itself the nickname "London-by-Sea." Attracting the most fashionable of visitors and residents, Brighton combines urban chic with flip-flops and salty air and, like London, is composed of many individual districts, each with its own unique vibe. Exploring the city, you could be in Amsterdam one minute, Greenwich Village the next; yet it's important to draw no such comparisons, for Brighton's personality is all its own.

Once a fishing port and small market town, Brighton's fortunes were transformed in the late 18th century, when the fashion for curative bathing in sea water took hold among the gentry. The patronage of the Prince Regent, who first visited Brighton in 1783, sealed the town's aristocratic credentials. Brighton's regal side can be seen today in its early 19th-century Regency architecture, and in the Royal Pavilion, an extravagant Asian-style royal palace.

The town has evolved from a royal summer resort to the year-round home of famous artists, musicians, and bright young creative things escaping the oppression of London

Main: Brighton's renowned Pier at sunset

Left (left to right): Regency townhouses in Brighton; the town's shingle beach

Right: Shopping in the Lanes

FURTHER DETAILS

BRIGHTON'S SIGHTS
The Royal Pavilion
This former palace, remodeled by John Nash from 1815 to 1823, contains Queen Victoria's apartments and lavish music and banqueting rooms. The gardens have recently been restored and replanted according to Nash's original vision; open Oct–Mar: 10am–5:15pm; Apr–Sep: 9:30am–5:45pm.
www.royalpavilion.org.uk

Brighton Festival
www.brightonfestival.org

The Lanes and North Laine
www.uniquebrighton.co.uk
www.northlaine.co.uk

Brighton Pier
Madeira Drive, Brighton. Iconic Victorian pleasure pier now packed with funfair-style attractions; open 10am–midnight daily; individual attractions close at varying times.
www.brightonpier.co.uk

WHAT ELSE TO SEE AND DO
Brighton Marina Village
The slick Marina Village development on the eastern edge of the town provides mooring for more than 1,500 boats and yachts as well as plenty of entertainment. Street performers, a boardwalk, shops, cafés and restaurants, a movie theater, and a casino and bowling complex draw plenty of visitors, many of whom make the short trip from Brighton on Volk's Electric Railway, the world's oldest operating electric railroad.
Marina Village: *www.brightonmarina.co.uk*
Marina shopping: *www.brightonmarinashopping.co.uk*
Volk's Electric Railway: *www.volkselectricrailway.co.uk*

The South Downs
A designated National Park and an Area of Outstanding Natural Beauty, the South Downs' chalk hills and clifftop paths stretch through Sussex into Hampshire. It's a short car trip to these superb walks and beautiful views; alternatively, you can take special "Breeze up to the Downs" buses from central Brighton.
www.visitsouthdowns.com

Charleston Farmhouse
Approximately 30 minutes' drive east of Brighton, beyond Lewes, this country residence was the meeting place of famed literary set the Bloomsbury Group in the early 20th century. There are tours of the house and grounds, and a busy events and workshop calendar.
www.charleston.org.uk

Below: The Royal Pavilion, inspired in part by the Taj Mahal

Exploring the city, you could be in Amsterdam one minute, Greenwich Village the next; yet it's important to draw no such comparisons, for Brighton's personality is all its own.

without leaving it far behind; a high-speed train connects the two cities in under an hour. The city's cultural scene punches well above its weight, most notably during the annual Brighton Arts Festival, a glossy celebration of traditional and fringe music, theater, literature, and art. Brighton is also home to a thriving gay scene and is famous for its relaxed atmosphere.

There is much in the way of retail therapy, too, much of it in the quirky independent specialty boutiques of The Lanes. Lose yourself in this maze of small shops and find retro gems and one-of-a-kind jewelry, or browse the antiques and flea market in the bohemian district of North Laine. To relax, take a stroll through arty Kemp Town "village", with its lively squares and cafés, and indulge in some people-watching. For traditionalists, the quintessential British seaside must-haves are certainly all in place: arcades and fairground rides on the Palace Pier, a huge shingle beach, and, most famously, sticks of delicious Brighton Rock.

THE ESSENTIALS

GETTING THERE AND AROUND
The Welsh Narrow-gauge Railways are concentrated in northwest Wales. The area is approximately 4 hours' drive from London. There are three main starting points for the narrow-gauge trains: Porthmadog, Caenarfon and Llanberis. Mainline rail services along the north Wales coast call at Porthmadog. The Sherpa bus service connects Porthmadog to Caenarfon and Llanberis, and runs buses to all the most popular tourist points in Snowdonia.

WEATHER
Spring is generally mild but windy, with rain showers. Daytime temperatures vary from 45 to 59°F (7–15°C) in the valleys and on the coast, and from 32 to 52°F (0–11°C) on Snowdon's summit.

ACCOMMODATIONS
Treat Yourself Tan-yr-Allt, just outside Porthmadog, was once the home of the Romantic poet Shelley.
www.tanyrallt.co.uk

On a Budget Lake View, in Llanberis, within the Snowdonia National Park, is a friendly family-owned hotel with lake views and good locally sourced food.
www.lakeviewhotel.co.uk

EATING OUT
Treat Yourself Bistro Moelwyn in Blaenau Ffestiniog is an excellent restaurant with views over the mountains and organic food.
www.bistromoelwyn.co.uk

On a Budget Russell Tea Room, in Porthmadog Station, is a classic old station café with mugs of tea and filling meals.
www.russelltearoom.co.uk

PRICE FOR A FAMILY OF FOUR
From $430 for accommodations, food, and train tickets.

WEBSITE
www.visitwales.com

National Slate Museum

The National Slate Museum at Dinorwig Quarry near Llanberis may not immediately fire the imagination, but this well-presented, award-winning attraction is quite a surprise – and since it's also based at the terminus of the Llanberis Lake Railway, built to transport the slate quarried here, you can arrive by steam train. Features of the museum include renovated buildings and workshops, and a row of reconstructed quarrymen's houses, furnished to illustrate three different eras.

FULL STEAM AHEAD

WALES HAS MORE THAN ITS FAIR SHARE of narrow-gauge steam railroads, especially in the northern region, around Snowdonia. These steam engines were used to transport slate from the area's world-famous slate quarries to the coast, for shipping around the British Empire during the 19th and early 20th centuries. No longer used for their original purpose, many have been renovated by enthusiasts and now offer short but evocative journeys through glorious countryside. All the trains travel at a delightfully modest speed, so you can gently soak up the wonderful views. In fact, by using Snowdonia's "Sherpa" bus services to plug the gaps, it's possible to travel from the sea to the summit of Mount Snowdon by steam train.

The Ffestiniog Railway heads east, climbing straight into the heart of Snowdonia, through glorious oakwoods and past magnificent lakes.

From Caernarfon on the Welsh coast you can take a Welsh Highland Railway train through stunning scenery to Pitt's Head, a starting point for a trek to the top of Snowdon, or travel on to Beddgelert before looping around, via a dramatic plunge through a hillside tunnel, for the return trip. Or disembark at Beddgelert and take the bus to nearby Llanberis, the starting point for two magical steam-train rides: one around tranquil twin lakes and through the Padarn Country Park, with great views of the peaks; the other chugging its way up the slopes of Snowdon itself to Hafod Eryri – the summit's new visitor center (see also pp62–3).

Buses connect Caernarfon with Porthmadog, farther up the coast, where there are another two trips to savor. From Porthmadog's Harbour Station the Ffestiniog Railway heads east, climbing straight into the heart of Snowdonia, through glorious oak woods and past magnificent lakes and waterfalls, clinging to the sides of the mountains or even tunneling through them, and up to Blaenau Ffestiniog station, at the head of the valley. The Welsh Highland Heritage Railway is a loop of line only 1-mile (1.6-km) long, starting and finishing at Porthmadog, but the stop at its engine sheds en route is a must for enthusiasts young and old. The line offers visitors over 18 the opportunity to drive a steam engine called "Gelert" – an experience likened to driving a car using bathtub faucets. While younger visitors may be disappointed at missing out, they can still clamber into the locomotive cabs in the engine sheds and learn how it all works. Each train has a wheelchair-accessible, stroller-friendly car, so this really can be a day out for the whole family.

Main: Welsh Highland Railway train **Inset:** Blaenau Ffestiniog Station
Below: Snowdon Mountain Railway train climbing the last section of rail before the summit

FURTHER DETAILS

WELSH NARROW-GAUGE RAILROADS
Great Little Trains of Wales
Ten of Wales's best steam railroads are grouped together under the Great Little Trains of Wales banner, with a website detailing all the routes. Each train line has its own schedules and prices, but you can buy a Great Little Trains Discount Card, which is valid for one year and gives you a 20 percent discount on all the trains. Many of the trains connect with mainline stations and bus services. Note that the steam-train services are less frequent in winter and may run on weekends only.
www.greatlittletrainsofwales.co.uk

Sherpa Buses
The Sherpa bus network covers the Snowdonia National Park, connecting Porthmadog, Caernarfon, Llanberis, and Betws-y-Coed. Winter services are reduced, but at Easter the summer schedule, with more frequent services, comes into operation.
www.visitcaernarfon.com/sherpa

National Slate Museum
Llanberis; open Easter–Oct: 10am–5pm daily; Nov–Easter: 10am–4pm Sun–Fri.
www.museumwales.ac.uk/en/slate

WHAT ELSE TO SEE AND DO
Caernarfon Castle
North Wales is home to some of the finest medieval castles in the world, and this is possibly the most impressive fortress in the British Isles.
www.caernarfon.com

Below (top to bottom): Snowdon Mountain Railway train pushing its single car up Snowdon; Ffestiniog Railway steam train

GREEN PARTY

ST. PATRICK'S DAY IS CELEBRATED AROUND THE WORLD, by Irish communities as far away as Australia, the US, and Tokyo. March 17 is an excuse for anyone with a drop of Irish blood – real or honorary – to don a shamrock, let down their dyed-green hair, and parade through the streets in the colors of the Emerald Isle. Nowhere is it celebrated more enthusiastically than in Ireland itself, where the liveliest celebration of its national holiday takes place in the capital, Dublin.

A week-long festival of culture and the *craic* – the Irish term for fun and entertainment – makes this party-loving city the place to be in springtime.

A week-long festival of culture and the *craic* – the Irish term for fun and entertainment – makes this party-loving city the place to be in springtime. It culminates with a grand parade on St. Patrick's Day that begins at noon in Parnell Square and wends its merry way through the downtown to St. Patrick's Cathedral. More than half a million people line the streets to watch the spectacle. Extravagant floats and pageants illustrate the theme of each year's parade, accompanied by marching bands. Colorfully costumed characters create a carnival atmosphere with dancing, singing, and acrobatic routines. Actors also portray St. Patrick himself, complete with flowing beard, staff, and shamrock. The parade passes by some of Dublin's most famous landmarks. It heads down O'Connell Street past the General Post Office, where the Republic of Ireland was proclaimed in 1916, and the Spire of Dublin, the city's millennium monument. After crossing the O'Connell Bridge, the procession turns west at the gates of Trinity College and heads along Dame Street, passing the stately Dublin Castle. At Christ Church Cathedral, Dublin's oldest building, it turns south toward St. Patrick's Cathedral – Ireland's largest church.

In the days leading up to the parade, the St. Patrick's Festival stages a range of events that celebrate Irish culture. There are music concerts and art exhibitions; numerous theater, film, comedy, and modern-dance performances; *céilí* – traditional Irish dancing; and family activities from funfairs to treasure hunts. Street performers from around the country fill Dublin's Georgian-era squares with free music and entertainment. When the festival comes to a close in a blaze of fireworks, you can't help thinking that old St. Patrick himself would approve.

Main: St. Patrick's Day Parade, O'Connell Street **Inset:** Party-goers decorated with shamrocks and wearing festive hats
Below: Revelers crowding the streets of Dublin during the parade

THE ESSENTIALS

GETTING THERE AND AROUND
Dublin is located halfway down the east coast of Ireland, and has its own international airport, 7 miles (11 km) north of the city. Driving in the city can be slow going, and most of the main sights can be easily reached on foot or by bus, or by using the excellent DART (Dublin Area Rapid Transit) train service.

WEATHER
Ireland is known for experiencing four seasons in one day, and that undoubtedly applies as much to Dublin as anywhere else. Average spring daytime temperatures range from 43 to 50°F (6–10°C).

ACCOMMODATIONS
Treat Yourself Dylan, in Eastmoreland Place, is a 5-star boutique hotel that offers the ultimate in comfortable accommodations.
www.dylan.ie

On a Budget The Charles Stewart, in Parnell Square, is a modest but cozy, centrally located bed and breakfast.
www.charlesstewart.ie

EATING OUT
Treat Yourself Patrick Guilbaud, on Upper Merrion Street, has 2 Michelin stars and serves extravagant modern cuisine prepared from Irish ingredients.
www.restaurantpatrickguilbaud.ie

On a Budget The Gotham Café, on St. Anne Street, is one of the city's most popular and atmospheric eating places, with great *craic* and great food.
www.gothamcafe.ie

PRICE FOR TWO PEOPLE
From $330 a day for accommodations, food, admission fees, and a pint or two of Guinness.

WEBSITE
www.visitdublin.com

Wearing of the Green

It may seem strange, but the tradition of celebrating St. Patrick's Day with raucous drinking and lively parades did not start in Ireland. In 1762 a small group of Irish New Yorkers marched to a Mount Pleasant inn to celebrate the feast day, thereby starting a growing tradition. Dublin held its first parade in 1931, but the pubs remained closed on March 17 until the mid-1990s, when the Irish government decided to relax its licensing laws and promote the day as a showcase for Irish culture.

FURTHER DETAILS

DUBLIN
St. Patrick's Day Festival
www.stpatricksfestival.ie

St. Patrick's Cathedral
Patrick's Close. St. Patrick was said to have baptized early Christians at this spot in the 5th century. The present cathedral was built on the site in 1191 and is the largest in the country; open Mar–Oct: 9am–5:30pm daily; Nov–Feb: 9am–5pm Mon–Sat, 9am–3pm Sun.
www.stpatrickscathedral.ie

Trinity College Library
College Street. Set within the lovely Trinity College campus, the college's old library is home to the Book of Kells, a beautiful medieval manuscript illustrated by 9th-century monks on the Scottish island of Iona; open 9:30am–5pm Mon–Sat, noon–4:30pm Sun (May–Sep: 9:30am–4:30pm Sun).
www.tcd.ie/library

Dublin Castle
Dame Street. Located at a strategic site in use since Viking times, the 13th-century castle was built by the invading Normans and remained the seat of English rule until 1922. Tours include the ornate State Apartments, the Chapel Royal, and the Undercroft; open 10am–4:45pm Mon–Fri, 2–4:45pm Sat–Sun.
www.dublincastle.ie

Christ Church Cathedral
Christchurch Place. The cathedral was founded by the Vikings in 1038, and rebuilt in stone by the Anglo–Norman warrior Richard de Clare – known as "Strongbow" – in 1169; open Sep–May: 9:45am–4:15pm Mon–Sat, 12:30–2:30pm Sun; Jun–mid-Jul: 9:45am–6:15pm Mon, Tue & Fri, 9:45am–4:15pm Wed, Thu & Sat, 12:30am–2:30pm and 4:30–6:15pm Sun; mid-Jul–Aug: 9:45am–6:15pm Mon–Fri, 9:45am–4:15pm Sat, 12:30am–2:30pm Sun.
www.cccdub.ie

Below: Marching band in parade; fireworks over Dublin's waterfront

THE ESSENTIALS

GETTING THERE AND AROUND
The West Highland Way is in western Scotland. It runs for 95 miles (152 km), from Milngavie in the south to Fort William in the north. Trains and buses travel between Glasgow and Milngavie (train trip around 30 minutes). Fort William can be reached by bus from the north, east, and south, and by train from Glasgow (travel time around 3 hours).

WEATHER
Spring weather along the trail is extremely changeable. Be prepared for anything from bright sun to gusty winds and driving rain. Average spring daytime temperatures range from 32 to 60°F (0–15°C). Warm, waterproof clothing is essential.

ACCOMMODATIONS
Treat Yourself Inverlochy Castle, near Fort William, is an opulent country-house hotel in the heart of the Highlands.
www.inverlochycastle.com

On a Budget Crianlarich Youth Hostel, in Crianlarich, is midway along the route, and has modern facilities and family rooms.
www.syha.org.uk

EATING OUT
Treat Yourself Crannog, on Waterfront Town Pier in Fort William, offers superb seafood dishes including locally caught lobster, crab, and scallops.
www.crannog.net

On a Budget Ben Nevis Inn, in Achintee, just outside Fort William, is a cozy walkers' inn serving hearty pub meals.
www.ben-nevis-inn.co.uk

PRICE FOR TWO PEOPLE
Around $200 a day for accommodations, picnic lunch, and evening meal.

WEBSITES
www.visitscotland.com
www.west-highland-way.co.uk

Faerie Folk

In the remote and atmospheric mountains and valleys of the Highlands of Scotland, myths and legends abound. There are tales of dozens of fantastical creatures that purportedly haunt the glens, forests, lakes, and rivers. The bestiary of mythical creatures includes brownies – invisible fairies who perform good deeds; evil water spirits called kelpies that take the form of horses; and the *Ghillie Dhu* – a shy elf who is kind to children and dresses in clothes made from moss and leaves.

Main: Dramatic Rannoch Moor on the West Highland Way

HIGHLAND HIKING

ONE OF THE GREAT JOYS OF SCOTLAND is the ease with which you can leave behind city life and plunge into wild open country. The West Highland Way is the perfect way to do this. Its southern end wends its way through the genteel suburbs of Glasgow and the rolling hills near Loch Lomond before traveling on over wild heather moors and through bleak but beautiful glens to the foot of Ben Nevis at Fort William. It's a challenging – but not too challenging – venture. Determined long-distance hikers can aim to complete its 95-mile (152-km) length in one assault of around a week, but the route can also be broken down into a series of sections that any reasonably fit walker can complete in a day's energetic stroll. It is well worth the effort; no other long-distance walk in Britain offers such stunning contrasts and beautiful scenery.

Most walkers set off from the quiet commuter village of Milngavie, where a granite obelisk on Douglas Street marks the southern end of the Way. There is a good reason for this: the gentle first section of the walk, skirting Loch Lomond's tranquil shores, lets you stretch your legs and warm up your walking muscles for the more demanding northern sections of the Way.

FURTHER DETAILS

WEST HIGHLAND WAY
There are two major tourist offices that cover the route of the West Highland Way, providing visitor information.
Southern sections (Milngavie–Bridge of Orchy):
www.visitscottishheartlands.com
Northern sections (Inveroran–Fort William):
www.visithighlands.com

Mountain Biking
It is possible to cycle along the Way, although you have to carry a bicycle over fences and any rough terrain. Certain sections are signposted as prohibited to bicycles, but these predate a change to the Scottish Outdoor Access Code in 2005, which now allows cycling.

Rob Roy's Cave
About 1 mile (1.5 km) northwest of Inversnaid, on the eastern shore of Loch Lomond, on the Inversnaid to Inverarnan section of the Way.
www.west-highland-way.co.uk

St. Fillan's Chapel
About 1 mile (1.5 km) from Tyndrum, on the Crianlarich to Tyndrum section of the Way.
www.west-highland-way.co.uk

WHAT ELSE TO SEE AND DO
Glengoyne Distillery
To reward yourself for a day's hard walking, pick up a bottle of fine malt whiskey at this pretty distillery near Strathblane, close to the start of the Way.
www.glengoyne.com

Ben Nevis
Britain's highest peak is close to the northern end of the Way. The ascent of the mountain begins around 2 miles (3 km) east of Fort William. Osprey Adventures, based in Inverness, offers guided trips to the summit.
Osprey Adventures: *www.osprey-adventures.com*

Below (top to bottom): Cyclists on the Devil's Staircase; Inverlochy Castle and Ben Nevis viewed from the West Highland Way

On the long day's walk across the wild peatlands of Rannoch Moor you may, with a little luck, see red deer grazing and golden eagles soaring.

The route is studded with landmarks from history and legend. Before leaving the shores of Loch Lomond, it passes "Rob Roy's Cave" – a crevice in the rock that was one of the legendary outlaw's many hideouts. Between Crianlarich and Tyndrum, the ruined shell of St. Fillan's Chapel is all that remains of a church endowed by Robert the Bruce in the 14th century.

But it is natural splendor, not human history, that makes the West Highland Way special. On the long day's walk across the wild peatlands of Rannoch Moor you may, with a little luck, see red deer grazing and golden eagles soaring, making it one of the few great adventures left in Britain. This deceptively easy hike, in the last third of the trip, covers a vast expanse of heather moor and peat bog. It calls for excellent trail skills if the weather closes in, as it can do at any time. The climax of the Way, stretching over the route's highest point – the 1,850-ft- (550-m-) high, aptly named "Devil's Staircase" – through the Lairigmor pass and on to Fort William by the sea, is breathtaking in every sense of the word.

THE ESSENTIALS

GETTING THERE AND AROUND
The British capital is served by five major airports; the largest two being Heathrow and Gatwick, 30 minutes by train to the west and south respectively. Northward, Stansted and Luton airports are farther out but still well connected by public transportation. London City Airport, in east London, serves the city's financial district. Once in London, the best way around is via the extensive Underground network or iconic red buses, although a London black cab should be experienced at least once.

WEATHER
Pack layers; shorts and T-shirts could be useful, but so could windbreakers, fleeces, and umbrellas. Spring daytime temperatures range from 42 to 60°F (6–14°C).

ACCOMMODATIONS
Treat Yourself Hotel 41, on Buckingham Palace Road, is a meticulously managed and excellently located boutique hotel.
www.41hotel.com

On a Budget EasyHotels have four no-frills properties (in Earls Court, Victoria, Paddington and South Kensington) in the center of London.
www.easyhotel.com

EATING OUT
Treat Yourself Gordon Ramsay at Claridge's, in Mayfair, offers fine gourmet dining.
www.gordonramsay.com/claridges

On a Budget Princi, in Wardour Street, Soho, offers delicious Italian food in a friendly atmosphere.
www.princi.co.uk

PRICE FOR TWO PEOPLE
$330–500 a day including food, accommodations, transportation, and admission fees.

WEBSITE
www.visitlondon.com

Bloomin' Hard Work

According to the proverb, April is showery and May flowery; but which came first, the folklore or the Chelsea Flower Show? May is indeed a flower-filled month in London, culminating in the amazing flower-fest that is the Royal Horticultural Society's annual five-day show at the Royal Hospital, Chelsea. Attracting over 150,000 visitors, this expo is the horticultural equivalent of a big-name fashion-show catwalk. It features around 20 exhibition gardens and launches horticultural trends.

LONDON CALLING

L ONDON – WHATEVER THE SEASON – IS A PHENOMENON. This vibrant, invigorating, and ardently cosmopolitan metropolis is among the world's truly great cities. Its historic architecture and vast, treasure-filled museums jostle for space with stylish Michelin-starred restaurants, world-class cultural events, effortlessly cool nightlife, and outstanding shopping. And when you need to slow down, its fresh green patchwork of public parkland brings the countryside to the heart of the capital. There are over 400 green spaces offering sanctuary in the city, from the spacious Royal Parks, such as Hyde Park and Green Park – havens from the bustling streets and perfect spots for a picnic – to botanical wonders such as Kew Gardens.

The capital celebrates spring with its biggest gardening festival – the Chelsea Flower Show – which bursts into bloom over five days in late May, astonishing visitors with its beautifully assembled show gardens. The London Marathon is another seasonal high point, when more than 35,000 runners – from professional athletes to fundraising amateurs and celebrities – are cheered on by thousands of spectators lining the route from Blackheath to The Mall. As the evenings draw out, even the arts events spill outside – Regent's Park's program of alfresco plays provides an unforgettable alternative to West End shows or Shakespeare at The Globe.

One way to appreciate just how much there is to see is to take a spin on the South Bank's London Eye and check off iconic views, from the Houses of Parliament, Big Ben, and the dome of St. Paul's Cathedral to Canary Wharf's skyscrapers and the bullet-shaped "Gherkin" building. You'll quickly realize that you need to plan a strategy to get the most out of London, a city that truly has something for everyone. Whether you're interested in art, science, music, finance, technology, or fashion, you can explore them here from their beginning to their projected future. From the Natural History and Victoria and Albert Museums to Tate Modern, a classy cocktail bar to a cozy Soho pub, and from Harrods department store to Topshop, London embraces life in all its forms and glory, and invites you to join in.

> This vibrant, invigorating, and ardently cosmopolitan metropolis is among the world's truly great cities.

Main: Houses of Parliament and the London Eye **Inset:** Millennium Bridge across the Thames
Below (left to right): Theaters on Shaftesbury Avenue in London's West End; Natural History Museum in South Kensington

FURTHER DETAILS

LONDON
The Royal Parks
www.royalparks.org.uk

Royal Botanic Gardens, Kew
Nearest Tube station: Kew Gardens; open
9:30am–6:30pm Mon–Fri; 9:30am–7:30pm Sat–Sun.
www.kew.org

The RHS Chelsea Flower Show
Nearest Tube station: Sloane Square; May.
www.rhs.org.uk/WhatsOn/Events

The London Marathon
Route runs from Blackheath to the Mall; April.
www.virginlondonmarathon.com

Regent's Park Open Air Theatre
Nearest Tube station: Baker Street.
www.openairtheatre.org

The Globe Theatre
Nearest Tube stations: Mansion House, London Bridge.
www.shakespeares-globe.org

London Eye
Nearest Tube stations: Waterloo, Embankment, Charing
Cross, Westminster; open Oct–Apr: 10am–8pm daily;
May–Jun and Sep: 10am–9pm daily; Jul–Aug:
10am–9:30pm daily.
www.londoneye.com

St. Paul's Cathedral
Nearest Tube stations: St. Pauls, Mansion House,
Cannon Street; open 8:30am–4pm Mon–Sat.
www.stpauls.co.uk

Natural History Museum
Nearest Tube station: South Kensington;
open 10am–5:50pm daily.
www.nhm.ac.uk

Victoria & Albert Museum
Nearest Tube station: South Kensington; open
10am–5:45pm Sat–Thu; 10am–10pm Fri.
www.vam.ac.uk

Tate Modern
Nearest Tube stations: Southwark, Mansion House, St. Paul's;
open 10am–6pm Sun–Thu; 10am–10pm Fri–Sat.
www.tate.org.uk/modern

Harrods
87–135 Brompton Road, Knightsbridge; open
10am–8pm Mon–Sat, 11:30am–6pm Sun.
www.harrods.com

Below: Spring daffodils in Green Park

THE ESSENTIALS

GETTING THERE AND AROUND
The Lake District is in northwestern England, to the south of the Scottish border. Manchester Airport and Newcastle International Airport are 97 miles (156 km) and 96 miles (154 km) respectively from Grasmere. The best way to explore the Lake District is by car, but there are good bus services between the major towns.

WEATHER
The Lake District is the wettest part of England, so be prepared for rain and hill fog at any time. Average spring daytime temperatures are 43–50ºF (6–10ºC).

ACCOMMODATIONS
Treat Yourself The Miller Howe Hotel, 8 miles (13 km) southeast of Grasmere by Windermere, is one of England's best country-house hotels.
www.millerhowe.com

On a Budget The How Foot Lodge Country Guest House, built in 1843, is a few seconds' stroll from Dove Cottage.
www.howfoot.co.uk

EATING OUT
Treat Yourself The restaurant at the Holbeck Ghyll Country House Hotel, a few minutes' drive from Grasmere, has a Michelin star and is not to be missed.
www.holbeckghyll.com

On a Budget The Jumble Room, in Grasmere, is an informal restaurant that serves top-quality food, and is rated by several food guides.
www.grasmererestaurants.co.uk

PRICE FOR A FAMILY OF FOUR
Around $330 a day for accommodations, food, and admission fees.

WEBSITE
www.golakes.co.uk

What's in a Name?

Only one of the lakes in the Lake District actually has the word "lake" in its name: Bassenthwaite Lake. You will hear many others referred to as lakes, especially "Lake Windermere," but this is incorrect; its proper name is simply Windermere. The word "mere" means a lake that is large but not very deep, so the word "lake" for places like Grasmere is redundant. All the other lakes use the word "water" to describe them, such as Derwent Water (which is also written as Derwentwater).

Main: Daffodils covering the shore of Ullswater
Right (top to bottom): Dove Cottage, home of William Wordsworth; Grasmere; red squirrel

GOLDEN DAFFODILS

IN THE SPRING OF 1802, WILLIAM WORDSWORTH and his sister Dorothy went for a walk at Gowbarrow Park, by the shore of Ullswater in the Lake District. They saw whole hillsides covered in bright yellow daffodils, and two years later Wordsworth published "I Wandered Lonely as a Cloud" – recently voted Britain's best-loved poem – immortalizing those "... golden daffodils; beside the lake, beneath the trees...". More than 200 years later, those hillsides are just as thickly swathed in daffodils in spring. It may be the vast, still beauty of the lakes and the dramatic grandeur of the mountains that attracts most people to the Lake District, but Wordsworth and other Lakeland writers also saw joy in nature's finer details.

When Wordsworth wrote his famous poem, he and Dorothy were living at Dove Cottage in the picturesque village of Grasmere – described by the poet as "the loveliest spot that man hath ever found." The cottage is open to visitors today, and remains much as it was when they called it home, from 1799 to 1808. To follow in Wordsworth's footsteps and discover Lakeland's daffodils, walk along the western side of Ullswater around Wordsworth Point. If you're lucky,

FURTHER DETAILS

EXPLORING WORDSWORTH'S LAKELAND
Much of the land around Ullswater and Grasmere is owned by the National Trust, and so can be enjoyed by everyone. The National Trust and local Tourist Information Centres sell leaflets and books that include information on Wordsworth and literary Lakeland walks.
www.nationaltrust.org.uk

Dove Cottage
Grasmere; open 9:30am–5:30pm daily (last admission 5pm).
www.wordsworth.org.uk

Wordsworth Point
This can be reached from the Glencoyne Bay National Trust parking lot on the A592 between Glenridding and Watermillock, 1 mile (1.6 km) north of Glenridding.
www.nationaltrust.org.uk

Aira Force Waterfall
There is a 1-mile (1.6-km) circular walk to the waterfall from the National Trust parking lot on the A592 between Glenridding and Watermillock, 330 ft (100 m) after the junction with the A5091 to Matterdale End and Troutbeck.
www.nationaltrust.org.uk

Hill Top Farm
Near Sawrey, Hawkshead, Ambleside; open mid-Feb–mid-Mar: 11am–3:30pm Sat–Thu; mid-Mar–Dec: 10:30am–4:30pm Sat–Thu.
www.nationaltrust.org.uk

Beatrix Potter Gallery
Main Street, Hawkshead; open mid-Feb–mid-Mar: 11am–3:30pm Sat–Thu; mid-Mar–Dec: 10:30am–4:30pm Sat–Thu.
www.nationaltrust.org.uk

WHAT ELSE TO SEE AND DO
Ullswater Lake Cruises
Ullswater Steamers run lake cruises year-round between the shoreside villages of Glenridding, Howtown, and Pooley Bridge, giving stunning views of the lake and surrounding mountains from the water.
www.ullswater-steamers.co.uk

Cumberland Pencil Museum
This unusual museum in Keswick showcases the history of pencil-making in the Lake District; it has a 26-ft (8-m) pencil that was, until 2005, the world's longest.
www.pencilmuseum.co.uk

Below: Hill Top Farm, the home of Beatrix Potter

If you choose a quiet day of the week and a secluded spot, it is still possible to find, as Wordsworth did, a "bliss of solitude" among these soaring mountains and cool, glassy lakes.

you might also see a red squirrel scampering through the trees; this charming and now-rare animal still thrives in these woodlands. While exploring the southern end of the lake, don't miss the spectacular waterfall Aira Force, which crashes through steeply sloping woodland.

No family outing in the Lake District is complete without a visit to Hill Top Farm near Windermere – the former home of another of its famous residents, Beatrix Potter, whose love of this landscape inspired her to write *The Tale of Peter Rabbit* and other cherished children's stories. The farmhouse is now a museum exhibiting her personal belongings. You can see many of her original drawings at the Beatrix Potter Gallery in nearby Hawkshead.

It may be harder these days to wander lonely in the ever-popular Lake District, but if you choose a quiet day of the week and a secluded spot, it is still possible to find, as Wordsworth did, a "bliss of solitude" among these soaring mountains and cool, rippling lakes.

THE SOUND OF MUSIC

Most evenings, the evocative strains of fiddle and bodhrán (an Irish drum) drift from pubs around the ancient city of Cork. Ireland's second city grew initially from a 7th-century monastery on the south bank of the River Lee, and the city today stands on an island created by two channels of the river. Cork's rich Gaelic heritage makes it a lively centre for all types of Irish music, and in spring it celebrates the Cork International Choral Festival.

Founded in 1954, this five-day festival in May is one of the leading events of its kind in Europe, attracting many of the world's finest amateur choirs. But there's more to their spirited singing than sheer love of music – this is a competitive event, with the winners taking home

The big public events take place in City Hall, Cork's finest public building and one of the best acoustic venues in the country.

the coveted Fleischmann International Trophy. In addition to the international choirs, up to 100 Irish adult and youth choirs attend the concurrent national competitions. With around 5,000 participants overall, music fills the air in a great heralding of spring. The competitions and the Opening Gala Concerts, which feature professional musicians, are ticketed events. But outside the contests, you can see the choirs in a variety of free public performances and fringe concerts, and experience a sweeping range of vocal styles. You might head to the Church of St. Anne Shandon, home of the famed Shandon Bells, at sunrise, to hear the glorious sound of the dawn chorus sung from its tower in an ancient May Day rite. Later on, in the atrium of the Clarion Hotel, you might choose to relax and enjoy an informal taster of international choirs, after browsing (and eating) at the delicious Food Fair outside.

The big public events take place in City Hall, Cork's finest public building and one of the best acoustic venues in the country. The international competitors are especially innovative, as each choir must present an *a capella* (unaccompanied) program that includes work from past and present composers. The national competition for church music is held in the spectacular Gothic landmark of St. Fin Barre's Cathedral, dedicated to Cork's patron saint. The many and varied highlights of the festival provide a great way to appreciate this most musical of cities.

Main: Shandon Tower, Church of St. Anne Shandon **Inset:** Participants in the festival
Below: Cork City Hall, site of many of the performances during the Cork International Choral Festival

FURTHER DETAILS

CORK INTERNATIONAL CHORAL FESTIVAL
The festival is held over the five days leading up to the May Day Bank Holiday each year.
www.corkchoral.ie

Church of St. Anne Shandon
Church St., Cork; open Easter–Oct: 9:30am–5pm daily; Nov–Easter: 10am–3pm daily.
www.shandonbells.org

The Clarion Hotel
The hotel is right beside the River Lee on Lapps Quay.
www.clarionhotelcorkcity.com

City Hall
Anglesea St., Cork. Home to the city's administration, the concert hall here is also Cork's main venue for concerts and festivals; open 9am–5:30pm Mon–Sat.
www.corkcity.ie

St. Fin Barre's Cathedral
Bishop St., Cork; open summer: 9:30am–5:30pm Mon–Sat, 12:30–5pm Sun; winter: 10am–12.45pm and 2–5pm Mon–Sat, 2–5pm Sun.
http://cathedral.cork.anglican.org

The English Market
Access via Princes St., Oliver Plunkett St., or Grand Parade, Cork; open 9am–5:30pm Mon–Sat.
www.corkenglishmarket.ie

WHAT ELSE TO SEE AND DO
Blarney Castle
Whether you see kissing the Blarney Stone as a silly custom or a must-do, it's worth the short drive out of town to visit its fascinating home, Blarney Castle.
www.blarneycastle.ie

Cork City Gaol
This castle-like jail on Sunday's Well Road recreates its grim 19th-century conditions with wax figures.
www.corkcitygaol.com

Below: Aerial view of Blarney Castle

THE ESSENTIALS

GETTING THERE AND AROUND
The Isles of Scilly are 30 miles (48 km) off the coast of Cornwall. You can fly here year-round by light aircraft from Land's End, Newquay, Exeter, Bristol, and Southampton, or by helicopter from Penzance. The *Scillonian* ferry runs daily from Penzance (Apr–Oct only). There are no rental cars on the islands, and virtually no buses, but plenty of taxis on St. Mary's; otherwise it's all by boat or foot.

WEATHER
The islands are generally sunnier and milder than the mainland. Average daytime temperatures in spring are 50–60°F (10–15°C), but are often above 68°F (20°C).

ACCOMMODATIONS
Treat Yourself St. Martin's on the Isle, in St. Martins, is a luxurious hotel masquerading as a cluster of granite cottages, set right on the beach.
www.stmartinshotel.co.uk

On a Budget Isles of Scilly Country Guest House, on St Mary's, is 25 minutes' walk from Hugh Town. It is a family-friendly B&B with a relaxed atmosphere.
www.scillyguesthouse.co.uk

EATING OUT
Treat Yourself The Boat Shed, in Porthmellon, St. Mary's, is a classy restaurant converted from a gig shed right on the beach.
www.the-boatshed.co.uk

On a Budget Dibble and Grub, on Porthcressa Beach, St. Mary's, is a cheap and cheerful seaside café.
Tel: 08715 286032

PRICE FOR A FAMILY OF FOUR
Around $410–460 a day for accommodations and food.

WEBSITE
www.simplyscilly.co.uk

Dipping the Oar

The traditional Scillonian six-oared rowing gigs (boats) were developed in the late-18th century to race pilots out to incoming sailing ships, although they were also used as lifeboats and for smuggling. Today, more than 2,000 rowers from across the West Country and beyond join the locals for the World Pilot Gig Championships in early May each year, racing in gigs of all ages – some over a century old. You can watch the small armada take to the water from land or boat.

SUNNY ISLES

LYING FAR OUT IN THE ATLANTIC off the western tip of Cornwall, the gloriously subtropical, unpolluted, and unspoiled Isles of Scilly don't really feel like part of England at all. There are virtually no cars on the smaller off-islands and no one locks their front doors; there are endless empty and secluded beaches and wonderful walks, often close to unique and largely undisturbed prehistoric sites, such as Bant's Carn, a neolithic dolmen (burial chamber). Late spring is one of the best times to visit, just before the main season gets underway, when the famous winter daffodils are still in bud, the rock pools are warm enough for children to explore, and the islanders still have the time, and the inclination, to chat.

Scilly comes awake after the long winter at Easter; this is still a largely church-going community, and at dawn on Easter Day crowds gather at the Buzza windmill above the harbor on the main island of St Mary's to see the sun rise. The biggest event in the islands' calendar,

The real charm of Scilly lies in its simplicity – boating, walking, splashing around in sheltered coves, or just admiring the extraordinary seascape.

the World Pilot Gig Championships *(see story box)*, takes place a week or two later, when you can join dozens of tripper boats filled with spectators for a long weekend of wonderful traditional rowing races, followed by a huge bonfire on the beach.

The main pastime for vacationers is island-hopping. Each morning, tripper boats leave St. Mary's quay for expeditions to the smaller off-islands: Tresco, with its exotic Abbey Gardens; St. Martin's and its beachside Caribbean-style hotel, where cocktails can be sipped beneath stunning sunsets while children wade in the azure water; and St. Agnes, the most southwesterly place in England, with its spectacular views over the Bishop's Rock Lighthouse.

There are specialty boat trips for diving and snorkeling, and to observe hundreds of gray seals basking in the sunshine on the Eastern Isles, or the puffins that come to Scilly at this time of year to breed on the granite outcrops of the northern coast. The real charm of Scilly lies in its simplicity – boating, walking, splashing around in sheltered coves, or just admiring the extraordinary seascape and rare wildlife. There are no hills or tall buildings here, so it's one of the few places in Britain where you can see the sun rise and set from the same spot.

FURTHER DETAILS

THE ISLES OF SCILLY

Bant's Carn and Halangy Down
Bant's Carn dolmen and the ancient village of Halangy Down are on the northwest coast of St. Mary's, 1 mile (2 km) north of Hugh Town.
www.english-heritage.org.uk

Buzza
This former windmill can be found by footpath from the eastern end of Porthcressa Beach, St. Mary's.

The World Pilot Gig Championships
The Championships are held every year over the first Bank Holiday weekend in May.
www.worldgigs.co.uk

Island-hopping
Boats leave St. Mary's quay for the other islands Apr–Oct, 10:15am daily (30 minutes' travel time).
www.scillyboating.co.uk

Tresco Abbey Gardens
These gardens feature more than 20,000 exotic plants; open 10am–4pm daily.
www.tresco.co.uk

Sealife and Shipwreck Tours
Island Sea Safaris offer 1- and 2-hour boat trips to view sealife and wrecks off the coast of St. Mary's, as well as 45-minute excursions to view gig races.
www.islandseasafaris.co.uk

WHAT ELSE TO SEE AND DO

Minack Theatre
This wonderful open-air theater in Porthcurno, just outside Penzance in Cornwall, was built into the cliffs overlooking the sea, adding extra drama to its performances of Shakespeare and other classics.
www.minack.com

Porthcurno Telegraph Museum
This fascinating museum in Porthcurno gives the history of what was once the world's most important cable station, connected to more than 100,000 miles (160,000 km) of cable radiating out under the oceans in a global network.
www.porthcurno.org.uk

St. Michael's Mount
The dramatic hilltop home of the St. Aubyn family in Marazion, Cornwall, is modeled on the monastery of Mont-Saint-Michel in Normandy on the coast of northern France. It is run by the National Trust and is accessible on foot at low tide.
www.stmichaelsmount.co.uk

Main: Aerial view of St. Martin's, Isles of Scilly

Left (top to bottom): World Pilot Gig Championships at Hugh Town in St. Mary's; Bishop's Rock Lighthouse

Above: Gray seal bull

Below: Tresco Abbey Gardens

Below: Vacationers on the beach at Tresco

THE ESSENTIALS

GETTING THERE AND AROUND
Oxford is in the area known as "the Heart of England," 55 miles (88 km) northwest of London (1–2 hours by car). The closest airport is London Heathrow (45 miles/ 72 km away). Trains run regularly from London Paddington (travel time 1 hour). Once there, you can explore the central city by bike or on foot, although a car is useful for visiting the surrounding countryside.

WEATHER
Oxford's weather in spring is variable; with luck you'll have bright skies and warm days, but be prepared for four seasons in one day. Average daytime temperatures range between 42 and 54°F (6–12°C).

ACCOMMODATIONS
Treat Yourself Malmaison, in Oxford Castle, is based in a converted prison, and now caters for a more discerning clientele. *www.malmaison.com*

On a Budget Keble, Queen's, University, Exeter and Trinity colleges offer fully refurbished student rooms during the university vacations. *www.universityrooms.co.uk*

EATING OUT
Treat Yourself The Cherwell Boathouse, on Bardwell Road, offers atmospheric riverside dining. *www.cherwellboathouse.co.uk*

On a Budget Pizza Mamma Mia, on South Parade, offers relaxed Italian food at great prices. *www.branca-restaurants.com*

PRICE FOR TWO PEOPLE
From $330 a day for food, accommodations, and admission fees.

WEBSITE
www.visitoxford.org

May Morning

Singing to the rising sun, the Magdalen College choristers get an early start every May 1. May Morning's gentle roots (probably stemming from the Masses sung for Henry VII, the college's patron, between his death in late April and burial in early May 1509) have given way to carousing and debauchery. Streets are closed to traffic, restaurants open from 5am, all-night revelers gather, and spectators can enjoy traditional morris dancing followed by a champagne breakfast.

A CLASS OF ITS OWN

ONE OF THE TWO TOWERING PILLARS OF ENGLISH EDUCATION, Oxford, like Cambridge, is home to punting, pedaling pedagogues, and earnest students in striped scarves. The home of the oldest university in the English-speaking world, Oxford is a city steeped in tradition, history, and – for the less highbrow – student revelry. All three are combined in the annual May Morning festivities, when the choir of Magdalen College heralds the dawn with the *hymnus eucharistus*, sung from the top of the college's tower to the onlookers below.

Matthew Arnold's "sweet city with her dreaming spires" may nowadays have its fair share of distinctly nonclassical chain stores, traffic jams, and coffee shops, but hidden behind the High Street or the Cornmarket – a stone's throw from a cappuccino machine or a sale rack – is another world: old Oxford is a Lewis Carroll–esque wonderland of ancient doorways and cobbled passageways, tranquil quads and bicycles leaning against golden limestone walls.

Don't be daunted; despite the city's intellectual heritage, Oxford's attractions don't all require a brain the size of a planet. To get a true feel for the place, a tour of the archaeological

FURTHER DETAILS

OXFORD

Oxford Colleges
Colleges can usually be visited 2–5pm daily all year, but check noticeboards outside each college for individual opening times. Admission fees apply.
www.ox.ac.uk

Ashmolean Museum
Beaumont Street, Oxford. The University's museum of art and archaeology displays everything from Chinese prints to coin collections, with a good café in the basement; open 10am–6pm Tue–Sat.
www.ashmolean.org

Pitt Rivers Museum
South Parks Road, Oxford. This anthropological gem is packed with over 500,000 artifacts from around the world. Entry is free; open 10am–4:30pm Tue–Sun, noon–4:30pm Mon.
www.prm.ox.ac.uk

Turf Tavern Public House
Hidden down an alley off New College Lane, Oxford, the foundations of this pub were laid in the 14th century.
www.theturftavern.co.uk

Eagle and Child Public House
St. Giles, Oxford. Locally known as the Bird and Brat, this has been a pub since the 1600s, when it lodged the Chancellor of the Exchequer during the English Civil War.
Tel: 01865 302925.

The Trout Inn
Lower Wolvercote, Oxford. A favored watering-hole of Colin Dexter's fictional detective Inspector Morse.
www.thetroutoxford.co.uk

Botanic Garden
Rose Lane, Oxford. Britain's oldest botanic garden, lying alongside the river opposite Magdalen College, in the heart of the city; open daily Mar–Apr and Sep–Oct: 9am–5pm; May–Aug: 9am–6pm; Nov–Feb: 9am–4.30pm.
www.botanic-garden.ox.ac.uk

Radcliffe Camera
The reading room of the University's Bodleian Library in Radcliffe Square is not open to visitors, but its beautiful domed exterior is a must-see tourist attraction.

WHAT ELSE TO SEE AND DO

The Cotswolds
A short trip from Oxford takes you to the impossibly pretty meadows and picture-perfect towns of the Cotswolds.
www.the-cotswolds.org

Below: Punts gathered by Magdalen College Bridge

Main: Aerial view of Oxford University buildings, including the Radcliffe Camera (center)

Left (left to right): Choristers singing at the top of Magdalen Tower on May Morning; students gathered to listen on Magdalen Bridge

Right: The Trout Inn on the banks of the Thames River

Old Oxford is a Lewis Carroll-esque wonderland of ancient doorways and cobbled passageways, tranquil quads and bicycles leaning against golden limestone walls.

displays of the university-owned Ashmolean Museum or the tribal treasures of the Pitt Rivers Museum should be swiftly followed by a pint of real ale in the tumbledown Turf Tavern – a hidden favorite of both "town" and "gown" (academia). Once on the pub trail, make a stop, too, at the Eagle and Child, the watering hole of choice for the Inklings – a regular group of drinkers and thinkers that counted C. S. Lewis and J. R. R. Tolkien among their number.

On a fine spring day, look upwards as you walk around the town, so you don't miss the more unusual architectural details such as the gargoyles on historic Queen's Lane. Take a boat trip on the Cherwell or the Thames rivers, stopping at riverside pubs such as the Trout Inn for a glass of ale, or take a picnic to Christ Church Meadow. Climb Carfax Tower for its sweeping views, browse the Covered Market, and amble through the spring flowers of the Botanic Garden. It's no surprise that large parts of the Harry Potter movies were shot in this magical city.

More Great Ideas for **Spring**

HISTORY AND HERITAGE

Atmospheric ruins of Laugharne Castle

LAUGHARNE CENTRAL WALES
Laugharne is the "lulled and dumbfound town" that Dylan Thomas wrote about in his 1954 play *Under Milk Wood*. He lived here for most of his adult life and it is where his body is buried. The little coastal town boasts a 12th-century castle, the boathouse where Thomas lived – now a museum, a fine Norman church, and walks around the estuary. There is also an annual award-winning spring festival celebrating Thomas and Celtic culture.
www.laugharne.co.uk

BEVERLEY MINSTER
NORTHEAST ENGLAND
One of the finest Gothic churches in England, the minster took two centuries to build, has a twin-towered west front, and has been described as "a symphony in stone."
www.beverleyminster.org

CULLODEN BATTLEFIELD HIGHLANDS AND ISLANDS
As the Battle of Culloden raged, the skies were leaden and gales drove sleet into the faces of the troops, so to evoke the awfulness of that tragic day on April 16, 1746, go in appalling weather. Visitors can roam the battlefield, visit the clan graves, and learn interactively about the rout of Bonnie Prince Charlie's exhausted Jacobite force by 9,000 government troops – a conflict that took less than an hour but changed the course of Scottish history.
www.nts.org.uk/culloden

DUN AENGUS
WESTERN IRELAND
This mysterious Iron Age fort on Inishmore, the largest of the Aran Islands, has stunning views from its clifftop position above the Atlantic Ocean.
www.nd.edu/~ikuijt/Ireland/Sites/acastela/site/index.html

TREVITHICK DAY
SOUTHWEST ENGLAND
Robert Trevithick's contribution to the industrial revolution is honored on the last Saturday in April, when the town band, dancers, and steam engines parade down the streets.
www.trevithick-day.org.uk

See also pp16–17, 26–7, 32–3.

WILDLIFE AND LANDSCAPE

River Rhaeadr plunging down lush slopes in Powys

PISTYLL RHAEADR WATERFALL NORTH WALES
The 19th-century author George Burrow likened Pistyll Rhaeadr to a great length of silk that is agitated by violent gusts of wind. At 240 ft (74 m), this magical waterfall is the highest in Wales. Its peaceful setting in the Berwyn Mountains in Powys is great walking country, and offers respite from a busy world. Look for the abundant bird life and the "fairy bridge," a natural stone arch over the River Rhaeadr, between two stages of the waterfall.
www.pistyllrhaeadr.co.uk

BLUE POOL SOUTHWEST ENGLAND
Tiny particles of clay suspended in the waters of this former clay pit, just north of the Purbeck Hills, account for its shimmering and seductive blue-green color. Rare fungi and mosses, and animals such as green sand lizards, sika deer, and even Dartford warblers, can been seen on its banks in spring. You can walk through the expanse of heathland around the pool, descend to the water's edge, and enjoy a delicious cream tea at the 1930s tea house next to the pool.
www.bluepooltearooms.co.uk

BALRANALD NATURE RESERVE
HIGHLANDS AND ISLANDS
Rare birds and unusual flowers thrive in this jewel in Scotland's natural crown in spring. Flocks of turnstones, purple sandpipers, sanderlings, dunlins, and the occasional endangered corncrake can be spotted. From the Greenland barnacle geese on the coast to the lapwings on the marshy grasslands, the air is filled with birdsong, and the ground is carpeted with sea rocket, sea sandwort, and silverweed.
www.rspb.org.uk

COTON MANOR GARDENS
WEST MIDLANDS
This 17th-century manor house is renowned for its landscaped gardens, but in spring it offers the added attraction of long walks in a large bluebell wood.
www.cotonmanor.co.uk

See also pp18–19, 30–31.

CITIES, TOWNS, AND VILLAGES

Cottages lining steep, cobbled Gold Hill in Shaftesbury

CANTERBURY
SOUTHEAST ENGLAND
You need to step inside Canterbury's 800-year-old cathedral to absorb its sheer splendor. At Easter, there are services throughout Holy Week, concerts and exhibitions.
www.canterbury-cathedral.org

SHAFTESBURY SOUTHWEST ENGLAND
Quintessentially English, beautiful Gold Hill is a highlight of Shaftesbury, one of the country's oldest and highest towns. Ancient cottages tumble down its cobbles toward Blackmore Vale, recalling a famous bread advertisement in which Gold Hill starred. The town is also proud of its links with the novelist Thomas Hardy, and two interesting museums chronicle the town's past. A few miles away is Old Wardour Castle, with an unusual 14th-century hexagonal tower house.
www.shaftesburydorset.com

BALLYCASTLE
NORTHERN IRELAND
Perfectly placed for touring the Causeway coast and the Glens of Antrim, this seaside town also offers temperate diving waters in late spring.
www.ballycastle.free-online.co.uk

BACUP
NORTHWEST ENGLAND
One of Britain's best-preserved historic mill towns, Bacup is also famous for its "Britannia Coco-Nut Dancers", who dress up and dance along the town boundaries on Easter Saturday.
www.coconutters.co.uk

STIRLING CENTRAL SCOTLAND
An historic and elegant town, Stirling stands at a strategic point of the River Forth – a location that has helped mold its past. It lies in Braveheart country, where the battles of the Scottish War of Independence were fought 700 years ago. Stirling also boasts a fabulous castle, perched high on a volcanic plug, which is a treasure house of history, having witnessed Scottish and Stuart kings, Mary Queen of Scots, wars, intrigue, and murders in its 600-year history.
www.stirling.gov.uk

See also pp20–21, 28–9, 36–7, 44–5, 52–3.

| OUTDOOR ACTIVITIES | FAMILY GETAWAYS | FESTIVALS AND EVENTS |

Tourists setting off for Ramsey Island

Discovering a letterbox in the wilderness of Dartmoor

Costumed revelers taking part in Helston's Furry Dance

ST. DAVIDS AND RAMSEY ISLAND CENTRAL WALES
St. Davids is the smallest city in Britain – in reality, a small village with a beautiful cathedral – but it is surrounded by vast and idyllic walking country, its sweeping coastlands dotted with prehistoric sites and tiny chapels. Offshore, its nutrient-rich sea waters ensure abundant sea life; porpoises, seals, whales and dolphins can be seen on boat tours. The nearby RSPB reserve of Ramsey Island is home to falcons and seabirds in spring, who build their nests among the flower-covered cliffs.
www.ramseyisland.co.uk

TARKA TRAIL SOUTHWEST ENGLAND
The Tarka Trail is a 30-mile- (48-km-) long disused rail line in rural Devon, which has been given a new lease on life as a cycling and walking trail. From Braunton in the north to Meeth in mid-Devon, users pass coastal cliffs, sandy bays, and the river estuaries where Henry Williamson's literary creation Tarka the Otter lived. As the trail wends south, it crosses wooded river valleys and rugged moorland. The route can be cycled in 4 hours or walked in 10.
www.devon.gov.uk/tarkatrail

KEYHAVEN'S SOLENT SHORE
SOUTHEAST ENGLAND
A delightful 15-minute ferry trip from Keyhaven to Hurst Castle takes you past a saltmarsh nature reserve rich in seabirds, unusual plant life, and brackish-water creatures. Crouching low and menacing at the end of Hurst Spit, in a perfect position to defend the western approach to the Solent, is Hurst Castle – part Tudor fortress, part Victorian battery – and a fascinating historical interlude for visitors.
www.new-forest-national-park.com

ARDNAMURCHAN PENINSULA
HIGHLANDS AND ISLANDS
The most westerly point of mainland Scotland has it all: wildlife, including red deer and eagles, hiking, cycling, fishing, boating, and beaches.
www.ardnamurchan.com

See also pp34–5, 42–3.

LETTERBOXING SOUTHWEST ENGLAND
Letterboxing began in 1854 when a Dartmoor guide left a bottle at Cranmere Pool and challenged hikers to make the long walk there and leave a calling card to mark their achievement. Today, clues are placed to help hikers locate letterboxes; on finding one, a rubber stamp in the box is used to record the find in a visitors' book and in the hunter's own book. There are many letterboxes hidden around Dartmoor, providing hours of orienteering fun.
www.dartmoorletterboxing.org

WOOLSACK RACES
SOUTHWEST ENGLAND
Thousands flock to the races and street fair in Tetbury every May to watch competitors carry heavy woolsacks on their backs for 240 yards (220 m) up the steep Gumstool Hill.
www.tetburywoolsack.co.uk

BEATRIX POTTER EASTER EGG HUNT
NORTHWEST ENGLAND
The World of Beatrix Potter attraction hides 100 eggs in Cumbria – finders are rewarded with great prizes, including Lake District breaks.
www.hop-skip-jump.com

CASTLE WARD NORTHERN IRELAND
Overlooking Strangford Lough, this quirky 18th-century house oozes personality. One half is built in the Classical style, while the side facing the lough is Gothic. The extensive grounds are crammed with interest, from a sunken garden and the Temple Water canal – built to reflect the ruins of Audley Castle – to woodlands, scenic views, an adventure play area, animals, and a wildlife center. Children can also dress up in Victorian clothes and play with Victorian toys.
www.nationaltrust.org.uk

SOUTH HARRIS BEACHES HIGHLANDS AND ISLANDS
Some argue that the beaches of South Harris are the best in the world. While the climate may not measure up to Hawaii, the stunning white sandy stretches, crystal-clear Atlantic waters, and shell-sand pasture called machair, spectacularly strewn with wild flowers, are without doubt some of nature's greatest triumphs. All this is set against a fabulous backdrop of dramatic mountains, notably Traigh Scarasta and Luskentyre.
www.scotland.org.uk

See also pp24–5, 38–9, 46–7, 50–51.

COAL-CARRYING CHAMPIONSHIP
NORTHEAST ENGLAND
Begun in the 1960s by two competitive friends, this race in Gawthorpe involves participants carrying coal sacks through the town every Easter Monday.
www.gawthorpe.ndo.co.uk

FURRY DANCE SOUTHWEST ENGLAND
Helston's Floral Dance – or The Furry Dance, as the locals call it – takes place on May 1 and features a dignified procession with men in morning suits and top hats and women in long dresses. It's a colorful occasion to welcome in the spring and the promise of summer, and sees the town decorated with greenery, bluebells, and gorse. Thousands descend on Helson for the revelry, with dancing from 7am to 5pm and partying that continues well into the night.
www.cornishlight.co.uk

OLIMPICK GAMES SOUTHWEST ENGLAND
Introduced in the early 17th century by Robert Dover, an extrovert lawyer, the Olympick Games take place on Dover's Hill, above Chipping Campden, in late May. The games involve traditional and less-common sports, such as falconry, hot-air ballooning, motorbike scrambling, and a shin-kicking contest. Fireworks and dancing end the day; the next morning, the Scuttlebrook Queen is crowned and there's a colorful display of costumes, maypole dancing, and a fair.
www.olimpickgames.co.uk

PAN CELTIC FESTIVAL SOUTHERN IRELAND
This lively festival promotes all things Celtic from six Celtic "nations" – Ireland, Scotland, Wales, Cornwall, Brittany, and the Isle of Man. Started in 1971, and held annually in the week following Easter, the event is hosted by different Irish towns and cities. Language, food, music, singing, and the *craic* – light-hearted mischief – are all embraced as the host town's streets come alive with pipe bands, ceilidhs, street entertainers, and competitions.
www.panceltic.ie

See also pp14–15, 22–3, 40–41, 48–9, 52–3.

SUMMER

Chesil Beach,
part of Dorset's
Jurassic Coast,
England

SUMMER IN GREAT BRITAIN AND IRELAND

Summer in the British countryside can be as close to perfection as it's possible to get.

AT ITS BEST, SUMMER IN THE BRITISH COUNTRYSIDE can be as close to perfection as it's possible to get. Wild flowers bloom along fencerows, wheat turns golden in vast fields, and flocks of swallows flit gracefully across azure skies. Sunlight dapples the woodlands of the New Forest and the rolling moors of Yorkshire, and sparkles on the still waters of the Lake District. But this lush perfection comes at a price: the British summer is notoriously unpredictable, and our fickle, ever-changing climate often leaves even professional meteorologists looking foolish. A dank and misty morning can easily turn into a gloriously sunny afternoon, which is why the weather is, famously and inescapably, one of the most popular topics of conversation all over England, Scotland, Wales and Ireland. But it is this constant mix of sunshine and showers that creates our "green and pleasant land", from the Highland forests to the humble village greens – the quintessentially British venue for local cricket matches, fêtes and morris dancers. Ireland would not be known as the "Emerald Isle" were it not for its forty shades of green, encouraged by the ever-changing weather. It's hard to imagine William Turner painting his breathtaking seascapes without the inspiration of England's shifting skies, and you need only visit the villages of the Stour Valley in summer to see how the fluctuating qualities of English summer light influenced Constable, whose work was inspired by the countryside around villages such as Clare and Dedham. British and Irish writers and poets, from Shakespeare to Shelley, Yeats to Keats, and Burns to Betjeman, have all sung the praises of this most capricious of seasons.

Summer is, of course, the ideal time to venture outside, whether to take part in energetic sports or merely laze around on a picnic rug, reading a book or newspaper. On thousands of village greens, the whack of leather on willow signals the beginning of the cricket season, when local sides compete for honor, batting as fiercely as their county and national counterparts do at legendary cricket grounds such as Lords and the Oval. In late June and early July, the eyes of the tennis world are on the Wimbledon Championships, while around the same time, the waters off the Isle of Wight are colored with the sails of more than 1,000 racing yachts and dinghies taking part in Cowes Week – the largest sailing regatta of its kind in the world. Many of the same boats will be seen in Irish waters during Cork Week, Ireland's biggest sailing event.

Below (left to right): Hiker admiring the view in the Lake District; yacht racing during Cowes Week

Away from the action, or, often, alongside it, people quietly enjoy another British summer tradition: the picnic. Ideally held under whispering oaks in grassy meadows, these casual feasts involve hampers packed to bursting with cucumber sandwiches, strawberries and cream, scones and a bottle or two of chilled Pimm's. At the seaside, the grand traditions of paper-wrapped fish and chips and a bracing stroll along the esplanade still thrive.

The summer sun might lull the south of England, but for those adventurous souls who prefer wide open spaces to neatly trimmed hedgerows and gardens, the lakes, moors and dales of northern England, the vast, empty Atlantic beaches of western Ireland and the wild sea lochs of northwest Scotland call out for exploration. The longest days of the year bring almost 18 hours of daylight to northern Scotland. Head out to sea in the choppy waters around the Isle of Mull, and there's an excellent chance of seeing dolphins, seals, basking sharks and even huge minke whales. Take a rod and line, and with any luck you can come back from a day's sea fishing with enough mackerel, gurnard or sea bass make the perfect summer barbecue. Further south, off Cornwall, Wales or the west coast of Ireland, a sea fishing trip may even yield a shark or other exotic fish. Inland, a summer day spent cycling in the Yorkshire Dales, sailing on the sublime Norfolk Broads, or scaling the breathtaking peaks of Snowdonia can be an idyllic experience. Even if the weather isn't always beautiful, it is never less than bracing, and striding out in the wide, windy open spaces of the Exmoor countryside or exploring a dramatic stretch of seashore, such as Dorset's "Jurassic Coast", can be exhilarating.

> The longest days of the year bring almost 18 hours of daylight to northern Scotland.

Summer's zenith is Midsummer's Eve, celebrated with music, bonfires, and dancing by modern pagans beside the ancient megaliths of Stonehenge, where thousands greet the dawn of Midsummer's Day, the longest day of the year. Watching the sun come up over equally ancient but less-frequented stone circles in Scotland and Ireland can be an even more moving and spiritual experience. The season's grand finale is perhaps the legendary Last Night of the Proms, which traditionally brings a summer programme of orchestral music at London's Royal Albert Hall to an exuberant crescendo. Linked to open air concerts in Scotland, Wales and Northern Ireland, these celebrations mark the end of the great British summer for another year.

Below (left to right): Wild flowers bloom in a Gloucestershire meadow; bottlenose dolphins off the coast of Scotland; village cricket match on Sarisbury Green in Hampshire

Beside the Sea

Above: Postcard of children enjoying donkey rides on the beach, posted at Blackpool in 1919
Right: National Rail poster for Morecambe

When the summer sun puts his hat on, few places are more fun than the British seaside. After all, it was the British who invented the seaside resort, complete with donkey rides, amusement piers, ice cream, and "bathing machines" – moveable changing rooms that could be wheeled into the water, concealing the lissom limbs of Victorian ladies from the public gaze. The expansion of the railroads in the mid- to late 19th century brought the masses to seaside towns, and by the 1930s, public-holiday trains would be heaving with city-dwellers flocking to the beach. Indeed, for most of the 20th century, British families looked no further than their own seaside for their annual vacation – until the advent of cheap travel to the Mediterranean and then even more exotic destinations.

In the 21st century, the British are rediscovering the charms of their coast. Some resorts have reinvented themselves: Brighton has embraced the arts, while Newquay has become Britain's preeminent surf resort. Others, such as Blackpool, remain fabulously brash. Piers, donkey rides, and fish and chips are still seaside staples, and few sights are more quintessentially British than a row of colorful beach huts. Childhood memories of rock pools and sand castles bring parents in search of these simple pleasures for their own children. It is nostalgia, as well as the beauty of much of the British coastline, that is drawing people back to the sea.

KINSALE

BRIGHTON

NEWQUAY

BRIDLINGTON

Arran, Southern Scotland Pebbly coves and sandy beaches ring the rugged shores of Scotland's most accessible island, and Brodick, its biggest village, has great pubs and fish-and-chip shops. *www.visitarran.net*

Largs, Southern Scotland For years, this great sweep of beach has been Glasgow's summer getaway. Much more sophisticated now than in its heyday, it boasts a shiny new marina. *www.largsonline.co.uk*

Kinsale, Southern Ireland Set on a superb natural harbor not far from Cork, Kinsale boasts great restaurants, charming hotels, and old-fashioned pubs, as well as pretty beaches nearby. *www.kinsale.ie*

Llandudno, North Wales This legendary Welsh resort's North Shore beach has a Victorian pier *(see p198)*, while the sandy West Shore is the place to be for fabulous sea views and sunsets. *www.llandudno.com*

Blackpool, Northwest England With its trams, sing-along pubs, and roller coasters, Blackpool is the epitome of the seaside resort. Despite attempts to go upscale, it's still gloriously tacky *(see pp124–5)*.

Morecambe Bay, Northwest England This resort is renowned for its abundant birdlife, fabulous sunsets, and fast-moving tides, which can rush in at the speed of "a good horse". *www.morecambebay.org.uk*

Scarborough, Northeast England Sweeping North Sea views, sandy bays, dramatic cliffs, and some of the freshest seafood in England are among the charms of this Yorkshire resort. *www.scarborough.co.uk*

Bridlington, Northeast England This town is home to a seaside museum and the John Bull World of Rock, celebrating the confectionery that is synonymous with seaside fun. *www.bridlington.net*

Filey, Northeast England Known since Victorian times for its bracing sea air, Filey is a fishing harbor with beaches overlooked by the chalk cliffs of Bempton *(see pp30–31)* and Flamborough Head. *www.filey.co.uk*

Southwold, Eastern England A swath of sea-smoothed pebbles, a long line of brightly painted beach huts, a brewery, and great fresh crab make this quirky Suffolk seaside village irresistible. *www.visitsouthwold.co.uk*

Brighton, Southeast England The Prince Regent (later King George IV) made this city fashionable in the early 19th century. A hub of the arts, it's still where London goes for a weekend by the sea *(see pp36–7)*.

Margate, Southeast England A favorite with Londoners for years, this bucket-and-spade resort on the Kent coast now has the Turner Centre – a gallery named after the famous English artist. *www.visitthanet.co.uk*

Weston Super Mare, Southwest England This resort has been famous for its donkey rides and arcades for almost a century. An observation wheel adds to its appeal. *www.weston-super-mare.com*

Newquay, Southwest England England's answer to Bondi Beach has become the southwest's party town *par excellence*, loved by surfers, yachties, and gap-year party animals *(see pp150–51)*.

St. Ives, Southwest England Gorgeous beaches and a heritage bequeathed by some of the 20th century's best British artists are the hallmarks of this Cornish fishing village. *www.stives-cornwall.co.uk*

Torquay, Southwest England Palm trees line the esplanade and sub-tropical blooms adorn the gardens of stylish Art Deco hotels in genteel Torquay. Don't miss the town's superb Devon cream teas. *www.torquay.com*

TORQUAY

ST. IVES

THE ESSENTIALS

GETTING THERE AND AROUND
Snowdonia National Park covers an area of 838 sq miles (2,170 sq km) in North Wales and is around 4 hours' drive from London. The main train station is Llandudno Junction, from where regular services run to Betws-y-Coed in the heart of the park. The Sherpa bus service covers the park; day passes are available.

WEATHER
Summer in Snowdonia is generally mild and wet, though sunny spells are not uncommon. Daytime temperatures average 48–52°F (9–11°C) on Snowdon's summit, but it can get considerably colder.

ACCOMMODATIONS
Treat Yourself Maes-y-Neuadd is an award-winning hotel set in a 14th-century manor house close to Harlech and well situated for both coast and mountains.
www.neuadd.com

On a Budget Pen-y-Gwryd Hotel, in the foothills of Snowdon, hosted the successful 1953 Everest team while they trained in the area – their signatures can be seen scrawled on the ceiling.
www.pyg.co.uk

EATING OUT
Treat Yourself Ty Gwyn, in Betws-y-Coed, is an award-winning restaurant in the heart of the mountains.
www.tygwynhotel.co.uk

On a Budget Pete's Eats, in Llanberis, is the classic mountaineer's café where you can stuff yourself after a hard day on the hill.
www.petes-eats.co.uk

PRICE FOR TWO PEOPLE
$300–370 a day for food and accommodations.

WEBSITE
www.snowdonia.org.uk

Rock Legends

Snowdonia's mountains have long been a training ground for mountaineers. George Mallory, who died on Everest in the 1920s (it's still not known for sure if he made the summit), climbed here; the pioneering 1953 Everest team trained at Snowdon; it was a testing ground for famous climbers such as Joe Brown, Don Whillans, and Chris Bonington in the 1950s; and today, world-class "rock stars," including Leo Houlding, still climb here when not making first ascents in exotic foreign ranges.

Main: Above the clouds at the summit of Mount Snowdon **Right (top to bottom):** Scrambling across Crib Goch Ridge; waterfall beside the Miners' Track route up the flanks of Snowdon

WHERE EAGLES DARE

ERYRI, THE WELSH NAME FOR SNOWDONIA, has its Celtic roots in the word for "eagle's nest." It is a fitting appellation for the most spectacular highland region and most celebrated national park in Wales. Breathtaking walks above the clouds, exhilarating scrambles to boulder-strewn summits, and enthralling views down onto icy lakes and razor-edged ridges are the highlights of a visit to the north of the region, where the rocky shoulders of Mount Snowdon dominate the landscape. Rising to 3,560 ft (1,085 m), Mount Snowdon is the highest point in Britain south of Scotland, but it is not reserved for eagles and dedicated mountaineers: many thousands of people make the 6-hour ascent every year.

Several routes of varying difficulty lead to the summit; if you're feeling intrepid, take the ridge walk along the "Snowdon Horseshoe," negotiating the jagged edge of Crib Goch Ridge, where the ground falls away dizzyingly on either side. At 8 miles (13 km) long and with 3,200 ft (975 m) of ascent, this route demands a head for heights, good fitness, and thorough preparation, even in the summer months. For less of a white-knuckle experience, try the

FURTHER DETAILS

SNOWDONIA NATIONAL PARK
The national park's many information centers can advise on events, activities, transportation, and accommodations. *www.eryri-npa.co.uk*

Snowdon Mountain Railway
Trains run regularly from Llanberis in late Mar–Nov; at the very beginning and end of the season, they may stop short of the summit, at Clogwyn, if the weather is bad. *www.snowdonrailway.co.uk*

WHAT ELSE TO SEE AND DO
Mountain biking
There are excellent mountain-biking trails within the national park; find mountain-bike rental and information centers in Betws-y-Coed and Coed-y-Brenin. *www.mbwales.com*

Rock-climbing
Some of the finest rock-climbing in southern Britain is to be had here. Renowned crags include Idwal Slabs on Glyder Fawr, and Dinas Mot, Dinas Wastad, and Dinas Cromlech at Llanberis Pass.
British Mountaineering Council: *www.thebmc.co.uk*

Watersports
The River Tryweryn is the best rafting and kayaking river in Wales. Visit the National Whitewater Centre near Bala to check out the action. You can also sail and windsurf on Lake Bala, Wales's biggest freshwater lake.
National Whitewater Centre: *www.ukrafting.co.uk*
Lake Bala: *www.bala-snowdonia.co.uk*

Below (top to bottom): Mountain-biking in Snowdonia; rock-climbing on the Snowdon Horseshoe at Capel Curig

popular "Miners' Track" from Pen-y-Pass, which extends for 4 miles (6.5 km) and ascends 2,400 ft (730 m), passing gushing waterfalls and the derelict buildings once used by the mountain's copper miners. This undemanding, well-made trail stops at Llyn Glaslyn – a lake colored blue by copper salts, set like a jewel 1,970 ft (600 m) up on the eastern flank – and only very experienced walkers should attempt the challenging ascent to the summit from here.

But by far the easiest way to conquer Snowdon is to hop aboard Britain's only rack-and-pinion railroad, the Snowdon Mountain Railway, which takes you on an enthralling ride through woodlands, across an impressive viaduct, and along high ridges to the summit, where a striking new visitor center offers welcome refreshments. On a clear day, views from the train and especially from the cairn right at the top of the mountain are astonishing: you can look across Snowdonia's many peaks to see the Isle of Man, the east coast of Ireland, the Lake District, the Yorkshire Dales, and even parts of southern Scotland.

But there's more to Snowdonia than this jewel in its crown. There is fine mountain walking across the park, especially farther south among the purple-tinged peaks of the Moelwyn range, and countless activities to suit the adventurous, such as biking, rafting, canyoning, and canoeing, as well as woodland and coastal walks for more gentle exercise and contemplation.

ALL ABOARD

A S THE WORLD'S PREMIER SAILING REGATTA, Cowes Week in August is a red-letter day for the small but perfectly formed Isle of Wight. With a huge program of daily races, the regatta attracts more than 1,000 boats, as seasoned professionals rub shoulders with amateur skippers, weekend sailors, Olympic veterans, celebrities, greenhorns, and some 100,000 enthusiastic spectators. Cowes Week may be the world's oldest regatta – dating back to 1826 – but it's totally up-to-date and alive with the latest nautical buzz. With a Ladies' Day running since 2006, Cowes Week also recognizes the growing number of serious women sailors.

Although it's ultimately a celebration of sailing, Cowes Week is also a crucial slot on the island's social calendar – a huge, week-long party. For extraordinary views, hop aboard one of the spectator boats and get closer to the action. The traditional fireworks celebrations on Friday evening are a pyrotechnic curtain-call on eight days of competition and festivities.

THE ESSENTIALS

GETTING THERE AND AROUND
The Isle of Wight is located in the English Channel, off the south coast of England. As many as 350 ferry sailings a day link the island to the mainland, including from Southampton to East Cowes (taking around 55 minutes). Ferries also sail from Portsmouth Harbour and Lymington to other points on the island. High-speed passenger catamarans run between Southampton and West Cowes (around 25 minutes). The island has a comprehensive bus network.

WEATHER
The Isle of Wight has a mild climate with daytime highs of 60–66°F (16–19°C). Always prepare for changeable weather.

ACCOMMODATIONS
Treat Yourself The Albert Cottage Hotel, in Cowes, is an imposing former royal residence that offers 10 luxurious rooms, or Queen Victoria's Indian Summer House in the garden, which you can rent exclusively for perfect seclusion. www.albertcottagehotel.com

On a Budget The Dorset Hotel, in Ryde, 6 miles (10 km) from Cowes, offers great-value bed and breakfast. www.thedorsethotel.co.uk

EATING OUT
Treat Yourself The Hambrough, in Ventnor, is a Michelin-starred restaurant with glorious sea views. www.thehambrough.com

On a Budget The Pierview Public House, in Cowes, is popular with thirsty sailors and spectators during Cowes Week. www.pierview.co.uk

PRICE FOR TWO PEOPLE
From $230 a day for accommodations, food, local transportation, and admission fees.

WEBSITE
www.iwight.com

The Needles

The Needles are an iconic row of three chalk stacks slicing into the waters of the English Channel at the western tip of the Isle of Wight. Their red-and-white automated lighthouse, sitting on the farthest point out to sea, marks their position for passing ships. Their name derives from the needlelike, 120-ft- (36-m-) tall fourth chalk tower – named Lot's Wife – that collapsed during a storm in 1764. Boat trips run from nearby Alum Bay for close-up viewings of the Needles in the summer months.

Ultimately a celebration of sailing, Cowes Week is also a crucial slot on the island's social calendar – a huge, week-long party.

If you get the sailing bug, enroll in the Cowes Sailing School, where you can learn how to tack and get the chance to race, and call in at the Cowes Maritime Museum to get some fascinating insights into the island's sailing history and shipbuilding industry.

Ever since the Victorians first started vacationing on the Isle of Wight, it has become a popular destination for mainlanders, and beyond the yachts there's no shortage of attractions. Osborne House, outside East Cowes, was Queen Victoria's main residence in her later years, and you can visit both its sumptuous state rooms and its private apartments. The island has several other historic treasures, such as the Brading Roman Villa, home to magnificent mosaics. Carisbrooke Castle, in the island's capital, Newport, has some intriguing exhibits detailing its history – including items belonging to King Charles I, who was incarcerated here before his execution in 1649. A visit to Yarmouth Castle, an artillery fort built during the reign of King Henry VIII, provides solid evidence of the island's strategic importance over the centuries. Finally, if you visit in early summer, don't overlook the Isle of Wight Festival in June – this popular music festival has always attracted international stars, from The Doors to The Pixies.

FURTHER DETAILS

ISLE OF WIGHT

Cowes Week
The regatta takes place in the first week of August. Races begin at 10am and run through the afternoons. Places on spectator boats can be booked online from June or on site (subject to availability).
www.cowesweek.co.uk

Cowes Sailing School
Gurnard Heights, Cowes. Two- and five-day theoretical and practical sailing courses are available.
www.cowessailingschool.co.uk

Cowes Maritime Museum
Cowes Library, Beckford Road; open 9:30am–5:30pm Mon, Tues, Fri, 11am–7pm Wed, 9:30am–4:30pm Sat.
www.iwight.com/museums

Osborne House
East Cowes; open Apr–Sept: 10am–6pm daily; Oct–Nov: 10am–4pm daily; Nov–Mar: 10am–4pm Wed–Sun (prebooked guided tours only).
www.english-heritage.org.uk

Brading Roman Villa
Brading; open 9:30am–5pm daily.
www.bradingromanvilla.org.uk

Carisbrooke Castle Museum
Newport; open 21 Mar–Sep: 10am–5pm daily; Oct–21 Mar: 10am–4pm daily.
www.carisbrookecastlemuseum.org.uk

Yarmouth Castle
Yarmouth; open Apr–Sep, 11am–4pm Sun–Thu.
www.english-heritage.org.uk

Isle of Wight Festival
Seaclose Park, Newport. The festival is held over the second weekend of June.
www.isleofwightfestival.com

The Needles
Alum Bay. Boat trips depart from Alum Bay *(see story box)* from Easter to late Oct, from 10:30am daily.
www.theneedles.co.uk

WHAT ELSE TO SEE AND DO

Isle of Wight Steam Railway
Take a trip back in time aboard the dark-green carriages of a steam train on this quaint old railroad. It runs along a 5-mile (8-km) route from Smallbrook Junction in the east of the island to Wootton in the north.
www.iwsteamrailway.co.uk

Blackgang Chine
This eccentric amusement park, near Blackgang, is a collection of pirate-, cowboy- and fairy-tale-themed rides, set within rambling Victorian gardens, and provides a great day out for families with younger children.
www.blackgangchine.com

Main: "Class 1" yachts taking part in a Cowes Week race

Far left (top to bottom): Dinghy race during Cowes Week; Osborne House, the family home of Queen Victoria and Prince Albert

Above: Isle of Wight Festival in full flow

Below: The Needles, stretching into the English Channel

THE ESSENTIALS

GETTING THERE AND AROUND
Powerscourt Estate lies near the town of Enniskerry, County Wicklow, about 22 miles (35 km) south of Dublin Airport and 14 miles (22 km) south of central Dublin. You can reach it by taking a combination of the DART train from Dublin and public buses, but a car is the best way to get there.

WEATHER
The summer weather can be beautiful, but you are close to the Wicklow Mountains so it can also be changeable, with average daytime temperatures of 52–66°F (11–19°C).

ACCOMMODATIONS
Treat Yourself The Ritz-Carlton Powerscourt is one of the best hotels in Ireland, complete with a Gordon Ramsay restaurant.
www.ritzcarlton.com

On a Budget Ferndale House, in Enniskerry, is a good-value, welcoming B&B in a preserved Victorian building.
www.ferndalehouse.com

EATING OUT
Treat Yourself The Gordon Ramsay restaurant at the Ritz-Carlton Powerscourt has to be the first choice for gourmets, with dining at the Chef's Table in the kitchen the ultimate indulgence.
www.gordonramsay.com/dublin

On a Budget Emilia's Ristorante, in Enniskerry, is a cheerful trattoria-style eaterie serving good thin-crust pizzas baked in a wood-burning oven.
www.emilias.ie

PRICE FOR TWO PEOPLE
From $270 a day for admission fees, food, and accommodations.

WEBSITE
www.wicklow.ie

Powerscourt Waterfall

Beyond the colorful gardens and leafy avenues surrounding the mansion, Powerscourt Estate contains a further surprise: Ireland's highest waterfall. Located 3 miles (5 km) from the house in a wooded glen, it plunges 390 ft (121 m), and is spectacular after a heavy rain. The falls are fed by the River Dargle, and in 1858 the seventh Viscount Powerscourt created a deer park around this beauty spot. Today it's a popular place for picnics, and there are hiking trails into the forest.

A GRAND GARDEN

H UMAN ENDEAVOR RARELY MATCHES the pure natural beauty of the Emerald Isle, but Powerscourt Estate is a happy exception. Set a few miles outside Dublin in County Wicklow, a region famed as the "garden of Ireland," the estate's breathtaking landscaped gardens are made all the more remarkable by the tragic story of the great house behind them.

In 1731 the renowned German architect Richard Cassels began converting a 13th-century Anglo-Norman castle into a Palladian mansion for the third Viscount Powerscourt, Richard Wingfield. A decade later this exquisite hilltop manor boasted the finest ballroom in the land, attracting nobles and royalty for the next two centuries. But in 1974, a terrible fire gutted the building, leaving a burned-out shell. Only the facade and the ballroom, which now houses a historical exhibition, have been restored to their former glory.

Thankfully, the magnificent gardens were spared, and this is what people come to see. There can be few finer views in the British Isles than that from Powerscourt's cobblestone balcony, sweeping down the terraced hillside and across the lake and woodlands to the distant

Main: Magnificent lake that lies in front of Powerscourt House **Below (top to bottom):** Powerscourt House, damaged by fire but retaining its splendor; dramatic Powerscourt Waterfall, the highest in Ireland

There can be few finer views in the British Isles than that from Powerscourt's cobblestone balcony, sweeping down the terraced hillside and across the lake and woodlands.

peak of Great Sugar Loaf Mountain. Much of this harmonious vista was created in the middle of the 19th century to the designs of landscape architect Daniel Robertson. Suffering from gout, he allegedly directed workers from a wheelbarrow while sipping sherry to dull his pain.

The formal terraces, decorative ironwork, and statuary reflect Robertson's love of Italianate garden design. Other generations added specimen trees, woodland paths, grottoes, Japanese gardens, and a pepper-pot tower. Earliest are the fragrant walled gardens, laid out at the same time as the original house. There's even a pet cemetery with engraved headstones.

The gardens are in their full glory in summer. There's much to explore, but if you do nothing else, walk down the monumental staircase to the lake, framed by two winged horses. In the center the Triton Fountain spurts a jet of water high in the air. Stroll around the lake and look back on the handsome mansion, with its impressive twin-domed round towers. You can almost imagine ballroom music drifting from the windows. For the more sedentary visitor, the Terrace Café offers its own astounding views.

FURTHER DETAILS

POWERSCOURT HOUSE AND GARDENS
Powerscourt Estate, Enniskerry, County Wicklow; open 9:30am–5:30pm daily.
www.powerscourt.ie

WHAT ELSE TO SEE AND DO
Bray
One of Ireland's oldest seaside resorts, Bray sits just to the east of Enniskerry, at the end of Killiney Bay between Bray Head and a sweeping shingle beach. Stroll along the ocean on the promenade, or take the 3-mile (5-km) scenic cliff walk to the fishing village of Greystones. Children can also enjoy the National Sea Life Centre, one of the country's largest marine zoos.
Bray Sea Life Centre *www.sealife.ie*

Killruddery House and Gardens
Killruddery has been the home of the Earls of Meath since 1618. The present house, built in the 1820s, contains many treasures, and the magnificent formal gardens are among the earliest in Ireland, with many original 17th-century features.
www.killruddery.com

Mount Usher Gardens
These wild, romantic gardens, just outside the town of Wicklow, are spread along the banks of the River Vartry. Laid out in naturalistic style in the 19th century, they contain many exotic species.
www.mountushergardens.ie

Russborough House
West of Enniskerry and over the Wicklow mountains near Blessington, Russborough is another Palladian mansion designed by Richard Cassels, considered by many to be Ireland's loveliest stately home.
www.russborough.ie

Below (top to bottom): Triton Fountain, framed by two statues of winged horses; vista of Powerscourt Estate with the Great Sugar Loaf Mountain in the background

THE ESSENTIALS

GETTING THERE AND AROUND
The Norfolk Broads are in Norfolk and
Suffolk in eastern England, 90 miles
(145 km) northeast of London. Norwich,
Norfolk's biggest city, is just 10 miles
(16 km) from the heart of the Broads and
has a small airport, as well as regular train
services from other parts of Norfolk and
from London. The Broads are accessible
by a network of small roads but are, of
course, best explored by boat.

WEATHER
The Broads are at their absolute best in
summer, when there should be plenty of
warm, sunny days and the least chance
of rain. Average daytime temperatures
range from 60 to 70ºF (16–21ºC).

ACCOMMODATIONS
Treat Yourself Fritton House, in Fritton,
is an 18th-century house that is also very
much a 21st-century boutique hotel.
www.frittonhouse.co.uk

On a Budget Black Horse Cottage, near
Hickling Broad, is a delightful thatched
cottage with three B&B bedrooms.
www.blackhorsecottage.com

EATING OUT
Treat Yourself The Lavender House, in
Brundall, is a superb restaurant with a
stunning menu and a great atmosphere.
www.thelavenderhouse.co.uk

On a Budget The Earsham Street Café,
in Bungay in Suffolk, serves Brancaster
mussels and other tasty local fare.
Tel: 01986 893103

PRICE FOR TWO PEOPLE
Around $260 a day for food,
accommodations, and admission fees.

WEBSITE
www.visitnorfolk.co.uk

Coot Club

In 1933 the children's author Arthur Ransome
rented a boat on the Norfolk Broads. He was so
charmed by the abundance of coots, grebes, swans,
and other wildlife that he was inspired to write the
book *Coot Club,* in his series of Swallows and
Amazons novels. He wrote four other novels in
the 1930s and 1940s that were set in the Broads,
including two in the village of Horning. The
picturesque waterside village depicted in *Coot
Club* or *The Big Six* is easily recognizable today.

Above (left to right) Horning village; kayaking on the Broads
Main: Hickling Broad from the air

BROAD HORIZONS

PURE SILENCE IS SO RARE, that when we experience it, we are compelled to stop and listen to the quiet. One place where it is possible to capture this elusive stillness is in a canoe on the Norfolk Broads. Although this watery region attracts millions of visitors every year, its 120 miles (200 km) of navigable lakes and gently moving rivers provide ample space to lose oneself and find those peaceful moments.

The Broads stretch from the historic city of Norwich to the eastern coastlines of Norfolk and Suffolk. Despite their stunning natural beauty, they are, in fact, a joint effort of man and nature – the result of the digging of peat for fuel and building materials over hundreds of years. The excavated areas slowly flooded as sea levels rose in the 13th century, creating the network of rivers and lakes that now form Britain's third-largest inland waterway.

The Broads is the nation's largest protected wetland, sheltering some of the UK's rarest birds, including bitterns and marsh harriers, as well as more common species such as swans and grebes. The birdwatcher's motto has always been "let the birds come to you," and if you take a moment to pause in your canoe, wildlife usually emerges from the reedbeds. To see a great crested grebe, with its tufted head and russet ruff, is always special, and if you're lucky you might spot a graceful heron in flight or a cormorant diving for fish. Kestrels and sparrowhawks circle the skies here too, and you will share the water with geese, ducks, moorhens, and coots.

If you prefer to stay on dry land, there are many other ways to enjoy summer in the Broads. There are over 200 miles (322 km) of paths and boardwalks along which to hike or cycle, or you can explore the region by car and find spots to relax by the water's edge. There are dozens of pretty villages, among them Horning, featured in the novels of Arthur Ransome *(see story box)*, and Hickling, with its 14th-century flint-and-stone church. But it's in a kayak that you can truly immerse yourself in this region's haunting landscape. The peace comes when you stop paddling, and let the immensity of the Broads and their strange beauty embrace you.

Below (left to right): Windmill at How Hill; greylag goose flying over reedbeds; sunset over the Broads

FURTHER DETAILS

THE NORFOLK BROADS
Broads Authority: *www.broads-authority.gov.uk*
Broads Tourism: *www.norfolkbroads.com*

Kayak Rental
Kayaks can be rented by the day or the half-day, and some companies run kayak safaris with guides to help you navigate. Kayaks and other boats can be rented at several locations, including Norwich, Beccles, Wroxham, Stalham, Wayford Bridge, and the Sutton Staithe Boatyard.
www.discoverthebroads.com

WHAT ELSE TO SEE AND DO
The Museum of the Broads
This award-winning museum in Stalham has enjoyable displays on life in the Broads, the people, the boats, the wildlife, and how the Broadland was created.
www.northnorfolk.org

Bure Valley Railway
This beautiful old steam-engine line follows an 18-mile (29-km) circular route between the market towns of Aylsham and Wroxham, at the heart of the Broads. The trains travel through the picturesque Bure Valley countryside, following the River Bure through meadowland and ancient pasture.
www.bvrw.co.uk

Somerleyton Hall and Gardens
Just outside Lowestoft on the Suffolk coast, the grand Somerleyton Hall and its beautiful gardens are open to the public and are well worth a visit.
www.somerleyton.co.uk

The peace comes when you stop paddling, and let the immensity of the Broads and their strange beauty embrace you.

DICKENS' RETREAT

Tucked between the resorts of Ramsgate and Margate on the Isle of Thanet (a peninsula of north Kent flatland that juts into the Strait of Dover), the pint-sized Victorian settlement of Broadstairs is hands-down the most delightful of the towns that fringe this sandy coastline. This tranquil, easy-going coastal town makes for a breezy escape from urban England. Its chalky clifftop perch overlooks Viking Bay, historically used by smugglers who also infested coves up and down the coast. The town's evocative name is said to derive from the wide steps that gave access to the sands below, which were cut from the rock in the 15th century. More importantly, Broadstairs finds itself indelibly marked on the

THE ESSENTIALS

GETTING THERE AND AROUND
Broadstairs is on the Kent coast, in southeastern England. Trains run daily to and from London Victoria to Broadstairs every half-hour (every hour on Sundays). The regular Thanet Loop bus service runs through Margate, Broadstairs, and Ramsgate.

WEATHER
In summer, Broadstairs is generally sunny and pleasant, with average daytime temperatures of 61–72°F (16–22°C). However, be prepared for rain.

ACCOMMODATIONS
Treat Yourself Charles Dickens was a regular visitor at the Royal Albion, on Albion Street, a classic Regency seafront hotel; the spacious superior rooms at the front look over Viking Bay.
www.albionbroadstairs.co.uk

On a Budget Number 68 B&B, on West Cliff Road, is a stylish but cozy little place near the seafront with themed rooms.
www.number68.co.uk

EATING OUT
Treat Yourself Osteria Posillipo Pizzeria, on Albion Street, was voted 4th best Italian restaurant in the UK by Antonio Carluccio, who called it "a little bit of Naples in Kent."
www.posillipo.co.uk

On a Budget Morelli's Cappuccino, on Victoria Parade, is a lovely family-run café and ice cream parlor on the seafront; great for snacking, coffee, sandwiches, hot dishes, and smashing sundaes.
Tel: 01843 862500.

PRICE FOR TWO PEOPLE
$130–180 a day for accommodations, food and admission fees.

WEBSITE
www.visitthanet.co.uk

The pint-sized Victorian settlement of Broadstairs is hands-down the most delightful of the towns that fringe this sandy coastline.

literary atlas for its associations with the towering genius of Charles Dickens, who found the town inspirational and penned *David Copperfield* here. A regular visitor between 1837 and 1859, the brilliant novelist is celebrated in the Dickens House Museum, and the house overlooking Viking Bay where Dickens lodged was perhaps unsurprisingly rechristened Bleak House. Summer is naturally the optimal season to dip your toes in the Broadstairs brine, especially as June sees enthusiasts trooping to the annual Dickens Festival *(see story box)*, which first took place in 1937. Later in summer there's the excitement of Broadstairs Folk Week, an enthusiastic celebration of folk music and dance. The festival attracts folk musicians from all over Britain, and hums with musical events and activities for adults and children. Handy workshops in a variety of musical instruments offer a chance for both novices and experts to play together.

The town's small size means Broadstairs is easily navigable on foot, leaving time for exploring other sights in the locality. After wandering the sands on Viking Beach, consider exploring Louisa Bay and Dumpton Gap to the south and the coastline toward Margate, where a string of quiet, secluded coves and bays extends north: Stone Bay, Joss Bay, Kingsgate Bay – overlooked by Kingsgate Castle, now converted into apartments – and Botany Bay.

Main: Viking Bay in Broadstairs, overlooked by Bleak House (top right) **Inset:** Sunbathers on Viking Bay beach
Below (left to right): Cliffs at Kingsgate Bay; bust of the town's most famous tourist, Charles Dickens

What the Dickens?

During Broadstairs' celebrated festival, there's a theatrical buzz in town, with Dickens enthusiasts dressing up in Victorian attire and sauntering along Viking Bay beach. Events include country fairs, historical walks, grand parades, dramatizations of the novelist's works, musical concerts, and a competition to judge the best-dressed Dickensian. Even Victorian-era cricket matches and bathing parties take place, with a grand gala ball bringing the curtain down on the event.

CHARLES DICKENS

FURTHER DETAILS

BROADSTAIRS
Broadstairs Dickens Festival
Various venues; late Jun.
www.broadstairsdickensfestival.co.uk

Broadstairs Folk Week
Various venues; mid-Aug.
www.broadstairsfolkweek.org.uk

Dickens House Museum
2 Victoria Parade; open Jul–Sep: 10am–5pm daily;
Easter–Jun and Oct: 2pm–5pm daily.
www.visitbroadstairs.co.uk

WHAT ELSE TO SEE AND DO
St. Peter's Village
A short walk inland from Broadstairs, the pretty village
of St. Peter's is an attractive diversion. The graveyard
of the church of St. Peter-in-Thanet is among the
largest to be found in England.
www.villagetour.co.uk

Margate
The Thanet resort town of Margate, to the north of
Broadstairs, is far better known than its sibling to the
south, but is consequently busier and less genteel.
Margate was one of the very first resorts to lure British
vacationers to paddle in the sea as a leisure activity.
A big reason to earmark Margate for exploration is the
presence of the new Turner Contemporary Art Gallery.

Ramsgate
Either hop on a bus or walk to Ramsgate, 2 miles (3 km)
south of Broadstairs. It's an attractive and much larger
resort situated on the top of a cliff, with an excellent crop
of Regency architecture.
www.portoframsgate.co.uk

Sandwich
The attractive town of Sandwich lies 9 miles
(12 km) south of Broadstairs. It once enjoyed fame
as a great medieval port.
www.discoversandwich.co.uk

Deal
This coastal town, 15 miles (24 km) southeast of
Broadstairs, has two Tudor castles: Deal and Walmer.
William Pitt the Younger (British Prime Minister,
1783–1801 and 1804–06) lived here with his niece,
Lady Hester Stanhope. An inspiration to Picasso and
friend of James Joyce, Lady Hester later became the
most famous woman traveller of her time.
www.aboutdeal.co.uk

Below: Beach and harbor at Broadstairs

THE ESSENTIALS

GETTING THERE AND AROUND
The Peak District is in central England, largely in the county of Derbyshire. The nearest international airport is Manchester Airport, 10 miles (16 km) northwest of the Peak District National Park boundary. Trains run regularly from London to main Peak District stations, such as Chesterfield, Derby, and Sheffield, with travel times of around 2 hours 30 minutes. The region is well served by buses.

WEATHER
Much of the Peak District experiences higher-than-average rainfall in summer, when daytime temperatures are highest, ranging from 57 to 61°F (14–16°C).

ACCOMMODATIONS
Treat Yourself Fischer's Baslow Hall, near Baslow, is a beautiful country-house hotel on the Chatsworth Estate that boasts a Michelin-starred restaurant.
www.fischers-baslowhall.co.uk

On a Budget Crown Cottage, on the Main Road in Eyam, is a 4-star bed and breakfast located in a 200-year-old building that was once an inn.
www.crown-cottage.co.uk

EATING OUT
Treat Yourself Rowley's, in Baslow, on the edge of the Chatsworth Estate, specializes in locally sourced food.
www.rowleysrestaurant.co.uk

On a Budget The Chequers Inn, in Froggatt, dates from the 16th century and is a great example of the Peak District's many "gastropubs."
www.chequers-froggatt.com

PRICE FOR TWO PEOPLE
From $250 a day for food, accommodations and entry fees.

WEBSITE
www.visitpeakdistrict.com

The First National Park

In 1951, the Peak District National Park became the first official national park in Britain. This was partly as a result of an incident that took place in 1932, known as the "Mass Trespass of Kinder Scout." Thousands of hikers willfully trespassed on private areas of the Peak District, and demanded the restoration of ancient rights of way, confronting gamekeepers who challenged them. The action was pivotal in changing the law, leading to large areas of private land being opened to the public.

WELL-DRESSED WELLS

T HE DERBYSHIRE PEAK DISTRICT has an air of mystery about it, and the origins of the region's time-hallowed and fascinating tradition of well-dressing are suitably obscure. From the end of April to mid-September, throughout Derbyshire – and to a lesser extent in neighboring Staffordshire – the inhabitants of over 60 towns and villages decorate the local village wells that have all but disappeared in other parts of rural England.

In pre-Christian Britain, all villages would have had access to a well or natural spring, and offerings – usually in the form of flowers and other plants – were placed beside them to thank the gods for the supply of fresh water. When Christianity arrived in Britain in the 4th century AD, this custom was condemned as a form of water worship. However, the tradition lingered on in this part of the Peak District, perhaps due to the region's isolation and lack of major roads.

In 1665, the bubonic plague that was sweeping the country arrived in the village of Eyam, in a bundle of cloth that had been sent from a tailor in London. In a noble act, the inhabitants of Eyam voluntarily quarantined themselves for 16 months to stop the plague from spreading further. They were naturally thankful for the fresh water provided by the village well, and the well-dressing ceremony as it is known today was born. Eyam's well-dressing lasts for a week in August, giving you enough time to explore Derbyshire's Peak District; you can tour its many pretty villages, and go hiking on nearby Eyam Moor and the green hills of the Derwent Valley.

Visitors to Eyam and other notable well-dressing places – such as Tissington, Bakewell, Hope, and Hathersage – have the chance to see for themselves how the dressings are created, and can admire the finished results. Boards are soaked in the local pond or river and then covered in clay, onto which a design is sketched. Then flowers, seeds, berries, and other natural materials are skillfully used to create an incredibly colorful collage that will be placed beside the well. These works of art last for up to a week – enough time to thank the ancient gods for their munificence in ensuring that this endearing tradition survives in our hectic modern world.

FURTHER DETAILS

DERBYSHIRE PEAK DISTRICT WELL-DRESSING
Well-dressing ceremonies take place in many villages around the Derbyshire Peak District between late April and mid-September.
www.welldressing.com

WHAT ELSE TO SEE AND DO
The Hope Valley Line
This is one of the most scenic train routes in the UK, traveling through the Peak District National Park to connect Sheffield and Manchester via a scattering of pretty villages in the beautiful Derwent, Hope, and Edale valleys. Many of them are "folk trains," featuring onboard musicians who will invite you to step off the train at one of the village stations and continue the festivities at a local pub.
www.hvhptp.org.uk

Peveril Castle
One of England's earliest Norman castles, Peveril Castle, in Castleton, was founded in 1066. Its high grounds provide some of the best views of Derbyshire's Peak District.
www.english-heritage.org.uk/peveril

Chatsworth House
Residence of the Duke and Duchess of Devonshire, Chatsworth House, near Bakewell, is one of Britain's most impressive country houses, containing an art collection that ranges from Roman sculptures to paintings by Rembrandt and Lucian Freud.
www.chatsworth.org

Haddon Hall
Overlooking the River Wye at Bakewell, Haddon Hall is a vast, fortified 12th-century manor house. The house was modified by each generation of its inhabitants until the 17th century, when it was abandoned and left to decay gracefully. Both the house and its Elizabethan gardens were lavishly restored in the 1920s.
www.haddonhall.co.uk

Below: Beautiful example of well-dressing at Coffin Well in Tissington

> Flowers, seeds, berries, and other natural materials are skillfully used to create an incredibly colorful collage that will be placed beside the well.

Main: Village of Hathersage, nestling in the Derwent Valley
Inset: Creating a traditional well-dressing **Below:** Chatsworth House, overlooking the River Derwent

THE ESSENTIALS

GETTING THERE AND AROUND
The Scottish Borders are in the southeast
of Scotland, along the national border
with England. They begin about 15 miles
(24 km) south of Edinburgh, where the
nearest international airport is situated.
There are bus and train connections from
Edinburgh, but with the Borders' beautiful
scenery and widely spaced towns, it is
best to travel the region by car.

WEATHER
While summer in the southeast of
Scotland is generally warmer and dryer
than in the Highlands, be prepared for rain
at any time. Average daytime temperatures
range from 64 to 72°F (18–22°C).

ACCOMMODATIONS
Treat Yourself The Roxburghe Hotel
& Golf Course, near Kelso, is a relaxed
country-house hotel on the wooded
Roxburghe estate.
www.roxburghe.net

On a Budget The Tontine Hotel, in
Peebles, is a historic hotel with an
excellent restaurant, a stone's throw from
lovely walks along the River Tweed.
www.tontinehotel.com

EATING OUT
Treat Yourself Bardoulet's Restaurant at
The Horseshoe Inn, in Eddleston, has won
awards for its innovative food featuring
local produce and Scottish specialties.

On a Budget The Waggon Inn Bar and
Restaurant, in Kelso, offers something for
everyone, from homemade pub classics
to steaks and seasonal specials.
www.thewaggoninn.com

PRICE FOR TWO PEOPLE
Around $330 a day for accommodations
and food.

WEBSITE
www.visitscottishborders.com

The Border Abbeys

In medieval times, four great abbeys were built
along Scotland's border, and their ruins are some
of the most atmospheric in the country. Melrose
Abbey is the best preserved, with much finely
carved detail still visible on its arches. Dryburgh
Abbey, the burial place of Sir Walter Scott, has a
peaceful setting on the banks of the River Tweed.
English forces destroyed part of Kelso Abbey, once
the richest in the region. The sheer size of Jedburgh
Abbey makes it the most impressive of them all.

Main: Standard Bearer at the Selkirk Common Riding **Right (top to bottom):** Traditional Scottish dancing; evening
festivities during the Langholm Common Ridings; mounted participants heading to the Ride Out in Langholm

RIDING OUT

As dawn approaches, the piper plays, summoning the townsfolk to an ancient duty. A
crowd gathers in anticipation, until at last the clatter of horses' hooves is heard, growing
louder as their flag-bearing riders approach the town square. The Common Ridings have begun.

Each summer this scene is played out in towns throughout the Scottish Borders. The ritual of
the Common Ridings dates back to the 14th century, when the region suffered constant turmoil
in the border wars with England. While kings and noblemen fought over territory, ordinary
families had to defend their livestock against *reiving* – cattle thieving – a common practice in
those lawless times. So the townspeople decided to gather together and patrol the boundaries
(or "marches") of their lands themselves, in a practice known as the "Ridings of the Marches".

The Common Ridings are a re-enactment of these patrols, and they have become a yearly
tradition, commemorating the Borders turbulent past. They take place in the Border towns
every summer and have grown to become great festive affairs, with parades, pageants, and
carnivals. Each town has its own unique agenda and ceremonial customs, but in each of the

FURTHER DETAILS

THE COMMON RIDINGS

Ridings take place annually in many of the border towns, and, from 2010, in Edinburgh, between June and August. Towns with the most extensive festivites are listed below. *www.returntotheridings.co.uk*

Hawick
Here the Ridings honor a group of young local men who routed an English raiding party near Hawick after the Battle of Flodden in 1514, capturing their flag.

Langholm
"Langholm's Great Day," as the Ridings are known, takes place on the last Friday in July. Three unusual emblems are carried aloft: the thistle, spade, and crown and barley banna (barley bread nailed to a platter with a salted herring).

Selkirk
In the largest of the Common Ridings, up to 400 riders set off on a 12-mile (19-km) ride, galloping back to the Market Place for the Casting of the Colours ceremony.

Galashiels
The "Braw Lad" leads riders to the Raid Stane – where the townsfolk massacred English plunderers in 1337 – before returning to the Old Town Cross for colorful ceremonies.

Melrose
Activities at this event include parades, Ride Outs, the ceremonial crowning of the Festival Queen, and the swearing-in of the "Melrosian," the town's representative.

Jedburgh
The Callants Festival lasts two weeks, celebrating the bravery of the Jedburgh ("Jethart") Callants during the Redeswire Raid – the last of the border skirmishes.

Peebles
The Riding of the Marches takes place during Beltane Week, in mid-June, which celebrates an even older pagan festival marking the return of summer.

Lauder
One of the original Common Ridings, this culminates with the Cornet leading the riders to the only surviving boundary stone in the Borders.

Below: Jedburgh Abbey in the Scottish Borders

These great displays of horsemanship often see hundreds of horses and riders thundering across the beautiful Borders landscape, in some of the largest mounted gatherings in Europe.

towns one man is chosen to lead the procession, and he is bestowed with an honorary title, such as Cornet (in Hawick and Langholm), Standard Bearer (in Selkirk), or Braw (fine) Lad (in Galashiels). A principal Lass ties a ribbon to the man's Burgh Flag, or Standard, just as a knight's lady would have attached her "favour" (such as a ribbon or veil) to his lance before battle. There are moving speeches, rousing songs, and marching pipe bands.

But the essence of every gathering is the "Ride Out." These great displays of horsemanship often see hundreds of horses and riders thundering across the beautiful Borders landscape, in some of the largest mounted gatherings in Europe. Horses are ridden proudly and passionately, whether owned or rented by their riders for this great day. There's a warm feeling of community pride as each crowd follows its riders to the edge of town. And as the townsfolk ride the marches, age-old boundaries are redrawn, and ties to a common history and culture once again renewed.

THE ESSENTIALS

GETTING THERE AND AROUND
The Stour Valley is in eastern England, on the coastal border of Essex and Suffolk. The nearest major airport is London Stansted, 40 miles (65 km) west of Dedham. The closest train station is at Manningtree, 5 miles (8 km) from Dedham. The area is best explored on foot or by bicycle, although a car is useful for longer trips.

WEATHER
The summer climate in the Stour Valley is generally mild, but be prepared for rain. Average summer daytime temperatures range from 59 to 64°F (15–18°C).

ACCOMMODATIONS
Treat Yourself Maison Talbooth, in Dedham, is a Victorian country-house hotel by the River Stour with 12 luxury suites, massage treatment rooms, and a restaurant.
www.milsomhotels.com

On a Budget May's Barn Farm, in Dedham, is a quiet B&B in a secluded location with views over Dedham Vale.
www.btinternet.com/~mays.barn

EATING OUT
Treat Yourself Le Talbooth, in Dedham, is part of the Maison Talbooth complex, and serves some of the best-quality food for miles around.
www.milsomhotels.com

On a Budget The Sun Inn, in Dedham, is a great local village pub that also serves tasty Italian food.
www.thesuninndedham.com

PRICE FOR TWO PEOPLE
From $240 a day for accommodations, food, and admission fees.

WEBSITE
www.visiteastofengland.com

A Painters' Landscape
The Stour Valley has always been a haven for painters – besides Constable, the renowned English landscape artist Thomas Gainsborough (1727–88) was born here in the town of Sudbury. Sir Alfred Munnings (1878–1959), famous for his paintings of horses and hunt scenes, lived in Dedham. Constable himself, one of Britain's best-loved artists, was more popular in France than in Britain during his lifetime, and was forced to take up portrait painting to subsidize his real love: landscape painting.

CONSTABLE COUNTRY

Iᴛ ᴍᴀʏ ꜱᴜʀᴘʀɪꜱᴇ ʏᴏᴜ ᴛᴏ ꜰɪɴᴅ ᴛʜᴀᴛ there is an area of England that has hardly changed in two centuries – yet is scarcely an hour's drive from London's suburbs. The Stour Valley lies along the River Stour, forming the border between the counties of Essex and Suffolk. It was the setting of many paintings by the renowned artist John Constable (1776–1837), who painted the Stour Valley region extensively in the early 1800s. He captured the majestic water meadows, the willowy bankside trees, and scenes of rural life along the lowland river valley in Dedham Vale: these quintessentially English countryside scenes are today preserved in an

> The Stour Valley… is a gentle landscape of lazy little rivers, quaint churches, country pubs, and cricket on the village green.

Area of Outstanding Natural Beauty. It's a gentle landscape of lazy little rivers, quaint English churches, country pubs, and cricket on the village green. Meanwhile, in the patchwork of fields, June's spectacular harvest of bright yellow rapeseed later gives way to crops of wheat, barley, and onions. Oxeye daisies, bee orchids, and clover flower in the ancient hedgerows bordering the quiet rural lanes and attract a flurry of butterflies in August.

In this warm summer glow, Constable painted some of his best-loved works. Born in East Bergholt in Suffolk, the son of a wealthy grain merchant, he was most inspired by the landscape in and around nearby Dedham. In 1802 he painted one of his most famous scenes, *Dedham Vale*, which captures the river winding toward the distant tower of Dedham Church. It was a view he returned to and painted again and again. Not far from here is Flatford Mill, where Constable composed perhaps the best known of his great works, *The Hay Wain*. The mill itself is not open to the public, although you can take Constable-related art courses at the Field Centre here, and you are allowed to walk past in order to view Willy Lott's Cottage, the building at the left-hand side of *The Hay Wain*. The cottage was built sometime in the 16th century, and was around 300 years old when Constable finished his painting in 1821. To see it still standing today, almost two centuries later, is just one of the spirit-lifting moments that you will experience in the quite literally "picturesque" landscapes of Constable Country.

Main: Willy Lott's Cottage near Flatford Mill **Inset:** *The Hay Wain* by John Constable
Below (left to right): Flatford Mill; fields of rapeseed in bloom near Dedham

FURTHER DETAILS

STOUR VALLEY CONSTABLE COUNTRY
The Flatford Mill Field Centre
Flatford Mill Field Centre, East Bergholt, Suffolk. The Field Studies Council, based at the Flatford Mill Centre, runs over 170 arts, crafts, and natural history short courses lasting from two days to a week – naturally including artistic explorations of Constable Country.
www.field-studies-council.org/flatfordmill

WHAT ELSE TO SEE AND DO
Flatford Bridge Cottage
Adjoining Flatford Mill is the lovely old thatched Bridge Cottage, which also features in many of Constable's paintings of the area. It has been restored and now houses an exhibition on the artist and a tea room. In summer guided walks can be booked here.
www.nationaltrust.org.uk

The Beth Chatto Gardens
The renowned gardening expert and author Beth Chatto has opened her gardens – in Elmstead Market, just over 5 miles (8 km) south of Dedham – for public viewing. Established in 1960, the gardens are most famous for the xeriscaped gravel section, where only truly drought-hardy plants survive. The "island planting" of the main gardens is inspirational.
www.bethchatto.co.uk

Sir Alfred Munnings Museum
Castle House, in Dedham, was the home of the artist Sir Alfred Munnings *(see story box)* – a former president of the Royal Academy of Arts. The house is now an art museum that displays over 200 of his works, and his studio has been preserved just as it was in his lifetime.
www.siralfredmunnings.co.uk

Below: Cows drinking from the River Stour

THE ESSENTIALS

GETTING THERE AND AROUND
Salcombe is on the Devon coast in southwest England. The nearest airports are Plymouth, 29 miles (47 km) to the northwest, and Exeter, 50 miles (80 km) to the northeast. Totnes has a train station, and there are trunk roads to within half an hour of Salcombe. Once there, ditch the car and explore using the town's buses and ferries, or on foot. Salcombe also operates a park-and-ride service.

WEATHER
Salcombe has a mild climate and in summer is routinely warmer than other parts of the UK, with average daytime temperatures of 59–64°F (15–18°C).

ACCOMMODATIONS
Treat Yourself H2O houseboats offer all-out luxury, including a hot tub and huge plasma TV; boats sleep up to eight people.
www.h2oresorts.co.uk.

On a Budget Waverley, on Devon Road, is a comfortable, family-friendly bed and breakfast with magnificent beach views.
www.waverleybandb.co.uk

EATING OUT
Treat Yourself The Oyster Shack, on Island Street, has a great atmosphere and serves delicious food.
www.oystershack.co.uk/salcombe

On a Budget Captain Flint's, on Fore Street, is a hugely popular pizza and pasta restaurant that's great for children.
Tel: 01548 842357

PRICE FOR A FAMILY OF FOUR
Around $500 a day for food, accommodations, and boat rental.

WEBSITES
www.salcombeinformation.co.uk
www.southhams.gov.uk

Shipwrecks

The untamed seas beyond the safety of the Salcombe Estuary have claimed many ships, among them a Bronze Age vessel near Gammon Head carrying weapons and jewelry, and an 18th-century East Indiaman laden with uncut diamonds. In 1917, the steamship *SS Maine* was torpedoed, and in 1992, the coaster *Demetrius* went aground at Prawle Point. Generations of smugglers have enjoyed rich pickings from the coastline, and today, despite protection zones, rogue divers continue to raid the wrecks.

A SUMMER PLAYGROUND

WITHIN MINUTES OF ESCAPING the thundering traffic of the A38 Devon Expressway, the air changes, life slows, and all becomes right with the world. Unspoiled villages welcome you along the network of narrow, high-banked lanes, many of which are drawn south toward a magnetic coastline of such beauty that you may never want to leave. At the heart of this ravishing haven, anchored between Torbay and Plymouth on the edge of a deeply wooded estuary, lies Salcombe, a glorious summer playground of flaxen sands and leisurely waves.

The small town's self-consciously smart Fore Street and Island Street – with its boatbuilders' workshops – are the focus of activity on shore, and there are dozens of pubs, restaurants, cafés and clothing shops. Away from retail heaven, difficult choices await the summer visitor – should it be the bare-faced indulgence of Salcombe Dairy ice cream, the fun of crabbing on the embankment, or the fascination of ancient tales of shipwrecks and smugglers at the Museum

At the heart of this
ravishing haven
lies Salcombe –
a glorious summer
playground of
flaxen sands and
leisurely waves.

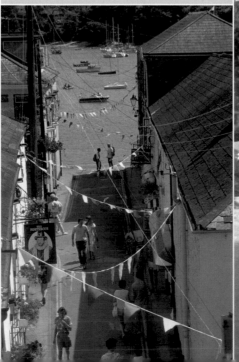

of Maritime and Local History? Of course, salty sea dogs just want to be on the water exploring the cobalt-blue estuary and its backwater creeks, where ferries, tourist cruisers, and fishing boats ply their routes between yacht races, dinghy lessons, and visiting sailboats. In August the week-long Salcombe Regatta takes over land and water, with lots of sailing and rowing races, but also crab-catching contests, treasure hunts, sand-castle competitions, mud races, torch-lit processions, and even daring aerial displays by planes and helicopters.

For those who don't want to take to the water, there are half a dozen clean and safe beaches for swimming, relaxing, and sandy fun, which also provide perfect vantage points for estuary-watching. One of the prettiest and most sheltered is Mill Bay, a short ferry ride from Salcombe. And as families wend their way home at the end of each day, the chances are they are already planning the next – perhaps a visit to the subtropical gardens created by the Edwardian eccentric Otto Overbeck, a ramble along the South West Coast Path's heart-stopping stretches with their sensational views, or – and why not? – another day on the beach. It's impossible to be bored in Salcombe in the summer.

FURTHER DETAILS

SALCOMBE
On the Water
Salcombe offers lots of ways to have fun on the water: you can learn to sail, kayak, or paddle-surf; charter your own boat; or go on a relaxing Rivermaid ferry cruise, with guides to help you spot seals and myriad sea birds.
Island Cruising Club: www.icc-salcombe.co.uk
South Sands Sailing: www.southsandssailing.co.uk
Salcombe Rib Charter: www.salcomberibcharter.com
Rivermaid Ferry Cruises: Tel: 01548 853525

Museum of Maritime and Local History
Market Street, Salcombe; open Easter–Oct:
10:30am–12:30pm & 2:30–4:30pm daily.
www.devonmuseums.net

Salcombe Regatta
Salcombe's colorful August water festival.
www.salcomberegatta.com

Overbeck's Museum and Garden
Sharpitor, Salcombe; opening times vary throughout the year; see website for details.
www.nationaltrust.org.uk

South West Coast Path
www.southwestcoastpath.com

WHAT ELSE TO SEE AND DO
Dartmoor
Wild, mysterious, and only 40 minutes' drive from Salcombe (see pp178–9).
www.dartmoornp.gov.uk

Bantham
Stunning sands not far from Bigbury and Burgh Island, where a sea-tractor crosses the causeway at high tide.
www.southhams.gov.uk

Slapton Ley National Nature Reserve
Slapton Ley is a beautiful freshwater lagoon, home to hundreds of species of flora and fauna. Nearby is Slapton Sands where, in 1944, hundreds of US troops died after German U-boats torpedoed a D-Day exercise.
www.slnnr.org.uk

Woodlands Leisure Park
Located just outside of Dartmouth, this theme park is perfect for boisterous youngsters.
www.woodlandspark.com

Main: Stunning Mill Bay, backed by rolling hills

Far left (top to bottom): Pastel-colored houses in Salcombe; Fore Street

Above: Crabbing, a popular pastime for children

Below: Salcombe viewed across the water

THE ESSENTIALS

GETTING THERE AND AROUND
The Dingle Peninsula, County Kerry, is on the southwest coast of Ireland, stretching west from Tralee. The nearest major airports are at Cork, about 80 miles (130 km) to the southeast, and Shannon, 78 miles (126 km) to the northeast. There are buses serving the area, but the best way to get around is by car or bicycle.

WEATHER
The Gulf Stream brings a mild climate, but there's a good chance of wind and rain even in summer, so come prepared. Daytime temperatures average 54–60°F (12–20°C).

ACCOMMODATIONS
Treat Yourself The Dingle Skellig Hotel and Peninsula Spa, on the harbor just outside Dingle Town, is a 4-star modern hotel with fantastic views over Dingle Bay. *www.dingleskellig.com*

On a Budget James G Ashes is a bright and clean B&B with downstairs bar and restaurant in the center of Dingle Town. *www.jamesgashe.com*

EATING OUT
Treat Yourself The Chart House, in Dingle Town, is an award-winning restaurant serving modern cuisine in an atmospheric old cottage. Dinner only.
Tel: 066 915 2255

On a Budget The Goat Street Café, in Dingle Town, serves healthy dishes, such as vegetarian tagine with couscous, and has a very relaxed atmosphere. *www.thegoatstreetcafe.com*

PRICE FOR TWO PEOPLE
From $270–300 a day for food, accommodations, and admission fees.

WEBSITE
www.dodingle.com
www.dingle-peninsula.ie

Fun with Fungi

In 1983 a young male bottle-nosed dolphin turned up in Dingle's harbor, and he has been there ever since. The locals named him Fungi, and even built a statue of him on the quayside. Although middle-aged by now (bottlenose dolphins live 35–40 years), he is still playful and greets many of the tour boats that take visitors out to see him. It's also possible to arrange to swim with Fungi early in the morning before the harbor gets too busy; several companies can arrange this for you.

Above (left to right): The Gallarus Oratory, an early Christian church; brightly painted Irish bars abound on the peninsula
Main: The Blasket Islands from Clogher Head on the Dingle Peninsula

THE END OF THE ROAD

THERE ARE FEW PLACES MORE ENCHANTING than Ireland's Dingle Peninsula. Its very name has a magical ring, and its chain of green hills, studded with ancient stone cottages and strange little beehive huts, just might make you believe in leprechauns. Though this slim finger of the western coast stretches just 35 miles (56 km) into the Atlantic, it encompasses idyllic beaches, high rugged mountains, stunning seascapes, and fascinating historical sites.

Magical too are the songs that you'll hear in the pubs of Dingle Town. It's renowned as a center for traditional Irish music, and lively "sessions" – both organized and impromptu – take place almost every night. In summer, the narrow streets of colorful shops and houses winding up from the harbor are packed with visitors who've come to enjoy the legendary *craic* (fun).

One of the best ways to see Dingle's wild and remote landscape is on a drive around the region. Head east out of town along Dingle Bay to one of Ireland's most heavenly beaches, Inch Strand, its 4 miles (6 km) of soft sand overlooked by the Slieve Mish mountains. To the west lies adventure, starting with the road signs: Dingle Peninsula is an Irish-speaking region, and there are few English translations. Follow Slea Head Drive for dramatic coastal views. The eerie ruins of Dunbeg Fort, a dramatic Iron Age promontory fort, cling to surf-pounded cliffs. Nearby, explore the curious stone *clochans* (beehive huts) at Fahan – dwellings built by prehistoric farmers. Around the peninsula's tip there are breathtaking views across the sound to the Blasket Islands. Now uninhabited, they were once known as "the last parish before America". Reaching toward them is Garraun Point, the most westerly spot on the mainland – perfect for sunset-watching.

A short detour inland brings you to the phenomenal Gallarus Oratory. Like the *clochans*, this early Christian church was built of stone without mortar, yet has remained watertight for centuries. To the north, Mount Brandon is Dingle's highest peak, rising 3,127 ft (953 m) high. From Brandon Bay below, the 6th-century navigator St. Brendan allegedly set sail for the New World. Modern-day explorers are more likely to end their journeys on the fine sandy beaches that stretch along Tralee Bay on Dingle's northern shore.

Below (left to right): Ancient remains of Dunberg Fort; Mount Brandon; dramatic drive around Slea Head

FURTHER DETAILS

THE DINGLE PENINSULA
Dunbeg Fort
Slea Head Drive, Fahan; open access.
www.dunbegfort.com

Fahan Beehive Huts
On private land; farmers often charge a small fee for up-close access.

Gallarus Oratory
Near Ballyferriter; tel: 066 915 5333; open Mar–Oct: 9am–9pm daily; Nov–Feb: 10am–5pm daily.

WHAT ELSE TO SEE AND DO
The Blasket Islands
These beautiful, windswept islands, 6 miles (9.5 km) off the tip of the Dingle Peninsula, were settled as far back as the Iron Age. Though they are now home only to a great variety of seabirds, the fascinating story of life as it was in this remote community is told in the Blasket Centre in Dunquin, a village on the mainland. Weather permitting, you can take a boat trip from Dunquin Pier to visit the picturesque Great Blasket Island.
Blasket Centre: tel: 066 915 6444
Blasket Islands Ferry: *www.blasketislands.ie*

Tralee
Kerry's county town puts on the Rose of Tralee International Festival each August, with a famous beauty pageant and a week of parades, funfairs, and other activities. The National Folk Theatre of Ireland is also based here and stages performances of traditional music and dance throughout the summer.
Rose of Tralee: *www.roseoftralee.ie*
National Folk Theatre: *www.siamsatire.com*

The eerie ruins of Dunbeg Fort, a dramatic Iron Age promontory fort, cling to surf-pounded cliffs.

THE ESSENTIALS

GETTING THERE AND AROUND
Bristol is in southwestern England. The nearest airport is Bristol International Airport, around 8 miles (13 km) from the city. Regular trains run to Bristol Temple Meads from London Paddington, and take just under 2 hours. Most of the central sights in the city can be seen on foot, with recourse to buses for outlying destinations.

WEATHER
Bristol has a mild climate with generally dry summers. Average summer daytime temperatures range from 55 to 72°F (13 to 22°C).

ACCOMMODATIONS
Treat Yourself Hotel du Vin & Bistro, in Narrow Lewins Mead, is situated in restored warehouse buildings, and offers style, comfort, and great food in a central location.
www.hotelduvin.com

On a Budget The Greenhouse B&B, on Greenbank Road, is a pretty Victorian cottage with modern interior styling.
www.thegreenhousebristol.co.uk

EATING OUT
Treat Yourself Riverstation, on The Grove, is a converted former police station that serves tasty modern European cuisine.
www.riverstation.co.uk

On a Budget El Puerto, on Prince Street, serves tasty tapas in a lively and fun atmosphere with flamenco dancing on Sundays and paella-cooking demonstrations.
www.el-puerto.co.uk

PRICE FOR TWO PEOPLE
From $260 a day for accommodations, food, and admission fees.

WEBSITE
www.visitbristol.co.uk

A Passage to the Indies

The 15th-century Italian navigator John Cabot (anglicized from "Giovanni Caboto") twice set out from Bristol in search of a "Northwest Passage" to the East Indies. After an unsuccessful first voyage, he departed Bristol on his second expedition in 1497 aboard the *Matthew*, reaching the coast of North America. He is presumed to have died at sea, and is commemorated in Bristol by the Cabot Tower on Brandon Hill and a replica of the *Matthew* alongside the *SS Great Britain*.

Main: Hot-air balloons over Clifton Suspension Bridge **Right (top to bottom):** Bristol Harbourside Marina at night; interior of Bristol City Museum and Art Gallery; aerial view of Bristol Floating Harbour with Queen Square at the center

ON THE WATERFRONT

STRADDLING THE RIVER AVON, the vital and dynamic inland port and university city of Bristol is the cultural nucleus of England's rural southwest. The city's longstanding relationship with sea trade – particularly the shipping of tobacco, wine, and slaves – survives in its pronounced historic port character. The Floating Harbour, so called because lock gates insulate it from the tides, celebrated its 200th anniversary in 2009. It is the city's focal point, an attraction for residents and visitors alike. In late July or early August, the area also hosts the exuberant Bristol Harbour Festival, when the water swarms with boats and the waterside comes alive with festivities, from music to dance, circus acts, and a cavalcade of fireworks that concludes the celebrations at the end of the long weekend.

Other summer events include August's Bristol International Balloon Fiesta, when dozens of hot-air balloons fill the skies above the city, and the "birthday party" of the *SS Great Britain*, held annually on July 19. This renowned vessel is forever associated with Bristol. Designed by the daring Victorian engineer Isambard Kingdom Brunel, and launched in Bristol in 1843, it

FURTHER DETAILS

BRISTOL

Bristol Harbour Festival
Held over a weekend in late July or early August.
www.bristolharbourfestival.co.uk

Bristol International Balloon Fiesta
Held over four days in mid–Aug.
www.bristolfiesta.co.uk

***SS Great Britain* Birthday Party**
Held annually on July 19, 6:30–10pm.

SS Great Britain
Bristol Dock. Tickets also include entry to the dry dock,
the replica of *The Matthew*, and the Maritime Heritage
Centre. Open Apr–Sep: 10am–5:30pm daily; Oct, Feb–Mar:
10am–4:30pm daily; Nov–Jan: 10am–4pm daily.
www.ssgreatbritain.org

Bristol Cathedral
College Green; open 8am–6pm Mon–Sat;
7:20am–5pm Sun.
www.bristol-cathedral.co.uk

Explore-at-Bristol
Anchor Road, Harbourside; open 10am–5pm
Mon–Fri: 10am–6pm Sat–Sun.
http://explore-at-bristol.org.uk

Theatre Royal
Bristol Old Vic, King Street.
www.bristololdvic.org.uk

City Museum and Art Gallery
Queens Road, West End; open 10am–5pm daily.
www.bristol.gov.uk/museums

St. Mary Redcliffe
Colstone Parade; open 9am–5pm Mon–Sat;
8am–7:30pm Sun.
www.stmaryredcliffe.co.uk

Arnolfini Arts Centre
Narrow Quay; open 10am–6pm Tue–Sun and Bank
Holiday Mon.
www.arnolfini.org.uk

Clifton Suspension Bridge
www.clifton-suspension-bridge.org.uk

WHAT ELSE TO SEE AND DO

Cheddar Caves and Gorge
Take in the amazing geological formations in the Mendip
Hills and explore the cavernous secrets of Cheddar Gorge.
www.cheddarcaves.co.uk

Glastonbury Abbey
Set in idyllic parkland, this sublime ruined abbey – once
the largest in England – is a highlight of the area.
www.glastonburyabbey.com

Below: Bristol Harbour Festival

was the first iron-hulled ocean-going vessel to be powered by propeller, transforming world travel. After a million miles at sea, it returned to Bristol in 1970 for restoration. Today it lies adjacent to a replica of another iconic vessel, *The Matthew (see story box)*.

Away from the waterfront, Bristol still has plenty to offer. The city's 12th-century cathedral is an outstanding example of a "hall church," where the nave, choir, and aisles all reach a uniform height. The streets off Park Street north of the cathedral boast some fabulous examples of Georgian architecture, while Explore-at-Bristol is an entertaining combination of hands-on science center and planetarium, perfect for children. Across Pero's Bridge, Queen Square is an elegant Georgian Square, north of which lies the cobbled 17th-century King Street, home of the Theatre Royal. If rain strikes, the City Museum and Art Gallery, alongside the Neo-Gothic Wills Memorial Tower, provides not just shelter but a first-rate collection of artifacts ranging from ancient Egyptian relics, dinosaurs, and fossils to art works by Old Masters and contemporary names. But if it's sunstroke you're escaping, seek refuge in the cool interior of St. Mary Redcliffe or chill out at the excellent waterfront Arnolfini Arts Centre. Finally, in Clifton, to the west of the downtown, you can admire the iconic Clifton Suspension Bridge – also designed by Brunel – that dramatically spans the River Avon.

THE ESSENTIALS

GETTING THERE AND AROUND
Bath is in Somerset, in southwestern
England. The nearest airport is Bristol
International, about 19 miles (30 km)
away. There is a regular train service
between Bath and London (travel time
90 minutes), and a fast and frequent train
service connecting Bath with Bristol. Buses
connect Bath with the nearby city of Wells.
Open-air bus tours of Bath are plentiful,
and in summer months river trips run
along the River Avon.

WEATHER
Bath enjoys a mild summer climate, with
average daytime temperatures ranging
from 59 to 63ºF (15–17ºC).

ACCOMMODATIONS
Treat Yourself The Bath Priory,
on Weston Road, is a fabulous historic
house with delightful gardens and
a Michelin-starred restaurant.

On a Budget Apsley House Hotel, on
Newbridge Hill, is an elegant Georgian
country house with outstanding service
and divine gardens.
www.apsley-house.co.uk

EATING OUT
Treat Yourself The Olive Tree at the
Queensberry Hotel, on Russell Street,
majors in modern British cooking using
local, seasonal ingredients.
www.thequeensberry.co.uk

On a Budget The Bathtub Bistro, on
Grove Street, is a popular bistro that
offers flavorsome food.
www.romanbath.co.uk/bathtub

PRICE FOR TWO PEOPLE
From $215 a day for food,
accommodations, and admission fees.

WEBSITE
www.visitbath.co.uk

John Wood and Son

Many of Bath's handsome streets and 18th-century
Georgian buildings were designed by the English
architect John Wood the Elder (1704–54) and his
son John Wood the Younger (1728–82), both
of whom promoted the Neo-Classical Palladian
crescents, terraces, and town houses that have
come to characterize the city. John Wood the
Elder's crowning achievements are the grandeur of
The Circus and elegant Queen Square, while his
son fashioned Bath's outstanding Royal Crescent.

MAKING A SPLASH

Named after its celebrated hot springs, which the Romans developed into a temple and bathing complex, Bath – a UNESCO World Heritage Site – is one of England's most elegant cities. The city's long history, Palladian-style crescent architecture, and ample parklands breed a languorous refinement that few newer towns can muster.

Summer sees the arrival of the Bath Music Festival in late May or early June, when a galaxy of musicians comes to town. The festival – 17 days of musical events from jazz to classical, world music, folk, and electronica – is celebrated at venues across town. Artists from across the musical spectrum come to perform, from Brian Eno to Branford Marsalis, the Charles Mingus Big Band, bluegrass star Ralph Stanley, and noted soprano Emma Kirkby. But it's not just about music: there's also dance, film, workshops, multimedia performances, lectures, free events, and a host of exhibitions, all bringing a cultural buzz to Bath.

Situated just southwest of the city's imposing abbey, the Roman Baths – work on which commenced around AD 60 – constitute some of England's most important Roman

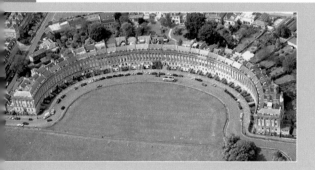

The city's long history, its Palladian-style crescent architecture and ample parkland breed a languorous refinement that few newer towns can muster.

architectural relics. A visit to the baths is a direct link to the Roman occupation of England: take your time exploring the Sacred Spring and the Great Bath or pop into the adjacent Pump Room and its excellent restaurant. For a more hands-on appreciation of Bath's thermal waters, immerse yourself in the luxurious new Thermae Bath Spa – the best possible conclusion to a day's walking. Overlooking the Roman Baths is the 16th-century Bath Abbey, parts of which date back to Norman times. In the 18th century, Bath became fashionable as a spa resort, and the city's grand Georgian buildings, built in the distinctive Bath stone, date from this era. Designed by John Wood the Younger in 1774, the elegant bow of Royal Crescent is Bath's best-looking slice of Georgian grandeur; you can visit No. 1 Royal Crescent's sumptuous interior. A further example of the city's Georgian heritage can be seen in the shop-lined elegance of Pulteney Bridge, designed by Scottish architect Robert Adam.

Main and inset: Magnificent Royal Crescent in Bath
Below (left to right): Roman baths with Bath Abbey in the background; Thermae Bath Spa

FURTHER DETAILS

BATH
Bath Music Festival
Various venues, Bath; late May/early Jun.
www.bathmusicfest.org.uk

Roman Baths
Abbey Church Yard, Bath; open Mar–Jun, Sep–Oct: 9am–6pm daily; Jul–Aug: 9am–9pm daily; Nov–Feb: 9:30am–5:30pm daily.
www.romanbaths.co.uk

Thermae Bath Spa
New Royal Bath open 9am–10pm daily (last entry 7:30pm); Cross Bath open 10am–8pm daily (last entry 6:30pm).
www.thermaebathspa.com

Bath Abbey
Open Apr–Oct: 9am–6pm Mon–Sat, 1–2:30pm and 4:30–5:30pm Sun; Nov–Mar: 9am–4:30pm Mon–Sat, 1–2:30pm and 4:30–5:30pm Sun.
www.bathabbey.org

No. 1 Royal Crescent
Open Feb–Oct: 10:30am–5pm Tue–Sun; Nov: 10:30am–4pm Tue–Sun.
www.bath-preservation-trust.org.uk

Walking Tours
Free 2-hour walking tours leave from Abbey Church Yard at 10:30am daily and 2pm Sun–Fri.

WHAT ELSE TO SEE AND DO
Bristol
The maritime city of Bristol (see pp82–3), a 15-minute train trip from Bath, has dozens of sights, including the 12th-century Bristol Cathedral, the Clifton Suspension Bridge, and the Steamship SS Great Britain.
www.visitbristol.co.uk

Wells
The compact city of Wells is most famous for its splendid cathedral, encasing a stunning English Gothic interior. Wells can also be used as a base for visiting Cheddar Gorge, Wookey Hole, and Glastonbury.
Wells Cathedral www.wellscathedral.org.uk

Below (top to bottom): Operatic production in the historic Roman Baths; Pulteney Bridge

THE ESSENTIALS

GETTING THERE AND AROUND
The Orkney Islands are 10 miles
(16 km) off the northern coast of
Scotland. Mainland Orkney has its
own airport at Kirkwall, with flights from
several Scottish city airports. Other
islands have smaller airports and there
are also connecting ferries for cars and
for foot passengers.

WEATHER
The summer climate in the Orkneys is
surprisingly mild, with very long daylight
hours and average summer daytime
temperatures of 54–61°F (12–16°C).

ACCOMMODATIONS
Treat Yourself The Orkney Hotel, in
Kirkwall on Mainland, is a restored but
still traditional 17th-century inn.
www.orkneyhotel.co.uk

On a Budget Berstane House, in
St. Ola on Mainland, offers superior
B&B accommodations set in woodland,
with breathtaking views over the sea.
www.berstane.co.uk

EATING OUT
Eating options in this remote place are
limited, with little price variation.

The Foveran Hotel's restaurant, near
Kirkwall on Mainland, overlooks Scapa
Flow and serves superb local dishes.
www.foveranhotel.co.uk

The Ferry Inn, in Stromness on Mainland,
offers tasty home-cooking with daily
specials and many vegetarian dishes.
www.ferryinn.com

PRICE FOR TWO PEOPLE
Around $330 a day for food,
accommodations, and admission fees.

WEBSITE
www.visitorkney.com

The Ays Have It

The names of the main Orkney islands, such as
Westray, Eday, Rousay, and Egilsay, all end in the
suffix "-ay," which is the Old Norse word for an
island. The main part of each name refers to an
island characteristic, such as the sand of Sanday.
"Orkney" itself is a slight variation on this; it derives
from the Viking *Orkneyjar*, "seal island," which was
shortened to "Orkney" by the islanders. The old
Gaelic name was *Insi Orc*, "the island of the wild
pigs," thought to refer to the islands' wild boars.

STONE-AGE SETTLEMENT

Britain has a wealth of prehistoric sites, but some of the oldest and most fascinating are scattered across the far-flung Orkney Islands. This archipelago of around 70 islands lies off the northern tip of Scotland, where the Atlantic Ocean merges into the North Sea. It's a meeting point of cultures, too, with a strong Scandinavian heritage that reflects its early Viking rulers as well as its Scottish ancestry.

But Orkney's human history goes back much farther. Its largest island, simply called Mainland, is home to the most complete Neolithic village in Northern Europe, Skara Brae. Inhabited between 3200 and 2500 BC, it lay buried in the dunes on the west coast of Mainland until a storm uncovered it in 1850. The 10 partly subterranean houses were built of dry-stone slabs, surrounded by midden (refuse) mounds and linked by covered passageways. With their turf and animal-skin roofs long gone, you can look down into these dwellings and marvel at their sophisticated comforts. Each had a hearth, stone beds, wall cupboards, and a stone dresser. The inhabitants' jewelry, pottery, and tools are now displayed in the site's visitor center.

Main: Ring of Brodgar on Mainland

Left (left to right): Walker surveying the islands of the Orkney archipelago; interior of a prehistoric house at Skara Brae

Right: Viking runes engraved on a stone in the chambered cairn at Maeshowe

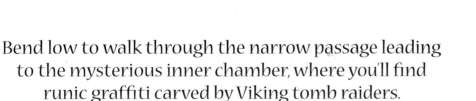

FURTHER DETAILS

UNESCO ORKNEY WORLD HERITAGE SITE
Skara Brae
19 miles (31 km) northwest of Kirkwall on the B9056 on Mainland; open Apr–Sep: 9:30am–5:30pm daily; Oct–Mar: 9:30am–4:30pm daily.
www.historic-scotland.gov.uk

Maeshowe Chambered Cairn
Admissions to the cairn are via Tormiston Mill Visitor Centre, 9 miles (14 km) west of Kirkwall on the A965 on Mainland; open Apr–Sep: 9:30am–5pm daily; Oct–Mar: 9:30am–4pm daily; twilight tours Jun–Aug at 6pm, 7pm and 8pm; advance reservations required.
www.historic-scotland.gov.uk

Ring of Brodgar
5 miles (8 km) northwest of Stromness on Mainland; open access.
www.historic-scotland.gov.uk

Stones of Stenness
Just over ¾ mile (1 km) southeast of the Ring of Brodgar; open access.
www.historic-scotland.gov.uk

WHAT ELSE TO SEE AND DO
St. Magnus Cathedral
Orkney's capital, Kirkwall, is home to Britain's most northerly cathedral, St. Magnus, named after the islands' martyred patron saint. The handsome red sandstone building dates back to 1137. The ornate interior features enormous Romanesque pillars and decorated stonework.
www.stmagnus.org

Italian Chapel
During World War II, Italian prisoners of war on Orkney converted two Nissen huts into this delightful memorial chapel on the tiny island of Lamb Holm. The interior is a work of creativity and imagination, decorated with frescoes and *trompe l'oeil* artwork.
www.undiscoveredscotland.co.uk/eastmainland/italianchapel

Walking Trips
Wilderness Scotland offers guided walking trips around the islands' coastal paths and famous geographical formations, such as the Old Man of Hoy and Cuilags on the island of Hoy. Tours of the Neolithic sites are also included.
www.wildernessscotland.com

Below: Stones of Stenness in late-afternoon sunlight

Bend low to walk through the narrow passage leading to the mysterious inner chamber, where you'll find runic graffiti carved by Viking tomb raiders.

Skara Brae is part of UNESCO's Heart of Neolithic Orkney World Heritage Site, together with three other sites on Mainland. The grassy mound at Maeshowe hides a monumental chambered cairn dating to around 2800 BC. Bend low to walk through the narrow passage leading to the mysterious inner chamber, where you'll find runic graffiti carved by Viking tomb raiders. The Ring of Brodgar is a huge stone circle some 340 ft (104 m) in diameter, surrounded by a deep ditch. Though only 36 of its original 60 standing stones remain, it is strikingly set on an isthmus (land bridge) between two lochs. The nearby Stones of Stenness, one of the earliest recorded stone circles, date from around 3100 BC. Five of the original 12 stones remain, the tallest standing 20 ft (6 m) high. These great megaliths are all the more dramatic in summer, looming up in stark contrast to Orkney's windswept, almost treeless terrain, their striking shadows creeping far across the ground in the long hours of daylight.

THE ESSENTIALS

GETTING THERE AND AROUND
The Yorkshire Dales National Park covers 680 sq miles (1,762 sq km) of northern England. The nearest international airports are Leeds Bradford Airport and Manchester Airport, 14 miles (22 km) and 50 miles (80 km) respectively from the park's southern boundary. There are good bus services in the Yorkshire Dales, but a car is convenient for more remote areas.

WEATHER
The weather in the Dales varies greatly. Summers can be glorious, but be prepared for showers. Average summer daytime temperatures range from 60 to 66°F (16–19°C).

ACCOMMODATIONS
Treat Yourself Swinton Park, near Masham, is a luxurious 30-room castle hotel set in 200 acres (80 hectares) of its own grounds in Wensleydale. *www.swintonpark.com*

On a Budget Beck Hall, in Malham, is a friendly guesthouse with log fires, four-poster beds, and fantastic breakfasts. *www.beckhallmalham.com*

EATING OUT
Treat Yourself The Burlington Restaurant, at the Devonshire Arms Hotel on the Bolton Abbey Estate, has won a Michelin star for its fantastic modern cuisine. *www.thedevonshirearms.co.uk*

On a Budget The George and Dragon, in Aysgarth, serves excellent food at reasonable prices in a great location near Aysgarth Falls in Wensleydale. *www.georgeanddragonaysgarth.co.uk*

PRICE FOR TWO PEOPLE
Around $285 a day for food and accommodations.

WEBSITE
www.yorkshire.com

Going Underground

The rock of the Yorkshire Dales is mainly limestone and porous, so many huge cave systems have formed. One of the best known is Ingleborough Cave, which has 350-million-year-old stalagmites and stalactites. It connects to Gaping Gill, whose main chamber is big enough to house St. Paul's Cathedral. On the May and August Bank Holidays, potholing clubs set up a winch above Gaping Gill's entrance so that the public can descend into the cave and experience its breathtaking magnificence.

Above (left to right): Barn surrounded by meadow buttercups; golden plover at home in the Yorkshire Dales
Main: Network of dry-stone walls running over the Dales

LIMESTONE LANDSCAPE

ONE OF BRITAIN'S BEST-LOVED LANDSCAPES, the Yorkshire Dales stretch across northwest Yorkshire and into Cumbria. Collectively, these "dales" – from the Norse for "valleys" – make up the vast and glorious Yorkshire Dales National Park. There are around 20 dales to explore, via footpaths, bike paths, and the tiny roads that wind their way through this pastoral upland region of limestone hills and glacier-carved river valleys. Most of the valleys here take their names from the rivers that run through them, such as Wharfedale, which is named after the River Wharfe.

Summer sees the national park at its most beautiful, when the sloping fields are at their brightest green and the rustic, gray, dry-stone walls march over the steep hills. Under the sun's golden glow, sheep and cattle graze contentedly in pastures dotted with charming old stone barns. Elsewhere the upland hay meadows are cleared of livestock, allowing them to burst spectacularly into flower from June through to July. The wildflowers provide a colorful habitat for a wide variety of animals, insects, and nesting birds, and include dozens of traditional, rarely seen British plant species, such as pignut, lady's mantle, meadow buttercup, wood cranesbill, and globeflower.

The Yorkshire Dales also contain vast stretches of moorland, at its best in August when the heather covering it is in full bloom, creating a sea of color. This is prime bird-watching country; the merlin – Britain's smallest bird of prey – can be seen here, as can other raptors, such as peregrines, kestrels, and buzzards. Look for golden plovers, lapwings, and yellow wagtails, too.

The national park's most celebrated features are its dramatic limestone landscapes. Aysgarth Falls in Wensleydale is a series of broad limestone steps in the river that create a stunning scenic waterfall. At Malham Cove, a massive, sheer white cliff towers over the head of the valley. It is topped by limestone pavement, a natural feature in which rainwater etches deep fissures, called "grykes." Nearby Gordale Scar is a rugged ravine that boasts two cascading waterfalls. There's a weird and wonderful landscape below ground too (*see story box*); don't miss an opportunity for an unforgettable underground adventure.

Below (left to right): Hikers following a footpath alongside a dry-stone wall; caver abseiling down a gorge at Alum Pot cave system; hawthorn tree on limestone pavement

(*see story box*)

FURTHER DETAILS

YORKSHIRE DALES NATIONAL PARK
National Park Centres
There are five National Park Centres within the Yorkshire Dales: Aysgarth Falls, Grassington, Hawes, Malham, and Reeth. They provide maps and bus schedules as well as information about walking routes, events, facilities, and accommodations; open Apr–Oct: 10am–5pm daily; Nov–Mar: 10am–4pm on varying days.
www.yorkshiredales.org.uk

Aysgarth Falls
Wensleydale, North Yorkshire.
www.yorkshire-dales.com/aysgarth-falls.html

Malham Cove and Gordale Scar
Malhamdale, North Yorkshire.
www.malhamdale.com

Alum Pot
Selside, North Yorkshire.
www.malhamdale.com

Gaping Gill
Ingleborough Mountain, near Ingleton, North Yorkshire.
www.bpc-cave.org.uk/gaping_gill.htm

WHAT ELSE TO SEE AND DO
Dales Countryside Museum
Housed in a former train station building in Hawes Station Yard, this museum celebrates the history, people, and landscapes of the Yorkshire Dales through many hands-on and interactive exhibits.
www.thedales.org.uk/dalescountrysidemuseum

Castle Bolton
You can visit the Great Hall, adjacent rooms, and the gardens of this battlemented 14th-century fortress near Leyburn, where Mary, Queen of Scots was imprisoned by her cousin Elizabeth I in 1568.
www.boltoncastle.co.uk

> The national park's most celebrated features are its dramatic limestone landscapes.

THE ESSENTIALS

GETTING THERE AND AROUND
Arundel is in West Sussex, in southeastern England. The nearest airport is London Gatwick, 28 miles (45 km) away. Regular trains take 90 minutes to travel from London Victoria to Arundel, and buses run between Arundel and Brighton. The castle is a 10-minute walk from the train station.

WEATHER
In summer the weather in Arundel is generally pleasant, with long days and average daytime temperatures of 57–70°F (14–21°C). However, always prepare for rain and changeable weather.

ACCOMMODATIONS
Treat Yourself Live literally like a lord at the sumptuous, 900-year-old Amberley Castle, just north of Arundel, and watch the portcullis being lowered at midnight. *www.amberleycastle.co.uk*

On a Budget April Cottage, in Crossbush Lane, is a peaceful cottage B&B with rural views and a friendly owner, around 1 mile (2 km) from the center of Arundel. *www.april-cottage.co.uk*

EATING OUT
Treat Yourself The Town House, on Arundel High Street, has spectacular views of the castle and boasts a top-tier menu. *www.thetownhouse.co.uk*

On a Budget The Bay Tree, in Tarrant Street, is an excellent family-owned restaurant with a winning British and European menu. *www.thebaytreearundel.com*

PRICE FOR TWO PEOPLE
$250–330 a day for accommodations, food, and admission fees.

WEBSITES
www.arundel.org.uk
www.arundelmuseum.org.uk

The Knucker
Pop into a local pub and sample a bottle of Arundel Brewery's Old Knucker. This strong, dark beer, which has a powerfully malty taste, is inspired by the legend of a ferocious water-serpent ("knucker" in Old English) that supposedly lived in a pond in Lyminster, between Arundel and Littlehampton. This monster would rampage through the countryside at night, slaughtering livestock and locals, until it was subdued by a knight in one version of the legend, or ate a pie laced with poison in another.

Main: Arundel Castle overlooking the River Arun
Right (top to bottom): Town buildings overlooking the Arun; aerial view of the castle and grounds

JEWEL OF THE SOUTH

THE CRENELLATED MEDIEVAL FORM OF ARUNDEL CASTLE, historic seat of the dukes of Norfolk, sits picturesquely on a hilltop in the South Downs. It towers above the charming West Sussex market town of Arundel and the winding River Arun. The river historically served as a vital link to the sea, and for centuries the town was a flourishing port. Wandering through Arundel's attractively cobbled streets and antique shops is a day out in itself, but it is the dominating presence of the castle that draws visitors to this historic town. Although its foundations originally date to Norman times, the castle has evolved dramatically during its 950-year existence. A combination of disrepair, fire, and wartime damage, compensated for with extravagant restoration and lavish embellishments over the centuries, has resulted in the majestic building that we see today.

Climb the castle's keep for simply stunning views of the South Downs, and look for marks on the walls caused by cannonballs fired during the English Civil War. Admire the magnificent collections of armor, paintings (including works by Van Dyck), china, tapestries,

FURTHER DETAILS

ARUNDEL

Arundel Castle
High Street, Arundel, West Sussex; open Apr–Oct only, Tue–Sun: castle rooms 12pm–5pm; castle keep 11am–4:30pm; Fitzalan Chapel, gardens and grounds 10am–5pm. Guided tours (75 minutes) run prior to the opening of the castle to the public, from 10:30am to 11:45am; advance reservations are essential.
www.arundelcastle.org

Arundel Cathedral
London Road; open 9am–6pm daily.
www.arundelcathedral.org

Carpet of Flowers Festival
Arundel Cathedral celebrates the Catholic feast of Corpus Christi with a carpet of flowers and a procession from the cathedral to the castle. Corpus Christi falls on a Thursday between late May and the middle of June.
www.arundelcathedral.org

Arundel Festival
Runs for around 10 days in late August.
www.arundelfestival.co.uk

WHAT ELSE TO SEE AND DO

Petworth House and Park
Petworth House is a magnificent 17th-century mansion famed for its lavish collection of art, including works by Turner, Bosch, and Titian. The house sits in 700 acres (280 hectares) of parkland landscaped by Capability Brown – England's most famous landscape gardener.
www.nationaltrust.org.uk

Bignor Roman Villa
Arundel has a few relics from the Roman era, but nothing compared to the excellently preserved Roman mosaics from the 2nd century at this celebrated heritage site in Bignor, 6 miles (10 km) north of Arundel. No buses run here, so you will need either your own car or a taxi.
www.bignorromanvilla.co.uk

Below: The "Carpet of Flowers" in Arundel Cathedral

and furniture on display, and allow time to wander around the fine gardens. Overflowing with heritage and history, the castle also has a gaggle of ghosts, obligatory perhaps for a bastion with this pedigree. Past dukes of Norfolk lie interred in the Fitzalan Chapel, located within the castle grounds. This Catholic chapel is attached to, but not part of, the Anglican Church of St. Nicholas; an unusual arrangement that allowed, albeit somewhat dangerously, the Catholic dukes to observe their faith in Protestant England during the Reformation.

Summer is without doubt the perfect season to visit: the beaches at Littlehampton and Worthing, or Brighton and Hove farther east, are not far away, and the town of Arundel celebrates two of its most popular and spectacular events. The renowned "Carpet of Flowers" festival takes place at Arundel Cathedral in late May or early June. The cathedral itself is a huge, awe-inspiring edifice in the Neo-French Gothic style, dating back to 1873. Its distinctive annual festival celebrates the Catholic festival of Corpus Christi, when a floral "carpet" – comprising more than 15,000 blooms – is laid out in a pattern stretching 90 ft (27 m) along the main aisle of the cathedral, to be trampled underfoot during mass. The Arundel Festival takes place later in the summer, toward the end of August, when the castle and town play hosts to top performers from the worlds of theater, dance, and music.

The National Eisteddfod

The National Eisteddfod is a celebration of Wales's
own language and culture. Held in the first week of
August, this folk festival alternates annually between
North and South Wales. Its first language is Welsh,
although non-Welsh-speakers are warmly
welcomed. You can see the great and good of
Wales in flowing druidic robes, and the festival
climaxes with the awarding of a ceremonial chair,
recalling the very first Eisteddfod in 1176, when the
winner was awarded a chair at Lord Rhys's table.

FESTIVAL OF SONG

THE SMALL WELSH TOWN OF LLANGOLLEN becomes a whirl of color for one week every
July. Take a stroll up the main street and you may encounter African dance troupes in
bright, flowing kaftans; women's choral groups from Eastern Europe, resplendent in their
richly embroidered tunics; and, from closer to home, members of traditional Welsh male-voice
choirs walking proudly in their immaculate, navy-blue blazers. All are in town for the
International Eisteddfod, one of Europe's largest multicultural musical events. Every year,
children and adults from more than 50 countries descend on Llangollen's festival field to
compete in a range of choral and musical disciplines. Many of the competitors, from solo
instrumentalists to folk-dance groups and barbershop quartets, remain in their national dress
throughout the festival, which begins with the colorful opening pageant.

The first Eisteddfod was held in Cardigan Castle, in 1176, when Lord Rhys invited poets
and musicians from all around Wales to perform there. The National Eisteddfod continues this
tradition, but Llangollen takes a more global approach. Since 1947 it has been hosting the

Main: The International Eisteddfod's lively opening pageant **Below (top to bottom):** Llangollen Railway Station;
male-voice choir performing at the International Eisteddfod; horse-drawn barge on the Llangollen Canal

International Eisteddfod, bringing together national folk traditions from all around the world. It was the brainchild of Harold Tudor, a journalist from nearby Wrexham, who wanted to promote reconciliation and mutual cultural understanding within postwar Europe. The inaugural event featured only a handful of choirs, with one group, from Hungary, hitchhiking across Europe to attend. Today, some 4,000 competitors and 50,000 spectators converge on Llangollen every summer, and the small market town is venerated by folk musicians worldwide.

The focus of the Eisteddfod rests on the Royal International Pavilion. A series of concerts takes place there during the evenings, but it is the pavilion's daytime competitions that really create excitement. The standard of performers is high, and you may be lucky enough to discover choral music's next big thing – in 1955, the then-unknown opera supremo Luciano Pavarotti experienced his first musical success here, as part of a male-voice choir. The contests culminate in the Choir of the World, a sing-off between all the winning choirs on the Saturday night, and the winners receive the Pavarotti Trophy, named after the Eisteddfod's most eminent supporter.

An eclectic mix of world-class acts are attracted here, such as Bryn Terfel, Joan Baez and José Carreras. Most fondly remembered is Pavarotti's 1995 concert – the 40th anniversary of his first appearance. But remember that potential stars are just as likely to appear on the festival field as in the pavilion, so take time to simply wander and enjoy the multicultural delights.

FURTHER DETAILS

EISTEDDFOD FESTIVALS
International Eisteddfod
Royal International Pavilion, Abbey Road, Llangollen; Tue–Sun in the second week of July.
www.international-eisteddfod.co.uk

National Eisteddfod
The Eisteddfod takes place in the first week of August; the venue changes each year *(see website for details).*
www.eisteddfod.org.uk

WHAT ELSE TO SEE AND DO
Plas Newydd
The "Ladies of Llangollen" were a pair of eccentric spinsters who turned their backs on their Anglo-Irish aristocratic background and took up residence together at Plas Newydd, near Llangollen. In the early 1800s the couple – Lady Eleanor Butler and Miss Sarah Ponsonby – were the toast of society. Their elegant Gothic house, with its formal gardens and woodland walk, now houses a small museum about the ladies and Regency society.
www.nationaltrust.org.uk

Horse-drawn Canal Trips
Llangollen Wharf is the departure point for horse-drawn boat trips along the beautiful Llangollen Canal. The quiet waterway – now a UNESCO World Heritage Site – offers the most relaxing way of traveling through the stunning Welsh mountains. The 45-minute cruises depart every half-hour during school holidays; every hour at other times.
www.horsedrawnboats.co.uk

Llangollen Railway
One of Britain's most scenic heritage lines, the Llangollen Railway runs steam and preserved-diesel trains through the beautiful Dee Valley, from Llangollen to Carrog. The timetable changes throughout the year, and offers special events such as family days and murder-mystery tours.
www.llangollen-railway.co.uk

Angling on the River Dee
The Llangollen Angling Association controls a 6-mile (10-km) stretch of the River Dee in and around Llangollen. The Dee is particularly renowned for salmon, brown trout, and grayling.
www.llangollenangling.net

Below: Plas Newydd, home of the "Ladies of Llangollen"

THE ESSENTIALS

GETTING THERE AND AROUND
The Lulworth Ranges are in Dorset, in southwestern England. The nearest airport is at Bournemouth, 25 miles (40 km) away. The nearest train station is at Wool (on the Dorchester/Poole line), 5 miles (8 km) away; buses run from Wool to Lulworth Cove. Please note that roads in the ranges are restricted during live firing exercises – call +44 (0) 1929 404819 for the latest information.

WEATHER
The summer climate in Dorset is pleasant and mild, with average daytime temperatures ranging from 57 to 63°F (14–17°C).

ACCOMMODATIONS
Treat Yourself Mortons House Hotel, in Corfe Castle, 5 miles (8 km) from Kimmeridge Bay, is a very pretty 16th-century manor house converted into an award-winning luxury hotel. *www.mortonshouse.co.uk*

On a Budget Cove House B&B, in West Lulworth, is a converted Victorian house with spacious rooms and amiable owners. *www.covehouse.net*

EATING OUT
Treat Yourself The restaurant at Mortons House Hotel, in Corfe Castle, spices up classic British ingredients with modern fusion flavors – but also serves up a traditional Sunday lunch. *www.mortonshouse.co.uk*

On a Budget Lulworth Cove Inn, in West Lulworth, offers dependably flavorsome seafood and shellfish dishes. *www.lulworth-cove.co.uk*

PRICE FOR TWO PEOPLE
From $170 a day for accommodations, food, and admission fees.

WEBSITE
www.lulworthonline.co.uk

Tyneham Ghost Village

Perhaps the quirkiest sight along the path is the ghost village of Tyneham, which was evacuated in 1943 after the Ministry of Defence requisitioned the area. It was not repopulated after the end of World War II, and much of the village has now either disappeared or fallen into ruin. The Elizabethan manor house was demolished in the 1960s, but St. Mary's Church and the schoolhouse have found a new lease of life as museums. The latter still has pupils' abandoned homework on display.

THE JURASSIC COAST

ONE OF ENGLAND'S FINEST SECTIONS OF COASTLINE, Dorset's Lulworth Ranges run from Kimmeridge Bay in the west to Lulworth Cove in the east. They offer spectacular hikes but are also home to firing ranges for the British army, so plan a visit when the paths are open and artillery practice has been put on hold. It's worth the wait – the stunning views from this heathland path include sweeping bays and rugged, folding white cliffs. The absorbing cliffside limestone geology and beauty of the Jurassic Coast has resulted in the Ranges being designated a UNESCO World Heritage Site and Area of Outstanding Natural Beauty (AONB). It's no walk in the park, however, and the cresting and falling path can be demanding in sections.

Before setting off, visit the Lulworth Heritage Centre, which has lots of useful information on the area and its geology. Then make your way to Lulworth Cove, a scenic, horseshoe-shaped bay formed over the millennia by persistent waves. The nearby Stair Hole is a cove-in-the-making where you can see "Lulworth Crumple" – the distinctive folded rock found in this area. A further geological marvel is the Fossil Forest, east of Lulworth Cove: weird, ring-shaped formations in the rock that are the 135-million-year-old petrified remains of Jurassic tree trunks.

A string of bays unfurls along the coast east of Lulworth Cove, including Mupe Bay and Arish Mell. Mupe Bay is overlooked by Bindon Hill (said to be haunted by a spectral Roman army), while Arish Mell, farther east, is a pretty, sheltered cove. Beyond this lies the ancient Iron Age hill fort and earthen burial mound of Flower's Barrow. To the east of Tyneham Village, the dark Jurassic shale layers of Kimmeridge Bay are worth exploring – there are thousands of amazing fossils embedded in the local rock. There is also an excellent marine wildlife reserve in the bay. The three-story Clavell Tower, just to the east above the bay, was built in 1830 as a folly; a few years ago, the tower was moved 80 ft (25 m) back from the crumbling cliff to stop it from falling into the sea. The exhilarating views, archaeological treasures, and potential fossil finds make the Lulworth Ranges one of the most exciting places to walk in summer.

FURTHER DETAILS

LULWORTH RANGES
The Lulworth Ranges are live-ammunition training grounds used by the army, so it is essential to coincide with public opening times: late Jul–Aug daily, plus most weekends, school vacations, and Bank Holidays. Red flags indicate that the firing range is in use. Do not leave the path.
www.lulworth.com/ranges.htm

Lulworth Heritage Centre
Lulworth Cove; open Apr–Sep: 10am–6pm; Oct: 10am–5pm; Nov–Mar: 10am–4pm daily.
www.lulworth.co.uk

Purbeck Marine Wildlife Reserve
Kimmeridge Bay; open Apr–Sep: 10:30am–5pm Tue–Sun, Oct–Mar: 12–4pm weekends and school vacations.
www.lulworth.co.uk

WHAT ELSE TO SEE AND DO
Durdle Door
A few miles west along the coast from West Lulworth, this well-known and iconic limestone arch is a geological highlight of the Jurassic Coast.

Corfe Castle
Magical castle ruins to explore, not far from Kimmeridge, with engaging exhibitions, activities, and family trails based on the castle's turbulent past.
www.nationaltrust.org.uk

Below (top to bottom): Tranquil Lulworth Cove; Durdle Door arched rock formation in Durdle Bay

The dark Jurassic shale layers of Kimmeridge Bay are worth exploring – there are thousands of amazing fossils embedded in the local rock.

Main: "Lulworth Crumple" rock strata at Stair Hole **Inset:** Ammonite fossils recovered at Kimmeridge
Below: Clavell Tower on the clifftops overlooking Kimmeridge Bay

THE ESSENTIALS

GETTING THERE AND AROUND
The Irish National Heritage Park is 3 miles
(5 km) west of Wexford on the N11, and
is best reached by car. The nearest airport
to Wexford is Waterford, 25 miles (40 km)
to the west, with flights from the UK. The
nearest international airport is at Dublin,
80 miles (130 km) north.

WEATHER
Summer is the best time to visit
County Wexford, with average daytime
temperatures of 55 to 64°F (13–18°C),
though as always in Ireland, be prepared
for rain.

ACCOMMODATIONS
Treat Yourself The Ferrycarrig Hotel
is a 4-star choice with stunning views
across the River Slaney, and is very
close to the Heritage Park.
www.ferrycarrighotel.ie

On a Budget Westgate House is a
simple but excellent family-run B&B
in a period home in Wexford.
www.wexford-online.com/westgate

EATING OUT
Treat Yourself Forde's Restaurant is one
of Wexford's top dining establishments,
with daily fish specials and a harbor view.
www.fordesrestaurantwexford.com

On a Budget La Dolce Vita, in Wexford,
is a good-value Italian restaurant; the
quality of the food is evident from its
popularity with the locals.
Tel: 053 917 0806

PRICE FOR A FAMILY OF FOUR
From $270 a day for admission
fees, food, and accommodations.

WEBSITE
www.wexfordtourism.com

The Sands of Time

Wexford's history has been affected, quite literally,
by the sands of time. It was once one of the most
important ports in southeast Ireland, with a natural
harbor and a short crossing distance to the British
mainland. However, due to the constant movement
of the tides and the waters of the River Slaney, the
harbor had to be regularly dredged to rid it of
the shifting sands. By the late 1960s this was no
longer economically viable, and today the harbor
is left to leisure craft and small fishing boats.

Main: Reconstruction of a *crannog*, or island settlement, built in the middle of a lake at the Irish National Heritage Park
Right (top to bottom): Replica of a dolmen, or portal tomb; Celtic cross painted with Biblical images

A JOURNEY TO THE PAST

IRELAND IS AN ANCIENT LAND, and traces of its early inhabitants are scattered across the
green hills like snapshots of history. Here, a massive dolmen (stone tomb) stands guard in a
lonely field; there, a grassy mound marks a prehistoric burial site. It can sometimes be hard to
understand the character of the people who built them, and how they must have lived.

The Irish National Heritage Park is like a time-trail into this past. Spread out through
reclaimed marsh and woodlands, 9,000 years of history are displayed in a series of reconstructed
dwellings. First you come across a Stone Age hut, its sapling frame covered in earth and animal
skins. Next is an early Irish farmstead with conical, thatched houses and animal shelters. As
you enter the dark, smoky interiors you start to imagine what life was like in these ancient
abodes. Costumed guides are on hand to demonstrate how people cooked and what they ate.

The park is an educational experience for young children and history buffs alike. You can
explore a Neolithic dolmen, see inside a Bronze Age cist (a box-shaped stone grave), and stand
within one of the mysterious stone circles that seem to watch over these ancient tombs.

FURTHER DETAILS

IRISH NATIONAL HERITAGE PARK
Ferrycarrig, County Wexford; open 9:30am–6:30pm daily.
www.inhp.com

WHAT ELSE TO SEE AND DO
Wexford Town
It's fun to wander through this attractive harbor town
founded by the Vikings. Explore its medieval lanes, ruined
Selskar Abbey, 18th-century Cornmarket, and the West
Gate Tower from the old city walls.
www.wexfordtourism.com

Kilmore Quay
This picturesque little village with its thatched cottages
is one of the main fishing ports in southeast Ireland.
June and July are good months to take a boat trip to the
Saltee Islands – one of Ireland's largest bird sanctuaries,
home to thousands of cormorants, puffins, gannets, and
other birds, as well as seals. A boat trip from Kilmore Quay
Marina with Saltee Cruises lasts about 90 minutes.
Saltee Cruises Tel: 053 912 9684

Wexford Wildfowl Reserve
In summer, wading birds and birds of prey can be
seen at this reserve, located on the mudflats, or
"slobs," 3 miles (5 km) northeast of Wexford Town.
www.wexfordwildfowlreserve.ie

Curracloe Beach
The closest place to spread your beach towel on a sunny
day is beyond the mudflats, 6 miles (10 km) northeast
of Wexford Town. The opening scenes of Steven Spielberg's
movie *Saving Private Ryan* were filmed here.

Below (top to bottom): Gannet colony at Great Saltee Island;
Kilmore Quay harbor, the starting point for many boat trips to
the Saltee Islands

You can explore a Neolithic dolmen, see inside a Bronze
Age grave, and stand within one of the mysterious stone
circles that seem to watch over these ancient tombs.

Each turn in the woods brings you into another era. Children love the Celtic ring fort with
its wooden stockade and secret underground passage. The brightly colored Celtic cross at
the monastic settlement may come as a surprise, but this is how the weathered high crosses
originally looked. Nearby is the drying kiln and water mill that the monks used to grind grain.

Perhaps the most striking homestead is the *crannog*, a medieval settlement located on a
man-made island in a reedy lake. You can also explore a Viking ship and walled household, and
an early Norman feudal castle, the whitewashed facade of which makes a gleaming contrast to
the rare stone ruins that are left in Ireland today. Each dwelling is recreated in fantastic detail.

The Irish National Heritage Park really comes to life on summer weekends, when living
history events are enacted throughout the grounds. A deeper understanding of so many of
Ireland's ancient heritage sites awaits you amid this lush and pleasant Wexford countryside.

EXPLORING EXMOOR

STRADDLING THE NORTH COAST OF SOMERSET AND DEVON, Exmoor National Park can present very different faces. The high moors evoke a bleak and haunting beauty when the mists roll in from the sea, while sunshine exposes a timeless rural idyll of green hillside pastures, divided by dry-stone walls and solitary farms that date back as far as the 11th century. In summer, you can cross fallow fields knee-deep in sun-burnished grass and wildflowers, and hike through the forested valleys of the rivers Exe and Barle, before cooling your feet in clear rushing water beside the stone arches of a packhorse bridge.

Though it covers just 267 sq miles (692 sq km), Exmoor is crisscrossed by more than 620 miles (1,000 km) of footpaths and bridleways. The park is also popular with cyclists, who can often be seen pedaling en masse up to Dunkery Beacon – Exmoor's highest point at 1,705 ft (520 m) – where there are sweeping views over the heather-covered moors to the sea. Here, and

THE ESSENTIALS

GETTING THERE AND AROUND
Exmoor National Park is in southwest England on the north coast of Somerset and Devon, around 30 miles (48 km) north of Exeter. The closest major airport is Bristol, 31 miles (50 km) northeast of the Exmoor boundary. The best way to explore the region is on foot or by bicycle, but a car is also recommended for more remote areas. There are buses between the main Exmoor villages.

WEATHER
Exmoor has a temperate climate and is warmest during the summer months, with average daytime temperatures ranging from 60 to 63°F (15–17°C).

ACCOMMODATIONS
Treat Yourself The Luttrell Arms, in Dunster, is a small and atmospheric hotel in a 15th-century building with an excellent bar and restaurant.
www.luttrellarms.co.uk

On a Budget Town Mills, in the beautiful Exmoor town of Dulverton, is a charming converted millhouse.
www.townmillsdulverton.co.uk

EATING OUT
Treat Yourself The Royal Oak Inn, in Luxborough, has several dining rooms that all share the same tasty menu, which includes unusual and innovative dishes.
www.theroyaloakinnluxborough.co.uk

On a Budget Cobblestones, in Dunster, is an old-fashioned restaurant with friendly staff that boasts a fantastic menu and reasonable prices.
Tel: 01643 821595

PRICE FOR TWO PEOPLE
Around $260 a day for food and accommodations.

WEBSITE
www.visit-exmoor.co.uk

Exmoor in Literature

Exmoor has played the muse to many writers. Local author R. D. Blackmore's novel *Lorna Doone* (1869) is a riveting tale of outlaws and romance on Exmoor. You can visit the church at Oare that plays a pivotal role in the plot. Samuel Taylor Coleridge wrote some of his finest poems, including *The Rime of the Ancient Mariner*, when he lived at Nether Stowey. In 1797 William Wordsworth and his sister Dorothy rented a house at nearby Holford, and the three regularly walked from Porlock Weir to Culbone.

> In summer, you can cross fallow fields knee-deep in sun-burnished grass and wildflowers, and hike through the forested valleys.

on the moor near Simonsbath to the west, you are likely to see wild Exmoor ponies, a rare and ancient breed that roams free in the park. England's only wild herd of red deer lives here too, numbering several thousand. Keep an eye out for their fawns, which are born in early summer.

Charming villages and hamlets with quaint churches and cozy pubs are scattered throughout the park. Favorite beauty spots include Selworthy, with its thatched cottages and whitewashed church, and Allerford with its double-arched packhorse bridge. Exford, in the heart of the park, is a stag-hunting center; packs of dogs and horses are a common sight in this pretty village around the River Exe. Nearby Winsford is a collection of thatched cottages, pubs, and picturesque bridges.

A handful of larger villages form the main tourist hubs. Dulverton is the starting point for fine walks along the River Barle. Overlooked by its turreted castle, Dunster is a lovely medieval wool-exporting village with an octagonal Yarn Market in the high street. There are more thatched cottages and an ancient parish church at Porlock, perhaps the most attractive village on the north coast. Lastly, perched on a high cliff, the Victorian resort of Lynton affords fine views over the beach at Lynmouth below, and across the Bristol Channel to Wales.

FURTHER DETAILS

EXMOOR NATIONAL PARK
The three main national park visitor centers at Dulverton, Dunster, and Lynmouth offer maps, trail guides, details of local events, and information about the park.
www.exmoor-nationalpark.gov.uk

Dulverton National Park Centre
Fore Street; open Mar 30–Nov 1: 10am–5pm daily; limited winter opening.

Dunster National Park Centre
Dunster Steep; open Mar 30–Nov 1: 10am–5pm daily; limited winter opening.

Lynmouth National Park Centre
Lyndale Car Park; open late Apr–Oct: 10am–5pm daily; also weekends in March.

WHAT ELSE TO SEE AND DO
Dunster Castle
A 13th-century gateway leads to this romantic fortress in Dunster, set on a hill with terraced gardens and splendid views over Exmoor and the Bristol Channel. It was the seat of the aristocratic Luttrell family for nearly 600 years.
www.nationaltrust.org.uk

Coleridge Cottage
Samuel Taylor Coleridge wrote *The Rime of the Ancient Mariner* and other works while living here in 1797–98. His cottage is on the Coleridge Way, a 36-mile (58-km) footpath named after him, and visitors can view the parlor, reading room, and a collection of personal mementoes.
www.nationaltrust.org.uk

The Cliff Railway
Take a delightful ride on the Cliff Railway, a remarkable Victorian hydraulic cable-car that is powered by counterbalanced water tanks. It has been transporting passengers between the clifftop resort of Lynton and the beach at Lynmouth since 1890.
www.cliffrailwaylynton.co.uk

Outdoor Activities
Exmoor has an abundance of varied terrain that is suitable for all manner of outdoor pursuits, including hiking, fishing, and mountain biking. You can also learn to canoe and windsurf on the reservoir at Wimbleball Lake.
www.activeexmoor.com

Main: Typical Exmoor cottage by the double-arched packhorse bridge in Allerford

Left (top to bottom): Yarn Market in Dunster; mountain bikers climbing past gorse bushes

Above: Wild ponies grazing on Exmoor

Below: Rolling Exmoor countryside

THE ESSENTIALS

GETTING THERE AND AROUND
Mull is an island in the Inner Hebrides, off the coast of northwest Scotland. The main ferry route (with a travel time of 45 minutes) operates from Oban on the mainland to Craignure on Mull. There are also ferries from Lochaline to Fishnish (taking 15 minutes) and Kilchoan to Tobermory (taking 35 minutes). Loch Lomond Seaplanes fly from Glasgow airport to Tobermory Harbour (35 minutes). There are buses, taxis, and car rentals available on Mull.

WEATHER
Summer weather on Mull is mild, with daytime highs of 59 to 73°F (15–23°C), but strong winds and choppy seas are normal. Weatherproof clothing is essential.

ACCOMMODATIONS
Treat Yourself Glengorm Castle, near Tobermory, offers luxury B&B rooms in a stunning family-owned mansion.
www.glengormcastle.co.uk

On a Budget Tobermory Youth Hostel, in Tobermory, has cheap dormitory accommodations and also offers private and family rooms.
www.syha.org.uk

EATING OUT
Treat Yourself Highland Cottage, in Tobermory, offers exceptional gourmet food in an elegant setting.
www.highlandcottage.co.uk

On a Budget Fisherman's Pier Chip Van, in Tobermory, is legendary for its fantastic fresh-fried fish and chips to take away.
www.tobermoryboatcharters.co.uk

PRICE FOR TWO PEOPLE
$300 a day for accommodations, food, trips, and admission fees.

WEBSITES
www.visitscottishheartlands.com
www.tobermory.co.uk

The Gulf Stream

On a chilly day it's hard to believe that the waters off Mull are warmed by currents flowing from the Caribbean. But the Gulf Stream, winding its way around the Atlantic, creates a range of microclimates on Scotland's west coast, making it possible for subtropical plants to flourish as far north as Ullapool in northern Scotland. If climate change ever weakens the Gulf Stream, as scientists fear, Mull's waters may no longer be able to support warm-blooded creatures like whales or dolphins.

Main: Minke whale, a regular visitor to the waters around Mull
Right (top to bottom): Colorful facades on the harbor-front in Tobermory, Mull; puffin colony

A WHALE OF A TIME

IT'S IMPOSSIBLE TO DECIDE which of Scotland's many islands is the most enchanting. Mull, with its miles of heather moorland, azure seas, and picture-postcard villages, is definitely a strong contender. But Mull is more than just a pretty face. Its hinterland and its waters are home to a vast array of wildlife, making it a nature-lover's paradise in the summer months.

Sea eagles soar above a rugged coastline where crags and rocky headlands are interspersed with coves of pristine white sand. Otters, recovering in numbers after decades of decline, patrol its silver streams and rock pools. Inquisitive seals pop their heads up as if to greet passing boats, or loll on seaweed-covered rocks at low tide. The waters around Mull and its smaller sister islands are also the home of permanent populations of bottlenose dolphins and harbor porpoises, and blooms of plankton attract huge, ponderous basking sharks – a little scary at first sight, but completely harmless. With a bit of luck and determination, you may be able to view many of these species on even a short visit to Mull. Stay for a week in summer, and it's almost guaranteed that you'll encounter one or more of these amazing creatures.

FURTHER DETAILS

MULL WILDLIFE
Wildlife Cruises
Sea Life Surveys offers 6-hour day cruises that visit the best areas to see whales, dolphins, porpoises, sharks, seals, and a variety of sea birds. Day cruises depart from Tobermory Apr–Oct, 9:30am daily; shorter boat trips are also available year-round. www.sealifesurveys.com

Overland Expeditions
Wild About Mull, in Pennyghael, offers minibus tours of the island, led by naturalists who know the best wildlife sites. www.wildaboutmull.co.uk

WHAT ELSE TO SEE AND DO
Torosay Castle and the Mull Railway
This Victorian mansion is worth visiting just for its beautiful gardens and for the 20-minute trip to the castle on the Mull Railway's miniature train, which departs from Craignure. www.torosay.com

Duart Castle
The ancestral seat of the Maclean clan – one of the most powerful families on Mull – was built in Lochdon, on Mull, in the 13th century. You can explore both the evocative castle and its grounds. www.duartcastle.com

Below (top to bottom): European otters play on seaweed along Mull's beaches; shimmering white shell-sand of the west-coast beaches

However, it's another summer visitor that can make a trip to this island very special. Huge minke whales – which can reach up to 36 ft (11 m) in length – are drawn to the west coast of Scotland by the nutrient-rich waters that well up from the Atlantic depths. In the summer months, it's possible to sight minke whales up to half-a-dozen times a day. Despite suffering centuries of whaling, the whales can be surprisingly fearless, swimming right up to small boats before rolling over to pass beneath. More commonly, they can be spotted as they breach, or surface, blasting out a spume of spray as they exhale before sliding back below the waves.

Minke are not the only whales seen in these waters: orcas (killer whales) are spotted occasionally in summer. Humpback whales have also been recorded, and there has been at least one sighting of a fin whale – second only in size to the blue whale – in recent years. Look also for sea birds such as puffins, razorbills, shearwaters, and kittiwakes. They prey on the same shoals of fish that feed the minke, so large flocks may indicate the presence of whales.

Mull has a thriving wildlife industry, with many companies offering day trips – and sometimes longer cruises – from various points on the island. There are also overland tours that allow you the chance to see such rare sights as golden eagles, red deer, and adders. A day out in Mull offers plenty of potential thrills: you just have to keep your eyes wide open.

CASTLES AND COASTLINE

WITH ITS LUSH GREEN VALLEYS and windswept mountains, South Wales is rich in natural beauty. There are few sights that beat the sunset at Rhossili, on the Gower Peninsula, or the rugged coastline of Cardigan Bay. But this ancient land has man-made wonders, too: a string of gray stone castles that stud the countryside like uncut gems. Some are crumbling ruins, providing a picturesque backdrop for family picnics and endless opportunities for games of hide and seek. Others look much as they did when they were first built – historic treasure troves ringed with battlements and containing grand halls and mighty towers. All have their own unique and compelling story to tell.

> This ancient land has man-made wonders, too: a string of gray stone castles that stud the countryside like uncut gems.

THE ESSENTIALS

GETTING THERE AND AROUND
South Wales lies on the western coast of Britain and shares a border with England. Cardiff International Airport is 14 miles (23 km) from Cardiff; there are direct train connections from Cardiff to London, Birmingham, and Manchester. South Wales's castles are best reached by car; most are located within a couple of hours' drive of Cardiff.

WEATHER
In summer the weather in South Wales is generally pleasant, with daytime temperatures averaging 63–72°F (17–22°C), but be prepared for rain too.

ACCOMMODATIONS
Treat Yourself St. David's Hotel and Spa, in Cardiff, is a luxury option and a favorite with visiting celebrities.
www.stdavidshotelcardiff.co.uk

On a Budget The Glynhir Estate, in Carmarthenshire, offers bed and breakfast or full meal service and is ideally situated for visiting the coastal castles of Dinefwr and Carreg Cennen.
www.theglynhirestate.com

EATING OUT
Treat Yourself
The Old Pharmacy, in Solva, is a quaint little restaurant – formerly an apothecary's shop – that specializes in local seafood.
www.theoldpharmacy.co.uk

On a Budget The Greendown Inn, in St.-Georges-Sur-Ely near Cardiff, is a friendly inn that serves simple local fare, including homemade beef pie.

PRICE FOR A FAMILY OF FOUR
$460–500 a day for accommodations, food, transportation, and admission fees.

WEBSITE
www.visitwales.com

Chepstow Castle is particularly dramatic. Stunningly situated above the River Wye, on the border with England, it is a brooding reminder of a turbulent past. Built by the Normans in 1067 just after the Conquest, it was the first stone castle in Britain – a strategic base for aggressive raids into Wales. Then there's Caerphilly, a little town dominated by a castle so imposing that the poet Lord Tennyson declared: "It isn't a castle – it's a town in ruins." Built in the 13th century, the castle was a medieval masterpiece of military engineering, with impenetrable walls and formidable water defenses. Cardiff Castle, by contrast, is noted for its flamboyant 19th-century interiors, created for the eccentric Marquis of Bute by William Burgess. Its rooms are a Gothic fantasy of gilded ceilings, mirrors, and elaborate carvings.

Travelers with an artistic streak will love the romantic ruins of Laugharne Castle, a favorite of the poet Dylan Thomas, while families with budding young historians might prefer Pembroke Castle. Founded by one of William the Conqueror's most trusted lords, and the birthplace of Henry VII, it is often used for energetic reenactments of historic events.

Perhaps the most striking sight of all is Carreg Cennen Castle, in rural Carmarthenshire. The castle is perched precariously on a crag above the River Cennen, and legend has it that one of King Arthur's knights lies asleep deep beneath it, ready to awaken when Wales is in peril.

Main: Visitors in the grounds of the impressive Laugharne Castle in Carmarthenshire **Inset:** Remains of Caerphilly Castle **Below:** Cardigan Island, lying in Cardigan Bay

A Rich Architectural Legacy

The castles of Wales were built in three distinct phases. The earliest castles were built by the Normans when they were trying to suppress the Welsh after the Norman Conquest – most of these are located in the south. In the 13th century, when many factions were struggling for control of the country, Welsh princes built fortresses on isolated hills, but few survive today. Finally, in the late 13th century, Edward I built a series of large castles to suppress rebellions in the north of the country.

FURTHER DETAILS

CASTLES OF SOUTH WALES

Chepstow Castle
Bridge Street, Chepstow, Monmouthshire;
open 9:30am–5pm daily.
www.chepstow.co.uk

Caerphilly Castle
Caerphilly; open 9:30am–5pm daily.
www.aboutbritain.com/CaerphillyCastle.htm

Cardiff Castle
Castle Street, Cardiff; open Mar–Oct: 9am–6pm daily;
Nov–Feb: 9am–5:30pm daily.
www.cardiffcastle.com

Laugharne Castle
King Street, Laugharne, Carmarthenshire;
open 9:30am–5pm daily.
www.aboutbritain.com/LaugharneCastle.htm

Carreg Cennen Castle
Llandeilo, Carmarthenshire; open Mar–Oct: 9:30am–6pm
daily; Nov–Feb: 9:30am–4pm daily.
www.carregcennencastle.com

WHAT ELSE TO SEE AND DO

Cardiff
In Cardiff, the lively Welsh capital, you can take a tour
of the Millennium Stadium, visit the Welsh Millennium
Centre – a stunningly modern center for the arts – or
head to the Museum of Welsh Life. The huge variety of
theaters, galleries, and nightspots provides a welcome
contrast to the region's historical architecture.
www.visitcardiff.com

Swansea and the Gower Peninsula
Try the famous cockles with vinegar and pepper at
Swansea Market, or savor an ice cream cone at the
Mumbles – a large village just outside of Swansea,
where you can also view the ruins of yet another castle,
Oystermouth. The nearby Gower Peninsula offers beautiful
scenery and spectacular sunsets over Rhossili Bay from its
headland, which is known as Worm's Head.
www.swansea.gov.uk

National Wetland Centre, Llanelli
Stretching over 450 acres (180 hectares) on the Burry
Inlet, this magnificent mosaic of lakes, pools, and lagoons
is home to countless wild species, from dragonflies to
egrets. You can explore the watery expanses in a canoe.
www.wwt.org.uk

Below: The Great Hall of Caerphilly Castle

THE ESSENTIALS

GETTING THERE AND AROUND
The Cheshire Ring is located in northwest England, near Manchester, Stoke-on-Trent, and Northwich. Manchester Airport is within half an hour's drive of the canals. Train stations close to boatyards include Manchester Piccadilly, Macclesfield, Sandbach, and Northwich.

WEATHER
At the height of summer, Cheshire can be pleasantly warm and dry (55–63°F/ 13–17°C), but be prepared for rain.

ACCOMMODATIONS
Treat Yourself The Place Hotel, in Manchester, provides comfortable and contemporary two-bedroom family apartments with kitchen and living room. www.theplacehotel.com

On a Budget Premier Inn Macclesfield South West is useful for a stopover at the beginning or end of your trip, with trains to Macclesfield and boatyards nearby. www.premierinn.com

EATING OUT
Treat Yourself Sutton Hall Hotel, near the Macclesfield Canal, is a splendidly converted 16th-century manor house now run as a dining pub, with an interesting changing menu. www.suttonhall.co.uk

On a Budget Dukes 92, in Castlefield, provides real ales, pizza, and good bar food. Children are welcome until 8:30pm. www.dukes92.com

PRICE FOR A FAMILY OF FOUR:
Around $300–415 a day including boat rental and food.

WEBSITE
www.waterscape.com

An Engineering Marvel

Near Northwich, the gigantic Anderton Boat Lift connects the River Weaver with the Trent and Mersey Canal. When it opened in 1875 it was the first device of its kind in the world. It dispensed with the need for a long flight of locks – instead, the boat enters a water-filled tank at the bottom and is lifted 50 ft (15 m) by the immense machinery. The experience of going up and down in the Lift, sometimes with a short cruise up the River Weaver, is available to visitors arriving by car or by boat.

Main: Narrowboat navigating the Bridgewater Canal at Walton
Right (top to bottom): Mills alongside the canal at Macclesfield; Anderton Boat Lift at Barnton, near Northwich

CANAL CRUISING

Taking to the water on Britain's historic canal network gloriously uncomplicates your lifestyle for a week or so, and in the heat of summer it can provide the perfect relaxation fix. One of the most diverse circular routes takes in six canals to form the 97-mile (156-km) Cheshire Ring, which is possible to navigate in about a week.

For families, this trip can be an unbeatable way of sharing the sheer pleasure of travel: the boat is your home, your kitchen, and your entire life, while the rest of the world glides effortlessly by. Added to that, it's a wonderful history lesson. Your children may be learning about the Industrial Revolution at school – here, they'll find out what travel was like in the brief heyday of the canal, before the coming of the railroads. They'll help open and close the 92 locks, and older children can take a turn at steering the craft. You'll head through tunnels and under packhorse bridges, and there's always the towpath for stretching your legs, on foot or by bicycle. If you start your journey on the lock-free Bridgewater Canal, you can travel right into central Manchester, where you can moor at Castlefield and explore. Some of the best

FURTHER DETAILS

CHESHIRE RING
You do not need a license to pilot a canal boat, and piloting is quickly learned. A full fuel tank is supplied at the start of the week and will easily last for the whole trip. It is often possible to take bicycles and pets on boats.
Blakes: www.blakes.co.uk
Alvechurch Boats: www.alvechurch.com
Claymoore Canal Holidays: www.claymoore.co.uk

Little Moreton Hall
Congleton. Cheshire's most iconic country house is considered to be one of the finest examples of English Tudor architecture. Built without foundations in 1450, and extensively added to over the following 120 years, it is spectacularly "crooked", with barely a straight vertical line; open mid-Mar–Oct: 11am–5pm Wed–Sun; end-Feb–mid-Mar and Nov–mid-Dec: 11am–4pm, Sat–Sun.

Museum of Science and Industry (MOSI)
Liverpool Road, Castlefield. The MOSI tells the fascinating story of Manchester's scientific and industrial past, present, and future; open 10am–5pm daily.
www.mosi.org.uk

Manchester United Museum and Stadium Tour
Old Trafford, Sir Matt Busby Way. Manchester United's stadium, Old Trafford, famously called the "Theatre of Dreams", offers a perfect day out for supporters, and enough to see even for those who aren't football fans; open 9:30am–5pm daily.
www.manutd.com

Anderton Boat Lift
Lift Lane, Anderton, near Northwich; trips on the lift run daily in the summer months. Check the website for days of operation outside the summer season.
www.andertonboatlift.co.uk

WHAT ELSE TO SEE AND DO
New Mills
A popular short add-on to a Cheshire Ring cruise is to take the Upper Peak Forest Canal to New Mills, where the town perches over the dramatic Torrs gorge, which is great fun to explore.
www.newmillstowncouncil.com

Below: Little Moreton Hall, a fine example of half-timbered architecture

An unbeatable way of sharing the sheer pleasure of travel: the boat is your home, your kitchen, and your entire life, while the rest of the world glides effortlessly by.

diversions are the Museum of Science and Industry and the tour of the Manchester United soccer club's huge stadium. You can then continue along the Rochdale Canal, winding between atmospheric backdrops of Victorian warehouses before rising steadily through the outskirts.

At Marple there are two spectacular canal features: the imposing Marple Aqueduct and an impressive flight of 16 locks. From there you skirt brooding Peak District hills as the Macclesfield Canal passes by old silk mills, before the 12 Bosley locks lower you on to the Cheshire Plain, where you can visit the eye-catching riot of half-timbering that is Little Moreton Hall. Turn right at Stoke to cruise up the Trent and Mersey Canal and, just before you rejoin the Bridgewater Canal, you'll pass an unmissable sight: the Anderton Boat Lift (*see story box*), which once carried working barges up to the River Weaver. You can park up your canal boat and join the Lift's own pleasure craft to experience this engineering marvel, a theme park ride from Britain's industrial past.

THE ESSENTIALS

GETTING THERE AND AROUND
Edinburgh is located in southeastern Scotland. The nearest airport is Edinburgh International, 10 miles (16 km) west of the city. Hourly trains (fastest 4 hours 20 minutes) run from London King's Cross to Waverley Station in Edinburgh. Trains also run to Edinburgh from other cities across the UK. Most of the downtown can be easily explored on foot.

WEATHER
Edinburgh enjoys summer daytime temperatures averaging 52–72°F (14–22°C). However, Scotland's weather is fickle, so be prepared for rain at any time.

ACCOMMODATIONS
It is essential to reserve accommodations for the festival up to 6 months in advance. Expect premium prices at this time of year.

Treat Yourself The Balmoral Hotel, on Princes Street, has a fantastic location, and offers excellent comfort and service. www.thebalmoralhotel.com

On a Budget Glendale House, in Craigmillar Park, 2 miles (3 km) from the downtown, is a clean, well-equipped B&B. www.glendaleguesthouse.co.uk

EATING OUT
Treat Yourself The Kitchin, in Commercial Quay, is an award-winning restaurant by the waterfront in Leith, with an inventive menu and great ambience. www.thekitchin.com

On a Budget Petit Paris, on Grassmarket, offers an authentic French menu. www.petitparis-restaurant.co.uk

PRICE FOR TWO PEOPLE
Around $400 a day for accommodations, food, and festival tickets.

WEBSITE
www.edinburgh.org

The Camera Obscura

Housed within the Outlook Tower, Edinburgh's Camera Obscura reveals an exact picture of the city outside, reflected and refracted through a series of mirrors and lenses before being projected on to a white concave table in a darkened room. The effect is similar to watching a film of the city. What makes it all the more fascinating is that, at 150 years old, this is Edinburgh's oldest attraction. The attached World of Illusions explores optical illusions, and is an excellent day out for children.

Main: Festival fireworks over Edinburgh's nighttime skyline
Above (left to right): Edinburgh Castle; *One Flew Over the Cuckoo's Nest* performed at the Edinburgh Fringe Festival

FUN AT THE FRINGE

WITH ITS GRAND ARCHITECTURE AND COSMOPOLITAN VIBE, Edinburgh has long been a center for enlightened thinking, earning it the title "the Athens of the North." Today, Scotland's capital city conserves this noble tradition by playing host to the world's biggest arts festival. The world-famous Edinburgh Festival is not one event, but rather a constellation of individual arts and culture festivities that bring a creative *frisson* to the city. The "original" event, the Edinburgh International Festival, boasts an inspiring program of classical music and theater productions, but it's the world-famous Edinburgh Fringe that steals much of the limelight, attracting performers from over 60 countries every year. Ranging across the full dramatic spectrum, from theater, mime, comedy, dance, and musicals to performances aimed exclusively at little ones, the Fringe sees almost 20,000 participants displaying their creative talents across the city – every available public space simply overflows with performers.

With so many concurrent events in town, something is bound to catch your interest: there's the Edinburgh International Film Festival, the Edinburgh Jazz and Blues Festival, the Edinburgh Art Festival, the Edinburgh Book Festival, the Edinburgh Annuale, and the Edinburgh Comedy Festival. The festival period is wildly popular, bringing in more visitors than the city's entire resident population, so you'll have to battle for every square foot of space. But summer is usually kind weather-wise, and the long days encourage extensive exploration.

When you have time to put aside your festival schedule, explore the city's melange of medieval, Gothic, and Georgian architecture. Both the medieval Old Town and the adjoining Georgian New Town are UNESCO World Heritage Sites. A trip to Edinburgh Castle, on its perch of Castle Rock, offers panoramic views over the city; during festival time, the spectacular Edinburgh Military Tattoo is performed here nightly. Admire the architecture of the Royal Mile and explore the exhaustive collection of Scottish heritage at the National Museum of Scotland. The National Gallery of Scotland and the Scottish National Gallery of Modern Art will surely satisfy art-lovers. The royal Abbey and Palace of Holyroodhouse, St. Giles Cathedral, the Scottish Parliament, and the Royal Yacht *Britannia* are all other excellent sights. If you get hooked in summer, you can always come back to the city for the New Year's Eve Hogmanay.

Below (left to right): Crowds gathering on the Royal Mile during the festival; Swan Lake performed at The Edinburgh International Festival; Edinburgh Tattoo

FURTHER DETAILS

EDINBURGH FESTIVAL
Edinburgh International Festival: *www.eif.co.uk*
Edinburgh Fringe Festival: *www.edfringe.com*
Edinburgh International Film Festival:
 www.edfilmfest.org.uk
Edinburgh Jazz and Blues Festival:
 www.edinburghjazzfestival.co.uk
Edinburgh Art Festival: *www.edinburghartfestival.org*
Edinburgh Book Festival: *www.edbookfest.co.uk*
Edinburgh Annuale:
 www.annuale.edinburghcontemporary.org
Edinburgh Comedy Festival: *www.edcomfest.com*

EDINBURGH
Edinburgh Castle
Castle Hill; open Apr–Sept: 9:30am–6pm daily;
Oct–Mar: 9:30am–5pm daily.
www.edinburghcastle.gov.uk

Edinburgh Military Tattoo
Performances in August: 9pm Mon–Fri, 7:30pm and
10:30pm Sun; fireworks display on Sat nights.
www.edintattoo.co.uk

National Museum of Scotland
Chambers Street; open 10am–5pm daily.
www.nms.ac.uk

National Gallery of Scotland
The Mound; open 10am–5pm Fri–Wed, 10am–7pm Thu.
www.nationalgalleries.org

Scottish National Gallery of Modern Art
Belford Road; open 10am–5pm daily.
www.nationalgalleries.org

Abbey and Palace of Holyroodhouse
Royal Mile; open Nov–Mar: 9:30am–4:30pm daily;
Apr–Oct: 9:30am–6pm daily.
www.royalcollection.org.uk

Royal Yacht Britannia
Leith; open Jan–Mar and Nov–Dec: 10am–3:30pm
daily; Apr–Jun and Sep–Oct 10am–4pm daily; Jul:
9:30am–4pm daily; Aug: 9:30am–4:30pm daily.
www.royalyachtbritannia.co.uk

Camera Obscura and World of Illusions
Castlehill; open Jul–Aug: 9:30am–7:30pm
daily; Sep–Oct: 9:30am–6pm daily; Nov–Mar:
10am–5pm daily; Apr–Jun: 9:30am–7pm daily.
www.camera-obscura.co.uk

WHAT ELSE TO SEE AND DO
Aberdour
The charming village of Aberdour on the Firth of Forth
has several sights, including Aberdour Castle, an extended
13th-century residence; the 12th-century St Fillan's
Church; two beaches; and a summer festival.
www.historic-scotland.gov.uk

More Great Ideas for **Summer**

HISTORY AND HERITAGE

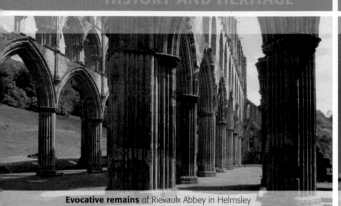

Evocative remains of Rievaulx Abbey in Helmsley

CHILTERN OPEN AIR MUSEUM
SOUTHEAST ENGLAND
Rescued and reerected local buildings, from an Iron Age house to a Victorian farm, bring history alive for visitors to Chalfont St. Giles.
www.coam.org.uk

RIEVAULX ABBEY NORTHEAST ENGLAND
A majestic and amazingly intact 900-year-old Cistercian abbey, Rievaulx is set in the stunning River Rye valley with sublime views of the dale. This atmospheric building once housed 650 monks and became one of the wealthiest abbeys in England. It was dissolved by Henry VIII in 1538, but much of the church and parts of the chapter house and refectory remain standing. The site houses an interesting interactive museum and there are wonderful walks nearby.
www.english-heritage.org.uk

TOLPUDDLE MARTYRS PROCESSION AND FESTIVAL SOUTHWEST ENGLAND
Every July, a three-day festival of music, performance, and debate, combined with a Trades Union Congress parade, celebrates the birthplace of trade unionism in the village of Tolpuddle. In the 1830s, six impoverished agricultural laborers started the Friendly Society of Agricultural Labourers to demand a minimum wage. They were deported to Australia, then returned following a public outcry.
www.tuc.org.uk

BARDSEY ISLAND
NORTH WALES
Bardsey, off the Llŷn Peninsula, was a place of pilgrimage for the early Celtic Christian Church. The abbey's 13th-century tower houses a 1,200-year-old stone carving.
www.enlli.org

FLOORS CASTLE
SOUTHERN SCOTLAND
Overlooking the River Tweed and the Cheviots, this fairy-tale castle is dotted with turrets and surrounded by beautiful grounds, where massed pipe bands play in late August.
www.roxburghe.net

See also pp66–7, 72–3, 86–7.

WILDLIFE AND LANDSCAPE

Red squirrel on Brownsea Island

BROWNSEA ISLAND SOUTHWEST ENGLAND
Brownsea Island, at the entrance to Poole Harbour, teems with flora and fauna in its mixed woodland, wetland, and heath nature reserve. There are rare plants, insects, and birds, such as the bar-tailed godwit, as well as red squirrels, sika deer, and shy water voles. Trail and tracker packs are available for lovely walks with beautiful views, and the island has an open air theatre. The Baden Powell Outdoor Centre allows you to camp on the site of the world's first scouting camp, held in 1907.
www.nationaltrust.org.uk

SLIEVENACLOY
NORTHERN IRELAND
Northern Ireland's newest nature reserve is home to many rare flora and fauna, including species of orchids and fungi, as well as Irish hares, curlews, and kestrels.
www.ulsterwildlifetrust.org

DOZMARY POOL
SOUTHWEST ENGLAND
Wild and desolate, Dozmary Pool is said to be the resting place of King Arthur's sword, Excalibur, thrown into the water by a loyal knight to be caught by the Lady of the Lake.
www.legendofkingarthur.co.uk

FETLAR
HIGHLANDS AND ISLANDS
"The Garden of Shetland" is a fertile haven for exquisite flowers and ground-nesting birds, including 90 percent of the British population of red-necked phalaropes.
www.iknow-scotland.co.uk

BOARSTALL DUCK DECOY SOUTHEAST ENGLAND
A duck decoy is an inventive device that was employed in the 17th–19th centuries to trap ducks. The Boarstall Duck Decoy is one of only four surviving in England and is still in working order. Regular demonstrations show how the ducks were coaxed by a fake duck, the "decoy," into a small patch of water and then corralled by man and dog into a wickerwork tunnel. Originally trapped for food, birds that are "caught" today are ringed and released into the wild.
www.nationaltrust.org.uk

See also pp76–7, 80–81, 88–9, 100–101.

CITIES, TOWNS, AND VILLAGES

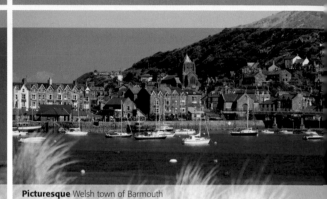

Picturesque Welsh town of Barmouth

BARMOUTH NORTH WALES
An attractive stone town set between an enormous sandy beach and the dramatic Mawddach Estuary, Barmouth backs onto a craggy hillside, on top of which is Dinas Oleu ("Fortress of Light"), the first piece of land acquired by the National Trust and a great viewing point. Once a major ship-building center, Barmouth is now a seaside resort hosting entertaining summer events, such as kite-flying festivals, and is the starting point of the Three Peaks Yacht Race.
www.barmouth.org.uk

PEEBLES
SOUTHERN SCOTLAND
Straddling the River Tweed, Peebles is famous as a centre of arts and for the Beltane Festival, a week-long celebration of legend, history, and tradition that takes place every June.
www.peebles.info

WHITSTABLE SOUTHEAST ENGLAND
A historic harbor and noisy fish markets draw the crowds to this small Kent coastal town. Pebbled beaches and colorful beach huts provide a flavor of traditional "Englishness", while restaurants offer delicious fresh seafood. The lively Oyster Festival in July celebrates Whitstable's history and heritage through music, art, and street theater. Delicious food and drink stalls abound, and the festival week kicks off with a ceremonial "landing of the oysters" on the beach.
www.seewhitstable.com

RYE SOUTHEAST ENGLAND
Once a coastal town, Rye now lies 2 miles (3 km) from the sea, leaving sheep to graze where boats once moored. The town became a cinque port in the 13th century, gaining trading and tax concessions for supporting the Plantagenet kings with ships, men, and safe harbor. Today, it has a thriving artistic community and its ancient buildings, cobbled streets, pubs, and shops are a tourist magnet. Look out for the entertaining summer Raft Race.
www.visitrye.co.uk

See also pp70–71, 82–3, 90–91, 98–9.

Traditional narrowboat crossing the Pontcysllte aqueduct

Landscape art at Groombridge Gardens

Horse racing on Laytown Beach

PONTCYSYLLTE AQUEDUCT NORTH WALES

For a memorably scary experience, take a narrowboat ride along the Llangollen canal from Llangollen Wharf to the Pontcysyllte Aqueduct. Built over the River Dee by Thomas Telford and William Jessop more than 200 years ago, the cast-iron, 126-ft- (38-m-) high structure has been given World Heritage status. With very little protection on one side except for a low iron "wall," crossing the 1,000-ft- (300-m-) long aqueduct in a boat gives the feeling of being suspended in mid-air.
www.attractionsnorthwales.co.uk

GROOMBRIDGE GARDENS SOUTHEAST ENGLAND

For horticulturists with kids, Groombridge has it all – award-winning gardens for adults and an enchanted forest for children. The formal gardens are organized into "rooms," including the "drunken" garden, the Asian garden, and glorious herbaceous borders. In the forest, youngsters will be amazed by unusual animals, such as the "zeedonk" – a rare zebra and donkey cross-breed. There is also a playground, as well as birds of prey and landscape art to admire.
www.groombridge.co.uk

LAYTOWN BEACH RACES EASTERN IRELAND

Turf meets surf at Laytown for the only officially approved beach strand race in Europe. These popular races have been taking place at the end of August on the beautiful Laytown Beach for 140 years, and thousands turn up every year to watch the spectacular sight of horses thundering across the sandy shore. A field above the beach is transformed for the one-day occasion into a racing enclosure with a ring, a weighing area, bookies, a grandstand, restaurants, and bars.
www.racingsight.co.uk

INNER HEBRIDES

HIGHLANDS AND ISLANDS
Summer ferries run trips to the smaller islands including the pretty Iona, and Staffa, home of the dramatic Fingal's Cave. The Treshnish Isles shelter thousands of sea birds.
www.staffatours.com

RUTLAND WATER

EAST MIDLANDS
This small county contains a reservoir the size of Lake Windermere. Perfect for fishing and sailing, the lake also hides the half-submerged Normanton Church Museum.
www.staffatours.com

THE HOPPINGS

NORTHEAST ENGLAND
Europe's largest traveling fair comes to Newcastle in June. There is a huge variety of white-knuckle rides to enjoy, as well as old favorites such as carousels and bumper cars.
www.newcastlegateshead.com

SPEYSIDE WAY

HIGHLANDS AND ISLANDS
The Way runs from the Moray Firth to the Cairngorms, but shorter treks between villages offer delights such as a folk museum, a castle or two, and the Glenfiddich distillery.
www.visitbritain.co.uk

SIDMOUTH FOLK WEEK

SOUTHWEST ENGLAND
Eight days of music, singing, dancing, ceilidhs, workshops, and performances in a lovely Devonshire Regency seaside town in August.
www.sidmouthfolkweek.co.uk

CALSHOT

SOUTHEAST ENGLAND
Calshot Activities Centre, on the Isle of Wight's Solent Coast, is one of the most popular water sports locations in Britain. It offers sailing, windsurfing, canoeing, and powerboating.
www.calshot.com

TATTON PARK NORTHWEST ENGLAND

There is something for everyone at this imaginatively presented visitor attraction. The magnificent house is full of historic treasures, including a Tudor great hall, complete with costumed guides. The estate also boasts a 1,000-acre (400-hectare) deer park, landscaped gardens, and a farm that still uses traditional methods. The park hosts over 100 events every year, including the Royal Horticultural Society's five-day Flower Show in July.
www.tattonpark.org.uk

FLYING LEGENDS AIR SHOW EASTERN ENGLAND

An international lineup of historic fighter aircraft awaits the thousands of spectators who attend this nostalgic two-day annual event, organized by the Imperial War Museum and the Fighter Collection. Every July, classic aircraft are displayed and flown at Duxford in Cambridgeshire. Airplanes from Britain, the US, Germany, Italy, and Russia, including famous models such as Spitfires, Hawkers, Mustangs, and Focke-Wulfs, take part in a mass takeoff and flyby.
www.fighter-collection.com

SCAFELL PIKE NORTHWEST ENGLAND

Soaring to 3,200 ft (980 m), Scafell Pike is the highest mountain in England. Its rough and rugged terrain is surrounded by a spectacular range of fells – Sca Fell, Kirk Fell, Pillar, and Great Gable – giving you a fantastic panorama of views as you tackle the long walk to the summit. Start your trip with a visit to the historic Wasdale Head Inn, Wasdale, a traditional starting point at the foot of Scafell Pike that has been offering sustenance and advice to climbers since the 19th century.
www.mountainwalk.co.uk/scafellpikewalk.html

MARBLE ARCH CAVES GLOBAL GEOPARK

NORTHERN IRELAND
This innovative geopark offers boat trips on an underground river and tours of the awe-inspiring natural caverns.
www.marblearchcaves.net

LAKE DISTRICT SHEEPDOG TRIALS

NORTHWEST ENGLAND
The one-day trials at Hill Farm, Ings, in August demonstrate the traditional skills of dog and shepherd moving sheep through a series of obstacles.
www.isds.org.uk

CORACLE RACES

CENTRAL WALES
Water-based frolics take place on the River Teifi for one day in August, including a race for novices, a non-swimmers' race, a water-polo match, and net-fishing displays.
www.coracle-fishing.net

See also pp62–3, 68–9, 94–5.

See also pp78–9, 96–7, 102–3, 104–5.

See also pp64–5, 74–5, 84–5, 92–3, 106–7.

FALL

Kilchurn Castle
on Loch Awe in
Argyll, Scotland

FALL IN GREAT BRITAIN AND IRELAND

Fᴀʟʟ, ɪɴ ʙʀɪᴛᴀɪɴ ᴀɴᴅ ɪʀᴇʟᴀɴᴅ is a long, mellow time between the two more extreme seasons of summer and winter. John Keats, in his ode *To Autumn*, called it the "season of mists and mellow fruitfulness." He was inspired by the River Itchen near Winchester, where autumnal mists rise from the river early in the morning and late in the afternoon, and the boughs of nearby orchards hang heavy with fruit. All around Britain, fruit trees are laden with plums, pears, and apples, and hedges are rich with wild blackberries. Occasionally, September brings an "Indian summer", when days are unusually warm, and in Scotland and northern England early fall can often be a gentler season than wet, windy, and unpredictable spring. Down on the coast of North Cornwall, the beginning of fall marks the start of the prime surfing season, when the big waves begin to roll onto the sandy shores just as the last summer visitors head for home.

> The honking of geese winging in from Scandinavia haunts the skies above wetlands.

A few late-blooming plants, such as the mauve and yellow Michaelmas daisy (so called because it flowers around St. Michael's feast day, on September 29), bring pretty dabs of color to cottage gardens. In fields and woodlands, connoisseurs of wild fungi have fun hunting for delicious edible versions, such as chanterelles and ceps. The leaves change color across the gardens of stately homes, city parks and rural woodlands, as far apart as Loch Lomond in Scotland and the spectacular Wye Valley on the Welsh border, creating great swathes of red and gold, punctuated by the scarlet splashes of rowan berries, haws and rosehips. Soon, these and other berries, nuts, and seeds will begin to attract Arctic migrant birds, such as vividly colored waxwings, rare, tiny redwings, and sociable fieldfares, which all spend winter in Britain. The honking of skeins of geese winging in from Scandinavia haunts the skies above wetlands, such as the Firth of Tay on the east coast of Scotland, in one of the characteristic sounds of fall.

Only a few miles inland, avid anglers bid for access to the choicest stretches of the River Tay, where the last few weeks of fall offer some of the best fishing of the season. Fall is the time, too, to seek out some of Britain's most spectacular wildlife, such as red deer stags, as they clash antlers during the rutting season on the heathlands of the New Forest, Hampshire or Richmond Park in London, or on the moors of Islay in the Inner Hebrides.

Below (left to right): Red deer stag roaring during rutting season, in Richmond Park, London; surfer in Newquay, Cornwall; Parade of fire on Bonfire Night in Lewes, Sussex

Fall is harvest time, and food festivals all over Britain celebrate the successful growing season. In Scotland, Braemar is the home of the Royal Highland Games, where kilted muscle-men toss cabers and fight to win the "tug-o-war," Highland dancers perform the Highland Fling, and the music of pipe bands and lone pibroch players fills the air. The event is always attended by the British Royal Family, who stay at their home in nearby Balmoral. For those with an interest in Britain's royal heritage, this is a wonderful time to visit Windsor Castle, a royal residence just outside London. Visitors gain access to five additional, magnificent chambers – the Semi-State Rooms – in fall and winter, complementing the State Apartments that are always open. Fallow deer stags roam free in Windsor Great Park, the vast, Saxon hunting forest that encircles the castle and is open to all comers for walking, cycling, and horse-riding.

Smuggler-costumed revellers tour the streets in noisy torchlit processions.

As fall moves inexorably towards winter, the days begin to dawn under a covering of frost, and all but the most stubborn of leaves fall from the trees. Hearts are gladdened, though, by a festival that occurs all over the world, and is celebrated here in a peculiarly British way. Halloween, or – to give its original Celtic name – Samhain, was a pre-Christian festival that marked the coming of winter on a night when spirits of the dead were thought to mingle with the living, held at bay only by masks and bonfires. It was incorporated into the Christian calendar more than 1,000 years ago as All Saints' Day, or All Hallows' Eve, and today it is celebrated on October 31 with fireworks displays and bonfires. In England it sometimes merges with Guy Fawkes Night – a festivity celebrating the failure of a Catholic plot to blow up King James I and the Houses of Parliament. Some of the most spectacular celebrations, held on the anniversary of the Gunpowder Plot each 5 November, take place in Lewes in Sussex, where smuggler-costumed revellers tour the streets in noisy torchlit processions, before ritually burning effigies upon bonfires. Public bonfires and fireworks displays take place all over England, and in recent years many of them have become more multicultural because the date sometimes overlaps with Diwali (Festival of Lights), a Hindu festival that is also celebrated with fireworks. Whether it is Halloween, Guy Fawkes Night, or Divali, all of these celebrations provide an exciting (if noisy) seasonal signpost, marking the end of fall and the coming of winter.

Below (left to right): Still, deep waters of Loch Lomond in Scotland; trees lining the Long Walk at Windsor Great Park

Food, Glorious Food

Above: *The Harvest Wagon* (c.1767)
by the English painter George Stubbs
Right: Wartime poster

With crops ripening in the fields – from the hops and barley that make English ale and Scotch whisky to the golden wheat that goes into our bread – the fall has long been a time to celebrate nature's bounty. Though pagan in origin, Harvest Festival is traditionally one of Britain's best-loved church festivals, when parishioners and schoolchildren give thanks for the harvest by bringing baskets of food to decorate their local churches and singing hymns. The event usually takes place in late September or early October, on the Sunday closest to the "harvest moon" – the full moon nearest to the autumn equinox.

Today, the fine quality of the food itself is likely to be celebrated as much as the provision of it. Those planning a trip to sample the best of Britain and Ireland's produce will find September and October packed with food festivals and events. Whether it's apples from the orchards of Herefordshire, venison from the Scottish Highlands, or oysters from the coast of Ireland, this time of year is an opportunity to celebrate the very best of seasonal and local fare. Unsurprisingly, many of the most attractive and exciting festivals take place in the heart of rural Britain, where farming is still a traditional way of life, but there are festivals and seasonal events in towns and cities too, often celebrating world influences and cosmopolitan cooking, as well as local produce.

CORNWALL FOOD FESTIVAL, TRURO

HARVESTING A CORN FIELD

GREAT BRITISH CHEESE FESTIVAL, CARDIFF

ABERGAVENNY FOOD FESTIVAL

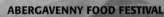

Shetland Food Festival, Highlands and Islands Britain's northernmost isles unveil an array of local delicacies at this event in early October, from seawater oatcakes to fudge. *www.shetlandfoodfestival.com*

Venison Season, Highlands and Islands The deer-stalking season in Scotland peaks in October; red deer, roe stags and hinds roam wild in the Highlands, so the quality of the meat is fantastic.

EatBute, Central Scotland This "slow food" event takes place in September and is devoted to food from the island of Bute, the farms of Argyll, and the waters of the Firth of Forth. *www.eatbute.com*

Aberfoyle Wild Mushroom Festival, Central Scotland Delicious wild fungi, including "penny buns" (ceps) and parasol mushrooms, appear in Scottish woodlands in October. *www.visitaberfoyle.com*

Carlingford Oyster Festival, Eastern Ireland The first shellfish of the season, fresh from the Irish Sea, are served up by the bucket in September in this welcoming fishing harbor. *www.carlongford.ie*

Welsh Food Festival, Central Wales Organic-food producers and microbrewers gather in the grounds of Glansevern Hall in the village of Berriew, Powys, in early September. *www.welshfoodfestival.co.uk*

Abergavenny Food Festival, South Wales Celebrity chefs, food writers, farmers, and beer-makers descend on Abergavenny every September for this popular foodie event. *www.abergavennyfoodfestival.co.uk*

Great British Cheese Festival, South Wales Cardiff Castle is the setting for this September event, where you can sample 400 cheeses made from cow, sheep, goat, and buffalo milk. *www.thecheeseweb.com*

Isle of Man Food Festival, Northwest England Sample everything from moorland lamb and local cheese to organic ice cream at this event, held in Douglas in September. *www.gov.im/tourism/events/food_festival.xml*

York Festival of Food and Drink, Northeast England Yorkshire is famous for its ale, cheese, beef, lamb, and seafood. Try them all in September in the center of historic York. *www.yorkfoodfestival.com*

The Big Apple, West Midlands Every October, Herefordshire villages celebrate their apple- and pear-growing heritage with tastings of local cider and perry (pear cider). *www.bigapple.org.uk*

Norwich Beer Festival, Eastern England Run by the Campaign for Real Ale, which champions the cause of traditional British beers, this October event celebrates more than 200 ales. *www.norwichcamra.org.uk*

Faversham Hop Festival, Southeast England This medieval town comes alive with street entertainment, dancing, and music at the annual hop-harvest festivities in September. *www.swale.gov.uk/hopfestival*

English Wine Festival, Southeast England Our warming climate has made it possible to produce very drinkable wines in southern England. Visit Glynde in September to taste the best of them. *www.glynde.co.uk*

Sturminster Newton Cheese Festival, Southwest England Cheese, chutney, and more than 30 kinds of beer, cider, and perry make this Dorset event, held in September, go with a bang. *www.cheesefestival.co.uk*

Cornwall Food Festival, Southwest England The best of Cornish food and drink is served up in September on Truro's quaysides, with an emphasis on seafood. *www.cornwallfoodanddrinkfestival.com*

WELSH FOOD FESTIVAL, BERRIEW

FAVERSHAM HOP FESTIVAL

SPECTACULAR COLOR

IF BRITAIN HAD A "FALL FOLIAGE" REGION to rival new england's, it would be the Lower Wye Valley gorge. The mixed native forest of ash, beech, and oak produces one of the country's best displays of fall color. The winding river and high slopes of the gorge make this an enticing landscape to explore, and the soaring roofless remains of Tintern Abbey are among the most evocative of ruins.

Leaving England, you're likely to approach the Lower Wye Valley by the M48 motorway, crossing the iconic 1966 suspension bridge over the River Severn – very much the gateway to Wales. Heading north from Chepstow, there's a real feeling of a change of pace and time as

The winding river and high slopes… make this an enticing landscape to explore, and the soaring roofless remains of Tintern Abbey rank among the most evocative of ruins.

THE ESSENTIALS

GETTING THERE AND AROUND
The Lower Wye Valley gorge marks the southern end of the border between England and Wales. Cardiff and London Heathrow airports are 60 miles (95 km) and 143 miles (230 km) from the valley respectively. There are trains to Hereford and Chepstow, and local buses run approximately hourly between the two along the Wye Valley, via Monmouth.

WEATHER
The Wye Valley often enjoys fine weather in fall, but be prepared for cool evenings and rain. Average daytime temperatures are around 43 to 54°F (6 to 12°C).

ACCOMMODATIONS
Treat Yourself The Old Court Hotel, in Symonds Yat West, is a characterful 16th-century house near the River Wye. *www.oldcourthotel.co.uk*

On a Budget The Nurtons, in Tintern, has spectacular views of the valley and offers organic breakfasts and evening meals. *www.thenurtons.co.uk*

EATING OUT
Treat Yourself The Crown at Whitebrook is an acclaimed Michelin-starred small restaurant with rooms, in a remote setting just off the Wye Valley. *www.crownatwhitebrook.co.uk*

On a Budget The Saracen's Head, in Symonds Yat East, is a riverside inn serving above-average pub grub made with local, seasonal produce, and has a children's menu. *www.saracensheadinn.co.uk*

PRICE FOR TWO PEOPLE
From around $280 a day for food, accommodations, and activities.

WEBSITES
www.visitwyevalley.com
www.wyevalleyaonb.org.uk

you are enfolded by the wooded landscape, passing from sunlight to dappled shade, with every turn in the winding road promising a new autumnal viewpoint.

Tintern village sits on a looping curve in the river, with Tintern Abbey occupying much of the flat land by the banks. Henry VIII dissolved the 14th-century Cistercian monastery here in 1536, and the buildings were rented out to locals: the great church was used for playing quoits. The area soon became part of the Industrial Revolution, when Tintern began to produce brass and wire. The ruins lay mostly forgotten until poets and artists of the Romantic movement sought them out: they inspired one of William Wordsworth's most celebrated works, "Lines Composed a Few Miles Above Tintern Abbey," and J. M. W. Turner painted the scene several times.

North of Monmouth, the main road swings away from the river, and it's worth exploring the lanes and paths around the spectacular Symonds Yat Rock, a towering viewpoint set high on a narrow neck of land. The village of Symonds Yat straddles the Wye; a hand-pulled rope ferry opposite the Saracen's Head Inn takes you across the river, and an easy 3-mile (5-km) circular walk returns over a wire suspension bridge. There's also level cycling between here and Monmouth on the Peregrine Path, which runs for 6 miles (10 km) along the line of a former railroad, and canoeing from the Wyedean Canoe and Adventure Centre.

Main: River Wye from Symonds Yat Rock **Inset:** Ruins of Tintern Abbey in Monmouthshire
Below (left to right): Fall color in the Lower Wye Valley; canoeing and kayaking on the River Wye

Birthplace of British Tourism

From the late 18th century, the Wye Valley became a place of pilgrimage for those in search of the "picturesque." One of the first travel guidebooks ever published, clergyman William Gilpin's *Observations on the River Wye* (1782), greatly helped develop the area's popularity. The first of Britain's landscapes to be "discovered," the gorge had everything the romantically minded traveler desired: brooding forests and cliffs punctuated by medieval ruins, all easily observed from the water.

FURTHER DETAILS

WYE VALLEY GORGE

Tintern Abbey
Tintern, Chepstow, Monmouthshire; open Apr–Oct: 9am–5pm daily; Nov–Mar: 9:30am–4pm Mon–Sat, 11am–4pm Sun.
www.cadw.wales.gov.uk

Wyedean Canoe and Adventure Centre
Symonds Yat East, Ross-on-Wye. Canoes are available to rent by the day, the half-day, or the hour.
www.wyedean.co.uk

WHAT ELSE TO SEE AND DO

Chepstow Museum
This local history museum, in an elegant 18th-century house, has exhibits detailing the development of Chepstow – a historic walled town and former port.
www.chepstow.co.uk

Chepstow Castle
This well-preserved medieval castle has a dramatic setting on slopes above the River Wye.
www.cadw.wales.gov.uk

Goodrich Castle
There are substantial remains of this 11th-century hilltop castle, which guarded the entrance to the north end of the Wye Valley gorge near Symonds Yat.
www.english-heritage.org.uk

River Cruises
The *Kingfisher* offers short cruises on the river, with commentary, from Symonds Yat East.
www.fweb.org.uk/kingfisher

The Kymin
Set high above Monmouth, this wooded hill has pleasure grounds to explore and a circular Georgian banqueting hall and Naval Temple memorial to visit.
www.nationaltrust.org.uk

Monmouth
This unspoiled old border town offers many sights: a remarkable gated medieval bridge, handsome Georgian buildings, and the Nelson Museum and Local History Centre, which has a tremendous collection of Admiral Nelson memorabilia.
www.monmouth.org.uk

Wye Valley Walk
This marked walking route runs from Chepstow to Monmouth and beyond; the full route runs 136 miles (220 km) to the remote mountain source of the Wye.
www.wyevalleywalk.org

Below: Imposing ruins of Chepstow Castle

THE ESSENTIALS

GETTING THERE AND AROUND
Braemar is 56 miles (90 km) west of Aberdeen, the site of the nearest international airport. Trains connect Aberdeen with London – with a travel time of around 7 hours – and with most Scottish and English cities. Buses run daily between Aberdeen and Braemar, with a travel time of around 2 hours. A car is useful for traveling in the remote countryside around Braemar.

WEATHER
Braemar's weather is usually mild in early September, but rain is always possible in the Scottish Highlands. Average daytime temperatures range from 59 to 63°F (15–17°C).

ACCOMMODATIONS
Treat Yourself Darroch Learg, in Ballater (15 miles/24 km from Braemar), is a mansion-house hotel with high-quality rooms, set in a beautiful location. www.darrochlearg.co.uk

On a Budget Braemar Youth Hostel, in Braemar, has comfortable accommodations located in a former shooting lodge. www.syha.org.uk

EATING OUT
Treat Yourself The Spirit Restaurant, in Ballater, is an excellent restaurant with a menu that features local produce such as lamb, venison, and rabbit. www.theauldkirk.com

On a Budget Gordon's, in Braemar, is a traditional restaurant and tearoom serving breakfast, full meals, and snacks. www.gordonsbraemar.com

PRICE FOR TWO PEOPLE
Around $300–400 a day for tickets to the games, food, and accommodations.

WEBSITE
www.visitscotland.com

Royal Balmoral

Balmoral's close connection with Britain's Royal Family goes back to 1848, when German-born Prince Albert, the Prince Consort, acquired the estate. He built a new castle on the site of the original 15th-century building – giving it an unmistakably Teutonic, fairy-tale appearance. Queen Victoria called the castle "my dear paradise in the Highlands," and her successors have been equally fond of it. Balmoral is the Queen's private property, rather than part of the Royal Estate.

Main: Highland dancing in full flow
Right (top to bottom): Tossing the caber at Braemar; tug-of-war; contestant in the stone-putting competition

FUN AND GAMES

PIPERS, HIGHLAND DANCERS, AND KILTED MUSCLE-MEN make the Royal Braemar Gathering the most dramatic and exciting of all Scotland's many Highland games events. This is Highland pageantry at its most spectacular. Only a spoilsport would point out that most of the "ancient" traditions celebrated here go back no farther than the early 19th century, when the romantic novels of Sir Walter Scott prompted a surge of interest in Highland life – a fascination that was shared by Queen Victoria, who first visited the Gathering in 1848, and later bestowed the title "Royal" onto the Highland Society and its games. Today, members of Britain's Royal Family are always in attendance at the Braemar games, usually dressed in their finest Highland attire. Their Scottish residence, Balmoral Castle (see story box), lies only a few miles away.

For many onlookers, the highlight of the Gathering is the fiercely contested Highland dancing competition. Various Scottish dances – reels, jigs, and strathspeys – are performed by teams of nimble dancers, accompanied by traditional music. The haunting strains of bagpipes are, of course, omnipresent, but to those who are only familiar with military bands, the eerie

FURTHER DETAILS

BRAEMAR

Braemar Highland Gathering
The Princess Royal and Duke of Fife Memorial Park, Braemar. Held on the first Sat in Sep; advance booking from Feb 1.
www.braemargathering.org

Balmoral Castle
Crathie, near Ballater. The Royal Family's Highland retreat since the reign of Queen Victoria is closed during the Gathering, but you can admire it from a distance.
www.balmoralcastle.com

WHAT ELSE TO SEE AND DO

Braemar Castle
This sturdy little stronghold in Braemar is steeped in history – it was garrisoned by British troops until 1831 – and has recently been restored to its full glory by community volunteers.
www.braemarscotland.co.uk/about_braemar/ braemar_castle.htm

Old Royal Station
This station in Ballater, with its luxurious waiting room, was built especially for Queen Victoria in the 19th century. A life-size replica of the royal train car used by Victoria and her many offspring stands outside.
www.aberdeen-grampian.com

Royal Lochnagar Distillery
This historic distillery, near Balmoral Castle in Crathie, offers tours and educational whiskey tastings.
www.discovering-distilleries.com

Lochnagar
One of Scotland's most spectacular summits, Lochnagar is 3,787 ft (1,154 m) high. It can only be reached by walking, taking a path that starts at the Spittal of Glen Muick. There are superb views all along the ascent, and it takes 7–8 hours to reach the summit. Proper walking footwear and waterproof clothing are essential.
www.cairngorms.co.uk

Golf Clubs
The Deeside region has a number of excellent golf clubs, including Braemar Golf Club – home of the highest 18-hole golf course in Britain. The upmarket Inchmarlo Golf Club, 39 miles (62 km) east of Braemar, boasts an excellent location and luxurious facilities.
Braemar Golf Club: *www.bracmargolfclub.co.uk*
Inchmarlo Golf Club: *www.inchmarlogolf.com*

Below: The Royal Family at the annual Braemar Highland Gathering

Strongmen from all over the world clash in a display of straining sinews, clenched teeth, and sweating muscle that is unique to Highland gatherings.

pibroch – a lament played by a lone piper – will be a revelation. The "heavy events" at the games, in which strongmen from all over the world clash in a display of straining sinews, clenched teeth, and sweating muscle that is unique to Highland gatherings, are an unmissable spectacle. The events – from tossing the caber (a telephone-pole-sized length of wood), putting the stone, and throwing the hammer to the strength-sapping hill race – all have their origins in the trials of prowess and martial skills practiced by the clan warriors of Scotland's past.

But it's not all deadly serious. Despite the extreme exertion required by each competitor, the tug-of-war is a good-humored event, and the children's sack race gives younger visitors a chance to shine. Whether you put your own skills to the test – anyone can enter – or just marvel at the displays of strength and endurance, the Braemar Highland Gathering is an experience you won't forget in a hurry.

MEMORY LANE

As children dust off their history books for the beginning of a new school year, Beamish Open Air Museum offers an alternative hands-on experience that will immerse them in the past. Spread over 300 acres (120 hectares) in the County Durham countryside, this historical park features homes, shops, and other buildings from the 19th and early 20th centuries, with costumed guides who tell you what life was like "way back when."

Behind the busy entrance hall you'll step into another world. Beamish focuses on two very different moments in history: 1825, when the lives of people in the northeast of England revolved around farming; and 1913, when the region was at its industrial peak. The first scene you come to is the 1913 Colliery Village, where you can take an underground tour of a real drift mine. At ground level, miners' cottages, with their vegetable gardens, show how the pitmen and their families lived, from the tin bathtubs in front of the hearth to baking demonstrations. The three-room schoolhouse also provides a fascinating trip down memory lane.

Miners' cottages… show how the pitmen and their families lived, from the tin bathtubs in front of the hearth to baking demonstrations.

Many buildings have been brought in from around the region and carefully reconstructed, but others, such as Pockerley Manor, have been here all along. The manor reveals the lifestyle of a yeoman farmer in the 1820s, and comprises a parlor, a kitchen pantry, and servants' quarters. The 1913 Home Farm has also been restored; the farmer's wife bustles around the kitchen, and the farm buildings house an array of animals and machinery. Electric trams trundle along the cobbled street in the 1913 Town, passing the newspaper office and the Co-op, stocked with vintage canned goods. The gruesome instruments in the dentist's surgery may help you resist the temptation of the old-fashioned candy for sale in the Jubilee Confectionery.

Beamish is huge, but there is a delightful range of historic vehicles to transport you around the site. Take a ride on a horse-drawn dogcart, a restored omnibus, or a steam-hauled carriage on the Pockerley Waggonway. Alternatively, the nearby woodlands and gentle fields are ideal for a peaceful walk, while casting a nostalgic eye on days gone by.

Main: Electric tram on the cobbled street of the 1913 Town **Inset:** Former coal mine in Beamish
Below: Products on display in the Co-op in the 1913 Town

FURTHER DETAILS

BEAMISH OPEN AIR MUSEUM

Beamish, County Durham; open Jan–Apr: 10am–4pm
Tue–Thu and Sat–Sun; Apr–Nov: 10am–5pm daily.
www.beamish.org.uk

WHAT ELSE TO SEE AND DO

Durham Cathedral

Dating from 1093, this cathedral, with its massive carved
stone pillars, rib-vaulted ceiling, and rose window, is one
of Europe's great architectural masterpieces. You can
see the former monastery cloister and climb the tower
for splendid views.
www.durhamcathedral.co.uk

Durham City

Browse the crafts and foodstuffs in the charming Indoor
Market alongside the central Market Place. Then rent a
rowboat beneath Elvet Bridge or take a sightseeing cruise
along the River Wear with Prince Bishop River Cruiser.
River Cruise: www.princebishoprc.co.uk
Durham Indoor Market: www.durhammarkets.co.uk

Crook Hall

This rare and atmospheric small medieval hall in Durham
dates from the 13th century. Hear tales of resident ghosts
and enjoy tea in the beautiful gardens.
www.crookhallgardens.co.uk

Auckland Castle

The medieval St. Peter's Chapel is the highlight of this
former hunting lodge in Bishop Auckland, County Durham.
www.auckland-castle.co.uk

Below (top to bottom): Re-enacting farming life on the 1913 Home
Farm; re-creation of an early-20th-century candy store at Beamish

THE ESSENTIALS

GETTING THERE AND AROUND
Windsor lies about 20 miles (32 km) west of London. The closest airport is London Heathrow, 8 miles (12 km) away. Regular direct trains run to Windsor & Eton Riverside from London Waterloo. It's possible to visit the main sights on foot, but for trips to Legoland you'll need to take a car or a bus from Windsor.

WEATHER
Windsor enjoys a mild fall climate with pleasant daytime temperatures of 48–57°F (8–14°C). Fall rains are possible.

ACCOMMODATIONS
Treat Yourself Harte & Garter, in Windsor, stands in a stunning location opposite Windsor Castle and is an elegantly refurbished historic building with very comfortable rooms.
www.foliohotels.com/harteandgarter

On a Budget Clarence Hotel, Windsor, is a friendly 3-star hotel in a central location close to Windsor Castle.
www.clarence-hotel.co.uk

EATING OUT
Treat Yourself The Fat Duck, in Bray (4 miles/6 km from Windsor) was voted Best Restaurant in the World in 2005 by the prestigious *Restaurant* magazine, and the cooking of its chef – Heston Blumenthal – continues to delight.
www.fatduck.co.uk

On a Budget Cornucopia Bistro on Windsor High Street is a reliable and unpretentious bistro with a great French menu.
www.cornucopia-bistro.co.uk

PRICE FOR A FAMILY OF FOUR
$280–415 a day for food, accommodations, and admission fees.

WEBSITE
www.windsor.gov.uk

Christopher Wren's Pillars

Begun in 1687, Windsor's Guildhall was originally designed by Sir Christopher Wren to be fully supported by columns that line the edges of the building. According to legend, the town burghers insisted that the architect install a set of four interior pillars to support the weight of the upper floor, while Wren argued these were superfluous. Wren was eventually overruled and the pillars were built, but he deliberately left a gap between the top of each pillar and the ceiling to prove a point.

Main: Fall view of the Long Walk, leading to Windsor Castle
Above (top to bottom): St. George's Chapel; Windsor Castle; Changing of the Guard of the Royal Household Division

A ROYAL RESIDENCE

THE ROYAL ENCLAVE OF WINDSOR is one of England's superlative destinations. For family fun and entertainment, majestic views, great walks, river trips, and extravagant pageantry, few places can compete. Windsor Castle sits high above the town, dominating the landscape, and its majesty provides a fascinating insight into the very heart of sovereign England. The earliest incarnation of the castle was built here by William the Conqueror around 1070, and today's iconic building, finished in the 1820s, still serves as one of the Queen's main residences.

Beyond its distinctive exterior, the castle's most captivating sights are the glorious State Apartments (furnished with masterpieces by artists such as Canaletto, Gainsborough, and Rubens), the quiet and hushed interior of St. George's Chapel, and the exquisite Queen Mary's Dolls' House. This exact replica of the castle rooms offers a unique glimpse of the past. It was designed by Lutyens during the 1920s and includes copies of the furniture, wallpaper, lights, and paintings of the state rooms and servant's quarters at that time. In fall, visitors to Windsor Castle are also given access to George VI's private apartments, offering a glimpse of the

FURTHER DETAILS

WINDSOR CASTLE
Windsor; open Mar–Oct: 9:45am–5:15pm daily;
Nov 1–Feb: 9:45am–4:15pm daily.
www.royal.gov.uk

Changing of the Guard
Usually 11am; Jun–Jul daily, Aug–Mar alternate days only;
check website for schedule.
www.royalcollection.org.uk

Windsor Great Park
Windsor; open from sunrise to sunset daily. Carriage
rides through the park leave from High Street, opposite
the statue of Queen Victoria, at 12:30pm daily.
www.theroyallandscape.co.uk

Boat Tours
Windsor Promenade. Dec–Oct: regular departures from
10am–5pm daily; Nov: 10am–4pm Sat–Sun only.
www.boat-trips.co.uk

Eton College
Eton, Windsor; open for guided visits only Mar–Nov;
times vary, see website for details.
www.etoncollege.com

Royal Windsor Wheel
This giant ferris wheel offers spectacular views over the
Windsor countryside; open Apr–Oct, 10am–10pm daily.
www.royalwindsorwheel.com

Legoland Windsor
Winkfield Road, Windsor; open mid-Mar–Oct from 10am,
closing times vary according to season.
www.legoland.co.uk

WHAT ELSE TO SEE AND DO
Hampton Court Palace
King Henry VIII's palace, 15 miles (24 km) southeast of
Windsor, is an astonishing monument to his extravagance.
The royal apartments, Great Hall, Privy Gardens, Chapel
Royal, and famous maze are open to visitors all year,
10am–6pm daily.
www.hrp.org.uk/hamptoncourtpalace

Runnymede
In 1215 King John finally agreed to the terms of the
Magna Carta at Runnymede, setting his seal to the
document during negotiations that took place on these
very meadows. Lying 9 miles (14 km) southeast of
Windsor, the site is also famous today for its rare wildlife,
beautiful oxbow lake and many memorials, including
some designed by Sir Edwin Lutyens.
www.nationaltrust.org.uk

Below: Red deer stag and hinds in Windsor Great Park

Ancient traditions for marking the sovereign's presence –
such as the Changing of the Guard and the raising of the
Royal Standard – can still be seen today.

monarch's semi-private life. The castle has been a working palace for over 900 years, and its
ancient traditions for marking the sovereign's presence – such as the Changing of the Guard
and the raising of the Royal Standard – can still be seen today. To the south of the castle, the
royal Norman hunting chase now known as Windsor Great Park stretches over 5,000 acres
(2,000 hectares). Its magnificent Long Walk is an awe-inspiring sight on a fine day.

The town itself also boasts a long history, and its old cobbled streets contain intriguing
buildings such as the Guildhall *(see story box)*, designed by Sir Christopher Wren in the 1680s.
The River Thames is a glistening waterway here, with flocks of swans and riverboats, and one
of England's most illustrious public schools, the 15th-century Eton College, lies just across
Windsor Bridge. But if you need to give the children a 21st-century experience, take a ride
on the giant Windsor Wheel or head for the thrilling rides of nearby Legoland.

THE ESSENTIALS

GETTING THERE AND AROUND
Blackpool is on the northwest coast of
England, 53 miles (85 km) northwest
of Manchester and 55 miles (89 km)
north of Liverpool. It has its own small
international airport, just to the south
of the town. You can easily tour the
downtown on foot, and can explore
the Promenade by tram.

WEATHER
Blackpool has a temperate climate but fall
sees the wettest months of the year, and
there can be cold sea breezes adding a
chill factor. Average daytime temperatures
range from 46 to 57°F (8–14°C).

ACCOMMODATIONS
Treat Yourself Number One, on
St. Luke's Road, in an enviably quiet
area on the South Shore, is one of
Blackpool's finest boutique B&Bs.
www.numberoneblackpool.com

On a Budget The Berwyn Hotel, on
the North Shore, is a traditional Blackpool
hotel with its own large, attractive gardens.
www.berwynhotel.co.uk

EATING OUT
Treat Yourself Kwizeen, on King Street,
offers original and interesting cooking,
including a "Lancashire market" menu
prepared from locally sourced produce.
www.kwizeenrestaurant.co.uk

On a Budget Harry Ramsden's, on the
Promenade, is a seaside institution that
serves some of the best fish and chips
you'll find anywhere in the country.
www.harryramsdens.co.uk/h_blackpool

PRICE FOR A FAMILY OF FOUR
Around $320 a day for accommodations,
food, and admission fees.

WEBSITE
www.visitblackpool.com

The Big Switch On

It's dazzling to be in town for the Big Switch On,
when BBC Radio 2 broadcasts live from Blackpool's
brightest occasion. A free concert, featuring live
performances by pop bands and comedians, helps
build excitement before the grand moment when
the Illuminations are turned on by a celebrity guest.
Over the years, the list of luminaries has included
pop bands, DJs, television personalities, and even,
in 1977, Red Rum – the first racehorse to win the
Grand National three times.

NORTHERN LIGHTS

AS THE DAYS DRAW IN, AN ELECTRIC RAINBOW of over a million light bulbs shines over
Blackpool – "the Las Vegas of Lancashire." The Blackpool Illuminations – lasting 66 days
and running a length of just over 6 miles (10 km) along the town's famous Promenade – have
been called "the greatest free light show on earth." You can become part of this awe-inspiring
display by hopping aboard one of the illuminated trams that run up and down the seafront – it's
the best way to enjoy this eye-popping extravaganza of color.

The Illuminations began in 1879, after Blackpool became the first town in the world to
install electric street lighting. In its first year, 100,000 people came from across Britain to see the
"artificial sunshine." Within a few years, entire Lancashire villages would close down and decamp
here for a week to enjoy their annual holiday. Today, the light show draws over 3.5 million visitors,

The light show draws over
3.5 million visitors, who throng here
to enjoy the bold and cheerful
attractions of this quintessentially
British seaside resort each year.

who throng here to enjoy the bold and cheerful attractions of this quintessentially British
seaside resort each year, from the "Big Switch On" in late August or early September to its
conclusion in early November. The Illuminations, like the city itself, have changed with the
times – they now feature a startling array of light displays, including neon, lasers, fiber optics,
three-dimensional scenes, and moving figures. New technologies that cut energy consumption,
from LED bulbs to wind turbines, are powering the lights in the new millennium.

Blackpool claimed another first in 1885, when trams were introduced along a stretch of
the Promenade, becoming part of the first fully functioning electric tramway in the world.
The network now extends for over 11 miles (17 km), and during the Illuminations the trams
themselves are decked out in glorious colors and boast impressive designs – from space rockets,
fishing trawlers, and steam trains to hovercraft and Mississippi paddle steamers.

Once you've had your fill of the town's dazzling lights, stroll along the North Pier with an
order of fish and chips, explore Blackpool Pleasure Beach, or admire the sharks in the Sea Life
aquarium. And what better way to end the day than a show at the iconic Blackpool Tower?

Main: Blackpool Tower at night during the Illuminations
Inset: A giant mirrorball on Blackpool's Promenade **Below:** Roller coasters at Blackpool Pleasure Beach

FURTHER DETAILS

BLACKPOOL

Blackpool Illuminations
The Promenade, Blackpool; late Aug/early Sep–Nov.
www.blackpool-illuminations.net

Blackpool Pleasure Beach
South Promenade, Blackpool. With a wealth of shows,
rides, indoor entertainment, and outdoor attractions, such
as the Pepsi Max Big One – the tallest roller coaster in
Europe – Blackpool Pleasure Beach promises fantastic
entertainment for the whole family; open Feb–Nov, with
seasonal and daily variations.
www.blackpoolpleasurebeach.com

Sea Life Blackpool
The Promenade, Blackpool. This aquarium is home to
Europe's biggest collection of tropical sharks. You can walk
through an underwater tunnel and see more than 1,000
sea creatures, including giant crabs and moray eels; open
from 10am daily; closing times vary.
www.sealife.co.uk

Blackpool Tower
The Promenade, Blackpool. Blackpool's famous tower is
as much an icon of the town as the Eiffel Tower – the
inspiration for its design – is of Paris. There are spectacular
views of the town from the top, and the tower also
includes an aquarium, a circus, a 3-D movie theater,
and a ballroom. The tower is open 10am–6:30pm daily;
opening times of the attractions within it vary.
www.theblackpooltower.co.uk

Below (top to bottom): Illuminated tram; Blackpool Tower
from the North Pier

THE ESSENTIALS

GETTING THERE AND AROUND
The Chilterns are a range of hills in the south of England, between Oxford and London. Heathrow airport is about 29 miles (47 km) southwest of Stokenchurch. The best way to get to kite-viewing locations is by car. Some, such as Stokenchurch and Chinmoor, can be visited by bus from High Wycombe, where the nearest train station – on the London Marylebone to Birmingham Snow Hill route – can be found.

WEATHER
In fall the weather in southern England is pleasant, with average daytime temperatures of between 45 and 57°F (7–14°C), but with a good chance of rain.

ACCOMMODATIONS
Treat Yourself The Fox Country Inn, in Ibstone, is 300 years old and set in beautiful countryside.
www.foxcountryinn.co.uk

On a Budget South Fields, in Cadmore End, High Wycombe, is a cozy B&B only 5 minutes' walk from the village pub.
www.bedbreakfastsouthfields.co.uk

EATING OUT
Treat Yourself The Hand and Flowers, in Marlow, serves award-winning food in warm and welcoming surroundings.
www.thehandandflowers.co.uk

On a Budget The Grouse and Ale, in High Wycombe, is a cheerful and homey pub serving good bar food as well as à la carte cuisine.
www.exasite.com/grouseandale

PRICE FOR TWO PEOPLE
Around $250 a day for accommodations and food.

WEBSITE
www.chilternsaonb.org

A "Chequered" Past

A walk along the Ridgeway National Trail near Wendover provides tantalizing glimpses of Chequers, the country residence of British Prime Ministers since 1921. The present house dates from the 16th century, but was built on the site of the 11th-century home of a member of the Court of the Exchequer, which is thought to account for its name. In past years the house has served as a hospital and a military convalescent home as well as a backdrop for visits by heads of state.

Main: Red kite in its characteristic swooping dive
Right (top to bottom): Kite with wings fully extended; at rest, but still watchful

LORDS OF THE AIR

JUST A SHORT TRIP NORTHWEST OF LONDON, the rolling, chalky Chiltern Hills provide a welcome refuge not just for London's stressed commuters but for a rich variety of wildlife. Chalk grasslands attract naturalists in search of orchids and other wild flowers, while the region's famous beech forests, the floors of which are carpeted with bluebells in the spring, turn into dazzling blurs of yellow and russet in the fall. Since the 1980s, a majestic former resident – the red kite – has taken back its rightful place over the bucolic hills of the Chilterns. With a huge wingspan of up to 6 ft (1.8 m), warm russet, black, and white plumage, and a deeply forked tail, the red kite is unmistakable when seen soaring and spiraling as it catches thermals and performs its aerial acrobatics.

The red kite is one of Britain's great conservation success stories. These magnificent birds had been hunted to near national extinction in the mistaken belief that they fed on lambs and gamebirds (whereas they in fact subsist mainly on carrion) and by the 1960s there were just 30 left in Great Britain, all of them resident in mid-Wales. A reintroduction program was

FURTHER DETAILS

THE CHILTERNS

Watlington Hill
Near Watlington, Oxfordshire.
www.nationaltrust.org.uk

Cowleaze Wood
Near Stokenchurch, Oxfordshire.
www.forestry.gov.uk

The Ridgeway National Trail
This ancient 87-mile (139-km) trail, possibly Britain's oldest road, has been in use since Neolithic times by herdsmen, soldiers, and travelers. Its picturesque route passes directly through the Chilterns, and offers great views for walkers and access for horse riders and cyclists along parts of its length.
www.nationaltrail.co.uk/ridgeway

WHAT ELSE TO SEE AND DO

The Hellfire Caves
Created by Sir Francis Dashwood, the founder of the notorious 18th-century Hellfire Club of aristocratic hedonists, the Hellfire Caves were both a meeting place and the site of much scandalous behavior. Today the caves provide an atmospheric day out; you can explore the passages and chambers running half a mile (1 km) under West Wycombe, and learn about the site's shady past.
www.hellfirecaves.co.uk

The Roald Dahl Museum and Story Centre
This museum celebrates the life and work of Roald Dahl, the author of *Charlie and the Chocolate Factory*, *James and the Giant Peach*, and *The BFG*, who lived in the Chilterns in the town of Great Missenden. It contains a biographical gallery as well as an interactive "story center," where you are encouraged to get creative.
www.roalddahlmuseum.org

Watlington
Reputedly Britain's smallest town, Watlington, near High Wycombe, is steeped in the history of the region and is packed with buildings dating from the 15th to the 17th centuries. It's also within half a mile (1 km) of the Ridgeway Trail.
www.watlington.org

Below: Early morning mist over the Chiltern Hills

> With its huge wingspan… the red kite is unmistakable when seen soaring and spiraling as it catches thermals and performs its aerial acrobatics.

launched in the 1980s, when 90 birds were brought over from Spain; the first successful breeding took place in 1992, and numbers have since grown to about 500 breeding pairs. Today, kites can be seen almost anywhere in the Chilterns, casting their giant shadows even over large towns such as High Wycombe. But for the best views, a good place to start is at Watlington Hill, about 1 mile (2 km) southeast of the tiny historical town of Watlington, or nearby Cowleaze Wood, about 3 miles (5 km) from Stokenchurch.

The Chilterns are a designated Area of Outstanding Natural Beauty (AONB), so it's easy to combine a morning's kite-watching with a trip to one of the region's pretty brick-and-flint villages or a ramble along the ancient Ridgeway Trail. The long line of hills that makes up the Chilterns is perfect for an afternoon ramble that may take you past sparkling chalk streams, through wooded valleys, and down quiet lanes.

| THE ESSENTIALS

GETTING THERE AND AROUND
Galway is situated on the west coast of Ireland, 135 miles (215 km) from Dublin. Galway Airport is 4 miles (6 km) from the city and is accessible by internal flights from Dublin. The city is well serviced by train and bus links. There are taxis and buses in the city and the center is small enough to cover easily on foot. Rent a car if you want to travel farther afield.

WEATHER
Fall in Galway is generally mild and often sunny, with average daytime temperatures ranging from 45 to 54°F (7–12°C), but rain is not unusual.

ACCOMMODATIONS
Treat Yourself The award-winning Twelve boutique hotel, in Barna, near Galway, often has special deals during the festival. *www.thetwelvehotel.ie*

On a Budget Sea Breeze Lodge, in Salthill near Galway, is an inexpensive but cozy guesthouse overlooking the beautiful Galway Bay.
www.seabreezelodge.org

EATING OUT
Treat Yourself St. Cleran's, in Craughwell, is a classy fine-dining restaurant situated in a magnificent 18th-century house that is now a hotel.
www.stclerans.com

On a Budget McDonaghs, on Quay Street in Galway, is a combined seafood restaurant and fish-and-chips carry-out that has a fantastic reputation in the city.
www.mcdonaghs.net

PRICE FOR TWO
$320–380 a day for accommodations, food, and festival tickets.

FURTHER INFORMATION
www.galwaytourism.ie

The Claddagh Ring

A Claddagh Ring is a piece of jewelry that has a distinctive design of two hands joined together to support a heart. The ring is a symbol of love and friendship, and how you wear it depends on the state of your love life. When worn on the right hand with the heart facing outward to the nail, it signifies the wearer is single. However, if the heart faces inward, the wearer is no longer available. The custom originated in the 17th century in the fishing village of Claddagh, just outside Galway.

A CRACKING GOOD TIME

OYSTERS AND GUINNESS form the staple diet of guests at the Galway Oyster Festival, which takes place in this charming Irish city at the end of every September – the official start of the oyster season. The festival has been running since 1954, and was the brainchild of Brian Collins, proprietor of Galway's Great Southern Hotel. He wanted to increase the number of fall guests to his establishment, and saw the oyster season as the perfect excuse to do so.

Today, the emphasis of the four-day-long Oyster Festival is on fun, food, and, of course, filling up with Guinness – the national drink. After months of summer festivals and *fleadhs* (music festivals), there is always more than enough *craic* (fun) to go around at the last festival of the season, with the highlight being the "cracking" Guinness World Oyster Opening Championships. The festival's lineup, which includes a Mardi Gras party complete with jazz bands, continues to draw crowds from overseas every year. All the events are guaranteed sellouts, and the entertainment is frequently described as some of the best in the world.

The oysters themselves are, of course, the focus of the festivities. They are carefully selected from beds beneath Galway Bay, where the native oyster still resides in the wild. After suffering at the hands of eager men frantically trying to beat the world record at the Oyster

Main: Hundreds of revelers enjoying the *craic* in the main marquee at the annual Galway Oyster Festival

Above: Festival staples – oysters and Guinness

Below: Competitors shuck piles of oysters at the World Oyster Opening Championship in Galway Town

Far right (top to bottom): Claddagh Quay in Galway Town; Twelve Ben mountain range in Connemara

The oysters themselves are, of course, the focus of the festivities. They are carefully selected from beds beneath Galway Bay, where the native oyster still resides in the wild.

Opening Championships on the Saturday afternoon, the oysters are served in all their glory in the festival marquee at the Claddagh, one of the oldest areas of the city. The marquee is erected on Nimmo's Pier, beside Galway Bay, and the festival's glamour is evident in the amount of *haute couture* you'll see making its way to the marquee via the Spanish Arch in Galway's Old Town.

Galway is conveniently located in the heart of western Ireland, and most of the 12,000 or so annual visitors to the festival make the most of their journey and venture beyond the folds of the marquee to search for a real sense of Irish life. The Aran Islands, Connemara, and The Burren are all on Galway's doorstep and await your discovery. Take the ferry over to Aran, an archipelago of three tiny islands where the primary language is Gaelic and life has a more traditional pace. A walk along the dramatic rocky coast will certainly awaken your Guinness-dulled senses as you stroll past fields that have been tamed over the years by the locals constantly working the craggy land. Or you can explore the eerie landscape of The Burren and the beauty of Connemara, and finish up in a cozy bar to start the *craic* all over again.

FURTHER DETAILS

GALWAY
Galway Oyster Festival
Various venues around Galway; four days in late Sep.
www.galwayoysterfest.com

Aran Islands
Europe's westernmost point, these austere islands offer stunning coastal views and large prehistoric stone forts. You can reach them by taking a short flight from Connemara Airport or a ferry from Rossavael.
www.irelandwest.ie

Connemara National Park
The unspoiled beauty of the Twelve Ben Mountains is home to a wealth of flora and fauna; open Mar–May and Sep–Oct: 10am–5.30pm daily; Jun–Aug: 9:30am–6.30pm daily.
www.heritageireland.ie

The Burren
This desolate area of County Clare is a unique region in which Mediterranean and alpine plants can thrive.
www.burrennationalpark.ie

WHAT ELSE TO SEE AND DO
Our Lady Assumed into Heaven and St. Nicholas
This magnificent cathedral, on the Galway Street called Nun's Island, was built in limestone and Connemara marble in 1965.

Galway Market
This eclectic market is located outside the Collegiate Church of St. Nicholas, the largest functioning medieval parish church in Ireland.
www.galwaymarket.net

THE ESSENTIALS

GETTING THERE AND AROUND
Portmeirion is situated on the coast of North Wales on the estuary of the River Dwyryd. By public transportation, travel to Porthmadog by train or bus, then take a train to Minffordd, which lies 1 mile (2 km) away from Portmeirion. You can walk from there, or catch a bus. The village is 230 miles (370 km) from London.

WEATHER
Fall in North Wales is often wet and windy, although spells of cool, dry, sunny weather are not uncommon. Daytime temperatures average 37–52ºF (3–11ºC) on the coast and 32–41ºF (0–5ºC) in the mountains.

ACCOMMODATIONS
Treat Yourself Castell Deudraeth, in Portmeirion, is a castellated Victorian mansion that is now a boutique hotel.
www.portmeirion-village.com

On a Budget The Travelodge in Porthmadog is only 2 miles (3 km) from Portmeirion. It is clean and comfortable, but has no dining facilities – guests use local restaurants and cafés for meals.
www.travelodge.co.uk

EATING OUT
Treat Yourself The Hotel Portmeirion Dining Room was designed by Clough Williams-Ellis in 1931 and redesigned in 2005 by Sir Jasper Conran. The menu features highlights of Welsh cuisine.
www.portmeirion-village.com

On a Budget Caffi Glas is an Italian-style restaurant in Portmeirion, offering pasta, pizzas, salads, and snacks.
www.portmeirion-village.com

PRICE FOR TWO PEOPLE
Around $500 a day for food, accommodations, travel, and admission fees.

WEBSITE
www.visitwales.com

The Prisoner

The extraordinary mixture of building styles and Portmeirion's beautiful landscape made it the ideal setting for the surreal 1960s TV series, *The Prisoner*. The programme featured the actor Patrick McGoohan, who starred as a secret agent – "Number Six" – who was held captive by a mysterious regime in a village where the inhabitants were brainwashed. The cult series still has huge numbers of fans, some of whom meet here every September for a "Prisoner Convention".

Main: Vllage of Portmeirion and the Dwyryd estuary **Right (top to bottom):** Black sheep sign above the wool shop; examples of Portmeirion's idiosyncratic style; Patrick McGoohan (left) in the TV series *The Prisoner*, set in Portmeirion

THE VILLAGE

THE IDIOSYNCRATIC VILLAGE OF PORTMEIRION is an extraordinary collection of Italianate buildings and sub-tropical gardens set high above the tranquil blue waters of the Dwyryd Estuary and against a background of the majestic mountains of Snowdonia. The village was built between 1925 and 1976 by an eccentric local architect, Sir Clough Williams-Ellis, who had vowed as a child to erect an ensemble of buildings that would represent his ideas on architecture, "and indeed be me". It is this sense of individual creativity that hits you very forcefully when you first see the surreal village he created and owned. How many architects would have thought to place together a collection of pastel-shaded, terracotta-roofed bungalows, colonnades, porticoes, and Corinthian columns and set them among palm trees and fountains in North Wales? This is a rare sight indeed.

Williams-Ellis used "endangered" buildings from all over Britain, which were brought to Portmeirion and rebuilt, so that the steep slopes above the estuary now sport every architectural theme from Neo-Classical to Jacobean, and Gothic to Oriental, with Italianate style

FURTHER DETAILS

PORTMEIRION VILLAGE
Portmeirion Village, Minffordd, Penrhyndeudraeth, Gwynedd; open Apr–Sep: 9:30am–7:30pm daily; Oct–Mar: 9:30am–5:30pm daily. www.portmeirion-village.com

WHAT ELSE TO SEE AND DO
Plas Brondanw
The family home of Sir Clough Williams-Ellis is not open to the public, but you can visit the extraordinary gardens, which are divided into "rooms" surrounded by hedges. Tel: 01766 770000

Ffestiniog Railway
The vintage steam trains of the world's oldest railroad company, established in 1832, run regular services from Porthmadog to Blaenau Ffestiniog, climbing over 700 ft (200 m) through the glorious Snowdonia landscapes (see pp62–3). Disembark at Minffordd for Portmeirion. www.ffestiniograilway.co.uk

Llechwedd Slate Caverns
There are 25 miles (40 km) of tunnels and 16 working levels at this massive slate mine near Blaenau Ffestiniog, which can be visited on one of two organized tours – the Miners' Tramway Tour or the more spectacular Deep Mine Tour on the very steep underground railroad. There's also a reconstructed Victorian mining village at ground level. www.llechwedd-slate-caverns.co.uk

Below (top to bottom): Beach at Portmeirion; steam train traveling down the Ffestiniog Railway

One moment a Jacobean town hall stands proudly in front of you, the next you find yourself walking through a Mediterranean piazza admiring a sculpture of Buddha.

dominating. There's an architectural surprise around every corner as you wend your way from the entrance down to the still, gray water of the Dwyryd Estuary – one moment a Jacobean town hall stands proudly in front of you, the next you find yourself walking through a Mediterranean piazza admiring a sculpture of Buddha, or Siamese figures atop Ionic columns. It all sounds a bit of a mish-mash of styles, but somehow it works, like a living museum of world architecture.

Wandering around Portmeirion is a chance to step away from real life for a few hours, and if you visit in the fall you'll avoid the often overcrowded cafés, shops, gardens, and woodland walks of summer. Consider an overnight stay at one of the hotels or cottages here; the village is "closed" to the public in the evening, so you'll get a more intimate feel for the place then. And to really revel in the other-worldly feel of Portmeirion, why not arrive by steam train on the Ffestiniog Railway (see pp38–9)? It's as near as you're likely to get to stepping back in time.

THE ESSENTIALS

GETTING THERE AND AROUND
The Mountains of Mourne are on the east coast of Northern Ireland, between Newcastle and Newry. The nearest airports are Belfast City Airport and Belfast International Airport, 30 miles (48 km) and 52 miles (84 km) north of Newcastle respectively. Once there, an Ulsterbus "Mourne Rambler" service provides good access to the mountains.

WEATHER
The weather varies enormously in and around the mountains. In fall, expect anything from sunny days to gales and pouring rain, with average daytime temperatures of 45–50°F (7–10°C).

ACCOMMODATIONS
Treat Yourself The Slieve Donard Resort and Spa, in Newcastle, has earned a reputation as one of the most luxurious hotels in Northern Ireland.
www.hastingshotels.com

On a Budget The Briers, in Newcastle, is a beautiful 18th-century country house at the foot of the Mountains of Mourne, set in its own gardens.
www.thebriers.co.uk

EATING OUT
Treat Yourself The Oak Restaurant, in the Slieve Donard Resort, has traditional decor and some of the best food for miles.
Tel: 028 4372 1066

On a Budget The Mourne Café, in Newcastle, offers tasty and fresh fish dishes in a family-friendly atmosphere.
Tel: 028 4372 6401

PRICE FOR TWO PEOPLE
From around $230 a day for food and accommodations.

WEBSITES
www.mournelive.com
www.armaghanddown.com

Musical Fame

"The Mountains of Mourne," the song that helped to make this area famous around the world, has proved to be very long-lived, with new versions still being recorded today. The song was written in 1896 by the Irish musician and song-writer Percy French, and it tells the story of an Irish migrant to London who misses his mountains and the girl who waits for him to return. French's other popular works include "Phil the Fluther's Ball," "A Sailor Courted a Farmer's Daughter," and "Abdul Abulbul Amir."

MISTY MOUNTAINS

THE LOVELY MOUNTAINS OF MOURNE really do "sweep down to the sea", as the famous song proclaims. As you drive along the coast road south from the resort of Newcastle, their rocky, wooded cliffs tower steeply above. When viewed from a distance inland, however, the grassy slopes appear deceptively gentle. It's only when you get up close that you can make out the rugged granite peaks and the steep flanks and moraines (glacial debris) leading up to them.

Tucked away in the southeast corner of Northern Ireland, between Carlingford Lough and the Irish Sea, the Mourne Mountains are designated as an Area of Outstanding Natural Beauty, and are excellent hiking country. They cluster together in a compact area stretching 15 miles (24 km) inland from the coast and measuring just over 7 miles (11 km) wide. The highest peak, Slieve Donard, rises 2,789 ft (850 m) above sea level. A relatively easy trail leads from the coast at Bloody Bridge up to the summit, where there are incredible views across the mountain terrain.

The best way to see beyond the mountains' perimeter is on foot, as only a few narrow roads penetrate the interior. Fall is the best time to take to the trails, when the grasses and heathers erupt in golden and purple hues, and the skies and slopes play host to an amazing variety of

Main: Walker looking over the Silent Valley from the summit of Slieve Bearnagh

> C. S. Lewis was so struck by these mountains' magical atmosphere that he declared that they made him feel that at any moment a giant might raise his head over the next ridge.

birdlife, from peregrine falcons and owls to skylarks, song thrushes, lapwings, and red grouse. The author C. S. Lewis was so struck by these mountains' magical atmosphere that he declared that they made him feel that at any moment a giant might raise his head over the next ridge. The Mountains of Mourne were the inspiration for Lewis's mythical kingdom of Narnia, and whether you go on one of the many challenging hikes to the high summits, or for a gentler walk in forest parks on the lower slopes, you can't help but be struck by the area's mysterious beauty.

Head inland from Annalong or Kilkeel, following signs to the Silent Valley, and you'll reach the starting point for the circular Viewpoint Walk, about 3 miles (5 km) long. This takes you around a reservoir and gives you magnificent views of the surrounding peaks. Here you'll also see the remarkable Mourne Wall, a drystone wall that was built to define land boundaries in the early 1900s. It runs for 22 miles (35 km) and connects over 15 mountains – passing near or over the summits of all but one – making for a challenging but extraordinary walk.

FURTHER DETAILS

THE MOUNTAINS OF MOURNE
The Silent Valley Mountain Park, situated in the high Mournes, has an information center and restaurant with impressive views over the mountain range. The visitor center is open Jul–Aug: 11am–6:30pm daily; Jun and Sep: 11am–6:30pm Sat–Sun only.
www.mournemountains.com

WHAT ELSE TO SEE AND DO
Newcastle Beaches
The popular seaside resort of Newcastle, at the foot of Slieve Donard, has a 5-mile (8-km) expanse of beach and a busy boardwalk. Nearby is beautiful Tyrella Beach, a conservation area of mature dunes and scenic walks.
www.discovernorthernireland.com

Tollymore Forest Park
Giant Gothic gateways mark the entrance to Northern Ireland's oldest forest park, in the foothills of the Mourne Mountains, 2 miles (3 km) from Newcastle on the B180.
www.forestserviceni.gov.uk

Castlewellan Forest Park
Lying on the outskirts of Castlewellan, near Newcastle, this park forms the grounds of a baronial castle. Its highlights are a magnificent arboretum, dating from 1740, and superb views of the Mourne Mountains across the castle's lake.
www.forestserviceni.gov.uk

Downpatrick
North of the mountains, Downpatrick has several religious sites associated with St. Patrick, including Down Cathedral, whose churchyard is reputed to be the burial place of Ireland's three patron saints: Patrick, Brigid, and Colmcille.
www.visitdownpatrick.com

Below (top to bottom): Male red grouse; Mourne Wall

THE ESSENTIALS

GETTING THERE AND AROUND
Fountains Abbey and Studley Royal are in North Yorkshire, 29 miles (47 km) northwest of York. The nearest airport is Leeds/Bradford International Airport, 24 miles (38 km) to the south. The nearest town is Ripon, 4 miles (6 km) to the northeast; buses run from here to the abbey's visitor center.

WEATHER
Fall in North Yorkshire is generally mild but can be chilly. Although the weather is usually fair, it's wise to prepare for rain at all times. The average daytime temperature ranges from 39 to 52°F (4–11°C).

ACCOMMODATIONS
Treat Yourself The Old Deanery, in Ripon, is a charming 17th-century hotel and restaurant with immaculate rooms opposite Ripon Cathedral.
www.theolddeanery.co.uk

On a Budget The Old Coach House, in North Stainley, offers faultless rooms at a snug lakeside retreat a few miles from Fountains Abbey.
www.oldcoachhouse.info

EATING OUT
Treat Yourself The Old Deanery, in Ripon, is a perfect place for atmospheric dining, with a grade-A menu and a splendid setting.
www.theolddeanery.co.uk

On a Budget Lockwoods, in Ripon, offers great food prepared using local produce, and has a relaxed vibe.
www.lockwoodsrestaurant.co.uk

PRICE FOR TWO PEOPLE
$250–330 a day for accommodations, food, and admission fees.

WEBSITE
www.yorkshire.com

Studley Royal

Fountains Abbey is part of the UNESCO World Heritage Site of Studley Royal, a stunning expanse of lake, lawns, gardens, woods, and temple architecture to the west, connected to the abbey ruins by a picturesque walk along the river. Standout features of Studley Royal, designed from 1720 by John Aislabie and his son William, are the Deer Park – home to over 500 deer and diverse wildlife – and the Water Garden, with its tranquil lake and Classical statues and follies.

BREATHTAKING RUINS

E NGLAND'S MOST SUBLIME ARCHITECTURAL RUIN, Fountains Abbey is also the largest and grandest of Britain's monastic sites. The roofless and skeletal abbey church with its staggeringly long nave – culminating in an arched window opening at each end – is the abbey's defining image, particularly at its eastern extremity where the Chapel of the Nine Altars stands. The nave is overlooked by the 160-ft- (50-m-) Perpendicular Tower, a sturdy and dramatic edifice dating from the early 16th century. The remarkable arched Cellarium to the south, in which goods were stored and lay brothers ate their meals, is testament to the ambitious nature of Fountains Abbey – it is 300 ft (90 m) long and was built over the Skell River.

Dating from 1132, and located within a North Yorkshire landscape wreathed in history, Fountains Abbey was founded by Benedictine monks – who later adopted the more frugal monastic rule of the Cistercian order – in an area described at the time as "more fit for wild beasts than men to inhabit." The monastery's 400-year working life was brought to an end during the Dissolution of the Monasteries in Henry VIII's reign, and it was sold to Sir Richard Gresham, a London merchant. The abbey's glass, lead, and stone were plundered: the building material for the neighboring Jacobean mansion Fountains Hall was sourced from the site. In 1767 Fountains Abbey was purchased by William Aislabie, who incorporated it into the grand landscaping plans for Studley Royal *(see story box)*, giving the ruins a new lease of life.

Fountains Abbey, set in over 800 acres (320 hectares) of prime North Yorkshire countryside, is an idyllic setting for lazy picnics and captivating walks. After you've spent the day exploring the monastery and its extraordinary countryside setting, in the midst of the autumnal blaze of reds and yellows, the complex begins to conjure up further magic at twilight. Saturdays in fall bring the highlight of Fountains' year, when you can experience the floodlit monastic ruins echoing to the sound of nocturnal choir music and Gregorian chants – a perfect end to a truly atmospheric trip.

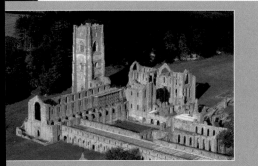

Saturdays in fall bring the highlight of Fountains' year, when you can experience the floodlit monastic ruins echoing to the sound of nocturnal choir music.

Main: Ruined nave of the abbey **Inset:** Aerial view of the ruins, surrounded by forest and fields
Below: Fountain Abbey's impressive, vaulted Cellarium

FURTHER DETAILS

FOUNTAINS ABBEY
Fountains Abbey, near Ripon, North Yorkshire; open Nov–Jan: 10am–4pm Mon–Thu and Sat–Sun; Feb: 10am–4pm daily; Mar–Oct: 10am–5pm daily. *www.fountainsabbey.org.uk*

Fountains Hall
A 16th-century mansion set in Studley Royal; opening times as for Fountains Abbey.

Fountains Abbey by Floodlight
In fall the abbey is floodlit in the evening, while recorded Gregorian chant fills the air. A choir sings sacred and classical music from 8–9pm. Sep–Oct: dusk–10pm Sat only; last admission 9pm.

Studley Royal
Georgian water gardens, ornamental lakes, and numerous follies; opening times as for Fountains Abbey. The Deer Park is open daily year-round during daylight hours. There are organized Deer Walks to watch the red, fallow, and sika deer in the rutting season (Aug–Nov).

WHAT ELSE TO SEE AND DO
Ripon
The North Yorkshire market town of Ripon is well worth exploring, especially for the small Ripon Cathedral and the nearby Market Place where the watchman sounds his horn every night at 9pm. For relaxation, walks along Ripon Canal are peaceful and attractive.
Ripon *www.ripon.org*
Ripon Cathedral *www.riponcathedral.org.uk*

Newby Hall
Lying southeast of Ripon, Newby Hall is an attractive 17th-century house set within 25 acres (10 hectares) of exquisite gardens. The interior of the house, designed by Scottish architect Robert Adam, is particularly stunning, and is beautifully accented by a lavish collection of paintings, porcelain, and furniture. *www.newbyhall.com*

Below: The Studley Royal Water Garden

THE ESSENTIALS

GETTING THERE AND AROUND
Lewes is in southeast England, 58 miles
(93 miles) from London. Trains run
between Lewes and London Victoria every
30 minutes from Monday to Saturday,
and every hour on Sunday (travel time
70 minutes). There are buses from
Brighton to Lewes (travel time 30 minutes)
every 15 minutes from Monday to
Saturday, and every hour on Sundays.
The town can be easily explored on foot.

WEATHER
In November the weather in Lewes is
relatively pleasant, but always be prepared
for rain and chilly winds, with daytime
temperatures from 39 to 50°F (4–10°C).

ACCOMMODATIONS
Treat Yourself The Shelleys, on Lewes
High Street in the heart of town, is a 4-star
17th-century manor-house hotel with
plenty of character.
www.the-shelleys.co.uk

On a Budget Berkeley House, in Albion
Street, is a late-Georgian 4-star town
house B&B with considerable charm.
www.berkeleyhouselewes.co.uk

EATING OUT
Treat Yourself Pelham House Restaurant,
on St. Andrews Lane, is a 16th-century
house with a gorgeous menu and fine
views of the Downs.
www.pelhamhouse.com

On a Budget John Harvey Tavern, on
Cliffe High Street, is a traditional cozy pub
with a great range of beers and pub food.
www.johnharveytavern.co.uk

PRICE FOR TWO PEOPLE
Around $250–330 a day for food,
accommodations, and admission fees.

WEBSITES
www.lewesonline.com
www.lewes.co.uk

Lewes Bonfire Societies

The first bonfire society was created in the mid-18th
century to help impose order on the Bonfire Boys,
groups of youths whose riotous celebrations every
November 5 led to clashes with the police. They
were dispersed to fields outside the town (now the
suburbs), where they formed seven societies, each
with distinct clothing and mottos. The societies
survive today, and on bonfire night each group's
members parade around their district before joining
the other societies in a procession through Lewes.

Main: Costumed revelers at the bonfire night procession in Lewes

ALL FIRED UP

Sitting on the river ouse and rising and falling with the gentle undulations of the
magnificent South Downs, the East Sussex county town of Lewes is a fetching vignette
of narrow lanes, time-warped wood-framed buildings, and all the tidy elegance of a historic
English market town. Lewes is charming all year, but its cultural calendar literally explodes
every November 5, when it hosts Britain's largest and most famous bonfire night.

Lewes's remarkable anti-Catholic bonfire traditions, managed by local bonfire societies
(*see story box*), honor the deaths of 17 Lewes Protestants martyred in the mid-16th century, as
well as celebrating the anniversary of Guy Fawkes's demise in 1605. The festivities are highly
tribal and religiously partisan, with smuggler costumes, riotous music, flying sparks, clouds
of smoke, and a tangibly martial flavor. The "Bonfire Boys" (and girls) of the seven societies
blacken their faces, don striped smuggler's jerseys, and raise flaming torches and crosses to
parade through the streets as one, before dividing into their separate societies and returning
to their respective "firesites" (home districts) to kindle bonfires and light fireworks. Effigies of
Guy Fawkes and Pope Paul V (made head of the Catholic Church in 1605), along with more

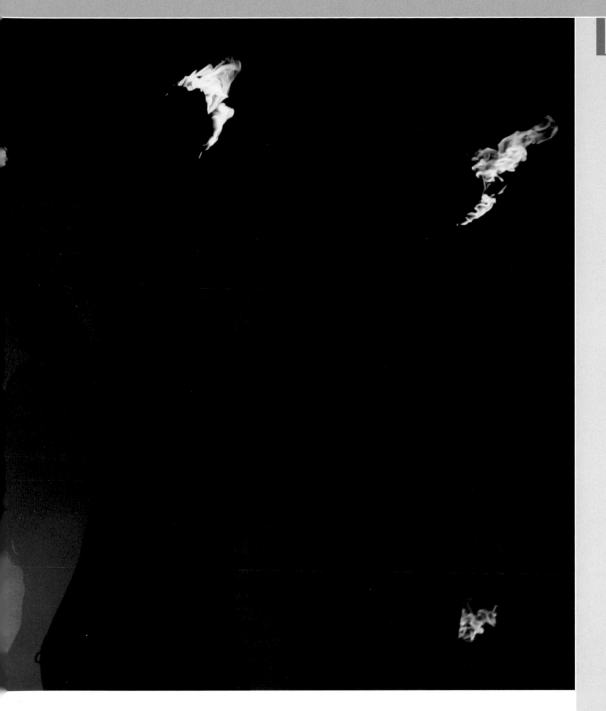

FURTHER DETAILS

LEWES

Lewes Bonfire Night
Bonfire Night takes place on November 5, unless this is a Sunday, in which case the celebrations are staged the night before; the first procession begins at around 5:30pm with the last one ending roughly at midnight. If you are planning to stay in Lewes on bonfire night, reserve your hotel room and restaurant table early. It can be wet and muddy at the bonfire sites, so wrap up and take rain gear and suitable footwear. It's best to arrive in Lewes by train, as the streets are closed for the processions and it's very difficult to park in town.
www.lewesbonfirecouncil.org.uk

Lewes Castle
Open 10am–5:30pm Tue–Sat; 11am–5:30pm Sun–Mon and Bank Holidays (closed Mondays in January).
www.sussexpast.co.uk/lewescastle

Anne of Cleves House
Wealden; open Mar–Oct: 10am–5pm Tue–Thu, 11am–5pm Sun, Mon and Bank Holidays; Nov–Feb: 10am–5pm Sat, 11am–5pm Sun.
www.sussexpast.co.uk/anneofcleves

WHAT ELSE TO SEE AND DO

Bluebell Railway
Taking its name from the bluebells that grow alongside the line in spring, this steam railroad runs on an old train line between Sheffield Park, just north of Lewes, and Kingscote, south of East Grinstead. Trains run regularly in summer and fall until November 15, and then for special events only in the winter months. Check the website for details.
www.bluebell-railway.co.uk

Brighton
A short bus or train trip takes you to the pebbly beaches, seaside charms, and Georgian buildings of Brighton *(see pp36–7)*. Visit the Royal Pavilion, amble to the tip of Brighton's famous Palace Pier, and don't overlook wandering the Lanes, where a medley of small antique, knickknack, and jewelry shops share space with restaurants and bars.
www.visitbrighton.com

Glynde House
A vast Elizabethan manor house 4 miles (6 km) from Lewes, with incredible views across the South Downs to the Weald. Treasures include art, craft, and furniture pieces collected by the family over three centuries. The large gardens offer captivating walks.
www.glynde.co.uk

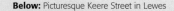

Below: Picturesque Keere Street in Lewes

> The celebrations are highly tribal and religiously partisan, with smuggler costumes, riotous music, flying sparks, clouds of smoke, and a tangibly martial flavor.

current "villains," are sent up in flames. Some bonfire societies still propel burning barrels of tar into the river, creating a truly dramatic sight. The town heaves with visitors; if you can't make the November 5 celebrations, check for others in the preceding and following weeks, both in Lewes and at the nearby villages of Battle, Newick, and Mayfield.

Much of the appeal of Lewes comes from its historic street layout and its timber-framed buildings and "twittens," the Sussex name for the narrow lanes seen in these parts. The town also serves as a useful starting point for walks in the South Downs, which can be seen in all their rolling glory from Lewes Castle, a fortification erected in 1087 on a man-made hill, the town's highest point. Other town highlights include the historic architecture and medieval charm of Keere Street – a steep and cobbled incline once famously navigated by the Prince Regent in his carriage – and Anne of Cleves House, a wood-framed Tudor building. The pretty Elizabethan gardens of Southover Grange provide a beautiful spot for a picnic.

POTTERY CENTRAL

T HE SPRAWLING CONURBATION OF STOKE-ON-TRENT – made up of six smaller towns in England's industrial heartland – is inextricably linked with the story of an entire industry. Ceramics have been made in the Potteries – the towns of Burslem, Fenton, Hanley, Longton, Stoke, and Tunstall – for centuries, and a visit to Stoke-on-Trent provides a chance to learn about the region's long and distinguished history of pottery-making. You can also browse the numerous factory shops and stock up on classy tableware, and fall is the ideal time to find that perfect Christmas gift of fine bone china, before the busy festive season begins.

Ceramics have been made in the Potteries for centuries, and a visit to Stoke-on-Trent provides a chance to learn about the region's long and distinguished history.

The Potteries boomed during the Industrial Revolution of the 18th and 19th centuries. The region, once covered with smoke from hundreds of brick bottle kilns – so named for their bottle shape – supplied ceramic goods across the British Empire. Stoke-on-Trent is unusual among British industrial cities in that its key industry is still going strong: it has hundreds of pottery firms and remains a world center for ceramic design and production.

To get a real feel for the grimy old days, visit the Gladstone Pottery Museum at Longton. This typical 19th-century bone-china pottery was saved from demolition in the 1970s, and it is the last surviving complete Victorian pottery in the country. It has plenty to offer: you can try your hand at pot-throwing and explore a huge collection of ceramic artifacts, including a display of antique toilets. Meanwhile, Ceramica, in Burslem's elegant Victorian town hall, tells the story of the social effects the pottery boom had on the area, with imaginative children's activities such as jewelry-making. Sandwiched between two of the city's canals is the Etruria Industrial Museum, home to a mill once used to crush bone and flint for the china industry.

Founded by Josiah Wedgwood in 1759, Wedgwood is the best-known china pottery company in the city, and its visitor center and museum at nearby Barlaston are worth a day out in themselves. You can try throwing a pot, and there's a wonderful array of priceless Wedgwood antiques on show, as well as contemporary jasper ware for sale.

Main: Red-brick interior of a bottle kiln at Gladstone Pottery Museum **Inset:** Pottery-making demonstration
Below (left to right): Gladstone Pottery Museum; statue of Josiah Wedgwood outside the pottery company he founded

THE ESSENTIALS

GETTING THERE AND AROUND
Stoke-on-Trent is 160 miles (260 km) northwest of London. Birmingham, Manchester, and East Midlands airports are all within 60 miles (100 km) of the city. Trains from London Euston to Stoke-on-Trent take approximately 90 minutes. Local buses run regularly from the station to the main attractions; otherwise there are well-signposted roads.

WEATHER
Fall often brings spells of fine weather to the area, but be prepared for some wind and rain, with average daytime temperatures ranging from 43 to 55°F (6–13°C).

ACCOMMODATIONS
Treat Yourself The Manor, at Hanchurch, is a secluded luxury retreat that's very convenient for Trentham and Wedgwood. www.hanchurchmanor.co.uk

On a Budget New Hayes Farm B&B, 4 miles from Stoke, is a Victorian farmhouse on a working farm that serves award-winning breakfasts. www.newhayesfarm.co.uk

EATING OUT
Treat Yourself Café Davide, on the Trentham Estate, serves delicious contemporary Mediterranean cuisine. www.cafe-davide.co.uk

On a Budget Ivy House Restaurant, at the Wedgwood Visitor Centre (but also open to non-visitors), is an open-plan restaurant that serves its home-cooked food on Wedgwood china. www.wedgwoodvisitorcentre.com

PRICE FOR TWO PEOPLE
From around $240 a day for food, admission fees, and accommodations.

WEBSITE
www.visitstoke.co.uk

Ceramic Evolution

Stoke's pottery trade started in the 17th century, when farmer-potters used the area's red and brown clays to make earthenware "butterpots". From the mid-18th century the potters wanted white clay, similar to china from the Far East, so they began to bring this up from Devon and Cornwall. Early innovators included Josiah Wedgwood, who developed the highly-collectible "creamware" and Joseph Spode, who invented bone china, the toughest form of porcelain.

FURTHER DETAILS

STOKE-ON-TRENT

Gladstone Pottery Museum
Uttoxeter Road, Longton, Stoke-on-Trent;
open 10am–5pm daily.
www.stokemuseums.org.uk

Ceramica
Old Town Hall, Market Place, Burslem, Stoke-on-Trent;
open 10:30am–4:30pm Mon–Sat.
www.ceramicauk.com

Etruria Industrial Museum
Lower Bedford Street, Etruria, Stoke-on-Trent;
open noon–4:30pm Wed–Sun.
www.stokemuseums.org.uk

Wedgwood Visitor Centre and Museum
Barlaston, Stoke-on-Trent; open 9am–5pm Mon–Fri,
10am–5pm Sat–Sun; closed Dec 24–Jan 1.
Visitor Centre: *www.wedgwoodvisitorcentre.com*
Museum: *www.wedgwoodmuseum.org.uk*

WHAT ELSE TO SEE AND DO

Emma Bridgewater Ltd
This contemporary working pottery, factory shop, and
decorating studio in Hanley allows you to paint your own
pieces, and offers guided tours (Tuesdays only) that give
you the opportunity to see a working pottery in action.
www.emmabridgewater.co.uk

The Potteries Museum and Art Gallery
This extensive free museum in Hanley is home to the
world's finest collection of Staffordshire ceramics.
There are also displays of pottery from across the world,
along with exhibits on local and natural history and fine
work by local artists.
www.stokemuseums.org.uk

Trentham Estate
First noted in the Domesday Book in 1086, this historic
estate offers stunning parkland, an Italian Garden, a lake,
a giant observation wheel, and lots of family activities.
www.trenthamleisure.co.uk

Below (top to bottom): The Potteries Museum and Art Gallery;
magnificent Italian Garden at the Trentham Estate

THE ESSENTIALS

GETTING THERE AND AROUND
Loch Lomond is 20 miles (32 km) –
less than an hour's drive – from Glasgow,
where the closest international airport
is located. The Trossach region is easily
reached from Stirling, 16 miles (26 km)
away via Callander, or from Aberfoyle
(20 miles/32 km away). You will need a
car to explore the many beautiful drives
throughout the national park. There are
also scenic boat trips on Loch Katrine and
Loch Lomond.

WEATHER
The weather can change rapidly here,
especially in the mountains, so prepare for
rain even on fine days. Average daytime
temperatures range from 43 to 54°F
(6–12°C).

ACCOMMODATIONS
Treat Yourself The Roman Camp Hotel,
in Callander, is a country-house hotel set
in extensive grounds by the River Teith and
has an acclaimed restaurant.
www.romancamphotel.co.uk

On a Budget The Glenbruach Country
House B&B, in Loch Achray, is a Victorian
mansion, the gardens of which are often
visited by local deer.
www.nationalparkscotland.com

EATING OUT
Treat Yourself The Restaurant at the
Roman Camp Hotel is simply named
but serves up stunning flavors.
www.romancamphotel.co.uk

On a Budget The Byre Inn, in Brig
o' Turk, produces adventurous locally
sourced food with a Scottish twist.
www.byreinn.co.uk

PRICE FOR TWO PEOPLE
$260 a day for food and accommodations.

WEBSITES
www.visitscottishheartlands.com
www.trossachs.co.uk

Rob Roy MacGregor

The Trossachs was home to one of Scotland's
most romantic figures, Rob Roy MacGregor. Born
at Glen Gyle in 1671 and named for his flaming
hair ("roy" comes from the Gaelic word for "red"),
MacGregor was a skillful swordsman and an
infamous cattle raider – an honorable profession
among the clans. When he was falsely accused of
stealing from the Duke of Montrose, he fled to the
hills and became an outlaw. He was later pardoned
and died peacefully in Balquhidder in 1734.

Main: Low fall clouds over Loch Lomond **Right (top to bottom):** Mountain biker exploring a trail on the eastern shore of
Loch Lomond; road winding through rugged countryside in the Trossachs; steam boat on Loch Katrine

TAKE THE HIGH ROAD

WITH ITS BONNIE, BONNIE BANKS immortalized in the classic Scottish ballad, Loch Lomond
is one of Scotland's most famous lochs. Less well-known, but equally beautiful, is the
Trossachs region that surrounds it. Together they make up Scotland's first national park,
which was established in 2002. Covering around 720 sq miles (1,865 sq km), the park is
like a miniature version of Scotland itself, encompassing its quintessential landscapes, from
mountains, lochs, and glens to forests and rolling lowlands.

At 23 miles (37 km) long, Loch Lomond is the largest expanse of fresh water in Great
Britain. Known as the Queen of Scottish Lochs, its narrow northern neck is bordered by steep
mountains, while its southern half spreads out into a wide watery blue cloak, encrusted with
dozens of jewel-like islands known as "inches." These privately owned islands, some of which
appear only when the water levels are very low, have, over the years, provided havens for
everyone from whiskey-runners to saintly hermits, and you can see them up close from the
pleasure boats that cruise the loch from several ports.

FURTHER DETAILS

LOCH LOMOND AND THE TROSSACHS
There is something for all tastes in the Loch Lomond
and Trossachs National Park: hill-walking, cycling, boating,
golf, and, for the more adventurous, canoeing, kayaking,
windsurfing, and mountain biking.
www.lochlomond-trossachs.org

Loch Lomond Shores
This shopping, dining, and activity complex is located at
Balloch on the southern end of Loch Lomond. The
Gateway Centre here is a visitor center for Loch Lomond
and Trossachs National Park. There are audio-visual shows,
woodland walks, bike and canoe rentals, cruises, and more.
www.lochlomondshores.com

Trossachs Discovery Centre
The visitor center on Aberfoyle's Main Street provides
an overview of the history and geography of the region.
Tel: 08707 200 604

Lake of Menteith
The romantic ruins of Inchmahome, a 13th-century
Augustinian priory, lie on an island in this scenic lake.
They are accessible by ferry from the Port of Menteith.
www.historic-scotland.gov.uk

WHAT ELSE TO SEE AND DO
Stirling Castle
There are fantastic views from the ramparts of this
impressive castle in Stirling, dating from 1496. It features
striking Renaissance architecture and some period rooms.
www.historic-scotland.gov.uk

Below: Port of Menteith Church reflected in the Lake of Menteith

> The Trossachs… is like a miniature version of Scotland itself,
> encompassing its quintessential landscapes, from mountains,
> lochs, and glens to forests and rolling lowlands.

Stretching north and east of Loch Lomond, the Trossachs has been a popular holiday spot since
the late 18th century. Its lowlands contain one of the few Scottish "lakes," the Lake of Menteith,
and the foothills around Aberfoyle mark the beginning of the Highlands. From here, a road
winds up through Queen Elizabeth Forest Park and over Duke's Pass to Loch Katrine; it's a drive
of exceptional beauty when the woodlands display their full autumn glory. Alternatively, a
minor road west from Aberfoyle leads you into the wild glens along the shores of Loch Lomond,
once the territory of the MacGregor clan. Some of the national park's most dramatic scenery lies
in the Breadalbane region to the north. The scenic road from Killin to Tyndrum is spectacular,
taking you past Ben More, the park's highest peak at 3,852 ft (1,174 m). More mountains
surround Argyll Forest Park, west of Loch Lomond. From Arrochar, drive up Glen Croe for
stunning views, before descending through the atmospheric forest of Hell's Glen to Lochgoilhead.

THE ESSENTIALS

GETTING THERE AND AROUND
The Great North Run takes place in
northeast England: it starts in Newcastle
upon Tyne and ends in South Shields.
Newcastle International Airport is 7 miles
(11 km) northwest of Newcastle. The
Tyne and Wear Metro links the airport
with Newcastle and South Shields. Buses
connect harbor and downtown areas.

WEATHER
In September the weather in Newcastle
is normally cool and relatively dry, with
average daytime temperatures ranging
from 48 to 60°F (9–16°C).

ACCOMMODATIONS
Treat Yourself Malmaison Newcastle,
on the quayside, has stunning views of
the waterfront and is a short distance
from the Millennium Bridge.
www.malmaison-newcastle.com

On a Budget Jurys Inn Newcastle, on
Scotswood Road, is a functional modern
hotel about 10 minutes' walk from central
Newcastle.
http://newcastlehotels.jurysinns.com

EATING OUT
Treat Yourself Café 21, in Newcastle's
Trinity Gardens, is a smart restaurant
in the heart of the quayside that offers
contemporary European food and classic
bistro dishes in stylish surroundings.
www.cafetwentyone.co.uk

On a Budget Panis Café, on High
Bridge, Newcastle, is a genuine Italian
establishment serving Sardinian and
other regional dishes.
www.paniscafe.co.uk

PRICE FOR TWO
$250–330 a day, including
food and accommodations.

WEBSITE
www.visitnortheastengland.com

Brendan Foster

The Great North Run is the brainchild of local
athletics hero Brendan Foster, who won a bronze
medal in the 10,000-m event at the 1976 Montreal
Olympics. Following a visit to New Zealand in 1979,
where he took part in the Round the Bays race,
Foster came up with the idea of creating a similar
event in his native northeast. The Great North Run
was launched as a "fun run" in 1981 and takes
place annually, attracting the biggest names in
distance running as well as many celebrities.

Above (left to right): Competitors in the Great North Run; Newcastle's Castle Keep and the Tyne Bridge
Main: Red Arrows pass over runners on the Tyne Bridge

ROAD RUNNERS

SINCE ITS INCEPTION IN 1981, the Great North Run has become one of the biggest days in the British sporting calendar. With 50,000 runners cheered on by 30,000 spectators lining the route, the half-marathon – now the largest in the world – celebrates both the determination of the athletes taking part and the rejuvenated cityscapes of Newcastle, Gateshead, and South Shields, which provide its backdrop. Elite runners tackling the 13-mile (21-km) route are joined by thousands of amateurs, many relying on sheer guts – rather than athleticism – to complete the route and raise millions of pounds for charity.

The tension builds as the competitors assemble at the starting point at Newcastle's Town Moor before the hooters sound to release the hordes of runners, their bobbing heads forming a rippling stream. The route takes the runners under the iconic arch of the Tyne Bridge, and those who have timed their run perfectly will cross from Newcastle to Gateshead just as the Red Arrows thunder overhead, leaving behind colored smoke trails. But inspiration soon turns to perspiration as the runners spread out, passing Gateshead International Stadium, and head east toward the sea and South Shields. A sharp downhill section leads to the coast, where bands and supporters gather to provide the encouragement needed to move aching limbs. Eventually, the runners catch sight of the finish gantry, where the electronic clocks record times and stewards prevent chaos as the runners, in various stages of exhaustion and exuberance, cross the line and head toward their belongings and loved ones.

Once the hurly-burly of the run is over, competitors and spectators have time to explore the diverse urban heart of Tyneside, where world-class arts venues such as the Sage Gateshead, with its astonishing curved glass structure, and the Baltic Centre, housed in a converted flour mill, vie for attention with Newcastle's famed nightlife. The city's tough face, which can be seen in the buildings that stand as memorials to the region's industrial past, has been softened by new architectural marvels, including the astonishing tilting Millennium Bridge over the Tyne, and public art along the quayside. Tyneside is a modern success story – a region that has successfully reinvented itself, some would say against the odds – and the Great North Run is the perfect symbol of its continued vitality.

Below (left to right): Baltic Centre for Contemporary Art; Millennium Bridge over the Tyne

FURTHER DETAILS

THE GREAT NORTH RUN
The run takes place in either Sep or Oct annually.
www.greatrun.org

The Sage Gateshead
St. Mary's Square, Gateshead Quays, Gateshead; open 9am–11pm daily, depending on performance times.
www.thesagegateshead.org

The Baltic Centre for Contemporary Art
Gateshead Quays, South Shore Road; open 10am–6pm Wed–Mon, 10:30am–6pm Tue.
www.balticmill.com

The Millennium Bridge
The Millennium Bridge links Newcastle to Gateshead, and tilts daily at noon.
www.gateshead-quays.com

WHAT ELSE TO SEE AND DO
Newcastle Castle Keep
Constructed in the 12th century to defend Newcastle from Scottish invasions, the castle keep is a must-see.
http://museums.ncl.ac.uk

St. James' Park Tour
Soccer fans will enjoy taking a tour of St. James' Park stadium, home of Newcastle United.
www.nufc.premiumtv.co.uk

Bamburgh Castle
Standing guard over miles of uncrowded Northumberland beaches, Bamburgh Castle is a dramatic starting point for any historical tour of the region.
www.bamburghcastle.com

The Alnwick Garden
These fabulous gardens in Alnwick were created by the Duchess of Northumberland.
www.alnwickgarden.com

Durham The beautiful medieval city of Durham features the UNESCO World Heritage Site of Durham Cathedral.
www.durhamtourism.co.uk

Tyneside is a modern success story – a region that has successfully reinvented itself, some would say against the odds – and the Great North Run is the perfect symbol of its continued vitality.

THE ESSENTIALS

GETTING THERE AND AROUND
Manchester is in northwestern England. Manchester Airport is 10 miles (16 km) to the south of the city, and trains from here to the city centre (Manchester Piccadilly station). Hourly trains run from London and half-hourly trains run from Liverpool. Most of central Manchester can be explored on foot, but there's also an extensive bus network.

WEATHER
Manchester enjoys a mild climate, with fall daytime highs of 41–59°F (5–15°C). The city gets less rain than many parts of the UK, but it's best to be prepared.

ACCOMMODATIONS
Treat Yourself Velvet, on Canal Street, is a stunning hotel with lavishly equipped rooms and an exceptional restaurant with superb service.
www.velvetmanchester.com

On a Budget Ivy Mount Guesthouse, in Eccles, 4 miles (6 km) from the city, is a 3-star B&B with neat rooms and handy transportation links to the city.
www.ivymountguesthouse.co.uk

EATING OUT
Treat Yourself Gaucho Grill, on St. Mary's Street, is a spacious Argentinian restaurant offering mouth-watering steaks and exceptional service.
www.gauchorestaurants.co.uk

On a Budget Lounge 10, on Tib Lane, has a tasty French menu and sterling service.
www.lounge10manchester.co.uk

PRICE FOR TWO PEOPLE
From $300 a day for food, accommodations, and admission fees.

WEBSITE
www.visitmanchester.com

Chinatown

England's second-largest Chinatown after London's famous community, Manchester's Chinatown is a lively and bustling district of shops, supermarkets, and Asian restaurants. Bounded by York Street, Mosley Street, Oxford Street, and Portland Street, Chinatown declares itself with a large and brightly colored memorial arch – Europe's largest and finest – on Faulkner Street. The festive high point for Chinatown is Chinese New Year, which is celebrated in late January or early February.

Main: Modern arched Merchants Bridge over the Bridgewater Canal sits among the city's older canal bridges
Right (top to bottom): Statue outside Old Trafford Football Stadium; sushi bar, example of Manchester's thriving gastronomic culture; entrance to Chinatown

INDUSTRIAL REVELATION

ONCE A MANUFACTURING GIANT processing more than 65 percent of the world's cotton, Manchester still enjoys international fame. The city that grew up at the forefront of the Industrial Revolution is home to Manchester United, the wealthiest and most popular soccer club in the world. Fans from Singapore to China make pilgrimages just to visit Old Trafford in the southwest of the city, for guided tours of the hallowed stadium. The city has also given rise to some groundbreaking popular music – Oasis, the Stone Roses, the Happy Mondays, the Smiths, and Take That are all on the roll-call of local bands.

Manchester's eclectic and stylish restaurant culture is also a great reason to visit. Although this cosmopolitan university city can be explored at any time of year, 250,000 people visit in fall to sample the gastronomic delights on offer at the Manchester Food and Drink Festival. All of the city's restaurants, bars, cafés, pubs and delis put on special tastings and talks, the festival pavilion hosts "mini" festivals, of wine, whisky, and real ale, and St. Anne's Square is abuzz with chef demonstrations and busy market stalls selling delicious local food.

FURTHER DETAILS

MANCHESTER

Manchester United Museum and Stadium Tour
Old Trafford; open 9:30am–5pm Mon–Sat;
tours every 10 minutes from 9:40am–4:30pm.
www.manutd.com

Manchester Food and Drink Festival
Held in early October at venues across the city.
www.foodanddrinkfestival.com

Manchester Art Gallery
Mosley Street; open 10am–5pm Tue–Sun.
www.manchestergalleries.org

Albert Memorial
Albert Square.

Manchester Town Hall Visitor Information Centre
Lloyd Street; open 10am–5:30pm Mon–Sat, 10:30am–
4:30pm Sun.
www.visitmanchester.com

Central Library
St. Peter's Square; open 9am–8pm Mon–Thu,
9am–5pm Fri–Sat.

Free Trade Hall
St. Peter's Square.

Manchester Cathedral
Victoria Street; open 8:30am–7pm Mon–Fri,
8:30am–5pm Sat, 8:30am–7:30pm Sun.
www.manchestercathedral.org

Museum of Science and Industry
Castlefield; open 10am–5pm daily.
www.msim.org.uk

The Lowry Arts Centre
Pier 8, Salford Quays; open 11am–5pm Sun– Fri,
10am–5pm Sat.
www.thelowry.com

WHAT ELSE TO SEE AND DO
Chester
Enclosed within ancient walls, the historic city of Chester
has a glut of sights. From the half-timbered Tudor and
Victorian buildings that line The Rows to the cathedral
and castle, Roman relics, and nearby Chester Zoo, this
city offers something for everyone.
www.visitchester.co.uk

Below: Lowry footbridge over the Manchester Ship Canal

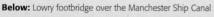

In between bouts of eating and drinking, turn your attention to the rest of what Manchester
has to offer. The impressive form of Manchester Art Gallery contains an abundant and varied
catalog of art, including a strong selection of Pre-Raphaelite oil paintings. The architecture,
too, is worthy of attention. The most magnificent structures owe much to the Mancunians'
allegiance to Queen Victoria: they demolished 100 buildings to erect Britain's first Albert
Memorial in 1865, and then built Albert Square around it, before adding the imposing
Neo-Gothic Town Hall and other Victorian gems. Neighboring St. Peter's Square boasts its own
architectural delights, including the Neo-Classical circular Central Library and the palazzo-style
Free Trade Hall. And Manchester Cathedral, near the River Irwell, is home to an extraordinary
Saxon carving, the 8th-century Angel Stone.

Don't overlook the canals and Victorian viaduct scenes of Castlefield, where fragments of a
Roman fort survive. On a rainy day, you can have a lot of fun exploring the Museum of Science
and Industry, or discovering more about Manchester's industrial past through the works of its
most famous painter, L. S. Lowry (1887–1976), at The Lowry Arts Centre in Salford Quays.
And if you're still full of energy at the end of a satisfying day of exploration, Manchester's
famous nightlife and bar scene offers limitless entertainment.

THE ESSENTIALS

GETTING THERE AND AROUND
The New Forest is in Hampshire, in southern England. The nearest airport is at Bournemouth, 17 miles (27 km) from Brockenhurst. Regular trains run to Brockenhurst from London Waterloo. Local buses run from both Brockenhurst and Lyndhurst to points within the forest; the New Forest Tour Bus runs from June to September between the forest's principal towns.

WEATHER
The New Forest enjoys a pleasant climate in fall, but prepare for changeable weather. Average daytime temperatures range from 45 to 57°F (7–14°C).

ACCOMMODATIONS
Treat Yourself Rhinefield House Hotel, in Brockenhurst, is a secluded and grand 4-star country-house hotel in the heart of the New Forest.
www.handpickedhotels.co.uk

On a Budget Whitemoor House Hotel, in Lyndhurst, is a well-liked bed and breakfast with a handy central location.
www.whitemoorhouse.co.uk

EATING OUT
Treat Yourself Lanes of Lymington, in Lymington, is a former schoolhouse converted into a stylish restaurant with a classy contemporary menu.
www.lanesoflymington.com

On a Budget Plummers, on High Street in Ringwood, is a friendly restaurant serving great snacks and light lunches, and more ambitious meals in the evening.
www.plummersbistro.co.uk

PRICE FOR TWO PEOPLE
$200–250 a day for accommodations, food, and local transportation.

WEBSITE
www.new-forest-national-park.com

Death of a King

King William II was hunting in the New Forest in August 1100 when he was fatally shot in the heart with an arrow. The details remain a mystery: the traditional tale blames Sir Walter Tirel for accidentally killing William. The Rufus Stone, near Brook, marks the spot where an oak tree supposedly deflected his arrow – aimed at a stag – into William's unprotected chest. Other versions of the story blame the king's brother Henry, who was also in the forest, and inherited the crown after the king's death.

A ROYAL FOREST

ORIGINALLY A HUGE SWATH of uninterrupted woodland, the New Forest – recorded as "Nova Foresta" in the Domesday Book – is a scenic sanctuary for stressed urbanites and wildlife enthusiasts. Ranging over an area of 145 sq miles (375 sq km), this national park is today far less a forest than a vast, diverse patchwork of heathland, grassland, wetland, and woodland, embracing a rich ecological diversity and a wonderful range of wildlife.

Deer have always populated the area, which was the principal reason why William the Conqueror designated it a "forest" – the medieval term for a royal hunting reserve – in the 11th century. Today, five species roam the forest; you'll need patience and a degree of luck to get close-up views of them, as they are extremely shy creatures. The largest and most impressive species is the red deer: the heftiest land mammal in the British Isles, the male is an imposing sight during the rutting (mating) season, which runs from mid-September to the end of October. Displaying their dense coats, muscular build, and huge, magnificent antlers, the stags square off against each other in their challenge. The contest is usually decided through a mixture of performance and posturing, but if there is a battle, it can be ferocious.

The forest is also home to sika deer, originally from Japan, and the shy, rare muntjac deer from China. You may also catch a glimpse of the small roe deer, whose rutting season finishes in late summer. Fallow deer are among the most common animals in the forest, and you should see plenty of their white-spotted bodies flashing among the trees of this ancient royal park. If all else fails, you're virtually guaranteed to see them gathered beneath the viewing platform at the Bolderwood Deer Sanctuary in the forest, where they are fed regularly. But by far the most conspicuous animals in the forest are domesticated cattle and pigs, and, of course, the semi-wild New Forest ponies. As you watch the iconic New Forest ponies wandering lazily around villages and even poking their noses into shops, you'd be forgiven for thinking that all the animals are friendly, but watch out for adders, which go slithering back to their hibernation sites in fall.

FURTHER DETAILS

NEW FOREST
New Forest Visitor Centre
Main car park, Lyndhurst; open 10am–5pm daily. There are also Visitor Information points scattered throughout the New Forest.
www.thenewforest.co.uk

The two main tourist towns in the New Forest are Lyndhurst and Brockenhurst.
Lyndhurst: *www.newforest-online.co.uk/lyndhurst.asp*
Brockenhurst: *www.brockenhurst-newforest.org.uk*

New Forest Tour Bus
The New Forest Tour offers one-day bus tickets that can be bought online, allowing you to hop on and off at will. Bicycles are allowed on board; runs mid-Jun–mid-Sep.
www.thenewforesttour.info

Bolderwood Deer Sanctuary
Deer are fed daily from April to September at this deer park, situated near the main Bolderwood car park. Several signposted, graded walks start here too, passing through ancient woodland.
www.new-forest-national-park.com/bolderwood-deer-sanctuary.html

WHAT ELSE TO SEE AND DO
Beaulieu
Lying within the New Forest, Beaulieu – pronounced "Bewley" – is a famous collection of sights, including the Palace House, home to the Montagu family since the 16th century; Beaulieu Abbey; the National Motor Museum; the World of Top Gear; and stunning gardens.
www.beaulieu.co.uk

Below: Rambling through the New Forest National Park

> This national park is today far less a forest than a vast patchwork of heathland, grassland, wetland, and woodland, embracing a rich ecological diversity.

Main: Red deer with bracken in its antlers **Inset:** Coiled adder, common in the New Forest
Below (left to right): Red deer stags tussle during a "rut"; New Forest ponies grazing on the forest floor

THE ESSENTIALS

GETTING THERE AND AROUND
Bunratty Castle is in the town of Bunratty, which is about 8 miles (13 km) east of Shannon Airport and 7½ miles (12 km) west of Limerick, in County Clare on the west coast of Ireland. There are buses between Limerick and the airport at Shannon, which go directly past the castle, but it is most easily visited by car.

WEATHER
The weather in Bunratty in the fall is usually mild, but can be changeable, with average daytime temperatures of 48 to 57°F (9–14°C).

ACCOMMODATIONS
Treat Yourself The Bunratty Castle Hotel is a luxury spa resort, offering a diverse range of rooms and facilities, a short stroll away from Bunratty Castle.
www.bunrattycastlehotel.com

On a Budget Bunratty Villa, in Bunratty, offers comfortable and affordable rooms set in elegant grounds, within walking distance of the castle.
www.bunrattyvilla.com

EATING OUT
Treat Yourself The Bunratty Castle Hotel's Round Room is an upscale restaurant serving excellent meals and fine wine.
www.bunrattycastlehotel.com

On a Budget The Original Durty Nelly's Pub boasts two reasonably priced restaurants, and there are cheaper bar meals available too.
www.durtynellys.ie

PRICE FOR A FAMILY OF FOUR
Around $500 a day for accommodations, food, and admission fees.

WEBSITE
www.shannonheritage.com

Durty Nelly

Bunratty was once a real, thriving town, but after the Potato Famine of 1845–52, which devastated the Irish economy, it fell into decline along with the castle. At one point the only building still occupied was Durty Nelly's pub, which had been built in about 1804. The pub was named after a local woman, who was allegedly the first person to brew poteen, the fierce Irish alcoholic drink. Whatever the truth, the pub, like the village, thrives again, and there are regular music sessions there.

WINDOWS ON THE PAST

THE SHANNON REGION OF WESTERN IRELAND is peppered with nearly 1,000 castles. While most stand in various stages of ruin and can only be glimpsed from a distance, Bunratty Castle is marvellously intact, and, together with its surrounding folk park, lets you experience history up close. Built on the site of a 10th-century Viking camp near the Shannon estuary, this imposing fortress dates back to 1425. It was sensitively restored in 1954 to its full medieval glory, inside and out, and now allows you to travel majestically back in time.

The castle is home to the extraordinary Bunratty Collection – some 450 pieces of medieval furniture, art, and artifacts. But this is no staid museum. While parents admire the vaulted

Imaginations will be fired by the castle's exciting features, such as "murder holes", gaps above passageways that were used to drop missiles or boiling liquids onto invaders.

ceilings, tapestries and other highlights such as the rare 17th-century harpsichord in the South Solar Room, young imaginations are fired by the castle's more exciting features, such as "murder holes", gaps above passageways that were used to drop missiles or boiling liquids onto invaders passing beneath. Actors in medieval costume bring the past to life with entertaining tours, and there are great views from the ramparts. In the evening, it's possible to attend a medieval feast in the castle's splendid banqueting hall, with its minstrels' gallery. On the menu are dishes such as roast beef, which you eat with your fingers and wash down with mugs of mead. Then you can sit back and enjoy medieval and traditional Irish music. Fall also boasts seasonal joys such as September's Traditional Harvest Day and spooky Halloween events.

In the grounds around the castle, Bunratty Folk Park features more than 30 buildings that re-create local life in the 19th century, ranging from a fisherman's cottage to a Georgian gentleman's residence. Blacksmiths, thatchers, potters, weavers, and other characters in period clothing demonstrate their skills. You can buy flour freshly ground at the watermill or try a slice of hot griddle bread baked by the farmer's wife. Along the village street you'll find the schoolhouse, printworks, hardware shop, and grocery. The pretty Walled Garden has been restored to a Regency style, and once again supplies fruit, vegetables, and flowers to the castle.

Main: South Solar Room at Bunratty Castle **Inset:** Medieval wood-carving in the Great Hall of Bunratty Castle
Below: Re-creations of 19th-century housing in the Folk Park, Bunratty

FURTHER DETAILS

BUNRATTY CASTLE AND FOLK PARK
Bunratty, Shannon, County Clare; open Sep–May:
9:30am–5:30pm daily; Jun–Aug: 9am–6:30pm daily;
closed 23–27 Dec.
www.bunrattycollection.com

WHAT ELSE TO SEE AND DO
Limerick
Sprawled at the head of the Shannon estuary, Ireland's
fourth-largest city has several attractions in its medieval
core. Visit King John's Castle, a Norman fortress boasting
historical and interactive exhibits, and 12th-century St. Mary's
Cathedral with its old tombs and carved oak misericords
(carvings under seats). Don't miss the outstanding Hunt
Museum, which houses an eclectic collection ranging from
Celtic treasures to medieval artifacts and fine art.
King John's Castle: *www.shannonheritage.com*
St. Mary's Cathedral: *www.cathedral.limerick.anglican.org*
Hunt Museum: *www.huntmuseum.com*

The Burren
For a scenic drive, head north into County Clare, where
you'll find the vast limestone plateau of the Burren –
one of the most unusual landscapes in Ireland. It's dotted
with tiny, rare plants as well as prehistoric dolmens and
medieval ruins. It stretches all the way to the sea, to one
of Ireland's prime beauty spots, the Cliffs of Moher.
www.cliffsofmoher.ie

Craggaunowen
Authentically reconstructed buildings at the archaeological
open-air museum of Craggaunowen, 10 miles (16 km)
north of Bunratty, demonstrate the lifestyle of the ancient
Celts. The exhibits include a ring fort, a *crannog* (island
settlement), and a medieval castle. There are also rare-
breed farm animals and the leather-hulled Brendan Boat,
used to reenact the 6th-century journey of St. Brendan.
www.shannonheritage.com/attractions/craggaunowen

Below: Bunratty Castle illuminated at night and Durty Nelly's Pub

THE ESSENTIALS

GETTING THERE AND AROUND
Cornwall is in southwestern England, about 5 hours' drive or train trip from London. The three main routes by car into the county are the A39 north coast road (which passes many good surf beaches), the A30 across Dartmoor, and the A38 over the River Tamar. There are regular flights from London and other UK cities to Newquay's small airport.

WEATHER
Fall daytime temperatures vary from 48 to 64°F (9–18°C), falling off considerably in late fall, when it may get close to freezing at night. Water temperatures vary from around 64°F (18°C) early in the season to around 55°F (13°C) later on.

ACCOMMODATIONS
Treat Yourself Watergate Bay Hotel, in Watergate Bay, is literally right beside the surf and alongside the "Extreme Academy" for high-adrenaline sports.
www.watergatebay.co.uk

On a Budget Reef Island, in Newquay, is a good option if you want to combine surfing and nightlife.
www.aquashacksurflodge.com

EATING OUT
Treat Yourself The Beach Restaurant, above Sennen Beach, overlooks the most consistent surf in Cornwall.
www.sennenbeach.com

On a Budget Godrevy Café is based in an attractive wooden chalet overlooking Gwithian Towans, near St. Ives.
Tel: 01736 757999

PRICE FOR TWO PEOPLE
From $250 a day for accommodations, food, and transportation.

WEBSITES
www.visitcornwall.com
www.magicseaweed.com

Big Waves

Not to be outdone by more famous surf resorts around the world, Newquay has its own "big wave." A 20-ft (6-m) wave known as "the Cribber" breaks only a few times each year off Towan Head. First tackled in the 1960s, for many years only the brave or foolish would take it on, but these days, with better equipment and surf forecasting, the Cribber is ridden quite regularly. You may not dare to ride it yourself, but it's fun to watch those who do from the safety of the headland.

Main: Surfing enthusiasts taking to the water off Newquay
Right (top to bottom): Riding the dramatic Atlantic surf off Fistral Beach, Newquay; blokarting on the beach near St. Ives

SURF'S UP!

B EACHES EMPTY OF SUMMER VISITORS, swells rolling in from the North Atlantic, and the warmest waters of the year make fall the best time to hit the surf in North Cornwall. With more than 80 surfing locations off magical bays and coves, and plenty of surf schools, this rugged coast is the perfect place to feed your surfing addiction or try exciting new activities, such as windsurfing, kite surfing, wave-skiing, and blokarting.

Newquay is the obvious starting point: not only does it boast several great surf beaches, but it is the center of the county's après-surf action. Watergate Bay, just up the coast, promises glassy waves and a quieter setting; and if you want spectacularly blue seas, white sands, and a chance to surf with dolphins, check out Sennen, near Land's End. Alternatively, just strap your surfboard onto the roof of your car, throw your wetsuit in the back, and go exploring as the fall sun warms the sand and reflects rainbows off the back of the breaking waves.

The sea is never far away in Cornwall, and its call is irresistible: try a fishing safari aboard one of the boats departing from Newquay and catch some mackerel for supper, or take a

FURTHER DETAILS

NORTH CORNWALL

Surfing and Water Sports
North Cornwall has many surf schools, including the
National Surfing Centre at Fistral Beach, Newquay.
Speedsail UK, based near St. Ives, offers lessons in
blokarting; the Extreme Academy on Watergate Bay offers
tuition and rentals for many water- and beach-based sports.
National Surfing Centre: www.nationalsurfingcentre.com
Speedsail UK: www.speedsailuk.com
Extreme Academy: www.watergatebay.co.uk

Eden Project
Bodelva, Cornwall; opens 10am daily; closing times vary
according to season (see p13).
www.edenproject.com

The Lost Gardens of Heligan
Pentewan, Cornwall; open 10am–6pm daily.
www.heligan.com

Tate St. Ives
Porthmeor Beach, St. Ives, Cornwall; open Mar–Oct:
10am–5:20pm daily; Nov–Feb: 10am–4:20pm daily.
www.tate.org.uk/stives

Barbara Hepworth Museum and Sculpture Garden
Barnoon Hill, St. Ives, Cornwall; open Mar–Oct: 10am–
5:20pm daily; Nov–Feb: 10am–4:20pm Tue–Sun.
www.tate.org.uk/stives/hepworth

Below (top to bottom): Tideflats at Newquay Harbour; aerial view
of the Eden Project site

Strap your surfboard onto the roof of your car,
throw your wetsuit in the back, and go exploring
as the fall sun warms the sand.

wildlife boat from the harbor in Padstow to spot peregrine falcons, seals and dolphins. On
wind-lashed days, when the sea's too wild for surfing or beach rambles, there's still plenty to see
and do; stroll around one of North Cornwall's impossibly pretty fishing villages, squeezing down
narrow lanes between whitewashed cottages to find tiny pubs once frequented by smugglers. Or
head south to the Eden Project and visit the giant geodesic domes housing exotic plants from
around the world. Nearby, the restored Lost Gardens of Heligan at Pentewan are often less
crowded than the Eden Project and just as rewarding, with superb kitchen gardens, a wildlife
blind, and a boardwalk through giant rhubarb and banana plantations. Culture vultures will
enjoy the arty enclave of St. Ives, where the light has attracted many artists over the years.
Here is the Cornish outpost of the Tate Gallery, a museum and garden housing the works of
sculptor Barbara Hepworth, and other galleries where you can browse and buy original artworks.

THE ESSENTIALS

GETTING THERE AND AROUND
Hereford is in western England, about
3 hours from London by train. Trains and
long-distance buses also link Hereford with
Worcester (26 miles/ 42 km away), and
Birmingham (67 miles/108 km away),
home of the nearest international airport.
Once in Herefordshire, cycling allows
freedom, versatility, and scenic enjoyment.

WEATHER
Herefordshire enjoys a mild and pleasant
climate, with average fall daytime
temperatures of 48–63°F (9–17°C).
Always be prepared for fickle weather,
however, especially if cycling or walking.

ACCOMMODATIONS
Treat Yourself The Feathers Hotel,
in Ledbury, is located within a historic
"black and white" coaching inn situated
in the heart of town.
www.feathers-ledbury.co.uk

On a Budget Lowe Farm Bed and
Breakfast, in Pembridge, is a working
farm with a welcoming, homey
atmosphere – a perfect escape in
the heart of rural England.
www.bedandbreakfastlowefarm.co.uk

EATING OUT
Treat Yourself The Malthouse Restaurant,
in Ledbury, is tucked away down a pretty
cobbled Lane, and its menu delights with
modern British and continental flavors.
www.malthouse-ledbury.co.uk

On a Budget The Stewing Pot, on Church
Street, Hereford, offers excellent value and
fine, locally sourced ingredients.
www.thestewingpot.co.uk

PRICE FOR TWO PEOPLE
From $200 a day for accommodations
and food.

WEBSITE
www.ciderroute.co.uk

Black and White Trail

Beginning and ending in Leominster, the 40-mile
(64-km) "black and white trail" runs through a
series of charming, ancient Herefordshire villages,
noted for their 16th- and 17th-century timber-
framed buildings. The buildings – some misshapen,
lopsided, leaning, or decorated with attractive
herringbone timber patterns – are splendid portraits
of England's past, and many have been restored to
their original glory. Villages on the trail include
Pembridge, Eardisley, Kinnersley, and Lyonshall.

Main: Apple orchards in Newton, near Leominster
Right (top to bottom): Demijohns of cider; cider press in action; "black and white" timber-framed cottages at Pembridge

CIDER COUNTRY

ITS FERTILE LAND LARGELY DEVOTED TO AGRICULTURE, Herefordshire – nudging up against the Welsh border – is famed for its Hereford beef cattle and, of course, its glorious fruit, especially apples. The county is home to an extraordinary number of orchards and hard cider makers, making its pastoral villages ripe for scrumptious exploration. In fall the cider apple harvest brings out the full richness, color, and flavor of the Herefordshire countryside.

Today's Herefordshire is still delightfully dappled with cider orchards, spreading over 15 sq miles (39 sq km), and the county is home to the world's largest cider mill (Bulmers). A portion of the annual 75 million gallons (286 million liters) of hard cider enriches the local cuisine with apple aromas. A host of cider festivals – from the Cider-Making Festival and The Big Apple Festival in Hereford to the Ross-on-Wye Cider Festival – add extra sparkle to a tour of the county, with much consumption of the cloudy drink, festive music, and a fair degree of merriment. At the Flavours of Hereford Food Festival in late October, apple pressing and tasting is just one part of a broader celebration of the outstanding local produce.

FURTHER DETAILS

HEREFORDSHIRE

Hereford Tourist Office
King St.; open mid-May–mid-Sep: 9am–5pm Mon–Sat;
Bank Holidays: 10am–4pm.
www.visitherefordshire.co.uk

Hereford Cider Museum
21 Ryelands St., Hereford; open Apr–Oct: 10am–5pm
Tue–Sat (and over the Cider-Making Festival weekend);
Nov–Mar: 11am–3pm.
www.cidermuseum.co.uk

Hereford Cider-making Festival
Demonstrations of traditional cider-making, usually held
in late October at the Hereford Cider Museum.
www.cidermuseum.co.uk

The Big Apple Festival
This harvest festival celebrates apples and pears in all their
incarnations, as raw fruit, juices, alcoholic drinks and even
teas. It takes place across several Herefordshire villages in
early October each year.
www.bigapple.org.uk

Ross-on-Wye Cider Festival
The festival is held in September at Ross-on-Wye Cider
and Perry Company, Broome Farm, Peterstow.
www.rosscider.com

Flavours of Hereford Food Festival
Usually held at Hereford Racecourse in late October; open
10am–4:30pm Sat–Sun.
www.visitherefordshire.co.uk/sense/sense_foodfestival.asp

Cycling Routes
Leaflets detailing cycle routes are available from the
Ledbury Tourist Information Centre (tel: 01531 636147)
and other tourist information centers.

Hereford Cathedral
College Cloisters, Hereford; open 9:15am–5:30pm daily.
www.herefordcathedral.org

Mappa Mundi and Chained Library
The Chained Library is the cathedral's collection of
manuscripts, many dated earlier than 1500. The Chained
Library and Mappa Mundi are now housed in the New
Library at Hereford Cathedral; open mid-Mar–late Oct:
10am–4:30pm Mon–Sat; late Oct–mid-Mar: 10am–
3:30pm Mon–Sat; also May–Aug: 11am–3:30pm Sun.

Church of St. Mary and St. David
Kilpeck, near Hereford.

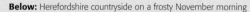

Below: Herefordshire countryside on a frosty November morning

Cycling through the rolling Herefordshire countryside is an ideal way to experience the rustic charms of this county – and you get to work off any weight you've accumulated from cider-drinking by getting from A to B. Hop on a pair of wheels and embark upon the 20-mile (32-km) Ledbury cycle route, which runs along tranquil lanes, through pretty villages, and past historic pubs. You can load up with fruit from farms along the way. Or try the 19-mile (30-km) Pembridge cycle route, which also winds its way through a rich cider-producing region and whisks you past Dunkertons Cider Mill, an organic cider-making farm.

Be sure not to overlook Herefordshire's other charms. On the western flank of the Malvern Hills, Ledbury is an attractive enclave of half-timbered Tudor and Stuart architecture, a highlight on the Herefordshire "Black and White" villages trail *(see story box)*. Perched on the River Wye, the city of Hereford is home to the eclectically styled Hereford Cathedral, dating from 1079, and the adjacent New Library is home of the Mappa Mundi, a 14th-century map of the world that ranks among the country's finest historical documents. The nearby village of Kilpeck has a well-preserved Norman church – the Church of St. Mary and St. David – that contains a variety of exquisite religious carvings. Finally, take a walk around Ross-on-Wye, a small town perfectly poised for scenic sojourns along the Wye River Valley.

THE ESSENTIALS

GETTING THERE AND AROUND
The River Tay runs for 120 miles (193 km) through central Scotland, reaching the sea outside the town of Perth. The nearest international airports are at Edinburgh and Glasgow, 41 miles (66 km) and 68 miles (110 km) from Perth. There are train connections from Glasgow and Edinburgh to Perth, then on to Dunkeld and Pitlochry. Car rental is available at the airports, and in Perth, Pitlochry, and larger towns.

WEATHER
Early fall weather on the Tay is often sunny, but mist, drizzle, and heavy rain are always possible, with average daytime temperatures of 43–52°F (6–11°C).

ACCOMMODATIONS
Treat Yourself Hilton Dunkeld House, in Dunkeld, is a luxury hotel and leisure club that offers a range of rooms and activities on a landscaped estate by the river.
www.hilton.co.uk/dunkeld

On a Budget The Kenmore Hotel, in Kenmore, claims to be the oldest inn in Scotland, in a great location overlooking the river as it flows out of Loch Tay. Its restaurant serves good Scottish fare.
www.kenmorehotel.com

EATING OUT
Treat Yourself Deans@Let's Eat, in Perth, is a fine modern restaurant with an emphasis on tasty local produce prepared with culinary flair.
www.letseatperth.co.uk

On a Budget The Courtyard at Mains of Taymouth, in Kenmore, has a good, mid-priced restaurant and deli-style café.
www.thecourtyard-restaurant.co.uk

PRICE FOR TWO PEOPLE
$250 a day for accommodations, activities, food, and admission fees.

WEBSITE
www.visitscotland.com/fish

Jewels of the River

The Tay is one of only a handful of rivers in Britain where pearl-bearing freshwater mussels can survive. Found on shallow stretches of the river north of Perth, the mussel beds produced pearls that were highly valued in medieval times, and the pearl fishery did a roaring trade until the 1970s. Sadly, freshwater mussels are highly sensitive to pollution. As a result their numbers have dwindled, and the pearl fishery is no longer financially viable, although you can still buy antique pearl jewelry.

Above (left to right): Canoeing on Loch Tay; leaping Atlantic salmon
Main: River Tay near Dunkeld at sunset

A QUEST FOR SILVER

Like silver blades slicing through the water, salmon carve a path from the North Sea to the headwaters of the Tay on an annual fall journey to their spawning grounds. It's a prospect to thrill the heart of any angler – for many, the chance to dip a line into Scotland's longest river is the fulfillment of a lifetime's ambition.

There are a variety of methods you can use here to catch salmon: trolling on the loch, which involves dragging a baited line through the water from a boat; fly-fishing from land beside the Tay's upper reaches; and bait-fishing from boats or the riverbanks. Each stretch of the Tay – from the mirror-calm waters of the loch to tree-lined stretches concealing deep underwater potholes, home to massive fish – calls for different angling skills and techniques, challenging even the most experienced of anglers. And the fish themselves are no easy catch; they are strong enough to swim upstream, leaping out of the rushing waters of rapids and waterfalls in their determination to return home. South of Perth, the River Earn – a tributary of the Tay that joins it at the wide Firth of Tay – is a great location to cast for hard-fighting sea trout, and also offers more opportunities for salmon fishing.

If you eventually sate your appetite for angling, pay a visit to Aberfeldy, where the Tay passes under the elegant Wade Bridge, designed by the Scottish architect William Adam in 1733. The little town has become a hub for adventure sports guaranteed to get the adrenaline flowing, from kayaking and slalom canoeing to white-water rafting on rapids. Sailing dinghies, motorboats, and fishing boats can also be rented at nearby Kenmore, where the river exits Loch Tay between thickly wooded banks. On land, the region boasts mountain-bike trails for novices and experienced riders, off-road ATV-riding, and 4WD wildlife safaris.

For the more laid-back visitor, there are plenty of golf courses to choose from. Perthshire has 40 courses, in glorious parkland, heathland, and Highlands settings. Some back right up to the Tay. Anglers will be absorbed by their quest for silver in Scotland's famous river, but for their friends and families, its banks and tranquil lochs also provide a fantastic experience.

Below (left to right): Salmon fishing at Kenmore; off-road ATV-riding; Kenmore and Loch Tay

FURTHER DETAILS

RIVER TAY
Tay Salmon Fisheries Company
Stockgreen Lodge, Lairwell, Kinfauns, Perth. You can fish for salmon on the river at Cargill and in the estuary near Perth, and for trout at the Willowgate fishery, home to rainbow, blue, and brown trout. The Tay District Salmon Fisheries Board urges anglers to return all female fish and all males weighing over 15 lb (7 kg) to the water; open for salmon fishing Jan 15–Oct 15, dawn until dusk Mon–Sat; open for trout fishing all year round, 8am–dusk daily. www.taysalmon.co.uk

Country Pursuits Scotland
Henderson Street, Bridge of Allan. Salmon- and trout-fishing trips are available on the upper, lower, and middle Tay, and on its tributary the Earn, where the salmon season lasts until the end of October. www.country-pursuits.com

WHAT ELSE TO SEE AND DO
Golf
The most popular golf course in the region is Dunkeld & Birnam Golf Club, a 100-year-old heathland course. www.dunkeldandbirnamgolfclub.co.uk

Pitlochry salmon ladder
Thousands of salmon battle their way up the 34 artificial pools of the world's first "salmon ladder" each year on the River Tummel, a tributary of the Tay at Pitlochry. www.scottish-southern.co.uk

Canoeing
The Scottish Canoe Association has a slalom site at the Grandtully rapids on the River Tay, and also maintains its own campsite near Grandtully village. www.canoescotland.com

Wildlife Safaris
Highland Safaris in Aberfeldy offer walking and 4WD safaris around the mountains and forests of Perthshire. http://highlandsafaris.net

ATV Rides and Mountain Biking
Activity Scotland offers ATV riding, mountain biking, climbing, abseiling, gorge-walking, and more from their base at the Dunalastair Hotel in Kinloch Rannon. www.activityscotland.com

> For many anglers, the chance to dip a line into Scotland's longest river is the fulfillment of a lifetime's ambition.

More Great Ideas for **Fall**

HISTORY AND HERITAGE

WILDLIFE AND LANDSCAPE

CITIES, TOWNS, AND VILLAGES

William the Conqueror's Battle Abbey in East Sussex

Red knot calidris flock over Snettisham in October

Inveraray, on the shores of Loch Fyne

BATTLE ABBEY SOUTHEAST ENGLAND

William the Conqueror, Duke of Normandy, built Battle Abbey on the site of the Battle of Hastings to commemorate his victory against the Saxon King Harold in 1066. The altar in the abbey church is said to mark the very spot where King Harold fell. Evocative audio tours pitch visitors into the bloody melee of the battlefield and "interviews" with monks, soldiers, and other witnesses bring the day-long conflict to life. In the fall, a battle reenactment takes place on the site.
www.english-heritage/battleabbey

WESTONBIRT ARBORETUM

SOUTHWEST ENGLAND
Heartwarming autumnal color from a collection of more than 18,000 trees and shrubs, in 600 acres (240 hectares) of glorious parkland.
www.forestry.gov.uk

INVERARAY CENTRAL SCOTLAND

Lying on the wooded shores of Loch Fyne, Inveraray is one of Scotland's most attractive towns in autumn, when the richly colored trees create a vivid backdrop to its fine castle. Home of the Dukes of Argyll, the castle was redesigned and the town rebuilt by the second Duke in the 1740s. Heavily influenced by French architecture, yet unmistakably Scottish, Inverary Castle houses magnificent interiors and a fascinating old jail that puts on ghost-hunting events.
www.inveraray-argyll.com

CROFT CASTLE

WEST MIDLANDS
With wonderful views over the Welsh Marches, this castellated late-17th-century house has a remarkable Georgian interior and is set in glorious parkland, which has miles of walking trails.
www.nationaltrust.org.uk

KILCHURN CASTLE

CENTRAL SCOTLAND
Abandoned after being struck by lightening in the 18th century, Kilchurn Castle sits on Loch Awe. It's a magnificent sight in fall, when the hills behind it turn a flaming red.
www.kilchurncastle.com

SNETTISHAM EASTERN ENGLAND

In the fall, thousands of thrushes and finches migrate over this RSPB reserve on the Wash in Norfolk, described as an "avian motorway service station." Waders, noisy wigeon, and Brent geese converge at Snettisham, while pink-footed geese roost on the Wash and fly inland at dawn to feed on sugar beet remnants. Look for the breathtaking spectacle of giant flocks of knot – a species of wading bird – taking off by the hundreds as the tide covers their roost.
www.rspb.org.uk

SELBORNE SOUTHEAST ENGLAND

This pretty village is famous for being the home of Gilbert White, the 18th-century naturalist who wrote the much-loved *The Natural History and Antiquities of Selborne*. His house hosts regular workshops and exhibitions, and is set against the backdrop of a beautiful beech wood, through which White built a steep zigzag path. You can also visit the Oates Museum, which charts Lawrence Oates' part in Scott's expedition to the South Pole in 1910–1913.
www.hampshirescountryside.co.uk

DEVIL'S BRIDGE CENTRAL WALES

Near Aberystwyth are three bridges that span both the River Mynach and 900 years. Unusually, these bridges are built on top of each other: the lowest bridge dates from the 12th century, the middle one from the 18th century, and, on top of that, an iron bridge built in 1901 carries the Vale of Rheidol narrow-gauge railroad. There are walks from the bridge to the 300-ft (90-m) Mynach Falls, the Devil's Punchbowl crater, and steps known as "Jacob's Ladder."
www.tourism.ceredigion.gov.uk

INVEREWE GARDENS HIGHLANDS AND ISLANDS

Inverewe Gardens lie on the same latitude as Canada's Hudson Bay, yet warm currents from the Gulf Stream ensure that the site is mild year-round, enabling temperate plants to grow. The 50-acre (20-hectare) woodland gardens, on a craggy hillside, were created in 1862, and contain 2,500 species of plants. Its walled sections contain many unusual and exotic plants, and elsewhere otters, pine martens, seals, and red deer can be found, along with marvelous views.
www.nts.org.uk

DUNMORE EAST

SOUTHERN IRELAND
Pretty cottages and a bustling harbor characterize this charming fishing village, which hosts the Dunmore East Autumn Leaves Golf Classic competition in September.
www.waterford-dunmore.com

TRAQUAIR HOUSE

SOUTHERN SCOTLAND
Visited by 27 kings and queens over its 900-year history, Scotland's oldest inhabited house exudes atmosphere. After a tour, sample Traquair House ales.
www.traquair.co.uk

BOG OF ALLEN

EASTERN IRELAND
A massive peat bog covering 370 sq miles (960 sq km) in the Irish Midlands, the Bog of Allen is rich in history, ecology, and walking routes, and there is also a nature center to visit.
www.forestry.gov.uk

KIELDER FOREST

NORTHEAST ENGLAND
Among the many events that take place in Britain's largest forest is the fall forest foray. Some interesting wildlife can also be found here, such as red squirrels and bats.
www.forestry.gov.uk

KENMARE SOUTHERN IRELAND

An upscale town boasting charming streets, gourmet restaurants, friendly pubs, and a huge sweep of sandy bay. Kenmare is a great place to stay, especially out of season, when the roads are less crowded. Take the 105-mile (170-km) circular tourist trail, known as the "Ring of Kerry," which has breathtaking views of Macgillycuddy's Reeks mountain range, a glaciated valley, and fantastic beaches. For a brush with history, search out the stone circle known as "The Shrubberries."
www.ringofkerrytourism.com

See also pp134–5, 152–3.

See also pp116–17, 126–7, 140–41, 146–7.

See also pp124–5, 130–31, 138–9, 144–5.

One of the statues of *Another Place*, on Crosby Beach

Tintagel Castle in Cornwall

Gothic fan enjoying the Goth Weekend in Whitby

ANOTHER PLACE NORTHWEST ENGLAND
The artist Antony Gormley put Crosby on the map when his installation *Another Place* was moved to the beach there. One hundred cast-iron, life-size statues, made from casts of the artist's own body, are set along 2 miles (3 km) of beach and ½ mile (1 km) out to sea. Previously exhibited abroad, the figures are now permanently placed at Crosby. A brisk beach walk offers a close encounter with the figures, which are best viewed at low tide.
www.visitsouthport.com

HOT-AIR BALLOON FESTIVAL NORTH WALES
Visit Llangollen in late summer and you'll see mass hot-air balloon launches and a night event, when the balloons are illuminated like giant light bulbs in the night sky.
www.hotairballoonfestival.co.uk

GOTH WEEKEND IN WHITBY NORTHEAST ENGLAND
Whitby has literary associations with Dracula – in the novel, it is where the vampire arrives in England – and so it is the perfect spot for a celebration of all things Gothic. The event takes place during the week of Halloween, with the main events on October 31, and attracts people of all ages. Most of the events take place at the 1,000-capacity Whitby Pavilion, and include a strange bazaar, music, and comedy acts, a charity soccer match, and many fringe events.
wgw.topmum.co.uk

SELF-GUIDED CYCLING TOURS
NORTHERN IRELAND
Cycling tours are offered around Ulster and Connaught until the end of October, in sparsely populated areas with frequently clear roads.
www.emeraldtrail.com

TINTAGEL CASTLE SOUTHWEST ENGLAND
Steep steps lead walkers to the romantic ruins of Tintagel Castle, set in a spectacular wave-lashed location on the cliffs of north Cornwall. Visitors have never let facts get in the way and they flock to this magical site eager to believe that it was, as legend has it, the birthplace of King Arthur. Splendid views can be enjoyed from the headland. Scramble down the rocks to Merlin's Cave, which lies just below Tintagel and leads on to a sandy cove.
www.tintagelcastle.co.uk

OYSTER AND WELSH FOOD FESTIVAL
NORTH WALES
A celebration of Anglesey's high-quality food and drink, this is a weekend for tantalizing the taste buds. Held at the Trearddur Bay Hotel in October, thousands come to this friendly fair, where celebrity chefs give demonstrations and food and drink producers ply their wares. There are also crafts, a "sausage competition," and live music. Delicious foodstuffs include oyster fritters, crab cakes, and laver bread.
www.angleseyoysterfestival.com

RAFT-BUILDING
CENTRAL WALES
Raft-building at Glasbury guarantees fun and a thorough soaking. Barrels, ropes, and planks are used to make rafts that are strong enough to race on the River Wye.
www.blackmountain.co.uk

SEVINGTON LAKES
SOUTHWEST ENGLAND
These spring-fed lakes have pitches for coarse fishing and offer day-long sessions and night fishing by arrangement. Fish stocks include carp, rudd, perch, tench, and roach.
www.go-fish.co.uk

HALLOWEEN AT WOOKEY HOLE
SOUTHWEST ENGLAND
For 50,000 years, the caves at Wookey Hole, set deep in the Mendip Hills, have been home to humans or animals. Evidence of this comes from archaeological artifacts, including flint tools and the bones of ice-age animals such as mammoths. Today the cavernous chambers are a major tourist attraction with a resident real-life "witch" and a circus, and at Halloween there are special spooky events.
www.wookey.co.uk

BARNSTAPLE OLD FAIR SOUTHWEST ENGLAND
Barnstaple's world-famous fair is thought to date from 930. Throughout the centuries its traditions have been honored, starting with toasts of spiced ale and a gloved hand being displayed from a window of the Guildhall to signify the hand of friendship to all comers. The fair continues with a grand procession and the reading of the proclamation. It's only then that the thousands who attend the four-day event can really let their hair down and enjoy the fairground rides.
www.barnstaple-history.co.uk

NORDIC WALKING SOUTHERN SCOTLAND
Nordic walking, also called "ski walking," involves the use of poles to increase the use of the upper body, turning walking into a full-body workout. Originating in Finland in the 1930s, it was designed to help competitive cross-country skiers stay in shape in the off-season, but it became a popular recreational activity during the 1980s, and is now a mainstream activity in Scotland's many hiking regions. The gentle landscapes of Dumfries and Galloway are perfect beginner country.
www.cndoscotland.com

STONE SKIMMING AT EASDALE ISLAND
CENTRAL SCOTLAND
Easdale is a 5-minute ferry ride from the adjacent island, Seil, off the west coast of Argyll. A car-free island without roads, it was once an important slate-mining community, as evidenced by the abandoned, water-filled quarries. Easdale is famous today as the location of the one-day World Stone Skimming Championships, which take place on a quarry here in September. Just turn up to register and take part.
www.stoneskimming.com

INVERNESS
CENTRAL SCOTLAND
Fireworks illuminate the skies above Inverness on Guy Fawkes Night. There's also a torch-light procession, huge bonfire, and funfair, all located in Bught Park.
www.scotland-inverness.co.uk

WASDALE HEAD SHOW
NORTHWEST ENGLAND
This October country show features country delights such as fell races, wrestling, vintage cars, and dog trials in a beautiful Lake District setting.
www.wasdaleweb.co.uk

See also pp118–19, 132–3, 142–3, 150–51, 154–5.

See also pp120–21, 122–3, 148–9.

See also pp128–9, 136–7.

Snow-covered
farmland in
Wiltshire,
England

WINTER IN GREAT BRITAIN AND IRELAND

WHEN DOES WINTER TRULY BEGIN? Some believe that it's marked by the end of British Summer Time in October, when the clocks are set back by an hour (ensuring that Britain and Ireland remain perpetually an hour out of step with countries in mainland Europe). But this would deny fall its rightful place, and ignores the seasonal change that occurs in the weather come December, when the days are at their shortest. Purists argue that the season's true beginning is the winter solstice, on December 22, the shortest day of the year and the date of a pagan festival traditionally celebrated at Stonehenge. It's certainly true that over most of Britain and Ireland, real winter conditions of snow and ice rarely take hold until after Christmas or the New Year. A "white Christmas" – even in northern Scotland – is an increasingly rare event. There has been widespread snow on Christmas Day only once since 1990, and bookmakers will happily take your money if you wish to bet that one snowflake will fall on the Meteorological Office on Christmas Day. But it wasn't always so. During the 17th and 18th centuries, the stretch of the River Thames that runs through London sometimes froze over completely, and "frost fairs" – complete with makeshift taverns, food stands, river skating, and other entertainment – took place on the ice. Most famously, the river froze solid for two whole months in the winter of 1683–84, and even King Charles II and his courtiers joined in the cavorting. Today's pre-Christmas Bankside Winter Festival in London has revived the tradition, with dog-sledding, market stands, and street theater.

Christmas markets offer unusual gifts and delicacies from all over the world.

Some of Britain's winter traditions are truly ancient. We still deck homes, churches, and public places with boughs of mistletoe and holly, one of the last relics of pagan tradition from the pre-Christian, Celtic winter solstice festival of December 25, which became the Christian festival of Christmas. Many other aspects of the "traditional" British Christmas are much more recent embellishments. The Christmas tree, with its lights and decorations, is a German tradition, unheard of in Britain until it was popularized by Queen Victoria's German consort, Prince Albert. The Christmas turkey is another innovation: until well into the 20th century, the traditional Christmas roast was a goose or ham.

Christmas markets are a tradition that temporarily disappeared under Oliver Cromwell's puritanical reign. They resurfaced in Victorian times, and today many cities, notably Dublin, Edinburgh, London, and Birmingham, host

Below (left to right): Christmas at Winchester Cathedral; Hogmanay fireworks, Edinburgh

colorful seasonal markets offering unusual gifts and delicacies from all over the world. The "switching on" of Christmas illuminations by local dignitaries is every town's official signal that the festive season has truly begun. Great excitement accompanies the illumination of the mighty fir tree in London's Trafalgar Square, which is donated each year by the people of Norway in remembrance of British support during World War II. But despite the older pagan and newer commercial traditions, Christmas Eve and Christmas itself remain the greatest of Christian festivals, celebrated with carol singing and candlelit midnight services at the great cathedrals, such as Canterbury, York, and Winchester, and in the tiniest of village churches. For children, Christmas Day is a private riot of unpacking stockings, ripping open presents, and eating too much.

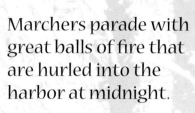

Marchers parade with great balls of fire that are hurled into the harbor at midnight.

If Christmas Day is the biggest family occasion of the year, New Year's Eve is the public party. Traditionally celebrated most gloriously in Scotland, Hogmanay has grown from an informal, one-night affair into a four-day festival that draws hundreds of thousands of visitors to Edinburgh to see out the old year. In Stonehaven, on the east coast of Scotland, marchers parade with great balls of fire that are hurled into the harbor at the stroke of midnight, while in smaller Scottish towns Hogmanay is a community party at which everyone is welcome – especially, according to tradition, a "tall, dark and handsome stranger." In London, revelers congregate in Trafalgar Square to hear the chimes of Big Ben and St. Martin-in-the-Fields herald the New Year, while in Wales, Cardiff's Calennig (New Year) celebrations include a funfair and fire show in the Civic Centre.

Once the partying is over, winter begins to tighten its grip. In the far north, with only six hours of daylight in midwinter, dark skies may be lit by the flickering glow of the "dancers" – the poetic, old-fashioned name for the Northern Lights, or aurora borealis. With luck, skiers can enjoy deep snow on the Scottish runs of Aviemore and Glen Shee, and – on rare occasions – even Londoners can go tobogganing on the slopes of city parks, such as Primrose Hill and Hampstead Heath. Ironically, our heaviest snowfall often comes just after St. Valentine's Day (February 14), the day that is held to signal the coming of spring, when songbirds choose their mates and human lovers become dewy-eyed and romantic. Everyone's hearts are thawing; winter is nearly over.

Below (left to right): Dawn on winter solstice at Stonehenge; aurora borealis rays arc over trees in Arran; skiers on the slopes of Glencoe

The Festive Season

Above: Artwork showing a traditional Christmas scene **Right:** Pantomime poster for *Jack and the Beanstalk* (1899)

Winter in Britain and Ireland ushers in a season of festivities ancient and modern. Some, such as the winter solstice fire festivals that take place in many parts, have roots that extend deep into our history, pre-dating the advent of Christianity. In the West Country, "wassailing", a pagan luck-bringing ritual, can still be witnessed on Twelfth Night, and in Ireland, troupes of "mummers" continue a medieval tradition, taking chaotic performances to the winter streets. Other seasonal highlights are celebrated with the lighting of candles – these include Hanukkah, the Jewish Festival of Lights, and Advent Sunday, the fourth Sunday before Christmas, which marks the beginning of the festive season.

But it is Christmas, with all its traditions and trappings, that truly dominates this time of year. While Christmas Day is, by and large, a family affair, the festive season builds for weeks before with the customary Christmas treats of carol concerts and nativity plays, pantomimes and office parties. In most parts of Britain and Ireland, New Year's Eve is the crescendo of the party season, and is marked with a night of revelry. This is followed, by some, with the decidedly more Puritan New Year's Day swim – an icy dip in the sea. In several cities, including London and Manchester, it is the colorful celebration of Chinese New Year at the end of January or in mid-February that brings the festive season to a close.

CHINESE NEW YEAR, LONDON

NORWEGIAN CHRISTMAS TREE IN TRAFALGAR SQUARE, LONDON

BRIGHTON WINTER SOLSTICE

Edinburgh's Hogmanay, Southern Scotland This is the biggest New Year's Eve celebration in the UK, with music, dancing, and fireworks as the clock strikes midnight. *www.edinburghshogmanay.org*

Burns Night Celebrated in Scotland and further afield as close to the great poet's birthday (January 25) as possible, the event kicks off with pipe music, the Selkirk Grace, and the address to the haggis.

Mumming, Northern Ireland Troupes of costumed players, or "mummers", perform ancient, rhyming, yuletide folk dramas in village halls or on house-to-house visits.

Twelve Days of Christmas Market, Eastern Ireland In the run-up to Christmas, St. George's Dock on Dublin's waterfront is lined with carnival rides and stalls selling stocking-fillers, hot drinks, and tasty snacks. *www.dublindocklands.ie/12daysofchristmas*

"Scroggling the Holly", Northeast England Children in Victorian costume, brass bands, and morris dancers welcome Father Christmas in Haworth, Yorkshire, over a weekend in mid-November.

King's College Cambridge, Eastern England A solemn Christmas Eve service, A Festival in Nine Lessons and Carols features readings from undergraduates and commissioned carols *(see pp196–7)*.

Advent Carol Service and Procession at St. Paul's Cathedral, London St. Paul's Cathedral choir ushers in the festive season every year on Advent Sunday, with an atmospheric candlelit procession as well as traditional and contemporary carols.

Chinese New Year, London Vivid red lanterns, lion dancers, and fireworks are highlights of Chinese New Year in London's Chinatown. *www.chinatownchinese.co.uk*

Norwegian Christmas Tree Ceremony, London The lights on this enormous tree in Trafalgar Square, an annual gift from the people of Norway to Londoners, are turned on in a ceremony close to Advent Sunday.

Harrods Winter Sale, London Bargain-hunters flock to this world-famous Knightsbridge store for its post-Christmas shopping frenzy, opened by A-list celebrities in a glitzy ceremony. *www.harrods.com*

Sung Eucharist at Canterbury Cathedral, Southeast England The Eucharist sung by the cathedral choir is the moving climax of a Christmas Day morning of worship at England's greatest cathedral.

Brighton Winter Solstice Fire Festival, Southeast England An evening parade through the city streets with homemade lanterns on December 21 ends on the beach with a spectacular firework display.

Whimple Wassailing, Southwest England Locals parade through this Devon village on "Old Twelvy Night" (January 17) in an age-old ritual thought to bring about a good apple harvest. *www.whimple.org*

New Year's Day Swim All over Britain and Ireland, from Achill on Ireland's west coast to Brighton in Sussex, hardy bathers plunge into chilly seas in a New Year's Day ritual, reputed to be the best cure for a hangover.

Hanukkah Jewish families all over Britain light the menorah for eight days and feast on *latkes* (potato pancakes) and doughnuts; the festival starts on the 25th day of Kislev in the Hebrew calendar, which falls any time from late November to late December.

Pantomime Season Plump men in drag, girls dressed as boys, and broad innuendos are the hallmarks of the great British panto. Performances take place nationwide.

PANTOMIME

YORK MINSTER

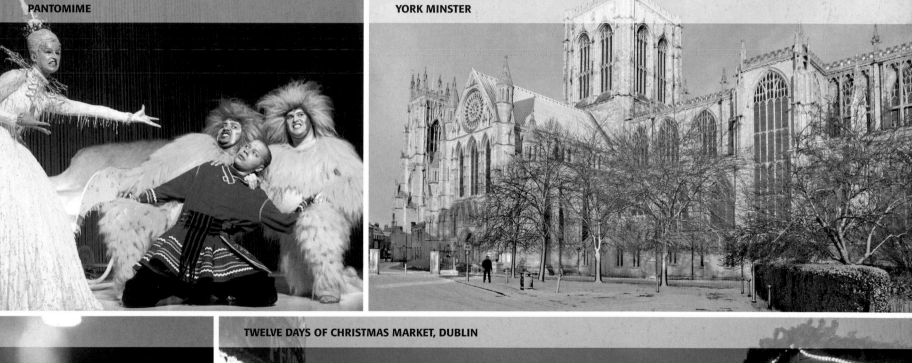

TWELVE DAYS OF CHRISTMAS MARKET, DUBLIN

THE ESSENTIALS

GETTING THERE AND AROUND
The Giant's Causeway is just over 2 miles (3 km) north of the town of Bushmills, and about 50 miles (80 km) north of Belfast International Airport. When visiting in winter you will need to have a car or take a taxi to visit the Causeway.

WEATHER
In Northern Ireland in winter you can expect average daytime temperatures of 34–45°F (1–7°C), with the biting sea breeze adding an extra wind chill. You should also be prepared for some rainfall.

ACCOMMODATIONS
Treat Yourself The Bushmills Inn is a one-time coaching inn with oak beams, oil lamps, and other characterful touches, as well as a fine restaurant.
www.bushmillsinn.com

On a Budget The Causeway Hotel has spacious rooms right by the Causeway and has been here since 1836.
www.giants-causeway-hotel.com

EATING OUT
Treat Yourself The Bushmills Inn, in the village of Bushmills, uses local produce and offers good seafood and Bushmills whiskey in its award-winning restaurant.
www.bushmillsinn.com

On a Budget The Harbour Bistro, on the waterfront in Portrush, has plenty of well-priced options including home-made burgers, salads, and pasta dishes.
www.ramorerestaurant.com

PRICE FOR A FAMILY OF FOUR
$300–330 a day for accommodations, food, and parking at the Causeway.

WEBSITE
www.northernantrim.com/
giantscauseway.htm

A Big Baby

According to Irish legend, Finn McCool was a giant who lived on the Antrim coast. After trading insults with the Scottish giant Benandonner, he built the Giant's Causeway so that his rival could cross the water for a test of strength. Finn had become so exhausted, however, that he was no match for his opponent. Finn's wife quickly wrapped him in a blanket and bonnet. When Benandonner saw the size of the "baby," he fled back to Scotland in terror, wondering how big the father must be!

Main: Giant's Causeway, dramatically situated on the coast of County Antrim
Right (top to bottom): Interlocking geometric shapes of the basalt columns; Organ rock formation

WALKING WITH GIANTS

There are few prettier or more dramatic drives in the British Isles than the narrow road that hugs the Antrim coast between the mountains and the sea. It leads to Northern Ireland's most visited attraction, the phenomenal Giant's Causeway. Here an army of narrow basalt columns – around 40,000 of them – gathers en masse at the shoreline and marches haphazardly out to sea. As the sea and winter mists swirl around their disappearing forms, it's almost possible to imagine the giants of Irish legend – allegedly the builders of the Causeway (see story box) – hurling insults at each other across the waves.

In fact, the Causeway is the work of geology, not giants. Around 60 million years ago, the explosion of an undersea volcano spewed molten lava into a depression along the shore. As it cooled, the shrinking and cracking produced tens of thousands of hexagonal columns of varying heights. The columns form stepping stones into the sea, and if you could follow them beneath the waves they would stretch along an underwater fissure, emerging in Scotland at the Isle of Staffa. In 1986 this geological marvel was named a UNESCO World Heritage Site.

FURTHER DETAILS

GIANT'S CAUSEWAY VISITOR CENTRE
Bushmills, County Antrim, Northern Ireland; open
Oct–Mar: 10am–5pm daily; Apr–Sep: 10am–7pm
daily; closed Dec 25–26.
www.giantscauseway.com

WHAT ELSE TO SEE AND DO
Old Bushmills Distillery
Located in Bushmills, this is the oldest legal distillery in
the world, dating its official production of whiskey back
to 1608, though alcohol was produced here for several
centuries before that. Children from 8 to 17 are welcome
on the tours, although younger children are excluded for
safety reasons.
www.bushmills.com

Dunluce Castle
Built in the 15th and 16th centuries, Dunluce is the most
impressive monument along the North Antrim coast, a
few miles west of Bushmills. It sits on a basalt outcrop,
the same stone that created the Giant's Causeway, and
is connected to the mainland by a bridge. Don't miss
the cave below the castle either, but be very careful if
scrambling down with children.
www.ehsni.gov.uk

Portrush
This seaside town on the North Antrim coast is famed
for its sandy beaches, and has many hotels, bars,
and restaurants. The town is also home to the Royal
Portrush Golf Club – the only club in Ireland to have
hosted the British Open Championship.
www.portrush.org.uk

Below (top to bottom): Bushmills distillery and reservoir;
13th-century ruins of Dunluce Castle, perched on an outcrop
of the rocky Antrim coast

> It's almost possible to imagine the giants of Irish legend –
> allegedly the builders of the Causeway – hurling insults
> at each other across the waves.

Down on the shoreline, the columns seem smaller than you might expect – the tallest are
around 40 ft (12 m) high – but it's the sheer mass of them that is so impressive. As you stand
atop them in the winter wind, watching the relentless pounding of the waves, you can
appreciate the ferocity of the storms that eroded them over the centuries. The lack of crowds
in this quieter season makes their lonely beauty more intense.

The Causeway is backed by dramatic cliffs rising to 330 ft (100 m). A variety of sea birds
make their home here. From the visitor center you can walk along a clifftop path leading to
other unusual rock formations, such as the Giant's Chimney. The Shepherd's Steps will take
you back down to the Causeway via 162 stone steps, making a circuit of about 2 miles (3 km).
Alternatively, continue on past the Organ, its long columns hugging the cliff face like cathedral
organ pipes, to the Port Reostan viewpoint. Here you can look back across a spectacular vista
of the Giant's Causeway, one of the most remarkable coastlines in the world.

A MEGALITHIC MARVEL

IT IS BRITAIN'S MOST IMPORTANT and well-known ancient monument – and its most mysterious. Rising out of Salisbury Plain, the megalithic circle of Stonehenge is an awesome and magical sight. Yet no one knows for sure who built it, and why. For centuries people have tried to unlock its secrets, theorizing that it was used as a religious temple, a royal palace, a Neolithic place of healing or a giant astronomical calendar – it is perfectly aligned with the points of sunrise and sunset on the winter and summer solstices.

Constructed in stages from around 3000 to 1500 BC, Stonehenge consists of colossal stones set in concentric circles, some linked by horizontal lintels, and all set within a larger earthwork of ditches and banks. The huge sandstones that form part of the original outer circle are local stones that stand over 21 ft (6 m) tall. But the smaller bluestones that formed the inner circle were transported here from Preseli in Wales, 150 miles (240 km) away.

THE ESSENTIALS

GETTING THERE AND AROUND
Stonehenge is on Salisbury Plain in Wiltshire, in southern England, about 7 miles (11 km) north of Salisbury itself. Salisbury is about 70 miles (110 km) southwest of London's Heathrow Airport. The Stonehenge Tour Bus departs from Salisbury, and it's even possible to walk the 2 miles (3 km) from Amesbury, but access is a lot easier with your own car. The site is located where the A303 and the A344 converge, just west of Amesbury.

WEATHER
Winter on Salisbury Plain can be bitter when cold winds are blowing, but there can also be crisp days when the stones look at their best. Average daytime temperatures are 34 to 43°F (1–6°C).

ACCOMMODATIONS
Treat Yourself Howard's House Country Hotel, in Teffont Evias, is 10 miles (16 km) from Stonehenge, and has luxurious accommodations and an exceptional restaurant.
www.howardshousehotel.co.uk

On a Budget The Victoria Lodge Guest House, in Salisbury, offers simple but fine accommodations.
www.victoria-guest-house.co.uk

EATING OUT
Treat Yourself The Ship Inn, in Burcombe, is a splendid "gastropub" dating from the 17th century.
www.theshipburcombe.co.uk

On a Budget Charter 1227, in Salisbury, offers good, wholesome British food at inexpensive prices.
Tel: 01722 333118

PRICE FOR TWO PEOPLE
Around $290 a day for food, accommodations, and admission fees.

WEBSITE
www.visitwiltshire.co.uk

Romancing the Stones

It is not well-known that visitors can gain access to the stones at Stonehenge, and spend up to an hour in the middle of the stone circle. Visits must be arranged in advance with English Heritage and are made before or after normal visiting hours. Naturally, these visits book up a long way ahead, and you will have to choose a specific date. A guide accompanies you into the circle, but will then leave you space and time to enjoy the unique experience in near solitude.

> Over the centuries, many myths and belief systems, from Arthurian tales to druidic traditions, have drawn inspiration from this enigmatic site.

Over the centuries, many myths and belief systems, from Arthurian tales to druidic traditions, have drawn inspiration from this enigmatic site. In 2008, after six years of excavations, archaeologists put forward the exciting new theory that Stonehenge was a monument to the dead. Evidence from cremation burials at the site and further dating of stone fragments revealed that the bluestones were the first to be erected, in 3000 BC, and that hundreds of people were buried here over the next 500 years. What's more, Stonehenge stands in a wider landscape of even older burial mounds, processional avenues and timber circles, indicating that rituals of life and death were celebrated here much earlier.

Today, more than one million people visit this UNESCO World Heritage Site each year. The circle itself is cordoned off – you can walk all around Stonehenge but not within it unless you join an organized tour or arrange a private visit *(see story box)*. It is, however, opened for a few hours at dawn on the solstices and equinoxes that mark the seasons. It is well worth making the effort to be there for dawn on the winter solstice (December 21 or 22). There are few sights more extraordinary than watching the sun rise above the frosted ground and over the mighty stones.

Main: Aerial view of Stonehenge in winter **Inset:** Circle at sunrise
Below: Interior of the megalithic circle

FURTHER DETAILS

STONEHENGE
Open daily except Dec 24 and 25. Opening hours vary and access may be reduced in bad weather. For all opening times, access times on the summer and winter solstices and spring and fall equinoxes, and details of small-group private visits, contact English Heritage. *www.english-heritage.org.uk*

WHAT ELSE TO SEE AND DO
Avebury
Only 25 miles (40 km) north of Stonehenge, one of the largest prehistoric earthworks in Europe lies near the village of Avebury. Slightly older than Stonehenge, its magnificent stone circle has been reerected and you can walk freely among the stones. *www.nationaltrust.org.uk*

Silbury Hill
This green hill, 5 miles (8 km) west of Marlborough in Wiltshire, is the largest human-made prehistoric mound in Europe. You can only view the hill from a distance – there is no access – but you can follow a footpath to the nearby West Kennet Long Barrow, a prehistoric chamber tomb. *www.english-heritage.org.uk*

Salisbury Cathedral
The finest 13th-century Gothic cathedral in Britain, Salisbury Cathedral is topped by a 404-ft (123-m) spire, the tallest in the country. Among its many highlights are Britain's largest cathedral cloisters and the chapter house, which contains an original copy of *Magna Carta*, one of only four still in existence. *www.salisburycathedral.org.uk*

Old Sarum
On the edge of Salisbury, the remains of this Iron Age fort and Norman settlement include prehistoric earthworks and the scant ruins of a Norman castle, royal palace, and cathedral. *www.english-heritage.org.uk*

Below (top to bottom): Neolithic monument of Silbury Hill; standing stones outside Avebury at dusk

THE ESSENTIALS

GETTING THERE AND AROUND
The Shetland Islands are 100 miles
(160 km) from the north coast of
Scotland. There are flights from Edinburgh,
Glasgow, Inverness, and Aberdeen to
Sumburgh Airport, 25 miles (40 km) from
Lerwick. Buses, taxis, and car rentals are
available at the airport. There are ferries
to Lerwick from Aberdeen and Kirkwall.
Flights (*www.directflight.co.uk*) connect
the island of Mainland with outlying
islands including Fair Isle, Foula, and Papa
Stour. Car ferries operate from Lerwick and
connect Mainland with outlying islands.

WEATHER
Winter daytime temperatures in Shetland
are between 38 and 41°F (3–5°C), and
strong winds and sleet or rain are likely in
winter. Shetland has less than 6 hours of
light a day in January.

ACCOMMODATIONS
Treat Yourself Brentham House, in
Lerwick, is a small but cozy and stylish
town-house hotel.
www.brenthamhouse.co.uk

On a Budget Glen Orchy House, in
Lerwick, is a comfortable guesthouse with
modern facilities in a central location.
www.guesthouselerwick.com

EATING OUT
Treat Yourself Hay's Dock Café
Restaurant, in Lerwick, is an attractive
modern waterside restaurant.
www.haysdock.co.uk

On a Budget Osla's Cafe, also in Lerwick,
is a pretty restaurant with a tasty and
inexpensive Italian-influenced menu.
www.oslas.co.uk

PRICE FOR TWO PEOPLE
Around $160 a day for
accommodations and food.

WEBSITE
www.visitshetland.com

Torchlit Tradition?

It may be a romantic spectacle, but the Up Helly Aa
fire festival is very far from being an age-old Viking
tradition. The name was invented by a group of
young Shetlanders in 1870, when the costumed
torchlight procession was added to less formal
festivities and bonfire parties that began earlier in
the 19th century. The "galley" first appeared in the
late 1880s, and the Guizer Jarl, who takes on the
character of a figure from Norse legend, has
presided over the event only since 1906.

Main: Northern Lights illuminating the sky over the Shetland Islands
Right (top to bottom): Gannet colony on a cliff edge; Scalloway harbour on the island of Mainland

FIRE AND LIGHT

SHETLANDERS CALL THEM THE "MERRY DANCERS" – wavering curtains of pale green and
white light that shimmer over the northern horizon on up to 100 nights a year, like a scene
from a science fiction movie. During the long days of a Shetland summer, when the sky never
gets truly dark, the Northern Lights – or aurora borealis – are unremarkable, but during the
long winter nights they can be truly spectacular, and on these distant islands there is little
urban light pollution to interfere with one of the most magical phenomena in the night sky.

Shetland is a land apart: not just one island, but an archipelago of more than 100 far-flung,
low-lying, and surprisingly verdant isles and skerries (rocky reefs) where sheep graze, otters
prowl for crabs in the rockpools, gannets soar over the clifftops, and seals bask at low tide.

Far from Scotland's shores, Shetland is home to the proud descendants of Viking
seafarers, and some Shetlanders have argued that, should Scotland ever achieve independence,
the islands might be better off opting to become part of Norway. It's true that the capital,
Lerwick, is closer to the Norwegian city of Bergen than to Edinburgh. Shetland's Viking

FURTHER DETAILS

SHETLAND
Lerwick Tourism Information Centre
Market Cross, Lerwick; open 9am–5pm Mon–Sat.
www.visitshetland.com

Up Helly Aa
Lerwick celebrates a huge fire festival throughout the town
on the last Tuesday of January.
www.uphellyaa.org

Sumburgh Airport Tourism Information Centre
Wilsness Terminal, Sumburgh; open 8am–5pm daily.
www.visitshetland.com

Shetland Museum and Archives
Hay's Dock, Lerwick. An outstanding new waterfront
museum and galleries in Lerwick house exhibits spanning
Shetland's history; open 10am–5:30pm Mon–Fri,
10am–5pm Sat, noon–5pm Sun.
www.shetland-museum.org.uk

Below (top to bottom): Rugged coastline of the Shetland Islands; torchlit procession during Lerwick's Up Helly Aa fire festival

heritage can be heard in the dialect spoken by islanders, which includes many Norse words, and seen in historic buildings dating back to the 9th century and the first Norse settlers.

Perhaps the most potent symbol of the islands' Scandinavian ancestry is an annual event that takes place on the last Tuesday in January. On this night, the streets of Lerwick are lit by the flames of torches brandished by bearded islanders, known as *guizers*, in the fearsome garb of their Viking forebears. This is Up Helly Aa, perhaps the largest fire festival in Europe, and the climax of a year of planning and preparation that involves almost everyone in Lerwick.

At the head of a procession of almost 1,000 torch-bearers, the leader, known as Guizer Jarl, stands at the prow of his Viking longship – the "galley." The ship is dragged through Lerwick, and finally meets a fiery end as hundreds of torches are hurled into its wooden hull to create a mighty bonfire. Only after the ship is well ablaze do the festivities really start. Revelers are welcomed into homes and halls throughout Lerwick, and a night of fiddle music, dancing, and drinking gathers pace, with the last stragglers struggling home just in time for breakfast. For obvious reasons, the following day is traditionally a holiday in Lerwick, but there are further, slightly more subdued festivities, known as the "Guizers' Hop," that night. Come to Shetland for the eerie majesty of the Northern Lights, but stay for the wonderful festivities.

THE ESSENTIALS

GETTING THERE AND AROUND
Glendalough is in eastern Ireland, 50 miles (80 km) south of Dublin. It is situated in Wicklow Mountains National Park, about 3 miles (5 km) west of the village of Laragh. It's about an hour's drive south from Dublin, but St. Kevin's Bus Service (www.glendaloughbus.com) runs daily to Glendalough from Dublin via Bray.

WEATHER
In winter, the average daytime temperature at Glendalough is 39–48°F (3–8°C), with sub-freezing temperatures early in the morning. Be prepared for rain and showers of light snow.

ACCOMMODATIONS
Treat Yourself Lynham's Hotel, in the nearby village of Laragh, offers modern rooms with beautiful river views and has a bar and restaurant.
www.lynhamsoflaragh.ie

On a Budget Glendalough River House, just outside Laragh, is a 200-year-old stone mill house offering comfortable B&B accommodations.
www.glendaloughriverhouse.ie

EATING OUT
Treat Yourself The Wicklow Heather, in Laragh, serves traditional Irish and continental cuisine using organic produce.
www.thewicklowheather.com

On a Budget Jake's Bar, in Lynham's Hotel, Laragh, serves good pub meals and family fare in the hotel restaurant.
www.lynhamsoflaragh.ie

PRICE FOR TWO PEOPLE
Around $225 a day for food, accommodations, and admission to the Visitor Centre.

WEBSITE
www.glendalough.connect.ie

Legends of St. Kevin

Kevin, the heir to one of the province of Leinster's ruling families, came to this remote spot seeking the life of a hermit. But his fame and followers grew, and Glendalough became known throughout Europe as a great center of learning. There are many legends about this gentle, reclusive soul. It is said that one day while Kevin was praying, a blackbird built a nest in his outstretched hands. He did not move until all of the birds hatched and flew away. Kevin died in 618 at the ripe old age of 120.

MONASTIC TRANQUILITY

IN A LAND SPRINKLED WITH MYSTERIOUS ROUND TOWERS and elaborate Celtic high crosses, Glendalough stands out as Ireland's finest early Christian monastic site. This "valley of the two lakes" has a timeless beauty, its sturdy stone ruins nestled at the base of two loughs that wind below forested folds in the Wicklow Mountains.

It's easy to love Glendalough in summer, when sunlight turns the loughs a sparkling blue, inviting pleasant strolls along their leafy shores. But in winter, when the crowds are gone and snow dusts the surrounding peaks, the dark towers of slate and granite rise starkly out of the valley into the crisp air and you can feel the mystical, magical pull of this tranquil place that attracted St. Kevin so many centuries ago.

Kevin established a monastery here in 570, and its ruins, though of a later date (8th–12th centuries), are evocative and well preserved. From a distance you can spot the monastery complex's slender round tower, perfectly intact and rising 98 ft (30 m) from the ground. This style of tower, which served not only as a belfry but also as treasury and watchtower, is rare outside Ireland. With its entrance about 13 ft (4 m) above the ground and accessible only by ladder, the tower was also a

Main: Frosty morning at Glendalough, with the round tower of the monastery visible beyond

In winter, when the crowds are gone and snow dusts the surrounding peaks, the dark towers of slate and granite rise starkly out of the valley into the crisp air and you can feel the mystical, magical pull of this tranquil place.

place of safety from invaders. The main entrance to the monastery complex is a double arched stone gateway. The largest building in the group is the 9th-century cathedral, now roofless but nonetheless impressive. In the surrounding cemetery, still used by local villagers, stands St. Kevin's Cross, with Celtic decorations; carvings on the nearby Priests' House suggest that it once held Kevin's shrine. St. Kevin's Church, an oratory or private chapel, is sometimes called St. Kevin's Kitchen because of its chimney-like tower. Across a footbridge, a path along the Lower Lough leads to more sites on the Upper Lough: tiny Reefert Church, the ruined beehive hut called St. Kevin's Cell, and, higher up in the cliffs, a hermit's cave known as St. Kevin's Bed.

Though Glendalough was raided by Vikings, Normans, and the English, it remained a place of pilgrimage until the mid-19th century. Before exploring the ruins, first take a moment to stop at the Visitor Centre, with its excellent film and exhibits, to discover why the historical site of Glendalough is as important as it is beautiful.

FURTHER DETAILS

GLENDALOUGH
Glendalough Visitor Centre
Glendalough, Bray, County Wicklow; open mid-Oct–mid-Mar: 9:30am–5pm daily; mid-Mar–mid-Oct: 9:30am–6pm daily.
www.heritageireland.ie

WHAT ELSE TO SEE AND DO
Wicklow Mountains National Park
Glendalough lies within this beautiful landscape of mountains, bogs, waterfalls, and woodlands. Open year-round, the park is a popular area for walking, with nine marked trails around the Glendalough valley, including the long-distance Wicklow Way. Winter weather needn't prevent a hike on the shorter trails as long as you are prepared for conditions with suitable clothing and footwear; indeed, the surrounding mountains are stunning when capped with snow. The Glendalough Visitor Centre (above) serves as an information point for the park in winter. Walking trails are described on the park website.
www.wicklowmountainsnationalpark.ie

Avoca Handweavers
Ireland is famous for its fine woven goods, and winter is the perfect time to buy a cozy sweater or wrap up in a soft scarf. Avoca Handweavers are known for their creative take on traditional designs. They are based in Avoca village at Ireland's oldest working mill, which dates from 1723. On weekdays, you can watch the weavers at work on a guided tour. It's a beautiful drive from Glendalough via Rathdrum through the Vale of Avoca to get there.
www.avoca.ie

Wicklow Town
On the coast east of Glendalough, Wicklow's county town overlooks a broad bay. Stroll along its harbor and pebble beach, backed by the Broad Lough wildfowl lagoon and the ruins of the Black Castle. In the town, visit Wicklow's Historic Gaol (jail).
Wicklow County: *www.visitwicklow.ie*
Wicklow's Historic Gaol: *www.wicklowhistoricalgaol.com*

Below (top to bottom): Oratory, or "St. Kevin's Kitchen"; graveyard at Glendalough

THE ESSENTIALS

GETTING THERE AND AROUND
The Isle of Man lies in the Irish Sea, between England, Scotland, and Northern Ireland. There are flights from all major British and Irish cities to Ronaldsway Airport, 10 miles (16 km) from the island's capital, Douglas. Ferries connect Douglas with Liverpool and Dublin. Buses link all towns on the island, operating from four main depots in Douglas, Peel, Ramsey, and Port Erin. Several car rental companies operate from Ronaldsway Airport.

WEATHER
The winter months are the wettest of the year, and strong winds are possible, with daytime temperatures of 32 to 50°F (0–10°C).

ACCOMMODATIONS
Treat Yourself The Hilton Isle of Man Hotel, in Douglas, has two restaurants, five bars, an indoor pool, and a casino. www.hilton.com

On a Budget Hydro Hotel, in Douglas, has a grandiose exterior that conceals comfortable rooms with modern facilities. www.hydrohotel.co.im

EATING OUT
Treat Yourself Ciapelli's, in Douglas, is a stylish restaurant and wine bar that serves produce from Manx farms and fisheries, prepared with an Italian twist. www.aperitivo.co.uk

On a Budget Welbeck Hotel Restaurant, also in Douglas, serves traditional island fare such as Manx lamb and locally raised beef, as well as seafood dishes. www.welbeckhotel.com

PRICE FOR A FAMILY OF FOUR
Around $400 a day for accommodations, food and tours.

WEBSITES
www.visitisleofman.com
www.manxbirdatlas.org.uk

The Oldest Parliament

The Isle of Man is ruled by its own parliament, the Tynwald, which was instituted in the 10th century by Viking settlers and celebrated its millennial anniversary in 1979. In 1266 Man became a Scottish possession, but in 1405 the island passed into English hands, and it has been a dependency of the British Crown since 1765. However, it is not part of the United Kingdom – hence its unusual legal code and its reputation as a haven for British tax-dodgers, who have taken advantage of its low taxes.

Main: Mountain bikers exploring the Isle of Man's coastline at sunset

AN ISLAND APART

I F YOU LIKE SWEEPING VISTAS AND BRACING SEA BREEZES, then the Isle of Man is definitely the place to visit. Lying in the Irish Sea, midway between Ireland and Britain, this rocky island has a history and culture all of its own. Winter sees Man at its best, when the coasts and countryside are delightfully uncrowded and the many species of wildlife roam undisturbed.

Small though it is, the Isle of Man boasts an impressive variety of landscapes. The rugged sea-pounded cliffs back onto dry sandy heathland at the Ayres National Nature Reserve, which is the perfect place for a bracing stroll. Rolling hills, moors, and wooded glens, where waterfalls tumble into narrow streams, give way to fertile farmland. Set dramatically amid these diverse landscapes are ancient stone monuments left by the island's past inhabitants, from the first Stone-Age settlers to later Celts and Vikings. More than 200 elaborately carved early Christian crosses, adorned with complex Celtic patterns, are also scattered around the island.

Man attracts a variety of bird life too, with Brent geese and Bewick's and whistler swans among the migrant species exchanging the harsh Arctic winter for Man's more clement

FURTHER DETAILS

ISLE OF MAN

Manx National Heritage
The Heritage Agency protects and maintains a portfolio of areas of natural beauty and special interest on the island. Most locations are freely accessible all year.
www.gov.im/mnh

Ayres National Nature Reserve
Near Bride. The reserve's bird species include gannets, oystercatchers, and ringed plovers. You can sometimes spot whales, basking sharks, and gray seals off the coast from here; open daily all year.
www.iomguide.com

Curraghs Wildlife Park
Ballaugh. More than 100 bird and animal species from around the world live in the natural wetland environment of this wildlife park and breeding center; open summer: Mon–Fri 10am–6pm; winter: school vacations only.
www.gov.im/wildlife

Cycle Rental
Sulby. Isle of Man Cycle Hire offers cycle rental and guided cycling vacations.
www.iomcyclehire.co.uk

Riding Stables
Little London, Cronk-y-Voddy. The Ballahimmin Riding Centre offers off-road riding in beautiful countryside, with a wide selection of ponies and horses available; open all year, reservations necessary.
www.ballahimmin.com

Boat Rental
Port Erin. I. B. Boat Charter operates fishing, bird- and wildlife-watching, and seal-spotting cruises; open year round (weather permitting).
www.ibboatcharter.iofm.net

Wildlife Tours
Douglas Sea Terminal. Isle of Man Wildlife Tours offers guided trips to the best spots for wildife-watching; tours start at 10am Sat–Sun, lasting around 5 hours.
www.iomtours.co.uk

Below (top to bottom): Rugged cliff formations; flock of Brent geese

> Winter sees Man at its best, when the coasts and countryside are delightfully uncrowded and the many species of wildlife roam undisturbed.

climate. Ballaugh Curraghs, a region of peat wetlands, willow, and bog myrtle scrub, is one of the best year-round wildlife sites. In winter it hosts the largest hen harrier roost in Europe and, if you're lucky, you might even spot one of its population of over 100 wild wallabies – the descendants of a pair that escaped from the nearby Curraghs Wildlife Park in the 1960s.

All you really need to explore the island is a good pair of walking boots, but if you prefer to travel on two wheels or four legs, there are several bicycle rental companies and riding stables around the island – and there are plenty of trails that you can explore. And for stunning views of the rugged coastline and the tiny neighboring island of the Calf of Man, along with opportunities to spot seals and a huge array of bird life, boat trips operate year-round from the Isle of Man's fishing harbors. Tour companies also offer guided driving and walking trips along the coast and inland, maximizing your chances of a great day of wildlife-watching.

THE ESSENTIALS

GETTING THERE AND AROUND
The Peak District National Park, the location of most of the caves, is in northwestern England. The nearest airport is Manchester International Airport, 16 miles (26 km) northwest of Buxton. A car is the best way to explore the area, although there are also good bus connections.

WEATHER
Much of the Peak District National Park experiences higher-than-average rainfall in winter, and the weather can be changeable. Average daytime temperatures range from 39 to 41°F (3–5°C).

ACCOMMODATIONS
Treat Yourself The Old Hall Hotel, in central Buxton, has been welcoming guests since the 16th century or earlier. www.oldhallhotelbuxton.co.uk

On a Budget Bargate Cottage, in Buxton, was built in 1650 below Peveril Castle and boasts cozy rooms with private bathrooms. www.bargatecottage.co.uk

EATING OUT
Treat Yourself The Columbine, in Buxton, combines sophisticated modern cuisine with the intimate feel of dining in a private home. www.buxtononline.net/columbine

On a Budget Ye Olde Cheshire Cheese Inn, in Castleton, was built in the 1600s and serves simple but delicious pub food in historic surroundings. www.cheshirecheeseinn.co.uk

PRICE FOR TWO PEOPLE
Around $330 a day for accommodations, food, and admission fees.

WEBSITES
www.visitpeakdistrict.com
www.visitbuxton.co.uk

Blue John

Unique to some of the Peak District caves, Blue John is the informal name of fluorite, a mineral composed of calcium fluoride. It is a vivid blue in color, with hints of yellow – the name "Blue John" is an anglicization of the French words *bleu et jaune*, or "blue and yellow." Its attractive colors make it very appealing to collectors, and you can buy Blue John when you visit the caves. However, due to its scarcity, the amount of the rock mined is now heavily restricted.

ROCK BOTTOM

THE UNSPOILED LANDSCAPE OF THE PEAK DISTRICT is green and rolling in some places and stark and rugged in others. In the depths of winter, only the intrepid venture onto the windswept higher hills, but there is another terrain of stunning scenery open year-round: the underground world of Derbyshire's cave networks. Over millions of years, water trickling through the limestone hills and peaks has carved out a fantasy land of stalactites, stalagmites, and crystal rock formations – a netherworld that is both beautiful and bizarre. Bad winter

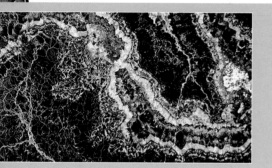

> A fantasy land of stalactites, stalagmites, and crystal rock formations – a netherworld that is both beautiful and bizarre.

weather is good news for cave visitors, as melting snows or rainfall increase the volume of underground waterfalls and rivers, making this hidden realm all the more magnificent.

Two cave sites that have special appeal are near the towns of Buxton and Castleton. The Romans turned Buxton into an attractive spa town, as it remains today. Yet even the works of these mighty builders were dwarfed by the two-million-year-old cave network at Poole's Cavern on the edge of the town. Roman remains have been found here, but it was the Victorians who christened its most evocative rock formation the "Frozen Waterfall." Other strange formations in the cavern include Derbyshire's largest stalactite, the "Flitch of Bacon"– so named because of its resemblance to a side of pork.

There are impressive underground waterfalls in the cave networks around Castleton, 10 miles (16 km) northeast of Buxton. Blue John Cavern takes its name from the colorful mineral that is unique to the area's caves *(see story box)*. Blue John is still mined in nearby Treak Cliff Cavern, where winter brings the added attraction of carol services held within the caves. You can also enjoy carol concerts in nearby Peak Cavern, which has the largest natural cave entrance in the British Isles and was once home to a whole village. Speedwell Cavern is the only show cave that you can explore by boat – and when you traverse its underground lake in the eerie half-lit darkness, you can see why it has been called the "Bottomless Pit." In winter, the subterranean world of Derbyshire's caves is every inch as awe-inspiring as the peaks above.

Main: Potholing in Peak Cavern **Inset:** Blue John stone, unique to the area
Below (left to right): Navigating through Speedwell Cavern; Poole's Cavern on the edge of Buxton

FURTHER DETAILS

THE CAVES OF CASTLETON AND BUXTON
Poole's Cavern
Green Lane, Buxton. This cavern has been a local attraction for centuries, and Mary, Queen of Scots is believed to have visited it in 1582; open Mar–Oct: 9:30am–5pm daily; Nov–Feb: 10am–4pm Sat–Sun.
www.poolescavern.co.uk

Blue John Cavern
Castleton. One of the many features of the Blue John Cavern is Lord Mulgrave's Dining Room, so called because the eponymous lord is said to have entertained miners to a meal here once; open from 9:30am daily, seasonal closing times vary.
www.bluejohn-cavern.co.uk

Treak Cliff Cavern
Cross Street, Castleton. Naturally occurring examples of Blue John stone can still be seen here; open 10am–5pm daily; carol services held on weekends throughout December at 11:30am and 2:00pm (until the weekend before Christmas).
www.bluejohnstone.com

Peak Cavern
Peak Cavern House, Peak Cavern Road, Castleton. The cave village here was inhabited until as recently as 1915, and its remains can still be seen; open Apr–Oct: 10am–5pm daily; Nov–Mar: 10am–5pm Sat–Sun; carol concerts are held in the caves in December on the three weekends before Christmas.
www.peakcavern.co.uk

Speedwell Cavern
Winnats Pass, Castleton. The deepest of the cave networks in the area, Speedwell Cavern is located some 600 ft (183 m) below ground; open 10am–5pm daily (later at peak times); guided boat tours take place daily.
www.speedwellcavern.co.uk

Below (top to bottom): The Crescent in Buxton; caver in a stream passage in Peak Cavern

THE ESSENTIALS

GETTING THERE AND AROUND
Glasgow is in southern Scotland. Glasgow Airport is 8 miles (13 km) from the downtown, connected by a frequent shuttle bus service. Glasgow Central rail station has services to London Euston and elsewhere. Many attractions lie within walking distance of each other; the quickest way around the city is by Subway, Glasgow's underground metro system.

WEATHER
Be prepared for rain, wintry showers, and daytime temperatures averaging 36–41°F (2–5°C) but often dipping below freezing.

ACCOMMODATIONS
Treat Yourself Hotel du Vin, in Devonshire Gardens, is a fine boutique hotel in the fashionable West End district. Its bistro serves modern European dishes.
www.hotelduvin.com/glasgow

On a Budget The Victorian House, on Renfrew Street, is a conveniently central guesthouse with 60 rooms, from singles to family suites.
www.thevictorian.co.uk

EATING OUT
Treat Yourself The Ubiquitous Chip, on Ashton Lane, offers modern Scottish cuisine and varied dining areas including a stylish courtyard, brasserie, and public bar.
www.ubiquitouschip.co.uk

On a Budget Babbity Bowster, on Blackfriars Street, offers a good blend of Scottish and international dishes, as well as a bar menu.
Tel: 0141 552 5055

PRICE FOR TWO PEOPLE
Around $250 a day for food, accommodations, local transportation, and Winterfest activities.

WEBSITE
www.seeglasgow.com

On the Trail of Mackintosh

The work of Glasgow's most famous architect, Charles Rennie Mackintosh, fused baronial, Art Nouveau, and Japanese elements. Two outstanding examples of his work are the Willow Tea Rooms, Sauchiehall Street, and The House for an Art Lover, in Bellahouston Park – a fascinating re-creation of a building that he designed, but that was not built in his lifetime. You can fully explore all his works in the city with a Rennie Mackintosh Trail ticket, available from *www.crmsociety.com*.

Main: Ice skaters enjoy Winterfest in George Square
Right (top to bottom): Glasgow's elegant, Neo-Classical Gallery of Modern Art; winter fireworks lighting up the City Chambers

WINTER WONDERLAND

OFFERING A PULSATING PROGRAM OF EVENTS, Glasgow's Winterfest easily justifies a visit to Scotland's biggest city, even at this chilly time of year. Winterfest is an umbrella organization that brings together all of Glasgow's winter festivities from mid-November to mid-January. Its hub is George Square, a great civic set piece in a city with an astonishing heritage of innovative Victorian architecture. Here you can don full winter garb and join the throng on what becomes the largest open-air ice-skating rink in Britain. There's also a festive market here in the lead-up to Christmas, with all kinds of tempting seasonal products for sale.

Glasgow is one of Britain's top shopping cities, and the Christmas lights and decorations spectacularly transform the main drags of Sauchiehall, Argyle, and Buchanan streets, as well as some huge indoor shopping malls, such as the Buchanan Galleries. The window displays can be eye-catching, especially at the House of Fraser department store on Buchanan Street. It's "panto" (musical comedy theater) season, and a clutch of theaters present their own takes on traditional seasonal offerings such as *Cinderella* or *Aladdin* – with an inimitable twist of Glaswegian humor.

FURTHER DETAILS

GLASGOW

Glasgow on Ice
George Square; late Nov–early Jan, 10am–10pm.
www.glasgowswinterfestivals.com

Festive Market
George Square; open late-Nov–Dec: 10am–7pm Mon–Fri,
9am–6pm Sat, 11am–5pm Sun and Bank Holiday Mondays.
www.glasgowswinterfestivals.com

Theatre Royal
Hope Street; performances throughout the year.
www.ambassadortickets.com/theatre-royal-glasgow

Glasgow Royal Concert Hall
Sauchiehall Street; musical performances all year.
www.glasgowconcerthalls.com

Hogmanay
George Square; Dec 31. Tickets available from Nov.
www.ticketmaster.co.uk

Celtic Connections
Various venues, Jan.
www.celticconnections.com

Glasgow Film Festival
Various venues, Feb.
www.glasgowfilmfestival.org.uk

WHAT ELSE TO SEE AND DO

City Chambers
These grandiose buildings were built in the 1880s, when
Glasgow was the "second city of empire."

Glasgow Museums
There are thirteen City of Glasgow Museums to visit; the
most popular is Kelvingrove Art Gallery and Museum.
www.glasgowmuseums.com

Glasgow Botanic Gardens
Renowned gardens, greenhouses, and arboretum.
www.glasgow.gov.uk

Below (top to bottom): Kibble Palace glasshouses
at Glasgow's Botanic Gardens; Kelvingrove Museum.

Offering a pulsating program of events, Glasgow's
Winterfest easily justifies a visit to Scotland's biggest
city, even at this chilly time of year.

If you're looking for higher culture, The Scottish Ballet always performs a family favorite, such as
Swan Lake or the *Nutcracker*, at the Theatre Royal, and the Royal Scottish National Orchestra puts
on several Christmas concerts, including one special evening at the Royal Concert Hall, when live
music is provided for a showing of the much-loved children's movie *The Snowman*.

The Winterfest continues into the New Year. On New Year's Eve, over 25,000 people pack
into George Square to celebrate Hogmanay, with a massive music party featuring chart-topping
bands and traditional pipers. It's ticket-only, but if you don't have tickets, there are street
performances, concerts, and ceilidhs throughout the city. January events continue with the huge
Celtic Connections festival, featuring all types of Celtic music and musicians from around the
world. In February, the Glasgow Film Festival provides opportunities to go to the UK premieres
of films of all genres, from blockbusters to more thoughtful shorts and documentaries.

THE ESSENTIALS

GETTING THERE AND AROUND
Dartmoor National Park is in the county of Devon, in southwestern England. The nearest airports are Plymouth City Airport or Exeter International Airport. A car is recommended in winter, when the park's buses do not run. There are free guided walks provided by the Dartmoor National Park Authority.

WEATHER
The weather on Dartmoor is notoriously fickle, so it is always important to be prepared for extreme weather, including sudden storms, rain, and snow, as well as thick mist and fog. Average winter daytime temperatures range from 36 to 41°F (2–5°C).

ACCOMMODATIONS
Treat Yourself The Horn of Plenty, in Gulworthy, Tavistock, offers the perfect location for a trip to Dartmoor, with gorgeous Tamar Valley views.
www.thehornofplenty.co.uk

On a Budget The Rosemont, in Yelverton, offers comfortable rooms and an excellent location in the southwestern part of the national park.
www.therosemont.co.uk

EATING OUT
Treat Yourself 22 Mill St, in Chagford, is a modern restaurant offering tasty European fare.
www.22millst.com

On a Budget The Rugglestone Inn, in Widecombe-in-the-Moor, is a traditional pub serving real ales and good pub grub.
www.rugglestoneinn.co.uk

PRICE FOR TWO PEOPLE
From $250 a day for accommodations, food, and admission fees.

WEBSITES
www.dartmoor.co.uk
www.dartmoor-npa.gov.uk

Clapper Bridges

Across Dartmoor, hundreds of clapper bridges – an ancient form of bridge technology – can be found crossing rivers and streams. They are constructed from long slabs of granite resting on stone piers, and some date from medieval times. The best-known clapper bridge is the large and ambitious one at Postbridge, which is thought to date back to the 14th century, with slabs weighing up to 8 tons each. Other examples include the Teignhead Farm Clapper and the Avon Clapper.

Main: Dramatic sunset over Saddle Tor on Dartmoor **Right (top to bottom):** Clapper bridge over the River Dart; Widgery Cross on Brat Tor near Lydford; prehistoric Merrivale Rows in Dartmoor National Park

GRANITE HILLTOPS

A SWATH OF LANDSCAPE WITH AUSTERE NATURAL GRANDEUR, Dartmoor National Park occupies a vast chunk of England's southwest. The "grim charm" of this unspoiled, sweeping granite moorland, as Sir Arthur Conan Doyle poetically described it, is the antithesis of Britain's claustrophobic urban sprawls. The Ministry of Defence has laid claim to a large northwestern segment of the national park, and there's a scattering of peaceful villages and a web of roads, but otherwise this is sensationally boundless and empty rambling territory.

The bleak appeal of Dartmoor's barren moorland and tors (granite hilltops) is compelling at any time of the year, but for many visitors it reaches its full stature in winter. The waterfalls of Dartmoor, such as the tumbling Whitelady Waterfall at Lydford Gorge, are in full flow in the wet winter months. The air at this time of year is crisp and clear, ideal for raw and refreshing hikes and long, penetrating views, especially from high points such as rocky Bellever Tor (1,453 ft/443 m), while winter dawns and sunsets create some fantastic panoramas. Rambling across the winter moorland – from Widgery Cross, a granite cross that sits high on Brat Tor,

FURTHER DETAILS

DARTMOOR NATIONAL PARK
The Dartmoor National Park Authority publishes a handy guide to events and guided walks on Dartmoor over fall and winter. It is essential to take a good map of Dartmoor and a compass with you when hiking. Don't underestimate the terrain, especially in winter: snow may make the landscape attractive, but it can also make it slippery underfoot. Always take water with you.
www.dartmoor-npa.gov.uk

Some of the highest tors in Dartmoor, such as Yes Tor (2,031 ft/619 m) and High Willhays (2,037 ft/621 m), are located within an army firing range and are off limits if red flags are flying (signifying the range is in use). For further information on Dartmoor's firing ranges, consult *www.dartmoor-ranges.co.uk*

National Park Information Centre
Princetown; open 10am–5pm daily.
www.dartmoor-npa.gov.uk

Whitelady Waterfall
Lydford Gorge; opening times vary during the wet winter months; visit the website for more information.
www.nationaltrust.org.uk

Castle Drogo
Drewsteignton; opening times are variable over the winter; visit the website for further details.
www.nationaltrust.org.uk

WHAT ELSE TO SEE AND DO
Plymouth
The maritime town of Plymouth offers a number of significant historical sights. You can seek out the Mayflower Steps, marking the point where the Pilgrim Fathers set sail for the New World in 1620; explore Plymouth Hoe; join boat trips along Plymouth Sound; or peruse the Barbican area, the town's main concentration of old buildings, including Elizabethan House.
Plymouth: *www.visitplymouth.co.uk*
Elizabethan House: *www.plymouth.gov.uk/ museumelizabethanhouse*

Buckland Abbey
Established in Yelverton in the 13th century by Cistercian monks, Buckland Abbey is the one-time residence of Sir Francis Drake, who allegedly still haunts the property. It is also the home of "Drake's Drum," which, according to legend, beats when England is in danger.
www.nationaltrust.org.uk

Museum of Dartmoor Life
The three floors of exhibits in this Okehampton museum give a fascinating insight into Dartmoor's social history.
www.museumofdartmoorlife.eclipse.co.uk

Below: Kayaking on the River Dart

to the cascading waters of Doe Tor Brook and Falls – can be spectacular. The Belstone Ring in north Dartmoor is a superb 4-hour circular walk that includes a climb to the summit of Cosdon Hill, where there are excellent views of Dartmoor, and encompasses Little Hound Tor, Oke Tor, and Belstone Tor. You can also join organized overnight winter tours of Dartmoor, which provide opportunities to camp out in the wilderness. White-water kayaking and canoeing is also a popular pastime, especially along the River Dart.

It's not just the awesome natural drama of Dartmoor that seduces travelers: the national park is also riddled with archaeological and prehistoric sites, with a host of stone circles, cairns, and burial chambers. Some prehistoric relics, such as the Bronze Age settlement at Grimspound and the lines of standing stones known as the Merrivale Rows, are clearly defined, but others are more inconspicuous until a light dusting of snow brings their features into relief. Winter also sees a considerable number of farmers' markets on Dartmoor, such as the excellent Tavistock Farmers' Market. Further rounding out the picture is a host of historic houses and castles in the region, supplying architectural grandeur to the natural landscape. Castle Drogo, in the northeast of Dartmoor, is a particularly special building; designed by Sir Edwin Lutyens and completed as recently as 1930, it was the last castle to be built in England.

THE ESSENTIALS

GETTING THERE AND AROUND
The Fens is a low-lying area of eastern England that stretches roughly from north of Cambridge to Spalding and Boston in Lincolnshire, and from Rutland to western Norfolk. Several airports surround the Fens, notably London Stansted, Norwich, and East Midlands, which is 25 miles (40 km) north of Leicester. Driving is the best way to get around, but you can also explore the Fens on foot.

WEATHER
The Fens can be damp and chilly in winter, with little shelter from cold winds, but heavy snow is uncommon. Average daytime temperatures range from 34 to 45ºF (1–7ºC).

ACCOMMODATIONS
Treat Yourself Congham Hall, in Grimston, is a luxury country house hotel with beautiful gardens and an acclaimed restaurant.
www.conghamhallhotel.co.uk

On a Budget The Old Rectory, in King's Lynn, is a friendly B&B in a fine Norfolk Georgian building.
www.theoldrectory-kingslynn.com

EATING OUT
Treat Yourself The Anchor Inn at Sutton Gault, near Sutton, was one of the country's first gastropubs, and its fish dishes are renowned.
www.anchorsuttongault.co.uk

On a Budget The Ship Inn, in Surfleet, has superb Fenland views and serves well-cooked steak, fish, and chicken.
www.shipinnsurfleet.com

PRICE FOR TWO PEOPLE
Around $250 a day for food and accommodations.

WEBSITE
www.visitthefens.co.uk

A Fen Tiger

When traveling around the Fens, you might hear someone refer to a local person as a "Fen Tiger." This is a term of respect for a man or woman who was born and bred here, and who knows the Fenland skills that were once used to make a living in the endless marshlands of the Fens. Fen Tigers keep these traditions alive, practicing skills such as trapping eels, catching wildfowl, and utilizing the area's unusual herbs and plants for medicinal purposes.

Above (left to right): Windmill on Wicken Fen near Ely in Cambridgeshire; barn owl, a frequent sight hunting over the Fens
Main: Pink-footed geese soaring over the Fens

BIG SKY COUNTRY

GREAT BRITAIN HAS MOUNTAINS AND MOORLAND, hills and dales, but of all its varied landscapes, one of the strangest is the Fens. In this low-lying region of eastern England, the sky seems to go on forever over the vast, flat, endless expanse. In winter it has a desolate beauty, when the wind whistles in from the east and the flooded plains and marshes become home to thousands of water birds.

In their natural state, the Fens were broad marshlands, formed when rivers running from central England to the sea dropped sediment as they hit the flat plain. It was a murky landscape of shifting channels, sand bars, sedge banks, and mires, with tufts of solid ground rising above standing pools thick with vegetation. But it was far from wasteland. Medieval fen-dwellers harvested reeds for thatching and cut peat for fuel. They had a plentiful diet of fish and wildfowl, and eels were so abundant here they were used as currency. This rich habitat was renewed by periodic flooding in winter.

Over the years, the low-lying land of the Fens was drained to create agricultural land. Attempts at drainage began in Roman times, but in the 17th century a Dutch engineer, Cornelius Vermuyden, was hired to undertake widespread drainage over thousands of acres. This caused the land to sink below sea level as the peat topsoil dried out, resulting in more flooding. Steam-driven pumps finally brought it under control in the 1820s, and the land became useable; today it produces over a third of all of Britain's vegetables and flowers.

The Fens are still a haven for birds and wildlife, particularly breeding barn owls. Wicken Fen is Britain's oldest nature reserve, established in 1899, and preserves one of the last few pockets of undrained fenland. The Ouse Washes form the largest area of washland, or flood plain, in the country. When this area of pasture floods each winter, it attracts thousands of birds – from ducks and swans to waders, such as lapwings and golden plovers, and peregrines, merlins, and other hunters – making winter the ideal time for nature-lovers to visit. The Great Fen Project, which aims to restore parts of the Fens to their natural state, will attract even more species back to this unique and atmospheric environment.

Below (left to right): Mute swans and pochard ducks, some of the diverse wildlife that, in winter, flocks to the Ouse Washes in Cambridgeshire; walkers on the Fens in Norfolk

FURTHER DETAILS

FENLAND NATURE RESERVES
Wicken Fen
The nature reserve is 9 miles (14 km) south of Ely, Cambridgeshire; open Jan–Oct: 10am–5pm Tue–Sun (and Apr–Oct: 10am–5pm Mon); Nov–Dec: 10am–4:30pm Tue–Sun.
www.wicken.org.uk

Ouse Washes
The RSPB visitor center is 3 miles (5 km) from Manea village, near Chatteris, Cambridgeshire; open 9am–5pm daily; birdwatching hides are open at all times.
www.rspb.org.uk/reserves/guide/o/ousewashes

WHAT ELSE TO SEE AND DO
Ely Cathedral
The monastery founded here by St. Ethelreda in the 7th century was one of the great religious houses of East Anglia, and this abbey church, which dates from the 1180s, is among the most impressive cathedrals in Britain. Highlights include the Octagon Tower and the fan-vaulted Lady Chapel.
www.elycathedral.org

Straw Bear Festival
Each year in mid-January, the market town of Whittlesea, near Peterborough, holds the Straw Bear Festival, an ancient Fenland tradition in which the person chosen to be the "bear" is paraded through town in a costume made from the best harvest straw, accompanied by music, traditional street dancing, and much merrymaking.
www.strawbear.org.uk

Butterfly and Wildlife Park
The Butterfly and Wildlife Park, in Long Sutton, Lincolnshire, has a range of wildlife attractions, including a large tropical butterfly and bird house and a bird-of-prey center.
www.butterflyandwildlifepark.co.uk

Below: Ely Cathedral's nave and the Octagon Tower

THE ESSENTIALS

GETTING THERE AND AROUND
York is in northeastern England. The closest airport is Leeds Bradford Airport, about 25 miles (40 km) southwest of York. Excellent rail connections link the city with other destinations throughout England and into Scotland. York itself is fairly compact and is easily explored on foot.

WEATHER
Sheltered in the Vale of York, the city's winter climate is temperate compared to the rest of Yorkshire, but rain or snow is still a possibility. Average winter daytime temperatures range from 39 to 43°F (4–6°C).

ACCOMMODATIONS
Treat Yourself Middlethorpe Hall and Spa, on Bishopthorpe Road, is a luxury hotel surrounded by acres of parkland. *www.middlethorpe.com*

On a Budget The Bar Convent, on Blossom Street, is the oldest working convent in England, with characterful and very comfortable bedrooms. *www.bar-convent.org.uk*

EATING OUT
Treat Yourself J Baker's, on Fossgate, serves modern French bistro-style food, with a fixed-price "grazing menu." *www.jbakers.co.uk*

On a Budget The Black Swan Pub, on Peasholme Green, is the oldest pub in York, built in 1417, and offers decent pub grub in an atmospheric setting. *www.blackswanyork.co.uk*

PRICE FOR TWO PEOPLE
Around $300–370 a day for food, accommodations, and admission fees.

WEBSITE
www.visityork.org

Gates and Bars

"York – where the streets are gates, the gates are bars, and the bars are pubs." This amusing saying attempts to explain the city's historic (and eccentric) place names, many of which are Viking in origin. More than 40 of its street names end in the word "gate," which comes from the Norse *gata*, meaning "street." The four actual gates in the city walls are Micklegate Bar on London Road; Bootham Bar on the site of a Roman gateway; Monk Bar, the tallest; and Walmgate Bar, the best-preserved.

Main: Intricate vaulted Chapter House ceiling of York Minster
Right (top to bottom): Participants at JORVIK Viking Festival; East End of York Minster in winter

VISITING THE VIKINGS

Each february, the city of york is overrun with Vikings, just as it was in days of old. This time, however, they're here not to conquer but to celebrate the city's heritage in the annual JORVIK Viking Festival. It's as if you've stumbled upon a gigantic costume party, with scores of bearded, helmeted characters marauding through the narrow medieval streets. Over the five days of the festival, history is brought to life: you can hear Norse ballads and sagas, watch trials of strength and agility or full-scale battle reenactments, and enjoy Viking crafts and food. A highlight is the longship races on the River Ouse.

While a visit to the festival is a great winter getaway, you can also see Vikings year-round at the JORVIK Viking Centre. This wonderful attraction arose from a downtown archaeological dig that helped uncover how these Scandinavian trader-warriors lived when they ruled York – which the Vikings called *Jorvik* – from 866 until 954. Travel back in time on an underground journey through accurate re-creations of the buildings, street life, sounds, and even smells of the city in its Viking heyday. The tableaux of people going about their daily life are all the more fascinating

FURTHER DETAILS

YORK

JORVIK Viking Centre and Festival
Coppergate; open winter: 10am–4pm daily; summer: 10am–5pm daily. The JORVIK Viking Festival takes place annually in the third week of February.
www.jorvik-viking-centre.co.uk

National Railway Museum
Leeman Road; open 10am–6pm daily.
www.nrm.org.uk

York Minster
Ogleforth; open 9:30am–5pm Mon–Sat, noon–3:45pm Sun.
www.yorkminster.org

WHAT ELSE TO SEE AND DO

Castle Museum
Founded by Dr. John L. Kirk, who collected items from his rural patients in place of fees, this museum is a treasure trove of everyday items and memorabilia from Georgian times to the mid-20th century. Exhibits include period costumes, furniture, toys, crafts, tools, period rooms, and even a recreation of a Victorian cobbled street.
www.yorkcastlemuseum.org.uk

York Art Gallery
A highlight of this fine art gallery on Exhibition Square is its extensive collection of British studio pottery. It also features paintings by 20th-century British artists, including L. S. Lowry's view of Clifford's Tower, as well as works by early Italian, Dutch, and other European painters.
www.yorkartgallery.org.uk

Yorkshire Museum and Gardens
Set in the grounds of the former St. Mary's Abbey on Museum Street, this is one of the country's best archaeological museums. It contains an impressive collection of Roman remains from everyday life to the grave, as well as Viking and Anglo-Saxon artifacts and the ruins of the city's Benedictine abbey.
www.yorkshiremuseum.org.uk

Below (top to bottom): York's city wall; National Railway Museum

> The city's most famous landmark is York Minster, one of Britain's finest cathedrals and its largest Gothic building, with magnificent stained-glass windows.

when you discover that their faces are based on computer regenerations of actual skulls discovered at the site, and the artifacts are in the exact positions in which they were found.

When you've had your fill of Vikings, travel to the more recent past at the National Railway Museum – the largest of its kind in the world, with over 100 locomotives. Exhibits range from Thomas the Tank Engine to sumptuous royal carriages, the sleek Japanese bullet train – the only one outside Japan – and Mallard, the world's fastest steam locomotive.

The city's most famous landmark is York Minster, one of Britain's finest cathedrals and its largest Gothic building, with magnificent stained-glass windows. Perhaps the most atmospheric feature of York, however, is the medieval wall that still encircles the city, measuring 2½ miles (4 km) in circumference, with four original gates intact. Today, you can walk along a footpath atop this wall – the best place from which to admire one of the most beautiful cities of the north.

THE ESSENTIALS

GETTING THERE AND AROUND
Pembrokeshire forms the southwestern tip of Wales. It is accessed by car via the M4 and A40 and is approximately 4½ hours' drive from London. The nearest airport to the Pembrokeshire coast is Cardiff, about 90 miles (145 km) to the east; car rental is available at the airport. To explore Pembrokeshire's coastline, a car is essential, as the best storm sites are not well serviced by public transportation.

WEATHER
Welsh winters tend to be wet and windy. Average temperatures in the daytime are 39–52°F (3–11°C), although they can drop below freezing. Snow is very infrequent on the coast.

ACCOMMODATIONS
Treat Yourself St. Brides Spa Hotel, in Saundersfoot, has a clifftop location with superb views and a spa with an infinity pool heated to body temperature. www.stbridesspahotel.com

On a Budget TYF Eco Lodge, in St. Davids, is based in an old windmill on the outskirts of the country's smallest city. www.tyf.com

EATING OUT
Treat Yourself Tregynon Farmhouse Restaurant, in Fishguard, offers excellent fine-dining dishes, such as their signature Pembrokeshire lamb, in a rustic setting. Tel: 01239 820531

On a Budget The Farmer's Arms, on Goat Street in St. Davids, serves hearty pub grub. Tel: 01437 721666

PRICE FOR TWO PEOPLE
From around $250 a day for accommodations and food.

WEBSITE
www.visitwales.com

Flotsam and Jetsam

Beachcombing after a big storm can be fun or even rewarding as you encounter flotsam and jetsam (flotsam is floating material, jetsam is material washed ashore). In recent years Pembrokeshire has seen everything from timbers to tugboats, dead whales, and thousands of bottles of sun-tan lotion washed onto beaches after big storms, not to mention the 10-ft- (3-m-) high, 400-yd (365-m) pebble bank at Newgale that blocked the main coast road for two days in 1989.

Main: Breathtaking breakers crashing on the wild and windy Pembrokeshire coast

STORM-WATCHING

A MIGHTY STORM IS HOWLING IN FROM THE ATLANTIC against the Pembrokeshire coast, flinging streams of sea spray and salty rain at shoreline cottage windows, sending dune sand whistling through the air, bending trees and bushes until they creak and groan, and smashing thundering steel-blue swells against towering, rain-lashed sea cliffs.

Pembrokeshire, jutting boldly out into the Atlantic, is hit by some of the most intense storms to batter the British Isles, and winter provides the best time for a breathtaking walk along the coast, into the teeth of a gale. This makes for an exhilarating expedition through what is possibly the only real wilderness environment left in Britain.

Few experiences are as raw and exciting as leaning into the screaming wind on a storm-swept beach to watch huge waves boom and break way offshore, or crash against cliffs and crags and hurl sea spray dozens of yards into the air to cascade back to sea level like a waterfall from the heavens. Winter is the prime time to see this phenomenon on a regular basis. Most of the low-pressure systems that bring these storms to British shores pass by quickly, so the chances

FURTHER DETAILS

PEMBROKESHIRE COAST NATIONAL PARK
Park Authority: *www.pcnpa.org.uk*

National Park Visitor Centre
St. Davids, Pembrokeshire; open Nov–Easter: 10am–4pm daily (closed Dec 21–28); Easter–Oct: 9:30–5:30pm daily. *www.orielyparc.co.uk*

Bear in mind that coastal storms can be dangerous as well as spectacular:
• Be wary of storm and tidal surges, and rogue waves on beaches and low cliffs, which could sweep you out to sea
• Look out for loose and crumbling cliff faces after a storm
• Daylight hours are very short in winter, so bear this in mind if you go for a long walk
• Always let someone know your intended walking route and when you expect to be back
• Wear good waterproof clothing and footwear
• In an emergency, call 999 and ask for the Coastguard. *www.metoffice.gov.uk*

WHAT ELSE TO SEE AND DO
Surfing in Mathry
Surfing lessons are available at Preseli Venture near Mathry, from about $80 per half-day including equipment. *www.preseliventure.com*

St. Davids
Britain's smallest city provides respite from the winter storms. You'll find sanctuary in the 11th-century St. Davids Cathedral or the city's numerous pubs.
City: *www.stdavids.co.uk*
St. Davids Cathedral: *www.stdavidscathedral.org.uk*

Below (top to bottom): Surfer riding the waves in Pembrokeshire; waves pound the dramatic, rocky coastline

Few experiences are as raw and exciting as leaning into the screaming wind on a storm-swept beach to watch huge waves boom and break way offshore.

are that if Saturday is windy and wet, Sunday will be breezy and sunny. Exposed coastlines such as Strumble Head and St. Davids Head in North Pembrokeshire, and the vast white limestone cliffs of the Castlemartin region of South Pembrokeshire, offer unforgettable views of Mother Nature at her most raw and elemental, with the added bonus of welcoming B&Bs and warm, cozy pubs to scurry back to when you've had enough of being buffeted and blasted by wind, waves, and sand.

The Pembrokeshire Coast National Park is Britain's only coastal national park, conserving over 240 sq miles (620 sq km) of this beautiful landscape. The park maintains the spectacular Pembrokeshire Coast Path – 186 miles (299 km) of trail you can follow around the peninsula, from St. Dogmaels on Cardigan Bay to Amroth on the south coast. If you need a weekend winter break, nothing will blow away the cobwebs like a walk along this coastline.

THE ESSENTIALS

GETTING THERE AND AROUND
Portsmouth is in southern England on the Hampshire coast, across the Solent channel from the Isle of Wight and 75 miles (120 km) from London. Regular trains run to Portsmouth from London Waterloo (journey time 90 minutes) and Southampton (journey time 50 minutes). Portsmouth is a major ferry port, with daily connections to ports in France, Spain and the Channel Islands.

WEATHER
Portsmouth enjoys a relatively mild winter climate, with daytime temperatures ranging from 36 to 48°F (2–8°C). Always prepare for rain and changeable weather.

ACCOMMODATIONS
Treat Yourself Florence House Hotel, in Portsmouth's Southsea district, is stylish, comfortable, and elegant, and offers excellent value and a seafront location.
www.florencehousehotel.co.uk

On a Budget Fortitude Cottage, in Old Portsmouth, offers pretty quayside lodgings with great panoramic views.
www.fortitudecottage.co.uk

EATING OUT
Treat Yourself Bistro Montparnasse, on Palmerston Road, is an elegant, stylish and uncluttered bistro with an imaginative British and European menu.
www.bistromontparnasse.co.uk

On a Budget Chez Choi Restaurant, in Southsea, is a popular Chinese Sichuan/Cantonese noodle bar.
www.chezchoinoodlebar.co.uk

PRICE FOR TWO PEOPLE
Around $250 a day for accommodations, food, and admission fees.

WEBSITE
www.visitportsmouth.co.uk

What Sank the *Mary Rose*?

Constructed in Portsmouth, the *Mary Rose* – the flagship of Henry VIII's fleet – sank in the Solent in 1545 during an engagement with French vessels. The cause of her demise remains uncertain, but theories point the finger at top-heaviness, or her open gun ports letting in water. A section of the ship was famously lifted from the seabed in 1982, and was put on display in the Historic Dockyard. However, due to conservation work the remains have been withdrawn from public view until 2012.

NAVAL HEROES

PORTSMOUTH IS ENGLAND'S ONLY TRUE ISLAND CITY, as most of it lies on Portsea Island, where the Solent joins the English Channel. Nicknamed "Pompey," Portsmouth is a historic naval base of vast importance and is home to the world's oldest dry dock. The city's powerful bond with the sea dates back to Roman times, but Portsmouth's great naval value made it a prime target for *Luftwaffe* bombing in World War II. The subsequent destruction led to some severe architectural reshaping, but the old town of Portsmouth maintains a historic charm, while a new, more innovative architectural impetus has given rise to the tall, graceful Spinnaker Tower – designed to resemble a spinnaker sail catching the wind.

It is Portsmouth's proud associations with the Royal Navy and British maritime history that truly define the city. Its Historic Dockyard is the resting place of three notable ships from very different periods: *HMS Victory*, *HMS Warrior*, and the ill-fated *Mary Rose (see story box)*.

It is Portsmouth's proud associations with the Royal Navy and British maritime history that truly define the city.

Nelson's ship, *HMS Victory*, sits today in dry dock, a world away from the roar and smoke of the Battle of Trafalgar. The imposing *HMS Warrior* entered service in 1861; it was Britain's first armor-plated battleship and the fastest vessel of its day, propelled by both steam engine and sails. You can admire a collection of fascinating objects retrieved from the wreck of the 16th-century warship *Mary Rose* in a purpose-built museum. The Dockyard also houses the Royal Naval Museum, which paints a detailed portrait of Portsmouth's role in British naval history, and Action Stations, a hands-on array of interactive games. A good way to get the city in full aerial perspective is to ascend the full 558 ft (170 m) of the elegant Spinnaker Tower.

Portsmouth can be visited in any season, but in late November and early December the atmosphere in the Historic Dockyard is at its most lively, when the Victorian Festival of Christmas brings the flavors of old Portsmouth to the fore. Join in the bustling festivities, when a host of street performers unite with Victorian characters, circus acts, policemen in period costume keeping order, traditional funfair attractions, marching bands, rides, shows, and a galaxy of market stands to re-create the vibrant traditions of this historic city.

FURTHER DETAILS

PORTSMOUTH HISTORIC DOCKYARD
In addition to tickets for individual attractions, an annual pass for the Historic Dockyard allows unlimited entry to *HMS Warrior*, the Royal Naval Museum, and Action Stations – the Royal Navy's interactive visitor attraction – but can be used once only for *HMS Victory*, the *Mary Rose*, and Harbour Tours.
www.historicdockyard.co.uk

HMS Victory, HMS Warrior, Mary Rose
Portsmouth Historic Dockyard; open Apr–Oct: 10am–6pm daily (last entry at 4:45pm); Nov–Mar: 10am–5:30pm daily (last entry at 4pm).
HMS Victory: www.hms-victory.com
HMS Warrior: www.hmswarrior.org
Mary Rose: www.historicdockyard.co.uk

Royal Naval Museum
Tickets to the museum can be bought separately or are included in the *HMS Victory* ticket or Dockyard annual pass; open summer: 10am–5pm daily; winter: 10am–4:15pm daily.
www.royalnavalmuseum.org

Spinnaker Tower
Portsmouth Harbour; open 10am–6pm daily.
www.spinnakertower.co.uk

Victorian Festival of Christmas
Tickets include entry to *HMS Victory*, *HMS Warrior* and the *Mary Rose*; open 10am–6pm (last admission 4:30pm) daily.
www.christmasfestival.co.uk

WHAT ELSE TO SEE AND DO
Southsea
The seaside resort of Southsea, to the south of Old Portsmouth, has a largely gravel beach. The D-Day Museum offers fascinating insights into Portsmouth's role in the Normandy landings of 1944. Longer than the Bayeux Tapestry, the Overlord Embroidery at the museum relates the story of the invasion force.
Southsea: www.southsea.co.uk
D-Day Museum: www.ddaymuseum.co.uk

Portchester Castle
Originally dating from the 3rd century, Portchester Castle is unique as the last surviving Roman fort in northern Europe with walls still standing to their full height. Stationed at the head of Portsmouth Harbour, the castle served as a jail for French prisoners during the Napoleonic Wars.
www.english-heritage.org.uk

Main: Stern of *HMS Victory*

Far left (top to bottom): Gun deck on *HMS Victory*; Prow of *HMS Victory*

Above: Ship figurehead of Admiral Horatio Nelson, alongside *HMS Victory*

Below: Spinnaker Tower at Gunwharf Quays, completed in 2005

Below: *HMS Warrior* seen from the top of the Spinnaker Tower

THE ESSENTIALS

GETTING THERE AND AROUND
The Brecon Beacons are in southeast Wales. The nearest international airport is Cardiff, 53 miles (87 km) south of Brecon. The nearest train station is at Abergavenny, served by London trains via Newport. Buses run from Abergavenny to Brecon, which has bus and taxi services. Driving within the National Park can be slow, but it's a great area for walking, cycling, and horse riding.

WEATHER
The Beacons experience bright, cold weather in winter, as well as periods of wind and rain. Average winter daytime temperatures are 36–41°F (2–5°C).

ACCOMMODATIONS
Treat Yourself Peterstone Court Country House and Spa, in Llanhamlach, offers luxurious spa and restaurant facilities with a mountainous backdrop.
www.peterstone-court.com

On a Budget The Bear, in Crickhowell, is an old-fashioned town coaching inn with antique furnishings and log fires.
www.bearhotel.co.uk

EATING OUT
Dining in the Beacons is limited to inns and pubs, so prices are quite consistent.

Nantyffin Cider Mill Inn, in Crickhowell, is a 16th-century inn serving high-quality British pub food in a bistro-style setting.
www.cidermill.co.uk

The Felin Fach Griffin Inn, near Brecon, has the motto of "simple things done well," which is reflected in its fantastic menu.
www.eatdrinksleep.ltd.uk

PRICE FOR TWO PEOPLE
Around $250 a day for accommodations and food.

WEBSITE
www.visitmidwales.co.uk

The Big Pit

High on the heather-covered moors close to Abergavenny, Wales's National Coal Museum is a real reminder of how South Wales was shaped by mining. At the Big Pit – a working coal mine until 1980 – former miners take visitors on a tour 295 ft (90 m) underground, telling stories of their working lives as they go. The museum and the nearby town of Blaenavon – famous for its historic ironworks – have together been designated a UNESCO World Heritage Site.

Main: Brecon Beacons from Pen y Fan
Right (top to bottom): Hikers exploring the winter wilderness; waterfall in the Beacons

PANORAMIC VIEWS

WITH THE HIGHEST PEAKS IN WALES outside of Snowdonia, the Brecon Beacons National Park makes a superb winter escape. Hewn from sandstone, the snow-dusted Beacons rise skyward to the twin high-points of Pen y Fan and Cribyn. They immediately invite you to climb, but these summits can be treacherous in winter, so stop off first to speak to the experts at the National Park Visitor Centre in Libanus, who know when it's safest to set off.

Limber up with a walk on Mynydd Illtyd Common, a protected area of grassland and wetland with stunning mountain vistas. Then pick a day with clear blue skies, wrap up warm to counter the inevitable biting wind, and set off for one of the adjacent summits. The journey is astounding. The grassy ridges give way to dizzying drops from sheer clifflike edges, and on a fine day a far-ranging panorama surrounds you, encompassing points over 100 miles (160 km) apart. To the north are the uplands of mid-Wales and pristine Snowdonia; to the east are the rolling Malverns and Cotswolds; the Bristol Channel and the heights of Exmoor in north Devon lie to the south, while the sea hides beyond the Black Mountains to the west.

FURTHER DETAILS

THE BRECON BEACONS
Brecon Beacons National Park Visitor Centre
Libanus, Brecon; open 9:30am–4:30pm daily.
www.breconbeacons.org

Mynydd Illtyd Common
Between Libanus and Brecon, Brecon Beacons
National Park.
www.breconbeacons.org

Sgwd yr Eira
Near Penderyn, Brecon Beacons National Park.
www.breconbeacons.org

The Big Pit: National Coal Museum
Blaenavon, Torfaen; open 9:30am–5pm daily; 50-minute
underground tours run between 10am and 3:30pm.
www.museumwales.ac.uk/en/bigpit

Blaenavon Ironworks
North Street, Blaenavon; open 9:30am–4pm
Fri–Sat, 11am–4pm Sun.
www.cadw.wales.gov.uk

WHAT ELSE TO SEE AND DO
Abergavenny Museum
Located in a ruined Norman castle, and its grounds, in
Abergavenny's Castle Street, this local history museum
is home to a re-created old Welsh kitchen and a grocer's
shop. The museum's displays tell the story of this
centuries-old market town from prehistoric times through
to the present day.
www.abergavennymuseum.co.uk

Brecknock Museum & Art Gallery
Housed in the former Assize Court, in Captain's Walk
in Brecon, this museum and gallery houses displays
on local history and has changing exhibitions featuring
contemporary artists from all over Wales.
www.powys.gov.uk

Llangorse Multi-Activity Centre
The largest riding and indoor climbing center in Wales is at
Gilfach Farm, Llangorse, near Brecon. It also offers sky-wire
rides, gorge-walking, and pony trekking (minimum trek
time 1 hour).
www.activityuk.com

Taff Trail
A largely traffic-free cycling route, the Taff Trail runs
55 miles (88 km) between Brecon and Cardiff, through
the center of the Brecon Beacons National Park.
www.tafftrail.org.uk

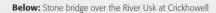

Below: Stone bridge over the River Usk at Crickhowell

Pick a day with clear blue skies, wrap up warm to
counter the inevitable biting wind, and set off for one
of the adjacent summits. The journey is astounding.

South of the peaks is Brecon Beacons Waterfall Country, where the rivers Nedd, Hepste and
Mellte carved their way through the land to form deep gorges during successive ice ages. The
gorges are now cloaked with forests, but the rivers still run their course, tumbling over a series
of tumultuous waterfalls. They are at their most dramatic after prolonged rain, so winter is an
ideal time to experience them. Perhaps the most breathtaking of all the falls is Sgwd yr Eira, where
an ancient route leads you along a rocky ledge and right beneath the curtain of the waterfall.

Once you've had your fill of the landscape, you might like to visit the compact, stone-built
towns of Abergavenny, Brecon, and Crickhowell, with their welcoming inns and traditional
shops that still serve the local farming communities. At the northeastern tip of the Beacons is
the quaint book town of Hay-on-Wye (*see pp14–15*), while toward Cardiff are the famous Welsh
"Valleys"– once scarred by mining and ironworking, but now a lush green landscape once again.

THE ESSENTIALS

GETTING THERE AND AROUND
The Burns Heritage Trail is in Ayrshire, on the southwest coast of Scotland. Alloway is 6 miles (10 km) south of Glasgow's Prestwick Airport and 42 miles (67 km) south of Glasgow's main international airport. The Burns sites are best visited by car, as public transportation is relatively limited.

WEATHER
The mild sea air makes this corner of Scotland fairly pleasant in winter. Temperatures can be higher than in eastern Scotland, averaging 39–48°F (4–9°C) on winter days.

ACCOMMODATIONS
Treat Yourself Glenapp Castle, in Ballantrae, 30 miles (48 km) south of Alloway, is a luxurious 5-star retreat in a magnificent restored baronial castle. *www.glenappcastle.com*

On a Budget Greenan Lodge, in Doonfoot, is a small and friendly guesthouse a few minutes' drive from Burns Cottage in Alloway. *www.greenanlodge.com*

EATING OUT
Treat Yourself The Linen Room, in Dumfries, has won many awards, including Scottish Restaurant of the Year for its contemporary Scottish cuisine. *www.linenroom.com*

On a Budget The Alloway Inn, in Doonfoot, is close to Burns Cottage and has good-quality pub food. *www.costley.biz*

PRICE FOR TWO PEOPLE
Around $310–330 a day for food, accommodations, car rental, and admission fees.

WEBSITES
www.visitdumfriesandgalloway.co.uk
www.visitscotland.com

Scotland's Book Town

If you want to buy some Burns poetry, Wigtown, in Dumfries and Galloway, is the place to go. Lying just outside the Heritage Trail, it was designated Scotland's National Book Town by the government in 1997. Second-hand bookshops can be found on and around the town square, many of them in Wigtown's pretty pastel-coloured buildings. Every fall there's an impressive Book Festival which brings internationally acclaimed authors to this pretty spot on the Solway Coast.

THE PLOWMAN POET

Scotland's best-loved native son is not a warrior or a king but a poet – Robert Burns. People the world over ring in the New Year with his lyrics to "Auld Lang Syne," while Scots everywhere traditionally celebrate his birthday on January 25 with boisterous Burns Suppers, featuring recitations of his works and consumption of his favorite fare: whiskey and haggis.

The Bard of Ayrshire was born in 1759 in a humble cottage built by his father's own hands in Alloway, near Ayr. The village became something of a place of pilgrimage after Burns's death, and much of it is now sequestered within the Burns National Heritage Park. His birthplace, Burns Cottage, has been restored to its original condition, and you can wander from here past places that formed the settings for his most famous poems, such as the eerie 16th-century kirk (church) and "Brig O'Doon," the medieval bridge that spans the beautiful river Doon. Climb to the Burns Monument at the edge of the village for far-reaching views over his beloved Ayrshire, before retreating to the cottage to read the great man's words again in his own hand – its museum contains the world's largest collection of his manuscripts and personal belongings.

Following in Burns's footsteps will take you through some of southwest Scotland's most beautiful scenery. Heading south through Galloway Forest Park, you'll travel through the ancient woodlands, lochs, and moorland surrounding the Galloway Hills, a haven for wildlife, from red deer to red kites. In 1788, Burns took a lease on Ellisland Farm, just outside Dumfries, and its idyllic river setting inspired his best nature poetry. You can visit the artists' colony of Kirkcudbright and the old mill town Gatehouse of Fleet, where the cotton mill owned by Alexander Birtwhistle – immortalized by Burns as "Roaring Birtwhistle" – still stands.

Burns moved to the county town of Dumfries in 1791, and died here five years later, at just 37 years old. There is a memorial statue of him on Dumfries High Street, and you can explore the simple house where he spent his final years, or – perhaps most fitting of all – visit the Globe Inn, his favorite pub, and raise a glass to the great poet, Rabbie Burns.

FURTHER DETAILS

THE BURNS HERITAGE TRAIL
Robert Burns National Heritage Park
Alloway, Ayr; Burns Cottage and visitor center open Oct–Mar: 10am–5pm daily; Apr–Sep: 10am–5:30pm daily.
www.burnsheritagepark.com

Galloway Forest Park
Near Newton Stewart and New Galloway, Dumfries and Galloway; open daily.
www.forestry.gov.uk/gallowayforestpark

Ellisland Farm
6 miles (10 km) north of Dumfries on the A76; open Oct–Mar: 2–5pm Tue–Sat; Apr–Sep: 10am–1pm and 2–5pm Mon–Sat, 2–5pm Sun.
www.ellislandfarm.co.uk

Burns House
Mill Road, Dumfries; open Oct–Mar: 10am–1pm and 2–5pm Tue–Sat; Apr–Sep: 10am–8pm Mon–Sat, 2–5pm Sun.
www.dumfriesmuseum.demon.co.uk

The Globe Inn
High Street, Dumfries; open 10am–11pm Mon–Wed, 10am–midnight Thu–Sun.
www.globeinndumfries.co.uk

WHAT ELSE TO SEE AND DO
Glenkiln Reservoir
A series of monumental sculptures by the artists Henry Moore, Rodin, and Jacob Epstein stand in atmospheric natural settings in the hills and woods surrounding Glenkiln Reservoir, near Shawhead. You can walk or drive along the sculpture trail.
www.visitsouthwestscotland.com

Sweetheart Abbey
The brooding ruins of the last great abbey built in Scotland lie just outside Dumfries. Sweetheart Abbey was named in honor of the undying love of its founder, Lady Dervorgilla, for her husband John Balliol, King of Scotland from 1292 to 1296. She is buried in front of the High Altar with a casket containing his embalmed heart.
www.dumfriesmuseum.demon.co.uk

Below (top to bottom): Burns Monument from the Brig O'Doon in Alloway; walkers at the summit of Craiglee in the Galloway Hills

The ancient woodlands, lochs, and moorland surrounding the Galloway Hills are a haven for wildlife.

Main: Loch Doon, Dumfries and Galloway **Inset:** Red deer stag in the Galloway Hills
Below (left to right): Birthplace of Robert Burns, Alloway; statue of Burns in Dumfries

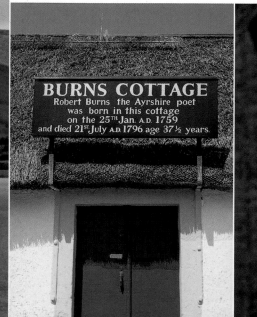

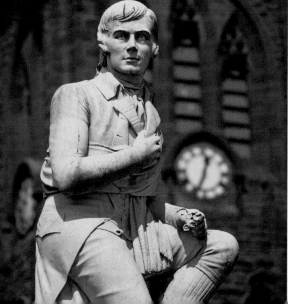

THE ESSENTIALS

GETTING THERE AND AROUND
Aviemore is in north-central Scotland.
The nearest airport is at Inverness,
36 miles (58 km) to the north. Aviemore
is also on the main train route to the
Highlands; trains here from Edinburgh
take 2 hours. Most of the Cairngorms
National Park is only accessible on foot, but
a number of Aviemore-based companies
offer ATV tours, 4WD trips, and pony
trekking on the fringes of the park.

WEATHER
You will encounter freezing temperatures
and must be prepared for sleet, rain, and
potential blizzard conditions, with low to
zero visibility from November until March.
Average daytime temperatures range
from 5 to 43°F (−15 to 6°C), but depend
greatly on altitude and exposure.

ACCOMMODATIONS
Treat Yourself Macdonald Aviemore
Resort, in Aviemore, is made up of four
separate up-market hotels that share
extensive leisure facilities.
www.aviemorehighlandresort.co.uk

On a Budget Aviemore Youth Hostel
in Aviemore offers dormitory bunks and
family rooms (some with private baths).
www.syha.org.uk

EATING OUT
Treat Yourself Aspects, in the Macdonald
Aviemore Resort, offers elegant fine dining
using Scottish foods.
www.macdonaldhotels.co.uk/aviemore

On a Budget The Old Bridge Inn, also
in Aviemore, offers hot soup and an
open fire in a quaint old building.
www.oldbridgeinn.co.uk

PRICE FOR TWO PEOPLE
From $300 a day for accommodations,
food, and leisure activities.

WEBSITE
www.visitaviemore.com

Whiter than White

The wild inhabitants of the Cairngorms have
evolved winter camouflage that allows them to
merge almost invisibly with the snow. The mountain
hare sheds its gray-brown summer coat for pure
white fur to conceal it from birds of prey, such as
the golden eagle. The ptarmigan grouse drops its
mottled summer plumage for snow white feathers.
One of Scotland's wiliest predators, the stoat, also
adopts winter camouflage, or "ermine"; this rich fur
has been prized since medieval times.

Main: Ice-climbing in the Cairngorms
Right (top to bottom): Ski range at Glenshee Ski Centre in Cairnwell; sunset over the Cairngorm mountains

CAIRNGORMS CHALLENGE

Visiting the Cairngorms in winter is like entering a dazzling white universe. This is
the largest wilderness area in Britain – a region of hills, moors, and steep-sided glens
that is home to birds and beasts found nowhere else in the country. Yet the gateways to this
otherworldly kingdom are just a couple of hours away from any of Scotland's major cities.

At the heart of the Cairngorms, 1,970 ft (600 m) above sea level, lies a unique Arctic world
where wildlife such as ptarmigan grouse, mountain hares, and stoats don their pure white
winter coats for concealment against the snow-covered landscapes (*see story box*). This can be
an unforgiving environment, which, in the depths of winter, calls for an array of mountain
survival skills in those who brave it. But if you dare, the Cairngorms National Park offers a
heart-lifting experience unique to this part of the British Isles. Nothing beats the sight of a
mighty golden eagle circling high in a brilliant, frosty blue sky, or the simple excitement of
being the first to break a trail across a pristine expanse of newly fallen snow. If you obey the
easily learned rules of survival, and have the right equipment and a modicum of common

FURTHER DETAILS

WINTER SPORTS IN THE CAIRNGORMS
Cairngorms National Park Authority
www.cairngorms.co.uk

Mountaineering Council of Scotland
The Old Granary, West Mill, Perth; open 9am–5pm
Mon–Fri.
www.mcofs.org.uk

Scotland's National Outdoor Activities Centre
Glenmore Lodge, Glenmore.
www.glenmorelodge.org.uk

British Association of Snowsports Instructors
The Square, Grantown on Spey; open 9am–5pm Mon–Fri.
www.basi.org.uk

Aviemore Sled Dog Rally
Aviemore; held annually in the last week of January.
www.siberianhuskyclub.com/aviemore

WHAT ELSE TO SEE AND DO
G2 Outdoor Centre
Winter survival skills training, snowboarding, skiing,
and other winter sports are offered at this training
center in Aviemore.
www.g2outdoor.co.uk

Glenshee Ski Centre
Based in Cairnwell, 22 miles (35 km) southeast
of Aviemore, the largest ski area in Britain offers
36 runs with an amazing diversity of natural terrain
for all skill levels of skiers and snowboarders.
www.ski-glenshee.co.uk

Rothiemurchus Estate
This private estate in Inverdruie, near Aviemore, offers a
huge number of outdoor activities, including hill-walking,
horse riding, ATV riding, canoeing, and wildlife-watching.
It is possible to stay on the estate's campsite.
www.rothiemurchus.net

Highland Wildlife Park
At this park, in Kincraig near Kingussie, 12 miles (20 km)
south of Aviemore, open-air enclosures house threatened
Highland wildlife, such as otters and wildcats. Also found
here are wolves and Arctic foxes – species that were once
native to the Highlands until they were sadly hunted into
near-extinction – and rather more unlikely guests such
as camels and Amur tigers.
www.highlandwildlifepark.org

Below: Golden eagle landing in snow

sense, an expedition in the hills can be a stroll in the park. At centers like Glenmore Lodge, Scotland's national outdoor training center, expert mountain climbers have passed on their hard-won expertise for more than 60 years, and today you can enroll in a course in one of many mountain sports. While taking a course at Glenmore can be a demanding and grueling learning experience, it can also be great fun, leaving you with an empowering sense of achievement, and skills that will last a lifetime.

With an array of places to stay, eat, drink, and be merry, the vacation village of Aviemore, on the northwest fringes of the national park, is a perfect base, offering a variety of outdoor activities, including skiing and ice- and rock climbing. In January, it hosts the Aviemore Sled Dog Rally, the largest of its kind in Britain, with more than 250 squads and more than 1,000 sled dogs competing. Unlike in Alaska or Canada, where the dogs pull real sleds, heavy snow cannot always be guaranteed in Scotland even at the height of winter – so the dog teams instead haul two-wheeled "sled-carts" over trails where the mud can often be deeper than the snow.

Whether you want to test your limits by learning the toughest of survival skills and taking on the fiercest mountain conditions, or would rather spend your time in the less demanding environs of Aviemore, a winter trip to the Cairngorms will certainly be an adventure.

CHRISTMAS CHEER

B IRMINGHAM'S STYLISHLY REGENERATED downtown comes as a very pleasant surprise to those who don't know it. At its heart lies Victoria Square, an exciting public space watched over by the elegant 19th-century domed Council House, and filled with fountains, weirs, and notable sculptures. Antony Gormley's *Iron Man* attracts visitors, but the locals' favorite is the friendlier *River Goddess* – also known as "the floozie in the Jacuzzi" – by Dhruva Mistry.

From mid-November to December 23, the square plays host to the Frankfurt Christmas Market, which is the largest authentic German winter market outside Germany or Austria, and is full of European delights. This busy festive fair symbolizes Birmingham's partnership with its twin city, and many vendors travel from Germany especially for the occasion. Crowds throng the area well into the evening, soaking up the atmosphere and sampling German delicacies, such as *glühwein* (mulled wine), grilled sausages, pretzels, and beer, accompanied by music from

THE ESSENTIALS

GETTING THERE AND AROUND
Birmingham is in the West Midlands of England, 120 miles (190 km) northwest of London and 95 miles (153 km) south of Manchester. Birmingham International Airport is 14 miles (22 km) east of the city. There are high-speed trains from London Euston, slower services from London Marylebone, and hourly buses from London Victoria. It's possible to walk between the main sites in central Birmingham.

WEATHER
Freezing temperatures are not common in Birmingham until after Christmas, but be prepared for wind, rain, and colder periods, with average daytime temperatures ranging from 36 to 41ºF (3–5ºC).

ACCOMMODATIONS
Treat Yourself Hotel du Vin, on Church Street, is a stylish hotel and bistro located in the Jewellery Quarter, converted from a Victorian hospital.
www.hotelduvin.com/birmingham

On a Budget Premier Inn Birmingham, on Broad Street, is a handily located and cheap downtown hotel.
www.premierinn.com

EATING OUT
Treat Yourself Purnell's, on Cornwall Street, is a fantastic Michelin-starred restaurant serving contemporary cuisine.
www.purnellsrestaurant.com

On a Budget Kushi Balti House, on Moseley Road in the heart of the "Balti Belt," serves "healthier" recipes alongside more traditional South Asian dishes.
www.kushibalti.co.uk

PRICE FOR TWO PEOPLE
Around $300–330 a day for food, accommodations, and admission fees.

WEBSITE
www.visitbirmingham.com

The Workshop of the World

Birmingham specialized in metalworking in the 19th and early 20th centuries, and was renowned as "the workshop of the world." Jewelry is still made today in the Jewellery Quarter; a must-see is the Museum of the Jewellery Quarter, set within the premises of the former jewelry manufacturers Smith and Pepper, and preserved in an antiquated state. To see how the metalworkers themselves lived, you can visit examples of their back-to-back housing, preserved by the National Trust.

Main: German Frankfurt Christmas Market in Victoria Square

Above: *River Goddess* fountain in Victoria Square

Below: Festive gingerbread for sale at a stand at the Christmas Market

the bandstand and a traditional fairground carousel. Among the colorful stalls are displays of traditional handmade toys, Christmas decorations, candles, gingerbread, marzipan, and craft items. Even the "floozie in the Jacuzzi" is lit up like a giant Christmas tree. And as if that were not enough, there's also local crafts and produce on sale at the nearby Christmas Craft Fair.

Central Birmingham offers a host of other attractions, and is surprisingly compact and easy to explore. Close to Victoria Square, the Birmingham City Museum and Art Gallery includes the finest collection of Pre-Raphaelite paintings in the world. Music is also central to city life here, and it's well worth visiting the Symphony Hall, home of the renowned Birmingham Symphony Orchestra. Their state-of-the art concert hall features a stunning auditorium and a 6,000-pipe organ, and is open for events and tours virtually every day.

For children, the nearby National Sea Life Centre has spectacular displays of exotic marine species. Then there are Birmingham's canals – famously outdoing Venice's in extent. A stroll along the canal paths, past converted former warehouses, takes you to Gas Street Basin, now home to a buzzing concentration of bars and cafés too good to resist at the end of the day.

FURTHER DETAILS

BIRMINGHAM

Frankfurt Christmas Market
Victoria Square, Birmingham; open mid-Nov–Dec 23, 10am–9pm daily.
www.birmingham.gov.uk/marketschristmas

Birmingham City Museum and Art Gallery
Chamberlain Square, Birmingham; open 10am–5pm Mon–Sat (from 10:30am Fri), 12:30–5pm Sun; closed Dec 25–26 and Jan 1.
www.bmag.org.uk

Birmingham Symphony Hall
Broad Street, Birmingham; open at varying times for public tours and a full concert program.
www.thsh.co.uk

National Sea Life Centre
The Waters Edge, Brindley Place, Birmingham; open 10am–4pm Mon–Fri, 10am–5pm Sat–Sun.
www.sealifeeurope.com

Museum of the Jewellery Quarter
The Smith and Pepper Building, Vyse Street, Hockley, Birmingham; open 10:30am–4pm Tue–Sat, closed Sun and Mon except Bank Holidays.
www.bmag.org.uk/museum-of-the-jewellery-quarter

Birmingham Back to Backs
Inge Street and Hurst Street, Birmingham; open 10am–5pm Tue–Sat and Bank Holidays, guided tours only (reservations advised); closed Jan.
www.nationaltrust.org.uk

WHAT ELSE TO SEE AND DO

The Bull Ring
Birmingham's commercial center since the Middle Ages, the Bull Ring is now the most-visited shopping complex outside London, and is easily recognizable due to the iconic aluminum-disc-clad Selfridges building. Its latest incarnation was opened in 2003, on the site of the unloved 1960s development.
www.bullring.co.uk

Below (top to bottom): St. Martin's Church and the futuristic Selfridges department store; Symphony Hall auditorium

THE ESSENTIALS

GETTING THERE AND AROUND
Cambridge is in eastern England, 60 miles (96 km) north of London. The nearest international airport is London Stansted, 30 miles (48 km) south of the city and connected to it by bus and train. Once in the city, walking is the easiest way to see the main colleges and museums, as the center is compact and pedestrianized.

WEATHER
Cambridge is in a very flat area of England and winter winds can be bitingly cold, though it only snows occasionally and not usually for long. Average winter daytime temperatures range from 36 to 46°F (2–8°C).

ACCOMMODATIONS
Treat Yourself The Doubletree by Hilton, in Granta Place, is an upscale luxury hotel on the banks of the River Cam, just a stroll from the center of town.
http://doubletree.hilton.co.uk

On a Budget Worth House, on Chesterton Road, a short walk north of the downtown, is a 4-star guesthouse with reasonably priced rooms.
www.worth-house.co.uk

EATING OUT
Treat Yourself Restaurant 22, also on Chesterton Road, is an old city favorite, serving consistently good cuisine with a *prix-fixe* menu.
www.restaurant22.co.uk

On a Budget The Anchor, on Silver Street in the center of town, is a historic and lively riverside pub serving great food.
www.cambridgeanchor.co.uk

PRICE FOR TWO PEOPLE
Around $250 a day for food, accommodations, and admission fees.

WEBSITE
www.visitcambridge.org

Head Boy

The severed head of Oliver Cromwell (1599–1658), the controversial 17th-century politician, is buried in Cambridge at his alma mater, Sidney Sussex College, although its exact location is a secret. Cromwell, who briefly overthrew the English monarchy after the English Civil War (1641–1651), lived in Ely, near Cambridge. After his death he was denounced as a traitor, and his head was displayed at Westminster Hall in London. The head later disappeared, but was eventually found and was reburied in 1960.

Main: King's College and its magnificent Chapel

CAROLS IN THE COLLEGE

T HE UNIVERSITY CITY OF CAMBRIDGE is one of the most beautiful in England. Its lofty spires and clock towers, ornately carved Tudor and Neo-Gothic facades, and colleges with neat courtyards and quadrangles contrast with its low, half-timbered and whitewashed city buildings that house charming shops, pubs, and restaurants. In summer its narrow streets are packed with tourists and there's a steady flotilla of flat-bottomed punts poling along the River Cam. But winter is really the most romantic time to visit this historic city.

This is the season for the finest views of the university along the Backs – the long swaths of lawns and gardens alongside the river behind the colleges. When the trees drop their leaves, the impressive architecture really stands out. Walk from the Backs across graceful arched bridges to explore the colleges and admire their architectural and historical highlights at close hand – Trinity College, which boasts the Tudor-era Great Court and a library designed by the great architect Sir Christopher Wren; Magdalene College, whose library contains Samuel Pepys's famous diary; and St. John's College with its picturesque Bridge of Sighs.

FURTHER DETAILS

CAMBRIDGE

College Tours
Guided tours of the colleges can be booked through the Visitor Information Centre, Wheeler Street, Cambridge; open 10am–5:30pm Mon–Fri, 10am–5pm Sat; also May–Sep: 11am–3pm Sun and Bank Holidays.

Trinity College
Trinity Street, Cambridge.
www.trin.cam.ac.uk

Magdalene College
Magdalene Street, Cambridge.
www.magd.cam.ac.uk

St. John's College
St. John's Street, Cambridge.
www.joh.cam.ac.uk

King's College Chapel
King's Parade, Cambridge.
www.kings.cam.ac.uk

Art and Craft Market
All Saints Garden, Trinity Street, Cambridge; open Jan–Nov: 10:30am–4:30pm Sat; Dec: 10:30am–4:30pm Wed–Sat.
www.cambridge-art-craft.co.uk

Cambridge Market
Market Hill, Cambridge. This daily market sells a mixture of goods Mon–Sat, and becomes a farmers' market on Sun.

Sidney Sussex College
Sidney Street, Cambridge.
www.sid.cam.ac.uk

WHAT ELSE TO SEE AND DO

Great St. Mary's
This Gothic building (the "university church") in Market Square has grand views from its 15th-century tower.
www.gsm.cam.ac.uk

Fitzwilliam Museum
The city's top museum, in Trumpington Street, contains a vast collection of European paintings, sculptures, drawings, and prints, as well as Egyptian and Greek antiquities, illuminated manuscripts, and Asian art and ceramics.
www.fitzmuseum.cam.ac.uk

Below: Art and Craft Market in All Saints Garden

The star attraction is undoubtedly King's College Chapel – a late-Gothic masterpiece with magnificent fan-vaulting and exquisite stained-glass windows.

The star attraction is undoubtedly King's College Chapel – a late-Gothic masterpiece with magnificent fan-vaulting and exquisite stained-glass windows. A special carol service, "A Festival in Nine Lessons and Carols," is performed here by the King's College choir on Christmas Eve. Wrap up warm and get in line before 9am if you hope to get a seat for the 3pm service; it's worth the long wait to hear traditional carols sung in such glorious surroundings.

Cambridge is also a delightful place to do your Christmas shopping. Visit the Art and Craft Market in All Saints Garden, where you can purchase quality gifts directly from the artists. Then browse the outdoor market, on Market Hill, which features everything from fashion to gourmet foodstuffs. A ramble down Cambridge's cobbled passages will lead you to quirky boutiques, cozy cafés, and great secondhand bookstores. Or take a break from shopping by visiting one of the city's many museums or simply unwinding in one of its quaint old pubs.

More Great Ideas for **Winter**

Rock of Cashel in Tipperary

Slavonian grebe at Dungeness

Cornish fishing village of Mousehole

ROCK OF CASHEL SOUTHERN IRELAND
A winter visit to this ancient ecclesiastical stronghold in Tipperary is wonderfully atmospheric. It was once the seat of the ancient Kings of Munster, although most of the surviving buildings date from the 12th and 13th centuries. It flourished for centuries until Oliver Cromwell laid siege in 1647 and killed thousands, and it was eventually abandoned in the 18th century. Cormac's Chapel is the best preserved of the ruins, but St. Patrick's Cathedral is the Rock's heart.
www.cashel.ie

DUNGENESS KENT
Bleak, weird, and strangely beautiful, Dungeness is the largest shingle expanse in Europe. The eerie landscape is interrupted by a shack "village," two nuclear power stations, two lighthouses, a miniature railroad, and fishing boats. The RSPB nature reserve here is a magnet for migrating birds, such as grebe, smew, and bittern. Geese, swans, and wigeons also visit in winter, as do several types of owls. Winter walks here will help blow the cobwebs away.
www.rspb.org.uk

MOUSEHOLE SOUTHWEST ENGLAND
Mousehole (pronounced "Mowzel") is an unspoiled coastal village looking out toward St. Michael's Mount and Mounts Bay. It was the home of Dolly Pentreath, the last Cornish-language speaker, who died 200 years ago. On December 23 the village celebrates "Tom Bawcock's Eve" with songs and a huge "stargazey" fish pie, commemorating a local fisherman whose fishing prowess once saved the village from starvation. The Christmas harbor lights are spectacular.
www.cornishlight.co.uk

CORFE CASTLE SOUTHWEST ENGLAND
The magnificent windswept ruins of 1,000-year-old Corfe Castle offer breathtaking views across the Isle of Purbeck. Silhouetted against a bare winter sky, the castle dominates Corfe village as it has done for centuries. It is most famous as the home of Lady Bankes, who bravely defended the castle from a siege during the Civil War. In late winter, the castle's renowned ravens can be seen roosting. Legend says that when the birds leave, the castle suffers ill fortune.
www.nationaltrust.org.uk

CHEVIOT HILLS
NORTHEAST ENGLAND
An isolated and romantic region of rounded hills and valleys, the Cheviot Hills are great walking country, with hundreds of ancient tracks and the chance to see timid otters.
www.cheviotwalks.co.uk

ROBIN HOOD'S BAY NORTHEAST ENGLAND
This pretty village consists of a jumble of cottages clinging to a cliff. A maze of narrow cobbled alleyways and secret passages summons up images of smugglers, and on the sandy and rocky beach below, fossil hunters search for ammonite treasures. The North Sea Trail guides walkers along the beautiful coastline. In December, there's a Victorian Weekend with carol singing, street entertainment, and 19th-century-style food and drink.
www.robin-hoods-bay.co.uk

WEST STOW VILLAGE
EASTERN ENGLAND
Set on an Anglo-Saxon site in a large country park, West Stow is a reconstruction of an Anglo-Saxon village. Living history events in winter bring the village to life.
www.oldcity.org.uk

CAITHNESS HIGHLANDS AND ISLANDS
A landscape of massive cliffs, tiny islands, bleak moorland, and sandy beaches, Caithness is as far north as you can get on mainland Britain. Rich in sea birds and rare plants, it feels like a world apart. In the winter months, there's an extra attraction – the Northern Lights, an extraordinary phenomenon that occurs when solar flares collide with Earth's magnetic field, producing a seemingly supernatural light show. One of the best places to view them is at Dunnett Head.
www.scotland-inverness.co.uk/caithness

ENNIS
SOUTHERN IRELAND
The charming county town of Clare has a reputation as "the boutique capital of Ireland," and its narrow streets provide delightful shopping – just the place for winter retail therapy.
www.visitennis.ie

PORTHDINLLAEN
NORTH WALES
This tiny, idyllic village, which sits beside a golden beach, has magnificent walks that promise beautiful views, providing you with the perfect backdrop for a romantic Valentine's day.
www.walesdirectory.co.uk

LLANDUDNO PIER NORTH WALES
This Y-shaped Victorian masterpiece is the longest pier in Wales. It was originally built in 1858, at a fraction of its present size, but storms damaged the structure the following year. A longer pier, measuring 1,234 ft (376 m), opened in 1877. Much of the original structure, including the promenade deck, the elaborate ironwork and the pavilion, still remains, and is classed as a Grade-II listed building. Visit for a reminder of the glory days of the seaside.
www.the-pier.co.uk

STOURHEAD GARDENS SOUTHWEST ENGLAND
Visiting Stourhead is like stepping into an 18th-century painting. Frosted ground, snowdrops, rhododendrons, and a tranquil lake make the gardens here a magical destination for winter visitors. Stourhead was laid out in the 1740s by Henry Hoare, who inherited the house and gardens. The fantastical landscape is beautifully choreographed to make the most of the splendid views across the lake to classical Italianate temples, grottoes, statues, and bridges.
www.nationaltrust.org.uk

CHESTER
NORTHWEST ENGLAND
Dating from Roman times, Chester is best seen by walking around the ancient city walls. The city's two-storey shopping streets, the Rows, lie inside the walls.
www.chester360.co.uk

See also pp166–7, 170–71, 186–7, 190–91, 196–7.

See also pp168–9, 174–5, 180–81, 188–9.

See also pp182–3, 194–5.

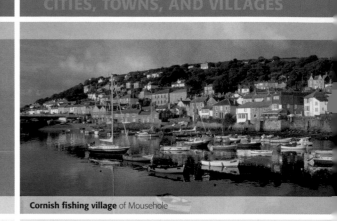

Mountain biking in the Dyfi Forest

Chinese dragon performance at London's Chinese New Year

Mad Maldon Mud Race

MOUNTAIN BIKING CENTRAL WALES
Machynlleth, on the southern side of Snowdonia, is the old capital of Wales, where Prince Owain Glyndwr held the first Welsh parliament. Today, it is a mountain-biking center, where enthusiasts can tackle a 9-mile (15-km) circuit of trails in the nearby Dyfi Forest. Gravity-defying maneuvers are required to tackle long descents and the "eye of the needle" jump, where cyclists have to land between two trees. "Design-your-own" routes are also available.
www.mbwales.com/machynlleth

CHINESE NEW YEAR SOUTHEAST ENGLAND
More than 50,000 people turn out to enjoy London's Chinese New Year, which falls between January 21 and February 21. It starts with a grand parade that travels from Trafalgar Square along the Strand to Leicester Square. This is superb family entertainment, with dragon and lion dances, martial arts displays, opera, and Chinese fireworks, and firecrackers. At dusk revellers flock to the food stalls in a decorated Chinatown, for more dancing and celebration.
www.chinatownchinese.co.uk

ROYAL WELSH WINTER FAIR
CENTRAL WALES
Livestock, poultry, and horses vie for attention with art and crafts at this popular fair at the South Glamorgan Hall in late November to early December.
www.rwas.co.uk

COTSWOLD WILDLIFE PARK
SOUTHEAST ENGLAND
Adults can become a keeper for a day at this wildlife park, where creatures including penguins, meerkats, and big cats need feeding and cleaning.
www.cotswoldwildlifepark.co.uk

TIME OF GIFTS
SOUTHWEST ENGLAND
The Eden Project's "Time of Gifts" Christmas event is a winter wonderland. Ice-skating discos, music, decorated trees, markets, and choirs are just some of the attractions.
www.edenproject.net

SIX NATIONS RUGBY SOUTH WALES
Catch some of the Six Nations rugby matches in Cardiff's Millennium Stadium in February; the competing teams are England, Scotland, Ireland, Wales, France, and Italy.
www.millenniumstadium.com

MAD MALDON MUD RACE EASTERN ENGLAND
Wet, messy, and sticky, this is a typically eccentric English event involving local men and women playing dirty. Competitors in fancy dress make a mad dash at low tide across the thick muddy bed of the River Blackwater, in Essex, in late December or early January to raise money for charities. It is a hugely popular piece of post-Christmas madness, which attracts up to 10,000 people and is a brilliant day out with the kids.
www.maldonmudrace.com

CURLING CENTRAL SCOTLAND
British interest in the sport of curling soared after the British team won a gold medal in the 2002 Winter Olympics, and courses on how to play this ancient game are now held at a number of venues in Scotland. An outside curling pond at the world's oldest curling center in Kilsyth is often used on colder days, but it's more likely that courses are held inside at the Dewar's Centre in Perth, where lessons are available on an eight-lane ice rink from the Olympic curling coach.
www.curlingscotland.com

CASTLE HOWARD NORTHEAST ENGLAND
Throughout most of December, Castle Howard, in North Yorkshire, opens from its winter break to show off in full Christmas regalia. The Great Hall and Long Gallery are decorated with garlands, roaring fires, and giant Christmas trees dressed with thousands of baubles, and are filled with candlelight. Musical performances take place daily, and Santa Claus welcomes visitors to his grotto, while in the stable courtyard, local and Christmas markets are held on set days.
www.castlehoward.co.uk

JORVIK VIKING FESTIVAL NORTHEAST ENGLAND
Around 1,000 years ago, York – then known as Jorvik – was the Vikings' capital in Britain. Each year, the city's Norse heritage is celebrated at this five-day festival, which takes over the streets in February and turns the city into a center of living history, as hundreds of "Vikings" invade for battle drills, training, and reenactments. There are also river events, saga-telling, lessons in sword-play, a food market, and Viking-era crafts and songs. There's even a "best beard" competition.
www.yorkfestivals.com

STORM-WATCHING SOUTHWEST ENGLAND
A relatively new tourist phenomenon, winter storm-watching is quickly catching on, especially along Cornwall's north coast. Watching the crashing waves, which have built up momentum over 3,000 miles (5,000 km) of open ocean, from cliffs above the wild sea, or at a safe distance on a beach, is always exciting and awe-inspiring. You can also watch experienced surfers catch the tail end of the storms on Newquay's beaches, such as Porthtowan *(see also pp184–5)*.
www.newquayguide.co.uk

SANTA EXPRESS WEST MIDLANDS
The Severn Valley Railway runs Christmas specials for youngsters in December. The vintage engines pull their packed carriages for a distance of 16 miles (26 km) through the wintry countryside, from Kidderminster in Worcestershire to Bridgnorth in Shropshire. The route, punctuated by several sleepy country stations, follows the picturesque River Severn. Santa Claus himself tours the carriages, greeting families and handing out presents to children.
www.svr.co.uk

UP HELLY AA
HIGHLANDS AND ISLANDS
The ingredients for this festival go back 12 centuries. Crowds flock to watch the burning of a Viking galley made by the men of Lerwick, then celebrate by dancing until dawn.
www.uphellyaa.org

PANCAKE RACE
SOUTHEAST ENGLAND
Competitors in this famous 500-year-old Shrove Tuesday pancake race must be local housewives, and dressed accordingly in skirts, aprons, and headgear.
www.olneytowncouncil.co.uk

See also pp178–9, 184–5, 192–3.

See also pp164–5, 172–3.

See also pp176–7.

Stornoway
Wick

Inverness
HIGHLANDS AND ISLANDS
Aberdeen

Fort William

Dundee
CENTRAL SCOTLAND

Edinburgh
Glasgow
SOUTHERN SCOTLAND

Dumfries

Derry
NORTHERN IRELAND
Bangor
Belfast
Newcastle upon Tyne
Sunderland
Lisburn
NORTHWEST ENGLAND
Middlesbrough
Armagh
NORTHEAST ENGLAND

Sligo
York
WESTERN IRELAND
Blackpool
Leeds
Hull
Drogheda
Blackburn
Athlone
Manchester
Galway
Liverpool
Sheffield
Dublin
Caernarfon
Llandudno
EAST MIDLANDS
EASTERN IRELAND
Stoke-on-Trent
Derby
Nottingham
NORTH WALES
Carlow
Norwich
WEST MIDLANDS
Limerick
Kilkenny
Peterborough
Llandrindod Wells
Birmingham
Coventry
Cambridge
SOUTHERN IRELAND
Waterford
CENTRAL WALES
Milton Keynes
EASTERN ENGLAND
Ipswich
Cork
Luton
Swansea
Newport
LONDON
SOUTH WALES
Swindon
London
Cardiff
Bristol
Maidstone
SOUTHEAST ENGLAND
SOUTHWEST ENGLAND
Southampton
Brighton
Exeter
Portsmouth
Bournemouth

Plymouth

REGIONAL DIRECTORY

THIS DIRECTORY offers further suggestions for travel within Great Britain and Ireland in a concise and easy-to-use way. The five nations are divided into 18 regions (*see facing page*), and for each region, entries are listed for eight types of activities: Local Food, Farmers' Markets, Pubs and Bars, Places to Stay, Festivals and Events, Museums and Galleries, Things to Do With Kids, and Spas and Health Resorts. Entries are located on detailed regional maps and include essential practical information. Note that we have not always given specific opening times for pubs that are open throughout the day; these pubs, "open daily," are generally open from around 11am to 11pm, with slightly shorter hours on Sundays to comply with licensing laws.

Above: Tower Bridge in London

HIGHLANDS AND ISLANDS, SCOTLAND

LOCAL FOOD

The Bay Owl ⑤
Fresh crab, lobster, and shellfish, all landed at nearby Dunbeath Harbour, are menu mainstays, with snacks and carry-outs too. *Dunbeath, Morven, Highland; tel: 01593 731356; open noon–2:30pm and 5–8pm Mon–Fri, noon–3pm and 5–8:30pm Sat, 12:30–3pm and 5–7:30pm Sun. www.thebayowl.net*

The River House Restaurant ⑭
Fine riverside restaurant with stunning views, serving local and seasonal cuisine. *1 Greig Street, Inverness; tel: 01463 222033; open noon–2:30pm and 5:30–9:30pm Tue–Sat. www.riverhouseinverness.co.uk*

The Stage Door ㉔
Scottish and European cuisine in a classy restaurant, close to His Majesty's Theatre. *26 North Silver Street, Aberdeen; tel: 01224 642111; open 5pm–late Mon–Sat. www.pbdevco.com*

Crannog at the Waterfront ㊵
Superb seafood on the menu here, including locally caught lobster and crab. *Town Pier, Fort William, Highland; tel: 01397 705589; open noon–2:30pm and 6–9pm daily. www.oceanandoak.co.uk*

Kinloch Lodge ㊻
The restaurant of a country hotel run by island aristocracy, serving delicious pies. *Sleat, Isle of Skye, Highland; tel: 01471 833333; open 8:30–9:30am, noon–2:30pm and 6:30–9:30pm daily. www.kinloch-lodge.co.uk*

The Seafood Restaurant ㊲
Solid Scottish home cooking, with an emphasis on locally caught seafood. *Plockton Station, Plockton, Highland; tel: 01599 544423. www.theseafoodrestaurant.com*

The Thai Café ㊾
Local seafood prepared with true Thai expertise in the Hebrides. *Church Street, Stornoway, Lewis, Outer Hebrides; tel: 01851 701127; open noon–3pm and 5pm–late Mon–Sat.*

The Creel Restaurant With Rooms ④
Much acclaimed for grills, roasts, and seafood, and a favorite with locals; three guest rooms are available. *St. Margaret's Hope, South Ronaldsay, Orkney; tel: 01856 831311; open Easter–mid-Oct: 7pm–late Wed–Sun. www.thecreel.co.uk*

Boath House ⑱
Acclaimed restaurant in a small country-house hotel, serving locally sourced seafood, game, and lamb. *Auldearn, Nairn, Highland; tel: 01667 454896; open 8:30–9:45am, 12:30–1:15pm and 7pm–late daily. www.boath-house.com*

The Bakehouse ⑲
Restaurant at the Findhorn Community eco-center, serving home-grown organic produce and local meats and fish. *Findhorn, nr Forres, Morayshire; tel: 01309 691826; open 10am–5pm Sun–Fri, 9am–5pm Sat. www.findhorn.org*

The Creel Inn ㉖
Clifftop gastropub with stunning sea views from Scotland's beautiful northeast coastline, offering a seafood menu that includes locally caught lobster. *Catterline, nr Stonehaven, Aberdeenshire; tel: 01569 750254; open noon–3pm and 6–11pm Mon–Thu, noon–3pm and 5pm–midnight Fri–Sat, noon–11pm Sun. www.thecreelinn.co.uk*

Eleven Restaurant ㊾
The restaurant of the Caladh Inn Hotel; a choice of carvery buffet, à la carte grill, and seafood menu. *Caladh Inn Hotel, James Street, Stornoway, Lewis, Outer Hebrides; tel: 01851 702740; open noon–3pm and 5–9pm Mon–Sat, noon–4pm and 5–9pm Sun. www.caladhinn.co.uk*

Riverside Bistro ㉒
Café-restaurant serving homemade pies and cakes by day and local lamb, game, venison, and seafood in the evening. *Lochinver, Highland; tel: 01571 844356; open Apr–Oct: 10am–8pm Mon–Sat, 10am–5pm Sun; Nov–Mar: 10am–5pm Mon–Sat.*

FARMERS' MARKETS

Dingwall Farmers' Market ⑧
Meats and poultry, baked goods, fresh fruit and vegetables, as well as pottery. *High Street, Dingwall, Highland; tel: 01349 866148; second Sat of every month, 9am–2:30pm. www.dingwall.org.uk*

Inverness Farmers' Market ⑭
Largest farmers' market in the Highlands, with a huge range of local produce. *Eastgate Precinct, High Street, Inverness, tel: 01309 651206; Feb–Jun and Oct–Nov: first Sat of every month; Jul–Sep and Dec: first and third Sat of every month, 8:30am–3pm.*

Lochaber Farmers' Market ㊱
Local arts and crafts, cheeses, seafood, pickles, preserves, pies, and cakes. *Lochaber Rural Complex, Torlundy, Highland; tel: 01397 701039; third Sat of every month, 9:30am–4:30pm. www.lochaberlarder.co.uk*

PUBS AND BARS

The Cawdor Tavern ⑰
Traditional country pub serving meals made from fresh local produce in the bar and in the à la carte restaurant. *Cawdor, nr Nairn, Morayshire; tel: 01667 404777; open daily.*

The Ship Inn ㉗
Authentic alehouse, the social hub of a thriving community of lobster-fishers. *The Square, Johnshaven, Aberdeenshire; tel: 01561 362257; open daily.*

The Clachaig Inn ㉟
Cheerful, busy pub and B&B in the legendary "Glen of Weeping." *Glencoe, Highland; tel: 01855 811252; open daily. www.clachaig.com*

Badachro Inn ㊴
Remote seaside pub in spectacular scenery, with a good menu, wine list, and choice of ales and whiskeys. *Badachro, nr Gairloch, Highland; tel: 01445 741255; open daily (from 4:30pm weekdays Jan–Mar). www.badachroinn.com*

King's House Hotel Bar ㉞
Strategically perched between the wilds of Rannoch Moor and the slopes of Glencoe; popular with walkers and climbers. *Glencoe, Highland; tel: 01855 851259; open daily. www.kingy.com*

The Lock Inn ㊲
Waterside pub on the bank of the Caledonian Canal, not far from the southwest end of Loch Ness. *Fort Augustus, Highland; tel: 01320 366302; open daily.*

Castlebay Bar ㊹
It's worth journeying to tiny Barra to spend an evening in this traditional island tavern. *Castlebay, Barra, Outer Hebrides; tel: 01871 810223; open daily. www.castlebayhotel.com*

The Old Forge ㊺
Claims be "the remotest pub in mainland Britain," with real ales and decent food. *Inverie, Knoydart, Highland; tel: 01687 462267; open daily. www.theoldforge.co.uk*

Seumas Bar ㊼
At the foot of the Black Cuillin ridge, this cozy hotel pub has its own microbrewery, the Cuillin Brewery, next door. *Loch Sligachan, Isle of Skye, Highland; tel: 01478 650204; open daily. www.sligachan.co.uk*

The Seaforth ㊽
Pub and brasserie offering more than 100 malt whiskeys as well as solid pub grub. *Quay Street (corner of Shore Street), Ullapool, Highland; tel: 01854 612122; open daily. www.theseaforth.com*

The Old Inn ㊵
Classic old-style Highland pub with traditional music in summer. *Old Bridge, Gairloch, Highland; tel: 01445 712006; open daily. www.theoldinn.net*

Kylesku Hotel Bar ㊽
A cozy bar in a remote, small hotel, set in some of the best walking territory in Britain. *Kylesku, by Lairg, Highland; tel: 01971 502231; open daily. www.kyleskuhotel.co.uk*

Marine Hotel ㉕
Award-winning tavern with rooms by the harbourside that serves Scottish real ales and tasty European imports. There is a gastropub restaurant upstairs that serves good Highland cuisine.
Shorehead, nr Stonehaven, Aberdeenshire; tel: 01569 762155; open daily. www.marinehotelstonehaven.co.uk

PLACES TO STAY

Aberdeen Youth Hostel ㉔
Located within a historic building, this hostel is close to the center of the city, and offers affordable private *en-suite* and family rooms as well as dormitory bunks.
8 Queen's Road, Aberdeen; tel: 01224 646988. www.syha.org.uk

Aberdeen Douglas Hotel ㉔
Comfortable, affordable hotel in the city's center with all the usual 3-star amenities.
43–45 Market Street, Aberdeen; tel: 01224 582255. www.aberdeendouglas.com

Rocpool Reserve ⑭
Stylish boutique hotel in the Highlands, with a bar and restaurant and 11 rooms.
14 Culduthel Road, Inverness; tel: 01463 240089. www.rocpool.com

Royal Hotel ㊾
Well-priced hotel in a central location with a bar serving alcohol on Sundays, which is rare in the town of Stornaway.
Stornoway, Lewis, Outer Hebrides; tel: 01851 702109. www.royalstornoway.co.uk

Ayre Hotel ①
Highly rated family-run Orkney hotel on the Kirkwall quayside; affordable as well as comfortable.
Kirkwall, Orkney; tel: 01856 873001. www.ayrehotel.co.uk

Eilean Iarmain ㊻
Cozy and relaxing island hostelry with breathtaking surroundings and spectacular views across the Knoydart Hills.
Sleat, Isle of Skye, Highland; tel: 01471 833332. www.eilean-iarmain.co.uk

Plockton Hotel ㊿
Pretty hotel and excellent village pub, with good-value rooms in the cottage annex.
Shore Street, Plockton, Highland; tel: 01599 544274. www.plocktonhotel.com

HIGHLANDS AND ISLANDS

Woodwick House ③
It's worth staying in this affordable country-house hotel for the views out to sea, but the food is tasty too.
Evie, Orkney; tel: 01856 751330.
www.woodwickhouse.co.uk

Carbisdale Castle Youth Hostel ⑥
Surely the world's grandest youth hostel, in a 19th-century castle with Classical statues in the foyer and portraits on the walls.
Culrain, nr Bonar Bridge, Highland;
tel: 0870 004 1109. www.carbisdale.org

Bunchrew House ⑪
Mansion house overlooking the waters of the Beauly Firth, and popular for weddings.
Bunchrew, Inverness; tel: 01463 234917.
www.bunchrew-inverness.co.uk

Culloden House ⑮
Ancestral home of the lairds of Culloden; now an opulent country-house hotel with a heated pool, huge Georgian rooms, and luxury suites.
Culloden, Inverness; tel: 01463 790461.
www.cullodenhouse.co.uk

The Station Hotel ㉑
Comfortable, small, family-run hotel in a tranquil fishing village on the south shore of the Moray Firth.
Portsoy, Aberdeenshire; tel: 01261 842237. www.stationhotelportsoy.co.uk

Linnhe Lochside Holidays ㉟
Luxury vacation chalets, set beside Loch Eil and surrounded by woodland.
Carpach, nr Fort William, Highland;
tel: 01397 772376.
www.linnhe-lochside-holidays.co.uk

The Three Chimneys ㊾
Delightful, reasonably priced hotel in a handy location on Skye.
Colbost, Isle of Skye, Highland; tel:
01470 511258. www.threechimneys.co.uk

Beaton's Croft House ㊿
A unique place to stay: from the outside, a traditional thatched cottage, but within, the National Trust for Scotland has introduced modern amenities.
Bornesketaig, nr Uig, Isle of Skye, Highland;
tel: 0131 243 9331. www.ntsholidays.com

The Torridon & Torridon Inn ㊳
Two hotels in one amid some spectacular Highland scenery. The Inn is cheaper, the nearby Torridon more luxurious.
Kinlochewe, Torridon, Highland; tel: 01445 791242. www.lochtorridonhotel.com

Pool House Hotel ㊲
Country-house hotel with seven gorgeous suites, ornamental gardens, a super restaurant, and a lovely location.
Poolewe, Highland; tel: 01445 781272.
www.poolhousehotel.com

Stoer Head Lighthouse ㊷
Two vacation apartments in a historic lighthouse-keeper's cottage.
Stoer Head, nr Lochinver, Highland;
tel: 0131 243 9331. www.ntsholidays.com

Altnaharra Hotel ㊺
One of the classic Scottish fishing hotels, with some of the most famous trout waters in the Highlands nearby.
Altnaharra, Highland; tel: 01549 411222.
www.altnaharra.com

FESTIVALS AND EVENTS

St. Magnus Festival ①
Orkney's 12th-century cathedral is the hub of this five-day midsummer festival of classical music and the arts, which often features symphony orchestras.
Kirkwall, Orkney; tel: 01856 871445;
mid-Jun. www.stmagnusfestival.com

Rockness ⑬
The biggest rock, pop, and dance weekend in the Highlands, located on the shores of Loch Ness and attracting top performers.
Dores Road, Dores, Loch Ness, Highland;
tel: 0131 220 3234; Jun.
www.rockness.co.uk

Tulloch Inverness Highland Games ⑭
Highland dancers, pipe bands, clan gatherings, and strong-man events, such as tossing the caber, attract crowds to this popular day of games in the Highlands.
Bught Park, Inverness; tel: 01463 663823;
Jul. www.invernesshighlandgames.com

Aberdeen's Winter Festival ㉔
A stunning fireworks display kicks off eight weeks of events culminating in Aberdeen's Hogmanay Street Party on New Year's Eve.
Various venues, Aberdeen; tel: 01224 523444; early Nov–Dec 31.
www.aberdeencity.gov.uk

Aberdeen International Jazz Festival ㉔
Two-week festival launched in 2003 and now a major event attracting top performers from all over the world.
Various venues, Aberdeen; tel: 01224 619769; Sep. www.jazzaberdeen.com

Doric Festival ㉔
This two-week-long festival celebrates the rich, broad Doric dialect, as well as Doric music and literature.
Various venues, Aberdeen and throughout Aberdeenshire; tel: 01771 653320; late Sep–mid Oct.
www.thedoricfestival.com

Stonehaven Fire Festival ㉕
Breathtaking event where marchers parade through the streets swinging giant balls of blazing tar before hurling them into the harbor on the stroke of midnight.
Stonehaven, Aberdeenshire; tel: 01569 767200; New Year's Eve (31 Dec).
www.stonehavenfireballs.co.uk

Johnshaven Fish Festival ㉗
A pipe-band parade, live music, street stands, fresh seafood, and a dramatic cross-harbor raft race are highlights of this two-day village festival.
Johnshaven, Aberdeenshire; tel: 01561 361969; first or second weekend in Aug.
www.johnshaven.com

Above: Up Helly Aa festival in Lerwick, Shetland

Royal Braemar Gathering ㉘
The most renowned "Highland" gathering attracts many visitors, including members of the British Royal family *(see pp118–9).*
Braemar Royal Highland Society, Braemar, Aberdeenshire; tel: 01339 741098; first Sat in Sep. www.braemargathering.org

Up Helly Aa ㊻
Torch-lit street procession by costumed "Vikings" culminates in a huge boat-burning bonfire and a night of drinking and dancing *(see pp168–169).*
Lerwick, Shetland; tel: 01595 693434;
last Tue in Jan. www.uphellyaa.org

MUSEUMS AND GALLERIES

Inverness Museum and Art Gallery ⑭
A fine array of clan tartans, silver, jewelry, claymores, dirks, and pistols, as well as traditional Highland dress.
Castle Wynd, Inverness; tel: 01463 237114; open 9am–5pm Mon–Sat.
http://inverness.highland.museum

Aberdeen Maritime Museum ㉔
Museum telling the story of Aberdeen's seaport, from the early days of the whaling industry to its decline in the 1980s.
Shiprow, Aberdeen; tel: 01224 337700; open 10am–5pm Tue–Sat, noon–3pm Sun. www.aberdeenships.com

Aberdeen Art Gallery ㉔
Varied collection of arts and crafts that includes an important portrait exhibition and extensive archaeological displays.
Schoolhill, Aberdeen; tel: 01224 523700; open 10am–5pm Mon–Sat, 2–5pm Sun. www.aagm.co.uk

Museum of Scottish Lighthouses ㉒
Many steps lead to the balcony of this historic lighthouse on the Moray Firth; it houses an extensive collection of glass lenses and lighting technology.
Kinnaird Head, Fraserburgh, Aberdeenshire; tel: 01346 511022; open 9am–5pm daily.
www.lighthousemuseum.org.uk

Highland Folk Museum ㉜
The Kingussie section of this open-air museum comprises farming equipment, traditional costumes, musical instruments, and more, while the Newtonmore annex contains a whole working farm township.
Newtonmore and Kingussie, Highland; tel: 01540 661307; open Apr–Aug: 10:30am–5:30pm daily; Sep: 11am–4:30pm daily; Oct: 11am–4:30pm Mon–Fri. www.highlandfolkmuseum.com

West Highland Museum ㊵
The best museum for anyone interested in the history of the Highland clans and the Jacobite cause.
Cameron Square, Fort William, Highland; tel: 01397 702169; open 10am–4pm Mon–Sat.
www.westhighlandmuseum.org.uk

Ullapool Museum and Visitor Centre ㊽
Museum highlighting the glory years of the local herring fishing industry and Ullapool's part in the great Highland emigrations of the 19th century.
West Argyle Street, Ullapool, Highland; tel: 01854 612987; open Apr–Oct: 10am–5pm Mon–Sat.
www.ullapoolmuseum.co.uk

Above: Pair of rare Amur tigers at the Highland Wildlife Park

Cromarty Courthouse Museum ⑦
Lifelike animatronic figures re-create the history of this village community.
Church Street, Cromarty, Highland; tel: 01381 600148; open Apr–Sep: 10am–5pm daily; Oct–Mar: 10am–4pm daily. www.cromarty-courthouse.org.uk

Regimental Museum of the Queen's Own Highlanders ⑯
Massive fortress built in 1769 to repel the French and the Highland clans, housing a collection of military paraphernalia.
Fort George, nr Inverness, Highland; tel: 01667 460232; open Apr–Sep: 9:30am–5:30pm daily; Oct–Mar: 9:30am–4:30pm daily. www.historic-scotland.gov.uk

Clan Cameron Museum ㊳
Museum painting a picture of Clan Cameron's support for the Jacobites and the history of the Cameron Highlanders.
Achnacarry, Spean Bridge, nr Fort William, Highland; tel: 01397 712090; open 1:30–5pm daily (Jul and Aug: 11am–5pm daily). www.clan-cameron.org

Glenfinnan Station Museum ㊶
The story of the famous West Highland Line, Britain's most spectacular railroad.
Glenfinnan Station, Glenfinnan, Highland; tel: 01397 722300; open Jun–Sep: 9:30am–4:30pm daily. www.glenfinnanstationmuseum.co.uk

Skye Museum of Island Life ㊽
Cottage-based museum that offers an entertaining re-creation of the lives of 19th-century crofter families.
Kilmuir, Isle of Skye, Highland; tel: 01490 522206; open Easter–Oct: 9:30am–5pm Mon–Sat. www.skyemuseum.co.uk

The Pier Art Centre ②
Work by contemporary artists, including Barbara Hepworth and Naum Gaba.
Stromness, Orkney; tel: 01856 850289; open 10:30am–5pm Mon–Sat. www.pierartscentre.com

Gairloch Heritage Museum (56)
Re-creation of village life in Gairloch, with the schoolhouse, village shop, and dairy.
Achtercairn, Gairloch, Highland; tel: 01445 712787; open Apr–Sep: 10am–5pm Mon–Sat; Oct: 10am–1:30pm Mon–Fri. www.gairlochheritagemuseum.org.uk

The Black House Village & Museum (60)
Remarkable re-created hamlet, comprising the thatched cottages the islanders lived in well into the 20th century.
Gearrannan, Lewis, Outer Hebrides; tel: 01851 643416; open Apr–Sep: 9:30am–5:30pm Mon–Sat.

THINGS TO DO WITH KIDS

Loch Ness Original Visitor Centre ⑫
Fun-filled activity center that reveals the stories behind the Loch Ness "monster."
Drumnadrochit, Loch Ness, Highland; tel: 01456 450342; open Nov–May: 9am–5pm daily; Jun–Aug: 9am–10pm daily; Sep–Oct: 9am–8pm daily. www.lochness-centre.com

Highland Wildlife Park ㉛
Wolves, bison, lynx, and other creatures that once roamed the Highlands can be seen in this excellent open-air zoo.
Kincraig, nr Kingussie, Highland; tel: 01540 651270; open Apr–Jun and Sep–Oct: 10am–5pm daily; Jul–Aug: 10am–6pm daily; Nov–Mar: 10am–4pm daily. www.highlandwildlifepark.org

Highland Museum of Childhood ⑨
Amusing collection of toys, games, and dolls from bygone times in a quaint old train station building.
The Old Station, Strathpeffer, Highland; tel: 01997 421031; open Apr–Oct: 10am–5pm Mon–Sat, 2–5pm Sun. www.highlandmuseumofchildhood.org.uk

North Kessock Dolphin and Seal Centre ⑩
Seals and dolphins can sometimes be seen from the shore here, and there are daily dolphin-spotting cruises too.
North Kessock, nr Inverness, Highland; tel: 01463 731866; open Jun–Sep: 9:30am–4:30pm daily. www.wdcs.org.uk

Archaeolink Prehistory Park ㉓
Ten millennia of regional history, from the Stone Age to the Roman invasion, re-enacted at this award-winning attraction.
Oyne, Insch, Aberdeenshire; tel: 01464 851500; open Apr–Oct: 9am–5pm daily. www.archeolink.co.uk

Waltzing Waters ㉝
Kitschy but colorful "light and water" show, with fountains lit by colored lasers and spotlights, all choreographed by computer.
Balavil Brae, Newtonmore, Highland; tel: 01540 673752; open Feb–mid-Dec: 10am–4pm daily. www.waltzingwaters.co.uk

Seaprobe Atlantis (51)
Trips in semi-submersible boats reveal the marine life teeming in the inshore waters of Scotland's west coast.
Kyle of Lochalsh, Highland; tel: 0800 980846; open Easter–Oct: at least five departures daily. www.seaprobeatlantis.com

Landmark Forest Adventure Park ㉚
This adventure park has lots of rides and activities, such as rock climbing and sky diving, offering hours of fun for adults and children of all ages.
Carrbridge, Highland; tel: 01479 841614; open Jul–Aug: 9am–7pm daily; Sep–Jun: 9am–5pm daily. www.landmarkpark.co.uk

Torosay Castle & the Mull Railway ㊷
A miniature train carries you from the harbor at Craignure, on the Isle of Mull, to this splendid Victorian mansion, home to some magnificent gardens.
Craignure, Isle of Mull, Argyll and Bute; tel: 01680 812421; open Apr–Oct: 10:30am–5pm daily. www.torosay.com

The Blackhouse at Arnol (61)
This primitive home (lived in until the 1960s) will fascinate children and provide a healthy reminder that the "simple life" was far from idyllic.
Arnol, nr Stornoway, Lewis, Outer Hebrides; tel: 01851 710395; open Mar–Sep: 9:30am–5:30pm Mon–Sat; Oct–Feb: 9:30am–4:30pm Mon–Sat. www.historic-scotland.gov.uk

SPAS AND HEALTH RESORTS

Best Western Inverness Palace Hotel and Spa ⑭
This comfortable hotel has an excellent leisure club with pool and offers a range of health and beauty treatments, as well as free car parking and WiFi internet access.
8 Ness Walk, Inverness; tel: 01463 223243. www.bw-invernesspalace.co.uk

Fantasia Health and Beauty Clinic ⑭
A hotel-based spa with highly qualified therapists, offering luxury packages including specialized laser treatments and aromatherapy massages.
Kingsmills Hotel Inverness, Culcabock Road, Inverness; tel: 01463 243244. www.fantasiabeauty.co.uk

Boath House Spa ⑱
Spa located in a country-house hotel, offering natural organic products and therapies such as massage and pure-light treatments.
Boath House Hotel, Auldearn, nr Nairn, Highland; tel: 01667 454896. www.boath-house.com/spa.htm

The Marcliffe Hotel & Spa ㉔
Five-star luxury hotel and spa with 42 rooms and two restaurants, widely regarded as one of the best places to stay in Aberdeen.
North Deeside Road, Pitfodels, Aberdeen; tel: 01224 861000. www.marcliffe.com

OTHER SIGHTS IN THE BOOK

Orkney Islands ① *(see pp86–7).* **Speyside** ⑳ *(see pp22–3).* **Highland Games** ㉘ *(see pp118–19).* **Cairngorms** ㉙ *(see pp192–3).* **Isle of Mull** ㊸ *(see pp100–1).* **Shetland** (66) *(see pp168–9).*

CENTRAL SCOTLAND

LOCAL FOOD

The Deep Sea ①
Traditional fish-and-chip restaurant with a great choice of fish from local harbors.
81 Nethergate, Dundee; tel: 01382 224449; open 11:30am–7pm Mon–Sat.

Dean's@Let's Eat ②
Vibrant Scottish menu based on local lamb, beef, salmon, scallops, and more.
77–79 Kinnoull Street, Perth; tel: 01738 643377; open noon–2pm and 6:30–9:30pm Tue–Sat. www.letseatperth.co.uk

Ostler's Close ⑧
The stunning dishes here range from fresh-picked wild chanterelles to game and seafood from the Fife fishing harbors.
25 Bonnygate, Cupar, Fife; tel: 01334 655574; open 7–9:30pm Tue–Fri, 12:15–1:30pm and 7–9:30pm Sat. www.ostlersclose.co.uk

The Peat Inn ⑨
This legendary restaurant, not far from St. Andrews, helped to launch Scotland's food renaissance and is still simply superb.
Nr St. Andrews, Fife; tel: 01334 840206; open 12:30–2pm and 7–9pm Tue–Sat. www.thepeatinn.co.uk

Anstruther Fish Bar ⑬
Rated by many as the best fish-and-chip shop in Scotland, this restaurant has stunning views over the Forth of Forth.
42–44 Shore Street, Anstruther, Fife; tel: 01333 310518; open noon–9pm Mon–Sat. www.anstrutherfishbar.co.uk

Sangster's ⑭
Michelin-starred restaurant where the menu is imaginative and the emphasis is on intense flavors.
51 High Street, Elie, Fife; tel: 01333 331001; open 12:30–1:30pm and 7–8:30pm Wed–Fri and Sun, 7–8:30pm Tue and Sat. www.sangsters.co.uk

An Lochan Tormaukin ⑳
Wild (not farmed) venison, hand-dived scallops, and homemade oatcakes to accompany local cheeses are just some of the delights here.
Glendevon, Perthshire; tel: 01259 781252; open noon–3pm and 5:30–9pm daily. www.anlochan.co.uk

Loch Fyne Seafood and Smokery ㉟
The original, legendary seafood restaurant (which has spawned a chain of franchises), serving superb local oysters, kippers, smoked salmon, and other fine seafood.
Clachan, Cairndow, Argyll and Bute; tel: 01499 600236; open 9am–8pm daily. www.lochfyne.com

Ee-Usk ㊲
Line-caught Atlantic halibut is among the specialties at this stylish seaside bistro.
North Pier, Oban, Argyll and Bute; tel: 01631 565666; open Sep–May: noon–2:30pm and 6–9pm daily; Jun–Aug: noon–3pm and 6pm–late daily. www.eeusk.com

Yann's at Glenearn House ⑥
Superb offerings, such as roast rump of lamb with four-bean casserole, blend French expertise with the best ingredients from Perthshire's hills and fields.
Perth Road, Crieff, Perth and Kinross; tel: 01764 650111; open noon–2pm and 6:30–9pm Wed–Sun. www.yannsatglenearnhouse.com

The Inn at Lathones ⑪
Game (such as hare and partridge), seafood (scallops, crab, and lobster), and other rich delights feature on the menu at this 17th-century coaching inn, which also offers comfortable bedrooms and live music.
Largoward, nr St. Andrews, Fife; tel: 01334 840494; food orders taken noon–9:30pm daily. www.theinn.co.uk

Loch Leven's Larder ⑱
Home-grown regional vegetables and locally sourced cheeses, bacon, and other foods appear on the menu in the café-restaurant of this working farm.
Channel Farm, Milnathort, Perth and Kinross; tel: 01592 841000; open 9:30am– 5pm daily. www.lochlevenslarder.com

The Lion and Unicorn ㉕
Unpretentious restaurant serving excellent steaks (with real ale from the bar), conveniently located for those exploring the landscapes of the Trossachs.
Thornhill, Lake of Menteith, Stirling; tel: 01786 850204; open noon–9pm daily. www.lion-unicorn.co.uk

Room With a View ⑯
The weekly menu here is dominated by fresh seafood from local harbors and foods sourced from nearby Fife farms. The river view is indeed spectacular.
Forth View Hotel, Aberdour, Fife; tel: 01383 860402; open noon–2:30pm and 6–9:30pm Wed–Sat, noon–2:30pm Sun. www.roomwithaviewrestaurant.co.uk

The Wee Restaurant ⑰
This tiny restaurant (it seats just 24) takes local culinary traditions and gives them a modern twist, and at a very affordable price.
17 Main Street, North Queensferry, Fife; tel: 01383 616263; open noon–2pm and 6:30–9pm Tue–Sat, noon–3pm Sun. www.theweerestaurant.co.uk

The Real Food Café ㉘
Café on a scenic road serving perfect crispy fish and chips, home-baked cakes, pies, and hearty breakfasts; ideal for those on a day's walking.
Tyndrum, Perth and Kinross; tel: 01838 400235; open 8am–10pm daily. www.therealfoodcafe.com

FARMERS' MARKETS

Perth Farmers' Market ②
Established in 1999, the oldest farmers' market in Scotland is held in Perth's traditional market street.
King Edward Street, Perth; tel: 01738 582159; first Sat of every month, 9am–2pm. www.perthfarmersmarket.co.uk

Cupar Farmers' Market ⑧
You'll meet friendly local producers at this bustling market in the heart of Fife's farming region.
Bonnygate, Cupar, Fife; tel: 01592 780246; third Sat of every month, 9am–1pm. www.fifefarmersmarket.co.uk

Kirkcaldy Farmers' Market ⑮
Fine local cheeses and meats for sale in this reinvented industrial town.
Town Square, Kirkcaldy, Fife; tel: 01592 780246; last Sat of every month, 9am–1pm. www.fifefarmersmarket.co.uk

Stirling Farmers' Market ㉒
Large and popular farmers' market in the town's pedestrian area, boasting a superb cross-section of Scottish producers.
Port Street, Stirling; tel: 01877 330151; second Sat of every month, 10am–3pm. www.scottishfarmersmarkets.co.uk

PUBS AND BARS

Taybridge Bar ①
A little-known gem of a bar, with a 1920s interior by the architect William Gauldie.
129 Perth Road, Dundee; tel: 01382 643973; open 11am–midnight Mon–Sat; 12:30pm–midnight Sun.

The Grange Inn ⑩
Cozy pub not far from St. Andrews that serves hearty meals. Reservations advised for lunch or dinner at weekends.
Nr St. Andrews, Fife; tel: 01334 472670; open lunch and eve Tue–Sat, lunch only Sun.

Above: Music fans at the T in the Park music festival

The Pitcairngreen Inn ④
Lively countryside pub, just outside Perth, offering real ales, mid-week acoustic music sessions, and good pub food.
Almondbank, Perth; tel: 01738 583022; open daily. www.thetaybank.com

The Dreel Tavern ⑬
This handsome old pub in a charming fishing village has a long history, and serves a wide variety of good ales and hearty pub meals.
16 High Street, Anstruther, Fife; tel: 01333 310727; open daily. www.thedreeltavern.co.uk

The Ship Inn ⑭
This pub, which has its own cricket team, boasts a great location overlooking the sea in one of Scotland's more picturesque east-coast villages.
Elie, Fife; tel: 01333 330246; open daily. www.ship-elie.com

The Portcullis ㉒
A few steps from Stirling Castle, the Portcullis serves pies, steaks, and other traditionally filling dishes, as well as a huge choice of real ales.
Castle Wynd, Stirling; tel: 01786 472290; open daily. www.theportcullishotel.com

The Lade Inn ㉖
In the heart of "Rob Roy Country," the Lade Inn brews its own humorously named ales ("Ladeback," for example), serves great food, and has its own shop stocked with Scottish brews and malts.
Kilmahog, nr Callander, Stirling; tel: 01877 330152; open daily. www.theladeinn.com

Skipinnish Ceilidh House ㊲
Fiddle music, Highland dancing, live bands, and a good range of ales and whiskeys are offered at the region's top folk-music venue.
34–38 George Street, Oban, Argyll and Bute; tel: 01631 569599; open 6pm–1am Mon–Sat. www.skipinnish.com

The Moulin Inn ㊹
A couple of miles from the center of town, this pub brews its own ales and has occasional live music on Sundays.
Pitlochry, Perth and Kinross; tel: 01796 472196; open daily. www.moulinhotel.co.uk

The Oak Tree Inn ㉗
This pub, in a quaint lochside village, is the ideal place for a heartening pint or dram before commencing an assault on the West Highland Way or a hike up nearby Conic Hill.
Balmaha, Loch Lomond, Stirling; tel: 01360 870357; open daily (from 12:30pm Sun). www.oak-tree-inn.co.uk

Bridge of Orchy Hotel ㊴
This welcoming small hotel bar offers outstanding views and good food.
Bridge of Orchy, nr Tyndrum, Stirling; tel: 01838 400208; open daily (from 12:30pm Sun). www.bridgeoforchy.co.uk

The Taybank ㊸
There are few better places for a pint on a sunny summer day in Perthshire than the tables outside this aptly named pub, well known for live music.
Tay Terrace, Dunkeld, Perth and Kinross; tel: 01350 727340; open daily. www.thetaybank.com

Fisherman's Tavern ㊾
Superb traditional pub with a good selection of ales on tap, and cozy bedrooms upstairs too.
Fort Street, Broughty Ferry, Dundee; tel: 01382 775941; open daily. www.fishermanstavern.co.uk

PLACES TO STAY

Salutation Hotel ②
Opened in 1699, this claims to be the oldest hotel in Scotland; famously, Bonnie Prince Charlie slept here.
34 South Street, Perth; tel: 01738 630066. www.strathmorehotels.com

St. Andrews Youth Hostel ⑦
Cheap single or double *en-suite* rooms within modern vacation apartments.
David Russell Apartments, Buchanan Gardens, St. Andrews, Fife; tel: 01334 476726. www.syha.org.uk

Osta ㉒
Stylish restaurant-with-rooms within walking distance of central Stirling.
78 Upper Craigs, Stirling; tel: 01786 430890. www.osta.uk.com

Stirling Youth Hostel ㉒
Hotel-style *en-suite* rooms as well as dorm bunks are available in this centrally located hostel within a converted historic church.
St. John Street, Stirling; tel: 01786 473442. www.syha.org.uk

Huntingtower Hotel ⑤
Very stylish rooms and good food, well located for an overnight stop en route between the Highlands and Lowlands.
Crieff Road, Perth and Kinross; tel: 01738 583771. www.huntingtowerhotel.co.uk

The Sheriffmuir Inn ㉓
Four comfortable bedrooms attached to an excellent restaurant make this strategically located establishment an excellent overnight stop on a tour of Scotland.
Sheriffmuir, nr Dunblane, Stirling; tel: 01786 823285. www.sheriffmuirinn.co.uk

Cromlix House ㉔
Serene country-house hotel set in a vast, wooded estate with its own fishing loch. Superb food and great atmosphere.
Cromlix Estate, Dunblane, Stirling; tel: 01786 822125. www.cromlixhouse.com

The Gigha Hotel ㉚
Choose from cozy rooms or self-catering cottages. The restaurant and bar serve excellent locally caught seafood.
Isle of Gigha, Argyll and Bute; tel: 01583 505254. www.gigha.org.uk

Port Charlotte Hotel ㉜
Unquestionably the finest place to stay and eat on the marvelous island of Islay. Great range of whiskeys at the bar and fresh local foods in the restaurant.
Port Charlotte, Islay, Argyll and Bute; tel: 01496 850360. www.portcharlottehotel.co.uk

Moor of Rannoch Hotel ㊵
Inexpensive hotel with a fine restaurant, the perfect jumping-off point for the Rannoch Moor section of the West Highland Way (see pp42–3).
Rannoch Station, Perth and Kinross; tel: 01882 633238. www.moorofrannoch.co.uk

Fortingall Hotel ㊶
Attractive 17th-century inn with a highly regarded restaurant, not far from picturesque Loch Tay.
Fortingall, Aberfeldy, Perth and Kinross; tel: 01887 830367. www.fortingall.com

Kenmore Hotel ㊷
Very pleasant country-house hotel in a picturesque village, overlooking the River Tay and Loch Tay.
The Square, Kenmore, Perth and Kinross; tel: 01877 830205. www.kenmorehotel.com

Glen Clova Hotel ㊺
Comfortable hotel with bunkhouse and *en-suite* rooms, a cozy bar, and good food, at the head of a picturesque glen.
Clova, Glen Clova, Angus; tel: 01575 550350. www.clova.com

Jura Hotel ㉛
This small, no-frills, affordable hotel is by far the best base for exploring the island's landscapes and sampling its malt whiskey. The views are spectacular.
Craighouse, Jura, Argyll and Bute; tel: 01496 820243. www.jurahotel.co.uk

FESTIVALS AND EVENTS

Scottish Game Fair ③
This annual three-day event celebrates all that's best in the world of game, tweed, tackle, shotguns, and gun dogs.
Scone Palace, Scone, Perth and Kinross; tel: 01828 650639; first weekend of Jul. www.scottishgamefair.com

T in the Park ⑲
Scotland's answer to Glastonbury is a healthy antidote to fake-traditional tartanry, with a line-up that includes the best contemporary bands over three days.
Balado, Perth and Kinross; second weekend of Jul. www.tinthepark.com

Cowal Highland Games ㉙
One of the largest Highland games in the world, this three-day event features pipers, caber-tossers, dancing, and local food.
Dunoon, Argyll and Bute; tel: 01369 703206; last weekend of Aug. www.cowalgathering.com

MUSEUMS AND GALLERIES

Dundee Contemporary Arts ①
Highly regarded modern arts center with an ever-changing calendar of cutting-edge exhibitions, a movie theater, a printmakers' workshop, and an excellent café-restaurant.
152 Nethergate, Dundee; tel: 01382 909900; open (galleries): 10:30am–5:30pm Tue–Sat (until 8:30pm Thu), noon–5:30pm Sun. www.dca.org.uk

Fergusson Gallery ②
Wonderful array of works by one of Scotland's most important 19th–20th century artists, J. D. Fergusson.
Marshall Place, Perth; tel: 01738 441944; open 10am–5pm Mon–Sat. www.scottishmuseums.org.uk

Black Watch Regimental Museum ②
Poignant museum following the history of one of Scotland's oldest regiments, from its foundation up to its present incarnation as 2nd Battalion, Royal Regiment of Scotland.
Balhousie Castle, Hay Street, Perth; tel: 0131 310 8530; open May–Sep: 10am–4pm Mon–Sat; Oct–Apr: 10am–3:30pm Mon–Fri. www.theblackwatch.co.uk

Scone Palace ③
An outstanding collection of portrait and landscape paintings, antiques, silverware, and porcelain in the former crowning place of the Kings of Scotland, including Macbeth and Robert the Bruce.
Scone, Perth and Kinross; tel: 01738 552300; open Mar–Oct: 9:30am–5:30pm daily. www.scone-palace.co.uk

Stirling Smith Museum & Art Gallery ㉒
Significant collection of rare and unique artifacts and works of art spanning several centuries, including some fine 18th- and 19th-century paintings.
Dumbarton Road, Stirling; tel: 01786 471917; open 10:30am–5pm Tue–Sat, 2–5pm Sun.
www.smithartgallery.demon.co.uk

Auchindrain Township Open Air Museum ㉝
Auchindrain is a unique example of a traditional Scottish farming settlement, with fields and buildings kept as they were more than 100 years ago.
Auchindrain, nr Inveraray; tel: 01499 500235; open Apr–Sep: 10am–5pm daily.
www.auchindrain-museum.org.uk

Inveraray Maritime Museum ㉞
Board the *Arctic Penguin*, a steel-hulled sailing ship built in 1911 and now permanently moored as a floating museum housing prints, charts, artifacts, photographs, and audiovisual displays.
The Pier, Inveraray, Argyll and Bute; tel: 01499 302213; open 10am–6pm daily.
www.inveraraypier.com

Broughty Castle Museum ㊾
Relics of Dundee's Arctic whaling heyday are displayed in this miniature castle, which also houses the Orchar Collection – an exhibition of works by prominent Scottish painters.
Castle Green, Broughty Ferry Harbour, Dundee; tel: 01382 436916; open Apr–Sep: 10am–4pm Mon–Sat, 12:30–4pm Sun; Oct–Mar: 10am–4pm Tue–Sat, 12:30–4pm Sun.
www.historic-scotland.gov.uk

THINGS TO DO WITH KIDS

Sensation ①
More than 80 hands-on exhibits, including interactive robots, bring children (and accompanying adults) into the world of the research scientist.
Dundee Science Centre, Greenmarket, Dundee; tel: 01382 228800; open 8am–5pm daily. www.sensation.org.uk

Discovery Point ①
Meet (through audiovisual displays) the whaling skippers who opened up the Antarctic, then go below decks aboard the Royal Research Ship HMS *Discovery*.
Discovery Quay, Dundee; tel: 01382 201245; open Apr–Oct: 10am–6pm Mon–Sat, 11am–6pm Sun; Nov–Mar: 10am–5pm Mon–Sat, 11am–5pm Sun.
www.rrsdiscovery.com

Verdant Works ①
An industrial museum where you can learn about the men and women who worked in the 19th-century jute mills that helped to make Dundee's fortunes.
5 Milne's Wynd, Dundee; tel: 01382 201245; open Apr–Oct: 10am–6pm Mon–Sat, 11am–6pm Sun; Nov–Mar: 10am–5pm Mon–Sat, 11am–5pm Sun.
www.rrsdiscovery.com

Scotland's Secret Bunker ⑫
Fans of *Dr. Who* will love this labyrinth of bombproof shelters, intended to save the country's elite from nuclear attack.
Nr Anstruther, Fife; tel: 01333 310301; open Apr–Nov: 10am–5pm daily.
www.secretbunker.co.uk

Scottish Fisheries Museum ⑬
Age-old boatbuilding skills are kept alive here, along with a fleet of 19 traditional wooden Scottish fishing boats.
Harbourhead, Anstruther, Fife; tel: 01333 310628; open Apr–Sep: 10am–5:30pm Mon–Sat, 11am–5pm Sun; Oct–Mar: 10am–4:30pm Mon–Sat, noon–4:30pm Sun. www.scotfishmuseum.org

Stirling Old Town Jail ㉒
The grim cells of this 19th-century jailhouse now house a scary visitor attraction, with actors taking on the roles of criminals and prisoners.
Old High Street, Stirling; tel: 01786 450050; open Jun–Nov: 10am–5pm daily. www.oldtownjail.com

Inveraray Jail ㉞
Actors play the parts of prisoners and jailers in this re-creation of life in a 19th-century prison. Excellent for older kids, but toddlers may find it frightening.
Church Square, Inveraray, Argyll and Bute; tel: 01499 302381; open Apr–Oct: 9:30am–6pm daily; Nov–Mar: 10am–5pm daily. www.inverarayjail.co.uk

Bannockburn Heritage Centre ㉑
Arms, armor, and a stirring audiovisual display take visitors back in time to the era of Robert the Bruce, at the site of a pivotal battle in Scotland's history.
Bannockburn, Stirling; tel: 0844 492 2100; open Mar–Oct: 10am–5:30pm daily.
www.nts.org

J. M. Barrie's Birthplace ㊻
The childhood home of the novelist and playwright, most famous for creating the children's story *Peter Pan*, now houses a museum dedicated to his life and works.
9 Brechin Road, Kirriemuir, Angus; tel: 0844 492 2100; open Apr–Jun and Sep–Oct: noon–5pm Wed–Sat; Jul–Aug: 11am–5pm daily. www.nts.org.uk

Pictavia ㊼
Ancient symbol stones and audiovisual displays bring to life the vanished world of the mysterious Pictish people of the northeast of Scotland.
Haughmuir, Brechin, Angus; tel: 01356 626241; open 9am–5pm Mon–Sat, 10am–5pm Sun. www.pictavia.org.uk

Angus Folk Museum ㊽
This hamlet of 18th-century cottages, in the shadow of Glamis Castle, explores how ordinary Scots villagers used to live.
Glamis, Forfar, Angus; tel: 0844 493 2100; open Apr–Jun and Sep–Nov: noon–5pm Fri–Sat; Jul–Aug: noon–5pm daily. www.nts.org.uk

Loch Lomond Aquarium ㉘
Get up close to sharks, rays, otters, starfish, and other sea and freshwater animals at this high-tech aquarium.
Loch Lomond Shores, Balloch, Dunbartonshire; tel: 0871 423 2110; open 9am–6pm daily. www.sealifeeurope.com

SPAS AND HEALTH RESORTS

Old Course Hotel, Golf Resort & Spa ⑦
This stylish spa has marvelous views of the world's most famous golf course, as well as health and beauty programs.
Old Course, St. Andrews, Fife; tel: 01334 477668. www.oldcoursehotel.kohler.com

Cameron House Hotel & Spa ㉘
This stylish mock-baronial mansion has a wealth of spa and fitness programs, plush rooms, and a fine-dining restaurant.
Loch Lomond, Dumbartonshire; tel: 01389 755565. www.devere-hotels.com

Loch Fyne Hotel and Spa ㉞
An array of therapies are offered here, plus a heated pool, whirlpool baths, a sauna, steam bath, and gym.
Inveraray, Argyll and Bute; tel: 0870 9306270. www.crearhotels.com/lochfyne

OTHER SIGHTS IN THE BOOK

River Tay ② *(see pp154–5)*. Loch Lomond ㉘ *(see pp140–41)*. West Highland Way ㊱ *(see pp42–3)*.

Below: Eighteenth-century State Drawing Room in Scone Palace

SOUTHERN SCOTLAND

LOCAL FOOD

21212 ①
A dazzlingly intelligent take on the best Scottish ingredients and genuinely friendly service. Amazingly affordable for this standard of food.
3 Royal Crescent, Edinburgh; tel: 0845 222 1212; open noon–2:30pm and 5:30–9:30pm Sun–Thu; noon–3pm and 5:30–10:30pm Fri–Sat. www.21212restaurant.co.uk

Oloroso ①
Steaks and beef from Scottish farms, plus freshly caught seafood from local harbors and, in season, game from nearby moors.
33 Castle Street, Edinburgh; tel: 0131 226 7614; restaurant open noon–2:30pm and 7–10:30pm daily; bar menu available noon–10pm daily. www.oloroso.co.uk

A Room in the Town ①
Offers a light-handed, modern take on Scottish fare, especially seafood.
18 Howe Street, Edinburgh; tel: 0131 225 8204; open noon–2:30pm and 5:30–9:30pm Sun–Thu, noon–3pm and 5:30–10:30pm Fri–Sat. www.aroomin.co.uk

Forth Floor ①
Visit the "Harvey Nicks" restaurant for some of Scotland's finest food.
Harvey Nichols, 30–34 St. Andrew Square, Edinburgh; tel: 0131 313 4404; open noon–3pm Mon, noon–3pm and 6–10pm Tue–Fri, noon–3:30pm and 6–10pm Sat, noon–3:30pm Sun. www.harveynichols.com

The Dining Room ①
Rich and hearty dishes are the hallmark of the Scotch Malt Whisky Society's own restaurant; fine single malts make a great aperitif and after-dinner drink.
Scotch Malt Whisky Society, 28 Queen Street, Edinburgh; tel: 0131 220 2014; open noon–3pm Mon–Tue, noon–3pm and 5pm–late Wed–Sat. www.smws.co.uk

The New Bell ①
Above the Old Bell pub in Edinburgh's university quarter, this restaurant serves the best of Scottish seasonal fare.
233 Causewayside, Edinburgh; tel: 0131 668 2868; open 5:30–10pm Mon–Thu, noon–2pm and 5:30–10pm Fri–Sun. www.thenewbell.com

Stac Polly ①
Stac Polly helped to reinvigorate Scottish cooking in the 1990s and manages to live up to its reputation for inventive modern and traditional cooking. There are also two further branches downtown, on Grindlay Street and St. Mary's Street.
29–33 Dublin Street, Edinburgh; tel: 0131 556 2231; open noon–2pm and 6–9:30pm Mon–Fri, 6–9:30pm Sat–Sun. www.stacpolly.com

Amber ①
Menu options here emphasize deep and smoky Scottish flavors to match the depth of Scotland's "water of life."
The Scotch Whisky Experience, 354 Castlehill, Edinburgh; tel: 0131 477 8477; open noon–3:45pm daily (and 7–9pm Tue–Sat). www.amber-restaurant.co.uk

The Sizzling Scot ①
Steak and more steak, culminating in the massive Aberdeen Angus T-bone – not a place for vegetarians.
103–105 Dalry Road, Edinburgh; tel: 0131 337 7744; open noon–2pm and 5–10:30pm daily. www.sizzlingscot.co.uk

The Brasserie at Oran Mor ㉖
The lively brasserie in this cultural center serves Scottish ingredients with French flair; the rack of lamb and the suckling pig are both highly recommended.
731–735 Great Western Road, Glasgow; tel: 0141 357 6226; open noon–3pm and 5–10pm daily. www.oran-mor.co.uk

Cail Bruich ㉖
The menu here emphasizes a small but well-chosen selection of Scottish seafood and fine steaks, and is unpretentious in the best possible way.
725 Great Western Road, Glasgow; tel: 0141 334 6265; open noon–3pm and 5–9:30pm Tue–Fri, 10am–3pm and 5–9:30pm Sat, 10am–9pm Sun. www.cailbruich.co.uk

Stravaigin ㉖
Well deserves its status as a local culinary legend with its imaginative take on Scots food and global influences – think crab cake with chili, braised fallow venison, pheasant with black kale, and much more.
28–30 Gibson Street, Glasgow; tel: 0141 334 2665; open 5–11pm Mon–Thu, 11am–11pm Fri–Sun. www.stravaigin.com

Roastit Bubbly Jocks ㉖
A "bubbly jock" is Scots dialect for a turkey, but there is much more than this on the menu at this cheery eatery, including free-range chicken from Ayrshire, venison from Perthshire, and Aberdeen Angus beef.
450 Dumbarton Road, Glasgow; tel: 0141 339 3355; open 5–9:30pm Mon–Fri, noon–2:30pm and 5–9:30pm Sat–Sun.

Blas ㉖
Blas is utterly committed to sourcing the best of Scotland, from Ullapool smoked salmon to Stornoway black pudding and lamb from the Borders.
139 Argyle Street, Glasgow; tel: 0141 357 4328; open noon–10pm Tue–Sun. www.blasrestaurant.com

An Lochan ㉖
The best and freshest of seafood from west-coast fisheries and farms, simply prepared and elegantly presented.
340 Crow Road, Glasgow; tel: 0141 338 6606; open noon–3pm and 6–9:30pm Tue–Sat, noon–3pm Sun. www.anlochan.co.uk

Arisaig ㉖
A classy eatery that comes top for fresh and smoked seafood, Scottish cheeses and classic desserts, such as cranachan.
1 Merchant Square, Glasgow; tel: 0141 553 1010; open 11am–midnight daily. www.arisaigrestaurant.co.uk

Duck's at Kilspindie House ③
Renowned chef Malcolm Duck has an outstanding way with seafood, including scallops, clams, sea bass, and oysters.
Main Street, Aberlady, East Lothian; tel: 01875 870682; open noon–3pm and 5–10pm Mon–Fri, noon–10pm Sat–Sun. www.ducks-aberlady.co.uk

Bass Rock Bistro ⑦
Fresh Scottish mussels, locally landed fish from North Berwick and Eyemouth harbors, and lamb from the Borders are among the offerings here.
37 Quality Street, North Berwick, Midlothian; tel: 01620 890875; open Jun–Aug: noon–2:30pm and 6:30–9pm daily; Sep–May: noon–2:30pm and 6:30–9pm Fri–Sun. www.bassrockbistro.co.uk

Creel Restaurant ⑧
Marvelous freshly caught seafood from nearby Eyemouth Harbour, simply presented and perfectly cooked.
25 Lamer Street, Dunbar, East Lothian; tel: 01368 863279; open noon–2pm and 6:45–9pm Thu–Sat, noon–2pm Sun. www.creelrestaurant.co.uk

Fouters Bistro ⑳
Scottish game and seafood, prepared with a deft modern touch, are served here, in the intimate surroundings of a former 18th-century bank vault.
2a Academy Street, Ayr, South Ayrshire; tel: 01292 261391; open noon–2pm Tue–Fri, noon–2pm and 6–9:30pm Sat. www.fouters.co.uk

SOUTHERN SCOTLAND

Fenton Barns ⑥
Farm shop café specializing in local produce, light meals, and tarts and scones.
Nr Drem, East Lothian; tel: 01620 850294; open 10am–4pm daily.
www.fentonbarnsfarmshop.com

The Garvald Inn ⑨
Cozy pub-restaurant that serves up an array of rich and tasty dishes.
Main Street, Garvald, nr Haddington, East Lothian; tel: 01620 830311; open noon–2:30pm and 6:30–8:30pm Tue–Fri, 12:20–2:45pm and 6:30–8:45pm Sat, 12:30–3pm Sun.

The Black Bull ⑪
Former coaching inn serving delicious beef sourced from nearby St. Boswells Market.
Market Place, Lauder, Borders; tel: 01578 722208; open noon–2:30pm and 5–9pm daily (till 11pm Sat–Sun).
www.blackbull-lauder.com

MacCallums of Troon ㉒
Probably the best fish and seafood on the southwest coast, freshly caught by the MacCallums' own boats and simply and brilliantly prepared.
The Harbour, Troon, South Ayrshire; tel: 01292 319339; open noon–2:30pm and 7–9:30pm Tue–Sat.

Creelers Seafood Restaurant ㉓
A legend in its own lunchtime, serving delicious locally sourced seafood.
Home Farm, Brodick, Arran, North Ayrshire; tel: 01770 302797; open Easter–Oct, 12:30–2:30pm and 6–9pm Tue–Sat, 1–3pm and 6–9:30pm Sun.
www.creelers.co.uk

Braidwoods ㉔
Michelin-starred restaurant that prepares the finest local foods, such as Wester Ross scallops, with cosmopolitan flair.
Saltcoats Road, Dalry, North Ayrshire; tel: 01294 833544; open 7–9pm Tue; noon–1:45pm and 7–9pm Wed–Sat; noon–1:45pm Sun. www.braidwoods.co.uk

Glenskirlie House ㉗
Seasonal Scottish ingredients dominate a modern-British menu in this restaurant at a boutique hotel.
Nr Banknock, Stirling; tel: 01324 840201; open noon–2pm Mon–Sat, 12:30pm–2pm Sun. www.glenskirliehouse.com

FARMERS' MARKETS

Edinburgh Farmers' Market ①
Seafood, organic bread, honey, cheeses, meats, and fruit wines are on sale here.
Castle Terrace, Edinburgh; tel: 0131 652 5940; every Sat, 9am–2pm.
www.edinburghfarmersmarket.com

Kelso Farmers' Market ⑬
Around 18 local producers, with the emphasis on sheep-related products, from organic lamb to sheepskin, wool, and tweed.
Kelso, Borders; tel: 01573 228276; last Sat of every month, 9:30am–1:30pm.
www.scottishfarmersmarkets.co.uk

Haddington Farmers' Market ④
Fine local cheeses, organic vegetables, North Sea line-caught fish and other seafood, lamb, game, and venison.
Corn Exchange, Court Street, Haddington, East Lothian; tel: 01368 863593; last Sat of every month, 9am–1pm.
www.haddingtonfarmersmarket.co.uk

Falkirk Farmers' Market ㉘
Vibrant market with much to offer including cakes, cuts of meat, smoked foods, and vegetables.
High Street, Falkirk; tel: 01560 484861; second Sun of every month, noon–4pm.
www.scottishfarmersmarkets.co.uk

PUBS

The Magnum ①
Spacious, gracious, and verging on grand, the Magnum is a great spot for a leisurely pint in the summer sun or a dram on a winter's night. Great food, too.
1 Albany Street, Edinburgh; tel: 0131 557 4366; open 11:30am–11:30pm Mon–Thu, 12:30pm–1am Fri–Sat, 11:30am–6pm Sun.

The Doric Tavern ①
Formerly a legendary rugby supporters' pub that traditionally opened earlier than any pub in town, the Doric pulls a mean pint as well as serving fine solid Scots cooking.
15–16 Market Street, Edinburgh; tel: 0131 225 1084; open daily.

Café Royal ①
Victorian pub, adorned with remarkable tiled portraits of great inventors, with excellent ales and a fine atmosphere.
17 West Register Street, Edinburgh; tel: 0131 556 1884; open daily.
www.caferoyal.org.uk/thebar.htm

Oxford Bar ①
Fine traditional Edinburgh pub favored by the fictional Detective Inspector Rebus and his creator, author Ian Rankin.
8 Young Street, Edinburgh; tel: 0131 539 7119; open 11am–1am Mon–Sat, 12:30pm–midnight Sun.
www.oxfordbar.com

The Sheep Heid ①
Dating back to 1360, this is a great place for a pint after walking up Arthur's Seat to enjoy the view of Edinburgh. It's also home to the world's oldest functional skittle alley.
Causeway, Duddingston Village, Edinburgh; tel: 0131 656 6951; open 11am–11pm Mon–Thu; 11am–midnight Fri–Sat, 12:30–11pm Sun.
www.sheepheid.co.uk

Joseph Pearce's ①
Bright, airy, and child-friendly bar with comfy sofas, WiFi access, a good choice of wines and beers, a Scandinavian-influenced bar menu, free newspapers, and friendly staff.
23 Elm Row, Leith Walk, Edinburgh; tel: 0131 556 4140; open 11am–midnight Mon–Fri, 11am–1am Sat–Sun.
www.bodabar.com

Above: The Balmoral hotel in Edinburgh

Kay's ①
Tucked away on a quiet corner on the edge of the New Town, Kay's is a gem of a pub with a great selection of ales.
39 Jamaica Street, Edinburgh; tel: 0131 225 1858; open 11am–midnight Mon–Thu (until 1am Fri, 1:30am Sat), 12:30–11pm Sun.

Poosie Nansie's ㉑
Immortalized in Robert Burns's *Tam O Shanter*, this Ayrshire pub is a classic. Little has changed here since Burns's day.
21 Loudoun Street, Mauchline, East Ayrshire; tel: 01290 550316; open daily.

The Horseshoe ㉖
This grand Victorian downtown pub claims to have the longest bar in Britain.
17 Drury Street, Glasgow; tel: 0141 229 5711; open 11am–midnight Mon–Sat, 12:30pm–midnight Sun.
www.horseshoebar.co.uk

The Scotia Bar ㉖
A favorite with local writers, poets, and musicians, this pub hosts live music on most evenings.
112 Stockwell Street, Glasgow; tel: 0141 552 8681; open 11am–midnight Mon–Sat, 12:30pm–midnight Sun.
www.scotiabar.net

Babbity Bowsters ㉖
Great pub in Glasgow's trendy Merchant City, with a French-Scottish restaurant upstairs, real ales, malt whiskeys, and live music downstairs, and a few tables outside for sunny days.
16–18 Blackfriars Street, Glasgow; tel: 0141 552 5055; open 11am–midnight Mon–Sat; 12:30pm–midnight Sun.

The Four Marys ㉙
Renowned real-ale pub close to the evocative ruin of Linlithgow Palace.
65–67 High Street, Linlithgow, West Lothian; tel: 01506 842171; open noon–11pm Mon–Wed, noon–midnight Thu–Sat, 12:30–11pm Sun.
www.thefourmarys.co.uk

PLACES TO STAY

The Balmoral ①
The *grande dame* of Edinburgh hotels, the Balmoral has a superb spa, as well as a Michelin-starred restaurant, a champagne bar and a central location in the city's main shopping area.
1 Princes Street, Edinburgh; tel: 0131 556 2414. www.thebalmoralhotel.com

The Scotsman ①
A three-level gym and health center and Scotland's largest stainless-steel swimming pool embellish this luxury hotel downtown.
20 North Bridge, Edinburgh; tel: 0131 556 5565. www.lhw.com/scotsman

The Grassmarket Hotel ①
Cheap and cheerful budget hotel with its own pub, Biddy Mulligan's, on the ever-popular Grassmarket, an area renowned for its nightlife.
94–96 Grassmarket, Edinburgh; tel: 0131 220 2299. www.festivalhotels.co.uk

The Lodge at Carfraemill ⑩
This roadside inn offers cozy rooms and good solid cooking. An excellent overnight stop while touring.
Carfraemill, nr Lauder, Borders; tel: 01578 750750. www.carfraemill.co.uk

Hotel du Vin ㉖
This pioneering boutique hotel, comprising a block of five Georgian town houses, boasts a classy bar and bistro.
1 Devonshire Gardens, Glasgow; tel: 0141 339 2001.
www.onedevonshiregardens.com

Malmaison ㉖
Stylish, comfortable boutique hotel with well-appointed rooms and lots of designer furniture, plus a good brasserie-style restaurant.
278 West George Street, Glasgow; tel: 0141 572 1000.
www.malmaison-glasgow.com

Above: Boat lift at the Falkirk Wheel

Abode Glasgow ㉖
Trendy town house hotel with an even trendier restaurant and bar. Bedrooms and suites are individually styled.
129 Bath Street, Glasgow; tel: 0141 572 6000. www.abodehotels.co.uk

St. Jude's ㉖
Tiny boutique hotel with five stylish, cozy rooms including plasma-screen televisions and WiFi. There is also a trendy Asian-fusion restaurant-bar.
190 Bath Street, Glasgow; tel: 0141 353 0800. www.saintjudes.com

The Victorian House ㉖
Centrally located hotel that's comfortable, but not ostentatiously so, and very good value for money.
212 Renfrew Street, Glasgow; tel: 0141 332 0129. www.victorianhouse.co.uk

Ednam House ⑬
Unpretentiously cozy hotel in the center of a pretty Borders market town, offering fine views of the River Tweed from its classy restaurant.
Bridge Street, Kelso, Borders; tel: 01573 224168. www.ednamhouse.com

Dakota Forth Bridge ㉛
Distinctive futuristic black glass monolith just off the motorway near the famous bridge, with king-size beds, cocktails, and an award-winning seafood restaurant.
A90 Forth Bridge Approach, South Queensferry, Midlothian; tel: 0870 423 4293. www.dakotaforthbridge.co.uk

The Black Bull ⑪
This inn offers eight *en-suite* rooms – including two family rooms – above a noted gastropub.
Main Street, Lauder, Borders; tel: 01578 722208. www.blackbull-lauder.com

Roxburghe Hotel ⑫
Aristocratic owners the Duke and Duchess of Roxburghe ensure that this country-house hotel lives up to its reputation for grandeur and fine dining.
Nr Kelso, Borders; tel: 01573 450331. www.roxburghe.net

Cringletie House ⑮
Comfortable rooms in the imposing surroundings of a 19th-century mock-baronial mansion in extensive grounds.
Nr Peebles, Borders; tel: 01721 725750. www.cringletie.com

Stobo Castle ⑰
Splendid baronial-style hotel, with service and facilities to match its grand exterior.
Stobo, Borders; tel: 01721 725300. www.stobocastle.co.uk

FESTIVALS AND EVENTS

Glasgow International Jazz Festival ㉖
Jazz musicians from all over the world gather in Glasgow to perform in concert halls, theaters, bars, and restaurants.
Various venues, Glasgow; tel: 0141 552 3552; last two weeks of Jun. www.jazzfest.co.uk

Glasgow Film Festival ㉖
A major fixture, attracting leading British and international actors, writers, and directors over ten days.
Various venues, Glasgow; tel: 0141 332 6535; mid–late Feb. www.glasgowfilmfestival.org.uk

Celtic Connections ㉖
Musicians and performers from all over the "Celtic Fringe" converge on Glasgow for this three-week celebration of contemporary and traditional music.
Various venues, Glasgow; tel: 0141 353 8000; Jan. www.celticconnections.com

Glasgow Festival on the Clyde ㉖
A weekend of fun events for people of all ages, on and around the lively waterfront.
Various riverside venues, Glasgow; tel: 0141 229 5420; last weekend of Jul. www.glasgowriverfestival.co.uk

Royal Highland Show ㉚
Celebration of all that is best from Scotland's farms and countryside, with a week of food and best-of-breed contests for rare breeds and traditional livestock.
Ingliston, nr Edinburgh; tel: 0131 335 6200; last week of Jun. www.royalhighlandshow.org

MUSEUMS AND GALLERIES

Museum of Scotland ①
Magnificent collection in a superb modern building displays the story of Scotland.
Chambers Street, Edinburgh; tel: 0131 225 7534; open 10am–5pm daily. www.nms.ac.uk

Scottish National Gallery of Modern Art and Dean Gallery ①
One of the world's finest collections of contemporary, Dadaist, and Surrealist art.
75 Belford Road, Edinburgh; tel: 0131 624 6200; open 10am–5pm daily. www.nationalgalleries.org

National Museum of Flight ⑤
Astounding collection of civil and military aircraft, including Concorde, at a historic airfield near Edinburgh.
Nr Haddington, Midlothian; tel: 01620 880308; open Apr–Jun: 10am–5pm daily; Jul–Aug: 10am–6pm daily; Sep–Mar: 10am–4pm Sat–Sun. www.nms.ac.uk

National Museum of Costume ⑱
Spectacular costumes from centuries of Scottish history, from kilts to ball gowns.
Shambellie House, New Abbey, Dumfries and Galloway; tel: 0131 247 4030; open Apr–Oct: 10am–5pm daily. www.nms.ac.uk

Kelvingrove Art Gallery and Museum ㉖
The largest civic museum and art gallery in Britain, recently completely renovated and boasting an impressive, eclectic collection.
Argyle Street, Glasgow; tel: 0141 276 9599; open 10am–5pm Mon–Thu and Sat, 11am–5pm Fri and Sun. www.glasgowmuseums.com

THINGS TO DO WITH KIDS

Scottish Storytelling Centre ①
Scottish stories old and new, told and reinterpreted for young and old.
43–45 High Street, Edinburgh; tel: 0131 556 9579; open Sep–Jun: 10am–6pm Mon–Sat; Jul–Aug: 10am–6pm daily . www.scottishstorytellingcentre.co.uk

Museum of Childhood ①
A collection of toys and games, guaranteed to delight children of all ages, and even the accompanying adults.
42 High Street, Edinburgh; tel: 0131 529 4142; open 10am–5pm Mon–Sat, noon–5pm Sun. www.edinburgh.gov.uk

Our Dynamic Earth ①
Journey through the hidden world of geology within this imaginative, interactive visitor attraction beneath Edinburgh's own extinct volcano.
Holyrood Road, Edinburgh; tel: 0131 550 7800; open 10am–5pm daily. www.dynamicearth.co.uk

Scottish Museum of Football ㉖
At Scotland's national stadium, this museum celebrates the country's soccer greats. A must for soccer-crazy youngsters.
Hampden Park, Glasgow; tel: 0141 616 6139; open 10am–5pm Mon–Sat, 11am–5pm Sun. www.scottishfootballmuseum.org.uk

Falkirk Wheel ㉘
This unique high-tech boat lift brings Scotland's 19th-century canal network back to life.
Lime Road, Tamfourhill, Falkirk; tel: 01324 61988; open 11am–3pm Mon–Wed, 10am–4:30pm Thu–Sun. www.thefalkirkwheel.co.uk

SPAS AND HEALTH RESORTS

Dalhousie Castle ②
Between Edinburgh and the Borders, this country-house hotel and spa has an excellent restaurant.
Bonnyrigg, Midlothian; tel: 01875 820153. www.dalhousiecastle.co.uk

Peebles Hotel Hydro ⑯
Historic spa hotel, built in 1907, which now offers top-quality modern treatments.
Peebles, Borders; tel: 01721 720602. www.peebleshydro.co.uk

Mar Hall ㉕
A superbly luxurious baronial house, with a spa offering a number of relaxing treatments, set in its own wooded grounds overlooking the Clyde and conveniently close to Glasgow Airport.
Earl of Mar Estate, Bishopton, nr Glasgow; tel: 0141 812 9999. www.marhall.com

OTHER SIGHTS IN THE BOOK

NORTHERN IRELAND

LOCAL FOOD

Deane's Deli ①
Superior snacks at Michelin chef Michael Deane's excellent deli, café, and wine bar. *44 Bedford Street, Belfast; tel: 028 9024 8800; open noon–3pm and 5–9pm Mon–Tue, noon–3pm and 5–10pm Wed–Sat. www.michaeldeane.co.uk*

Aldens in the City ①
Deli-style café offshoot of a top restaurant, with some of the best sandwiches in town. *8–14 Callendar Street, Belfast; tel: 028 9024 5385; open 8am–5:30pm Mon–Wed, 8am–6pm Thu, 9:30am–6pm Fri. www.aldensinthecity.com*

Café Conor ①
Irish breakfasts, home-baked scones, and a full menu in a place that's always busy. *11A Stranmillis Road, Belfast; tel: 028 9066 3266; open 9am–11pm daily. www.cafeconor.com*

Cargoes Café and Deli ①
One of the best-known cafés and delis in Belfast; winner of a Best Breakfast Award. *613 Lisburn Road, Belfast; tel: 028 9066 5451; open 9am–4:30pm Mon–Fri, 9am–5pm Sat, 10am–3pm Sun*

Swantons Gourmet Foods ①
One of Belfast's best delis; the home-made desserts are an irresistible treat. *639 Lisburn Road, Belfast; tel: 028 9068 3388; open 9am–5pm Mon–Sat. www.swantons.com*

Long's Fish Restaurant ①
The oldest – and many say the greatest – fish-and-chip shop in Belfast. A classic! *39 Athol Street, Belfast; tel: 028 9032 1848; open 11:45am–6:30pm Mon–Fri, noon–6pm Sat.*

Bay Tree Coffee House ②
Great café, considered to have the best cinnamon scones in the UK. *118 High Street, Holywood, County Down; tel: 028 9042 1419; open 8am–9:30pm Mon, Wed–Fri; 8am–5pm Tue; 9:30am–9:30pm Sat. www.baytreeholywood.com*

Coyle's Bistro ④
Michelin-rated menus with local produce, such as organic salmon steamed in dill, with live music in the bar Thu, Fri, and Sun. *44 High Street, Bangor, County Down; tel: 028 9127 0362; open 5–9pm Tue–Sat, 5–8pm Sun. www.coylesbistro.co.uk*

Yellow Door Deli, Bakery and Café ⑲
Homemade chutneys, jams, and ice cream at this wonderful award-winning bakery. *74 Woodhouse Street, Portadown, County Armagh; tel: 028 3835 3528; open 9am–5pm Tue–Sun.*

Donnelly's Bakery and Coffee House ㉟
Beautiful Irish breads, such as wheaten bread and potato bread, baked in-house. *Ann Street, Ballycastle, County Antrim; tel: 028 2076 3236; open 7am–6pm Mon–Sat. www.donnellysbakery.co.uk*

Picnic ⑦
Homemade fare and good local food in this quaint-looking deli-café across from Killyleagh Castle. *47 High Street, Killyleagh, County Down; tel: 028 4482 8525; open 7am–6pm Mon–Fri, 10am–4pm Sat.*

Mourne Seafood Bar ⑬
You know you'll get the best fresh shellfish and seafood here, as the owner also runs an oyster farm on Carlingford Lough. *10 Main Street, Dundrum, County Down; tel: 028 4375 1377; open noon–late Mon–Sat, noon–8:30pm Sun. www.mourneseafood.com*

Seasalt Delicatessen and Bistro ⑮
Irish cheeses and foodstuffs from around the world for the perfect picnic. *Central Promenade, Newcastle, County Down; tel: 028 4372 5027; open 9am–6pm Sun–Thu, 9am–9pm Fri–Sat. www.seasaltnewcastle.co.uk*

Deli on the Green ㉑
Nothing but the best local foods can be purchased in the deli or from the menu of this stylish brasserie. *The Linen Green, Moygashel, County Tyrone; tel: 028 8775 1775; open 8:30am–5:30pm Mon–Wed, 8:30am–5:30pm and 6–9:30pm Thu–Sat.*

FARMERS' MARKETS

Belfast Farmers' Market ①
Every other Saturday, local food producers add their stands to the ever-lively mix of this regular market. *St. George's Street, Belfast; tel: 028 3834 9100; first and third Sat every month, 8am–1pm.*

Lisburn Farmers' Market ⑩
Some of the best regional products, plus entertaining street performers. *15 Lisburn Square, Lisburn; tel: 028 9266 0038; first Sat of every month, 10am–4pm.*

Portadown Farmers' Market ⑱
The number and quality of local growers and makers selling here has won this market a "Best Farmers' Market" award. *Craigavon, nr Portadown, County Armagh; tel: 021 733 0178; last Sat of every month, 10am–4pm.*

Templepatrick Farmers' Market ㊲
Locally grown and produced foods, including fruit and vegetables, meats, artisan breads, and cheeses. *Coleman's Garden Centre, Ballyclare Road, Templepatrick, County Antrim; tel: 028 9443 2513; fourth Sun of every month, 11am–6pm.*

Tyrone Farmers' Market ㉒
Only around 15 stands, but a great mix of meats, fruit and vegetables (some organic), baked goods, jams, and local crafts. *Tesco's parking lot, Dungannon, County Tyrone; tel: 028 3752 3752; first Sat of every month, 8:30am–12:30pm.*

PUBS AND BARS

The Crown Bar ①
Historic watering hole, dating back to 1849, with Arabian-themed saloons. *46 Great Victoria Street, Belfast; tel: 028 9027 9901; open daily. www.crownbar.com*

The Spaniard ①
Fashionable pub offering a large variety of food and drink, great music, good *craic*, and quirky decor. *3 Skipper Street, Belfast; tel: 028 9023 2448; open daily.*

McHugh's Bar and Restaurant ①
Housed in the oldest building in Belfast, McHugh's has centuries of atmosphere behind it, and also puts on live music at night in its basement bar. *29–31 Queen's Square, Belfast; tel: 028 9050 9999; open noon–3pm and 5–11pm Mon–Fri, noon–1:30am Sat, noon–10pm Sun. www.mchughsbar.com*

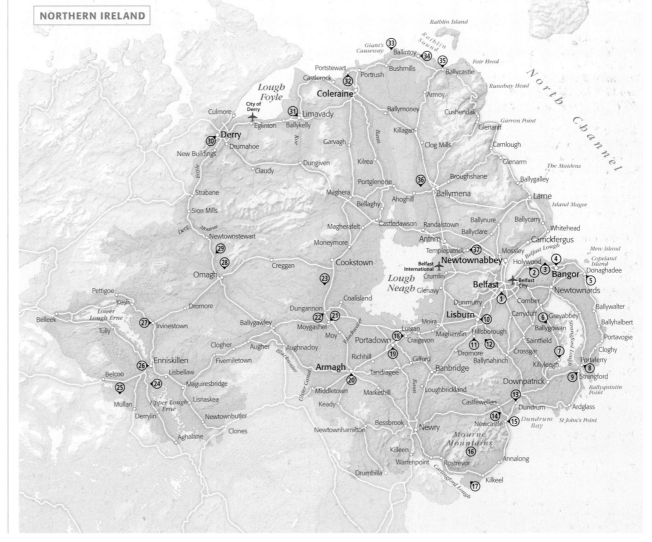

NORTHERN IRELAND

The Old Inn ③
Founded in about 1600, this inn has a large, traditional bar with an open fire, and a great, award-winning restaurant.
11–15 Main Street, Crawfordsburn, County Down; tel: 028 9185 3255; open daily. www.theoldinn.com

Grace Neill's ⑤
Ireland's oldest pub has a lounge bar held up by old ship timbers, and two "snugs" decorated with the booty of long-dead smugglers. The food is great too.
33 High Street, Donaghadee, County Down; tel: 028 9188 4595; open daily. www.graceneills.com

The Pheasant ⑫
With its atmospheric old Highland Bar and a Neo-Gothic restaurant, the Pheasant has character galore.
410 Upper Ballynahinch Road, Annahilt, County Down; tel: 028 9263 8056; open daily. www.the-pheasant-restaurant.co.uk

Blakes of the Hollow ㉖
The most famous pub in town, a Victorian classic rated as one of the best in Ireland.
6 Church Street, Enniskillen, County Fermanagh; tel: 028 6632 0918; open daily, noon–late.

PLACES TO STAY

Malmaison ①
A boutique hotel in stylishly converted warehouses in the center of Belfast.
34–38 Victoria Street, Belfast; tel: 028 9022 0200. www.malmaison.com

Anna's House ⑥
Peaceful retreat describing itself as a "luxury B&B," overlooking a pretty lake and serving its own organically grown food.
Tullynagee, 35 Lisbarnett Road, Comber, County Down; tel: 028 9754 1566. www.annashouse.com

Portaferry Hotel ⑧
Its loughside location and fine food make this one of Ireland's best small hotels. There are spacious rooms with ample beds (a couple of bedrooms have four-posters).
The Strand, Portaferry, County Down; tel: 028 4272 8231. www.portaferryhotel.com

The Cuan ⑨
The heart of Strangford life – a restaurant, pub, and fish-and-chip shop with superb, affordable accommodations.
Strangford Village, County Down; tel: 028 4488 1222. www.thecuan.com

Carriage House ⑬
Charming, family-run B&B that serves a great traditional breakfast in a sun room overlooking a walled garden.
71 Main Street, Dundrum, County Down; tel: 028 4375 1635. www.carriagehousedundrum.com

Burrenwood Farm ⑭
A working organic vegetable farm with rooms (no meal services) at the foot of the Mountains of Mourne.
38 Burrenbridge Road, Castlewellan, County Down; tel: 028 4377 0241. www.burrenwood.com

Lurganconary Organic Farms ⑰
Award-winning, 5-star cottages stunningly set in 100 acres (40 hectares) by the Mountains of Mourne.
25 & 27 Lurganconary Road, Kilkeel, County Down; tel: 028 3025 4595. www.lurganconaryfarms.com

Tullylagan Country House Hotel ㉓
Rural Ireland with modern conveniences; a manor hotel in 30 acres (12 hectares) of grounds and two award-winning restaurants.
40b Tullylagan Road, Cookstown, County Tyrone; tel: 028 8676 5100. www.tullylagan.com

Westville Hotel ㉖
Chic boutique hotel in the center of Enniskillen, with a stylish restaurant and open kitchen.
14–20 Tempo Road, Enniskillen, County Fermanagh; tel: 028 6632 0333. www.westvillehotel.co.uk

Omagh Hostel ㉘
Exceptionally good hostel on a quiet family farm with views of the Sperrin Mountains.
Glenhordial Farm, 9a Waterworks Road, Omagh; tel: 028 8224 1973. www.omaghhostel.co.uk

Beech Hill Country House Hotel ㉚
Four-star country retreat with many attractions, including the acclaimed Ardmore Restaurant, that serves great signature dishes, such as Finnebrogue Venison Wellington.
32 Ardmore Road, Derry; tel: 028 7134 9279. www.beech-hill.com

FESTIVALS AND EVENTS

The Belfast Festival at Queen's ①
Ireland's biggest arts festival brings world-class musicians, dancers, dramatists, and comedians to the city for two weeks.
Various venues; Belfast; tel: 028 9097 1197; last two weeks of Oct. www.belfastfestival.com

Festival of Fools ①
Wonderfully bizarre three-day mix of international comedy and street theater.
Various venues, Belfast; tel: 028 9023 6007; first May Bank Holiday weekend. www.foolsfestival.com

St. Patrick's Day ①
Although more associated with Dublin *(see pp40–41)*, the celebrations in Belfast are also a day of parades, music, and fun.
Belfast city centre; 17 Mar.

Cathedral Quarter Arts Festival ①
Week-long festival of the arts, including theater, dance, comedy, music, literature, visual arts, and events for children.
Cathedral Quarter, Belfast; tel: 028 9023 2403; May. www.cqaf.com

Open House Festival ①
Everything from traditional Irish ballads to bluegrass at this five-day folk-music event.
Cathedral Quarter, Belfast; tel: 028 9024 6609; Sep. www.openhousefestival.com

The Feile Festival ①
This 10-day festival grew up in response to the Troubles, and is now one of Europe's biggest community festivals.
Various venues, Belfast; tel: 028 9031 3440; Jul–Aug. www.feilebelfast.com

Hillsborough Oyster Festival ⑪
Four-day-long World Oyster Eating Championships, plus a masquerade ball.
Hillsborough, County Down; tel: 028 9268 9717; Sep. www.hillsboroughoysterfestival.com

Apple Blossom Festival ⑳
Four-day festival in Northern Ireland's orchard capital, home of the Bramley apple.
Armagh, County Armagh; tel: 028 3752 1800; May.

Banks of the Foyle Halloween Carnival ㉚
Music and parades are just part of this vibrant week-long festival by the river.
Various venues, Derry; tel: 028 7137 6545; last week of Oct. www.derrycity.gov.uk/halloween

International North West 200 ㉜
Ireland's biggest one-day outdoor sporting event attracts 150,000 motorcycle fans.
Portstewart, County Derry; May. www.northwest200.org

Ould Lammas Fair ㉟
One of the oldest surviving fairs in Ireland; two days of music and entertainment.
Ballycastle, County Antrim; last Mon and Tue of Aug.

Below: St. Patrick's Day celebrations in Belfast

MUSEUMS AND GALLERIES

The Ulster Museum ①
One of the best local collections of archaeology, art, and historical artifacts, this revamped museum reopened in 2009 with a new interactive learning zone. *Stranmillis Road, Belfast; tel: 028 9042 8428; open 10am–6pm Mon–Sat, 11am–6pm Sun. www.ulstermuseum.org.uk*

Ormeau Baths Gallery ①
The best place to see work by contemporary Irish artists and photographers. *18a Ormeau Avenue, Belfast; tel: 028 9032 1402; open 10am–5:30pm Tue–Sat. www.ormeaubaths.co.uk*

Ulster Folk and Transport Museum ②
Voted Museum of the Year in 2007, this joint museum is home to the largest transportation collection in Ireland and a reconstructed village from the early 1900s. *Cultra, Holywood, County Down; tel: 028 9042 8428; open Mar–Aug: 10am–5pm Tue–Sun; Sep: 10:30am–6pm daily; Oct–Feb: 10am–4pm Tue–Fri, 11am–4pm Sat–Sun. www.uftm.org.uk*

Armagh County Museum ⑳
Eclectic collection of local artifacts, art, and natural-history, and local-history displays. *The Mall East, Armagh, County Armagh; tel: 028 3752 3070; open 10am–1pm and 2–5pm Mon–Fri, 10am–5pm Sat. www.nmni.com*

Royal Irish Fusiliers Museum ⑳
Archives, uniforms, weapons, and other exhibits tell the story of this brave and historic regiment that served in many conflicts, including the Napoleonic Wars. *Sovereigns House, The Mall, Armagh, County Armagh; tel: 028 3752 2911; open 10am–12:30pm and 1:30–4pm Mon–Fri. www.rirfus-museum.freeserve.co.uk*

The Navan Centre and Fort ⑳
Excellent center offering modern multimedia and interactive insights into the ancient fort of the Kings of Ulster. *Killylea Road, Armagh, County Armagh; tel: 028 3751 0180; open Jul–Sep: 10am–7pm daily; Oct–Dec: 10am–4pm daily. www.navancentre.com*

Enniskillen Castle and Museums ㉖
An impressive 600-year-old castle incorporating two museums. *Castle Barracks, Enniskillen, County Fermanagh; tel: 028 6632 5000; open 2–5pm Mon, 10am–5pm Tue–Fri; May–Jun: also open 2–5pm Sat; Jul–Aug: also open 2–5pm Sat–Sun. www.enniskillencastle.co.uk*

Ulster American Folk Park ㉙
This fascinating museum brilliantly tells the story of Irish migration to America. *Castletown, Omagh, County Tyrone; tel: 028 8224 3292; open Mar–Sep: 10am–5pm Tue–Sun; Oct–Feb: 10am–4pm Tue–Fri, 11am–4pm Sat–Sun. www.folkpark.com*

Sheelin Antique Irish Lace Museum ㉔
The finest collection of antique lace in the country, with a tempting shop. *Bellanaleck, Enniskillen, County Fermanagh; tel: 028 6634 8052; open 10am–6pm Mon–Sat. www.irishlacemuseum.com*

Tower Museum ㉚
Award-winning museum exploring Derry's turbulent history, complete with treasures recovered from Spanish Armada wrecks. *Union Hall Place, Derry; tel: 028 7137 2411; open Jul–Aug: 10am–5pm Mon–Sat, 11am–3pm Sun; Sep: 10am–5pm Mon–Sat; Oct–Jun: 10am–5pm Tue–Sat. www.derrycity.gov.uk/museums/tower.asp*

Harbour Museum ㉚
Listed building with a collection that includes a replica of St. Columba's boat. *Harbour Square, Derry; tel: 028 7137 7331; open 10am–1pm and 2–5pm Mon–Fri. www.derrycity.gov.uk/museums/harbour.asp*

Workhouse Museum ㉚
See workhouse conditions and more on Derry's history – but watch out for ghosts! *23 Glendermott Road, Waterside, Derry; tel: 028 7131 8328; open 10am–5pm Mon–Thu and Sat. www.derrycity.gov.uk/museums/workhouse.asp*

THINGS TO DO WITH KIDS

Belfast Zoo ①
A wonderful collection of over 1,200 exotic animals, from agoutis to zebras. *Antrim Road, Belfast; tel: 028 9077 6277; open Apr–Sep: 10am–7pm daily; Oct–Mar: 10am–4pm daily. www.belfastzoo.co.uk*

The Belfast Wheel ①
Travel 200 ft (60 m) above the city for spectacular views, especially at night. *Donegall Square East, Belfast; tel: 028 9031 0607; open 10am–9pm Sun–Thu, 10am–10pm Fri, 9am–10pm Sat. www.worldtouristattractions.co.uk/wta_wheel_belfast.php*

Belfast Botanic Gardens ①
Children's playground, giant bird feeders, and plenty of space for racing around among exotic plant species. *Botanic Avenue, Belfast; tel: 028 9032 4902; open dawn–dusk daily.*

W5 ①
Science museum with lots of interactive fun and educational things to do. *W5@Odyssey, Queen's Quay, Belfast; tel: 028 9046 7700; open 10am–5pm Mon–Thu, 10am–6pm Fri–Sat, noon–6pm Sun. www.w5online.co.uk*

Titanic Boat Tours ①
Take a boat trip around Belfast's shipyards, where the ill-fated *Titanic* was constructed. *Lagan Boat Company, 48 St. John's Close, 2 Laganbank Road, Belfast; tel: 028 9033 0844; trips Mar–Oct daily; Nov–Dec weekends only. www.laganboatcompany.com*

Above: Palm House in Belfast Botanic Gardens

St. Patrick's Trian Visitor Complex ⑳
Exhibitions include the scenes of a Viking raid, the funeral of an Irish High King, and the Land of Lilliput, where a 20-ft (6-m) giant describes *Gulliver's Travels*. *40 English Street, Armagh, County Armagh; tel: 028 3752 1801; open Jul–Aug: 10am–5:30pm Mon–Sat, 2–6pm Sun; Sep–Jun: 10am–5pm Mon–Sat, 2–5pm Sun. www.saintpatrickstrian.com*

Armagh Astropark ⑳
An amazing scale model of the universe is set in the grounds of the excellent Armagh Observatory. *College Hill, Armagh, County Armagh; tel: 028 3752 2928; park open dawn–dusk daily. www.arm.ac.uk*

Armagh Planetarium ⑳
Exhibitions, rocket-building activities, and demonstrations, together with special events such as talks and films about space and astronauts. *College Hill, Armagh, County Armagh; tel: 028 3752 3689; open 11:30am–5pm daily, plus 7:30–9pm on the last Thu of each month. www.armaghplanet.com*

Marble Arch Caves ㉕
Take a boat trip then walk through an awe-inspiring cave network, with underground rivers and waterfalls. *Marlbank, Florencecourt, County Fermanagh; tel: 028 6634 8855; open Mar–Sep daily. www.marblearchcaves.ne*

Castle Archdale Country Park ㉗
Deer herds, a butterfly garden, bike rentals, and pony rides are just a few of the activities to keep children amused here. *Irvinestown, County Fermanagh; tel: 028 6862 1588; open 9am–dusk daily. www.ni-environment.gov.uk/archdale.shtml*

Carrick-a-Rede Rope Bridge ㉞
The simple pleasures are sometimes the best, and kids love taking the rope bridge to a little island here. *119a Whitepark Road, Ballintoy, County Antrim; tel: 028 2076 9839; Sep–May: open 10am–6pm daily; Jun–Aug: open 10am–7pm daily. www.nationaltrust.org.uk/main/w-carrickarede*

SPAS AND HEALTH RESORTS

Culloden Estate and Spa ②
This 5-star estate, built in the Holywood Hills for the Bishops of Down, has breathtaking country views as well as modern spa facilities. *Bangor Road, Holywood, County Down; tel: 028 9042 1066. www.hastingshotels.com*

The Slieve Donard Resort and Spa ⑮
One of Europe's finest spas in a 4-star resort overlooking the County Down coast. *Downs Road, Newcastle, County Down; tel: 028 4372 1066. www.hastingshotels.com*

Killyhevlin Hotel and Health Club ㉖
A health club and Elemis Spa in a hotel that has been voted as one of the top places to stay in Northern Ireland by UTV (Ulster TV) viewers. *Killyhevlin, Enniskillen, County Fermanagh; tel: 028 6632 3481. www.killyhevlin.com*

Lough Erne Golf Resort ㉖
Northern Ireland's newest resort, offering a Thai spa and two championship golf courses. It's refreshingly eco- and child-friendly too. *Belleek Road, Enniskillen, County Fermanagh; tel: 028 6632 3230. www.lougheregolfresort.com*

Radisson Roe Park Resort ㉛
The north coast's most deluxe resort, with a £1-million Roe Spa and its own golf course. *Limavady, County Derry; tel: 028 7772 2222. www.radissonroepark.com*

Galgorm Resort and Spa ㊱
With 163 acres (66 hectares) of lush parkland, the Galgorm is a rural retreat within 30 minutes' drive of Belfast. *136 Fenaghy Road, Galgorm, County Antrim; tel: 028 2588 1001. www.galgorm.com*

OTHER SIGHTS IN THE BOOK

Mountains of Mourne ⑯ *(see pp 132–3)*. **Derry** ㉚ *(see pp28–9)*. **Giant's Causeway** ㉝ *(see pp164–5)*.

WESTERN IRELAND

LOCAL FOOD

The Green Man ①
A wonderful deli that stocks food and drink from around the world, but is especially renowned for its local foods, including farmhouse cheeses, honey, and bacon.
Main Street, Dunfanaghy, County Donegal; tel: 074 910 0800; open 9:30am–6pm Mon–Sat, 10am–2pm Sun. www.greenmandunfanaghy.com

Aroma Coffee ②
This unpretentious little café features home-baked items, good local ingredients, and gives a nod to the chef's Mexican roots.
The Craft Village, Donegal, County Donegal; tel: 074 972 3222; open 9:30am–5:30pm Mon–Sat.

The Blueberry Tea Room ⑨
From sandwiches to home-baked pastries and cakes, this is the kind of perfect tea room every town should have.
Castle Street, Donegal, County Donegal; tel: 074 972 2933; open 9am–7pm Mon–Sat.

Moran's Oyster Cottage ㉙
A 300-year-old thatched cottage houses an award-winning restaurant, renowned for its delicious local oyster dishes.
The Weir, Kilcolgan, County Galway; tel: 091 796113; open noon–10pm daily. www.moransoystercottage.com

Anton's ㉛
A simple family-run café that has a loyal local following due to its good-value, home-cooked food.
12 Father Griffin Road, Galway, County Galway; tel: 091 582067; open 9am–6pm Mon–Fri.

Goya's ㉛
One of Galway's best delis and bakeries, which has a café too. The indulgent chocolate cakes are not to be missed.
2–3 Kirwan's Lane, Galway, County Galway; tel: 091 567010; open 9am–6pm Mon–Sat. www.goyas.ie

Cullen's at the Cottage ㉞
Café in the grounds of the Ashford Castle Hotel, serving less formal food from the hotel's superb kitchen.
Ashford Castle, Cong, County Mayo; tel: 094 954 5332; 11:30am–9:30pm daily. www.ashford.ie

Hungry Monk Café ㉞
A friendly eatery offering both home-baked snacks and wholesome meals.
Abbey Street, Cong, County Mayo; tel: 094 954 5842; open Mar–Oct: 10am–5:30pm Mon–Sat, 11am–5pm Sun; Nov–Dec: 10am–5:30pm Sat, 11am–5pm Sun.

McCormacks at the Andrew Stone Gallery ㊵
Fantastic Irish cooking; all the food is local and the homemade desserts are excellent.
Bridge Street, Westport, County Mayo; tel: 098 25619; open 10:15am–4:45pm Mon–Tue and Thu–Sat.

Lyons Café ⑮
The café in Sligo's traditional department store may be one of the oldest in town, but it is modern in outlook and serves some of the best organic snacks and meals around.
Lyons Department Store, Quay Street, Sligo, County Sligo; tel: 071 914 2969; open 9am–noon and 12:30–2pm daily.

Brigit's Garden Café ㉜
The gardens here are some of the best in the Galway area, and in season their produce is used in the café's menu.
Brigit's Garden, Pollagh, Roscahill, County Galway; tel: 091 550905; open May–Sep: 10:30am–5pm daily; Apr: 10:30am–5pm Sun; Oct–Mar: by arrangement. www.galwaygarden.com

Market Kitchen ㊻
A popular new restaurant situated in an historic building above Brennan's Lane Bar, with a gluten-free take on local dishes.
Brennans Lane, Garden Street, Ballina, County Mayo; tel: 096 74971; open 3pm–late daily.

FARMERS' MARKETS

Ballybofey Farmers' Market ⑧
Busy weekly market offering the best local foods of eastern Donegal.
GAA Grounds, Ballybofey, County Donegal; tel: 086 817 8854; every Fri, noon–4pm.

Donegal Farmers' Market ⑨
A typical array of products, with live music!
The Diamond, Donegal, County Donegal; tel: 087 973 0539; third Sat of every month, 10am–2pm.

Athenry Farmers' Market ㉚
The fields of Athenry are well represented at this weekly organic farmers' market.
Market Cross, Athenry, County Galway; tel: 087 627 2017; every Fri, 9:30am–4pm.

Galway Farmers' Market ㉛
Good organic produce and local seafood at this busy market held every weekend.
Beside St. Nicholas's Church, Galway, County Galway; tel: 091 231 1580; 9am–5pm Sat, 2–6pm Sun and Bank Holidays.

Boyle Farmers' Market ㉑
An award-winning market that sells a huge range of food, plus very good crafts.
Main Street, Boyle, County Roscommon; tel: 071 966 3033; every Sat, 10am–2pm. www.unabhan.net/farmersmkt.htm

Roscommon Farmers' Market ㉕
Find freshly baked bread, fish caught that morning, and organic meats among the produce on sale every week.
Market Square, Roscommon, County Roscommon; every Fri, 10am–2pm.

Ballinasloe Farmers' Market ㉖
One of the best markets in the area, with dozens of excellent stalls.
Croffey Centre, Ballinasloe, County Galway; tel: 087 256 3167; every Fri, 10am–3pm.

Kinvara Farmers' Market ㉘
A great cross-section of food, from shellfish to award-winning cheeses.
Johnston's Hall, Main Street, Kinvara, County Galway; tel: 08728 35425; every Fri, 10am–2pm.

WESTERN IRELAND

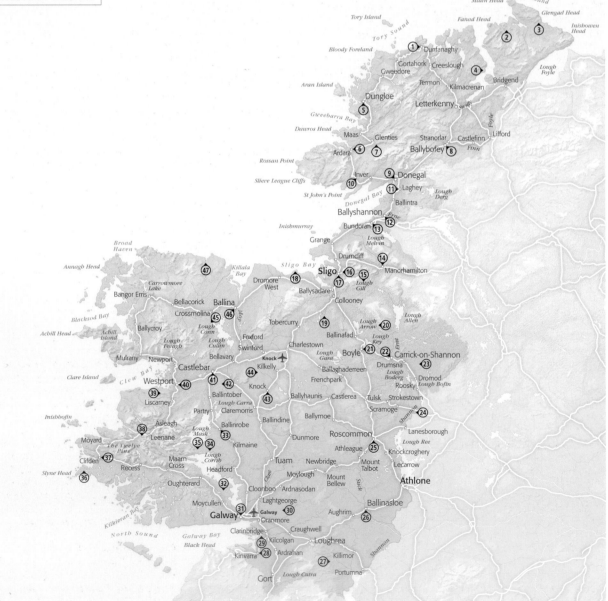

Manorhamilton Farmers' Market ⑭
At this enterprising cross-border market you can buy artisan cheeses, soda bread, and other home-baked goodies, plus local honey, yogurts, olive oil, and craft items.
Bee Park Resource Centre, New Line, Manorhamilton, County Leitrim; tel: 071 985 6935; every Fri, 10am–2pm.

Sligo Farmers' Market ⑯
Here you'll find freshly caught fish, organic local meats, cheeses, fruit and vegetables, delicious home-baked bread, and, in summer, a selection of crafts stands too.
IT College Car Park, Ballinode, County Sligo; tel: 071 914 7007; every Sat, 9am–1pm.

PUBS AND BARS

McGrory's of Culdaff ③
Whether you're after a bar, live music, a guesthouse, or a highly rated restaurant, this is an essential port of call in Culdaff.
Culdaff, County Donegal; tel: 074 937 9104; open daily. www.mcgrorys.ie

Nancy's Bar ⑥
Brilliant family-owned Irish bar that attracts some of the best local session musicians, and serves good pub food in summer too.
Front Street, Ardara, County Donegal; tel: 074 954 1187; open daily.

The Bridge Bar ⑬
Whether you want good food, a few drinks, music, or the chance to hang out with surfers, the Bridge Bar is the place to be.
West End, Bundoran, County Donegal; tel: 071 984 2050; open daily. www.maddensbridgebar.com

The Beach Bar ⑱
A 17th-century pub, that is also now a B&B and live-music venue, with an excellent reputation for its food.
Aughris Head, Templeboy, County Sligo; tel: 071 917 6465; open Apr–Oct: 1–late daily; Nov–Mar: 1–late Sat–Sun www.thebeachbarsligo.com

The Oarsman ㉒
Regarded as one of the best pubs in western Ireland, gaining plaudits for its fine food, with dishes such as Kettyle lamb.
Bridge Street, Carrick-on-Shannon, County Leitrim; tel: 071 962 1733; open daily. www.theoarsman.com

Keogh's ㉘
This fine family-run pub has a bar and separate dining area serving traditional food, such as local salmon or black pudding.
The Square, Kinvara, County Galway; tel: 091 637145; open daily. www.kinvara.com/keoghs

Cronin's Sheebeen ㊵
Who could resist a drink in a thatched pub with a name like this? Good food too, from Thai fishcakes to loin of venison.
Rosbeg, Westport, County Mayo; tel: 098 26528; open mid-Mar–Oct: noon–midnight daily; Nov–mid-Mar 4:30–12:30pm Mon–Thu, noon–midnight Fri–Sun. www.croninssheebeen.com

Matt Molloy's ㊵
This music bar is owned by Matt Molloy of the folk band The Chieftains, and features live artists every night of the week.
Bridge Street, Westport, County Mayo; tel: 098 26655; open daily, hours flexible. www.mattmolloy.com

Sheridan's on the Docks ㉛
One of Galway's oldest pubs; although it's been refurbished and now has a great new restaurant, it retains its old dockside charm.
New Dock Street, Galway, County Galway; tel: 091 564905; open 4:30–11:30pm Mon–Thu, 12pm–1am Fri–Sat. www.sheridansonthedocks.com

J J Gannons ㉝
A new-style Irish pub offering luxury accommodation and gastropub food, and serving champagne as well as Guinness.
Ballinrobe, County Mayo; tel: 094 954 1008; open daily. www.jjgannons.com

John J Burke ㉟
A family-run pub and restaurant, with wonderful home-cooked food and lovely views from the restaurant balcony.
Mount Gable House, Clonbur, County Galway; tel: 094 954 6175; open daily www.burkes-clonbur.com

Crockets on the Quay ㊻
An old-fashioned bar overlooking the River Moy, serving superb traditional dishes.
The Quay Village, Ballina, County Mayo; tel: 096 75930; open daily. www.crocketsonthequay.ie

PLACES TO STAY

Woodhill House ⑥
A characterful 17th-century coastal manor house offering occasional music events and an excellent restaurant which uses local Irish produce in French-style cuisine.
Ardara, County Donegal; tel: 074 954 1112. www.woodhillhouse.com

Donegal Organic Farm ⑦
Biodynamic farm set in idyllic Donegal countryside, offering accommodations in the farmhouse and in separate flats.
Doorian, Glenties, County Donegal; tel: 074 955 1286. www.donegalorganic.ie

Ard Na Breatha ⑨
A country house on a working farm, only a short walk from Donegal, Ard Na Breatha recently won a prestigious EU award for ecotourism.
Drumrooske Middle, Donegal, County Donegal; tel: 074 972 2288. www.ardnabreatha.com

Donegal Manor ⑨
Donegal Manor combines 4-star luxury with the friendliness of a family B&B, so it's no surprise this hotel has won all kinds of awards.
Letterkenny Road, Donegal, County Donegal; tel: 074 972 5222. www.donegalmanor.com

Above: Street performers at the Galway Arts Festival

Water's Edge ④
Boutique comfort on the edge of Lough Swilly. The modern glass-fronted restaurant has spectacular views over the water.
Rathmullan, County Donegal; tel: 074 915 8182. www.watersedgedonegal.com

Coxtown Manor ⑪
Award-winning Georgian country-manor hotel. Superb food, mainly local, but the Belgian proprietor also provides a renowned "Belgian fry" breakfast.
Laghey, County Donegal; tel: 074 973 4575. www.coxtownmanor.com

Ard Nahoo ⑰
An eco-retreat and health farm in stunning Yeats country, with accommodations in three Scandinavian-inspired eco-cabins.
Mullagh, Dromahair, County Leitrim; tel: 071 913 4939. www.ardnahoo.com

Keenan's ㉔
A boutique hotel, bar, and restaurant, dating back to 1838, that combines modern style and luxury with a healthy respect for Irish tradition.
Tarmonbarry, County Roscommon; tel: 043 26098. www.keenans.ie

Caheroyan House and Farm ㉚
Eighteenth-century manor house and organic farm offering accommodations, nature walks, and the chance for children to feed newborn farm animals.
Athenry, County Galway; tel: 091 844858. www.caheroyanhouseathenry.com

The Twelve ㉛
Voted "Best Boutique Hotel in Ireland 2008" (Hospitality Ireland Awards), this hotel's location in a village close to the centre of Galway adds to its chic appeal.
Barna Village, Galway, County Galway; tel: 091 597000. www.thetwelvehotel.ie

Ben View House ㊲
Stylish yet inexpensive family-run B&B in an 1848 town house with original features.
Bridge Street, Clifden, County Galway; tel: 095 21256. www.benviewhouse.com

Wyatt Hotel ㊵
Successfully blends a traditional setting with modern stylish comfort; the brasserie has won awards for both its food and its traditional music sessions.
The Octagon, Westport, County Mayo; tel: 098 25027. www.wyatthotel.com

Enniscoe ㊺
A country house with fantastic views of the breathtaking Mayo countryside, offering B&B and vacation apartments.
Castlehill, Ballina, County Mayo; tel: 096 31112. www.enniscoe.com

FESTIVALS AND EVENTS

Mary from Dungloe Festival ⑤
A huge eight-day festival with international music acts celebrating the famous Irish folk song "Mary from Dungloe."
Dungloe, County Donegal; Jul–Aug; tel: 074 910 2107. www.maryfromdungloe.com

Yeats Festival ⑮
Two-week period of events in Sligo and across the county celebrating one of Ireland's leading literary figures, W. B. Yeats.
County Sligo; tel: 071 914 2693; Jul. www.yeats-sligo.com

Ballinasloe October Fair and Horse Festival ㉖
The biggest horse fair in Ireland takes place over two weeks, offering music, parades, horse auctions, and other entertainment.
Ballinasloe, County Galway; Oct; tel: 090 96 44793. www.ballinasloeoctoberfair.com

Cruinniu na mBád ㉘
The three-day "Gathering of the Boats" in Galway Bay features the traditional sailing boats of the west coast.
Kinvara, County Galway; tel: 086 251 0922; Aug. www.kinvara.com

Fleadh na gCuach ㉘
The "Cuckoo Festival" is a long weekend of traditional Irish music and the arts held every year on the early May Bank Holiday weekend.
Kinvara, County Galway; tel: 091 63 7131; May. www.kinvara.com

Galway Arts Festival ㉛
For two weeks Galway welcomes theater, spectacle, street art, music, and comedy in a huge, exciting celebration.
Galway, County Galway; tel: 091 509700; Jul. www.galwayartsfestival.ie

Galway Film Fleadh ㉛
Ireland's leading film festival brings stars, glamour, and thought-provoking films to Galway for six days each July.
Various venues, Galway; tel: 091 751655; Jul. www.galwayfilmfleadh.com

Galway International Oyster Festival ㉛
One of Ireland's most famous food festivals has been running for almost 60 years (see pp128–9).
Galway, County Galway; tel: 091 522066; Sep. www.galwayoysterfest.com

Ballyshannon Folk and Traditional Music Festival ⑫

A three-day festival that has been bringing some of Ireland's top music acts to this estuary town for over 30 years.
Ballyshannon, County Donegal; tel: 086 252 7400; Aug Bank Holiday weekend. www.ballyshannonfolkfestival.com

Connemara Pony Show ㉔

A one-day gathering for those who want to admire the semi-wild Connemara ponies in all their splendor.
Clifden, County Galway; tel: 095 21863; Aug. www.cpbs.ie

Croagh Patrick Pilgrimage ㊴

More than 15,000 pilgrims climb Mayo's third-highest peak, the name of which means "Patrick's Stack" in English, to honor Ireland's patron saint, St. Patrick.
Croagh Patrick, County Mayo; tel: 098 64114; last Sun in Jul. www.croagh-patrick.com

Westport International Sea Angling Festival ㊵

The longest-running and biggest sea angling festival in Ireland runs for four days.
Clew Bay, Westport, County Mayo; tel: 098 27297; Jun. www.westportseaanglingfestival.eu

Castlebar Blues Festival ㊶

For one weekend every year, Castlebar hosts the longest-running blues festival in Ireland, with concerts, a blues trail, and a CD and record fair.
Castlebar, County Mayo; tel: 094 902 3111; May–Jun. www.castlebarblues.com

Ballina Salmon Festival ㊼

Held in the "salmon capital of the world," this huge 10-day festival also celebrates local arts, culture, and communities.
Ballina, County Mayo; tel: 096 79814; Jul. www.ballinasalmonfestival.ie

MUSEUMS AND GALLERIES

Galway City Museum ㉛

A range of good exhibitions telling the intriguing story of the city of Galway.
Spanish Parade, Galway, County Galway; tel: 091 532460; open Jun–Sep: 10am–5pm daily; Oct–May: 10am–5pm Tue–Sat. www.galwaycitymuseum.ie

Nora Barnacle House Museum ㉛

The former home of Nora Barnacle, who married James Joyce, now restored to the way it was when she lived there as a child.
Bowling Green, Galway, County Galway; tel: 091 564743; open summer only, call to join a tour. www.norabarnacle.com

Claddagh Ring Museum ㉛

Tiny museum in the Claddagh Gold shop with a fascinating collection of traditional Irish lovers' rings (*see p128*), including some of the oldest and smallest ever made.
1 Quay Street, Galway, County Galway; tel: 091 566365; open 10am–5:30pm Mon–Sat, noon–4pm Sun. www.claddaghring.ie

Above: Bogwood tree at the Céide Fields Visitor Centre

Sligo County Museum ⑮

Strong on local history, but the main interest here is the W. B. Yeats Memorial Room, which contains items relating to the poet's life and works, including his 1923 Nobel Prize for Literature medal.
Stephen Street, Sligo, County Sligo; tel: 071 914 1623; open Jun–Oct: 10am–noon and 2–4:30pm Tue–Sat; Nov–May: 2–4:30pm Tue–Sat. www.sligotown.net/librarymuseum.shtml

Knock Museum ㊸

Learn the story of the apparition of the Virgin Mary in Knock, experienced by two women near the village church in 1879.
Knock, County Mayo; tel: 094 938 8100; open May–Oct: 10am–6pm daily; Nov–Apr: noon–4pm daily. www.museumsofmayo.com

Kiltimagh Museum ㊹

Excellent local museum in a former train station, exploring the history of the town and its inhabitants.
Kiltimagh, County Mayo; tel: 094 938 1132; open Jun–Sep: 2–6pm daily. www.museumsofmayo.com

Enniscoe Museum ㊺

This museum and family history center displays household and farm artifacts, and you can also explore the grounds and Victorian walled garden.
Mayo North Heritage Centre, Castlehill, Ballina, County Mayo; tel: 096 31809; open Apr–Oct: 9am–6pm Mon–Fri, 2–6pm Sat–Sun; Nov–Mar: family history section only, 9am–4pm Mon–Fri. www.museumsofmayo.com

Céide Fields Visitor Centre ㊼

This startling pyramid-shaped visitor center has won an architectural award; inside, it tells the story of the unusual surrounding landscape and blanket bogs.
Ballycastle, County Mayo; tel: 096 43325; open mid-Mar–May and Oct–Nov: 10am–5pm daily; Jun–Sep: 10am–6pm daily; Dec–mid-Mar: bookings only. www.museumsofmayo.com

THINGS TO DO WITH KIDS

Deane's Farm Equestrian Centre ⑩

Deane's 100-acre (40-hectare) farm on the Donegal coast offers pony rides, horse-trekking trips, and riding lessons.
Darney, Bruckless, County Donegal; tel: 074 973 7160; open 10am–4pm Tue–Sun. www.deanesequestrian.ie

Eagles Flying ⑲

Ireland's largest center for birds of prey and owls is a must-see, with daily hour-long flying demonstrations and a Pet Zoo.
Ballymote, County Sligo; tel: 071 918 9310; open Apr–Nov: 10:30am–12:30pm and 2:30–4:30pm daily. www.eaglesflying.com

Slieve Aughty Centre ㉗

This riding center and guesthouse offers riding vacations in summer, working stays at the stables, and pony-walking breaks.
Kylebrack West, Loughrea, County Galway; tel: 090 974 5246. www.riding-centre.com

Ireland's School of Falconry ㉞

Falconry school in the grounds of Ashford Castle offering classes in hawk-flying within the gardens and woodlands.
Ashford Castle, Cong, County Mayo; tel: 094 954 6820; open 9:30am–4:30pm daily, booking essential. www.falconry.ie

An Trá Mhóir ㊱

A 3-mile (5-km) popular surfing beach, "The Great Beach" is the perfect place to be when the sun is shining.
Creggoduff, Bunowen, Ballyconneely, County Galway.

Killary Adventure Company ㊳

Older children will love the adventure sports here, such as bungee-jumping, kayaking, and abseiling. There is also an activity-based summer camp.
Leenane, County Galway; tel: 095 43411. www.killaryadventure.com

Westport House ㊵

An 18th-century country house, built on the ruins of the castle where the 16th-century pirate Grace O'Malley lived.
Westport, County Mayo; tel: 098 27766/25430; open Mar: 10am–4pm Sat–Sun; Apr–Jun and Sep: 10am–4pm daily; Jul–Aug: 10am–5:30pm daily. www.westporthouse.ie

Mayo Horsedrawn Caravan Holidays ㊷

Hire a traditional Irish horse-drawn caravan and explore the area at a leisurely pace, staying overnight at prearranged farm sites.
Belcarra, Castlebar, County Mayo; tel: 094 903 2054. www.horsedrawncaravan.com

SPAS AND HEALTH RESORTS

Kee's Hotel and Leisure Club ⑧

This family-run hotel has its own leisure club with fitness room, pool, steam room, sauna, and in-house beauticians.
Stranorlar, Ballybofey, County Donegal; tel: 074 913 1018. www.keeshotel.ie

Jackson's Hotel and Leisure Centre ⑧

On the banks of the River Finn, Jackson's is an award-winning hotel with a sauna, Jacuzzi, swimming pool, and gym, offering yoga classes, massages, and treatments.
Ballybofey, County Donegal; tel: 074 913 1021. www.jacksons-hotel.ie

Villa Rose Hotel and V-Spa ⑧

Boutique hotel with an award-winning contemporary spa offering a thermal suite and a wide range of therapies, massages, and other spa treatments.
Main Street, Ballybofey, County Donegal; tel: 074 913 2266. www.villarose.net

Ballyliffin Lodge and Spa ②

A 4-star hotel with spectacular views of Malin Head. Its Rock Crystal Spa has nine treatment rooms, a pool, gym, 12-seater Jacuzzi, and a dry flotation chamber.
Shore Road, Ballyliffin, County Donegal; tel: 074 937 8200. www.ballyliffinlodge.com

Kilronan Castle Estate and Spa ⑳

This majestic, modernized castle retreat on the shores of Lough Meelagh has a new spa for the ultimate in luxurious pampering and individualized treatments.
Ballyfarnon, County Roscommon; tel: 071 961 8000. www.kilronancastle.ie

Lough Rynn Castle ㉓

This castle hotel by Lough Rynn boasts spa and leisure facilities, as well as a golf course designed by the golfer Nick Faldo.
Mohill, County Leitrim; tel: 071 963 2700. www.loughrynn.ie

Abbey Hotel ㉕

An 18th-century manor house set in large, pretty gardens, this 4-star luxury hotel has a big indoor pool, treatment room, gym, sauna, Jacuzzi, and steam room.
Galway Road, Roscommon, County Roscommon; tel: 090 666 6200. www.abbeyhotel.ie

Raheen Woods Hotel ㉚

A luxurious contemporary haven, with a "Tranquility" spa offering yoga and gym classes, massage and spa therapies, and a steam room, sauna, pool, and Jacuzzi.
Athenry, County Galway; tel: 091 875888. www.raheenwoodshotel.ie

Downhill House Hotel ㊻

This family hotel's Eagles Leisure Club offers a swimming pool, steam room, Jacuzzi, and exercise classes.
Ballina, County Mayo; tel: 096 21033. www.downhillhotel.ie

Mount Falcon Country House Hotel and Spa ㊻

Mount Falcon is hidden away in 100 acres (40 hectares) of woodland, with a gym, pool, steam room, sauna, and spa.
Ballina, County Mayo; tel: 096 74473. www.mountfalcon.com

OTHER SIGHTS IN THE BOOK

Galway Oyster Festival ㉛ (*see pp128–9*).

EASTERN IRELAND

LOCAL FOOD

Chapter One ①
Michelin-starred restaurant at the Dublin Writers Museum, known for its imaginative contemporary use of Irish ingredients. *Basement of the Writers Museum, 18 Parnell Square, Dublin; tel: 01 873 2266; open 12:30–2pm and 6–11pm Tue–Fri, 6–11pm Sat. www.chapteronerestaurant.com*

Chapterhouse Café ①
The café of the Dublin Writers Museum, offering less expensive, but exceptionally fine, food from the same kitchen as its parent restaurant, Chapter One *(above). 18 Parnell Square, Dublin; tel: 01 872 2077; open 10am–5pm Mon–Sat, 11am–5pm Sun. www.writersmuseum.com*

Blazing Salads ①
Amazing deli that makes everything on the premises except for bread, which is baked in an organic bakery. Several soups and dishes, such as vegetarian stews and shepherd's pie, are made daily. *42 Drury Street, Dublin; tel: 01 671 9552; open 10am–4pm Mon–Fri, 9am–5pm Sat. www.blazingsalads.com*

Queen of Tarts ①
Specializing in tarts, this café also sells home-baked breads, muffins, scones, cheesecakes, pastries, and other treats. *4 Cork Hill, Dame Street, Dublin; tel: 01 670 7499; open 7:30am–7pm Mon–Fri, 9am–7pm Sat–Sun. www.queenoftarts.ie*

The Gourmet Store ㉓
Deli selling delicious local cheeses, meats, and homemade sandwiches, paninis, wraps, and bagels. The hot bacon, sausage, and white-pudding sandwich is a specialty. *56 High Street, Kilkenny, County Kilkenny; tel: 056 777 1727; open 9am–6pm daily. www.thegourmetstorekilkenny.com*

Bradbury's Bakery ㉙
In business since 1938, this deli makes everything from fresh bread to wedding cakes and even the local school lunches – try one of the diet or spelt breads. *Leinster Street, Athy, County Kildare; tel: 059 863 1845; open 8am–6pm Mon–Sat, 8am–5pm Sun. www.bradburys.ie*

The Kitchen and Foodhall ㉛
Bakers, butchers, delis, and other food providers sell items sourced locally or made on the premises. *Hynds Square, Portlaoise, County Laois; tel: 057 866 2061; open 9am–5:30pm daily. http://kitchenfoodhall.com*

Ramparts Coffee Shop ㊹
Ireland is known for its wonderful baking, and this is a great place to sample homemade breads, scones, sandwiches, bagels, and more substantial meals too, close to the entrance to Trim Castle. *Castle Street, Trim, County Meath; tel: 046 943 7227; open 9:30am–5:30pm Mon–Sat.*

Donnybrook Village Market ②
Fine produce includes organic meats, fruit and veg, fresh fish, and farmhouse cheeses. *St. Mary's Church, Donnybrook, nr Dublin; tel: 01 284 1197; every Thu, 11am–7pm.*

Monkstown Village Market ③
Friendly market featuring a wide range of fresh Irish products. *Parish Church, Monkstown, County Dublin; tel: 087 234 9419; every Sat, 10am–4pm.*

Poppies ⑤
From a cup of tea or a carry-out salad to delicious traditional dishes, such as homity pie, Poppies prides itself on its country cooking. Unmissable if you're in the area. *The Square, Enniskerry, County Wicklow; tel: 01 282 8869; open 8:30am–6pm daily. www.poppies.ie*

Avoca ⑥
One of the best-known names in Ireland for crafts and foods, Avoca serves up some of the tastiest dishes around, including a Wicklow Blue cheese salad. *Kilmacanogue, Bray, County Wicklow; tel: 01 286 7466; open 9am–6pm Mon–Fri, 9:30am–6pm Sat–Sun. www.avoca.ie*

The Bakery Restaurant ⑩
Homemade soup, Wexford mussels, Wicklow lamb, and more exotic dishes feature on the menu at this former bakery. *Church Street, Wicklow Town, County Wicklow; tel: 0404 66770; open 5–9:30pm Tue–Sat, noon–9:30pm Sun. www.thebakeryrestaurantwicklow.com*

Avenue Café ㊲
Stylish café-restaurant in a university town serving cheap and cheerful options, such as Irish-beef burgers, and local dishes, such as Bantry Bay mussels. *Main St, Maynooth, County Kildare; tel: 01 628 5003; open noon–10pm (last orders 9:45pm) Mon–Sat, 1–8pm Sun. www.avenuecafe.ie*

Malahide Market ㊵
Very popular market offering arts, crafts, and fashion indoors, with fresh fish and local farm produce outside. *GAA Club, Church Road, Malahide, nr Dublin; tel: 087 611 5016; every Sat, 10am–4pm.*

FARMERS' MARKETS

Dublin Docklands Farmers' Market ①
Fashion and design items as well as fresh breads and homemade desserts at this popular market in Ireland's capital. *Excise Walk, International Financial Services Centre, Dublin; every Wed, noon–2:30pm. www.dublindocklands.ie*

Ranelagh Farmers' Market ①
Typically tempting array of breads, cakes, fruit, vegetables, meats, and local cheeses. *Multi Denominational School, Ranelagh, Dublin; tel: 086 868 2283; every Sun, 10am–4pm. www.irishfarmersmarkets.ie*

Kilkenny Farmers' Market ㉓
One of the best in the area with producers of honeys, meats, breads, cakes, and jams. *The Market Yard, Kilkenny, County Kilkenny; tel: 086 859 7716; every Thu, 9am–2pm.*

Portlaoise Farmers' Market ㉛
Only a handful of local stands, but they offer a range of top-quality local products. *Shaws Centrepoint parking lot, Portlaoise, County Laois; tel: 057 866 1900; every Fri, 9am–3pm.*

Ballymun Farmers' Market ㊴
Organic produce, homemade breads, cakes, and jams, as well as arts and crafts. *Ballymun Plaza, Ballymun, nr Dublin; tel: 087 698 1093; first Thu of every month, 11am–4pm. www.ballymunmarket.ie*

Wexford Farmers' Market ⑯
Excellent local market selling a range of local products, such as bacon, sausages, organic chicken and lamb, fish, yogurt, honey, butter, and bread. *Mallin Street, Cornmarket, Wexford, County Wexford; tel: 051 428375; every Fri, 9am–2pm. www.wexfordfarmersmarkets.com*

Howth Fishermen's and Farmers' Market ㊶
Especially good for fish and seafood, with many fishermen's stalls alongside bakers, farmers, butchers, and other food and drink stands. *West Pier, Howth Harbour, Howth, nr Dublin; tel: 087 611 5016; every Sun, 10am–5pm.*

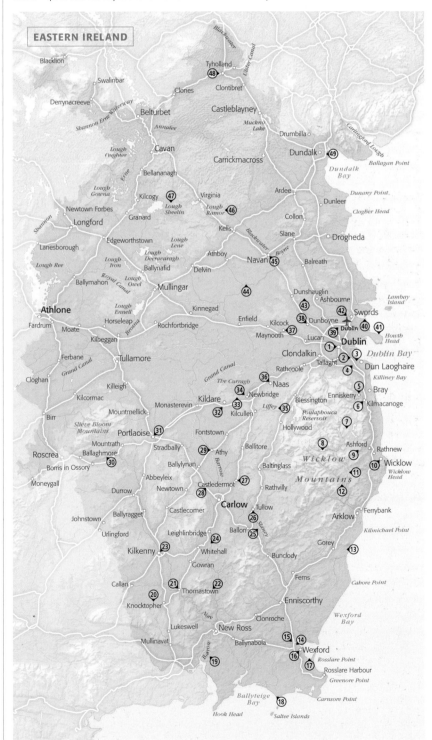

PUBS AND BARS

Davy Byrnes ①
Legendary Dublin pub, famous for its appearance in James Joyce's *Ulysses,* and the place to be on June 16 for Bloomsday *(see Festivals and Events).*
21 Duke Street, Dublin; tel: 01 677 5217; open daily. www.davybyrnes.com

McDaids ①
Famous pub popular in the 1950s with Brendan Behan and other Dublin literary figures, though it dates from 1779.
3 Harry Street, Dublin; tel: 01 679 4395; open daily.

The Coach House ⑦
Award-winning pub with great food, in an ideal location for tourists.
Main Street, Roundwood, County Wicklow; tel: 01 281 8157; open daily. www.thecoachhouse.ie

The Lobster Pot ⑬
Country pub specializing in the freshest of seafood – the Wexford cockles and mussels are very popular.
Ballyfane, Carne, County Wexford; tel: 053 913 1110; closed Mon (except Bank Holidays when closed Tue) and also Jan and first week Feb.

Kehoe's Pub and Parlour ⑱
With a nautical theme and a Maritime Heritage Centre on-site too, Kehoe's is the place for seafood: feast on the catch of the day, or the ocean pie.
Kilmore Quay, County Wexford; tel: 053 912 9830; open daily. www.kehoespubandparlour.ie

Kyteler's Inn ㉓
The oldest inn in Kilkenny serves good traditional food, such as Irish stews, Irish lamb and boiled bacon and cabbage, and puts on a variety of entertainment.
St. Kieran's Street, Kilkenny, County Kilkenny; tel: 056 772 1064; open daily. www.kytelersinn.com

Ballymore Inn ㉟
Renowned for its good country food, ranging from simple bar fare to fancier steaks and fish dishes.
Ballymore, Eustace, County Kildare; tel: 045 864585; open 12:30–9pm daily. www.ballymoreinn.com

Thomas Fletcher ㊱
One of the best-loved pubs in the area, Thomas Fletcher dates back to the 1800s and remains unspoiled by modern times.
Commercial House, Main Street, Naas, County Kildare; tel: 045 897328; open 4pm–late Sun–Fri, noon–late Sat.

Andy's Bar and Restaurant ㊽
Family pub in the center of town; a great place if you just want a drink, but it would be a shame not to sample the superb food.
12 Market Street, Monaghan, County Monaghan; tel: 047 82277; open from 4pm Tue–Fri, noon Sat, 3:30pm Sun. www.andysmonaghan.com

Above: "James Joyce" and "Molly Bloom," Bloomsday

Marble City Bar ㉓
Recently made over, this historic bar now has stylish modern touches, but it is the quality of the food that draws people here.
66 High Street, Kilkenny, County Kilkenny; tel: 056 776 1143; open daily until 10pm.

The Hanged Man's ㉞
Gastropub noted for creative Irish cuisine, especially the local fish and seafood, though its steak is also rightly renowned.
Milltown, Newbridge, County Kildare; tel: 045 431515; open 5–11pm Mon–Sat, noon–10pm Sun. www.hangedmans.ie

Fitzpatrick's Bar and Restaurant ㊾
With several bars, a beer garden, a bistro, and a restaurant, there's something for every budget at this very popular pub.
Rockmarshall, Jenkinstown, Dundalk, County Louth; tel: 042 937 6193; open Apr–Oct: daily; Nov–Mar: Tue–Sat. www.fitzpatricks-restaurant.com

PLACES TO STAY

Brooks Hotel ①
One of the best boutique hotels in Dublin, with a fashionable restaurant and bar.
Drury Street, Dublin; tel: 01 670 4000. www.brookshotel.ie

Quay House ⑱
In the heart of a delightful fishing village, Quay House and its helpful owners offer simple but comfortable accommodation.
Kilmore Quay, County Wexford; tel: 053 912 9988. www.kilmorequay.net

Ballindrum Farm ㉙
Only an hour's drive from Dublin but in the middle of rolling Kildare countryside, this farm has won awards for its hospitality.
Athy, County Kildare; tel: 059 862 6294. www.ballindrumfarm.com

Highfield House B&B ㊹
Lovely 18th-century house in a great location overlooking Trim Castle and the River Boyne, with beautiful private gardens.
Maudlins Road, Trim, County Meath; tel: 046 943 6386. www.highfieldguesthouse.com

Killiane Castle ⑰
Working farm and B&B, built in the ruins of a 13th-century Norman castle, and set in beautiful Wexford countryside.
Drinagh, County Wexford; tel: 053 915 8885. www.killianecastle.com

Croan Cottages ⑳
Four-star cottages hidden in the grounds of the 18th-century Croan House, a small farm next to a forest.
Dunamaggan, County Kilkenny; tel: 056 776 6868. www.croancottages.com

Ballyduff House ㉑
Built in 1760, this is an active farm as well as a B&B and is set in beautiful parkland, overlooking the River Nore.
Thomastown, County Kilkenny; tel: 056 775 8488. www.ballyduffhouse.com

Lorum Old Rectory ㉔
Luxury manor house built in 1863 in the Barrow Valley, at the foot of the Blackstairs Mountains. Exceptional home cooking includes home-grown organic produce.
Kilgreaney, Bagenalstown, County Carlow; tel: 059 977 5282. www.lorum.com

Ballin Temple ㉕
Set deep in the Carlow countryside, this private house has cottages to rent and acres of woodland to explore.
Ardattin, County Carlow; tel: 059 915 5037/086 817 9238. www.ballintemple.com

Kilkea Lodge Farm ㉗
This small, child-friendly family farm has just a handful of rooms and sometimes runs music and painting courses.
Castledermot, County Kildare; tel: 059 914 5112. www.kilkealodgefarm.com

Coolanowle Cottages ㉘
Enjoy a peaceful vacation in these cottages on a working organic farm an hour's drive from Dublin, with simple B&B or apartment options also available.
Ballickmoyler, Carlow, County Laois; tel: 059 862 5176. www.coolanowle.com

The Mill House ㊻
Vacation apartments with fishing rights on adjacent Mullagh Lake. You can buy produce from the owners' organic farm.
Lakeview Organic Farm and Gardens, Mullagh, County Cavan; tel: 046 924 2480.

Ross House ㊼
A working farm and equestrian center right on the shores of Lough Sheelin, described as the perfect rural Irish retreat.
Mountnugent, County Cavan; tel: 0498 540218. www.ross-house.com

FESTIVALS AND EVENTS

The Jameson Dublin International Film Festival ①
This 10-day event brings movie premieres and leading Irish filmmakers and actors to Ireland's capital.
Various venues, Dublin; tel: 01 662 4260; Feb–Mar. www.jdiff.com

Dublin Theatre Festival ①
Irish writers have produced remarkable drama, and for almost three weeks each year the city's theaters put on a wide range of plays celebrating their work.
Various venues, Dublin; tel: 01 677 8439; Sep–Oct. www.dublintheatrefestival.com

Bloomsday ①
Dublin brings alive the day on which James Joyce's *Ulysses* was set in 1904, with events all over the city, especially in bars.
Various venues, Dublin; 16 June. www.jamesjoyce.ie

Taste of Dublin ①
Spread over four days and held in pretty Iveagh Gardens, this festival celebrates the best of Dublin's food and drink.
Iveagh Gardens, Dublin; tel: 01 210 9290; Jun. www.tastefestivals.ie

The Wicklow 200 ⑪
Ireland's biggest bicycle race is a huge fixture in the calendar, and attracts over 1,000 cyclists hoping to cover 125 miles (200 km) over the course of a day.
Rathdrum (main checkpoint), County Wicklow; tel: 059 648 1350; Jun. www.wicklow200.ie

Wexford Opera Festival ⑯
One of the world's biggest festivals of opera, this 12-day event has been going since 1951 and boasts a huge array of performances in a variety of operatic styles.
Wexford Opera House, Wexford, County Wexford; tel: 053 912 2400; late Oct. www.wexfordopera.com

Town of Books Festival ㉒
Readers and writers unite in this little town for a weekend in late September, with readings, workshops, and music events.
Various venues, Graiguenamanagh, County Kilkenny; Sep. www.booktownireland.com

The Cat Laughs ㉓
An international selection from the world's top stand-up comedians livens up Kilkenny over a long weekend.
Various venues, Kilkenny, County Kilkenny; tel: 056 776 3837; May–Jun. www.thecatlaughs.com

Kilkenny Arts Festival ㉓
Art and music are celebrated over 10 days in Kilkenny, including street theater and special events for children.
Kilkenny, County Kilkenny; tel: 056 775 2175; Aug. www.kilkennyarts.ie

Kildare Derby Festival ㉝
The biggest festival in Kildare provides a 10-day build-up to the Irish Derby.
Curragh Racecourse, County Kildare; late Jun. www.kildare.ie/DerbyFestival

Irish Grand National ㊸
This two-day race meeting rivals only the Irish Derby in the horse-racing calendar.
Fairyhouse Racecourse, Ratoath, County Meath; tel: 01 825 6167; Mar/Apr. www.irish-grand-national.com

MUSEUMS AND GALLERIES

National Museum of Ireland ①
This fascinating museum is home to a huge collection of Irish historical artifacts, art, and natural-history displays.
Kildare Street, Dublin; tel: 01 677 7444; open 10am–5pm Tue–Sat, 2–5pm Sun. www.museum.ie

National Gallery of Ireland ①
Displays on W. B. Yeats and other Irish writers and artists, as well as a wide European collection – unmissable.
Merrion Square West and Clare Street, Dublin; tel: 01 661 5133; open 9:30am– 5:30pm Mon–Wed, Fri, Sat; 9:30am– 8:30pm Thu; noon–5:30pm Sun. www.nationalgallery.ie

Chester Beattie Library ①
A fine museum, with a breathtaking collection of rare books and manuscripts.
Dublin Castle, Dublin; tel: 01 407 0750; open May–Sep: 10am–5pm Mon–Fri, 11am–5pm Sat, 1–5pm Sun; Oct–Apr: 10am–5pm Tue–Fri, 11am–5pm Sat, 1–5pm Sun. www.cbl.ie

Irish Museum of Modern Art ①
A delightful and thought-provoking gallery housed in the restored former hospital.
Royal Hospital, Kilmainham, Dublin; tel: 01 612 9900; open 10am–5:30pm Tue and Thu–Sat, 10:30am–5:30pm Wed, noon–5:30pm Sun. www.imma.ie

Dublin Writers Museum ①
Excellent displays comprising manuscripts by many fine Irish writers.
18 Parnell Square, Dublin; tel: 01 872 2077; open Sep–May: 10am–5pm Mon– Sat, 11am–5pm Sun; Jun–Aug: 10am– 5pm Mon–Sat, 11am–6pm Sun. www.writersmuseum.com

Dublin City Gallery The Hugh Lane ①
Lovely gallery featuring modern European art and the studio of Francis Bacon.
Charlemont House, Parnell Square North, Dublin; tel: 01 222 5550; open 10am– 6pm Tue–Thu, 10am–5pm Fri–Sat, 11am–5pm Sun. www.hughlane.ie

The Guinness Storehouse ①
Imaginative displays and interactive exhibits designed to appeal to all ages tell the story of the national tipple (adults get a free one at the end).
St. James's Gate, Dublin; tel: 01 408 4800; open Sep–Jun: 9:30am–5pm daily; Jul–Aug: 9:30am–7pm daily. www.guinness-storehouse.com

The Irish National Stud ㉜
The best place to see racing thoroughbreds at rest. Also on site are the National Horse Museum, Saint Fiachra's Garden, and extensive Japanese Gardens.
Tully, County Kildare; tel: 045 521251; open Feb–Dec: 9:30am–6pm. www.irish-national-stud.ie

THINGS TO DO WITH KIDS

Dublin Zoo ①
From African hunting dogs and Arctic foxes to tigers, wolves, and zebras, Dublin Zoo has a large collection of animals in simulated natural environments.
Phoenix Park, Dublin; tel: 01 677 1425; open Mar–Sep: 9:30am–6pm daily; Oct: 9:30am–5:30pm daily; Nov–Dec: 9:30am–4pm daily; Jan: 9:30am–4:30pm daily; Feb: 9:30am–5pm daily. www.dublinzoo.ie

Dublinia and the Viking World ①
This heritage center brings early and medieval Dublin to life with detailed models and audiovisual displays.
St. Michael's Hill, Christchurch, Dublin; tel: 01 679 4611; open Apr–Sep: 10am–5pm daily; Oct–Mar: 11am–4pm Mon–Sat, 10am–4pm Sun. www.dublinia.ie

Viking Splash Tours ①
Guided tours around Dublin by land and water in amphibious World War II vehicles, taking in Viking and more recent historical sites. Tours finish with a splashy drive around the Grand Canal Docklands.
St. Stephen's Green North, Dublin; tel: 01 707 6000; tours operate all year, departing every 30 min in summer. www.vikingsplash.ie

Airfield House and Farm ④
Working farm with horses, cows, sheep, and goats and a vintage car display.
Upper Kilmacud Road, Dundrum, nr Dublin; tel: 01 298 4301; open 10am– 5pm daily. www.airfield.ie

Wexford Wildfowl Reserve ⑭
Bird reserve famous for the thousands of geese it attracts in the winter.
North Slob, County Wexford; tel: 053 912 3406; open 10am–5pm daily.

Irish National Heritage Park ⑮
Educational open-air museum covering 9,000 years of Irish history *(see pp96–7)*.
Ferrycarrig, County Wexford; tel: 053 912 0733; open Apr–Sep: 9:30am–6:30pm daily; Oct–Mar: 9:30am–5:30pm daily. www.inhp.com

Kilkenny Castle ㉓
Set in huge grounds and with many rooms and corridors to explore, this is one of the most fascinating castles in Ireland.
The Parade, Kilkenny, County Kilkenny; tel: 056 770 4100; open Oct–Feb: 9:30am–4:30pm daily; Mar: 9:30am– 5pm daily; Apr–May and Sep: 9:30am– 5:30pm daily; Jun–Aug: 9am–5:30pm daily. www.kilkennycastle.ie

Kilvahan Horse-Drawn Caravans ㉚
Rent a traditional horse-drawn caravan for a week and sample life in the slow lane.
Tullibards Stud, Coolrain, County Laois; tel: 057 873 5178. www.horsedrawncaravans.com

Malahide Castle ㊵
A "haunted" castle and model railroad in huge grounds, just north of Dublin.
Malahide, County Dublin; tel: 01 846 2184; open 10am–5pm daily. www.malahidecastle.com

SPAS AND HEALTH RESORTS

La Stampa Hotel and Spa ①
Hip combination of boutique hotel and spa right in the center of Dublin.
35 Dawson Street, Dublin; tel: 01 677 4444. www.lastampa.ie

Ballycullen Lodge and Yoga Retreat ⑨
Reflexology, acupuncture, massage, *reiki*, and homeopathy; other healthy options include forest walks and organic food.
Birch Hill, Ballycullen, Ashford, County Wicklow; tel: 0404 40000. www.ballycullenlodge.com

Brook Lodge and Wells Spa ⑫
The wells in the name of this hotel provide the spa water used in the flotation rooms, Finnish baths and pools.
Macreddin Village, County Wicklow; tel: 0402 36444. www.brooklodge.com

Kilmokea Country Manor and Gardens ⑲
The small spa in this 18th-century rectory includes an indoor pool, sauna, and gym, and offers aromatherapy treatment.
Great Island, Campile, County Wexford; tel: 051 388109. www.kilmokea.com

Mount Juliet Golf and Spa Hotel ㉑
Spa and health club with a swimming pool, sauna, steam room, and gymnasium.
Thomastown, County Kilkenny; tel: 056 777 3000. www.mountjuliet.ie

Mount Wolseley Hotel Spa and Country Club ㉖
Set in green rolling hills, this has a championship golf course and tennis courts, as well as a Sanctuary Spa.
Tullow, County Carlow; tel: 059 918 0100. www.mountwolseley.ie

Osprey Hotel and Spa ㊱
Features a sauna, steam room, salt grotto, and full- and half-day spa packages.
Devoy Quarter, Naas, County Kildare; tel: 045 881111. www.osprey.ie

Dunboyne Castle Hotel and Spa ㊳
Historic Dunboyne Castle has extensive mature gardens and is the perfect location for a spa; handy for Dublin Airport.
Dunboyne, County Meath; tel: 01 801 3500. www.dunboynecastlehotel.com

Castleknock Hotel and Country Club ㊷
The Tonic Health and Day Spa here offers yoga and Pilates classes, an indoor pool, sauna, steam room, and Jacuzzi.
Porterstown Road, Castleknock, Dublin; tel: 01 640 6300. www.castleknockhotel.com

Bellinter House ㊺
Georgian house, home to the Bellinter Bathhouse, which specializes in seaweed baths and other spa indulgences.
Navan, County Meath; tel: 046 903 0900. www.bellinterhouse.com

OTHER SIGHTS IN THE BOOK

Left: Malahide Castle

SOUTHERN IRELAND

LOCAL FOOD

The Sage Café ①
Serving everything from sandwiches to delicious Dingle crab risotto, and with a deli counter doing carry-outs too, the Sage Café is understandably always busy. *67–68 Catherine Street, Limerick, County Limerick; tel: 061 409458; open 9am–6pm Mon–Sat. www.thesagecafe.com*

The Pantry ②
From big breakfasts to afternoon teas and early suppers, the Pantry serves everything from a sandwich to daily specials such as salmon in a white wine and chive sauce. *12 Quentin's Way, Nenagh, County Tipperary; tel: 067 31237; open 8:30am–6:30pm Mon–Sat.*

Café Lucia ⑦
For breakfast, lunch, or an early dinner, this is one place you'll find locals visiting for good home-cooked food at good prices. *2 Arundel Lane, Waterford; tel: 051 852553; open Mon–Sat 9:30am–5pm (until 7pm Fri).*

Quealy's Café Bar ⑫
As the name says, Quealy's is part-café and part-bar, and has a lively atmosphere; make a pit stop here for inexpensive but exceptionally good local food, such as a seafood platter or smoked haddock pie. *82 O'Connell Street, Dungarvan, County Waterford; tel: 058 24555; open noon–9pm daily.*

Farm Gate Café and Restaurant ⑲
You won't find fresher produce or better local eating than at this café-restaurant in Cork's famous English Market. *English Market, Cork; tel: 021 427 8134; open 9am–4pm Mon–Sat. www.corkenglishmarket.ie*

Crawford Gallery Café ⑲
The café at Crawford's Art Gallery is run by the granddaughter of the acclaimed Irish chef Myrtle Allen, and the menu focuses on local dishes and local foods. *Emmet Place, Cork; tel: 021 427 4415; open 8:30am–3pm Mon–Fri, 9am–3pm Sat.*

Delicious Gourmet Food Store ⑲
One of a small chain of stores selling gluten-free breads and cakes made naturally with local ingredients. *Well Road, Douglas, Cork; tel: 021 487 5780; open 9:30am–6:45pm Tue–Fri, 9:30am–5:30pm Sat. www.delicious.ie*

Fishy Fishy Café ㉑
Friendly quayside restaurant serving beautifully fresh local fish and seafood, run by the same people who own a fine fish-and-chip shop nearby. *Crowley's Quay, Kinsale, County Cork; tel: 021 470 0415; open noon–8pm Tue–Fri, noon–4:30pm Sat–Mon. www.fishyfishy.ie*

Cathleen's Country Kitchen ㉟
Good local produce, inexpensive home-cooked food, with delicious local dishes such as bacon and cabbage. *17 New Street, Killarney, County Kerry; tel: 064 6633778; open 9am–6pm Mon–Sat.*

Murphy's Ice Cream ㊳
With its fine dairy products, it's not surprising Ireland produces some good ice cream, and here at Murphy's it's all made in Dingle with milk from Kerry cows. *Strand Street, Dingle, County Kerry; tel: 066 915 2644; open 11am–6:30pm daily (until 10pm in summer). www.murphysicecream.ie*

Annie May's ㉔
All-day restaurant-bar serving breakfast, lunch, and dinner using local produce, with lots of Irish favorites on the menu. *11 Bridge Street, Skibbereen, County Cork; tel: 028 22930; open 8:30am–9pm daily.*

Glebe Gardens and Café ㉕
Seasonal produce from the gardens is used in wonderful dishes, such as the elderflower pannacotta. *Glebe Gardens, Baltimore, County Cork; tel: 028 20232; open Easter–Sep, 10am–10pm Wed–Sat, 10am–6pm Sun. www.glebegardens.com*

FARMERS' MARKETS

Limerick Farmers' Market ①
Seaweed is one of the more unusual foods you can buy here, along with seafood, breads, cheeses, sausages, and jams; one of the best markets in southern Ireland. *Market Square, Limerick; every Sat, 8am–1:30pm. www.visitlimerick.com/milkmarket.asp*

Cahir Farmers' Market ④
An exceptionally good market highlighting the rich variety of local foods, including organic wines, juices, breads, meats, fish, and, of course, fruit and vegetables. *Craft Granary parking lot, Church Street, Cahir, County Tipperary; every Sat, 9am–1pm. www.cahirnews.cahirda.com/gpage8.html*

Dunhill Farmers' Market ⑨
Small, select monthly market with a chance to buy local specialty cheeses, eggs, vegetables, meats, and breads baked fresh on site. *Parish Hall, Dunhill, County Waterford; tel: 051 396 234; last Sun of every month, 11:30am–2pm.*

Carrick-on-Suir Farmers' Market ⑥
There are only a few stands here, but the produce is excellent and there's a chance to chat with the producers. *Heritage Centre, Main Street, Carrick-on-Suir, County Tipperary; every Fri, 10am–2pm.*

Dungarvan Farmers' Market ⑫
Here you can find farmhouse cheeses, traditional and not-so-traditional breads and cakes, organic meats, fruits, and vegetables, and tempting desserts. *Scanlon's Yard, Dungarvan, County Waterford; tel: 086 394 0564; every Thu, 9:30am–2pm.*

Midleton Farmers' Market ⑯
A small, select market with only a handful of stands, but offering top products, including seafood, shellfish, organic pork, vegetables, and local cheeses. *Hospital Road, Midleton, County Cork; tel: 021 463 1096; every Sat, 9am–1pm. www.midletonfarmersmarket.com*

Clonakilty Farmers' Market ㉓
Held twice a week: on Thursday it comprises mainly food stands and offers the chance to buy the local specialty, Clonakilty black puddings; on Saturdays it also features arts and crafts. *McCurtain Hill, Clonakilty, County Cork; tel: 023 48749; every Thu and Sat, 10am–2pm.*

Skibbereen Farmers' Market ㉔
The smell of fresh bread and pastries fills the air at this thriving market, where cheeses, honey, organic vegetables, and arts and crafts are also on sale. *The Fairfield, Skibbereen, County Cork; tel: 087 285 1897; every Sat, 9:30am–1:30pm. www.skibbereenmarket.com*

Country Market ㉖
From burgers to herbal teas, sushi to pizzas, the range sold here, in this lovely harbor village on the southwest coast, is enormous. *Pier car park, Schull, County Cork, tel: 028 27824; every Sun, 11am–3pm. www.schullmarket.com*

Listowel Farmers' Market ㊶
Cheeses and chutneys, breads and patisserie, seafood, vegetables, pies, and herbs – all sold at this busy little market. *The Square, Listowel, County Kerry; every Fri, 10am–2pm. www.listowelfoodfair.com/food-market-page.html*

PUBS AND BARS

Henry Downes ⑦
Quirky, very Irish pub – in business since 1759 – that bottles its own whiskey and, bizarrely, has its own squash court – just what you hope to find, if you can find it (second right after the Bridge Hotel). *8–10 Thomas Street, Waterford; tel: 051 874118; open from 5pm daily.*

Left: Picturesque harbor village of Schull

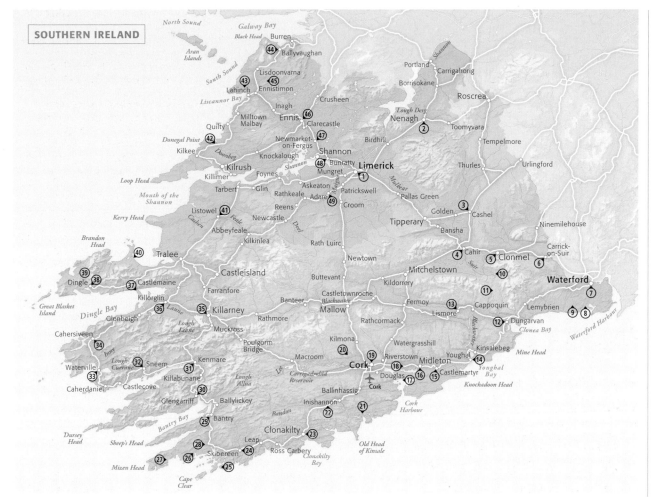

SOUTHERN IRELAND

Aulber House ③
Grand modern guesthouse with a sumptuous period feel, just a few minutes' walk from the center of Cashel. *Golden Road, Cashel, County Tipperary; tel: 062 63713. www.aulberhouse.com*

Kilmaneen Farmhouse ⑤
On land farmed by the same family for six generations, this 200-year-old farmhouse has apartments and B&B accommodation. *Newcastle, Clonmel, County Tipperary; tel: 052 613623. www.kilmaneen.com*

Glenorney ⑧
Beautiful house overlooking Tramore Bay on the Waterford coast, with comfortable rooms; the Irish breakfasts using local ingredients are outstandingly good. *Newtown, Tramore, County Waterford; tel: 051 381056. www.glenorney.com*

Glasha Farmhouse B&B ⑩
Welcoming B&B set in the lovely Nire Valley, offering packed lunches for walkers and a tasty home-cooked evening meal. *Via Clonmel, Ballymacarbry, County Waterford; tel: 052 36108. www.glashafarmhouse.com*

Sliabh gCua Farmhouse ⑪
A real rural retreat with breathtaking views and remarkable food, and with four championship golf courses nearby. *Ballynamult, nr Dungarvan, County Waterford; tel: 058 47129. www.sliabhgcua.com*

An Bohreen ⑫
Located in a deceptively plain bungalow, this guesthouse offers some of the area's finest cooking. It's worth staying here for dinner alone; the bedrooms are comfortable and the views are fabulous. *Killineen West, Dungarvan, County Waterford; tel: 051 291010. www.anbohreen.com*

Hagal Farm ㉙
A farm stay like no other, with holistic treatments and massages in a 150-year-old farmhouse set in 5 acres (2 hectares). *Coomleigh West, Bantry, County Cork; tel: 027 66179. http://hagalholistichealth.com*

Kingfisher Lodge ㉟
One of the best B&Bs in Killarney; generous breakfasts, a lovely garden, and just a few minutes' stroll to the town's center. *Lewis Road, Killarney, County Kerry; tel: 064 663 7131. www.kingfisherkillarney.com*

Drumcreehy Guesthouse ㊹
With views over Galway Bay, friendly hosts, open fires, and complimentary tea, coffee, and cakes, this is a dream of a guesthouse in which to stay while exploring the Burren. *Ballyvaughan, County Clare; tel: 065 707 7377. www.drumcreehyhouse.com*

The Fairways Bar ②
Country pub with a cozy "snug" bar, with cushion-strewn banquettes and, in winter, an open fire. There is a large bar–dining area with an upmarket menu and a fancier gourmet restaurant, the Orchard, attached. *Kilruane, Nenagh, County Tipperary; tel: 067 41444; open daily. www.thefairwaysbar.ie*

Dalton's ㉑
This Kinsale mainstay has been popular for years, and combines exceptionally good pub lunches with a typical Irish bar atmosphere in the evenings. *3 Market Street, Kinsale, County Cork; tel: 021 477 7957; open daily. www.ireland-guide.com*

The Poachers Inn ㉒
Local seafood is the draw here at what looks like an ordinary, cozy little pub – but which also happens to have a marvelous menu created by a top chef. *Clonakilty Road, Bandon, County Cork; tel: 023 884 1159; open daily; restaurant 7–10pm Thu–Sat, noon–3:30pm Sun.*

An Súgán ㉓
There's no missing this busy, brightly colored and cheerful pub, and the food and drink is some of the best in town, from smoked salmon to the local Clonakilty black pudding. *41 Wolfe Tone Street, Clonakilty, County Cork; tel: 023 883 3498. www.ansugan.com*

Mary Ann's Bar and Restaurant ㉔
A 19th-century pub in a 15th-century building, but the menu, including crab, salmon, and the catch of the day, is as fresh and modern as they come. *Castletownshend, Skibbereen, County Cork; tel: 028 36146; open daily. www.westcorkweek.com/maryanns*

Levis's Bar ㉘
This 150-year-old bar-cum-grocery store, now run by just one of the two Levis sisters, is exactly the kind of Irish pub that visitors hope to find – a warm welcome and a wonderful, traditional interior full of people having a good time. *Corner House, Main Street, Ballydehob, County Cork; tel: 028 37118; open daily*

The Horseshoe ㉛
It's almost impossible to resist this place, with an outside adorned with colorful flowers; the unpretentious interior belies an award-winning menu and wine list. *3 Main Street, Kenmare, County Kerry; tel: 064 664 1553; open daily. www.horseshoebarkenmare.com*

The Smugglers Inn ㉝
This inn was once a farmhouse and has almost 200 years of history, plus stunning views and a highly rated seafood restaurant, with fresh lobsters a specialty. *Cliff Road, Waterville, County Kerry; tel: 066 947 4330; open daily. www.the-smugglers-inn.com*

O'Neill's ㉞
In the same family for 150 years, this simple but very hospitable pub is at the tip of the Iveragh peninsula; the summer seafood bar has made this place a legendary spot. *Renard Point, Cahirciveen, County Kerry; tel: 066 947 2165; open daily; food served Apr–Oct only.*

Morrissey's Seafood Bar and Restaurant ㊷
With a lovely setting by the River Cree, the waterside terrace of this family-run bar is the perfect spot to enjoy everything from a refreshing pint to fish and chips. *Doonbeg, County Clare; tel: 065 9055304; open daily. www.morrisseysdoonbeg.com*

Vaughans Anchor Inn ㊸
Near the stunning Cliffs of Moher, this multi-award-winning pub serves superb seafood but remains a family establishment with a shop attached. *Main Street, Liscannor, County Clare; tel: 065 708 1548; open daily. www.vaughans.ie*

Vaughans Pub ㊺
One of the best music venues in southern Ireland, in a homey bar with an open fire and hearty food, such as beef and Guinness pie. What could be better? *Main Street, Kilfenora, County Clare; tel: 065 708 8004; open daily, food served 10am–9pm in summer only. www.vaughanspub.ie*

Fortview House ㉗
Working farm in a glorious location near Mizen Head, offering both apartment and B&B accommodation; the breakfasts are outstandingly good.
Gurtyowen, Toormore, Goleen, County Cork; tel: 028 35324.
www.fortviewhousegoleen.com

The Shores Country House B&B ㊵
Many rooms, furnished in period style, have panoramic views of Brandon Bay on the Dingle Peninsula. It offers much-acclaimed breakfasts and dinners.
Cappatigue, Castlegregory, County Kerry; tel: 066 713 9196.
www.shorescountryhouse.com

Newpark House ㊻
Farmhouse on a grand country-house scale surrounded by beech and oak trees; some rooms have canopied beds.
Roslevan, Ennis, County Clare; tel: 065 682 1233.
homepage.eircom.net/~newparkhouse/

Spraoi ⑦
Waterford's annual Spraoi Festival takes over the city for three days and includes street parades with bands and buskers from all over the world.
Various venues, Waterford; tel: 051 841808; Aug Bank Holiday weekend.
www.spraoi.com

Waterford Imagine Arts Festival ⑦
This 10-day annual festival includes music, dance, literature, theater, film, visual arts, and special events for children.
Various venues, Waterford; tel: 087 662 2086; late Oct or early Nov.
www.imagineartsfestival.com

Cork Film Festival ⑲
Spread over eight days, Ireland's biggest and oldest film festival has premieres of documentaries and short films, and attracts famous actors and directors.
Various venues, Cork; tel: 021 427171; Nov.
www.corkfilmfest.org

Cork Folk Festival ⑲
The four-day Cork Folk Festival has been going for over 25 years, with numerous stage performances, masterclasses, and impromptu sessions in the pubs too.
Various venues, Cork; early Oct.
www.corkfolkfestival.com

Cork Jazz Festival ⑲
Four days of the world's top musicians turn Cork into a jazz-lover's dream, with some drama productions thrown in.
Various venues, Cork; tel: 021 427 8979; late Oct. www.corkjazzfestival.com

Killorglin Puck Fair ㊱
Ireland's oldest fair is held, without fail, for three days on the same dates every year: see parades, music, street theater, and the crowning of a goat as King Puck.
Killorglin, County Kerry; tel: 066 976 2366; 10–12 Aug. www.puckfair.ie

Above: Lismore Heritage Centre

Cobh Peoples Regatta ⑰
Historically one of the biggest sailing regattas in Europe, this three-day event is still going strong in Cobh Harbour.
Cobh, County Cork; tel: 021 481 1347; Aug. www.cobhpeoplesregatta.com

Baltimore Fiddle Fair ㉕
For four days in May, some of the country's finest fiddle-players bring Baltimore to life with concerts and countless sessions.
Baltimore, County Cork; tel: 086 375 3380; early May. www.fiddlefair.com

Baltimore Seafood Festival ㉕
Cork is renowned for its seafood, and this three-day festival is the chance to join in and celebrate it, with rowing races, net-mending competitions, and more.
Baltimore, County Cork; tel: 028 20125; late May. www.baltimore.ie

Killarney Summerfest ㉟
This eclectic festival lasts for over two weeks, and has arts and outdoor events, as well as activities for children.
Scotts Garden, Killarney, County Kerry; tel: 064 667 1560; Jul. www.killarneysummerfest.com

Dingle Races ㊳
For a weekend in August, a Dingle field is transformed into a racecourse, with over 20 races and tens of thousands of people from all over Ireland and beyond.
Ballintaggart, Dingle, County Kerry; tel: 087 682 9255; Aug. www.dingleraces.ie

Dingle Regatta ㊳
A day of boat races in the harbor and carousing in the evening, all celebrating the skills of local sailors and boatmen.
Dingle Harbour, Dingle, County Kerry; tel: 066 915 1907; Aug.

Cork Butter Museum ⑲
This unique and entertaining museum tells the fascinating story of one of Ireland's most famous products.
The Tony O'Reilly Centre, O'Connell Square, Cork; tel: 021 4300 600; open Mar–Oct: 10am–5pm daily (till 6pm Jul–Aug). www.corkbutter.museum

The Hunt Museum ①
Picasso, Renoir, and Henry Moore are just some of the famous names in this extensive private art collection.
Rutland Street, Limerick; tel: 061 312833; open 10am–5pm Mon–Sat, 2–5pm Sun. www.huntmuseum.com

Nenagh Heritage Centre and Museum ②
Housed in what was the Governor's House and the gatehouse for the town jail, this museum includes a re-created school room, dairy, kitchen, condemned cells, and the execution area.
The Governor's House, Kirkham Street, Nenagh, County Tipperary; tel: 067 33850; open 9:30am–5pm Mon–Fri; May–Aug: also open 10am–5pm Sat. www.nenagh.ie

Brú Ború Cultural Centre ③
Found at the foot of the Rock of Cashel, this is a wonderful multimedia exploration of Irish culture and, in particular, its music, with evening shows.
Cashel, County Tipperary; tel: 062 61122; open mid-Jun–mid-Sep: 9am–9pm Tue–Sat; mid-Sep–mid-Jun: 9am–5pm Mon–Fri. http://comhaltas.ie/locations/detail/bru_boru/

South Tipperary County Museum ⑤
This museum, which tells the story of the county of Tipperary, has won several awards for its imaginative displays, and houses visiting exhibitions too.
Mick Delahunty Square, Clonmel, County Tipperary; tel: 052 34550; open 10am–5pm Tue–Sat. www.southtippcoco.ie/en/museum/

Carrick-on-Suir Heritage Centre ⑥
This former church now combines an interesting heritage museum with the town's Tourist Information Centre, making it any visitor's first port of call.
Main Street, Carrick-on-Suir, County Tipperary; tel: 051 640200; open 10am–5pm Mon–Fri; Jun–Sep: also open 10am–5pm Sat–Sun. www.carrickonsuir.ie

Waterford Treasures at the Granary Museum ⑦
Waterford's main museum contains exceptionally good and imaginative displays that tell the city's story using many impressive multimedia techniques.
Merchants Quay, Waterford; tel: 051 304500; open Jun–Aug: 9:30am–9pm daily; Apr, May, and Sep: 9:30am–6pm daily; Oct–Mar: 10am–5pm daily. www.waterfordtreasures.com

Waterford County Museum ⑫
Run by enthusiastic volunteers, this interesting museum houses fascinating artifacts, including coins and militaria. There's also maritime history, a shop, and genealogical information.
St. Augustine Street, Dungarvan, County Waterford; tel: 058 45960; open 10am–5pm Mon–Fri. www.waterfordcountymuseum.org

Lismore Heritage Centre ⑬
There was a monastery in Lismore as long ago as AD 636, and this excellent center tells the town's story through to the present day with entertaining audiovisual displays.
Main Street, Lismore, County Waterford; tel: 058 54975/54855; open 9:30am–5:30pm Mon–Fri; May–Oct: also open 10am–5:30pm Sat, noon–5:30pm Sun. www.discoverlismore.com

Fox's Lane Folk Museum ⑭
One of those fascinating little museums that displays all sorts of everyday items from the past – from sewing machines to glove stretchers – showing how previous generations lived.
Youghal, County Cork; tel: 024 91145; open Jul–Sep: 10am–1pm and 2–6pm Tue–Sat; other times by appointment. http://tyntescastle.com/fox/index.html

Cork Public Museum ⑲
Everything from ancient archaeology to modern sports in the city is presented in this first-class and sizable museum.
Fitzgerald Park, Cork; tel: 021 427 0679; open 11am–1pm and 2:15–5pm Mon–Fri, 11am–1pm and 2:15–4pm Sat; Apr–Sep: also open 3–5pm Sun. www.corkcity.ie/tourism/buildingsandtouristattractions

Crawford Municipal Art Gallery ⑲
Here you can view an extensive permanent collection of art by important 19th- and 20th-century Irish and international artists, as well as frequent visiting exhibitions.
Emmet Place, Cork; tel: 021 490 7855; open 10am–5pm Mon–Sat (till 8pm Thu). www.crawfordartgallery.ie

Kinsale Regional Museum ㉑
This comprehensive collection covers everything to do with Kinsale, including the story of the Kinsale Giant, the Battle of Kinsale, and the sinking of the Cunard liner *Lusitania* off the coast here in 1915.
Market Square, Kinsale, County Cork; tel: 021 477 7930; open 10:30am–1pm and 2–5:30pm Mon–Sat, 2–5pm Sun. http://homepage.eircom.net/~kinsalemuseum/index.html

Fota Wildlife Park ⑱
Spread over 70 acres (28 hectares), this park is designed to allow the animals to roam as freely as possible; the cheetahs' feeding time is not to be missed.
Carrigtwohill, County Cork; tel: 021 481 2678; open 10am–5pm Mon–Sat, 11am–5pm Sun. www.fotawildlife.ie

Cork City Gaol Heritage Centre ⑲
One of the city's major visitor attractions, this atmospheric center really brings home what prison conditions were like for the inmates.
Convent Avenue, Sunday's Well, Cork; tel: 021 430 5022; open Mar–Oct: 9:30am–5pm daily; Nov–Feb: 10am–4pm daily. www.corkcitygaol.com

Mitchelstown Cave ④
One of the finest show caves in Europe; guided tours lead visitors through just a fraction of the enormous underground network to see some of the most unusual shapes and structures.
Burncourt, Cahir, County Tipperary; tel: 052 67246; open Apr–Sep: 10am–5:30pm daily; Oct–Mar: from 10am daily, closing times vary. www.mitchelstowncave.com

Cahir Castle ④
Dating from 1142, Cahir Castle is one of the biggest and best-preserved castles in Ireland, thanks to 19th-century restoration work. There are plenty of nooks, crannies, and rooms for children to explore.
Cahir, County Tipperary, tel: 052 41011; open mid-Jun–mid-Sep: 9am–7pm daily; mid-Sep–Mar: 9:30am–4:30pm daily; Apr–mid-Jun: 9:30am–5:30pm daily. www.cahirtourism.ie

West Cork Model Railway Village ㉓
There are road-train rides that run around Clonakilty town, as well as the delightful and detailed scale model of the West Cork Railway as it would have looked in the 1940s.
The Station, Inchydoney Road, Clonakilty, County Cork; tel: 023 33224; open 11am–5pm daily. www.modelvillage.ie

Schull Planetarium ㉖
Amazingly, the Republic of Ireland's only planetarium is situated in the little Cork town of Schull. It is run through the Community College and offers a variety of shows throughout the summer months.
Community College, Schull, County Cork; tel: 028 28315/28552; open Jun–Sep: show times vary. www.westcorkweb.ie/planetarium/index.html

Fungi the Dolphin ㊳
Take the children to the harbor in Dingle and look for its most famous resident, Fungi the bottlenose dolphin, or admire his bronze sculpture. Rent a boat from the pier to see Fungi up close *(see pp80–81).*
The Harbour, Dingle, County Kerry. www.dodingle.com

Celtic and Prehistoric Museum ㊳
Mammoth fossils, dinosaur eggs, and skeletons: there's a lot to entertain both children and adults at this museum, which tells the intriguing story of ancient Dingle and its environs.
Kilvicadownig, Dingle, County Kerry; tel: 066 915 9191; open Mar–Nov: 10am–5:30pm daily. www.celticmuseum.com

Dingle Oceanworld Aquarium ㊳
Plenty of hands-on experiences for children in this top-class modern aquarium, which explores maritime life both locally and internationally. At the Touch Tank, friendly rays swim up to be petted.
The Wood, Dingle, County Kerry; tel: 066 915 2111; open 10am–5pm daily. www.dingle-oceanworld.ie

International Sailing Centre ⑰
Older children have the chance to learn sailing skills or surfing in this sheltered harbor; youngsters can join in supervised sessions of canoeing and water fun.
East Hill, Cobh, County Cork; tel: 021 481 1237; courses available to book all year round. www.sailcork.com

Blarney Castle ⑳
Famous for its Stone of Eloquence, kissed by millions, but also a magical place for exploring ruins and curious rock formations, including the Wishing Steps and the Witch's Kitchen.
Blarney, County Cork; tel: 021 438 5252; open May and Sep: 9am–6:30pm Mon–Sat, 9am–5:30pm Sun; Jun–Aug: 9am–7pm Mon–Sat, 9am–5:30pm Sun; Oct–Apr: 9am–sundown daily. www.blarneycastle.ie

Glengarriff Nature Reserve ㉚
Take the children out to this lovely wooded nature reserve to look for otters, stoats, bats, owls, and more.
Glengarriff, County Cork; tel: 027 63636; open access daily. www.glengarriffnaturereserve.ie

Inch Strand Beach ㊲
The most famous and beautiful beach in Ireland is a movie star in its own right – it famously featured in the 1970 film *Ryan's Daughter* – and has huge stretches of beautiful sand to explore.
Inch, south of Dingle, County Kerry.

SPAS AND HEALTH RESORTS

Radisson Blu Hotel and Spa Limerick ①
In a handy location between the city of Limerick and Shannon Airport, this hotel's spa has its own steam room, tropical rain shower, and outdoor hot tub, among other indulgences.
Ennis Road, Limerick; tel: 061 456200. www.radissonblu.ie/hotel-limerick

Coolbawn Quay Lakeshore Spa ②
On the shores of Lough Derg, this spa is modeled on an Irish village, and has luxurious "cottages." Its facilities include a natural spring-water pool, a eucalyptus steam room, and a sauna.
Coolbawn, Nenagh, County Tipperary; tel: 067 28158. www.coolbawnquay.com

Hayfield Manor Hotel ⑲
A 5-star hotel right in the center of Cork, with mature gardens, nine spa treatment rooms, an acclaimed restaurant, and many "Hotel of the Year" awards to its name.
Perrott Avenue, College Road, Cork; tel: 021 484 5900. www.hayfieldmanor.ie

Dingle Skellig Hotel and Spa ㊳
This 4-star hotel is situated on the most westerly tip of Europe, in an area that *National Geographic* magazine described as the most beautiful place on Earth.
Dingle, County Kerry; tel: 066 915 0200. www.dingleskellig.com

Castlemartyr ⑮
The luxury 5-star Castlemartyr opened in 2007 in 220 acres (50 hectares) of woodland and has a stunning modern spa, a championship golf course, archery, heritage trails, and many other activities right in the grounds.
Castlemartyr, County Cork; tel: 021 421 9000. www.castlemartyrresort.ie

Carlton Kinsale Hotel and Spa ㉑
This 4-star resort lies in 90 acres (36 hectares) and has extensive views over Oysterhaven Bay; its spa boasts ten treatment rooms, plus a swimming pool, sauna, and gym.
Rathmore Road, Kinsale, County Cork; tel: 021 470 6000. www.carltonkinsalehotel.com

Inchydoney Island Lodge and Spa ㉓
This has been voted Ireland's leading spa resort, and with its views over the ocean and two sweeping beaches, it is certainly one of the most idyllic retreats to be found in the country.
Clonakilty, County Cork; tel: 023 883 3143. www.inchydoneyisland.com

Park Hotel Kenmare ㉛
This 5-star spa hotel retreat is a short walk from the center of Kenmare, and boasts a lap-pool and sauna as well as tennis, t'ai chi courses, aquaerobics, and even a 12-seat movie theater.
Kenmare, County Kerry; tel: 064 664 1200. www.parkkenmare.com

Parknasilla Resort ㉜
Spa resort with its own 12-hole golf course; previous guests have included Charlie Chaplin and Robert Graves.
Sneem, County Kerry; tel: 064 75600. www.parknasillahotel.ie

Dromoland Castle Hotel ㊼
This medieval fortress can trace its history back 1,000 years, but today it is a 5-star, fabulously furnished luxury resort hotel with a spa set within the castle grounds.
Newmarket-on-Fergus, County Clare; tel: 061 368144. www.dromoland.ie

Bunratty Castle Hotel ㊽
This luxury hotel has its own spa, and there's also a leisure club, pool, sauna, and steam room.
Bunratty, County Clare; tel: 061 478700. www.bunrattycastlehotel.com

Adare Manor Hotel and Golf Resort ㊾
An 18th-century manor house by the River Maigue, transformed into a luxury spa resort and championship golf course.
Adare, County Limerick; tel: 061 605200. www.adaremanor.com

OTHER SIGHTS IN THE BOOK

Cork ⑲ *(see pp48–9).* **Dingle Peninsula** ㊴ *(see pp80–81).* **Bunratty Castle** ㊼ *(see pp148–9).*

Below: Cahir Castle in County Tipperary

NORTH WALES

LOCAL FOOD

The Little Deli ①
A wide choice of locally produced food and drink, including homemade fudge. *133 Mostyn Street, Llandudno, Conwy; tel: 01492 872114; open 10am–5pm Mon–Wed (until 6pm Apr–Sep), 10am–6pm Thu–Sat, noon–4pm Sun (until 6pm Apr–Sep). www.thelittledeli.co.uk*

Edwards of Conwy ④
Traditional, award-winning master butcher renowned for its Welsh lamb and beef. *18 High Street, Conwy; tel: 01492 592443; open 8am–5:30pm Mon–Sat. www.edwardsofconwy.co.uk*

The Rainbow Inn ⑭
Coaching inn serving traditional dishes such as fish and chips, lamb, and rabbit. *Ruthin Road, Gwernymyndd, Mold, Flintshire; tel: 01352 752575; open noon–9pm daily. www.therainbowinn.co.uk*

The Sun Trevor ㉓
Scenic, family-friendly inn close to the Llangollen Canal, offering substantial meals. *Sun Bank, Llangollen, Denbighshire; tel: 01978 860651; bar menu: noon–2:30pm Mon–Fri, noon–5:30pm Sat, noon–7:30pm Sun; evening menu: 6–9pm Sun–Thu, 6–9:30pm Fri–Sat. www.suntrevor.co.uk*

Penhelig Arms ㉗
Stylish, highly regarded restaurant serving fresh local seafood in an 18th-century seafront inn. *Aberdyfi, Gwynedd; tel: 01654 767215; open noon–2pm and 6–9:30pm daily. www.penheligarms.com*

Leonardo's Delicatessen ⑮
Choose from a wide selection of freshly made sandwiches here, as well as quiches and cakes. *4 Well Street, Ruthin, Denbighshire; tel: 01824 707161; open 9:30am–5:30pm Mon–Fri. www.leonardosdeli.co.uk*

Ruthin Produce Market ⑮
A wide range of local food is offered here in this pretty market town, including fresh fruit, vegetables, meats, and cheeses. *Old Gaol Courtyard, St. Peter's Square, Ruthin, Denbighshire; tel: 07798 914721; Apr–Sep: last Sat of the month, 10am–3pm. www.ruthinproducemarket.co.uk*

Yr Hen Fecws ㉛
Try imaginative local specialties with an international twist at this popular restaurant with seven guest rooms. *16 Lombard Street, Porthmadog, Gwynedd; tel: 01766 514625; open 6–10pm daily. www.henfecws.com*

Iechyd Da Delicatessen ㊷
Buy local cheeses, smoked fish, honey, chocolates, and a range of international delicacies here. *Station Road, Betws-y-Coed, Conwy; tel: 01690 710994; open 9:30am–5.30pm daily. www.delinorthwales.co.uk*

Rhiwafallen Restaurant ㊾
Intimate restaurant serving local beef, lamb, fish, and shellfish, with five comfortable guest rooms to collapse in. *Llandwrog, Caernarfon, Gwynedd; tel: 01286 830172; open 7pm–late Tue–Sat, 12:30–2pm Sun. www.rhiwafallen.co.uk*

Blas ar Fwyd ㊸
Deli with a huge range of cheeses, chutneys, preserves, cakes, and more, with a restaurant opposite. *25 Heol yr Orsaf, Llanrwst, Conwy; tel: 01492 640215; deli open 9am–5:30pm Mon–Sat; restaurant open 10:30am–8pm Mon–Fri, 10:30am–9pm Sat, 10:30am–4:30pm Sun. www.blasarfwyd.com*

Lle Hari Restaurant ㊸
Try local lamb, venison, pork, and fish at this smart and popular hotel restaurant. *The Meadowsweet Hotel, Station Road, Llanrwst, Conwy; tel: 01492 642111; open 6pm–9pm Tue–Sat, 6pm–8pm Sun–Mon. www.wales-snowdonia-hotel.co.uk*

Hooton's Homegrown ㊿①
Pick your own strawberries, raspberries, and vegetables in season at two sites with views of Mount Snowdon. *Gwydryn Hîr, Brynsiencyn, Anglesey; tel: 01248 430344; open from mid-Jun. www.hootonshomegrown.com*

The Lobster Pot ㊼
Long-established seafood restaurant serving fresh local crab, lobster, oysters, and scallops, as well as meat dishes. *Church Bay, Anglesey; tel: 01407 730241; open noon–1:30pm and 6pm–late Tue–Sat, noon–2pm Sun. www.lobster-pot.net*

Sarah's Delicatessen ㊽
Buy Welsh cheeses at the deli and tuck into tapas at the adjoining coffee house. *Church Street, Beaumaris, Anglesey; tel: 01248 811534; open 9am–5pm Mon–Sat. www.sarahsdelicatessencoffeehouse.co.uk*

The Courtyard Restaurant ㊽
Sample Welsh and international dishes, including lamb, steak, salmon, and pasta. *Regent House, 17 Church Street, Beaumaris, Anglesey; tel: 01248 810565; open 11:30am–3pm and 6–9:30pm Wed–Mon. www.courtyardcuisine.com*

The Old Boathouse Café & Restaurant ㊽
Enjoy sea views and a menu featuring salads, grills, fish, lamb, and lobster. *Red Wharf Bay, Anglesey; tel: 01248 852731; open from 7–10am, noon–2pm and 7–9:30pm daily. www.boathouserestaurantanglesey.co.uk*

FARMERS' MARKETS

Mold Farmers' Market ⑬
Buy locally produced organic meats and produce, as well as handmade crafts. *St. Mary's Church Hall, King Street, Mold, Flintshire; tel: 01745 561999; first Sat of every month, 9am–2pm. www.celynfarmersmarket.co.uk*

Wrexham Farmers' Market ⑳
Local producers sell everything from meats and eggs to cakes and honey. *Queen's Square, Wrexham; tel: 01978 292540; third Fri of every month, 9am–3pm. www.wrexham.gov.uk*

Glyndwr Farmers' Market ㉔
Produce, preserves, cheeses, and more are sold at this market on a working farm. *Rhug Estate, Corwen, Denbighshire; tel: 01691 860357; May–Oct: first Sun of every month, 10am–4pm. www.fmiw.co.uk*

Dolgellau Farmers' Market ㉖
Plenty of local food and drink is available at this busy monthly market in the Snowdonia National Park. *Eldon Square, Dolgellau, Gwynedd; tel: 01341 450211; third Sun of every month, 10am–2pm. www.fmiw.co.uk*

Menai Bridge Farmers' Market ㊽
Local fruit, veggies, and much more at this popular monthly market. *David Hughes School, Pentraeth Road, Menai Bridge, Anglesey; tel: 01248 712287; third Sat of every month, 9:30am–2:30pm.*

PUBS AND BARS

George & Dragon ④
Historic pub full of character near Conwy Castle, with beer garden, restaurant, and guest rooms. *21 Castle Street, Conwy; tel: 01492 592305; open daily. www.georgeanddragonconwy.co.uk*

Y Pentan ⑬
Modern restaurant-bar in a charming old building dating to 1820, serving cocktails and coffees as well as real ales. *3 New Street, Mold, Flintshire; tel: 01352 755665; open daily (until 1am Fri–Sat). www.y-pentan.com*

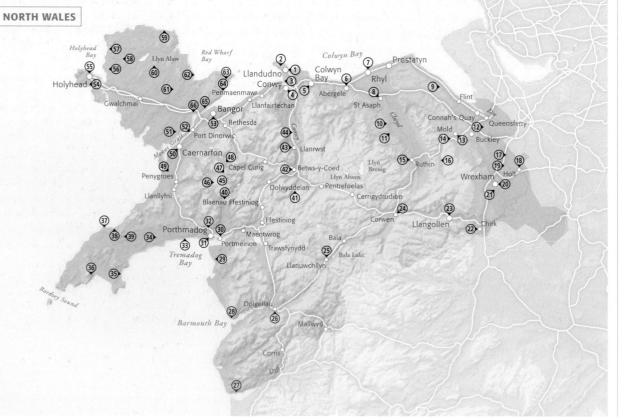

NORTH WALES

Glan Yr Afon Inn ⑨
Picturesque village pub with microbrewery ales, restaurant, and guest rooms.
Dolphin, Milwr, Hollywell, Flintshire; tel: 01352 710052; open daily.
www.glanyrafoninn.co.uk

Hope & Anchor ⑩
Traditional, sociable pub with a big beer garden and quiz and live music nights.
94 Vale Street, Denbigh, Denbighshire; tel: 01745 816707; open noon–2:30pm and 6–11pm Mon–Fri, noon–11pm Sat, noon–10:30pm Sun.

Pant-Yr-Ochain ⑲
Sample a wide range of real ales at this pub built into a historic manor house.
Old Wrexham Road, Gresford, Wrexham; tel: 01978 853525; open daily.
www.brunningandprice.co.uk/ pantyrochain

Ty Coch Inn ㊲
Quaint red-brick village inn on the Lleyn Peninsula that serves real ales and food in friendly surroundings.
Porthdinllaen, Gwynedd; tel: 01758 720498; open 11am–11pm Mon–Sat, 11am–4pm Sun. www.tycoch.co.uk

Cwellyn Arms ㊻
A popular pub in the heart of Snowdonia, with a range of dormitory, B&B, and campsite accommodations.
Rhyd Ddu, Gwynedd; tel: 01766 890321; open daily. www.snowdoninn.co.uk

The Black Boy Inn ㊾
The oldest pub in town, this is a cozy stop for local ales.
Northgate Street, Caernarfon, Gwynedd; tel: 01286 673604; open daily.
www.black-boy-inn.com

The Ship Inn ㊻
Historic, award-winning pub on the shore, serving regional real ales and 48 whiskeys.
Red Wharf Bay, Anglesey; tel: 01248 852568; open daily.
www.shipinnredwharfbay.co.uk

Ye Olde Bull's Head Inn ㉔
Historic 15th-century inn with oak-beamed ceilings, log fire, restaurant, brasserie, and elegant guest rooms.
Castle Street, Beaumaris, Anglesey; tel: 01248 810329; open daily.
www.bullsheadinn.co.uk

Four Crosses Inn ㉖
Family-friendly pub with an extensive menu and views of the Menai Strait.
Pentraeth Road, Menai Bridge, Anglesey; tel: 01248 712230; open daily.
www.fourcrossesinn.co.uk

PLACES TO STAY

Bodysgallen Hall Hotel ①
Historic mansion with a fine restaurant, 15 spacious rooms, and 16 cottage suites in the extensive grounds.
Llandudno, Conwy; tel: 01492 584466.
www.bodysgallen.com

Above: St. Deiniol's Library in Hawarden

The Quay Hotel ③
Luxurious waterfront hotel that boasts smart rooms and suites, a gym, and an excellent restaurant.
Deganwy Quay, Deganwy, Conwy; tel: 01492 564100. www.quayhotel.com

The Kinmel Arms Hotel ⑥
Choose from four individually designed suites, with balconies or patios.
The Village, St. George, Abergele, Conwy; tel: 01745 832207.
www.thekinmelarms.co.uk

The Pier Hotel ⑦
Seafront adults-only hotel with a choice of cozy rooms, plus bar and restaurant.
23 East Parade, Rhyl, Denbighshire; tel: 0871 271 1199.
www.thepierhotel.co.uk

The Talardy Hotel ⑧
Attractive, child-friendly boutique hotel with 16 imaginatively themed rooms, two restaurants, a wine bar, and a pub.
The Roe, St. Asaph, Denbighshire; tel: 01745 584957. www.talardy.co.uk

St. Deiniol's Library ⑫
Grand Victorian residential library, with 30 peaceful *en-suite* rooms, a restaurant, and 250,000 books to browse.
Church Lane, Hawarden, Flintshire; tel: 01244 532350. www.st-deiniols.com

The Beaufort Park Hotel ⑬
Large modern hotel and conference center with fresh rooms and suites, restaurant, and coffee house.
Mold, Flintshire; tel: 01352 758646.
www.beaufortparkhotel.co.uk

Rossett Hall Hotel ⑰
Attractive Georgian house with 50 tasteful *en-suite* rooms and an upmarket restaurant.
Chester Road, Rossett, Wrexham; tel: 01244 571000.
rossetthallhotel.co.uk

The Hand Hotel ㉒
Welcoming 17th-century coaching inn with *en-suite* rooms, restaurant, and bar.
Church Street, Chirk, Wrexham; tel: 01691 773472. www.thehandhotelchirk.co.uk

Cartref Guest House ㉗
Peaceful Edwardian house not far from the beach, with five neat rooms and a garden.
Aberdovey, Gwynedd; tel: 01654 767273.
www.cartref-aberdovey.co.uk

Ty'r Graig Castle ㉘
Grand, cliff-top Victorian mansion boasting 11 period-style rooms with views of Cardigan Bay.
Llanaber Road, Barmouth, Gwynedd; tel: 01341 280470. www.tyrgraigcastle.co.uk

Snowdon Lodge ㉜
Busy, friendly hostel with a range of dormitory accommodations and private rooms, plus a cozy lounge. *Lawrence House, Church Street, Tremadog, Porthmadog, Gwynedd; tel: 01766 515354. www.snowdonlodge.co.uk*

Venetia ㉟
Trendy boutique hotel with five chic, individually designed rooms and a classy seafood restaurant.
Lon Sarn Bach, Abersoch, Gwynedd; tel: 01758 713354. www.venetiawales.com

Caeau Capel Hotel ㊳
Homey, old-fashioned country-house hotel in large gardens near the coast, with 17 restful rooms.
Rhodfa'r Mor, Nefyn, Gwynedd; tel: 01758 720240.
www.caeaucapelhotel.com

The Old Rectory ㊴
Homey B&B rooms in a Georgian house and a separate cottage in the heart of the Llyn Peninsula.
Boduan, nr Pwllheli, Gwynedd; tel: 01758 721519. www.theoldrectory.net

Swallow Falls Complex ㊷
Beautifully located Edwardian hotel with smart modern rooms, high-quality hostel dorms, and a campsite.
Holyhead Road, Betws-y-Coed, Conwy; tel: 01690 710796.
www.swallowfallshotel.co.uk

Plas Maenan Country House ㊹
Tastefully furnished rooms and large suites are available in this welcoming mansion with mountain views.
Conwy Valley, nr Llanrwst, Conwy; tel: 01492 660232.
www.plas-maenan-hotel.co.uk

Ben's Bunkhouse ㊽
Simple dorm rooms, with kitchen and lounge, at the foot of Mount Snowdon.
Nant Peris, Llanberis, Gwynedd; tel: 07989 500657. www.bensbunkhouse.co.uk

Eryl Môr Hotel ㊾
Country-house hotel overlooking the Menai Strait with neat *en suite* rooms and a restaurant. *2 Upper Garth Road, Bangor, Gwynedd; tel: 01248 353789.*
www.erylmorhotel.co.uk

The Trearddur Bay Hotel ㊿
Family-run hotel on a great beach, with spacious rooms, pool, and restaurant.
Lon Isallt, Trearddur Bay, Anglesey; tel: 01407 860301.
www.trearddurbayhotel.co.uk

Penrhyn Farm ㊉
Choose apartment, B&B, or camping accommodations at this seaside farm.
Llanfwrog, Anglesey; tel: 01407 730134.
www.angleseyfarms.com

Drws-y-Coed Farm ㉟
Working cattle and sheep farm offering spacious *en-suite* rooms in a peaceful rural setting.
Llanerch-y-Medd, Anglesey; tel: 01248 470473. www.angleseyfarms.com

The Liverpool Arms Hotel (64)
Attractively renovated Georgian inn, with 10 stylish rooms, some with four-poster beds, and a traditional tavern.
Castle Street, Beaumaris, Anglesey; tel: 01248 810362.
www.liverpoolarms.co.uk

Auckland Arms Hotel (65)
Cozy B&B accommodations in a family-run hotel with a bar and pleasant garden.
Water Street, Menai Bridge, Anglesey; tel: 01248 712545.
www.anglesey-hotel.co.uk

Plas Cadnant (65)
Stay in one of five beautifully restored cottages set in private parkland.
Cadnant Road, Menai Bridge, Anglesey; tel: 01248 717007.
www.plascadnant.co.uk

FESTIVALS AND EVENTS

Conwy River Festival (4)
Major yachting festival with nine days of competitions, live music, RAF displays, and a children's procession.
Conwy Quay, Conwy; tel: 01492 596253; Aug. www.conwyriverfestival.org

Conwy Seed Fair (4)
This 700-year-old, day-long fair boasts stalls selling plants, seeds, and honey.
High Street and Lancaster Square, Conwy; tel: 01745 832812; Mar.
www.conwybeekeepers.org.uk

Gwledd Conwy Feast (4)
Popular two-day food festival featuring produce stalls, cooking demonstrations, and entertainment.
Quayside, Conwy; tel: 01492 593874; Oct.
www.conwyfeast.co.uk

Wrexham Science Festival (20)
Ten days of hands-on exhibits and shows covering aspects of science, technology, and the natural world.
Glyndwr University, Wrexham; tel: 01978 293473; Mar–Apr. www.wrexhamsf.com

Llangollen Food Festival (23)
Two-day international culinary festival, with numerous producers exhibiting their cheeses, meats, wine, and chocolate.
Llangollen Royal International Pavilion, Llangollen, Denbighshire; tel: 0870 2324256; Oct.
www.llangollenfoodfestival.co.uk

Barmouth Festival of Walking (28)
Ten-day exploration of local scenery; guided walks along the coast or inland. *Barmouth, Gwynedd; tel: 01341 280787; Sep.*
www.barmouthwalkingfestival.co.uk

Snowdonia Walking Festival (42)
Explore Snowdonia's beautiful scenery on a three-day series of guided walks, with evening entertainment.
Betws-y-Coed & District Tourism Association, Conwy; tel: 01690 710190; Oct. www.snowdoniawalkingfestival.co.uk

Above: Caernarfon Castle, a UNESCO World Heritage Site

Abersoch Jazz Festival (35)
Annual four-day festival with performers from across the UK and overseas.
Various venues, Abersoch, Gwynedd; tel: 01758 712929; Jun.
www.abersoch.co.uk/jazzfestival

Bangor New Music Festival (53)
Annual four-day showcase for contemporary and experimental music, with concerts and workshops.
Bangor University, Bangor, Gwynedd; tel: 01248 382181; Mar. www.bnmf.co.uk

Anglesey Oyster & Welsh Produce Festival (54)
Local producers exhibit their food and drink, with cooking demonstrations, talks, and music over two days.
Trearddur Bay Hotel, Lon Isallt, Trearddur Bay, Anglesey; tel: 01248 725700; Oct.
http://angleseyoysterfestival.com

Copperfest (59)
Three-day, free music festival, featuring Welsh and international pop artists.
Various venues, Amlwch, Anglesey; tel: 01407 831599; Aug. www.copperfest.co.uk

MUSEUMS AND GALLERIES

Conwy Castle (4)
One of the great medieval Welsh castles, with eight towers and a dramatic setting.
Conwy; tel: 01492 592358; open Apr–Oct: 9am–5pm daily; Nov–Mar: 9:30am–4pm Mon–Sat, 11am–4pm Sun.
www.cadw.wales.gov.uk

Plas Mawr (4)
The UK's best-preserved Elizabethan town house, with elaborate carvings, plaster ceilings, and furnishings. *High Street, Conwy; tel: 01492 580167; open Apr–Sep: 9am–5pm Tue–Sun; Oct: 9:30am–4pm Tue–Sun. www.cadw.wales.gov.uk*

Great Orme Mines (2)
Take a guided tour through this fascinating Bronze Age copper mine and museum.
Great Orme, Llandudno, Conwy; tel: 01492 870447; open Mar–Oct: 10am–4:30pm daily. www.greatormemines.info

Chirk Castle (22)
Explore the sumptuous rooms, galleries, and gardens of this 14th-century castle.
Chirk, Wrexham; tel: 01691 777701; open Apr–Sep: 10am–6pm Wed–Sun (also Tue Jul–Aug); Mar and Oct: 10am–5pm Wed–Sun. www.nationaltrust.org.uk

Harlech Castle (29)
Picturesque 13th-century castle with exhibitions on its tumultuous history.
Castle Square, Harlech, Gwynedd; tel: 01766 780552; open Apr–Oct: 9am–5pm daily; Nov–Mar: 9:30am–4pm Mon–Sat, 11am–4pm Sun.
www.cadw.wales.gov.uk

Sygun Copper Mine (40)
Explore the old mines and local geology on a guided tour with a museum.
Beddgelert, Gwynedd; tel: 01766 810202; open Mar–Oct: 9:30am–5pm daily.
www.syguncoppermine.co.uk

Tŷ Mawr Wybrnant (41)
A Tudor farmhouse, birthplace of Bishop Morgan, translator of the first Welsh Bible.
Penmachno, Betws-y-Coed, Conwy; tel: 01690 760213; open Mar–Sep: noon–5pm Thu–Sun; Oct–Nov: noon–4pm Thu–Sun. www.nationaltrust.org.uk

National Slate Museum (48)
See demonstrations and tour old workshops and quarrymen's houses *(see p38)*.
Padarn Country Park, Llanberis, Gwynedd; tel: 01286 870630; open Easter–Oct: 10am–5pm daily; Nov–Easter: 10am–4pm Sun–Fri. www.museumwales.ac.uk

Erddig Hall (21)
Georgian stately home with original furnishings, extensive parkland, coach rides, and servants' outbuildings.
Wrexham; tel: 01978 315151; open Mar and Oct: 11am–4pm Sat–Wed; Apr–Jun and Sep: 11am–5pm Sat–Wed; Jul–Aug: 11am–5pm Sat–Thu; Nov–Dec: 11am–4pm Sat–Sun. www.nationaltrust.org.uk

The Lloyd George Museum (33)
Displays on the life and times of the World War I Prime Minister, at his boyhood home.
Llanystumdwy, Criccieth, Gwynedd; tel: 01766 522071; open Apr–May: 10:30am–5pm Mon–Fri; Jun: 10:30am–5pm Mon–Sat; Jul–Sep: 10:30am–5pm daily; Oct: 11am–4pm Mon–Fri.
www.gwynedd.gov.uk

Plas Yn Rhiw (36)
Charming Tudor manor house with landscaped gardens and woodland walks.
Rhiw, Pwllheli, Gwynedd; tel: 01758 780219; open late Mar–early May: noon–5pm Thu–Sun; May–Jun and Sep: noon–5pm Thu–Mon; Jul–Aug: noon–5pm Wed–Mon; Oct–Nov: noon–4pm Thu–Sun. www.nationaltrust.org.uk

Caernarfon Castle (50)
Wales's most impressive medieval castle is a UNESCO World Heritage Site, with exhibitions on its 700-year history.
Castle Ditch, Caernarfon, Gwynedd; tel: 01286 677617; open Apr–Oct: 9am–5pm daily; Nov–Mar: 9:30am–4pm Mon–Sat, 11am–4pm Sun. www.cadw.wales.gov.uk

Swtan Cottage (57)
Visit Anglesey's last remaining thatched cottage, restored to its circa-1900 appearance, with displays on rural life.
Porth Swtan, Church Bay, Anglesey; tel: 01407 730186; open noon–4pm Fri–Sun.
www.swtan.co.uk

Holyhead Maritime Museum ⑤⑤
Wales's oldest lifeboat station houses displays on Holyhead's seafaring history and model ships.
Beach Road, Holyhead, Anglesey; tel: 01407 769745; open Apr–Oct: 10am–4pm daily (may be closed Mon out of high season).
www.holyheadmaritimemuseum.co.uk

Llynnon Mill ⑤⑧
Visit Wales's only working windmill, with a reconstructed bakery and Iron Age roundhouses.
Llanddeusant, Anglesey; tel: 01407 730407; open Apr–Sep: 11am–5pm Tue–Sat, 1–5pm Sun.
www.llansadwrn-wx.co.uk/gwynt/llynnon.html

Oriel Ynys Mon ⑥①
Exhibitions from local artists, including the Sir Kyffin Williams collection.
Rhosmeirch, Llangefni, Anglesey; tel: 01248 724444; open 10:30am–5pm daily. www.kyffinwilliams.info

Plas Newydd ⑥⑥
Beautiful country home of the Marquess of Anglesey, with a collection of fine art.
Llanfairpwll, Anglesey; tel: 01248 715272; open Mar–Nov: noon–5pm Sat–Wed.
www.nationaltrust.org.uk

THINGS TO DO WITH KIDS

Great Orme Tramway ①
View the Great Orme headland on the UK's only cable-hauled tramway.
Victoria Station, Church Walks, Llandudno, Conwy; tel: 01492 879306; open Apr–Sep: 10am–6pm daily; Mar–Oct: 10am–5pm daily. www.greatormetramway.co.uk

Welsh Mountain Zoo ⑤
A beautifully sited zoo with tigers, snow leopards, chimps, sea lions, and more.
Flagstaff Estate, Colwyn Bay, Conwy; tel: 01492 532938; open Apr–Oct: 9:30am–6pm daily; Nov–Mar: 9:30am–5pm daily.
www.welshmountainzoo.org

Rhyl SeaQuarium ⑦
Get close to sharks, rays, conger eels, sea lions, and more at this modern seafront aquarium.
East Parade, Rhyl, Denbighshire; tel: 01745 344660; open 10am–5pm daily.
www.seaquarium.co.uk

Rhyl Sun Centre ⑦
Fun seaside waterpark with indoor pools, slides, rides, and an outdoor sundeck.
East Parade, Rhyl, Denbighshire; tel: 01745 344433; open Apr–Oct; days and times vary, phone for details.
www.rhylsuncentre.co.uk

Pen-y-Ffrith Bird Gardens ⑯
Lovely woodland gardens inhabited by waterfowl, pheasants, owls, and rheas.
Llandegla Road, Llanarmon-yn-Ial, Denbighshire; tel: 01824 780501; open Mar–Nov: 10:30am–5:30pm daily.
www.pen-y-ffrithbirdgardens.co.uk

Horse-Drawn Canal Boat Trips ㉓
Take a trip along the Llangollen Canal in a horse-drawn canal boat *(see pp92–3). Llangollen Wharf, Llangollen, Denbighshire; tel: 01978 860702; trips run Easter–Oct from 11am.*
www.horsedrawnboats.co.uk

Bala Lake Railway ㉕
A 9-mile (15-km) steam-train journey takes in the stunning scenery of Lake Bala.
The Station, Llanuwchllyn, Gwynedd; tel: 01678 540666; open May–Oct: see website for departure times.
www.bala-lake-railway.co.uk

Ffestiniog Railway ㉛
This vintage steam train takes the scenic route from Porthmadog to Blaenau Ffestiniog *(see pp38–9). Harbour Station, Porthmadog, Gwynydd; tel: 01766 516000. Trains run all year; see website for timetables.*
www.ffestiniograilway.co.uk

Glasfryn Activity Park ㉞
Go-karting, ATV-riding, archery, bowling, and fishing are offered at this busy activity center, with toddlers' play area.
Y Ffôr, Pwllheli, Gwynedd; tel: 01766 810202; open from 10am daily.
www.glasfryn.co.uk

The Fun Centre ㊿
Younger children love the slides, ball pools, maze, and mini-cars at this play center.
Christchurch, Bangor Street, Caernarfon, Gwynedd; tel: 01286 671911; open Fri–Sun 10am–5pm; also during school holidays: noon–5pm Mon–Thu.
www.thefuncentre.co.uk

Anglesey Sea Zoo ㊿①
See everything from sea horses to sharks at Wales's largest aquarium.
Brynsiencyn, Llanfairpwll, Anglesey; tel: 01248 430411; open Mar–Oct: 10am–6pm daily; Nov–Feb: 10am–4pm Sat–Sun. www.angleseyseazoo.co.uk

Foel Farm Park ㊿①
Take a tractor tour of the farm, feed the animals, and see chocolate-makers at work.
Brynsiencyn, Anglesey; tel: 01248 430646; open Mar–Oct: 10:30am–5:30pm daily.
www.foelfarm.co.uk

Greenwood Forest Park ㊿②
Ride the world's only eco-friendly roller coaster, or try the mini-tractors, boardwalk maze, or forest theater.
Y Felinheli, Gwynedd; tel: 01248 670076; open Feb half-term: 11am–5pm daily; mid-Mar–early Sep: 10am–5:30pm daily; early Sep–Oct: 11am–5pm daily.
www.greenwoodforestpark.co.uk

Pili Palas Nature World ㊿⑤
A fascinating artificial jungle, home to butterflies, exotic birds, and reptiles.
Penmynydd Road, Menai Bridge, Anglesey; tel: 01248 712474; open 10am–5:30pm daily. www.pilipalas.co.uk

SPAS AND HEALTH RESORTS

The Wild Pheasant Hotel & Spa ㉓
Charming Victorian country house with spacious rooms and suites, and a separate modern spa center.
Berwyn Road, Llangollen, Denbighshire; tel: 01978 860629.
www.wildpheasanthotel.co.uk

St. Dyfnog Springs ⑪
Luxurious spa using "healing water" from St. Dyfog's well. The spa offers beauty treatments and gym, yoga, and pilates classes in relaxing surroundings.
The Coach House, Stable Yard, Llanrhaeadr, Denbighshire; tel: 01745 539922. www.stdyfnogsprings.co.uk

The Secret Spa ⑱
Beauty treatments, holistic therapies, massages and reflexology sessions to give you the "feel-good factor."
Lilac Cottage, The Cross, Holt, Wrexham; tel: 01829 271693.
www.thesecretspa.co.uk

Tre-Ysgawen Country House Hotel & Spa ⑥①
Pool, sauna, beauty treatments, gym, and yoga in the converted stables of a Victorian mansion.
Capel Coch, Llangefni, Anglesey; tel: 01248 753270.
www.treysgawen-hall.co.uk

Anglesey Healing Centre ⑥③
Small, private retreat offering *reiki*, reflexology, and aromatherapy treatments and workshops.
Llangoed, Anglesey; tel: 01248 490814.
www.angleseyhealingcentre.co.uk

OTHER SIGHTS IN THE BOOK

International Eisteddfod ㉓ *(see pp92–3).* **Portmeirion** ㉚ *(see pp130–31).* **Snowdonia** ㊺ *(see pp62–3).* **Welsh Narrow-Gauge Railways** ㊼ *(see pp38–9).*

Below: Great Orme Tramway in Llandudno

CENTRAL WALES

LOCAL FOOD

The Pilgrims Tearooms ⑱
Award-winning tearoom serving traditional home cooking using local ingredients.
Cathedral Close, Brecon, Powys; tel: 01874 610610; open 10am–5pm daily (until 4pm in winter). www.pilgrims-tearooms.co.uk

Caffi Salvador ㉖
Delicious Mediterranean tapas-style snacks at this cozy café, with full English and Welsh breakfasts on Sunday morning.
3 King Street, Llandeilo, Carmarthenshire; tel: 01558 822908; open 9am–4pm Mon–Sat, 6–8:30pm Wed–Thu, 6–9:30pm Fri–Sat, 10am–1:30pm Sun.

The Treehouse (61)
Popular organic food shop and café, with lots of fresh local foods on the menu.
14 Baker Street, Aberystwyth, Ceredigion; tel: 01970 615791; open 9am–5pm Mon–Sat. www.treehousewales.co.uk

Ultracomida Delicatessen (61)
A vast range of Welsh, French, and Spanish cheeses, cured meats, olives, and more.
31 Pier Street, Aberystwyth, Ceredigion; tel: 01970 630686; open 10am–6pm Mon–Sat. www.ultracomida.co.uk

Llanelli Market ㉛
Find Welsh delicacies such as cockles, laver bread, and the haggis-like "Felinfoel faggots" at this friendly covered market with over 50 family-run stands.
Market Precinct, Llanelli, Carmarthenshire; open 9am–5pm Mon–Sat. www.visit.carmarthenshire.gov.uk

The Blue Ball Restaurant ㊲
Relaxed, trendy restaurant offering a menu of local seafood and international dishes.
Upper Frog Street, Tenby, Pembrokeshire; tel: 01834 843038; open 5–9pm Tue–Sat, 12:30–2:30pm Sun. www.theblueballrestaurant.co.uk

Martha's Vineyard Restaurant ㊸
Overlooking the Cleddau Estuary, Martha's offers a varied menu of fresh local seafood.
Milford Marina, Milford Haven, Pembrokeshire; tel: 01646 697083; open noon–2pm and 6–9:15pm daily. www.marthas-vineyard.co.uk

The Harbour Inn ㊽
Local seafood and traditional pub meals, with picturesque views over the harbor.
Main Street, Solva, Pembrokeshire; tel: 01437 720013; restaurant open noon–3pm and 6–9pm daily. www.harbourinnsolva.com

Rhyd Country House (53)
Countryside hotel offering delicious meals prepared with fresh local ingredients.
Blaenannerch, Cardigan, Ceredigion; tel: 01239 810566; open 11am–2pm and 6:30–10pm Tue–Sat, noon–4pm Sun. www.rhydcountryhouse.co.uk

Llwynhelyg Farm Shop (54)
Local vegetables and cheeses, meats, and jams are sold at this award-winning shop.
Sarnau, Llandysul, Ceredigion; tel: 01239 811079; open 9am–6pm Mon–Sat, 9:30am–1pm Sun. www.llwynhelygfarmshop.co.uk

The Hungry Trout (55)
Seafood restaurant offering a creative menu of fresh local fish and shellfish.
2 South John Street, New Quay, Ceredigion; tel: 01545 560680; open 10am–3pm and 6–9pm Mon–Sat, 10:30am–3pm and 6–9pm Sun. www.thehungrytrout.co.uk

New Quay Honey Farm (55)
See working bees and sample Welsh mead at this honey-themed tearoom.
Cross Inn, New Quay, Ceredigion; tel: 01545 560822; open Easter–Oct 10am–5:30pm Tue–Sat; Nov–Christmas 11am–4:30pm Tue–Sat. www.thehoneyfarm.co.uk

Penlanlas Golf Club (60)
Pick your own strawberries, raspberries, blueberries, carrots, and beans.
Rhydyfelin, Aberystwyth, Ceredigion; tel: 01970 625319; open 10am–7pm daily in season. www.penlanlas.co.uk

FARMERS' MARKETS

Welshpool Farmers' Market ①
Buy local fruit, vegetables, cheeses, and more at this monthly market.
Market Hall, High Street, Welshpool, Powys; tel: 01686 626606; first Fri of every month, 9am–2pm. www.fmiw.co.uk

Knighton Farmers' Market ⑥
Farmers and small producers from across the region offer fruit, veggies, and more.
Community Centre, Knighton, Powys; tel: 01547 520096; second and fourth Sat of every month, 9am–2pm. www.fmiw.co.uk

Brecon Farmers' Market ⑱
A tempting array of home-baked cakes, farmhouse cheeses, fruits, and veggies.
Market Hall, Brecon, Powys; tel: 01874 636169; second Sat of every month except Aug, 10am–2pm. www.breconfarmersmarkets.wordpress.com

Carmarthen Farmers' Market ㉝
All manner of local produce is on sale at this bi-monthly food and drink market.
Carmarthen town center; first and third Fri of every month, 9am–1pm. www.fmiw.co.uk

Fishguard Farmers' Market (51)
Local fruit, vegetables, fish, poultry, honey, cheeses, butter, cakes, and more.
Town Hall, Fishguard, Pembrokeshire; tel: 01239 851419; every Sat Jun–Aug, every other Sat Sep–May, 9am–1pm. www.pembrokeshire.gov.uk

Lampeter Farmers' Market (57)
Local food and drink direct from the producers at this popular market.
Market Street, Lampeter, Ceredigion; tel: 01570 423200; every other Fri, 9am–2pm. www.fmiw.co.uk

PUBS

The Dragon Hotel ④
Try potent local real ales in the cozy bar of this 17th-century coaching inn and hotel in the Welsh Marches.
Montgomery, Powys; tel: 01686 668359; open daily. www.dragonhotel.com

Kilvert's Inn ⑫
Busy family-run inn in the foothills of the Brecon Beacons, serving several local ales. There is also a restaurant and regular live music nights.
The Bullring, Hay-on-Wye, Powys; tel: 01497 821042; open daily. www.kilverts.co.uk

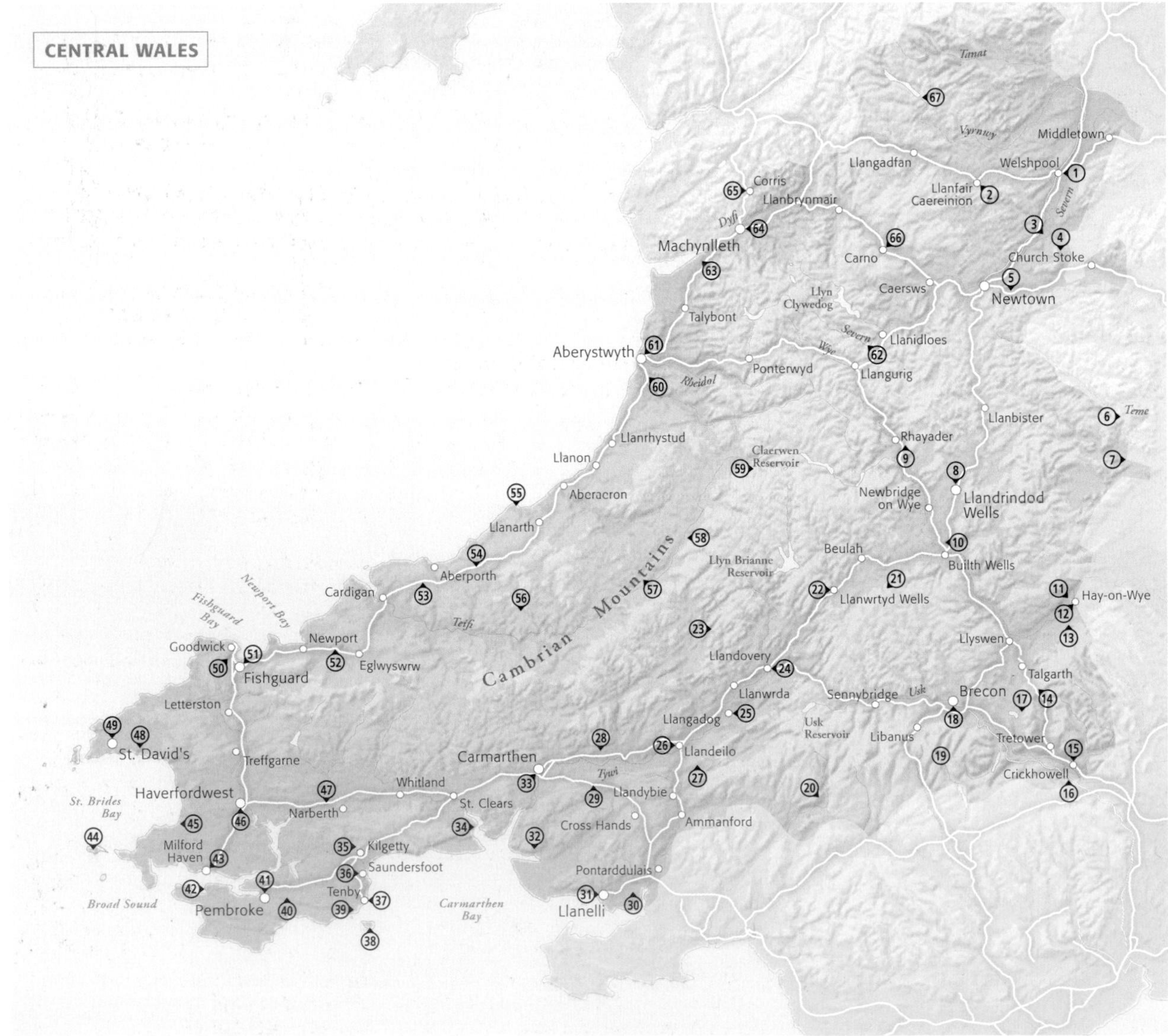

Above: Gwesty Cymru hotel in Aberystwyth

The Bear ⑮
Medieval pub recommended by the Campaign for Real Ale serving serving a range of local ales in historic surroundings.
High Street, Crickhowell, Powys; tel: 01873 810408; open 11am–3pm and 6–11pm Mon–Sat, noon–3pm and 7–10:30pm Sun. www.bearhotel.co.uk

The Red Lion ㉕
Award-winning village pub with an excellent restaurant and B&B rooms.
Church Street, Llangadog, Carmarthenshire: tel: 01550 777357; open daily. www.redlioncoachinginn.co.uk

White Hart Thatched Inn and Brewery ㉙
Picturesque 14th-century thatched village pub, with a range of ales brewed on site, a beer garden, and a restaurant.
Llanddarog, Carmarthenshire; tel: 01267 275395; open 11:30am–3pm and 6:30–11pm Mon–Sat, noon–3pm and 7–10:30pm Sun. www.thebestpubinwales.co.uk

The Crown Inn ㊲
Traditional family-run pub, with regular live music and special events.
Lower Frog Street, Tenby, Pembrokeshire; tel: 01834 842796; open daily. www.thecrowninn-tenby.co.uk

The Aleppo Merchant Inn ㊻
Historic rural pub with a large beer garden, restaurant, and a few guest rooms.
Carno, Caersws, Powys; tel: 01686 420210; open daily. www.thealeppo.co.uk

The Castle ㊺
Friendly Victorian pub and restaurant in a stunning coastal location, with two rooms.
1 Grove Place, Little Haven, Pembrokeshire; tel: 01437 781445; open 10:30–12am daily. www.littlehavencastle.co.uk

The Grove Hotel ㊾
Sample regional real ales and Welsh spirits at this attractively restored old inn set in idyllic grounds just outside the little cathedral city of St. Davids.
High Street, St. Davids, Pembrokeshire; tel: 01437 720341; open 8am–11pm daily. www.grovestdavids.co.uk

Penwig ㊻
Friendly, family-run pub overlooking Cardigan Bay, serving home-cooked meals in a bright, modern bar-restaurant.
South John Street, New Quay, Ceredigion; tel: 01545 560910; open daily. www.penwig.co.uk

The Nag's Head ㊿
A small, traditional, old-fashioned pub, popular with a friendly crowd of locals.
23 Bridge Street, Aberystwyth, Ceredigion; tel: 01970 624725; open daily.

Inn on the Pier ㊿
Party on the pier at the only all-night-long pub in Ceredigion, a lively nightspot with great sea views.
The Royal Pier, Marine Terrace, Aberystwyth, Ceredigion; tel: 01970 636101; open 11am–1:30am Mon–Wed, 11am Thu–3am Fri, 11am Fri–5am Sat, 11am Sat–1:30am Mon. www.royalpier.co.uk

PLACES TO STAY

Royal Oak Hotel ①
Renovated historic coaching inn with 25 tasteful rooms and a restaurant in a pleasant small market town.
The Cross, Welshpool, Powys; tel: 01938 552217. www.royaloakhotel.info

The Forest Country House ⑤
Five *en-suite* rooms are offered in this peaceful family-run Victorian country house, with tennis court and garden.
Gilfach Lane, Kerry, Newtown, Powys; tel: 01686 621821. www.bedandbreakfastnewtown.co.uk

The Metropole ⑧
Long-established family-run hotel in the center of town, with smart rooms and excellent facilities.
Temple Street, Llandrindod Wells, Powys; tel: 01597 823700. www.metropole.co.uk

Baskerville Hall Hotel ⑪
Imposing Gothic country mansion, with ornate rooms, indoor pool, campsite, and dorms.
Clyro Court, Hay-on-Wye, Powys; tel: 01497 820033. www.baskervillehall.co.uk

The Old Post Office Bed & Breakfast ⑬
Converted post office in an excellent location for the Hay Festival.
Llanigon, Hay-on-Wye, Powys; tel: 01497 820008. www.oldpost-office.co.uk

The Castle Inn ⑭
Four comfortable rooms in the inn, plus dorm accommodations and a campsite.
Pengenffordd, nr Talgarth, Powys; tel: 01874 711353. www.thecastleinn.co.uk

The Old Rectory Country Hotel ⑯
Attractive 16th-century countryside mansion with stylish *en-suite* rooms, restaurant, and nine-hole golf course.
Llangattock, Crickhowell, Powys; tel: 01873 810373. www.rectoryhotel.co.uk

The Beacons Guest House ⑱
Georgian town house with lots of period charm and neat modernized rooms.
16 Bridge Street, Brecon, Powys; tel: 01874 623339. www.thebreconbeacons.co.uk

Warpool Court Hotel ㊾
Attractive Victorian hotel with a popular restaurant. It has 25 modern bedrooms, many with sea views.
St. Davids, Pembrokeshire; tel: 01437 720300. www.warpoolcourthotel.com

The Black Lion Hotel ㊻
This hotel has a restaurant, bar, and garden, as well as nine spacious rooms overlooking scenic Cardigan Bay.
New Quay, Ceredigion; tel: 01545 560209. www.blacklionnewquay.co.uk

The New White Lion ㉔
Elegant preserved historic building with six stylish bedrooms, a restaurant, and regular music and poetry nights.
43 Stone Street, Llandovery, Carmarthenshire; tel: 01550 720685. www.newwhitelion.co.uk

Middle Mill Guest House ㉜
Rustic guesthouse with neatly furnished rooms, set in large grounds with a private river for fishing.
Middle Mill, Carmarthen Road, Kidwelly, Carmarthenshire; tel: 01554 228207. www.middlemillguesthouse.co.uk

Seaview ㉞
The former home of poet Dylan Thomas, this guesthouse offers smart rooms with sea views.
Market Lane, Laugharne, Carmarthenshire; tel: 01994 427030. www.seaview-laugharne.co.uk

St. Brides Spa Hotel ㊱
Light, airy rooms, many with sea views, in this classy hotel equipped with a restaurant and spa.
St. Brides Hill, Saundersfoot, Pembrokeshire; tel: 01834 812304. www.stbridesspahotel.com

Penally Abbey Country House Hotel ㊴
With views of Caldey Island, this is a peaceful coastal hotel with an excellent restaurant.
Penally, Pembrokeshire; tel: 01834 843033. www.penally-abbey.com

Nantgwynfaen Organic Farm ㊶
Three restful rooms are offered on this working organic farm, with on-site farm shop.
Penrhiwllan Road, Croeslan, Llandysul, Ceredigion; tel: 01239 851914. www.organicfarmwales.co.uk

Coed Parc Farm ㊷
Homey B&B accommodations are available at this friendly working farm that overlooks a lovely wooded valley.
Lampeter, Ceredigion; tel: 01570 422402. www.coedparcfarm.co.uk

Brynheulog Bed & Breakfast ㊸
Make yourself at home in the private guest annex of this tranquil B&B.
Llandewi Brefi, Tregaron, Ceredigion; tel: 01570 493615. www.brynheulog.com

Gwesty Cymru ㊿
Trendy modern hotel on the seafront, with eight stylish rooms and terrace restaurant.
19 Marine Terrace, Aberystwyth, Ceredigion; tel: 01970 612252. www.gwestycymru.co.uk

Ynyshir Hall ㊿
This grand country-house hotel set in lush landscaped gardens was once owned by Queen Victoria.
Eglwysfach, Machynlleth, Powys; tel: 01654 781209. www.ynyshirhall.co.uk

FESTIVALS AND EVENTS

Welsh Food Festival ③
Local producers sell their wares at this weekend event, with cooking demonstrations and family activities.
Glansevern Hall Gardens, Berriew, Welshpool, Powys; tel: 01686 640916; Sep. www.welshfoodfestival.co.uk

Presteigne Festival ⑦
A six-day celebration of classical music, including some by contemporary composers, in a countryside location.
Various venues, Presteigne, Powys; tel: 01544 267800; Aug. www.presteignefestival.com

Llandrindod Wells Victorian Festival ⑧
For a week, costumed locals and visitors re-create the spa town's Victorian heyday, with street entertainment and fireworks.
Various venues, Llandrindod Wells, Powys; tel: 01597 823441; Aug. www.victorianfestival.co.uk

Royal Welsh Show ⑩
One of the UK's biggest agricultural and country shows, with livestock competitions and entertainment over 4 days.
Royal Welsh Showground, Llanelwedd, Builth Wells, Powys; tel: 01982 553683; Jul. www.rwas.co.uk

Brecon Jazz Festival ⑱
Wales's premier jazz festival, with big-name acts from across the world performing over a weekend around town.
Various venues, Brecon, Powys; tel: 0870 9901299; Aug. www.breconjazz.org

Man Versus Horse Marathon ㉒
Annual 22-mile (35-km) countryside race between runners and horse-riders, only once won by a human.
Llanwrtyd Wells, Powys; tel: 01591 610850; Jun. www.green-events.co.uk

World Bog Snorkelling Championships ㉒
Bizarre swimming competition held in bog trenches, attracting numerous international participants over two days.
Waen Rhydd Bog, Llanwrtyd Wells, Powys; tel: 01591 610850; Aug. www.green-events.co.uk

Tenby Arts Festival ㊲
A week of amateur dramatics, classical and jazz music, dancing, talks, and poetry readings.
Various venues, Tenby, Pembrokeshire; tel: 01834 845277; Sep. www.tenbyartsfest.co.uk

Pembrokeshire Fish Week ㊸
This week-long celebration of fish and the seaside opens in Milford Haven harbor and continues across Pembrokeshire, with barbecues, cooking demonstrations, fishing competitions, and music.
Various locations, Pembrokeshire; tel: 01437 776168; late Jun/early Jul. www.pembrokeshirefishweek.co.uk

Above: Dylan Thomas Boathouse at Laugharne

Pembroke Festival ㊶
Live music, dancing, drama, and fireworks bring the community together at this annual four-day event.
Various locations, Pembroke; tel: 01646 680090; Jul. www.pembrokefestival.org.uk

Fishguard International Music Festival ㊿①
Prestigious eight-day music festival featuring classical concerts, operatic performances, string quartets, and soloists.
Various venues, Fishguard and St. Davids, Pembrokeshire; tel: 01348 875538; Jul. www.fishguardmusicfestival.co.uk

MUSEUMS AND GALLERIES

Powys Castle and Garden ①
Dramatic medieval castle housing a fine collection of paintings, plus Italian gardens.
Welshpool, Powys; tel: 01938 551944; open Mar–Sep: 1–5pm Thu–Mon (Jul–Aug: also open Wed); Oct: 1–4pm Thu–Mon. www.nationaltrust.org.uk

Powysland Museum ①
Exhibitions covering Montgomeryshire's prehistoric, Roman, and Viking past, and displays on local crafts.
The Canal Wharf, Welshpool, Powys; tel: 01938 554656; open May–Sep: 10am–1pm and 2–5pm Sat–Sun; Oct–Apr: 11am–2pm Sat. www.powys.gov.uk

The Judge's Lodging ⑦
Award-winning museum in this plush Victorian judge's residence, with re-created interiors, including servants' quarters.
Broad Street, Presteigne, Powys; tel: 01544 260650; open Mar–Oct: 10am–5pm daily; Nov: 10am–4pm Wed–Sun; Dec: 10am–4pm Sat–Sun. www.judgeslodging.org.uk

The Old Bell Museum ④
Displays on local archaeology and social history can be found at this museum, run entirely by volunteers, in an evocative 16th-century former inn.
Arthur Street, Montgomery, Powys; tel: 01686 668313; open Apr–Jul and Sep: 1:30–5pm Wed–Fri and Sun, 10:30am–5pm Sat and Bank Holiday Mondays; Aug: 1:30–5pm Sun–Fri, 10:30am–5pm Sat. www.oldbellmuseum.org.uk

Radnorshire Museum ⑧
Displays on the local history of this small spa town, as well as Neolithic and Roman artifacts, can be seen here.
Temple Street, Llandrindod Wells, Powys; tel: 01597 824513; open Apr–Sep: 10am–4pm Tue–Fri, 10am–5pm Sat, 1–5pm Sun; Oct–Mar: 10am–4pm Tue–Fri, 10am–1pm Sat. www.powys.gov.uk

Kidwelly Castle ㉜
Well-preserved and outstanding example of a 12th-century Norman castle, with exhibitions on its long and fascinating military history.
Castle Street, Kidwelly, Carmarthenshire; tel: 01554 890104; open Apr–Oct: 9am–5pm daily; Nov–Mar: 9:30am–4pm Mon–Sat, 11am–4pm Sun. www.kidwelly.gov.uk

The Dylan Thomas Boathouse at Laugharne ㉞
An exhibition on the famous Welsh poet's life, including his writing shed, at the house where he wrote *Under Milk Wood*.
Dylan's Walk, Laugharne, Carmarthenshire; tel: 01994 427420; open May–Oct: 10am–5:30pm daily; Nov–Apr: 10:30am–3:30pm daily. www.dylanthomasboathouse.com

The Cambrian Woollen Mill ㉒
Explore the history of weaving on a guided tour through this working wool mill, on the outskirts of the smallest town in Britain.
Llanwrtyd Wells, Powys; tel: 01591 610363; open 9am–5pm daily. www.cambrian-mill.co.uk

Dolaucothi Gold Mines ㉓
Underground tours of this unique Roman gold mine and exhibition in a stunning countryside setting.
Pumsaint, Llanwrda, Carmarthenshire; tel: 01558 825146; open Mar–Nov: 10am–5pm daily. www.nationaltrust.org.uk

Carreg Cennan Castle ㉗
One of Wales's best medieval castles *(see pp102–3)*, with magnificent views over the Carmarthenshire countryside.
Tir Y Castell Farm, Trap, Llandeilo, Carmarthenshire; tel: 01558 822291; open Apr–Oct: 9:30am–6:30pm daily. www.cadw.wales.gov.uk

Haverfordwest Town Museum ㊻
Varied displays on local history including paintings, vintage costumes, and archaeological artifacts.
Castle House, Haverfordwest, Pembrokeshire; tel: 01437 763087; open Apr–Oct: 10am–4pm Mon–Sat. www.haverfordwest-town-museum-org.uk

Ceredigion Museum ㉛①
In a restored Edwardian theater, the Ceredigion Museum houses exhibitions on local culture and industry.
Coliseum, Terrace Road, Aberystwyth, Ceredigion; tel: 01970 633088; open Apr–Oct: 10am–5pm Mon–Sat; Nov–Mar: noon–4:30pm Mon–Sat. www.ceredigion.gov.uk

Castell Henllys Iron Age Hill Fort 52

Reconstructed Iron Age roundhouses, prehistoric livestock breeds, costumed villagers, craft workshops, and storytelling.
Meline, nr Crymych, Pembrokeshire; tel: 01239 891319; open Apr–Oct: 10am–5pm daily; Nov–Mar: 11am–3pm daily. www.castellhenllys.com

Strata Florida Abbey 59

View the picturesque ruins of this 12th-century Cistercian abbey, with an on-site museum.
Ystrad Meurig, Ceredigion; tel: 01974 831261; open Apr–Oct: 10am–5pm daily. www.cadw.wales.gov.uk

Museum of Modern Art Wales 64

The four galleries of this museum feature 20th-century and contemporary Welsh paintings and sculpture.
The Tabernacle, Heol Penrallt, Machynlleth, Powys; tel: 01654 703355; open 10am–4pm Mon–Sat. www.momawales.org.uk

THINGS TO DO WITH KIDS

Welshpool and Llanfair Light Railway 2

Hop aboard a vintage narrow-gauge steam train for a trip across beautiful countryside.
The Station, Llanfair Caereinion, Welshpool, Powys; tel: 01938 810441; open Apr–Nov: see website for full timetable. www.wllr.org.uk

Gigrin Farm Red Kite Feeding Station 9

A rare chance to see wild red kites up close on this family-run farm, which has its own feeding station for the birds of prey.
Gigrin Farm, Rhayader, Powys; tel: 01597 810243; open 1–4pm daily (feeding time 3pm summer, 2pm winter). www.gigrin.co.uk

National Showcaves Centre for Wales 20

Tours around a spectacular series of caves, plus a dinosaur park and draft horse center for younger children.
Abercrave, Swansea; tel: 01639 730284; open Apr–Oct: 10am–3pm daily. www.showcaves.co.uk

National Wetland Centre Wales 30

Nature reserve with bird-watching blinds, lakes, lagoons, discovery center, canoe safari, and bike trail.
Llwynhendy, Llanelli, Carmarthenshire; tel: 01554 741087; open 9:30am–5pm daily. www.wwt.org.uk

Folly Farm 35

As well as an adventure playground and Europe's largest undercover vintage funfair, there are animals galore in this country park, farm, and zoo.
Begelly, Kilgetty, Pembrokeshire; tel: 01834 812731; open Jan–mid-Mar and Nov–Dec: 10am–4pm Sat–Sun; mid-Mar–Sep: 10am–5:30pm daily; Oct: 10am–5pm daily. www.folly-farm.co.uk

Skomer Island 44

Take a day trip to this nature reserve and discover dolphins, seals, puffins, and Manx shearwaters.
Pembrokeshire; tel: 01646 636800; day trips depart from Martin's Haven Apr–Oct: 10am–noon Tue–Sun. www.welshwildlife.org

Oakwood Theme Park 47

Fun for kids of all ages, with a huge selection of funfair rides and roller coasters, plus calmer boat rides for parents.
Canaston Bridge, Narberth, Pembrokeshire; tel: 01834 891373; open Apr–Nov: 10am–5pm (until 6pm Aug) daily in school holidays, weekends at other times. www.oakwoodthemepark.co.uk

Mount Severn Outdoor Activity Centre 62

Try kayaking, archery, orienteering, fishing, caving, and more in the extensive grounds of this activity center on the banks of the River Severn.
Glan-y-Nant, Llanidloes, Powys; tel: 01686 412344; see website for course details. www.mountsevern.co.uk

Corris Railway and Museum 65

Ride this 150-year-old steam railroad through the picturesque Dulas Valley and visit the railroad museum.
Station Yard, Corris, Machynlleth, Powys; tel: 01654 761303; open weekends May–Sep: trains hourly from 11am. See website for full timetable. www.corris.co.uk

Llangorse Multi Activity Centre 17

Wales's largest indoor climbing center, plus horse-riding and outdoor obstacle courses.
Gilfach Farm, Llangorse, Powys; tel: 01874 658584; open 9am–5pm daily. www.activityuk.com

Caldey Island 38

Picturesque island owned by Cistercian monks, with an abbey, churches, a museum, and a long sandy beach.
Pembrokeshire, tel: 01834 844453; boats sail from Tenby, May–Sep from 10am Mon–Sat; Apr and Oct from 10:30am Mon–Fri. www.caldey-island.co.uk

SPAS AND HEALTH RESORTS

Lake Country House and Spa 21

A range of spa treatments and a lakeside hot tub are offered at this peaceful hotel, which is in the perfect location for a truly relaxing, luxury break.
Llangammarch Wells, Powys; tel: 01591 620202. www.lakecountryhouse.co.uk

Four Seasons Health and Leisure 28

A heated indoor pool, Jacuzzi, steam room, and gym in a tranquil rural location.
Cwmtwrch Farm, Nantgaredig, Carmarthenshire; tel: 01267 290238. www.fourseasonswales.co.uk

Three Rivers Hotel & Spa 33

State-of-the-art spa with swimming pool, Jacuzzi, sauna, steam rooms, and gym.
Ferryside, Carmarthen; tel: 01267 267270. www.threerivershotel.co.uk

Monks Health Club & Spa 31

Spa and gym at a luxurious country club with pool, sauna, and numerous treatments.
Machynys Peninsula Golf & Country Club, Nicklaus Avenue, Machynys, Llanelli, Carmarthenshire; tel: 01554 744666. www.machynys.com/monks

Lamphey Court Hotel & Spa 40

Peaceful Georgian mansion offering modern luxury, including heated pool, sauna, gym, tennis courts, and various therapies and treatments.
Lamphey, nr Tenby, Pembrokeshire; tel: 01646 672273. www.lampheycourt.co.uk

The Ivybridge Spa 50

Day and overnight packages are available and numerous massages, facials, and body treatments are offered.
Drim Mill, Goodwick, Pembrokeshire; tel: 01348 875345. www.ivybridgespa.co.uk

Lake Vyrnwy Hotel & Spa 67

A luxury 4-star hotel and spa resort with fitness centre, spa pool, sauna, gym, and fine views over the beautiful Lake Vyrnwy nature reserve.
Llanwddyn, Powys; tel: 01691 870259. www.lakevyrnwy.com

OTHER SIGHTS IN THE BOOK

Hay Festival 12 *(see pp14–15)*. **The Brecon Beacons** 19 *(see pp188–9)*. **Pembrokeshire Coast** 42 *(see pp184–5)*.

Below: Puffin feeding on Skomer Island

SOUTH WALES

LOCAL FOOD

The Chandlery ⑩
Once the location of a 19th-century ship-building company, this restaurant offers a warm welcome and modern food. *Lower Dock Street, Newport; tel: 01633 256622; open noon–2pm and 7–10pm Tue–Fri, 7–10pm Sat, noon–2pm Sun. www.thechandleryrestaurant.com*

Baldocks ⑩
Historic delicatessen in a busy market with a wide range of fresh local and imported foods and wines. *The Provisions Market, High Street, Newport; tel: 01633 257312; market open 9am–5pm Mon–Sat. www.baldocks-deli.co.uk*

Berry Hill Fruit Farm ⑩
Pick your own pears, plums, berries, rhubarbs, beans, and peas in season at this well-stocked farm. *Coedkernew, Newport; tel: 01633 680938; open 9am–5pm Tue–Sat, 9am–1pm Sun. www.berryhillfruitfarm.co.uk*

The Farmer's Daughter Restaurant ⑪
Try traditional home-cooked fare or exotic dishes such as zebra or kangaroo at this working-farm-based restaurant. *Croescarneinion Farm, Bassaleg, Newport; tel: 01633 892800; open 6:30pm–late Wed–Sun. www.thefarmersdaughter.co.uk*

Prince's Cafe ⑰
Historic establishment offering home-made cakes and pies to carry out, and traditional meals upstairs. *74 Taff Street, Pontypridd, Rhondda Cynon Taf; tel: 01443 402376; open 9am–5pm Mon–Sat.*

Zerodegrees ⑳
A modern restaurant and microbrewery, serving British and European cuisine. *27 Westgate Street, Cardiff; tel: 029 2022 9494; open noon–midnight Mon–Sat, noon–11pm Sun. www.zerodegrees.co.uk*

Wally's Delicatessen ⑳
Cardiff institution selling a huge variety of cheeses, meats, and sweet treats. *42–44 Royal Arcade, Cardiff; tel: 029 2022 9265; open 8am–5:30pm Mon–Sat. www.displaysites.com/wallysdeli*

Cardiff Market ⑳
There are regional cheeses, meats, fish, fruit, and vegetables, and much more at this bustling market. *Entrances on Trinity Street and St. Mary Street, Cardiff; tel: 029 2087 1214; open 8am–5:30pm Mon–Sat. www.cardiff-market.co.uk*

Armless Dragon ⑳
Enjoyable contemporary Welsh cuisine made with fresh local foods. *97 Wyeverne Road, Cathays, Cardiff; tel: 029 2038 2357; open noon–2pm and 7–9pm Tue–Thu, noon–2pm and 7–9:30pm Fri, 7–9:30pm Sat. www.armlessdragon.co.uk*

Gelynis Farm ㉔
Pick your own strawberries, blackberries, and raspberries in season, and buy the farm's wine, honey, and preserves. *Morganstown, Cardiff; tel. 029 2084 4440; open Jun–Aug: 11am–5pm Tue–Sun; Sep: 11am–5pm Sat–Sun. www.gelynisfarm.co.uk*

Farthings At Home Delicatessen ㉙
Fresh home-made quiches, pastries, and sandwiches plus Welsh and Spanish cheeses are sold here. *31 High Street, Cowbridge, Vale of Glamorgan; tel: 01446 773545; open 8:30am–5:30pm Mon–Sat. www.farthingsofcowbridge.co.uk*

La Plie Restaurant ㉜
Top-class French cuisine by the seaside, made with fresh local ingredients. *52 Beach Road, Southerndown, Bridgend; tel: 01656 880127; open 12:30–2pm and 7–9:30pm Tue–Sun. www.laplierestaurant.co.uk*

Franklin's Café Bar ㉝
A cheerful bayside café-bar with a good-value brasserie-style menu that offers great food and a fine selection of beers and wines. *87 Main Road, Ogmore-by-Sea, Bridgend; tel: 01656 880661; open 9am–7pm Mon, Tue, Thu and Sun, 9am–2pm Wed, 9am–9pm Fri–Sat. www.franklinscafebar.co.uk*

The Courthouse Café Bar ㉞
Popular gastropub with stylish decor and a well-priced menu that features grills, chicken, salads, and more. *Hunters Ridge, Bridgend; tel: 01656 664042; open noon–11pm Sun–Thu, noon–2am Fri–Sat.*

Sidoli's Fish Restaurant ㉟
The place to go for traditional fish and chips and a variety of seafood dishes. *13 Well Street, Porthcawl, Bridgend; tel: 01656 783766; open 11am–3pm Mon–Sat. Also 55 New Road, Porthcawl; tel: 01656 783716; open 10am–7pm Mon–Sat.*

Swansea Market ㊴
Try the famous local cockles, laverbread (seaweed), and Welsh cakes in Wales's largest indoor market. *Oxford Street, Swansea; tel: 01792 654296; open 8am–5:30pm Mon–Fri, 7:30am–5:30pm Sat. www.swanseaindoormarket.co.uk*

The Chattery ㊴
Relaxed restaurant, with local produce on the menu and occasional music nights. *59 Uplands Crescent, Uplands, Swansea; tel: 01792 473276; open 10am–5pm Mon–Sat; open later for live music nights. http://homepage.ntlworld.com/thechattery*

Nicholaston Farm ㊶
Pick your own strawberries, raspberries, and gooseberries at this working farm and campsite, with farm shop and café. *Penmaen, Gower, Swansea; tel: 01792 371209; shop open 8am–6pm daily, PYO open mid-Jun–Jul. www.nicholastonfarm.co.uk*

Hurrens Inn on The Estuary ㊸
Enjoy fresh, organic local foods and a view of the spectacular north Gower coast. *13 Station Road, Loughor, Swansea; tel: 0845 838 0267; open noon–2:30pm and 7–9:30pm Tue–Sun. www.hurrens.co.uk*

The Walnut Tree Restaurant (51)
High-quality regional and international cuisine is on the menu at this highly regarded countryside restaurant. *Llanddewi Skirrid, Abergavenny, Monmouthshire; tel: 01873 852797; open noon–2:30pm and 7–10pm Tue–Sat. www.thewalnuttreeinn.com*

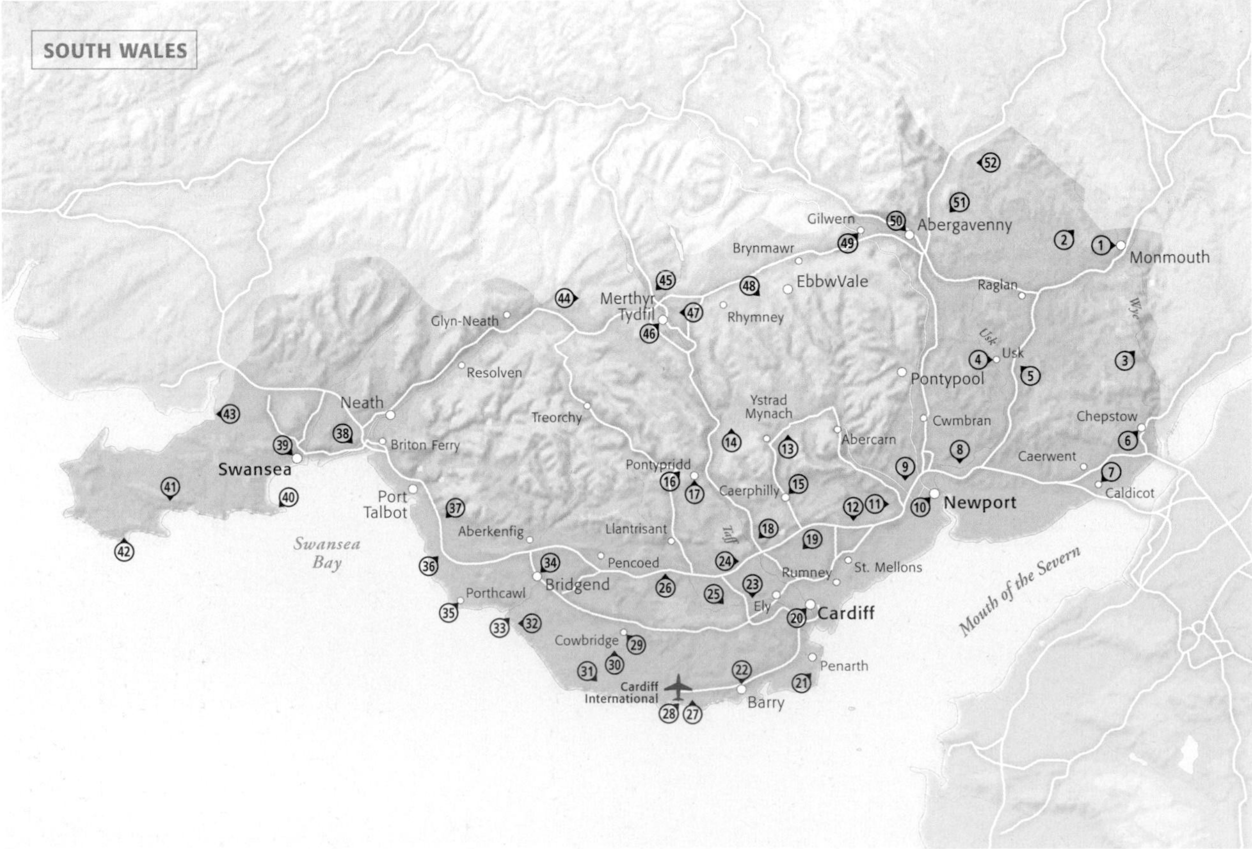

FARMERS' MARKETS

Monmouth Farmers' Market ①
Farmers, bakers, and brewers sell their produce on a medieval bridge in this historic border town. *The Monnow Bridge, Monnow Street, Monmouth; tel: 0845 610 6496; last Sat of every month, 10am–1pm. www.fmiw.co.uk*

Cowbridge Farmers' Market ㉙
Locally produced cheeses, bread, fruit, and vegetables can be bought at this twice-monthly market. *Arthur Johns Car Park, 43 High Street, Cowbridge, Vale of Glamorgan; tel: 01446 771033; first and third Sat of every month, 10am–1pm. www.valefarmersmarkets.co.uk*

Abergavenny Farmers' Market ㊿
A good range of food and drink produced in the area, along with occasional cooking and crafts demonstrations. *Market Hall, Cross Street, Abergavenny, Monmouthshire; tel: 01873 860271; second and fourth Thu of every month, 9:30am–2:30pm. www.abergavennyfarmersmarket.co.uk*

Penderyn Farmers' Market 44
A variety of local food, drink, and crafts on sale, opposite the Welsh Whisky Company. *Penderyn Community Centre, Penderyn, Rhondda Cynon Taf; tel: 01685 812545; last Sun of every month, 10am–2pm.*

PUBS

The Punch House 1
Historic inn with alleged resident ghost, live music on Fridays, and popular Sunday roasts. *4 Agincourt Square, Monmouth; tel: 01600 713855; open daily.*

The Queen's Head 1
This welcoming Tudor pub plays host to regular live jazz sessions and also offers accommodations and meals. *St. James' Street, Monmouth; tel: 01600 712767; open daily. www.queensheadmonmouth.co.uk*

The Church Inn 19
Quaint and sociable medieval pub in a picturesque setting, with quiz nights and live music. *Ty-Glas Road, Llanishen, Cardiff; tel: 029 2076 3601; open daily. www.churchinn.org.uk*

The Goat Major 20
This traditional pub, with dark wood paneling and black leather sofas and seats, serves a good choice of regional real ales. *33 High Street, Cardiff; tel: 029 2033 7161; open daily. www.cardiffpubs.co.uk*

The Maltsters Arms 20
Possibly dating back to 1310, this is believed to be Cardiff's oldest pub. *42–44 Cardiff Road, Llandaff, Cardiff; tel: 029 2033 3097; open daily. www.cardiffpubs.co.uk*

The Woodville 20
Lively Victorian pub in the heart of Cardiff's student neighborhood, popular with a younger crowd. *1–5 Woodville Road, Cathays, Cardiff; tel: 029 2064 9991; open daily. www.cardiffpubs.co.uk*

Terra Nova 20
Large, modern, trendy pub on the bay with an outdoor terrace and a good menu. *Mermaid Quay, Stuart Street, Cardiff Bay, Cardiff; tel: 029 2045 0947; open daily (until 2am Fri–Sat). www.terranovacardiff.com*

The Plymouth Arms 23
Atmospheric former Victorian hunting lodge, complete with oak beams, fireplaces, and a large garden. *Crofft Y Genau Road, St. Fagans, Cardiff; tel: 029 2057 1121; open daily. www.cardiffpubs.co.uk*

Three Horse Shoes Inn 25
Rustic, family-run countryside pub with a beer garden and a menu featuring plenty of traditional, hearty food. *Main Road, Peterston-Super-Ely, Vale of Glamorgan; tel: 01446 760388; open daily. www.sabrain.com*

Duke of Wellington 29
Award-winning medieval pub with open fires, pleasant beer garden, and traditional pub food. *48 High Street, Cowbridge, Vale of Glamorgan, tel: 01446 773592; open daily. www.cowbridgetown.co.uk*

No Sign Wine Bar 39
This fashionable downtown pub was one of Dylan Thomas's favorite drinking spots; it hosts music and comedy nights. *56 Wind Street, Swansea; tel: 01792 465110; open daily.*

The Pumphouse 39
Modern pub in an attractive quayside building with an outside terrace and a wide range of ales. *Pumphouse Quay, Maritime Quarter, Swansea; tel: 01792 651080; open daily.*

Salt at the George 40
Modern, airy, and family-friendly seaside pub with an outdoor terrace and good wine selection. *Southend, Mumbles, Swansea; tel: 01792 368129; open daily. www.saltmumbles.com*

PLACES TO STAY

Ciderhouse Cottage 2
Vacation apartments in a restored barn with modern conveniences, on a peaceful Monmouthshire farm. *Penylan Farm, The Hendre, Monmouthshire; tel: 01600 716435. www.penylanfarm.co.uk*

Llancayo Windmill 4
For a vacation home with a difference, try this rural five-story windmill deep within beautiful Monmouthshire countryside. *Morspan Holdings Ltd, Beech Hill Farm, Usk, Monmouthshire; tel: 01291 672539. www.llancayowindmill.com*

Rat Trap Hotel 5
Countryside hotel just outside Usk, with elegant rooms and a restaurant. *Chepstow Road, Llangeview, Usk, Monmouthshire; tel: 01291 673288. www.rattraphotel.co.uk*

The Kings Hotel 10
Good-quality central hotel with tasteful *en-suite* rooms and a restaurant. *High Street, Newport; tel: 01633 842020. www.kingshotelnewport.co.uk*

Heritage Park Hotel 16
A comfortable modern hotel with restaurant and spa, opposite the Heritage Park Museum. *Coed Cae Road, Trehafod, Pontypridd, Rhondda Cynon Taf; tel: 01443 687057. www.heritageparkhotel.co.uk*

The Big Sleep Hotel 20
In a converted office block, this is a modish, simply furnished central hotel. *Bute Terrace, Cardiff; tel: 029 2063 6363. www.thebigsleephotel.com*

Above: Terra Nova, in Cardiff's trendy bay area

NosDa Hostel 20
Smart backpacker hostel in central Cardiff, with *en-suite* rooms and a gym. *53–59 Despenser Street, Riverside, Cardiff; tel: 029 2037 8866. www.nosda.co.uk*

Jolyons Hotel 20
Elegant six-room boutique hotel in the Cardiff Bay area with king-size beds and whirlpool baths. *Bute Crescent, Cardiff; tel: 029 2048 8775. www.jolyons.co.uk*

Acorns Guest House 22
Comfortable seaside guesthouse near the downtown, with neat *en-suite* rooms. *17 Romilly Road, Barry, Vale of Glamorgan; tel: 01446 743238. www.cardiffbedandbreakfasts.co.uk*

Llanerch Vineyard 26
Apartments and B&B accommodations in farm buildings on Wales's largest vineyard. *Hensol, Pendoylan, Vale of Glamorgan; tel: 01443 225877. www.llanerch-vineyard.co.uk*

Egerton Grey Country House Hotel 27
Grand 17th-century manor house full of period features, set in landscaped gardens with sea views. *Porthkerry, Barry, Vale of Glamorgan; tel: 01446 711666. www.egertongrey.co.uk*

Fontygary Leisure Park 28
Popular seafront campsite with an entertainment and leisure center, a gym, and restaurants. *Rhoose, Barry, Vale of Glamorgan; tel: 01446 710386. www.fontygaryparks.co.uk*

Plas Llanmihangel 30
Tranquil and atmospheric 16th-century manor house, complete with baronial hall, log fires, and historic gardens. *Llanmihangel, nr Cowbridge, Vale of Glamorgan; tel: 01446 774610. www.plasllanmihangel.co.uk*

Bramble Cottage Bed & Breakfast 31
A 17th-century cottage with *en-suite* rooms and an attractive garden. *Flanders Road, Llantwit Major, Vale of Glamorgan; tel: 01446 795838. www.bramble-cottage.co.uk*

Rossett Guest House 35
Welcoming Victorian town house with neat rooms, close to the seafront. *1 Esplanade Avenue, Porthcawl, Bridgend; tel: 01656 771664. www.welcometoporthcawl.co.uk*

Seabank Hotel 35
Grand 19th-century hotel near the beach; most rooms enjoy spectacular sea views. *The Promenade, Porthcawl, Bridgend; tel: 01656 782261. www.seabankhotel.co.uk*

Trecco Bay Holiday Park 35
Family-friendly campsite on a blue-flag beach, with a pool and golf course. *Porthcawl, Bridgend; tel: 01656 774360. www.parkdeanholidays.co.uk*

Protea Guest House 35
Smart Edwardian town house near the seafront, with tastefully furnished and reasonably priced rooms. *25 Esplanade Avenue, Porthcawl, Bridgend; tel: 01656 786526. www.proteaguesthouse.com*

Above: Chepstow Castle in Gwent

The Dragon Hotel ㊴
Swansea's swankiest hotel, with 106 stylish rooms, two restaurants, a health club, and a pool.
The Kingsway, Swansea;
tel: 01792 657100.
www.dragon-hotel.co.uk

Port Eynon Youth Hostel ㊷
Fresh modern dorms and rooms in a restored lifeboat station, just off the beach.
Old Lifeboat House, Port Eynon, Gower, Swansea; tel: 0845 3719135.
www.yha.org.uk

Llwyn Onn Guesthouse ㊺
Pleasant rural guesthouse in the Brecon Beacons with simple airy rooms.
Llywyn Onn, Cwmtaf, Merthyr Tydfil;
tel: 01685 384384. www.llwynonn.co.uk

Chaplins Hotel ㊻
Neat, family-run hotel in the center of town with a popular bistro downstairs.
30–31 High Street, Merthyr Tydfil;
tel: 01685 387272.
www.chaplinshotel.co.uk

The Wenallt Bed & Breakfast ㊾
Restored Tudor longhouse on a working sheep farm in the Brecon Beacons, serving fresh local foods.
Gilwern, nr Abergavenny, Monmouthshire;
tel: 01873 830694. www.thewenallt.co.uk

The Old Rectory ㊼
Three elegant rooms in a 17th-century former rectory, set in a charming hamlet.
Llangattock Lingoed, Monmouthshire;
tel: 01873 821326.
www.rectoryonoffasdyke.co.uk

FESTIVALS AND EVENTS

Monmouth Music Festival ①
Week-long free music festival, featuring established and upcoming acts from a variety of musical genres.
Various venues, Monmouth; Jul.
www.monmouthfestival.co.uk

Welsh National ⑥
Join in the festivities at Wales's most prestigious horse-racing meeting on the Monday after Boxing Day.
Chepstow Racecourse, Chepstow, Monmouthshire; tel: 01291 622260;
Dec. www.chepstow-racecourse.co.uk

The Big Cheese ⑮
Caerphilly's rich heritage is celebrated with three days of street theater, music, reenactments, funfair rides, and fireworks. *Owain Glyndwr Playing Fields, Twyn Square, Caerphilly;*
tel: 029 2088 0011; Jul.
www.caerphilly.gov.uk/bigcheese

Porthcawl Elvis Festival ㉟
Europe's biggest gathering of Elvis Presley tribute artists, with three days of shows and singing competitions.
Various venues, Porthcawl, Bridgend; Sep.
www.elvies.co.uk

Cardiff Festival ⑳
City-wide festivities on weekends in the summer, including open-air theater performances, concerts, comedy, acrobats, and a carnival.
Various venues, Cardiff;
tel: 029 2087 2087; Jul–Aug.
www.cardiff-festival.com

Welsh Proms ⑳
Annual musical festival in the heart of Cardiff, featuring 16 days of performances, including classical, folk, and world music, and the Children's Proms.
St. David's Hall, The Hayes, Cardiff;
tel: 029 2087 8444; Jul.
www.stdavidshallcardiff.co.uk

Swansea Festival of Music and The Arts ㊴
Long-running musical festival featuring classical music, opera, jazz, gospel, and musical comedy over three weeks.
Various venues, Swansea; tel: 01792 411570; Sep–Oct.
www.swanseafestival.org

Abergavenny Food Festival ㊿
Major two-day culinary festival, with food stalls, cooking demonstrations, and entertainment (see p115).
Various venues, Abergavenny, Monmouthshire;
tel: 01873 851643; Sep.
www.abergavennyfoodfestival.com

MUSEUMS AND GALLERIES

Nelson Museum & Local History Centre ①
One of the world's best collections of Admiral Nelson memorabilia.
New Market Hall, Priory Street, Monmouth; tel: 01600 710630;
open Mar–Oct: 11am–1pm and 2–5pm Mon–Sat, 2–5pm Sun; Nov–Feb: 11am–1pm and 2pm–4pm Mon–Sat, 2–4pm Sun.
www.monmouthshire.gov.uk

Usk Rural Life Museum ④
Displays recall rural life in Monmouthshire, with a reconstructed farm kitchen and agricultural equipment.
The Malt Barn, New Market Street, Usk, Monmouthshire; tel: 01291 673777; open Apr–Oct: 10am–5pm Mon–Fri, 2–5pm Sat–Sun. www.uskmuseum.org.uk

Chepstow Castle ⑥
Dating from 1067, this is one of Britain's earliest stone castles. It commands spectacular views over the River Wye.
Chepstow, Monmouthshire; tel: 01291 623772; open Apr–Oct: 9am–5pm daily; Nov–Mar: 9:30am–4pm Mon–Sat, 11am–4pm Sun. www.cadw.wales.gov.uk

Caldicot Castle ⑦
Take an audio tour around this stunning Norman castle and its extensive parkland.
Church Road, Caldicot, Monmouthshire; tel: 01291 420241; open Apr–Oct: 11am–5pm daily. www.caldicotcastle.co.uk

National Roman Legion Museum ⑧
See Britain's best-preserved Roman amphitheatre, legionary barracks, countless artifacts, and a recreated Roman garden.
High Street, Caerleon, Monmouthshire; tel: 01633 423134; open 10am–5pm Mon–Sat, 2–5pm Sun.
www.museumwales.ac.uk/en/roman

Fourteen Locks Canal Heritage Centre ⑨
Discover the history of the Brecon and Monmouthshire Canal, and go for a boat trip on the waterway.
Cwm Lane, Rogerstone, Newport; tel: 01633 894802; open 9:30am–4:30pm daily. www.fourteenlocks.co.uk

Tredegar House ⑩
Explore this grand 17th-century mansion with costumed guides. Regular themed events are also held. *Duffryn, Newport; tel: 01633 815880; open Apr–Sep: 11am–4pm daily; guided tours 11am–4pm Wed–Sun. www.newport.gov.uk*

Llancaiach Fawr Manor ⑭
Costumed guides take you back in time at this 16th-century manor house. *Gelligaer Road, Nelson, Treharris, Caerphilly; tel: 01443 412248; open Mar–Oct: 10am–5pm daily; Nov–Feb: 10am–5pm Tue–Sun. www.caerphilly.gov.uk/llancaiachfawr*

Rhondda Heritage Park ⑯
A reconstructed mining village street and tours of the old buildings at the pit's head. *Lewis Merthyr Colliery, Coed Cae Road, Trehafod, Rhondda Cynon Taf; tel: 01443 682036; open Mar–Oct: 10am–6pm daily; Nov–Feb: 10am–6pm Tue–Sun. www.rhonddaheritagepark.com*

Castell Coch ⑱
Victorian "fairy-tale" castle in medieval style, with lush Neo-Gothic interiors.
Castle Hill, Tongwynlais, Cardiff; tel: 029 2081 0101; open Apr–Oct: 9am–5pm daily; Nov–Mar: 9:30am–4pm Mon–Sat, 11am–4pm Sun. www.cadw.wales.gov.uk

Butetown History & Arts Centre ⑳
Discover the history of Cardiff's docklands at this unique community center.
5 Dock Chambers, Bute Street, Cardiff; tel: 029 2025 6757; open 10am–4pm Tue–Fri, 11am–4:30pm Sat–Sun. www.bhac.org

National Museum of Wales ⑳
Fascinating displays on natural history, archaeology, social history, and art.
Cathays Park, Cardiff; tel: 029 2039 7951; open 10am–5pm Tue–Sun. www.museumwales.ac.uk

Bay Art ⑳
Stylish gallery, situated in Cardiff's bay area, regularly hosts major exhibitions of works by contemporary Welsh and international artists.
54B/C Bute Street, Cardiff Bay; tel: 029 2065 0016; open noon–5pm Tue–Sat. www.bayart.org.uk

Cosmeston Medieval Village ㉑
Faithfully reconstructed 14th-century village, complete with costumed villagers and rare farm animals.
Cosmeston, Lavernock Road, Penarth, Vale of Glamorgan; tel: 029 2070 1678; open Apr–Oct: 11am–4pm daily; Nov–Mar: 11am–3pm daily. www.valeofglamorgan.gov.uk

St. Fagans Museum of Welsh Life ㉓
Visit restored historic buildings brought here from across Wales, and watch traditional craftspeople at work.
St. Fagans, Cardiff; tel: 029 2057 3500; open 10am–5pm daily. www.museumwales.ac.uk

National Waterfront Museum ㊴
Explore Wales's industrial and maritime heritage with fascinating displays.
Oystermouth Road, Maritime Quarter, Swansea; tel: 01792 638950; open 10am–5pm daily. www.museumwales.ac.uk/en/swansea

Dylan Thomas Centre ㊴
Displays on the life and works of the poet, plus a café and bookshop.
Somerset Place, Swansea; tel: 01792 463980; open 10am–4:30pm daily. www.dylanthomas.com

Ynysfach Engine House ㊻
Once part of the 19th-century Cyfarthfa Ironworks, this building houses displays on local industrial heritage.
Ynysfach Road, Merthyr Tydfil; tel: 01685 382356; open 10am–4pm Mon–Fri. www.visitmerthyr.co.uk

Cyfarthfa Castle Museum & Art Gallery ㊻
A Regency-era mansion house, home to displays on local industrial history.
Brecon Road, Merthyr Tydfil; tel: 01685 723112; open Apr–Sep: 10am–5:30pm daily; Oct–Mar: 10am–4pm Tue–Fri, noon–4pm Sat–Sun. www.visitmerthyr.co.uk/attractions

Bedwellty House and Park ㊽
Restored Regency mansion and gardens with displays on local history.
Tredegar, Blaenau Gwent; tel: 01495 355937; open 2–5pm daily. www.blaenau-gwent.gov.uk

THINGS TO DO WITH KIDS

Chaos For Kids ⑩
Trampolines, slides, and ball games are offered in this fun indoor play venue.
18–19 Queensway Meadows, Estuary Road, Newport; tel: 01633 271001; open 9:30am–6pm Tue–Fri, 10:30am–6pm Sat–Sun. www.chaosforkids.co.uk

Cefn Mably Farm Park ⑫
Younger kids will love the pony rides, indoor and outdoor play areas, and petting the animals at this farm.
Began Road, Cefn Mably, nr Castleton, Newport; tel: 01633 680312; open 10am–5pm daily. www.cefnmablyfarmpark.com

Techniquest ⑳
Here kids can get hands-on with a variety of interactive science experiments.
Stuart Street, Cardiff Bay, Cardiff; tel: 029 2047 5475; open 9:30am–4:30pm Mon–Fri, 10am–5pm Sat–Sun. www.techniquest.org

Doctor Who Exhibition ⑳
Costumes and props from the BBC TV series here – watch out for the Daleks!
The Red Dragon Centre, Atlantic Wharf Leisure Centre, Hemingway Road, Cardiff Bay; tel: 029 2048 9257; open 10am–6:30pm daily. www.doctorwhoexhibition.com

Below: Interactive exhibits at Techniquest in Cardiff

Barry Island Pleasure Park ㉒
Wales's premier amusement park will provide thrills for the whole family.
Friars Road, Barry Island, Vale of Glamorgan; tel: 01446 732844; open May–Sep: 12:30pm–6pm Sat–Sun; late May and mid-Jul–Aug: also open 12:30pm–6pm Mon–Fri. www.barryislandpleasurepark.co.uk

Welsh Hawking Centre ㉒
Get close to over 200 birds of prey and watch displays of falconry in 25 acres (10 hectares) of attractive parkland.
Weycock Road, Barry, Vale of Glamorgan; tel: 01446 734687; open 10:30am–5pm daily. www.welsh-hawking.co.uk

Ogmore Farm Riding Centre ㉝
Saddle up a horse for a guided trek along wide beaches, sand dunes, and open countryside. *Ogmore Farm, Ogmore-by-Sea, Bridgend; tel: 01656 880856. www.rideonthebeach.co.uk*

Ocean Quest ㉟
A water-sports center that offers kayaking, surfing and power-boating lessons.
49 New Road, Porthcawl, Bridgend; tel: 01656 783310; see website for course details. www.ocean-quest.co.uk

Margam Country Park ㊲
Explore the magnificent Gothic mansion, orangery, narrow-gauge railroad, adventure playground, deer park, and bike trails in glorious country parkland.
Margam, Port Talbot; tel: 01639 881635; open Apr–early Sep: 10am–5pm daily; mid-Sep–Mar: 1pm–4:30pm Mon–Tue, 10am–4:30pm Wed–Sun. www.neath-porttalbot.gov.uk

Kenfig National Nature Reserve ㊱
The coastal dunes and wetlands here are ideal for bird-watching or just enjoying countryside walks.
Ton Kenfig, Bridgend; tel: 01656 743386; open daily (visitor center open 2–4:30pm Mon–Fri, 10am–4:30pm Sat–Sun). www.meadowgarden.co.uk

Brecon Mountain Railway ㊼
Take a steam-train ride through the stunning landscape of the Brecon Beacons.
Off Heads of the Valleys trunk road, Merthyr Tydfil; tel: 01685 722988; open Mar–Oct: trains depart from 11am (see website for full timetable). www.breconmountainrailway.co.uk

Parc Bryn Bach ㊽
Several instructor-led activities are available here, including mountain-biking, kayaking, and archery, with on-site accommodations.
Merthyr Road, Tredegar, Blaenau Gwent; tel: 01495 711816; phone for details. www.blaenau-gwent.gov.uk

SPAS AND HEALTH RESORTS

The Celtic Manor Resort ⑩
Luxurious resort with two spas offering various facial and body treatments.
Coldra Woods, Newport; tel: 01633 413000. www.celtic-manor.com

Bryn Meadows Spa ⑬
Luxurious boutique spa with pool, sauna, Jacuzzi, and sun terrace.
Maes-y-Cwmmer, nr Ystrad Mynach, Caerphilly; tel: 01495 225590. www.brynmeadows.co.uk

Laguna Health & Spa ⑳
A wide variety of beauty treatments and massages in the heart of Cardiff.
Park Plaza Hotel, Greyfriars Road, Cardiff; tel: 029 2011 1110. www.lagunahealthandspa.com

The St. Davids Hotel & Spa ⑳
A top-class spa and restaurant in a modern 5-star hotel overlooking Cardiff Bay.
Havannah Street, Cardiff Bay, Cardiff; tel: 029 2045 4045. www.stdavidshotelcardiff.co.uk

The Towers Hotel & Spa ㊳
A sauna, swimming pool, and various beauty treatments are available here.
Jersey Marine, Swansea Bay, Swansea; tel: 01792 814155. www.thetowersswanseabay.com

Nant Ddu Lodge ㊺
Relax and be pampered at this country hotel in the Brecon Beacons.
Cwmtaf, Merthyr Tydfil; tel: 01685 377088. www.nant-ddu-lodge.co.uk

OTHER SIGHTS IN THE BOOK

LOCAL FOOD

Earth Café ⑯
Buddhist-inspired, alcohol-free vegetarian café that has its (healthy) heart in the right place.
16–20 Turner Street, Northern Quarter, Manchester; tel: 0161 834 1996; open 9am–7pm Tue–Fri, 10am–5pm Sat. www.earthcafe.co.uk

Nawaab ⑯
Palatial Indian restaurant with an extensive and mouthwatering menu of dishes.
1008 Stockport Road, Levenshulme, Manchester; tel: 0161 224 6969; open 5:30–11pm Mon–Thu, 5–11pm Fri–Sat, 1–11pm Sun. www.manchester.nawaab.com

Manchester Real Food Market ⑯
Full of seasonal fare and local products, from cakes to cheeses and real ale.
Piccadilly Gardens, Manchester; tel: 0161 234 7357; second and fourth Fri and Sat of every month, 10am–5:30pm.

The Quarter ㉓
Splendid pizzas, pasta, salads, and homemade cakes at this relaxing bistro.
7–11 Falkner Street, Liverpool; tel: 0151 707 1965; open 8am–11pm Mon–Fri, 10am–11pm Sat, 10am–10:30pm Sun. www.thequarteruk.com

Below: "The Beats" pose at Liverpool's Cavern Club

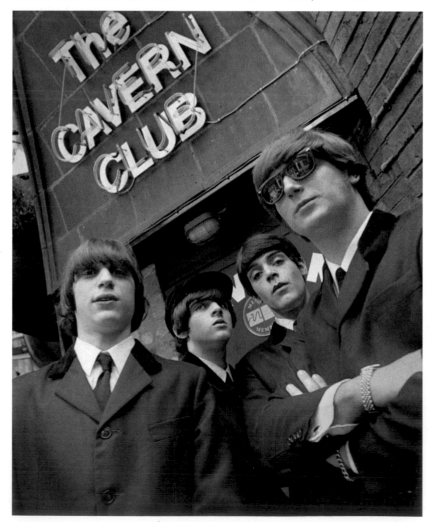

Village Bakery ③
Over three decades of organic experience is on display at this increasingly well-known bakery that uses local ingredients. There's also a lovely café attached.
Melmerby, Cumbria; tel: 01768 898437; open 8:30am–5pm Mon–Sat, 9:30am–5pm Sun and Bank Holiday Mondays. www.village-bakery.com

G.A.L. ⑳
Enjoyable, strikingly contemporary wine bar and restaurant with a modern, well-priced British and international menu.
13 Frodsham Street, Chester; tel: 01244 342384; open noon–9pm Mon–Sat, noon–6pm Sun.

Chez Jules Restaurant ⑳
Located within a lovely half-timbered building, this busy French eatery is one of Chester's most popular.
71 Northgate Street, Chester; tel: 01244 400014; open noon–3pm and 6–10:30pm Mon–Sat, noon–4pm Sun. www.chezjules.com

Seniors ㉘
Every day, apart from Sunday, is "fryday" at this fish-and-chip shop, which has a loyal following. Note that it closes early.
106 Normoss Road, Blackpool, Lancashire; tel: 01253 393529; open 11:30am–2pm and 4:30–7:30pm Mon–Thu and Sat, 11:30am–2pm and 4:30–8pm Fri. www.seniorsfishexperience.com

Steadman's ⑨
Award-winning Cumbrian butcher shop famed for its top-quality pork.
2 Finkle Street, Sedbergh, Cumbria; tel: 015396 20431; open 7am–5pm Mon–Sat. www.steadmans-butchers.co.uk

Brough's ㉕
Celebrated butchers with award-winning sausages and local meats.
581 Liverpool Road, Ainsdale, Southport, Merseyside; tel: 01704 574069; open 8am–5pm Mon–Fri; 8am–4pm Sat. http://broughs.com

FARMERS' MARKETS

Penrith Farmers' Market ⑤
A must for anyone on the trail of fresh produce, local specialties, and crafts, in a colorful setting.
Market Square, Penrith, Cumbria; tel: 01768 212147; third Tue of every month, 9:30am–3pm.

Colne Farmers' Market ⑩
Small market with an appetizing spread of vegetables, meats, and other organic fare.
Market Street, Colne, Lancashire; tel: 01282 661240; third Sat of every month, 9am–2pm.

Lancaster Charter Farmers' & Producers' Market ㉙
Bustling outdoor market with a cornucopia of fresh and tasty local foods.
Market Square, Lancaster; tel: 01524 66627; second Sat of every month, 9am–5pm.

Orton Farmers' Market ㊾
Mind-boggling range of local Cumbrian food and produce in the deliciously picturesque village of Orton.
Orton, Cumbria; second Sat of every month, 9:30am–2:30pm. www.ortonfarmers.co.uk

PUBS AND BARS

Peveril of the Peak ⑯
Traditional and distinctive-looking early-19th-century pub with a green-tiled exterior and a healthy range of real ales.
127 Great Bridgewater Street, Manchester; tel: 0161 236 6364; open noon–3pm and 5–11pm Mon–Sat, 7–11pm Sun.

The Metropolitan ⑯
Gorgeous red-brick railroad tavern full of period charm; bar and restaurant menus.
2 Lapwing Lane, West Didsbury, Manchester; tel: 0161 438 2332; open daily. www.the-metropolitan.co.uk

Cavern Club ㉓
Eternally associated with the Fab Four, the Cavern Club is an iconic spot for a drink and for catching live bands.
10 Mathew Street, Liverpool; tel: 0151 236 1965; open from 11am daily; closes 8pm Mon–Wed, late Thu–Sun (with evening admission charges for live performances). Families welcome before 7pm. www.cavernclub.org

The Greyhound Hotel ⑧
Hotel and pub with 17th-century roots and much-championed dining and drinking.
Main Street, Shap, Cumbria; tel: 01931 716474. www.greyhoundshap.co.uk

The Three Fishes ⑬
Lovely outpost of fine cuisine and real ale in the Ribble Valley.
Mitton Road, Mitton, nr Whalley, Lancashire; tel: 01254 826888; open daily. www.thethreefishes.com

Alma de Cuba ㉓
An altar-equipped church conversion that is dedicated to fine food and drink.
St. Peter's Church, Seel Street, Liverpool; tel: 0151 702 7394; open daily. www.alma-de-cuba.com

The Water Witch ㉙
Perched on the side of the Lancaster Canal, these converted stables provide an excellent place to slake a thirst.
Canal Tow Path, Aldcliffe Lane, Lancaster; tel: 01524 63828; open daily. www.thewaterwitch.co.uk

The Drunken Duck Inn ㊸
This magnificently named inn is a classic watering hole, set in massive grounds in the heart of the Lake District.
Barngates, Ambleside, Cumbria; tel: 015394 36347; open daily. http://drunkenduckinn.co.uk

The Bitter End ㊿
Traditional Lake District pub with on-site brewery, serving mussels in white wine and other delicious dishes.
15 Kirkgate, Cockermouth, Cumbria; tel: 01900 828993; open lunch and evening Mon–Fri and Sun; all day Sat. www.bitterend.co.uk

PLACES TO STAY

Warwick Lodge Guesthouse ①
Very clean and comfortable: large rooms, superb breakfasts, and friendly proprietors.
112 Warwick Road, Carlisle; tel: 01228 523796. www.warwicklodgecarlisle.co.uk

Hard Day's Night ㉓
Highly modish Beatles-dedicated accommodations in a lovely historic building in the heart of Liverpool.
North John Street, Central Buildings, Liverpool; tel: 0151 236 1964. www.harddaysnighthotel.com

Malmaison Liverpool ㉓
Carbon-gray and black industrial decor at this hotel, with stylish rooms, smooth dining, and entertainment facilities.
William Jessop Way, Princes Dock, Liverpool; tel: 0151 229 5000. www.malmaison-liverpool.com

Lilies Guesthouse ㉓
Lovely, well-kept, good-value Victorian B&B in a private square, overlooking a green.
4 Derwent Square, Old Swan, Liverpool; tel: 0151 284 4932. www.liliesguesthouse.co.uk

The Rampsbeck Country Manor Hotel ⑥
In an absolutely stunning lakeside position by Ullswater, and set in attractive grounds, this magnificent country-house hotel makes for a memorable stay.
Watermillock, Ullswater, Cumbria; tel: 07684 86442. www.rampsbeck.co.uk

Appleby Manor Country House Hotel ⑦
Delightfully located 19th-century house in the Eden Valley, with considerate staff and excellent dining.
Roman Road, Appleby in Westmorland, Cumbria; tel: 01768 351571. www.applebymanor.co.uk

The Welbeck ⑲
Just off the Central Promenade in Douglas, this hotel offers comfy, clean rooms, sea views, and attentive service.
Mona Drive, Douglas, Isle of Man; tel: 01624 675663. www.welbeckhotel.com

Green Bough ⑳
Highly welcoming B&B with the emphasis on comfort and a fabulous restaurant.
60 Hoole Road, Chester; tel: 01244 326241. www.chestergreenboughhotel.com

The Chester Grosvenor ⑳
The height of luxury in Chester, this gorgeous-looking historic hotel has everything you might need, including an invigorating spa.
Eastgate, Chester; tel: 01244 324024. www.chestergrosvenor.co.uk

Higher Huxley Hall ⑳
Fine-looking manor house dating back to the 13th century, with huge grounds.
Red Lane, Huxley, Chester; tel: 01829 781484. www.huxleyhall.co.uk

Ash Farm ㉑
This handsome 18th-century farmhouse, set in gorgeous Cheshire countryside, is a perfect romantic getaway.
Park Lane, Little Bollington, Altrincham, Cheshire; tel: 0161 929 9290. www.ashfarm.co.uk

The Big Blue ㉘
Guests are full of praise for the modern, roomy accommodations and family-oriented facilities at this hotel right next to the Pleasure Beach.
Ocean Boulevard, Blackpool Pleasure Beach, Blackpool, Lancashire; tel: 0845 367 3333. www.bigbluehotel.com

Winder Hall Country House ㊿
This stunning Lakeland Jacobean country manor house, with beautifully decorated rooms, is set in a tranquil village location.
Low Lorton, Cockermouth, Cumbria; tel: 01900 85107. www.winderhall.co.uk

New House Farm ㊿
Hidden away within 15 acres (6 hectares) of scenic Lakeland, this 17th-century house has the added allure of a garden hot tub.
Lorton, Cockermouth, Cumbria; tel: 07841 159818. http://newhouse-farm.com

Number 43 ㉚
Lovingly designed and cared-for Victorian boutique B&B overlooking the Kent Estuary, with more than a measure of style and up-to-date flair.
The Promenade, Arnside, Cumbria; tel: 01524 762761. www.no43.org.uk

The Pennington ㊵
Very relaxing seafront hotel in Ravenglass with modern, comfortable rooms and excellent dining.
Muncaster Castle, Ravenglass, Cumbria; tel: 01229 717222. www.penningtonhotels.com

The Archway ㊶
Truly charming B&B with Victorian charm; grade-A breakfasts, and packed lunches.
13 College Road, Windermere, Cumbria; tel: 015394 45613. www.the-archway.com

The Old Dungeon Ghyll Hotel ㊹
Hotel in a 300-year-old building with a perfect location in the Langdale Valley.
Great Langdale, Ambleside, Cumbria; tel: 015394 37272. www.odg.co.uk

Beck Allans Bed & Breakfast ㊼
Lovely Lakeland B&B with delightful views over the River Rothay.
College Street, Grasmere, Cumbria; tel: 01539 435563. www.beckallans.com

The Cottage in the Wood Country House Hotel & Restaurant ㊽
With welcoming owners, a great restaurant, a cozy feel, and a secluded mountain forest location overlooking Skiddaw, this is a great place for a relaxing break.
Whinlatter Forest, Braithwaite, nr Keswick, Cumbria; tel: 017687 78409. www.thecottageinthewood.co.uk

FESTIVALS AND EVENTS

Cumberland County Show ①
One-day celebration of food and farming with games, rides, and performances.
Rickerby Park, Carlisle, Cumbria; tel: 016977 47397; Jul. www.cumberlandshow.co.uk

Potfest ⑤
Two separate three-day gatherings for creative potters from all over Europe to show off their creations.
Penrith, Cumbria; Potfest in the Park at Hutton-in-the-Forest, Potfest in the Pens at Skirsgill Auction Mar; Jul; Aug. www.potfest.co.uk

The Great British R&B Festival ⑩
Three-day gathering of seasoned blues musicians, from Steve Cropper to The Yardbirds, Chicken Shack, and beyond.
Colne, Lancashire; tel: 01282 661234; Aug. www.bluesfestival.co.uk

Manchester International Festival ⑯
Biennial festival celebrating new and original performance art, visual arts, and music events over two weeks.
Various venues, Manchester; tel: 0161 238 7300; every other Jul. www.mif.co.uk

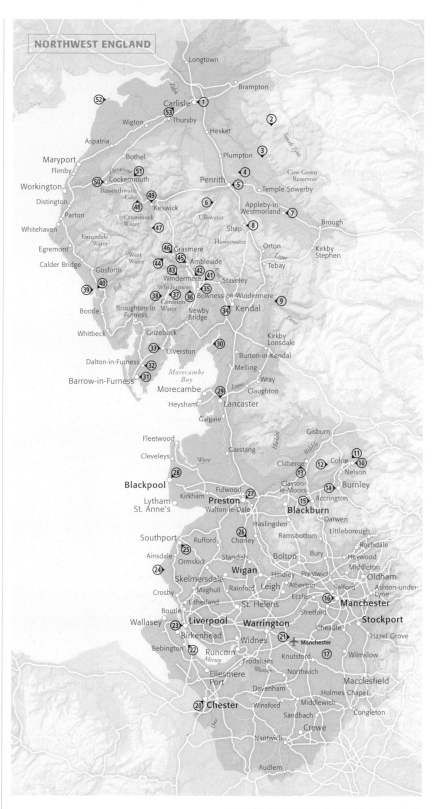

Liverpool Irish Festival ㉓
Music, art, theater, literature, Gaelic football, and dance at a two-week festival.
Various venues, Liverpool; tel: 07804 286145; Oct–Nov. www.liverpoolirishfestival.com

Grasmere Rushbearing Festival ㊻
Traditional bearing of rushes to St. Oswald's Church by local children; the festival dates back hundreds of years to when rushes were strewn on the floor of local churches.
Grasmere, Cumbria; Sat closest to St. Oswald's Day (Aug 5). www.grasmereandrydal.org.uk

Left: Burnley Balloon Festival

Grasmere Lakeland Sports and Show ㊼
Largest meeting for traditional Lakeland sports, such as fell-running, hound trails, and bouts between the inimitably dressed Cumberland wrestlers. Military bands provide accompaniment.
Grasmere, Cumbria; Aug Bank Holiday Sun. http://grasmeresportsandshow.co.uk

Appleby Horse Fair ⑦
Attracting thousands of travelers and a constellation of caravans and wagons, this week-long festival is an annual highlight.
Appleby in Westmorland, Cumbria; first Thu in Jun (unless first Thu is Jun 1, when it is held on Jun 8). www.applebyfair.org

Coniston Water Festival ㊲
Duck races, boat cruises, kayaking, and all things waterborne over two days.
Coniston Water, Cumbria; Jul. www.conistonwaterfestival.org.uk

Lakeland Country Fair ㊳
One-day celebration of traditional country crafts and skills, with sheepdog shows, fell races, and children's activities.
Torver, nr Coniston, Cumbria; Aug. www.lakelandcountryfair.co.uk

Windermere Air Show ㊶
Attention shifts from the lakes to the skies with a two-day host of aviation-related attractions including aerial displays.
Windermere, Cumbria; Jul. www.windermereairshow.co.uk

Burnley Balloon Festival ⑭
Hot-air balloons of all descriptions fill the Lancashire skies in this annual weekend-long extravaganza.
Towneley Park, Burnley, Lancashire; tel: 01282 424213; Jul or Aug. www.visitlancashire.com

Lancashire Food Festival ⑮
A two-day celebration of Lancashire gastronomy, including cooking demonstrations, food, music and dance.
Town Hall, Accrington, Lancashire; Apr. www.lancashirefoodfestival.co.uk

Ambleside Christmas Lights Festival ㊺
Heart-warming procession with paper lanterns through the winter streets of Ambleside one evening in November, with fireworks and other seasonal events.
Ambleside, Cumbria; mid-Nov. www.amblesidechristmaslights.co.uk

Keswick Beer Festival ㊽
The North's largest beer festival is a two-day exercise in real-ale indulgence.
Keswick Rugby Club, Davidson Park, Keswick, Cumbria; tel: 017687 73200; Jun. www.keswickbeerfestival.co.uk

Solway Festival ㊿
Annual summer Cumbrian music festival with a strong program of bands over the August Bank Holiday weekend.
Silloth, West Cumbria; late Aug. www.solwayfestival.co.uk

Pendle Walking Festival ⑪
Guided walks, pub walks, and the Pendle Way Challenge – a five-day hike.
Pendle, Lancashire; tel: 01282 661981; Sep. www.walkinginpendle.co.uk

Ulverston Walking Festival ㉝
For all who appreciate the scenic Lakeland outdoors – on foot – with walks led by experienced volunteers.
Ulverston, Cumbria; Apr or May.

Cyclefest ㉞
Races, stunts, bicycle-skills training, and a bicycle disco at this week-long event.
Abbot Hall Park, Kendal, Cumbria; May–Jun. www.cyclefest.org.uk

MUSEUMS AND GALLERIES

Whitworth Art Gallery ⑯
Superb collection including rare Turner and Pre-Raphaelite watercolors.
Oxford Road, Manchester; tel: 0161 275 7450; open 10am–5pm Mon–Sat, noon–4pm Sun. www.whitworth.manchester.ac.uk

The Imperial War Museum North ⑯
Dramatic Daniel Libeskind–designed modern museum with an extensive collection of military artifacts.
The Quays, Trafford Wharf Road, Manchester; tel: 0161 836 4000; open Mar–Oct: 10am–6pm daily; Nov–Feb: 10am–5pm daily. http://north.iwm.org.uk

Tullie House Museum and Art Gallery ①
Fascinating glimpses into the history, natural history, arts, and culture of Carlisle.
Castle Street, Carlisle; tel: 01228 618718; open Nov–Mar: 10am–4pm Mon–Sat, noon–4pm Sun; Apr–Jun and Sep–Oct: 10am–5pm Mon–Sat, noon–5pm Sun; Jul–Aug: 10am–5pm Mon–Sat, 11am–5pm Sun. www.tulliehouse.co.uk

The Manx Museum ⑲
Displays exploring Manx culture and heritage, including works by local artists.
Crellins Hill, Douglas, Isle of Man; tel: 01624 648000; open 10am–5pm Mon–Sat. www.iomguide.com/manxmuseum.php

Grosvenor Museum ⑳
Superb collection of Chester-related artifacts and displays including a first-rate range of Roman exhibits.
27 Grosvenor Street, Chester; tel: 01244 402033; open 10:30am–5pm Mon–Sat, 1–4pm Sun. www.grosvenormuseum.co.uk

Magical Mystery Tour ㉓
Essential Beatles bus tours where the streets become museum exhibits, organized by the Cavern Club, where the band first played *(see Pubs and Bars)*.
Cavern City Tours, Liverpool; tel: 0151 236 9091. www.cavernclub.org

Walker Art Gallery ㉓
Sumptuous collection of paintings from Pre-Raphaelite masters to Impressionist visionaries, as well as Turner and Hockney.
William Brown Street, Liverpool; tel: 0151 478 4199; open 10am–5pm daily. www.thewalker.org.uk

Laurel and Hardy Museum ㉝
Stan Laurel was born in Ulverston and this absorbing museum is dedicated to the sheer comic genius of the famous duo.
Roxy Cinema, Brogden Street, Ulverston, Cumbria; tel: 01229 582292; open Feb–Dec: 10am–4:30pm daily. www.laurel-and-hardy-museum.co.uk

Ruskin Museum ㊲
Art and artifacts associated with John Ruskin, plus a selection of items relating to Donald Campbell and his record-breaking speedboat, *Bluebird*, which crashed on Coniston Water in 1967.
Coniston, Cumbria; tel: 015394 41164; open mid-Mar–mid-Nov: 10am–5:30pm daily; mid-Nov–mid Mar: 10:30am–3:30pm Wed–Sun. www.ruskinmuseum.com

Keswick Museum and Art Gallery ㊽
Victorian-era museum crammed with oddities, from a mummified cat to musical stones, a mantrap, and Napoleon's teacup. Ranked as "one of the world's strangest museums."
Station Road, Keswick, Cumbria; tel: 017687 73263; open Mar–Oct: 10am–4pm Tue–Sat. www.allerdale.gov.uk

Lady Lever Art Gallery ㉒
A fantastic collection of Victorian art with a large selection of Pre-Raphaelite works. *Port Sunlight Village, Wirral, Merseyside; tel: 0151 478 4136; open 10am–5pm daily. www.liverpoolmuseums.org.uk*

The National Football Museum ㉗
This unfettered celebration of the "beautiful game" is a must for all soccer fans, young and old. *Sir Tom Finney Way, Preston, Lancashire; tel: 01772 908442; open 10am–5pm Tue–Sat, 11am–5pm Sun. www.nationalfootballmuseum.com*

Dock Museum ㉛
Built over a former dry dock, with an emphasis on the shipbuilding and maritime history of Barrow-in-Furness. *North Road, Barrow-in-Furness, Cumbria; tel: 01229 876400; open Easter–Oct: 10am–5pm Tue–Fri, 11am–5pm Sat–Sun; Nov–Easter: 10:30am–4pm Wed–Fri, 11am–4:30pm Sat–Sun. www.dockmuseum.org.uk*

Blackwell, The Arts and Crafts House ㉟
House near Lake Windermere associated with the Arts and Crafts movement and designed by M. H. Baillie Scott. *Bowness-on-Windermere, Cumbria; tel: 015394 46139; open Apr–Oct: 10:30am–5pm daily; Nov–Mar: 10:30am–4pm daily. www.blackwell.org.uk*

Hill Top Farm ㊱
Beatrix Potter's 17th-century Lake District bolthole, perfectly preserved and managed by the National Trust. *Nr Sawrey, Ambleside, Cumbria; tel: 015394 36269; open 14 Feb–12 Mar: 11am to 3:30pm Sat–Thu; 14 Mar–1 Nov: 10:30am–4:30pm Sat–Thu. www.nationaltrust.org.uk*

THINGS TO DO WITH KIDS

South Tynedale Railway ②
Scenic steam-train trips run along Northern England's highest narrow-gauge railroad – 2 miles (3.2 km) of line stretch from Alston to Kirkhaugh. *The Railway Station, Alston, Cumbria; tel: 01434 381696 (talking timetable 01434 382828); operating hours vary: see website or contact for details. www.strps.org.uk*

World Museum Liverpool ㉓
Fascinating fun for wide-eyed kids, from the Ancient Egypt Gallery to the fish-filled aquarium, plus plenty of ongoing events. *William Brown Street, Liverpool; tel: 0151 478 4393; open 10am–5pm daily. www.worldmuseumliverpool.org.uk*

Doctor Who Museum ㉘
An A–Z of the Doctor, for all Tardis- and Time Lord–obsessed little ones. *The Golden Mile Centre, Central Promenade, Blackpool, Lancashire; tel: 01253 299982; open 10:30am–5pm daily. www.doctorwhoexhibitions.com*

Dewa Roman Experience ⑳
Family-run attraction featuring re-creations of Roman street scenes and relics from Roman Empire-era Chester, and offering Roman soldier patrol tours around the city. *Pierpoint Lane, off Bridge Street, Chester; tel: 01244 343407; open Feb–Nov: 9am–5pm Mon–Sat, 10am–5pm Sun; Dec–Jan: 10am–4pm daily. www.dewaromanexperience.co.uk*

The World of Beatrix Potter Attraction ㉟
Potter's magical world brought colorfully to life, with a much-loved tea room. *Bowness-on-Windermere, Cumbria; tel: 015394 88444; open 10am–4:30pm daily. www.hop-skip-jump.com*

Ravenglass and Eskdale Railway ㊴
Hop aboard one of the steam trains running between Ravenglass and Dalegarth for a scenic journey. *Ravenglass, Cumbria; tel: 01229 717171; trains run at least six times per day mid-March–Nov 1. www.ravenglass-railway.co.uk*

The Bond Museum ㊾
007's Aston Martin DB5, amphibious Lotus Esprit S1, and Thunderball Jet Pack – they're all here, plus much more. *Southey Hill Trading Estate, Keswick, Cumbria; tel: 01768 774044; open 10am–5pm daily. www.thebondmuseum.com*

Eden Ostrich World ④
Children will be birds of a feather flocking to this colony of ostriches on a working farm that also boasts a play area. *Langwathby Hall Farm, Langwathby, Penrith, Cumbria; tel: 01768 881771; open Mar–Oct: 10am–5pm daily; Nov–Feb: 10am–5pm Wed–Mon. www.ostrich-world.com*

Camelot Theme Park ㉖
Medieval fun with jousting competitions, rides, and a farm filled with animals. *Park Hall Road, Chorley, Lancashire; tel: 01257 455001; open Easter–Sep, times vary according to season. www.camelotthemepark.co.uk*

South Lakes Wild Animal Park ㉜
From its white rhinos to red kangaroos and Colombian spider monkeys, this beautifully designed zoo is a joy. *Broughton Road, Dalton-in-Furness, Cumbria; tel: 01229 466086; open Easter–Nov: 10am–5pm daily; Nov–Easter: 10am–4:30pm daily. www.wildanimalpark.co.uk*

SPAS AND HEALTH RESORTS

Holbeck Ghyll Country House Hotel ㊶
With gorgeous Lake Windermere views and a Michelin-starred restaurant, this excellent hotel boasts a fantastic health spa, designed for total pampering. *Holbeck Lane, Windermere, Cumbria; tel: 015394 32375. www.holbeckghyll.com*

Formby Hall Golf Resort and Spa ㉔
All-around winner on the Golf Coast with soothing spa and great fitness packages. *Southport Old Road, Formby, Southport, Merseyside; tel: 01704 875699. www.formbyhallgolfclub.co.uk*

Low Wood Hotel ㊷
This Lake Windermere shoreside hotel has a lovely location, great for family getaways. *Ambleside Road, nr Windermere, Cumbria; tel: 015394 33338. www.elh.co.uk*

Lodore Falls Hotel ㊼
Highly relaxing getaway with health treatments that include waterfall therapy. *The Lodore Falls Hotel, Borrowdale, Keswick, Cumbria; tel: 017687 77285. www.lakedistricthotels.net/lodorefalls/*

Armathwaite Hall Hotel ㊿
Stately luxury near Bassenthwaite Lake; spectacular scenery and a marvelous spa. *Bassenthwaite Lake, Keswick, Cumbria; tel: 017687 76551. http://armathwaite-hall.com*

OTHER SIGHTS IN THE BOOK

Pendle Hill ⑫ *(see pp26–7)*. **Manchester** ⑯ *(see pp144–5)*. **Cheshire Ring** ⑰ *(see pp104–5)*. **Isle of Man** ⑱ *(see pp172–3)*. **Liverpool** ㉓ *(see pp20–21)*. **Blackpool** ㉘ *(see pp124–5)*. **Lake District** ㊻ *(see pp46–7)*.

Below: Ravenglass and Eskdale Railway

NORTHEAST ENGLAND

LOCAL FOOD

Brasserie Black Door ①
An art gallery and café serving imaginative British cooking with local ingredients.
The Biscuit Factory, 16 Stoddart Street, Newcastle; tel: 0191 260 5411; open noon–2pm and 7–10pm Mon–Sat, noon–2pm Sun. www.blackdoorgroup.co.uk

Bistro Hotel du Vin ①
Simple dishes, expertly prepared, with a menu that changes seasonally and is based on local seafood, meats, and veg.
Allan House, City Road, Newcastle; tel: 0191 229 2200; open noon–1:45pm and 6–10pm Mon–Thu, noon–1:45pm and 6–10:30pm Fri, 12:30–2:30pm and 6–10:30pm Sat, 12:30–2:30pm and 6–10pm Sun. www.hotelduvin.com

Helmsley Market ⑦
This weekly market is worth a visit just for a stroll around the picturesque square, but you can also browse fresh local food.
Helmsley, North Yorkshire; tel: 01653 600666; every Fri, 9am–3pm. www.yorkshiremoorsandcoasts.com

Melton's Too ⑪
Fresh-picked watercress, freshly caught mackerel, York ham, and rare-breed lamb, beef, and pork are on the menu here.
25 Walmgate, York; tel: 01904 629222; open 10:30am–midnight Mon–Sat, 10:30am–11pm Sun. www.meltonstoo.co.uk

Lanterna ⑬
This Italian restaurant is a Scarborough highlight, serving tasty local seafood.
*33 Queen Street, Scarborough, North Yorkshire; tel: 01723 363616; open 7–9:30pm Mon–Sat.
www.lanterna-ristorante.co.uk*

The Star Inn at Harome ⑧
This old-fashioned inn, with its thatched roof, is now a gastropub, acclaimed for its superb way with fresh local foods.
Harome, nr Helmsley, North Yorkshire; tel: 01439 770397; open 6:30–9:30pm Mon, 11:30am–2pm and 6:30–9:30pm Tue–Sat, noon–6pm Sun. www.thestaratharome.co.uk

The Pipe and Glass Inn ⑮
This 15th-century inn serves local Burdass lamb, beef, and sausages, game in season, and freshly caught local seafood.
West End, South Dalton, Beverley, East Yorkshire; tel: 01430 810246; open noon–2pm and 6:30–9:30pm Tue–Fri; noon–11pm Sat; noon–4pm Sun. www.pipeandglass.co.uk

The Old Vicarage ⑰
Tessa Bramley's Michelin-starred menu is embellished by ingredients from the restaurant's own kitchen garden.
Ridgeway, nr Sheffield; tel: 0114 247 5814; open 12:30–3pm and 6:30–11pm Tue–Fri, 6:30–10:30pm Sat. www.theoldvicarage.co.uk

Brasserie Blanc ㉝
Famed chef Raymond Blanc's downtown brasserie in Leeds offers his modern approach to classic French cooking.
28 Sovereign Street, Leeds; tel: 0113 220 6060; open 9am–6pm Mon–Sat. www.brasserieblanc.com

Kirkgate Market ㉝
Kirkgate is Europe's largest indoor market, with 400 stands in the market building and, on most days, 200 more outside.
George Street, Leeds; tel: 0113 242 5252; 9am–5pm Mon–Sat (indoor market Wed only). www.leedsmarket.com

The Three Acres ㉓
Superb pub-restaurant serving classic dishes; seafood is a specialty.
Roydhouse, Shelley, Huddersfield; tel: 01484 602606; open noon–3pm and 6–11pm daily. www.3acres.com

Box Tree Restaurant ㊴
Chef Simon Gueller's sumptuous menu puts the emphasis on local produce.
35–37 Church Street, Ilkley, West Yorkshire; tel: 01943 608484; open noon–2pm and 7–9:30pm Fri–Sun, 7–9:30pm Tue–Thu. www.theboxtree.co.uk

Knaresborough Market ㊶
Caters for the everyday needs of locals, not just visiting gourmets; stands are piled with locally sourced fruit and vegetables.
Knaresborough, North Yorkshire; tel: 01423 556055; every Wed, 9am–4pm. www.knaresborough.co.uk

General Tarleton ㊸
The signature dish in this quaint old coaching inn is the chef's "little moneybags" (seafood parcels in lobster sauce), but the menu changes daily.
Ferrensby, Knaresborough, North Yorkshire; tel: 01423 340284; open 6–9:15pm Mon–Sat, noon–1:45pm Sun. www.generaltarleton.co.uk

The Blue Lion ㊾
Romantic, candlelit restaurant priding itself on the wide variety of local Yorkshire ingredients used. Good vegetarian options.
East Wilton, nr Leyburn, North Yorkshire; tel: 01969 624273; open noon–2:30pm and 6–9:30pm Mon–Sat, noon–2:30pm Sun. www.thebluelion.co.uk

The Bridge Inn ㊳
Fine pub and restaurant in a picturesque village, with real ales and dishes based on seasonal produce from local farms.
Whorlton, County Durham; tel: 01833 627341; open noon–2pm and 7–10pm Wed–Sat, noon–2pm and 5:30–9pm Sun. www.thebridgeinnrestaurant.co.uk

FARMERS' MARKETS

Hartlepool Farmers' Market ⑤
Hand-reared meats, game, and poultry, and homemade chutneys, cheeses, and jams.
Historic Quay, Hartlepool, County Durham; tel: 01748 884965; second Sat of every month, 8am–1pm. www.ndfm.co.uk

Grassington Farmers' Market ㊽
Great for locally baked cakes, tea loaves and curd tarts, cheeses, and unusual preserves, such as blueberry and lavender jam.
Grassington, Upper Wharfedale, North Yorkshire; third Sun of every month, 9:30am–1:30pm. www.ndfm.co.uk

Hexham Farmers' Market ㊻
Look out for Northumberland hill lamb at this award-winning market.
Hexham, Northumberland; tel: 01434 270393; second and fourth Sat of every month, 9am–1:30pm. www.hexhamfarmersmarket.co.uk

Northallerton Farmers' Market ㊽
Everything from cheeses and organic dairy products to pork, lamb, and even buffalo.
Northallerton, North Yorkshire; tel: 01748 884965; fourth Wed of every month, 8am–1pm. www.ndfm.co.uk

PUBS

The Bacchus ①
Busy and popular downtown pub with a big choice of local microbrewery beers and cask ales and a long wine list.
42–48 High Bridge, Newcastle; tel: 0191 261 1008; open all day Mon–Sat, lunch and eve Sun.

The Victoria ④
The plain exterior of this family-run pub conceals a cozy interior with an open fire.
86 Hallgarth Street, Durham; tel: 0191 386 5269; open noon–3pm and 6pm–midnight Mon–Sat, noon–3pm and 7–10:30pm Sun.

The Golden Fleece ⑪
More than 400 years old, this pub in the historic heart of York is said to be haunted.
Pavement Lane, York; tel: 01904 625171; open daily. www.goldenfleece.yorkwebsites.com

The Kelham Island Tavern ⑱
The Campaign for Real Ale's (CAMRA) "Pub of the Year" in 2008, with ten hand-drawn ales.
62 Russell Street, Sheffield; tel: 0114 272 2482; open daily. www.kelhamislandtavern.co.uk

Whitelocks ㉝
Classic Leeds pub serving authentic ales on this site for almost 300 years.
Turk's Head Yard, Briggate, Leeds; tel: 0113 245 3950; open daily.

The Cross Keys ㉝
Fine real-ale pub in the center of Leeds, with beers by Rooster's Brewery at Knaresborough and a selection of stouts.
107 Water Lane, Leeds; tel: 0113 243 3711; open daily.

The Bingley Arms ㊵
With its "priest's hole," original Dutch oven, and "snug" bars, this country pub is one of the oldest in Britain.
Church Lane, Bardsley, nr Leeds; tel: 01937 572642; open daily.

The Old Fleece ㊽
Charles Dickens enjoyed a drink in this venerable pub in the center of a busy North Yorkshire market town.
89 High Street, Northallerton, North Yorkshire; tel: 01609 773345; open daily. www.carling.com

The Lister Arms ㊿
Classic Yorkshire country inn with bags of atmosphere, good home cooking, and cozy rooms, as well as local ales.
Malham, nr Skipton, North Yorkshire; tel: 01729 830330; open daily. www.listerarms.co.uk

Below: Interior of the Kirkgate Market in Leeds

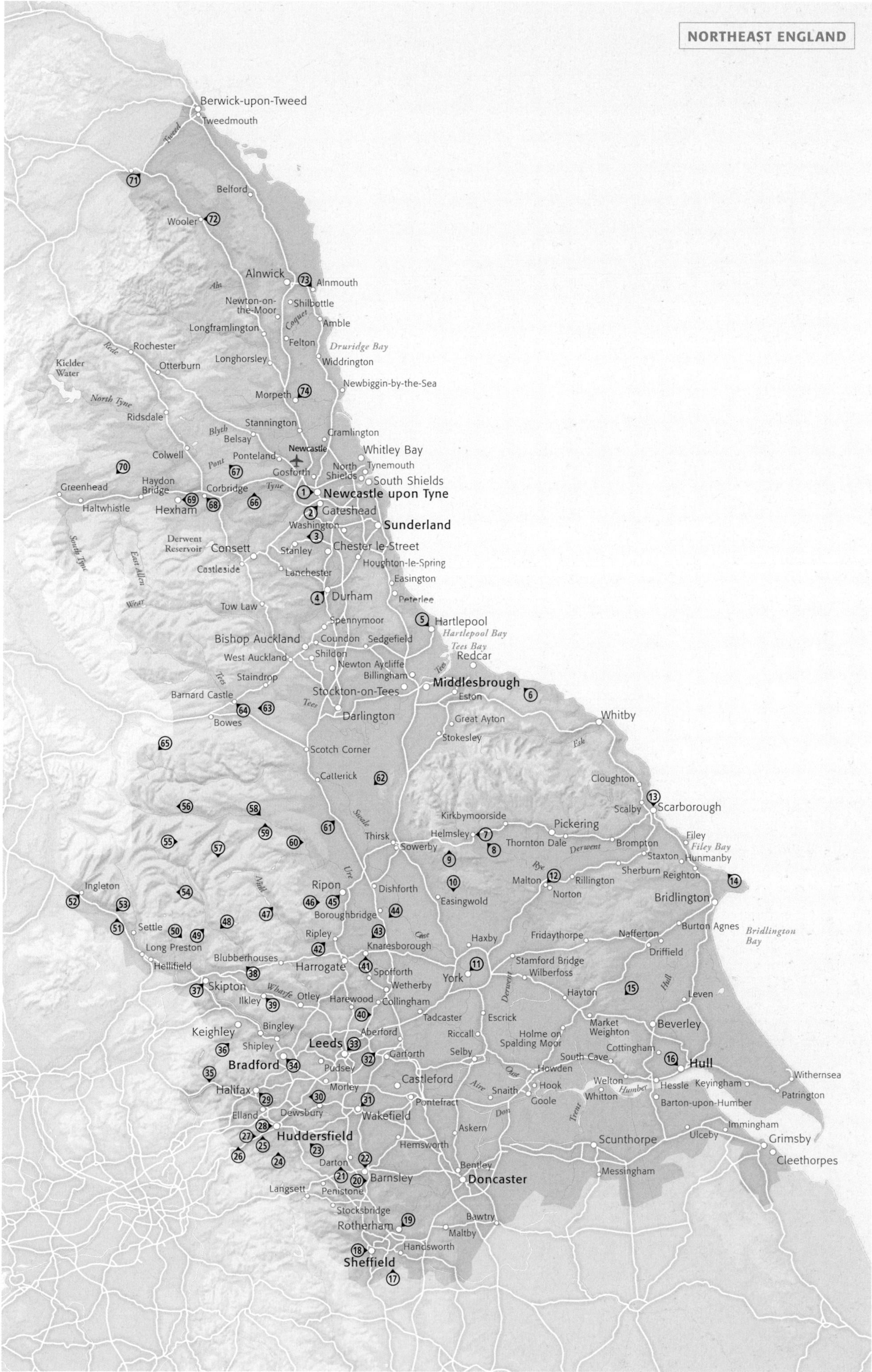

The Durham Ox ⑩
Award-winning pub and restaurant with three centuries of history.
Crayke, North Yorkshire; tel: 01347 821506; open daily.
www.thedurhamox.com

The Farmer's Arms ㉔
This pub has won awards for its choice of ales and wines and its excellent menus.
Holmfirth, West Yorkshire; tel: 01484 683713; open daily (but closed 31 Dec–14 Jan).

The Rat and Ratchet ㉘
Downtown pub acclaimed for its array of real ales and ciders.
40 Chapel Hill, Huddersfield, North Yorkshire; tel: 01484 542400; open daily.

The Woolley Sheep ㊲
This pub is favored by locals for its excellent range of real ales, including those from regional brewery Timothy Taylor.
38 Sheep Street, Skipton, North Yorkshire; tel: 01756 700966; open daily.

Ye Olde Punch Bowl ㊹
Good pub food and a selection of real ales from this inn's microbrewery.
Marton cum Grafton, North Yorkshire; tel: 01423 322519; open daily.
www.yeoldepunchbowl.co.uk

The One Eyed Rat ㊺
Local fruit wines, mulled wine in winter, and a fine range of English real ales.
Ripon, North Yorkshire; tel: 01484 683713; open daily.

The Old Hall Inn ㊾
Dignified, traditional Yorkshire country inn on the edge of Grassington National Park.
Threshfield, North Yorkshire; tel: 01756 752441; open daily.

Falcon Inn (54)
The Falcon Inn is the very epitome of a rustic Yorkshire Dales tavern, with a well-deserved reputation for its home cooking.
Arncliffe, nr Skipton, North Yorkshire; tel: 01756 770205; open daily.

The White Lion (55)
Claiming to be the highest pub in Wharfedale, this is an excellent place for a pint after tackling nearby Buckden Pike.
Cray, North Yorkshire; tel: 01756 760262; open daily (but closed Jan).

The Green Dragon Inn (61)
Cozy, classic country pub with a good range of traditional ales and a more than adequate menu, just off the A1 motorway.
Exelby, Bedale, North Yorkshire; tel: 01677 422233; open daily.
www.thegreendragonexelby.com

The Tan Hill Inn (65)
Way up in the Yorkshire Dales, this inn claims to be the highest pub in Britain, and offers rooms and cottages.
Tan Hill, Reeth, Swaledale, North Yorkshire; tel: 01833 628246; open daily.
www.tanhillinn.co.uk

The Boathouse ⑥⑥
With at least eight guest beers at any given time, the Boathouse is also the "brewery tap" for the local Wylam microbrewery. *Wylam, Northumberland; tel: 01661 853431; open 11am–11pm Mon–Sat, noon–3pm and 7–10:30pm Sun.*

Dipton Mill ⑥⑨
Delightful pub in an old mill building with ales from the local Hexhamshire Brewery. *Hexham, Northumberland; tel: 01434 606577; open noon–2:30pm and 6–11pm Mon–Sat, noon–4pm and 7–10:30pm Sun.*

The Red Lion Inn ⑦③
Good food and drink at this friendly 18th-century coaching inn in the prettiest village on the Northumberland coast. *22 Northumberland Street, Alnmouth, Northumberland; tel: 01665 830584; open daily. www.redlionalnmouth.com*

PLACES TO STAY

Jesmond Dene House ①
A grand and spacious Arts and Crafts mansion with 40 comfortable rooms. *Jesmond Dene Road, Newcastle; tel: 0191 212 3000. www.jesmonddenehouse.co.uk*

Hotel du Vin ①
Boutique hotel offering monsoon showers and plasma screen TVs in the rooms, and a bistro with *al fresco* dining. *Allan House, City Road, Newcastle; tel: 0191 229 2200. www.hotelduvin.com*

The Pheasant Hotel ⑧
Lovely country-house hotel on a charming village green, perfectly located for exploring the North Yorkshire countryside. *Harome, nr Helmsley, North Yorkshire; tel: 01439 771241. www.thepheasanthotel.com*

Byland Abbey Inn ⑨
Uniquely romantic inn with just three rooms and a fine-dining restaurant opposite the evocative Cistercian ruins of Byland Abbey. *Byland, North Yorkshire; tel: 01347 868204. www.bylandabbeyinn.com*

The Calls ㉝
This hotel by the River Aire, within walking distance of central Leeds, is everything a boutique town-house hotel should be. *42 The Calls, Leeds; tel: 0113 244 0099. www.42thecalls.co.uk*

Yorebridge House ㊺
A traditional stone building with classy facilities and an outstanding restaurant. *Bainbridge, Wensleydale, North Yorkshire; tel: 01969 652060. www.yorebridgehouse.com*

Ashfield House ㊲
Cozy haven on the main street of a pretty village, yards from a cobbled market square. *Grassington, Upper Wharfedale, North Yorkshire; tel: 01756 752584. www.ashfieldhouse.co.uk*

Above: Sheep-racing at the Masham Sheep Fair

Boar's Head ㊷
Opposite Ripley Castle, this "olde worlde" inn's aristocratic owner has furnished the bedrooms luxuriously. *Ripley, nr Harrogate, North Yorkshire; tel: 01423 771858. www.boarsheadripley.co.uk*

Yorke Arms ㊼
Michelin-starred restaurant with rooms, two of which are in the charming Ghyll Cottage, a short walk away. *Ramsgill-in-Nidderdale, Pateley Bridge, nr Harrogate, North Yorkshire; tel: 01423 755243. www.yorke-arms.co.uk*

The Austwick Traddock ㊾
Elegant small guesthouse with just 10 rooms, all *en suite*, set in the beautiful Dales countryside. *Austwick, nr Settle, North Yorkshire; tel: 01524 251224. www.austwicktraddock.co.uk*

Swinton Park ㉒
Outstanding, grand castle hotel, set in 200 acres (80 hectares) of grounds, with luxurious bedrooms. See falconry displays at the hotel's own Birds of Prey Centre. *Masham, North Yorkshire; tel: 01765 680900. www.swintonpark.com*

Burgoyne Hotel ㉕
A late-Georgian house set in an idyllic village. Bedrooms have four-posters and drawing rooms have open log fires. *The Green, Reeth, Swaledale, North Yorkshire; tel: 01748 884292. www.theburgoyne.co.uk*

The Angel Inn ㉘
Stylish coaching inn (the oldest in historic Corbridge) with a fine restaurant, a good bar, and bright, well-appointed bedrooms. *Corbridge, Northumberland; tel: 01434 631119. www.theangelofcorbridge.com*

The Collingwood Arms ㉛
Historic coaching inn on the banks of the River Tweed, popular with anglers. *Cornhill on Tweed, Northumberland; tel: 01890 882424. www.collingwoodarms.com*

Eshott Hall ㉔
Set in 500 acres (200 hectares), this fine 17th-century mansion is now a country-house hotel. A kitchen garden provides organic produce for the restaurant. *Morpeth, Northumberland; tel: 01670 787777. www.eshottreds.co.uk*

FESTIVALS AND EVENTS

JORVIK Viking Festival ⑪
A week of reenactments, river events, music, and arts and crafts *(see pp182–3)*. *JORVIK Viking Centre, York; tel: 01904 543403; mid-Feb. www.jorvik-viking-centre.co.uk*

York Festival of Food and Drink ⑪
Sample local food and drink in venues throughout the city, from street stands to gourmet restaurants and gastropubs, during this 10-day festival. *Various venues, York; tel: 01904 635149; Sep. www.yorkfoodfestival.com*

Huddersfield Carnival ㉘
This huge and popular community event is a boisterous, Afro-Caribbean-inspired weekend of "freedom and friendship." *Huddersfield, West Yorkshire; tel: 01484 536542; mid-Jul. www.huddersfieldcarnival.com*

Leeds CAMRA Beer, Cider and Perry Festival ㉝
Real ale, beers, and hard ciders from all over Britain and the world, live music, and local food, held by the Campaign for Real Ale (CAMRA) over three days in spring. *Various venues, Leeds; tel: 07940 006415; Mar. www.leedsbeerfestival.co.uk*

Bradford International Film Festival ㉞
This major 10-day event in Yorkshire's official "City of Film" is now established as a leading international fixture. *National Media Museum, Bradford; tel: 0870 701 0200; mid-Mar. www.bradfordfilmfestival.org.uk*

Ilkley Literature Festival ㊴
Ilkley's 17-day "wordfest" has become a top literary event attracting leading authors and poets, as well as new talent. *Various venues, Ilkley, West Yorkshire; tel: 01943 816714; early Oct. www.ilkleyliteraturefestival.org.uk*

Masham Sheep Fair ㉒
Local farmers bring their prize ewes and rams to compete for coveted prizes over two days. There is even a sheep race. *Masham, North Yorkshire; tel: 01765 680200; last weekend in Sep. www.visitmasham.com*

Masham Steam Engine and Fair Organ Rally ㉒
Two days of steam-traction engines and wagons, fair organs, and opportunities to sample local food and drink. *Masham, North Yorkshire; tel: 01765 680200; third weekend in Jul. www.visitmasham.com*

Slaithewaite Moonraking Festival ㉗
A week of storytelling, music, and dancing culminates with a lantern parade and a firework display. *Slaithewaite, West Yorkshire; mid-Feb. www.slaithewaitemoonraking.org*

Wakefield Festival of Food, Drink & Rhubarb ㉛
Celebrates the very best local food and produce, including the local specialty. *Wakefield, West Yorkshire; tel: 0845 601 8353; third weekend in Feb. www.experiencewakefield.co.uk*

Bradford Mela ㉞
Multicultural celebration with street theater and dance, live music, events for children, great street food, and market stalls. *Various venues, central Bradford; tel: 01274 432422; second weekend in Jun. www.bradfordmela.org.uk*

Hebden Bridge Arts Festival ㉟
Two enjoyable weeks of comedy, performance, music, and literary events. *Hebden Bridge, West Yorkshire; tel: 01422 842684; early Jul. www.hebdenbridge.co.uk*

Haworth Christmas Festival ㊱
Six weekends of Christmas events, traditions, shopping, and festive fun in a picturesque Yorkshire village. *Haworth, West Yorkhire; tel: 01536 642626; mid-Nov–24 Dec. www.haworthvillage.co.uk*

Dales Festival of Food and Drink ㊺
Three days of "food, farming, and fun": plenty of opportunities to sample local ales, cheeses, organic meats, and more. *Leyburn, Wensleydale, North Yorkshire; tel: 01748 828747; first weekend in May. www.dalesfestivaloffood.org*

Glendale Show ㊻
Northumberland's major annual agricultural show: a day of sheepdog trials, equestrian events, food and drink, and competitions for livestock breeders and producers. *Wooler, Northumberland; tel: 01668 283868; last Mon in Aug. www.glendaleshow.com*

MUSEUMS AND GALLERIES

Great North Museum ①
Newcastle's newest museum is exciting and eclectic; displays range from a large-scale interactive model of Hadrian's Wall to a *Tyrannosaurus rex* skeleton and a collection of Egyptian mummies. *Barras Bridge, Newcastle; tel: 0191 222 6765; open 10am–5pm Mon–Sat, 2–5pm Sun. www.twmuseums.org.uk*

Discovery Museum ①
This interactive museum celebrates Newcastle's shipbuilding and engineering heritage, and highlights inventions that changed the world. *Blandford Square, Newcastle; tel: 0191 232 6789; open 10am–5pm Mon–Sat, 2–5pm Sun. www.twmuseums.org.uk*

Baltic Centre for Contemporary Art ②
Dynamic center for contemporary visual arts in a landmark converted industrial building on the south bank of the Tyne.
Gateshead Quays, Gateshead, Tyne and Wear; tel: 0191 478 1810; open daily. www.balticmill.com

National Railway Museum ⑪
Three giant halls crammed with railroad history, including the world's fastest steam locomotive, "Mallard", and the legendary "Flying Scotsman".
Leeman Road, York; tel: 0844 815 3319; open 10am–6pm daily. www.nrm.org.uk

Eden Camp Modern History Theme Museum ⑫
Award-winning museum dedicated to Britain's role in the major conflicts of the 20th century.
Malton, North Yorkshire; tel: 01653 697777; open 10am–5pm daily (closed Dec 23–Jan 11). www.edencamp.co.uk

Millennium Galleries ⑱
This marvel of glass and white concrete houses cutting-edge contemporary art.
Arundel Gate, Sheffield; tel: 0114 278 2660; open 8am–5pm Mon–Sat. www.museums-sheffield.org.uk

Leeds Art Gallery ㉝
An outstanding collection of works by 20th-century British artists and a brand-new multimedia exhibition gallery.
The Headrow, Leeds; tel: 0113 247 8256; open 10am–5pm Mon–Tue and Thu–Sat, noon–5pm Wed, 1–5pm Sun. www.leeds.gov.uk/artgallery

Royal Armouries ㉝
Awe-inspiring collection of weaponry, from axes, swords, and daggers to muskets, modern pistols, and machine guns. Outdoor events in summer include medieval jousting.
Armouries Drive, Leeds; tel: 0870 034 4344; open 10am–5pm daily. www.royalarmouries.org

National Media Museum ㉞
Behind-the-scenes tours, two world-class cinemas, an IMAX giant-screen experience, and an exhibition dedicated to the history of TV are among the attractions here.
Bradford; tel: 0870 701 0200; open 10am–6pm Tue–Sun. www.nationalmediamuseum.org.uk

Brontë Parsonage Museum ㊱
Set amid desolate moorland, Haworth Parsonage was the lifelong home of Charlotte, Emily, and Anne Brontë.
Church Street, Haworth, West Yorkshire; tel: 01535 642323; open daily (but closed Jan). www.bronte.info

The Bowes Museum ㊽
A truly magnificent French-château-style building housing stunning collections of fine and decorative arts, but with family-friendly features too.
Barnard Castle, County Durham; tel: 01833 690606; open 10am–5pm daily. www.thebowesmuseum.org.uk

Cleveland Ironstone Mining Museum ⑥
Within Britain's first ironstone mine, this museum focuses on mining history, with a tour into deep underground galleries.
Deepdale, Skinningrove, North Yorkshire; tel: 01287 642877; open Apr–Oct: 10:30am–3:30pm Mon–Fri, 1–3:30pm Sat. www.ironstonemuseum.co.uk

Worsbrough Mill Museum ⑳
This museum comprises a working water mill dating from the 17th century and a powered mill from the 19th century.
Worsbrough Bridge, Barnsley, South Yorkshire; tel: 01226 774527; open Apr–Oct: 11am–4pm Sat–Wed; Nov–Dec and Mar: 11am–4pm Sun (but closed Dec 21–Mar 5). www.barnsley.gov.uk

Cannon Hall Museum, Park and Gardens ㉑
Georgian mansion housing outstanding furniture, porcelain, glassware, and art, and the regimental museum of the 13th and 18th Royal Hussars and Light Dragoons.
Bark House Lane, Barnsley, South Yorkshire; tel: 01226 790270; open Apr–Oct: 11am–5pm Sat–Wed; Nov–Dec and Mar: 11am–4pm Sun. www.barnsley.gov.uk

Cooper Gallery ㉒
Fine collection of oil and watercolor paintings, drawings, and prints.
Church Street, Barnsley, South Yorkshire; tel: 01226 242905; open 10am–4pm Mon–Fri, 10am–3pm Sat. www.barnsley.gov.uk

THINGS TO DO WITH KIDS

The Deep ⑯
Spectacular aquarium with 3,500 fish – including 40 sharks – viewed from an underwater tunnel and a glass elevator.
Tower Street, Hull; tel: 01482 381000; open 10am–6pm daily. www.thedeep.co.uk

Eureka! The National Children's Museum ㉙
More than 400 interactive exhibits, with lots of special events and activities on weekends and during school vacations.
Discovery Road, Halifax, West Yorkshire; tel: 01422 330069; open 10am–5pm daily. www.eureka.org.uk

Ripley Castle ㊷
A children's play trail is an attraction at this 700-year-old castle, along with beautiful walled gardens, lakes, and a deer park.
Ripley, nr Harrogate, North Yorkshire; tel: 01423 770152; open daily, tours hourly 11am–3pm. www.ripleycastle.co.uk

Housesteads Roman Fort ㊵
Explore the dramatic ramparts of Hadrian's Wall *(see pp34–5)* from one of the most accessible of its frontier fortresses.
Nr Bardon Mill, Northumberland; tel: 01434 344363; open Apr–Sep: 10am–6pm daily; Oct–Mar: 10am–4pm daily. www.visitnorthumberland.com

Magna Science Adventure Centre ⑲
Launch rockets, fire water cannons, board an airship, and enjoy Europe's largest science and technology playground.
Sheffield Road, Rotherham, South Yorkshire; tel: 01709 720002; open 10am–5pm daily. www.visitmagna.co.uk

Standedge Tunnel ㉖
Take a glass-roofed-barge cruise through the longest and deepest tunnel in Britain – 3-mile- (5-km-) long Standedge Tunnel.
Waters Road, Marsden, Huddersfield, West Yorkshire; tel: 01484 844298; tours run daily Apr–Nov. www.standedge.co.uk

Ponderosa Rare Breeds Farm ㉚
See exotic, rare-breed domestic animals in the lakes and gardens here.
Smithies Lane, Heckmondwike, West Yorkshire; tel: 01924 235276; open Easter–Oct 10am–5pm daily; Nov–Easter 10am–4pm daily. www.ponderosa-centre.org

Yorkshire Dales Falconry Centre ㊶
Eagles, falcons, owls, and hawks can be seen in three separate daily flying displays.
Crows Nest Barn, nr Settle, North Yorkshire; tel: 01729 822 832; open 10am–6pm daily. www.falconryandwildlife.com

White Scar Cave ㊷
Spectacularly located in the Yorkshire Dales National Park; the tour of the longest show-cave in Britain takes 80 minutes.
Ingleton, North Yorkshire; tel: 01524 241244; open Feb–Oct: 10am–4pm daily; Nov–Jan: 10am–4pm Sat–Sun. www.whitescarcave.co.uk

SPAS AND HEALTH RESORTS

Titanic Hotel & Spa ㉕
The UK's first "eco-spa," with an emphasis on organic products, in the unlikely surroundings of a Victorian textile mill.
Low Westwood Lane, Linthwaite, Huddersfield, West Yorkshire; tel: 0845 410 3333. www.titanicspa.com

Thorpe Park Hotel & Spa ㉜
A touch of the Mediterranean in Yorkshire with its glass atrium, stylish bedrooms, and seven spa treatment rooms.
1150 Century Way, Thorpe Park, Leeds; tel: 0113 264 1000. www.thorpeparkhotel.com

The Devonshire Arms ㊳
Aristocratic 18th-century exterior conceals 21st-century comforts, including a health, beauty, and fitness club with a pool, whirlpool, steam room, and sauna.
Bolton Abbey, Skipton, North Yorkshire; tel: 01756 710441. www.thedevonshirearms.co.uk

Matfen Hall ㉖
Spacious country-house hotel and spa with a fine restaurant and its own 27-hole and 9-hole golf courses.
Matfen, Northumberland; tel: 01661 886400. www.matfenhall.com

OTHER SIGHTS IN THE BOOK

Right: Bowes Museum at Barnard Castle

WEST MIDLANDS

LOCAL FOOD

Siam Corner Ma Ma Thai ④
First-rate menu with vegetarian dishes and outstanding service.
*17 Bird Street, Lichfield, Staffordshire;
tel: 01543 411911; open noon–11pm
Mon–Thu, noon–11:30pm Fri–Sat,
noon–3pm and 6–10:30pm Sun.
www.siamcornerthai.co.uk*

City Café ⑨
Very nifty modern café with a
contemporary international menu.
*1 Brunswick Square, Brindleyplace,
Birmingham; tel: 0121 643 1003; open
noon–2:30pm and 6–10pm Mon–Fri,
1–2:30pm and 6–10pm Sat, 1–3pm
and 6–10pm Sun.*

Rupali Tandoori Restaurant ⑪
Much-admired Indian restaurant with
a full-flavored, authentic menu.
*337 Tile Hill Lane, Coventry; tel: 02476
422500; open 5–11pm daily.
www.rupali.co.uk*

Kakooti ⑪
Authentic and delicious Italian cuisine
in a quaint old half-timbered building.
*16 Spon Street, Coventry; tel: 02476
221392; open 6pm–late Mon–Sat.
www.kakooti.com*

The Clive Bar and Restaurant ㉗
A former farmhouse that serves delicious
dishes made from locally sourced foods.
*Bromfield, Ludlow, Shropshire; tel: 01584
856565; open 11am–11pm Mon–Sat,
noon–10:30pm Sun. www.theclive.co.uk*

Deli on the Square ㉗
A fabulous range of cheeses, meats,
and hampers awaits visitors to this
award-winning establishment.
*4 Church Street, Ludlow, Shropshire;
tel: 01584 877353; open 9:30am–5pm
Mon–Fri, 9am–5pm Sat.
www.delionthesquareludlow.co.uk*

Mr. Underhills ㉗
A Michelin-starred seven-course set dinner
menu in a beautiful riverside location.
*Dinham Weir, Ludlow, Shropshire; tel:
01584 874431; orders taken 7:15–8:15pm
Wed–Sun. www.mr-underhills.co.uk*

Café Catalan ⑬
Serves tapas at lunchtime and in the
afternoon and Catalan dishes at night.
*6 Jury Street, Warwick; tel: 01926 498930;
open noon–3pm and 6–9:30pm Mon–
Thu, noon–3pm and 6–10pm Fri,
noon–10pm Sat. www.cafecatalan.com*

Puccini's ⑱
Much-loved Italian eatery with great pizzas,
a pleasant ambience, and polite staff.
*12 Friar Street, Worcester; tel: 01905
27770; open 12:30–2:30pm and 6–10pm
Wed–Thu, 12:30–2:30pm and 6–10:30pm
Fri, noon–10:30pm Sat.*

Pepper & Oz, The Brasserie ⑳
A stylish and intimate environment that
scores full points for food and service with
a jaw-dropping wine list.
*23 Abbey Road, Malvern, Worcestershire;
tel: 01684 562676; open noon–2:30pm,
6–7pm and 8:15–9:30pm Mon–Sat,
1–2:30pm Sun. www.pepperandoz.co.uk*

Frank Café Bar ㉞
Relaxing half-timbered restaurant and bar
with an addictive tapas menu.
*165–167 Frankwell, Shrewsbury;
Shropshire; tel: 01743 354422; open
5–11pm Mon–Tue, 5pm–midnight
Wed–Thu, 5pm–1am Fri, noon–1am Sat.
www.frank.uk.com*

FARMERS' MARKETS

Warwick Farmers' Market ⑬
A selection of fresh and organic products,
all from local farmers.
*Market Square, Warwick; tel: 01789
267000; third Fri and fifth Sat of the
month (if applicable), 9am–2pm.
www.warwickshirefarmersmarkets.co.uk*

Stratford-upon-Avon Farmers' Market ⑰
Warwickshire's largest farmers' market,
with a plethora of meats, cheeses,
beverages, eggs, breads, and cakes.
*Rother Street, Stratford-upon-Avon,
Warwickshire; tel: 01608 664659; first
and third Sat of the month, 9am–2pm.
www.warwickshirefarmersmarkets.co.uk*

Ross-on-Wye Farmers' Market ㉓
A wholesome spread of tasty local foods
sourced from local farmers.
*High Street, below the Market House,
Ross-on-Wye, Herefordshire; tel: 01886
821237; first Fri of the month, 9am–1pm.*

Hereford Farmers' Market ㉕
Excellent opportunity to get your hands on
bundles of the very freshest local foods.
*High Town, nr Buttermarket, Hereford;
first Sat and third Thu of every month,
9am–2pm.*

PUBS AND BARS

The Manor Arms ⑤
Claims to be one of England's oldest pubs
(12th century), in a perfect scenic position
by the Rushall Canal.
*Park Road, Walsall, West Midlands;
tel: 01922 642333; open daily.*

The Jam House ⑨
Easy-going and popular over-21s venue
for live jazz and rhythm-and-blues music,
aimed at a smart-casual audience.
*St. Pauls Square, Jewellery Quarter,
Birmingham; tel: 0121 200 3030;
open 6pm–late Tue–Sat.
www.thejamhouse.com*

The Lord Clifden ⑨
A magnificent meeting of urban artwork –
including pieces by Banksy – and real ale,
generating a trendy student vibe.
*34 Great Hampton Street, Hockley,
Birmingham; tel: 01215 237515; open
10am–2am Sun–Thu, 10am–4am Fri–Sat.
www.thelordclifden.com*

The Town Wall Tavern ⑪
Historic pub oozing with character, charm,
and traditional pub coziness.
*Bond Street, Coventry; tel: 02476 220963;
open daily.*

The Old Swan ⑧
Excellent Black Country pub – nicknamed
Ma Pardoe's after a long-serving landlady –
with home-brewed beer, including
"Old Swan" itself.
*87 Halesowen Road, Netherton, Dudley,
West Midlands; tel: 01384 253075;
open daily.*

The Prince of Wales ㉒
Fantastic hard ciders, draft pear cider, real
ales, and a lovely location.
*Church Lane, Ledbury, Herefordshire;
tel: 01531 632250; open daily.
www.powledbury.com*

The Mill Race ㉔
First-rate food and excellent ale, and
hard cider; its own farm supplies many
of the ingredients.
*Walford, nr Ross-on-Wye, Herefordshire;
tel: 01989 562891; open 11am–3pm
and 5–11pm Mon–Fri, 10am–11pm Sat,
noon–10:30pm Sun.
www.millrace.info*

The Harp Hotel ㉛
Friendly music venue/pub with traditional
jazz sessions on Tuesdays and Sundays.
*40 High Street, Albrighton, nr
Wolverhampton; tel: 01902 374381;
open daily. www.jazzclub90.supanet.com*

The Inn at Grinshill ㉟
Steeped in historic character, with some
tempting accommodations and an
extensive menu from the kitchen.
*The High Street, Grinshill, nr Shrewsbury,
Shropshire; tel: 01939 220410; open
11am–3pm and 6–11pm Mon–Sat,
noon–4pm Sun.
www.theinnatgrinshill.co.uk*

PLACES TO STAY

Prince Rupert Hotel ㉞
Historic charm and medieval elegance,
with a range of rooms including the
12th-century "Mansion House" suites.
*Butcher Row, Shrewsbury, Shropshire;
tel: 01743 499955.
www.prince-rupert-hotel.co.uk*

Albright Hussey Manor ㉞
Magnificently restored Tudor country
house in superb Shropshire countryside
with wonderful food and service.
*Shrewsbury, Shropshire; tel: 01939
290523.
www.albrighthussey.co.uk*

Netherstowe House ④
Tremendous Georgian boutique hotel with
bags of charm, up-to-date furnishings, and
lovely, individually named rooms.
*Lichfield, Staffordshire; tel: 01543 254270.
www.netherstowehouse.com*

Malmaison ⑨
Former Royal Mail sorting office given
a luxurious and trendy renovation to
the top-tier hotel market.
*One Wharfside Street, Birmingham;
tel: 0121 246 5000.
www.malmaison-birmingham.com*

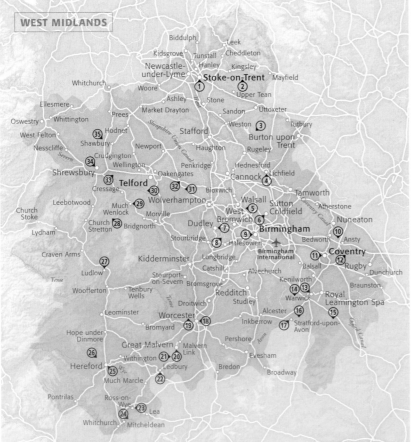

WEST MIDLANDS

Above: Fireworks display at Birmingham's annual Artsfest

Hyatt Regency Birmingham ⑨
Comfortable rooms and excellent service – the full range of top-notch Hyatt facilities in a central location.
Bridge Street, Birmingham; tel: 0121 643 1234. www.hyatt.com

Church Hill Farm B&B ⑮
Charming farmhouse in a tranquil rural location southeast of Warwick; with only three rooms, booking is advised.
Lighthorne, Warwickshire; tel: 01926 651251. www.churchhillfarm.co.uk

Stratford-upon-Avon Youth Hostel ⑯
Wide range of decent rooms at a Georgian mansion in huge grounds in Alveston, a short distance from Stratford-upon-Avon.
Hemmingford House, Alveston, Stratford-upon-Avon, Warwickshire; tel: 0845 371 9661. www.yha.org.uk

Riverside Caravan Park ⑰
Lovely campsite on the banks of the River Avon, with friendly staff, good facilities, and access to Stratford-upon-Avon by river taxi.
Tiddington Road, Stratford-upon-Avon, Warwickshire; tel: 01789 292312.

Copper Beech House ⑳
Tons of Victorian charm, a gorgeous garden, and comfortable rooms in the setting of the Malvern Hills.
32 Avenue Road, Malvern, Worcestershire; tel: 01684 565013.
www.copperbeechhouse.co.uk

Barnacle Hall ⑩
Ancient farmhouse B&B pressing all the right buttons: charm, comfort, time-worn textures, and a friendly owner.
Shilton Lane, Shilton, Coventry; tel: 02476 612629. www.barnaclehall.co.uk

Coombe Abbey Hotel ⑫
Stately Warwickshire former abbey surrounded by stunning parkland.
Brinklow Road, Binley, Coventry; tel: 02476 450450.
www.coombeabbey.com

Colwall Park Hotel ㉑
Exemplary service, fantastic food, and very comfy rooms in a handsome hotel; the perfect base for walks in the Malvern Hills.
Colwall, Malvern, Worcestershire; tel: 01684 540000. www.colwall.co.uk

The Barn House ㉒
Half-timbered former farm, full of history and charm, at the heart of the market town of Ledbury.
New Street, Ledbury, Herefordshire; tel: 01531 632825.
www.thebarnhouse.net

The Feathers Hotel ㉒
Gorgeous Elizabethan black-and-white former coaching inn with a relaxing spa and fine dining.
High Street, Ledbury, Herefordshire; tel: 0800 074 9377.
www.feathers-ledbury.co.uk

Linden House ㉓
Appealing and great-value B&B with comfy rooms and tasty breakfasts.
14 Church Street, Ross-on-Wye, Herefordshire; tel: 01989 565373.
www.lindenguesthouse.com

Castle House ㉕
Elegant and grand Georgian 4-star town-house hotel two minutes' walk from Hereford Cathedral.
Castle Street, Hereford; tel: 01432 356321.
www.castlehse.co.uk

New Priory Hotel ㉖
Fabulous former rectory with plenty of period character and comfort.
Priory Lane, Stretton Sugwas, Herefordshire; tel: 01432 760264.
www.hotelpriory.co.uk

Fishmore Hall ㉗
High degree of comfort, service, cuisine, and countryside views from a boutique hotel in a restored Georgian house.
Fishmore Road, Ludlow, Shropshire; tel: 01584 875148.
www.fishmorehall.co.uk

The Library House Guest House ㉚
Welcoming and comfy B&B in a beautiful Grade II-listed Georgian building just along from the Iron Bridge.
Severn Bank, Ironbridge, nr Telford, Shropshire; tel: 01952 432299.
www.libraryhouse.com

Wilderhope Manor ㉘
National Trust–managed Elizabethan manor; all you need as a base for hikes in the surrounding landscape.
Longville in the Dale, Shropshire; tel: 0845 371 9149. www.nationaltrust.org.uk

The Raven Hotel & Restaurant ㉙
Handsome 17th-century coaching inn with large rooms and a popular restaurant.
Barrow Street, Much Wenlock, Shropshire; tel: 01952 727251.

FESTIVALS AND EVENTS

Abbots Bromley Horn Dance ③
Highly distinctive ancient folk dance where the dancers carry reindeer antlers.
Abbots Bromley, Staffordshire; Wakes Monday, day after Wakes Sunday (first Sunday after 4 Sep).
www.abbotsbromley.com/horn_dance

Lichfield Festival ④
Excellent four-day international festival of music, theater, dance, poetry, and more.
Lichfield, Staffordshire; tel: 01543 306270; Jul. www.lichfieldfestival.org

Warwick Folk Festival ⑬
Festive celebration of folk music, with three days of dance, workshops, and a full schedule of folk-music performances.
Warwick School, Warwick; tel: 01926 614932; late Jul.
www.warwickfolkfestival.co.uk

Black Country Boating Festival ⑧
Hundreds of vessels congregate along the canal for a long weekend of fun. *Bumble Hole Nature Reserve, Windmill End, Netherton; tel: 0844 800 5076; Sep. www.bcbf.com.*

ArtsFest ⑨
Birmingham's leading cultural festival, bursting with talent and innovation across the creative spectrum over 13 days. *Various venues, Birmingham; tel: 0121 464 5678; Sep. www.artsfest.org.uk*

Birmingham Jazz Festival ⑨
A diverse 10-day appreciation of jazz, in which hundreds of musicians perform. *Various venues, Birmingham city centre; tel: 0121 454 7020; Jul. www.birminghamjazzfestival.com*

Ludlow Festival ㉗
Two-week-long celebration of the arts from theater to classical music, jazz, and dance and a dazzling fireworks display. *Various venues, Ludlow, Shropshire; tel: 01584 875070; Jun. www.ludlowfestival.co.uk*

MUSEUMS AND GALLERIES

Selly Manor Museum ⑨
Charming Tudor half-timbered house dating from the 16th century, with a great collection of historic furniture. *Maple Road, Bournville, Birmingham; tel: 0121 472 0199; open 10am–5pm Tue–Fri (also Apr–Sep: 2–5pm Sat–Sun and Bank Holiday Mondays). www.bvt.org.uk/sellymanor*

Coventry Transport Museum ⑪
A veritable A–Z of British and Coventry-built motor vehicles plus activities for speed-obsessed children. *Millennium Place, Hales Street, Coventry; tel: 02476 234270; open 10am–5pm daily (last admission at 4:30pm). www.transport-museum.com*

Royal Worcester Porcelain ⑱
The world's largest collection of Worcester porcelain, dating from the 18th century to the present day. *Severn Street, Worcester; tel: 01905 21247; open 10am–5pm Mon–Sat. www.worcesterporcelainmuseum.org*

The Commandery ⑱
Attractive half-timbered museum that chronicles the history of Worcester. *Sidbury, Worcester; tel: 01905 361821; open 10am–5pm Mon–Sat, 1:30–5pm Sun. www.worcestercitymuseums.org.uk*

Malvern Museum ⑳
Explore the curative properties of Malvern spring water and the Victorians' fascination with its healing powers, as well as the origins of the Morgan automobile. *The Priory Gatehouse, Abbey Road, Malvern, Worcestershire; tel: 01684 576811; open Easter–31 Oct: 10:30am–5pm daily (closed Wed in term time). www.malvernmuseum.co.uk*

The Elgar Birthplace Museum ⑲
The life and music of Sir Edward Elgar is celebrated in this cottage, which is full of mementoes and personal effects. *Crown East Lane, Lower Broadheath, Worcester; tel: 01905 333224; open 11am–5pm daily. www.elgarfoundation.org*

Hereford Museum and Art Gallery ㉕
Delve into local Hereford history at this collection of local art and artifacts housed within a magnificent Victorian building. *Broad Street, Hereford; tel: 01432 260692; open 10am–5pm Tue–Sat (also Apr–Sep: 10am–4pm Sun and Bank Holiday Mondays).*

Museum of the Gorge ㉚
Absorbing museum detailing the history and industrial culture of the Ironbridge Gorge World Heritage Site. *Ironbridge, Shropshire; tel: 01952 884391; open 10am–5pm daily. www.ironbridge.org.uk*

Museum of Iron ㉚
History of iron-smelting with fine examples of cast iron from the Coalbrookdale company, located in the old iron foundry. *Coalbrookdale, Ironbridge, Shropshire; tel: 01952 884391; open 10am–5pm daily. www.ironbridge.org.uk*

Coalport China Museum ㉚
Fantastic collection of richly glazed Coalport ceramics, with a range of workshops for young potters. *Coalport, Ironbridge, Shropshire; tel: 01952 884391; open 10am–5pm daily. www.ironbridge.org.uk*

Wroxeter Roman City ㉝
Roman Britain's fourth-largest city – known then as Viroconium – with an on-site museum detailing its appearance. *Wroxeter, Shropshire; tel: 01743 761330; open Mar–Oct: 10am–5pm daily; Nov–Feb: 10am–4pm Wed–Sun. www.english-heritage.org.uk/wroxeter*

THINGS TO DO WITH KIDS

Thinktank, Birmingham Science Museum ⑨
Interactive, hands-on educational displays and scientific exhibits for young Einsteins (and their parents), plus a state-of-the-art digital planetarium and IMAX theatre. *Millennium Point, Curzon Street, Birmingham; tel: 0121 202 2222; open 10am–5pm daily (last admission 4pm). www.thinktank.ac*

Ludlow Castle ㉗
Fantastic day out for the children at this 11th-century castle ruin, which also boasts vacation apartments. *Castle Square, Ludlow, Shropshire; tel: 01584 874465; open Dec–Jan: 10am–4pm Sat–Sun; Feb–Mar: 10am–4pm daily; Apr–Jul: 10am–5pm daily; Aug: 10am–7pm daily; Sep: 10am–5pm daily; Oct–Nov: 10am–4pm daily. www.ludlowcastle.com*

Above: Water ride at the Alton Towers theme park

Alton Towers ②
Staggeringly popular amusement park and resort with thrilling rides, a water park, and a spa for all-in-one family entertainment. *Alton, Staffordshire; tel: 0870 520 4060; open late Mar–early Nov, times vary through the year. www.altontowers.com*

Dudley Zoo and Castle ⑦
History, heritage, and wildlife all combined in an educational and fun experience. *Dudley, West Midlands; tel: 01384 215313; open Sep–Easter: 10am–3pm (grounds close at 4pm); Easter–Sep: 10am–4pm (grounds close at 5pm). www.dudleyzoo.org.uk*

Green Frog Pottery ⑳
Pottery painting, glazing, and firing for young potters at a Malvern studio. *117 Barnards Green Road, Malvern, Worcestershire; tel: 01684 561778; open 10am–5:30pm Tue–Sat. www.greenfrogpottery.co.uk*

Blists Hill Victorian Town ㉚
Victorian-themed town, situated in the Ironbridge Gorge complex, that is perennially popular with school children. *Madeley, Shropshire; tel: 01952 884391; open Apr–Oct: 10am–5pm daily; Nov–Mar: 10am–4pm daily. www.blistshill.org*

Royal Airforce Museum Cosford ㉜
Huge museum with a wealth of war planes and ever-changing displays and exhibits. *Shifnal, Shropshire; tel: 01902 376200; open 10am–5pm daily. www.rafmuseum.org.uk*

SPAS AND HEALTH RESORTS

Fairlawns Hotel and Spa ⑤
Ideal for spa breaks, with excellent packages and highly professional service, set in beautiful grounds. *Little Aston Road, Aldridge, nr Walsall, West Midlands; tel: 01922 455122. www.fairlawns.co.uk*

New Hall Hotel & Spa ⑥
Beautiful 800-year-old manor-house hotel (with moat) set in exquisite grounds. *Walmley Road, Sutton Coldfield, nr Birmingham; tel: 0845 458 0901. www.handpickedhotels.co.uk*

Amala Spa and Club ⑨
A range of packages tailored to meet individual health needs, including massages and skin treatments. *Hyatt Regency Birmingham, 2 Bridge Street, Birmingham; tel: 0121 643 1234. www.birmingham.regency.hyatt.com*

Ardencote Manor Hotel, Country Club and Spa ⑭
Fully equipped with health facilities and a golf course, this hotel is set in splendid and peaceful surroundings. *Lye Green Road, Claverdon, Warwickshire; tel: 01926 843111. www.ardencote.com*

OTHER SIGHTS IN THE BOOK

EAST MIDLANDS

LOCAL FOOD

The Old Bakery Restaurant ①
Homey restaurant in the historic Uphill area, serving tasty dishes with ingredients sourced from its own vegetable garden.
26–28 Burton Road, Lincoln; tel: 01522 576057; open noon–2pm and 7–9pm Tue–Sat. www.theold-bakery.co.uk

The Wheatsheaf Inn ⑧
This Boston restaurant is much celebrated for its wide range of fine food and real ales.
Hubberts Bridge, Boston, Lincolnshire; tel: 01205 290347; open noon–2:30pm and 5–9pm Tue–Sat, noon–2:30pm and 5–8pm Sun, 5–9pm Mon. www.thewheatsheafinn.org

The Church Restaurant ⑮
Swish modern dishes served up in the ecclesiastical setting of a former church.
67–83 Bridge Street, Northampton; tel: 01604 603800; open noon–late Mon–Sat. www.thechurchrestaurant.com

Cini Restaurant and Bar ⑲
Well-presented contemporary and innovative Italian dishes, made using locally sourced produce, are on offer here. Sleep off your meals in modern bedrooms.
26 High Street, Enderby, Leicester; tel: 0116 286 3009; open noon–2pm and 6:30–10pm Mon–Thu, noon–2pm and 6:30–10:30pm Fri–Sat. www.cinirestaurant.co.uk

Dickinson & Morris Ye Olde Pork Pie Shoppe ㉒
Delicious range of pork pies, sausages, cheeses, and bacon from this 160-year-old establishment.
10 Nottingham Street, Melton Mowbray, Leicestershire; tel: 01664 482068; open Mar–Dec: 8:30am–5pm Mon–Sat; Jan–Feb: 8:30am–4pm Mon–Sat. http://porkpie.placement.co.uk

World Service ㉗
A stylish fine-dining restaurant that offers outstanding food in the beautiful setting of 17th-century Newdigate House.
Newdigate House, Castlegate, Nottingham; tel: 0115 847 5587; open noon–2pm and 7–10pm Mon–Sat, noon–2:30pm and 7–9pm Sun. www.worldservicerestaurant.com

Thanal ㉙
Tasty South Indian cuisine focusing on the distinctive flavors of Kerala cooking.
19 St. Marks Lane, Newark, Nottinghamshire; tel: 01636 706230; open noon–3pm and 6–10:30pm Mon–Sat, noon–3pm Sun. www.thanalrestaurant.com

The Old Original Bakewell Pudding Shop ㊵
Tasty Bakewell puddings, jams, chutneys, marmalades and biscuits are sold here; there is also a restaurant on the first floor.
The Square, Bakewell, Derbyshire; tel: 01629 812193; open 9am–5:30pm daily. www.bakewellpuddingshop.co.uk

The Original Farmers' Market Shop ㊵
Small, independent shop that uses farmers' market principles, with as much sourced from local producers as possible.
3 Market St, Bakewell, Derbyshire; tel: 01629 815814; open 9am–5pm Mon–Sat, 11am–4pm Sun. www.thefarmersmarketshop.co.uk

Rose Cottage Restaurant and Tearooms ㊾
A snug and cozy Peak District cottage ambience, lovely garden, and great food.
Cross Street, Castleton, Derbyshire; tel: 01433 620472; open 10am–5pm Sat–Thu. www.rosecottagecastleton.co.uk

Columbine Restaurant ㊿
Popular Buxton restaurant with ample servings and considerable culinary flair.
7 Hall Bank, Buxton, Derbyshire; tel: 01298 78752; open 7–10pm Mon–Sat. www.buxtononline.net/columbine

FARMERS' MARKETS

Bakewell Farmers' Market ㊵
An accent on organic products, selling everything from chocolate to sausages.
Bakewell, Derbyshire; tel: 01629 813777; last Sat of every month, 9am–2pm.

Buxton Farmers' Market ㊿
A huge variety of local produce in Buxton's fantastic Pavilion Gardens.
St. John's Road, Buxton, Derbyshire; tel: 01298 23114; first Thu of every month, 10am–3pm. www.paviliongardens.co.uk

PUBS

The Strugglers Inn ①
Cozy pub at the foot of the walls of Lincoln Castle, named after prisoners who would struggle on the way to the nearby gallows.
83 Westgate, Lincoln; tel: 01522 535023; open daily.

The Tobie Norris ⑪
A fabulous range of brews are available at this stylish pub, located in a building dating from 1280, and containing seven uniquely decorated rooms.
12 St. Pauls Street, Stamford, Lincolnshire; tel: 01780 753800; open daily. www.tobienorris.com

The King's Head ⑭
Scenic riverside location with the Nene Way long-distance footpath right outside.
Church Street, Wadenhoe, Northamptonshire; tel: 01832 720024; open daily (noon–5pm Sun). www.kingsheadwadenhoe.co.uk

Ye Olde Trip to Jerusalem ㉗
"The oldest inn in Britain" and the assembly point for Crusading knights.
Brewhouse Yard, Nottingham; tel: 0115 947 3171; open daily. www.triptojerusalem.com

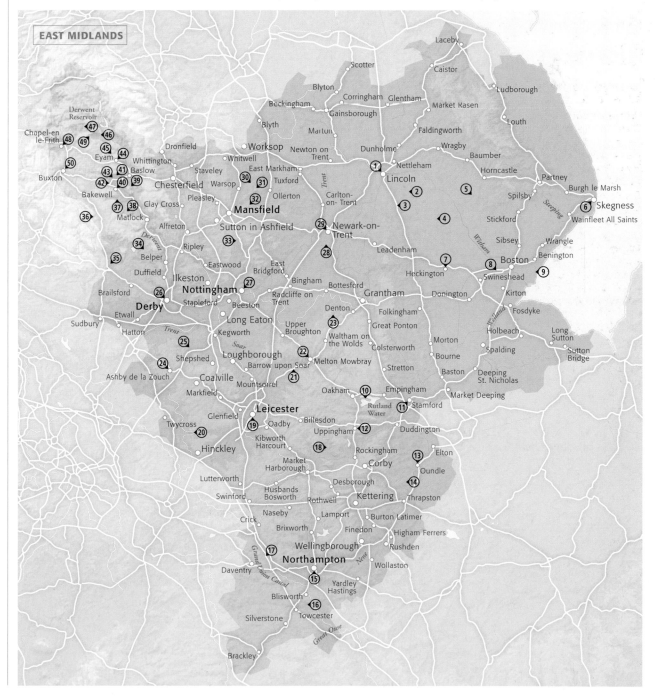

Above: RAF Waddington International Air Show

The Plough Inn 27
Traditional Nottingham brewery pub with a friendly atmosphere and a wide range of excellent beers and hard ciders.
17 St. Peter's Street, Radford, Nottingham; tel: 0115 970 2615; open daily. www.nottinghambrewery.com

Chequers at Woolsthorpe 23
Snug Vale of Belvoir pub with a focus on relaxation and excellent food. Plush accommodations also available.
Main Street, Woolsthorpe by Belvoir, Grantham, Lincolnshire; tel: 01476 870701; open daily. www.chequersinn.net

The Boat Inn 16
In the same family since the 19th century, this stone-floored pub has excellent canal views and offers trips on the pub's narrowboat, *Indian Chief*.
Shutlanger Road, Stoke Bruerne, Northamptonshire; tel: 01604 862428; open daily. www.boatinn.co.uk

The Druid Inn 38
Located in a building dating back to the early 17th century, this atmospheric pub is famed for its excellent restaurant.
Main Street, Birchover, Matlock, Derbyshire; tel: 01629 650302; open 11am–3:30pm and 5:30–11pm Mon–Thu, 11am–11pm Fri–Sat, 11am–4:30pm Sun. www.thedruidinn.co.uk

Eyre Arms 41
Dating back to the mid-18th century, the haunted Eyre Arms is a traditional pub with a seasoned interior and a quaint beer garden.
Hassop, Bakewell, Derbyshire; tel: 01629 640390; open 11am–3pm and 6:30–11pm (–10:30pm Sun) daily. www.eyrearms.com

The Crispin 43
Welcoming traditional Peak District pub near Bakewell serving cask-conditioned ales from Cheshire brewer Robinson's.
Main Road, Great Longstone, Derbyshire; tel: 01629 640237; open noon–3pm and 6–11pm Mon–Fri, noon–11pm Sat–Sun. www.thecrispin.co.uk

The Barrel Inn 45
Spend the night or just pop in for a drink at this charming building that claims to be the highest pub in Derbyshire.
Bretton, Eyam, Hope Valley, Derbyshire; tel: 01433 630856; open daily. www.thebarrelinn.co.uk

The Old Nag's Head 47
Dating back to the 16th century, this pub stands invitingly at the beginning of the Pennine Way.
Grindsbrook Booth, Edale, Hope Valley, Derbyshire; tel: 01433 670291; open daily.

PLACES TO STAY

Washingborough Hall Hotel 2
Magnificent Georgian country house with particularly good-value rooms and a gorgeous garden.
Church Hill, Washingborough, Lincolnshire; tel: 01522 790340. www.washingboroughhall.com

Kildare Hotel 6
This popular and very well-kept Skegness B&B is a short stroll from the beach.
80 Sandbeck Avenue, Skegness, Lincolnshire; tel: 01754 762935. www.kildare-hotel.co.uk

Plummers Place Guesthouse 9
With a lovely location in the Lincolnshire fens, this B&B is bursting with historic character and charm.
Shore Road, Freiston Shore, Boston, Lincolnshire; tel: 01205 761490. www.plummersplace.co.uk

The George of Stamford 11
Marvelous old hotel with particularly congenial service, excellent dining, and a variety of comfy rooms.
71 St. Martins, Stamford, Lincolnshire; tel: 01780 750750. www.georgehotelofstamford.com

Lake Isle Hotel & Restaurant 12
Elegant 18th-century house with outstanding dining and 12 fine rooms.
16 High Street East, Uppingham, Rutland; tel: 01572 822951. www.lakeisle.co.uk

The Regency Hotel & Restaurant 19
Impressive-looking Victorian town house with modest prices, decent rooms, and murder-mystery dinners.
360 London Road, Leicester; tel: 0116 270 9634. www.the-regency-hotel.com

Hotel Maiyango 19
Neat and effortlessly cool boutique hotel at the heart of Leicester offering a superlative dining experience and a rooftop terrace bar.
13–21 St. Nicholas Place, Leicester; tel: 0116 251 8898. www.maiyango.com

Bridge House B&B 28
Comfortable and very well-run Edwardian establishment with first-rate breakfasts.
4 London Road, New Balderton, Newark, Nottinghamshire; tel: 01636 674663. www.arnoldsbandb.co.uk

Harts Hotel 27
Delightful chic modern-looking boutique hotel with first-rate service.
Standard Hill, Park Row, Nottingham; tel: 0115 988 1900. www.hartshotel.co.uk

Hartington Hall Hostel 36
Excellent-value former manor house and youth hostel with accommodating staff.
Hall Bank, Hartington, nr Buxton, Derbyshire; tel: 0845 371 9740. www.yha.org.uk

Harthill Hall 37
Handsome group of historic buildings including a barn and chapel, with spa, indoor swimming pool, and other facilities.
Alport, Bakewell, Derbyshire; tel: 01629 636190. www.harthillhall.co.uk

Bagshaw Hall 40
Imposing 350-year-old building with a Queen Anne interior, gorgeous grounds, and great views.
Bagshaw Hill, Bakewell, Derbyshire; tel: 01629 810333. www.bakewellholidayapartments.com

Riverside House 42
Serene and relaxing Peak District retreat on the banks of the River Wye.
Ashford-in-the-Water, Bakewell, Derbyshire; tel: 01629 812475. www.riversidehousehotel.co.uk

Swiss House 49
Excellent B&B lodgings in the Peak District, with helpful owners and great breakfasts.
How Lane, Castleton, Hope Valley, Derbyshire; tel: 01433 621098. www.swiss-house.co.uk

The Chateau and Wye House Suites 50
First-rate one-, two-, and three-bedroom serviced apartments located in stunning surroundings.
Corbar Road, Buxton, Derbyshire; tel: 07595 482169. www.wyehouse.com

FESTIVALS AND EVENTS

RAF Waddington International Air Show 3
The RAF's largest air show, held over two days, with spectacular aerial displays and many events on the ground.
Waddington, Lincoln; tel: 01522 726102; Jul. www.waddingtonairshow.co.uk

Northampton Balloon Festival 15
Hot-air balloons galore make for a thrilling and memorable three-day spectacle.
Billing Aquadrome, Crow Lane, Great Billing, Northampton; tel: 01604 784948; mid-Aug. www.northamptonballoonfestival.net

Hare Pie Scramble and Bottle Kicking 18
This tradition, which involves scrambling for pieces of hare pie and then kicking bottles of beer between two streams, is over 200 years old.
Hallaton, Leicestershire; Easter Mon.

East Midlands Food & Drink Festival 21
A lavish spread of pies, cheeses, wines, and other delights, with live cooking demonstrations and celebrations of all things gastronomic over a food-filled weekend.
Brooksby Hall, Melton Mowbray, Leicestershire; tel: 01673 828764; Oct. www.eastmidlandsfoodfestival.co.uk

CAMRA Summer Beer Festival 26
Five-day celebration of beer organized by the Campaign for Real Ale, with live music.
Assembly Rooms, Market Place, Derby; Jul. www.derbycamra.org.uk

Robin Hood Festival 31
This week-long celebration of the life of Robin Hood and his Merry Men is perfect for little ones.
Sherwood Forest Visitor Centre, Edwinstowe, Nottinghamshire; tel: 01623 821338; Aug. www.nottinghamshire.gov.uk/ robinhoodfestival

International Byron Festival 33
Fans of Lord Byron flock to his family home at Newstead Abbey for a ten-day reflection on his life and poetic legacy.
Newstead Abbey, Nottingham; tel: 0115 963 9633; Jul. www.internationalbyronsociety.org

Wirksworth Festival 34
Popular arts festival with a focus on everything from performance art to poetry, visual arts, film, and sculpture – with workshops.
Wirksworth, Derbyshire; tel: 01629 824003; Sep. www.wirksworthfestival.co.uk

Royal Shrovetide Football 35
Dating from the 12th century, this game of soccer takes place across the whole town.*Ashbourne, Derbyshire; Shrove Tue and Ash Wed. www.ashbourne-town.com/events/ football.html*

Gilbert & Sullivan Festival 50
Each year the town of Buxton celebrates the work of Gilbert & Sullivan with three weeks of operatic performances.
Buxton Opera House, Buxton, Derbyshire; tel: 01422 323252; Aug. www.gs-festival.co.uk

Buxton Festival 50
Major event that attracts opera-goers, musicians, poets, writers, and other admirers for two weeks of festivities.
Opera House and various venues, Buxton, Derbyshire; tel: 01298 70395; Jul. www.buxtonfestival.co.uk

Buxton Festival Fringe 50
Offshoot of the Buxton Festival, with an emphasis on drama, comedy, poetry, film, and music over two weeks.
Various venues, Buxton, Derbyshire; tel: 01298 79351; Jul. www.buxtonfringe.org.uk

MUSEUMS AND GALLERIES

Battle of Britain Memorial Flight Visitors Centre ④
A nostalgic hangar tour displays World War II planes, including Spitfires and Hawker Hurricanes, up close.
RAF Coningsby, Dogdyke Road, Coningsby, Lincolnshire; tel: 01526 344041; open 10am–5pm Mon–Fri. www.raf.mod.uk/bbmf/visitorscentre

The Cottage Museum ⑤
This quaint museum outlines the history of the attractive village of Woodhall Spa.
Iddesleigh Road, Woodhall Spa, Lincolnshire; tel: 01526 353775; open Easter–Oct: 10am–5pm Mon–Fri, 10:30am–4:30pm Sat–Sun. www.woodhallspa-museum.co.uk

Stamford Museum ⑪
Absorbing collection of exhibits illustrating the history of this charming limestone Lincolnshire town.
Broad Street, Stamford, Lincolnshire; tel: 01780 766317; open 10am–4pm Mon–Sat. www.lincolnshire.gov.uk

Northampton Museum & Art Gallery ⑮
Outstanding historic collection of footwear in a famous shoe museum and gallery.
4–6 Guildhall Road, Northampton; tel: 01604 838111; open 10am–5pm Tue–Sat, 2–5pm Sun. www.northampton.gov.uk

National Waterways Museum Stoke Bruerne ⑯
Fascinating waterways exhibition housed in a former corn mill alongside the canal.
Stoke Brucrne, Towcester, Northamptonshire; tel: 01604 862229; open Apr–Oct: 10am–5pm daily; Nov–Mar: 11am–3pm Wed–Fri, 11am–4pm Sat–Sun. http://nwm.org.uk

New Walk Museum & Art Gallery ⑲
Magnificent museum, with collections from the natural world to art and beyond.
53 New Walk, Leicester; tel: 0116 225 9400; open 10am–5pm Mon–Sat, 11am–5pm Sun. www.leicester.gov.uk

Derby Museum and Art Gallery ㉖
Intriguing museum housing a collection of paintings by local artist Joseph Wright.
The Strand, Derby; tel: 01332 641901; open 10am–5pm Tue–Sat, 11am–5pm Mon, 1–4pm Sun. www.derby.gov.uk

Harley Gallery ㉚
Excellent venue showcasing work from contemporary craftspeople and artists.
Welbeck, Worksop, Nottinghamshire; tel: 01909 501700; open 10am–5pm daily. www.harleygallery.co.uk

Chatsworth House ㊳
Spectacular 17th-century estate and gardens with a wealth of antiquities.
Bakewell, Derbyshire; tel: 01246 565300; open Mar–Oct: 10:30am–6pm daily. www.chatsworth.org

Diana Exhibition ⑰
Six rooms of the magnificent stately home of Althorp House have been given over to a heartfelt celebration of the life and works of the late Princess Diana.
Althorp, Northamptonshire; tel: 01604 770107; open Jul–Aug: 11am–5pm. www.dianaexhibition.com

Nottingham Castle ㉗
Seventeenth-century mansion, on the site of the original castle, stuffed with history and culture, including the Castle Museum.
Off Friar Lane, Maid Marian Way, Nottingham; tel: 0115 915 3700; open Mar–Sep: 10am–5pm Tue–Sun; Oct–Feb: 10am–4pm Tue–Sun. www.nottinghamcity.gov.uk

Eyam Museum ㊹
Explore the ins and outs of this "plague village," which quarantined itself to contain the bubonic plague in 1665.
Hawkhill Road, Eyam, Derbyshire; tel: 01433 631371; open Mar–Nov: 10am–4:30pm Tue–Sun. www.eyammuseum.demon.co.uk

THINGS TO DO WITH KIDS

Lincoln Castle ①
An 11th-century castle offering a host of summer events, from jousting to drama.
Castle Hill, Lincoln; tel: 01522 511068; open Oct–Mar: 10am–4pm daily; Apr and Sep: 10am–5pm daily; May–Aug: 10am–6pm daily. www.english-heritage.org.uk

National Space Centre ⑲
The UK's largest planetarium and interactive space center, dedicated to the story of the universe.
Exploration Drive, Leicester; tel: 0116 261 0261; open 10am–4pm Tue–Fri, 10am–5pm Sat–Sun; school holidays: 10am–5pm daily. www.spacecentre.co.uk

Heckington Windmill ⑦
Dating back to 1830, England's sole surviving intact eight-sailed windmill is a fantastic sight.
Hale Road, Heckington, Sleaford, Lincolnshire; tel: 01529 461919; open Easter–mid-Jul: noon–5pm Thu–Sun; mid-Jul–mid-Sep: noon–5pm daily; mid-Sep–Easter: 2–5pm Sun. www.lincolnshire.gov.uk

Bosworth Battlefield Heritage Centre and Country Park ⑳
Medieval history gruesomely brought to life, plus nature walks for the squeamish.
Sutton Cheney, nr Market Bosworth, Nuneaton, Warwickshire; tel: 01455 290429; open Apr–Oct: 10am–5pm daily; Nov–Mar: 10am–4pm daily. www.bosworthbattlefield.com

Ashby-de-la-Zouch Castle ㉔
Famous ruin often hosting children's events, such as a medieval-style combat in August.
Ashby-de-la-Zouch, Leicestershire; tel: 01530 413343; open Apr–Jun and Sep–Oct: 10am–5pm Thu–Mon; Jul–Aug: 10am–5pm daily; Nov–Mar: noon–4pm Thu–Mon. www.english-heritage.org.uk

Donington Park Grand Prix Exhibition ㉕
Give young racing fans something to roar about with the world's largest collection of Grand Prix race cars.
Donington Park, Castle Donington, Derby; tel: 01332 810048; open 10am–5pm daily. www.donington-park.co.uk

Sherwood Forest Natural Nature Reserve ㉛
Great hiking opportunities in historic parkland that is forever associated with Robin Hood and his Merry Men.
Edwinstowe, Mansfield, Nottinghamshire; tel: 01623 823202; open Mar–Oct: 10am–5pm daily; Nov–Feb: 10am–4:30pm daily. www.nottinghamshire.gov.uk

World Conker Championship ⑬
A truly international battle of the conkers, with events for men and women plus junior competitions.
New Lodge Fields, nr Oundle, Northamptonshire; tel: 01832 272735; second Sun in Oct. www.worldconkerchampionships.com

Go Ape ㉜
High-wire adventures, zip lines, and obstacle courses up in the trees in a specially designed adventure park.
Sherwood Pines, Nottinghamshire; tel: 0845 643 9215; open Mar–Oct: daily; Nov: Sat–Sun. www.goape.co.uk

Chestnut Centre Otter, Owl and Wildlife Park ㊽
Inspiring wildlife park in the Peak District National Park, home to otters, polecats, red foxes, deer, and more.
Chapel-en-le-Frith, High Peak, Derbyshire; tel: 01298 814099; open Mar–Sep: 10:30am–5:30pm daily; Oct–Feb: 10:30am–dusk daily. www.chestnutcentre.co.uk

SPAS AND HEALTH RESORTS

Barnsdale Hall Hotel ⑩
Country house equipped with spa and leisure facilities in a fabulous location.
Stamford Road, Barnsdale, Oakham, Rutland; tel: 01572 757901. www.barnsdalehotel.co.uk

Losehill House Hotel & Spa ㊻
Lovely Peak District hotel in a secluded location, with swimming pool and spa.
Edale Road, Hope, Derbyshire; tel: 01433 621219. www.losehillhouse.co.uk

OTHER SIGHTS IN THE BOOK
Derbyshire Peak District ㊹ *(see pp72–3).*
Caves of Castleton and Buxton ㊾ *(see pp174–5).*

Below: National Space Centre in Leicester

EASTERN ENGLAND

LOCAL FOOD

Cotto ③①
Fantastic European menu using a wide variety of local ingredients – a large proportion of which is sourced from Cambridge Market – with a heavy bias toward organic produce.
183 East Rd, Cambridge; tel: 01223 302010; open 9am–3pm Tue–Wed, 9am–3pm and 7pm–late Thu–Sat. www.cottocambridge.co.uk

Midsummer House ③①
A Michelin-starred restaurant, housed in a quaint old building, that sources ingredients from local suppliers to create fantastic contemporary cuisine.
Midsummer Common, Cambridge; tel: 01223 369299; open 7–9:30pm Tue, noon–1:45pm and 7–9:30pm Wed–Sat. www.midsummerhouse.co.uk

The Last Wine Bar & Restaurant ①
Award-winning restaurant with a relaxed vibe; delicious English fare and fine wine.
76 St. George's Street, Norwich; tel: 01603 626626; open noon–2:30pm and 5pm–12:30am Mon–Fri, noon–2:30pm and 6pm–12:30am Sat. www.lastwinebar.co.uk

Caley's Cocoa Cafe ①
Tempting teas and chocolate treats housed in a 15th-century courtroom building.
The Guildhall, Gaol Hill, Norwich; open 9am–5pm Mon–Sat. www.caleys.com

The Old Fire Engine House ③③
Handsome restaurant and art gallery with a focus on traditional English dishes.
25 St. Mary's Street, Ely, Cambridgeshire; tel: 01353 662582; open 10:30–11:30am, 12:15–2pm, 3:30–5:15pm and 7:15–9pm Mon–Sat, noon–2pm and 3:30–5:15pm Sun. www.theoldfireenginehouse.co.uk

The Lifeboat Inn ④⑦
Delightful seafood restaurant, pub, and charming hotel in a superb coastal setting.
Ship Lane, Thornham, Norfolk; tel: 01485 512236; restaurant open 7–9:30pm Mon–Sat, noon–2:30pm and 7–9:30pm Sun; bar food noon–9:30pm daily. www.maypolehotels.com

The Hoste Arms ⑤⓪
Pretty former coaching inn offering locally sourced food and the catch of the day.
The Green, Burnham Market, Norfolk; tel: 01328 738777; open noon–2pm and 6–9pm daily. www.hostearms.co.uk

Wiveton Hall ⑤⑤
Gorgeous Jacobean house where you can pick your own fruit and eat in a lovely café.
Wiveton Hall, Holt, Norfolk; tel: 01263 740525; open Easter–Christmas, 9:30am–5pm daily. www.wivetonhall.co.uk

The Westleton Crown ⑧
Historic former coaching inn dating back to the 12th century, with log fires and an award-winning restaurant.
The Street, Westleton, Southwold, Suffolk; tel: 01728 648777; open 7–10am, noon–2:30pm and 7–9:30pm Mon–Fri, 7:30–10:30am, noon–2:30pm and 7–9:30pm Sat–Sun. www.westletoncrown.co.uk

Emmett's of Peasenhall ⑩
Scrumptious range of hams, organic wines, cheeses, chocolates, olives, and chutney.
Peasenhall, Saxmundham, Suffolk; tel: 01728 660250; open 8:30am–5:30pm Mon–Fri, 8:30am–5pm Sat. www.emmettsham.co.uk

Reckford Farm Shop ⑪
Locally produced goodies – from homemade pies to fish and cheeses – sourced from responsible producers.
Reckford Farm, Westleton Road, Middleton, Saxmundham, Suffolk; tel: 01728 648253; open 9am–5pm daily. www.onesuffolk.co.uk

Railway Farm Market Garden & Farm Shop ⑬
Bursting with homegrown and locally sourced goodies from vegetables to honey and free-range eggs.
Main Road, Benhall, Saxmundham, Suffolk; tel: 01728 605793; open 8:30am–5:30pm Mon–Sat, 9am–2pm Sun. www.4fusion.co.uk/railwayfarmshop

The Lighthouse Restaurant ⑭
Agreeable Aldeburgh restaurant with a very dependable English and European menu.
77 High Street, Aldeburgh, Suffolk; tel: 01728 453377; open noon–2pm and 6:30–10pm Mon–Fri, noon–2:30pm and 6:30–10pm Sat–Sun. www.lighthouserestaurant.co.uk

Butley Orford Oysterage ⑮
Superb seafood is on the menu here, with oysters from the restaurant's oyster bed.
Market Square, Orford, Suffolk; tel: 01394 450277; open noon–2:15pm daily; also Apr–May and mid-Sep–Oct: 6:30–9pm Wed–Fri, 6–9pm Sat; Jun–mid-Sep: 6:30–9pm daily (from 6pm Sat); Nov–Apr: 6:30–9pm Fri, 6–9pm Sat. www.butleyorfordoysterage.co.uk

The Whistlestop Café ⑱
Glorious food and coffee – all in the former Woodbridge train station, with bedrooms available upstairs.
Woodbridge Station Guesthouse, Station Road, Woodbridge, Suffolk; tel: 01394 384831; open 7am–5pm Mon–Fri, 9am–5pm Sat–Sun. www.woodbridgestationguesthouse.co.uk

Salthouse Eaterie ㉑
Delicious British and Mediterranean food served up in a stunning waterside location.
Salthouse Harbour Hotel, Neptune Quay, Ipswich, Suffolk; tel: 01473 226789; open 7am–10pm daily. www.salthouseharbour.co.uk/eaterie

EASTERN ENGLAND

The Company Shed ㉔
Simple, no-frills seafood eatery; the oysters alone are worth the trip out here.
129 Coast Road, West Mersea, Colchester, Essex; tel: 01206 382700; open 9am–4pm Tue–Sat, 10am–4pm Sun. www.west-mersea.co.uk/Mersea_Island_Company_Shed.htm

FARMERS' MARKETS

Aldeburgh Farmers' Market ⑭
Wholesome spread of locally produced edibles and drinks in a pleasant Suffolk coastal town.
Church Hall, Victoria Road, Aldeburgh, Suffolk; third Sat of every month, 9am–12:30pm.

Lavenham Farmers' Market ㉙
Huge and wholesome range of local produce in this delightful village near Bury St. Edmunds.
Lavenham Village Hall or Market Place, Church St, Lavenham, Suffolk; fourth Sat of every month, 10am–1pm.

Ely Farmers' Market ㉝
Small, friendly market featuring excellent local products, from traditional fruit and vegetables to farmed ostrich meat.
Off Market Square, Ely, Cambridgeshire; tel: 01353 665555; second and fourth Sat of every month, 8:30am–2pm.

Wayland Farmers' Market ㊱
Diverse range of locally reared, grown, and prepared products at a small market town in the heart of Norfolk.
Watton High Street, Watton, Norfolk; tel: 01953 883915; first Sat of every month except Jan, 8:30am–12:30pm. www.wayland.org.uk

Aylsham Farmers' Market ㊷
A bounty of locally reared meats, locally grown vegetables, and other products.
Market Place, Aylsham, Norfolk; tel: 01263 733354; first and third Sat of every month, 9am–1pm.

PUBS

Adam and Eve ①
A historic Norwich alehouse, thought to date from the 12th century, offering good food, charm, and a delightful garden.
Bishopsgate, Norwich; tel: 01603 667423; open daily. www.adamandevenorwich.co.uk

The Rumbold Arms ③
Great wine list, a host of real ales, an extensive menu, and huge back garden (once a bowling green).
107 Southtown Road, Great Yarmouth, Norfolk; tel: 01493 653887; open daily. www.therumboldarms.co.uk

The Ship Inn ⑨
This nautically flavored inn at the once-flourishing port of Dunwich is a joy.
St James Street, Dunwich, Saxmundham, Suffolk; tel: 01728 648219; open daily. www.shipatdunwich.co.uk

Above: Historic windmill at Cley, now converted into vacation accommodations

The Anchor ⑦
An emphasis on beach views, fresh local ingredients, and organic produce matched by an ambitious range of beers.
Main Street, Walberswick, Suffolk; tel: 01502 722112; open 11am–4pm and 6–11pm Mon–Fri, all day Sat–Sun. www.anchoratwalberswick.com

Land of Liberty, Peace and Plenty ㉖
A splendid range of real ales greets customers at this atmospheric pub in a 19th-century house with a great garden.
Long Lane, Heronsgate, Hertfordshire; tel: 01923 282226; open daily. www.landoflibertypub.com

The Old Cannon ㉚
Fantastic brew-pub in a converted brewery at the heart of Bury St Edmunds, with fine food and own-brewed beer.
86 Cannon Street, Bury St. Edmunds, Suffolk; tel: 01284 768769; open lunch and evening Mon–Fri, all day Sat–Sun. www.oldcannonbrewery.co.uk

The Eagle ㉛
Former coaching inn associated with Francis Crick and James Watson, who celebrated their discovery of the DNA double helix here.
8 Bene't Street, Cambridge; tel: 01223 505020; open daily.

Free Press ㉛
Great food and ale and a traditional vibe that's a pleasant contrast to modern pubs.
Prospect Row, Cambridge; tel: 01223 368337; open daily. www.freepresspub.com

The Sun Inn ㉓
Sleepy former coaching inn, steeped in real-ale aromas, with a lovely garden.
High Street, Dedham, Essex; tel: 01206 323351; open daily. www.thesuninndedham.com

The Cock ㉜
Much-loved quaint pub with an admirable European menu, good-value set meals, and bucketloads of character, right at the heart of the village.
47 High Street, Hemingford Grey, Huntingdon, Cambridgeshire; tel: 01480 463609; open 11:30am–3pm and 6–11pm Mon–Sat, noon–4pm and 6:30–10:30pm Sun. www.cambscuisine.com

The Rose and Crown ㊺
Stuffed with nooks, timber beams, uneven floors, and 14th-century charm, this pub has its own bedrooms if you simply can't pull yourself away.
Old Church Road, Snettisham, Norfolk; tel: 01485 541382; open daily. www.roseandcrownsnettisham.co.uk

The White Horse ㊽
Stunningly situated on the North Norfolk coastline with fantastic sea views: eat, drink, stay overnight, and enjoy the unique atmosphere. *Brancaster Staithe, Norfolk; tel: 01485 210262; open daily. www.whitehorsebrancaster.co.uk*

PLACES TO STAY

Dedham Hall ㉓
Fifteenth-century manor house deep in the heart of Constable Country *(see pp76–7)*, complete with a celebrated restaurant and luxury rooms.
Brook Street, Dedham, Essex; tel: 01206 323027. www.dedhamhall.co.uk

Lavenham Priory ㉙
Gorgeous, half-timbered, 13th-century B&B with a lovely, large garden, in the middle of a pretty village.
Water Street, Lavenham, Sudbury, Suffolk; tel: 01787 247404. www.lavenhampriory.co.uk

Cathedral House ㉝
Fine Georgian period B&B with charming owners, breakfast cooked to order, and a fabulous location in the shadow of Ely Cathedral.
17 St. Mary's Street, Ely, Cambridgeshire; tel: 01353 662124. www.cathedralhouse.co.uk

Killiney House Bed & Breakfast ㉞
En-suite rooms and excellent breakfasts at a truly handsome B&B.
18 Barkhams Lane, Littleport, Ely, Cambridgeshire; tel: 01353 860404. www.killineyhouse.co.uk

Elme Hall Hotel ㊵
Particularly spacious rooms in a large Georgian-style mansion offering both luxury and budget accommodations.
69 Elm High Road, Wisbech, Cambridgeshire; tel: 01945 475566. www.elmehall.co.uk

The Old Rectory ㊶
Former Georgian rectory swishly converted with comfy, good-value *en-suite* rooms and a terrace, courtyard, and garden.
33 Goodwins Road, King's Lynn, Norfolk; tel: 01553 768544. www.theoldrectory-kingslynn.com

Deepdale ㊾
Hostel accommodations and campsite at a fun and atmospheric spot on the north Norfolk coast.
Deepdale Farm, Burnham Deepdale, Norfolk; tel: 01485 210256. www.deepdalefarm.co.uk

Vine House ㊿
Elegant Georgian boutique hotel with a cozy study area, rooms that boast a flawless attention to detail, and butler service in the evenings.
The Green, Burnham Market, Norfolk; tel: 01328 738777. www.vinehouseboutiquehotel.co.uk

Above: Sandringham House

The Crown ⓐ

Excellent former coaching inn with rooms, on a Georgian square in a quintessential seaside town with long Norfolk views; the food is first-rate. *The Buttlands, Wells-next-the-Sea, Norfolk; tel: 01328 710209. www.thecrownhotelwells.co.uk*

Cley Windmill ⓔ

Bedrooms in a fabulous historic windmill and in converted stables and boathouses. *Cley-next-the-Sea, Holt, Norfolk; tel: 01263 740209. www.cleywindmill.co.uk*

<!-- FESTIVALS AND EVENTS -->

FESTIVALS AND EVENTS

Norfolk and Norwich Festival ①

Music, theater, dance, and the arts – including original commissions – celebrated with gusto over 16 days. *Various venues, Norwich and Norfolk; tel: 01603 877750; May. www.nnfestival.org.uk*

Ely Folk Festival ㉝

Folk fans converge on the cathedral town of Ely for three days of music, dance, merrymaking, and festive fun. *Ely Outdoor Centre, Ely, Cambridgeshire; tel: 07500 527334; Jul. www.elyfolk.co.uk*

Aldeburgh Festival ⑭

Five-day event focussing on classical music by past and contemporary composers, in a charming Suffolk seaside town. *Various venues, Aldeburgh, Suffolk; tel: 01728 687100; Jun. www.aldeburgh.co.uk*

Aldeburgh Poetry Festival ⑭

Three-day celebration of the written and spoken word complete with poetry workshops and open mic events. *Various venues, Aldeburgh, Suffolk; tel: 01986 835950; Nov. www.aldeburghpoetryfestival.org*

Debenham Arts Festival ⑯

Festival that celebrates music, drama, arts, crafts, and literature over three days. *Various venues, Debenham, Suffolk; Jul. www.debenhamartsfestival.co.uk*

Essex Poetry Festival ㉕

A month of poetry readings, workshops, open-mic events, and poetry competitions. *The Cramphorn Theatre, Fairfield Road, Chelmsford, Essex; tel: 01245 606505; Sep–Oct. www.essex-poetry-festival.co.uk*

King's Lynn Festival ㊶

A varied two-week program of music, including classical, jazz, and folk, with special celebrity guests. *Various venues, King's Lynn, Norfolk; tel: 01553 767557; Jul. www.kingslynnfestival.org.uk*

Holkham Country Fair ㊶

Two-day celebration of rural England held every other year (in odd-numbered years, such as 2011) in the dazzling grounds of this Palladian hall. *Holkham Hall, Wells-next-the-Sea, Norfolk; tel: 01328 821821; Jul. www.countryfairoffice.co.uk*

MUSEUMS AND GALLERIES

Castle Museum and Art Gallery ①

Appealing museum housed in an 11th-century castle, with artworks from the Norwich School, displays on Norfolk's history, and the largest collection of ceramic teapots in the world. *Castle Meadow, Norwich; tel: 01603 493625; open 10am–4:30pm Mon–Fri, 10am–5pm Sat, 1–5pm Sun. www.museums.norfolk.gov.uk*

Sainsbury Centre for the Visual Arts ①

Superb permanent collection of art, ranging from Yüan dynasty effigies to works by Francis Bacon and Henry Moore. *University of East Anglia, Norwich; tel: 01603 593199; open 10am–5pm Tue and Thu–Sun, 10am–8pm Wed. www.scva.org.uk*

Dunwich Museum ⑨

Displays about the once-magnificent medieval town of Dunwich, now reduced to a tiny coastal village because of erosion. *St James Street, Dunwich, Suffolk; tel: 01728 648796; open Apr–Sep: 11:30am–4:30pm. www.visit-dunwich.co.uk*

Bawdsey Radar Museum ⑳

The world's first radar station is a must for all World War II and Battle of Britain fans. *Bawdsey Quay, Suffolk, tel: 07821 162879; open some Sundays in Apr–Aug, 12:30–4:30pm; see website for details. www.bawdseyradargroup.co.uk*

Aldeburgh Museum ⑭

Delightful old timbered Tudor building exhibiting local artifacts and exploring legends such as the "Aldeburgh Witches" *Moot Hall, Aldeburgh, Suffolk; tel: 01728 454666; open Apr–May and Sep–Oct: 2:30–5pm daily; Jun–Aug: noon–5pm daily. www.aldeburghmuseum.org.uk*

Sutton Hoo Exhibition Hall ⑲

Celebrated collection of artifacts from the excavated burial mounds of the Anglo-Saxon kings of East Anglia. *Tranmer House, Sutton Hoo, Woodbridge, Suffolk; tel: 01394 389700; opening times vary according to season, check website for details. www.nationaltrust.org.uk*

Bridge Cottage ㉒

Thatched cottage by the River Stour, devoted to Constable (see pp76–7). *Flatford, Suffolk; tel: 01206 298260; open Jan–Feb: 11am–3:30pm Sat–Sun; Mar–Apr: 11am–5pm Wed–Sun; May–Sep: 10:30am–5:30pm daily; Oct: 11am–4pm daily; Nov–Dec: 11am–3:30pm Wed–Sun. www.nationaltrust.org.uk*

Duxford Imperial War Museum ㉗

Tremendous fleet of aircraft, including crowd-pulling Spitfires and Concorde. A great day out for aviation buffs. *Duxford, Cambridgeshire; tel: 01223 835000; open mid-Mar–Oct: 10am–6pm daily; Nov–mid-Mar: 10am–4pm daily. http://duxford.iwm.org.uk*

Gainsborough's House ㉘

Splendid collection of the works of Sudbury's most notable artistic resident, the portrait-painter Thomas Gainsborough, in his place of residence. *46 Gainsborough Street, Sudbury, Suffolk; tel: 01787 372598; open 10am–5pm Mon–Sat. www.gainsborough.org*

Bury St Edmunds Art Gallery ㉚

Inspirational displays of contemporary British and international art located within a delightful building. *The Market Cross, Cornhill, Bury St Edmunds, Suffolk, tel: 01284 762081; open 10:30am–5pm Tue–Sat. www.burystedmundsartgallery.org*

Whipple Museum of the History of Science ㉛

A great variety of fascinating models, instruments, and contraptions from the archives of scientific endeavor. *Free School Lane, Cambridge; tel: 01223 330906; open 12:30–4:30pm Mon–Fri. www.hps.cam.ac.uk/whipple*

Sedgwick Museum of Earth Sciences ㉛

A compendium of fossils, minerals, dinosaurs, and other geological exhibits from around the world. *University of Cambridge, Downing Street, Cambridge; tel: 01223 333456; open 10am–5pm Mon–Fri, 10am–4pm Sat. www.sedgwickmuseum.org*

Babylon Gallery ㉝
Waterside art gallery located in a former warehouse, with a wide range of works.
Waterside, Ely, Cambridgeshire; tel: 01353 616993; open 10am–4pm Tue–Sat, 11am–5pm Sun.
www.babylongallery.co.uk

Stained Glass Museum ㉝
An interesting little museum based in Ely Cathedral, offering a colorful look at the history of stained-glass manufacture.
The South Triforium, Ely Cathedral, Ely, Cambridgeshire; tel: 01353 660347; open 10:30am–5pm Mon–Fri, 10:30am–5:30pm Sat, noon–6pm Sun.
www.stainedglassmuseum.com

Ely Museum ㉝
Intriguing museum packed with local relics and housed in a 13th-century building that was once the Bishop's Gaol.
The Old Gaol, Market Street, Ely, Cambridgeshire; tel: 01353 666655; open Mar–Nov: 10:30am–5pm Mon–Sat, 1–5pm Sun; Oct–Feb: 10:30am–4pm Mon–Sat, 1–4pm Sun.
www.elymuseum.org.uk

Castle Rising ㊸
This Norman castle, not far from Sandringham, dates from 1140. It is surrounded by a defensive mound, and boasts seasonal events and guided tours.
Kings Lynn, Norfolk; tel: 01553 631330; open Apr–Oct: 10am–6pm daily; Nov–Mar: 10am–4pm Wed–Sun.
www.castlerising.co.uk

Sandringham House and Museum ㊹
Simply magnificent stately home and gardens – the retreat for four generations of British royals – with a museum containing a huge collection of keepsakes.
Sandringham, Norfolk; tel: 01553 612908; open Apr–Oct: 11am–5pm daily.
www.sandringhamestate.co.uk

THINGS TO DO WITH KIDS

Norwich Dragon Festival ①
A celebration of the fire-breathing serpent, its place in myth, and its links with Norwich.
Various venues, Norwich; tel: 01603 599576; Jan–Feb. www.norwich12.co.uk

Pleasure Beach ③
Vast seaside amusement park with thrilling rides, activities, and amusements.
South Beach Parade, Great Yarmouth, Norfolk; tel: 01493 844585; open May–Sep, see website for details.
www.pleasure-beach.co.uk

Duxford Airshows ㉗
Historic aircraft from the Duxford Imperial War Museum take to the skies.
Duxford Imperial War Museum, Duxford, Cambridgeshire; tel: 01223 835000; museum open daily, airshows in Sep and Oct. http://duxford.iwm.org.uk

Strawberry Fair ㉛
Family-oriented arts and crafts festival offering samba bands, circus acts, face-painting, locally made films, and more.
Midsummer Common, Cambridge; tel: 07984 230377; first Sat in Jun.
www.strawberryfair.org.uk

Snettisham Park ㊺
Kids will love the deer safari and bottle-feeding lambs at this huge park farm.
Snettisham, King's Lynn, Norfolk; tel: 01485 542425; open 10am–5pm daily (lambing season Feb–May).
www.snettishampark.co.uk

Wells and Walsingham Steam Railway ㉜
Board a steam train from Wells to Walsingham and enjoy the glorious views.
Stiffkey Road, Wells-next-the-Sea, Norfolk; tel: 01328 711630; open Apr–Nov.
www.wellswalsinghamrailway.co.uk

Lowestoft Air Festival ⑤
Popular weekend seafront air festival with mesmerizing flyovers from generations of planes, ranging from World War II Spitfires to the acrobatic Red Arrows.
Lowestoft, Suffolk; tel: 01502 587027; mid Aug.
www.lowestoftairfestival.co.uk

Southwold Pier ⑥
Bundles of amusements, including the fantastic "Under the Pier Show," plus fish and chips and gift shops.
Southwold, Suffolk; tel: 01502 7221055; open Nov–Mar: 10am–5pm daily; Apr–Oct: 10am–7pm daily.
www.southwoldpier.co.uk
www.underthepier.com

Bircham Windmill ㊻
Children and adults alike will fall in love with this wonderfully restored 19th-century windmill set in the pastoral fields of Norfolk.
Bircham Windmill, Great Bircham, Norfolk; tel: 01485 578393; open Apr–Sep, 10am–5pm daily.
www.birchamwindmill.co.uk

Blakeney Seal Trips ㊾
One-hour boat trips to view seals and birds in their natural habitat on Blakeney Point on the North Norfolk coast.
Morston Quay, Morston, Norfolk; tel: 01263 740505; Apr–Oct: daily; see website for winter trips.
www.norfolksealtrips.co.uk

Dinosaur Adventure Park ㊲
A hundred acres (40 hectares) of evocative woodland dedicated to all things Jurassic and Neanderthal. There are also displays about prehistoric life and a playground.
Weston Park, Lenwade, Norfolk; tel: 01603 876310; open Mar–mid-Jul and Sep–Oct: 10am–5pm daily; mid-Jul–Aug: 10am–6pm daily; Nov–Feb: 10am–4pm daily.
www.dinosauradventure.co.uk

Bressingham Steam Museum & Gardens ㉟
Museum of all things train-related, from gleaming engines built during the age of steam, to Thomas the Tank Engine rides for kids and train journeys for all ages.
Low Road, Bressingham, Norfolk; tel: 01379 686900; open Mar–Nov: from 10:30am daily. www.bressingham.co.uk

Sacrewell Farm & Country Centre ㊳
Children will love visiting this farm, which offers camping and party facilities from March to October.
Thornhaugh, Peterborough; tel: 01780 782254; open Mar–Sep: 9:30am–5pm daily; Oct–Feb: 10am–4pm daily.
www.sacrewell.org.uk

SPAS AND HEALTH RESORTS

Sprowston Manor Hotel Spa ①
Seven treatment rooms boasting a vast range of beauty and holistic treatments, in beautiful woodland surroundings.
Sprowston, Norwich; tel: 01603 410871.
www.marriott.co.uk

Hopton Holiday Village ④
Sporty family getaway in a sandy beach setting, with swimming pools, sauna, and sports courts.
Hopton-on-Sea, nr Great Yarmouth, Norfolk; tel: 0871 230 1922.
www.haven.com/parks/norfolk_essex/hopton

Potters Leisure Resort ④
Five-star vacation village with private beach and an impressive range of spa and sports facilities.
Coast Road, Hopton-on-Sea, nr Great Yarmouth, Norfolk; tel: 0870 112 9631.
www.pottersholidays.com

Best Western Ufford Park Golf, Hotel and Spa ⑰
Sweeping parkland, an 18-hole golf course and excellent health and spa facilities: relaxation is the watchword.
Yarmouth Road, Melton, Woodbridge, Suffolk; tel: 01394 383555.
www.uffordpark.co.uk

Greens Health and Fitness ㉛
Extensive treatments for both men and women, plus a gym and poolside spa.
213 Cromwell Road, Cambridge; tel: 01223 248100.
www.greensfitness.co.uk

Congham Hall Hotel ㊷
Idyllically situated, luxury Georgian manor finely attuned to the art of pampering and relaxation, with Sandringham nearby.
Congham Hall, Grimston, King's Lynn, Norfolk; tel: 01485 600250.
www.conghamhallhotel.co.uk

OTHER SIGHTS IN THE BOOK

Norfolk Broads ② *(see pp68–9).* **Suffolk Heritage Coast** ⑫ *(see pp18–19).* **Stour Valley** ㉒ *(see pp76–7).* **Cambridge** ㉛ *(see pp196–7).* **The Fens** ㊲ *(see pp180–81).*

Below: Seals on a sandbank at Blakeney Point in Norfolk

LONDON

LOCAL FOOD

Chutneys Indian Vegetarian Restaurant ⑨
Inexpensive, authentic north- and south-Indian cuisine near Euston station, with a popular lunchtime buffet.
124 Drummond Street, Camden, NW1; tel: 020 7388 0604; open noon–11:30pm daily. www.chutneyseuston.co.uk

Number Twelve Restaurant ⑩
Well-presented, good-value modern Italian cuisine; very handy for the British Museum.
12 Upper Woburn Place, Camden, WC1; tel: 020 7693 5425; open noon–3pm and 5:30–10:30pm Tue–Fri, 5:30pm–10:30pm Sat. www.numbertwelverestaurant.co.uk

North Sea Fish Restaurant ⑪
Family-run fish-and-chip restaurant with cozy decor in Bloomsbury, serving a good range of fish in huge portions.
7/8 Leigh Street, Bloomsbury, WC1; tel: 020 7387 5892; open noon–2:30pm and 5:30–11pm Mon–Sat. www.northseafishrestaurant.co.uk

Simpson's-in-the-Strand ㊹
Classic British dining in a Victorian setting; roast beef is carved at the table.
100 Strand, Westminster, WC2; tel: 020 7836 9112; open 12:15pm–2:45pm and 5:45pm–10:45pm Mon–Sat, 12:15–3pm and 6–9pm Sun. www.simpsonsinthestrand.co.uk

Rules Restaurant ㊺
Allegedly London's oldest restaurant, established in 1798; traditional British food including beef from their own estate.
35 Maiden Lane, Covent Garden, WC2; tel: 020 7836 5314; open noon–11:30pm Mon–Sat, noon–10:30pm Sun. www.rules.co.uk

Gay Hussar ㊾
A Soho institution with tremendous atmosphere, serving hearty and authentic Hungarian food.
2 Greek Street, Soho, W1; tel: 020 7437 0973; open 12:15–2:30pm and 5:30–10:45pm Mon–Sat. www.gayhussar.co.uk

Veeraswamy (51)
Britain's oldest surviving Indian restaurant, with delicious food and opulent decor evoking a maharajah's palace.
Mezzanine Floor, Victory House, 99 Regent Street, Westminster, W1; tel: 020 7734 1401; open noon–2:15 pm and 5:30–10:30pm Mon–Fri, 12:30–2:30pm and 5:30–10:30pm Sat, 6–10:30pm Sun. www.veeraswamy.com

Bentley's Oyster Bar & Grill (54)
Classy fish restaurant, grill, and oyster bar off Piccadilly, opened in 1916.
11–15 Swallow Street, Westminster, W1; tel: 020 7734 4756; oyster and champagne bar open noon–midnight Mon–Sat, noon–10pm Sun; restaurant open noon–3pm and 6–11pm Mon–Sat, 6–10pm Sun. www.bentleys.org

Konstam at the Prince Albert ⑭
Fresh seasonal cooking, with most of the ingredients sourced from Greater London.
2 Acton Street, WC1; tel: 020 7833 5040; open noon–2:30pm Mon–Fri, 6:30–10pm Mon–Wed, 6:30–10:30pm Thu–Sat, 10:30am–4pm Sun. www.konstam.co.uk

Brick Lane Beigel Bake ㉕
An East End institution: clubbers line up with locals for fresh bagels.
159 Brick Lane, Tower Hamlets, E1; tel: 020 7729 0616; open 24 hours a day.

Borough Market ㉝
London's oldest food market; a huge range of stands in a Dickensian setting.
Off Southwark Street, Southwark, SE1; open 11am–5pm Thu, noon–6pm Fri, 9am–5pm Sat. www.boroughmarket.org.uk

Oxo Tower Restaurant and Brasserie ㊱
Modern European food and spectacular Thames views from a London landmark.
Oxo Tower Wharf, Barge House Street, South Bank, SE1; tel: 020 7803 3888; open noon–2:30pm and 6–11pm Mon–Sat, noon–2:30pm and 6:30–10pm Sun. www.harveynichols.com

Porters English Restaurant ㊻
Good-value restaurant with a menu featuring hearty pies and English puddings, such as syrup sponge and Eton Mess.
17 Henrietta Street, Covent Garden, WC2; tel: 020 7836 6466; open noon–11:30pm Mon–Sat, noon–10:30pm Sun. www.porters.uk.com

Parlour Restaurant ㊿
Viennese cakes, hot chocolate, and ice cream treats for children of all ages.
First floor, Fortnum and Mason, 181 Piccadilly, W1; tel: 0845 602 5694; open 10am–7:30pm Mon–Sat, noon–5pm Sun. www.fortnumandmason.com

Kelly's Eel and Pie Shop (82)
Classic pies, mash, and jellied eels in an East End street market, established in 1937.
526 Roman Road, Bow, E3; tel: 020 8980 3165; open 10am–3pm Mon–Thu, 10am–7pm Fri, 10am–5:30pm Sat. www.gkellypieandmash.co.uk

Billingsgate Market (83)
Get up early to see the largest selection of fresh fish in the UK. The market also offers great fish-preparation and cooking classes.
Trafalgar Way, Poplar, E14; tel: 020 7987 1118; open 5–8:30am Tue–Sat. www.billingsgate-market.org.uk

Bibendum (89)
Classic French cuisine in a light and spacious restaurant housed in a converted Art Deco building.
Michelin House, 81 Fulham Road, Fulham, SW3; tel: 020 7581 5817; open noon–2:30pm and 7–11pm Mon–Fri, 12:30–3pm and 7–11pm Sat, 12:30–3pm and 7–10:30pm Sun. www.bibendum.co.uk

FARMERS' MARKETS

Marylebone Farmers' Market ⑥
One of London's largest, surrounded by many individual shops and cafés.
Cromer Street, off Marylebone High Street, Westminster, W1; every Sun, 10am–2pm. www.lfm.org.uk/mary.asp

Pimlico Road Farmers' Market (67)
Held in a leafy square and serving prosperous Chelsea and Belgravia.
Orange Square, off Pimlico Road and Ebury Street, Westminster, SW1; every Sat, 9am–1pm. www.lfm.org.uk/pimlico.asp

Notting Hill Gate Farmers' Market (75)
Plenty of organic produce at this market, very close to Notting Hill Tube station.
Kensington Place, junction of Kensington Church Street, Kensington, W8; every Sat, 9am–1pm. www.lfm.org.uk/nott.asp

Below: View over the Thames from the Oxo Tower Restaurant and Brasserie

Islington Farmers' Market (80)
Serving stylish Islington, and near its boutiques and antique shops.
William Tyndale School, Upper Street, Islington, N1; every Sun, 10am–2pm. www.lfm.org.uk/isling.asp

Blackheath Farmers' Market (86)
Close to the up-market shops and airy parkland of Blackheath village.
Blackheath train station parking lot, 2 Blackheath Village, SE3; every Sun, 10am–2pm. www.lfm.org.uk/black.asp

Clapham Farmers' Market (88)
In a popular residential area close to the green expanse of Clapham Common.
Bonneville Primary School, Bonneville Gardens, SW4; every Sun, 10am–2pm. www.lfm.org.uk/clapham.asp

Hammersmith Farmers' Market (91)
Wide range of fresh carry-out food as well as regional products.
King Street, Hammersmith, W6; tel: 020 8392 0631; every Thu, 11am–3pm. www.weareccfm.com/hammersmith

PUBS

The George Inn ㉜
National Trust–owned former coaching terminus, with a striking 16th-century galleried courtyard.
Off Borough High Street, Southwark, SE1; tel: 020 7407 2056; open daily. www.nationaltrust.org.uk

The Market Porter ㉝
Busy Victorian pub, open very early on weekdays for Borough Market workers.
9 Stoney Street, London Bridge, SE1; tel: 020 7407 2495; open 6am–8:30am and 11am–11pm Mon–Fri, noon–11pm Sat, noon–10:30pm Sun. www.markettaverns.co.uk

The Holly Bush (79)
Little-changed Hampstead village local with old-fashioned rooms and alcoves.
22 Holly Mount, Hampstead, NW3; tel: 020 7435 2892; open noon–11pm Mon–Sat, noon–10:30pm Sun. www.hollybushpub.com

The Spaniards Inn (79)
Good food and a large garden at this former tollhouse on Hampstead Heath.
Spaniards Road, Hampstead, NW3; tel: 020 8731 8406; open noon–11pm Mon–Fri, 11am–11pm Sat–Sun. http://thespaniardshampstead.co.uk

The Cutty Sark Tavern (85)
Lovely old tavern offering a good range of food made from locally sourced ingredients.
4–6 Ballast Quay, Greenwich, SE10; tel: 020 8858 3146; open daily. www.cuttysarktavern.co.uk

The Dove (91)
William Turner painted from the riverside terrace of this 17th-century pub.
19 Upper Mall, Chiswick, W6; tel: 020 8748 9474; open daily.

Heathfield Farmers' Market ㊶
Market in a South Downs town in the heart of the Sussex Weald country.
Co-op parking lot, 110 High Street, Heathfield, East Sussex; tel: 01435 862798; third Sat of every month, 9am–12:30pm. www.heathfield.net/Farmers-Market

Ryde Farmers' Market (60)
Market recently set up to bring fresh, local produce to Isle of Wight customers and tourists alike.
Town Square, Ryde, Isle of Wight, Hampshire; every Sat, 8:30am–12:30pm. www.islandfarmersmarket.co.uk

Southsea Farmers' Market (63)
All featured produce is from Hampshire or within 10 miles (16 km) of its border.
Palmerston Road Precinct, Southsea, Hampshire; tel: 01420 588671; third Sun of every month, 10am–2pm. www.hampshirefarmersmarkets.co.uk

Andover Farmers' Market (74)
One of the 14 Hampshire Farmers' Market locations, with guaranteed local foods.
High Street, Andover, Hampshire; tel: 01420 588671; third Sun of every month, 10am–2pm. www.hampshirefarmersmarkets.co.uk

Hungerford Farmers' Market (80)
Fresh local food to sample, as well as the chance to chat with the suppliers.
High Street, Hungerford, Berkshire; tel: 01865 820159; fourth Sun of every month, 9am–1:30pm. www.tvfm.org.uk

Newbury Farmers' Market (81)
Most produce here is grown or made within 30 miles (48 km) of west Berkshire.
Market Place, Newbury, Berkshire; tel: 07501 580032; first and third Sun of every month, 9am–1pm. www.tvfm.org.uk

Woodstock Farmers' Market (89)
Popular market conveniently located for Oxford, Blenheim, and the Cotswolds.
By Town Hall, Woodstock, Oxfordshire; tel: 01295 276771; first Sat of every month, 8:30am–1pm. www.tvfm.org.uk

Chipping Norton Farmers' Market (90)
All produce here is sourced from within a 50-mile (80-km) radius.
Town centre, Chipping Norton, Oxfordshire; tel: 01295 276771; third Sat of every month, 8:30am–1pm. www.tvfm.org.uk

PUBS AND BARS

The Cricketers Arms ㊹
Classic South Downs village pub, with flint walls and traditional beamed and paneled interiors.
Berwick Village, East Sussex; tel: 01323 870469; open 11am–11pm Mon–Sat, noon–10:30pm Sun (closed 3pm–6pm Oct–Mar). www.cricketersberwick.co.uk

The Old Queens Head ⑦
Characterful 17th-century inn, carefully reinvented as a classy dining pub.
Hammersley Lane, Penn, High Wycombe, Buckinghamshire; tel: 01494 813371; open daily. www.oldqueensheadpenn.co.uk

The Harrow Inn ⑳
A civilized and friendly country-dining pub with an extensive range of food and an attractive garden terrace.
Common Road, Ightham Common, Kent; tel: 01732 885912; open noon–3pm and 6–11pm Tue–Sat, noon–3pm Sun.

The Royal Oak ㊼
Old-fashioned and welcoming pub, with beer from the cask and country food.
Wineham Lane, Wineham, Henfield, West Sussex; tel: 01444 881252; open 11am–2:30pm and 6–11pm Mon–Sat, noon–5pm and 7–10:30pm Sun.

The Harrow (54)
This 17th-century pub, tucked away in the Hampshire countryside, has changed very little over the centuries.
Harrow Lane, Steep, Hampshire; tel: 01730 262685; open noon–2:30pm and 6–11pm Mon–Fri, 11am–11pm Sat, noon–3pm and 7–10:30pm Sun (closed Sun evening late Sep–May).

The Anchor Bleu (57)
Harborside views from a cozy beamed old bar, which serves local fish dishes.
High Street, Bosham, West Sussex; tel: 01243 573956; open Mar–Oct: 11:30am–11pm daily; Nov–Feb: 11:30am–3pm and 6pm–11pm Mon–Thu, 11:30am–11pm Fri–Sun. www.bosham.org/anchor

The Three Horsehoes (77)
Cheerful local in the Surrey hills, owned by villagers; good walking country.
Dye House Road, Thursley, Surrey; tel: 01252 703268; open noon–3pm and 5–11pm daily. www.3hs.co.uk

The Bell (83)
Unspoiled village pub with simple food, in the same family for 200 years.
Bell Lane, Aldworth, Reading, Berkshire; tel: 01635 578272; open 11am–3pm and 6pm–11pm Tue–Sat, noon–3pm and 7–10:30pm Sun.

The Swan Inn (88)
Riverside Cotswold dining pub with a menu of imaginative contemporary food.
Swinbrook, nr Burford, Oxfordshire; tel: 01993 823339; open 11am–3pm and 6–11pm Mon–Fri, 11am–11pm Sat–Sun. www.theswanswinbrook.co.uk

The Falkland Arms (91)
Traditional thatched and ivy-hung pub and restaurant in an unspoiled estate village.
Great Tew, Chipping Norton, Oxfordshire; tel: 01608 683653; open 11:30am–3pm and 6–11pm Mon–Fri; 11:30–midnight Sat, noon–10:30pm Sun. www.falklandarms.org.uk

Above: Spectators at the Henley Royal Regatta

The Royal Oak ㉟
Romney Marsh inn mixing original features with modern design; good bar food.
High Street, Brookland, Kent; tel: 01797 334215; open noon–3pm and 6–11pm Tue–Sat, noon–3pm Sun–Mon. www.royaloakbrookland.co.uk

The Three Chimneys ㉝
A traditional country pub with beers and local hard cider served from the cask, and a reputation for great modern British food.
Hareplain Road, Biddenden, Kent; tel: 01580 291472; open 11:30am–3pm and 5:30–11pm Mon–Fri, 11:30am–4pm and 5:30–11pm Sat, noon–4pm and 6–10:30pm Sun. www.thethreechimneys.co.uk

PLACES TO STAY

The Five Arrows ②
A striking Victorian hotel, built by the Rothschild family for craftsmen working on Waddesdon Manor.
High Street, Waddesdon, Aylesbury, Buckinghamshire; tel: 01296 651727. www.thefivearrows.co.uk

Gravetye Manor ⑯
Luxurious hotel in an Elizabethan manor house on its own wooded estate.
Nr East Grinstead, West Sussex; tel: 01342 810567. www.gravetyemanor.co.uk

Cathedral Gate Hotel ㉕
A 15th-century building near Canterbury's cathedral; oak beams and sloping floors.
36 Burgate, Canterbury, Kent; tel: 01227 464381. www.cathgate.co.uk

The Royal Hotel ㉘
Nautical-themed beachside guesthouse, run by the Kent brewer Shepherd Neame.
Beach Street, Deal, Kent; tel: 01304 375555. www.theroyalhotel.com

Seaview Hotel (59)
Stylish waterside accommodation with the warm atmosphere of a genuine pub.
High Street, Seaview, Isle of Wight, Hampshire; tel: 01983 612711. www.seaviewhotel.co.uk

Elvey Farm ㉜
Quality accommodations and seasonal food on a medieval farm in rural Kent.
Elvey Lane, Pluckley, Kent; tel: 01233 840442. www.elveyfarm.co.uk

Jeakes House ㊲
A 17th-century building with cozy and comfortable rooms that commemorate local literary figures, such as Conrad Aiken.
Mermaid Street, Rye, East Sussex; tel: 01797 222828. www.jeakeshouse.com

Sandy Balls Holiday Centre (68)
Peaceful, long-established resort with New Forest cabins and outdoor activities.
Godshill, Fordingbridge, New Forest, Hampshire; tel: 01425 653042. www.sandy-balls.co.uk

The Peat Spade Inn (73)
A rural retreat with stylish rooms lying in the heart of the Test Valley, the fly-fishing capital of the world.
Village Street, Longstock, Stockbridge, Hampshire; tel: 01264 810612. www.peatspadeinn.co.uk

The Elephant (83)
Quirky hotel with an Indian/colonial theme throughout its individually styled rooms, and models of elephants everywhere.
Church Road, Pangbourne, Berkshire; tel: 0118 984 2244. www.elephanthotel.co.uk

The Kings Arms (89)
Sitting on the edge of the Cotswolds, this hotel is a stone's throw from Blenheim Palace, home of the Duke of Marlborough and birthplace of Winston Churchill.
19 Market Street, Woodstock, Oxfordshire; tel: 01993 813636. www.kings-hotel-woodstock.co.uk

FESTIVALS AND EVENTS

Henley Royal Regatta ⑩
Dressing up for this five-day festival of rowing is part of the "society calendar."
Henley-on-Thames, Oxfordshire; tel: 01491 572153; Jun–Jul. www.hrr.co.uk

South of England Show ⑰
Massive three-day annual showcase for agriculture, equestrianism, and countryside activities, with arena entertainments.
The South of England Centre, Ardingly, West Sussex; tel: 01444 892700; Jun. www.seas.org.uk

Winchester Hat Fair (72)
This long-running street festival is four days of outdoor events and art installations.
Various venues, Winchester, Hampshire; tel: 01962 849841; Jul. www.hatfair.co.uk

Didcot Railway Centre Steamdays (84)
Old steam locomotives from the former Great Western Railway in action.
Didcot, Oxfordshire; tel: 01235 817200; Jul–Aug: weekends; also some school holidays. www.didcotrailwaycentre.org.uk

Above: Legendary race car driver Sir Stirling Moss at the Goodwood Festival of Speed

Kent County Show ㉒
Kent's largest outdoor event, with country pursuits and forestry, food, and farming exhibits over three days.
Kent Showground, Detling, Maidstone, Kent; tel: 01622 630975; Jul. www.kentshowground.co.uk

Battle of Hastings Reenactment ㊴
A two-day annual event with living-history demonstrations, culminating in a reenactment of the famous battle of 1066 that changed English history.
Battle Abbey, Battle, East Sussex; tel: 01424 775705; Oct. www.english-heritage.org.uk/1066

Airbourne ㊷
Eastbourne's free international aerial fair is the world's largest seaside airshow, with 4 days of synchronized flying displays and historic aircraft to admire.
Seafront, Eastbourne, East Sussex; tel: 0871 663 0031; Aug. www.eastbourneairshow.com

Goodwood Festival of Speed (53)
World-renowned celebration of motor sports and classic vehicles over three days on the famous Goodwood circuit.
Goodwood House, Goodwood, Chichester, West Sussex; tel: 01243 755000; Jul (booking required). www.goodwood.co.uk

Chichester Festivities (56)
An eclectic summer festival that offers music, talks, comedy, exhibitions, and outdoor events over 17 days.
Various venues, Chichester, West Sussex; tel: 01243 785718; Jun–Jul. www.chifest.org.uk

Isle of Wight Walking Festival (61)
Over 300 walking trips for all tastes, from easy family rambles to ghost-hunting and dinosaur fossil walks.
Various venues, Isle of Wight, Hampshire; tel: 01983 823070; two weeks in May, plus a weekend in late Oct. www.isleofwightwalkingfestival.co.uk

New Forest and Hampshire Agricultural Show (66)
Three-day country show in the New Forest, with vintage farm machinery on display alongside livestock.
The Showground, New Park, Brockenhurst, Hampshire; tel: 01590 622400; Jul. www.newforestshow.co.uk

Grange Park Opera (75)
Classy opera festival, where performances take place over two months in a theater built in the grounds of a ruined mansion.
The Grange, nr New Alresford, Hampshire; tel: 01962 737366; Jun–Jul. www.grangeparkopera.co.uk

Surrey County Show (78)
One-day agricultural show bringing the country into the center of Guildford, including best-of-breed competitions and working dog trials.
Stoke Park, Guildford, Surrey; tel: 01483 890810; late May Bank Holiday Mon. www.surreycountyshow.co.uk

Royal County of Berkshire Show (82)
Two-day county agricultural show that ends with a mass hot-air balloon ascent.
Newbury Showground, Priors Court Road, Hermitage, Thatcham, Berkshire; tel: 01635 247111; Sep. www.newburyshow.co.uk

MUSEUMS AND GALLERIES

Bletchley Park National Codes Centre ①
A fascinating exploration of how those who worked here cracked wartime Nazi codes.
The Mansion, Bletchley Park, Milton Keynes, Buckinghamshire; tel: 01908 640404; open Apr–Oct: 9:30am–5pm Mon–Fri, 10:30am–5pm Sat–Sun; Nov–Mar: 10:30am–4pm daily. www.bletchleypark.org.uk

Chiltern Open Air Museum ⑥
Working Victorian farm featuring endangered old buildings that have been saved and reerected here.
Newland Park, Gorelands Lane, Chalfont St. Giles, Buckinghamshire; tel: 01494 872163; open 10am–5pm daily. www.coam.org.uk

Brooklands Museum ⑭
Vintage race cars and planes displayed around this 1930s racing circuit.
Brooklands Road, Weybridge, Surrey; tel: 01932 857381; open Apr–Oct: 10am–5pm daily; Nov–Mar: 10am–4pm daily. www.brooklandsmuseum.com

Rochester Guildhall Museum ㉑
Fine 17th-century building, with displays on local history and exhibits relating to Charles Dickens, who lived nearby.
High Street, Rochester, Kent; tel: 01634 848717; open 10am–4:30pm Tue–Sun. www.medway.gov.uk/tourism

Towner Art Gallery ㊷
A striking new gallery of modern and contemporary art, opened in 2009.
Devonshire Park, College Road, Eastbourne, East Sussex; tel: 01323 434660; open 10am–6pm Tue–Sun. www.eastbourne.gov.uk/leisure/museums–galleries/towner

How We Lived Then Museum of Shops ㊷
A quirky personal collection that recreates old shops with thousands of nostalgic products.
20 Cornfield Terrace, Eastbourne, East Sussex; tel: 01323 737143; open daily from 10am; closing times vary according to season. www.sussexmuseums.co.uk

Weald and Downland Open Air Museum (53)
Rescued and relocated old local buildings, with farm animals and craftspeople.
Singleton, Chichester, West Sussex; tel: 01243 811363; open Jan–Feb: 10:30am–4pm Wed, Sat and Sun; Feb–Mar and Nov–Dec: 10:30am–4pm daily; Apr–Oct: 10am–6pm daily. www.wealddown.co.uk

Pallant House Gallery (56)
A Queen Anne town house housing a collection of 20th-century British art.
9 North Pallant, Chichester, West Sussex; tel: 01243 774557; open 10am–5pm Tue–Wed and Fri–Sat, 10am–8pm Thu, 12:30pm–5pm Sun. www.pallant.org.uk

Tunbridge Wells Museum ⑲
Includes costumes, toys, and the decorative wooden boxes known as Tunbridge Ware.
Civic Centre, Mount Pleasant, Royal Tunbridge Wells, Kent; tel: 01892 554171; open 9:30am–5pm Mon–Sat, 10am–4pm Sun. www.tunbridgewellsmuseum.org

Hastings Museum and Art Gallery ㊳
Richly eclectic collection including displays on distinguished Hastings residents, such as John Logie Baird, inventor of television.
Johns Place, Bohemia Road, Hastings, East Sussex; tel: 01424 451052; open Apr–Sep: 10am–5pm Mon–Sat, 11am–5pm Sun; Oct–Mar: 10am–4pm Mon–Fri, 11am–4pm Sat–Sun. www.hmag.org.uk

Shipwreck and Coastal Heritage Centre ㊳
Seafront museum telling the story of how local shipwrecks are being explored.
Rock-a-Nore Road, Hastings, East Sussex; tel: 01424 437452; open Apr–Oct: 10am–5pm daily; Nov–Mar: 11am–4pm varying days. www.shipwreck-heritage.org.uk

Petworth House (51)
The National Trust's finest art collection, including works by Turner and Van Dyck.
Petworth, West Sussex; tel: 01798 342207; open Mar–Oct: 11am–5pm Sat–Wed. www.nationaltrust.org.uk

Tangmere Military Aviation Museum (55)
A great collection of aircraft memorabilia, based around a former RAF station.
Tangmere Road, Tangmere, West Sussex; tel: 01243 790090; open Mar–Oct: 10am–5:30pm daily; Feb and Nov: 10am–4:30pm daily. www.tangmere-museum.org.uk

National Motor Museum (65)
Over 250 vehicles from every motoring era, plus motorcycles and a 1930s garage reconstruction.
Beaulieu, Brockenhurst, Hampshire; tel: 01590 612345; open 10am–6pm daily. www.beaulieu.co.uk

Christ Church Picture Gallery (86)
An important 18th-century collection of old masters in one of Oxford's grandest university colleges.
Christ Church College, Oxford; tel: 01865 276492; open 9am–5pm Mon–Sat, 2pm–5pm Sun. www.chch.ox.ac.uk

THINGS TO DO WITH KIDS

Roald Dahl Museum and Story Centre ⑤
Fun-filled interactive galleries that commemorate the great storyteller and promote creative writing.
81–83 High Street, Great Missenden, Buckinghamshire; tel: 01494 892192; open 10am–5pm Tue–Fri, 11am–5pm Sat–Sun. www.roalddahlmuseum.org

Bekonscot Model Village ⑧
Enchanting miniature landscape with six 1930s villages linked by a model railroad.
Warwick Road, Beaconsfield, Buckinghamshire; tel: 01494 672919; open mid-Feb–Oct: 10am–5pm daily. www.bekonscot.com

Ashdown Forest Centre ⑱
"Winnie the Pooh" country; the forest is perfect for picnics and children's games.
Wych Cross, Forest Row, East Sussex; tel: 01342 823583; open Apr–Sep: 2–5pm Mon–Fri, 11am–5pm Sat–Sun; Oct–Mar: 11am–4pm Sat–Sun. www.ashdownforest.org

Diggerland ㉑
Kids over 5 can ride on – and even drive – real dump trucks and giant diggers.
Roman Way, Medway Valley Leisure Park, Strood, Kent; tel: 0871 227 7007; open mid-Feb–Oct: 10am–5pm Sat–Sun and daily during school holidays (except Christmas). www.diggerland.com

Museum of Canterbury with Rupert Bear Museum ㉕
Family-focused museum, with well-loved children's characters and activities including a medieval discovery gallery.
Stour Street, Canterbury, Kent; tel: 01227 475202; open 11am–4pm Mon–Sat (and Jun–Sep: 1:30–4pm Sun). www.canterbury.gov.uk

Kent and East Sussex Railway ㉞
Take a vintage train ride on this rural light railroad, and end up exploring medieval Bodiam Castle.
Tenterden Town Station, Station Road, Tenterden, Kent; tel: 01580 765155; timetables vary, see website for details. www.kesr.org.uk

Observatory Science Centre ㊵
Astronomy demonstrations and giant outdoor interactive exhibits at a world-famous observatory, home to six historical telescopes that the public can try out
Herstmonceux, East Sussex; tel: 01323 832731; open Feb–Mar and Oct–Nov: 10am–5pm daily; Apr–Sep: 10am–6pm daily. www.the-observatory.org

Drusillas Park ㊸
Thoroughly child-friendly zoo and park where visitors can interact with a large variety of animals up close; there is also a huge adventure playground.
Alfriston, East Sussex; tel: 01323 874100; open Apr–Oct: 10am–5pm daily; Nov–Mar: 10am–4pm daily. www.drusillas.co.uk

Fort Nelson ⑥④
Napoleonic-era fort with underground tunnels to explore, and huge cannons fired daily. *Portsdown Hill Road, Fareham, Hampshire; tel: 01329 233734; open Apr–Oct: 10am–5pm Thu–Tue, 11am–5pm Wed; Nov–Mar: 10:30am–4pm Thu–Tue, 11:30am–4pm Wed. www.royalarmouries.org/visit-us/fort-nelson*

Camber Sands ㊱
A vast, safe, sandy seashore, backed by dunes, excellent for a family day out; a cycle path runs here from Rye.
Nr Rye, East Sussex. www.camber.east-sussex.co.uk

Chichester Harbour Water Tours ㊿⑧
Cruise Chichester Harbour in a former lifeboat, and see the yachts and wildfowl.
12 The Parade, East Wittering, West Sussex; tel: 01243 670504; times vary, see website for up-to-date timetables. www.chichesterharbourwatertours.co.uk

Marwell Wildlife ⑦⓪
Rolling parkland where animals roam in huge enclosures; evening safaris and accommodations are also on offer.
Thompsons Lane, Colden Common, Winchester, Hampshire; tel: 01962 777407; open from 10am daily, closed from 4pm to 6pm depending on season. www.marwell.org.uk

Winchester Cathedral ⑦②
An imaginative children's program includes free tours around the cathedral, workshops, and summer-vacation activities.
The Close, Winchester, Hampshire; tel: 01962 857224; open 8:30am–6pm Mon–Sat, 8:30am–5:30pm Sun; activity times vary. www.winchester-cathedral.org.uk/education

Below: Camber Sands

Port Lympne Wild Animal Park ㉚
Zebras, giraffes, and wildebeest in a vast park, where visitors can enjoy evening and overnight safaris.
Lympne, nr Hythe, Kent; tel: 01303 264647; open Apr–Oct: 10am–6pm daily; Nov–Mar: 10am–5pm daily. www.totallywild.net

SPAS AND RESORTS

Hartwell House and Spa ③
Seventeenth-century country-house hotel, with an elegant spa building modeled on an orangery.
Oxford Road, Aylesbury, Buckinghamshire; tel: 01296 746500. www.hartwell-house.com

Donnington Valley Hotel ⑧①
A contemporary hotel with an affordable spa offering a range of treatments, plus access to an 18-hole private golf course.
Old Oxford Road, Donnington, Newbury, Berkshire; tel: 01635 551199. www.donningtonvalley.co.uk

Vineyard Hotel and Spa ⑧①
Pampering with Balinese massage and chocolate-, wine- and truffle-themed treatments, as well as gourmet food at a Michelin-starred restaurant.
The Vineyard at Stockcross, Stockcross, Newbury, Berkshire; tel: 01635 528770. www.the-vineyard.co.uk

Pennyhill Park Hotel and The Spa ⑬
Super-spacious and relaxing luxury spa with eight indoor and outdoor pools.
London Road, Bagshot, Surrey; tel: 01276 486100. www.thespa.uk.com

Ashdown Park Hotel and Country Club ⑱
Victorian Gothic hotel in its own parkland, with an 18-hole golf course and a spa.
Wych Cross, Forest Row, East Sussex; tel: 01342 820254. www.ashdownpark.com

Tor Spa Retreat ㉖
Indian-inspired, down-to-earth spa emphasizing healthy vegetarian food and Ayurvedic treatments.
Ickham, Canterbury, Kent; tel: 01227 728500. www.torsparetreat.com

Bailiffscourt Hotel & Health Spa ㊾
Spacious, airy spa in an oak-framed building with an outdoor pool.
Climping, West Sussex; tel: 01903 723511. www.hshotels.co.uk

Aquila Health Spa ㊾②
Scandinavian-style spa in the grounds of a historic coaching inn; good value.
Spread Eagle Hotel, South Street, Midhurst, West Sussex; tel: 01730 816911. www.hshotels.co.uk

New Park Manor Hotel's Bath House Spa ⑥⑥
Old country manor with a spa, outdoor hot tub, and forest views.
Lyndhurst Road, Brockenhurst, Hampshire; tel: 01590 624964. www.newparkmanorhotel.co.uk

SenSpa at Careys Manor ⑥⑥
Hotel near the New Forest with an extensive Thai-themed spa, ice room, and large hydrotherapy pool.
Careys Manor Hotel, Brockenhurst, Hampshire; tel: 01590 624467. www.senspa.co.uk

Chewton Glen Hotel & Spa ⑥⑦
Country-house luxury spa resort near the New Forest and the coast.
New Milton, Hampshire; tel: 01425 275341. www.chewtonglen.com/spa

Grayshott Spa ⑦⑦
Country-house health spa that offers fitness programs alongside natural spa treatments.
Headley Road, Grayshott, Hindhead, Surrey; tel: 01428 602020. www.grayshottspa.com

OTHER SIGHTS IN THE BOOK

Red Kites, the Chilterns ⑨ *(see pp126–7).* **Windsor** ⑫ *(see pp122–3).* **Broadstairs** ㉗ *(see pp70–71).* **Dover Castle** ㉙ *(see pp16–17).* **Lewes** ㊺ *(see pp136–7).* **Brighton** ㊻ *(see pp36–7).* **Arundel** ㊿ *(see pp90–91).* **Cowes Week, Isle of Wight** ⑥② *(see pp64–5).* **Portsmouth** ⑥③ *(see pp186–7).* **New Forest** ⑥⑨ *(see pp146–7).* **Alresford** ⑦⑥ *(see pp24–5).* **Oxford** ⑧⑥ *(see pp52–3).*

SOUTHWEST ENGLAND

The Old Butcher's ①
Friendly, modern brasserie that serves modern cuisine using local ingredients. *Park Street, Stow on the Wold, Cheltenham, Gloucestershire; tel: 01451 831700; open noon–3:30pm and 6–9:15pm Mon–Sat (until 9:45pm Sat), noon–3:30pm and 7–9pm Sun. www.theoldbutchers.com*

Stroud Market ⑥
Popular multi-award-winning market with up to 60 regular and guest stands. *Cornhill Market Place, Stroud, Gloucestershire; tel: 01453 758060; every Sat, 9am–2pm.*

The Rectory Kitchen and Cellar ⑦
Add-on to an acclaimed hotel, selling local, seasonal, and sustainable foods. *2 Templar Mews, Black Jack Street, Cirencester, Gloucestershire; tel: 01285 644700; open 9am–5:15pm Mon–Sat. www.therectoryhotel.com*

Swindon Market ⑫
Highly regarded market with tastings of seasonal and local products. *Swindon Designer Outlet, Kemble Road, Swindon, Wiltshire; tel: 01453 758060; every Sun, 10am–4pm. www.fresh-n-local.co.uk*

Riverstation ⑭
A contemporary riverside restaurant with stylish but informal à la carte dining. *The Grove, Bristol; tel: 0117 914 4434; open noon–2:30pm and 6–11pm Mon–Sat, noon–3pm and 6–9pm Sun. www.riverstation.co.uk*

Wednesday Market ⑭
An award-winning market in Bristol, offering local honey, cheeses, and fruit. *Corn Street and Wine Street, Bristol; tel: 0117 922 4016; every Wed, 9:30am–2:30pm. www.bristol.gov.uk*

Bath Market ⑮
An established market, priding itself on sustainability and fresh, seasonal produce. *Green Park Station, Green Park Road, Bath; tel: 01761 490624; every Sat, 8:30am–1:30pm. www.bathfarmersmarket.co.uk*

Sally Lunn's Refreshment House and Museum ⑮
The oldest house in Bath and home to the original Bath Bun. Too famous to miss. *Sally Lunn's House, 4 North Parade Passage, Bath; tel: 01225 461634; open 10am–10pm Mon–Sat, 11am–6pm Sun. www.sallylunns.co.uk*

Britford Farm Shop ㉒
Award-winning shop in sight of Salisbury Cathedral selling first-rate local food. *Bridge Farm, Britford, Salisbury, Wiltshire; tel: 01722 413400; open 8am–6pm Mon–Sat, 10am–4pm Sun. www.britfordfarmshop.co.uk*

Pitney Farm Shop ㉝
Award-winning organic food, such as specialty sausages from local pigs. *Glebe Farm, Woodsbirdshill Lane, Pitney, Langport, Somerset; tel: 01458 253002; open 9am–5:30pm Mon–Tue and Thu–Sat. www.pitneyfarmshop.co.uk*

Museum Inn ㊳
Fabulous local foods, such as game from neighboring estates; luxury rooms too. *Farnham, Dorset; tel: 01725 516261; open noon–3pm and 6–11pm Mon–Sat, noon–3pm and 7–10:30pm Sun. www.museuminn.co.uk*

Crab House Café ㊽
Beachside wooden shack serving varied and inventive seafood and farmed oysters. *Ferryman's Way, Portland Road, Wyke Regis, Dorset; tel: 01305 788867; open noon–2pm and 6–9pm Wed–Thu; noon–2:30pm and 6–9:30pm Fri–Sat; noon–3:30pm Sun. www.crabhousecafe.co.uk*

Bakery at Lacock ⑱
Highly tempting and picturesque bakery; bread is made on the premises. *8 Church Street, Lacock, Chippenham, Wiltshire; tel: 01249 730457; open 10am–5pm daily.*

Wells Market ㉚
An all-year market with weekly variations of sellers and produce. *The Market Place, Wells, Somerset; tel: 01458 83080; every Wed, 9am–2:30pm. www.somersetfarmersmarket.co.uk*

Newton Abbot Market ㊿③
This central market has a reputation for quality and variety. *Courtenay Street, Newton Abbot, Devon; tel: 01626 25426; every Tue, 9am–3pm. www.teignbridge.gov.uk*

Truro Market ㊼①
County-town market with heaps of delicious local temptations. *The Piazza, Lemon Quay, Truro, Cornwall; tel: 01326 376244; every Sat, 8:30am–4pm. www.visitcornwall.com*

Lizard Pasty Shop ㊀⑦
Anne Mullen's famous pasties, freshly made. Don't visit late, as they often sell out. *Beacon Terrace, The Lizard, Helston, Cornwall; tel: 01326 290889; open 10am–3pm Tue–Sat.*

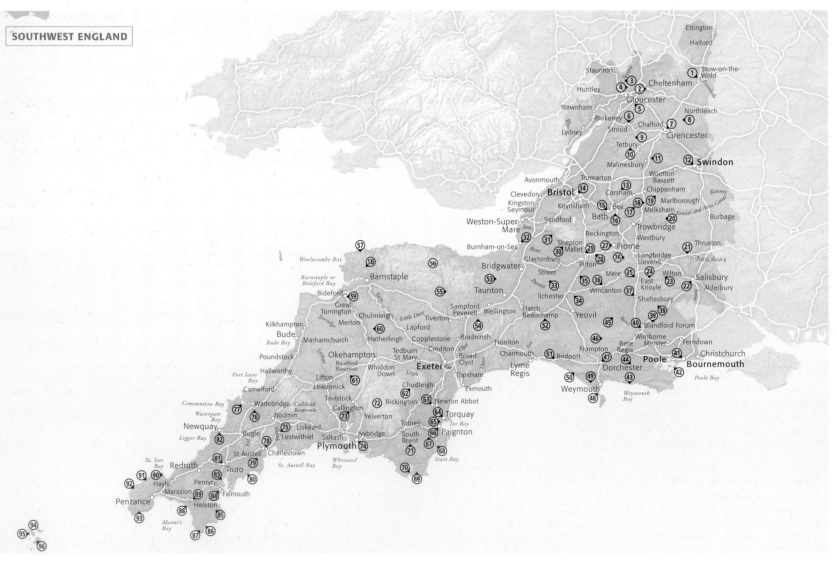

SOUTHWEST ENGLAND

New Angel (68)
Locally sourced ingredients are key at this top-notch Anglo-French-style restaurant.
2 South Embankment, Dartmouth, Devon; tel: 01803 839425; open 9–11am, noon–2:30pm and 6:30pm–9:30pm Tue–Sat. www.thenewangel.co.uk

South Devon Chilli Farm (71)
Thousands of chili pepper varieties and extensive growing information.
Wigford Cross, Loddiswell, Devon; tel: 01548 550782; open 10–4pm daily (closed Sat–Sun between Christmas and Easter). www.southdevonchillifarm.co.uk

Relish Food and Drink (76)
Popular deli and café with lovely staff and a passion for Cornish organic food.
Foundry Court, Wadebridge, Cornwall; tel: 01208 814214; open 9am–5pm Mon–Sat. www.relishwadebridge.co.uk

Lobbs Farm Shop (79)
Cornish cheeses, including nettle yarg and Heligan Slab, and other delights such as hog's pudding and saffron cake.
Heligan, St. Ewe, St. Austell, Cornwall; tel: 01726 844411; open Mar–Sep: 9:30am–5:30pm Mon–Sat, 10:30am–4:30pm Sun; Oct–Dec: 9:30am–5pm Mon–Sat, 10:30am–4.30pm Sun, Jan–Feb: 9:30am–5pm Mon–Sat. www.lobbsfarmshop.com

Quayside Fish (88)
Selling from Newlyn's sustainable catches only; voted Best British Fishmonger.
The Harbourside, Porthleven, Cornwall; tel: 01326 562008; open 9am–5pm Tue–Fri, 9am–1pm Sat. www.quaysidefish.co.uk

C3 Restaurant (89)
A welcoming café-bistro that serves traditional food with a contemporary twist.
3 Coinagehall Street, Helston, Cornwall; tel: 01326 565633; open Jun–Oct: 10am–5pm Mon–Sat; Nov–May: 10am–3pm and 6–9pm Thu–Sat.

Porthminster Beach Café (90)
Serves the freshest seafood direct from sea to plate in a stunning beach location.
Porthminster Beach, St. Ives, Cornwall; tel: 01736 795352; open noon–4pm and 6–10pm daily. www.porthminstercafe.co.uk

FARMERS' MARKETS

Cirencester Farmers' Market ⑦
Independently run market, selling treats such as Old Spot organic sausages.
Market Place, Cirencester, Gloucestershire; tel: 01453 834777; second and fourth Sat of every month, 9am–1pm.

Wincanton Farmers' Market ㊱
Indoor market with huge variety, from bison meat to peppers; parking available.
The Memorial Hall, High Street, Wincanton, Somerset; tel: 01458 830801; first Fri of every month, 9am–1pm.

Stow on the Wold Farmers' Market ①
Trout from nearby lakes and locally reared meats are offered at this Cotswold market in a picture-postcard town.
Market Square, Stow on the Wold, Gloucestershire; tel: 01453 758060; second Thu of every month, 9am–1pm. www.fresh-n-local.co.uk

Cheltenham Farmers' Market ②
Products on 40 stands include handmade Scotch eggs and charcuterie at this award-winning market.
The Promenade, Cheltenham, Gloucestershire; tel: 01608 652556; second and fourth Fri of every month, 9am–3pm. www.cheltenham.gov.uk

Devizes Farmers' Market ⑳
Outdoor market with a great range of locally produced fresh and seasonal foods.
Market Place, Devizes, Wiltshire; tel: 07775 614790; first Sat of every month, 9am–1:30pm. www.local-farmers-markets.co.uk

Frome Farmers' Market ㉗
One of Somerset's largest markets, with 30 stands and nearby parking.
Market Yard, Frome, Somerset; tel: 01373 455420; second and fourth Sat of every month, 9am–1pm. www.somersetfarmersmarkets.co.uk

Blandford Farmers' Market ⑩
Heaps of local food including handmade fishcakes and Dorset Blue Vinney cheese.
Market Place, Blandford Forum, Dorset; tel: 01258 454510; every second Fri, 9am–1:30pm. www.dorsetfarmersmarkets.co.uk

Poundbury Farmers' Market ㊼
Large market selling some of Dorset's best local products.
Brownsword Hall and Pummery Square, Poundbury, Dorchester, Dorset; tel: 01258 454510; first Sat of every month, 9am–1pm. www.dorsetfarmersmarkets.co.uk

Bridport Farmers' Market (51)
Award-winning market where British celebrity chef Hugh Fearnley-Whittingstall often sells produce from River Cottage.
The Arts Centre, South Street, Bridport, Dorset; tel: 01258 454510; second Sat of every month, 9am–1pm. www.dorsetfarmersmarkets.co.uk

Ilfracombe Farmers' Market (57)
Wide range of products including dairy, fish, meats, and preserves.
The Lantern Centre, Ilfracombe, Devon; second and fourth Sun of every month, 10am–12:30pm. www.discoverdevon.com

St. Mary's Farmers' Market (96)
Selection of fresh local foods, including shellfish, preserves, and dairy products.
Town Hall or on Holgates Green (depending on weather), St. Mary's, Isles of Scilly; tel: 01720 424355; first Thu of every month, 10am–2pm.

Above: Floating pontoon at the Pandora Inn

Plymouth Farmers' Market (74)
Central market selling ostrich meat, strawberries, vegetables, cheeses, and pies.
The Piazza, Plymouth, Devon; tel: 01752 306551; second and fourth Sat of every month, 9am–4:30pm.

Lostwithiel Farmers' Market (75)
All produce comes from within a 35-mile (56-km) radius of the town.
Community Centre, Lostwithiel, Cornwall; tel: 01840 250586; every other Fri, 10am–3pm. www.cgos.co.uk

Helston Farmers' Market (89)
Organic eggs, pasties, and herbs are among the local products on offer here.
Cattle Market Building, Boating Lake, Helston, Cornwall; tel: 01209 61406; first Sat of every month, 9:30am–1:30pm.

PUBS

The Boat ③
Delightful riverside pub that has belonged to the same family for 350 years.
Ashleworth Quay, Gloucestershire; tel: 01452 700272; open 11:30am–2:30pm and 6:30–11pm Tue–Fri, (6:30–11pm only Wed), 11:30am–3pm and 6:30–11pm Sat, noon–3pm and 7–10:30pm Sun. http://boatinn.wordpress.com

The Weighbridge Inn ⑨
Stylish pub serving "2-in-1" pies (half filling of your choice, half cauliflower and cheese).
Longfords, Minchinhampton, Gloucestershire; tel: 01453 832520; open daily. www.2in1pub.co.uk

The Gumstool Inn ⑩
Imaginative food in a traditional pub, sibling of the grander Calcot Manor Hotel.
Calcot Manor Hotel, Tetbury, Gloucestershire; tel: 01666 890391; open daily. www.calcotmanor.co.uk

The George Inn ⑱
Busy, child-friendly pub with lots of cozy corners in a National Trust village.
4 West Street, Lacock, Chippenham, Wiltshire; tel: 01249 730263; open daily.

The Fox and Hounds ㉕
Pretty pub offering fabulous views of Blackmore Vale, an imaginative menu, and good beers.
The Green, East Knoyle, Wiltshire; tel: 01747 830573; open daily. www.foxandhounds-eastknoyle.co.uk

The Half Moon Inn ㊲
Large edge-of-town pub, with helpful staff and more than decent food.
Salisbury Road, Shaftesbury, Dorset; tel: 01747 852456; open daily.

The Brace of Pheasants ㊻
Smart old thatched village pub with excellent food in lovely walking country.
Plush, Dorset; tel: 01300 348357; open noon–3pm and 7–11pm Tue–Sat, 7–10:30pm Sun. www.braceofpheasants.co.uk

The Lord Poulett (52)
Idyllic inn serving tasty food, and boasting lovely views and a *petanque* piste.
Hinton St. George, Somerset; tel: 01460 73149; open noon–3pm and 6:30–11pm daily. www.lordpoulettarms.com

The Culm Valley Inn (54)
"Olde worlde" appeal and good food in a charmingly scruffy pub that originally served as a railroad house.
Culmstock, Tiverton, Devon; tel: 01884 840354; open noon–3pm and 6:30–11pm Mon–Sat, noon–3pm and 7–10:30pm Sun.

Woods (55)
Very Exmoor – stuffed animals, hunting prints, and wood-burning stoves, as well as great food and drink.
4 Bank Square, Dulverton, nr Minehead, Somerset; tel: 01398 323366; open daily.

The Duke of York (60)
A rare find – a proper pub, simply furnished, friendly, and unspoiled, offering homey food.
Iddesleigh, Winkleigh, Devon; tel: 01837 810253; open daily.

The Millbrook Inn (69)
Tiny, historic creekside pub in an idyllic village setting.
South Pool, Kingsbridge, Devon; tel: 01548 531581; open daily. www.millbrookinnsouthpool.co.uk

The Pandora Inn (83)
Gorgeous waterside setting and tables on a floating pontoon – one of Cornwall's most endearing inns.
Restronget, Mylor Bridge, Falmouth, Cornwall; tel: 01326 372678; open daily. www.pandorainn.com

Cadgwith Cove Inn (86)
An unfussy, old-fashioned inn with a great atmosphere and good, straightforward food on the menu.
Cadgwith, nr Helston, Cornwall; tel: 01326 291018; open daily. www.cadgwithcoveinn.com

PLACES TO STAY

Thirty Two ②
Exclusive boutique hotel overlooking a garden square near the center of town. *32 Imperial Square, Cheltenham, Gloucestershire; tel: 01242 771110. www.thirtytwoltd.com*

Bibury Court Hotel ⑧
Jacobean mansion with four-poster beds and an award-winning restaurant menu. *Bibury, Gloucestershire; tel: 01285 740337. www.biburycourt.co.uk*

The Catherine Wheel ⑬
Friendly B&B and inn in a splendid building located in a quiet village near Bath. *High Street, Marshfield, Chippenham, Wiltshire; tel: 01225 892220. www.thecatherinewheel.co.uk*

The Pear Tree ⑰
Lovely rustic-chic farmhouse hotel offering inventive food sourced from local suppliers. *Top Lane, Whitley, Melksham, Wiltshire; tel: 01225 709131. www.maypolehotels.com*

Baverstock Manor ㉓
Age-old graceful B&B complete with bags of character, creaky floorboards, and antique furnishings. *Dinton, Salisbury, Wiltshire; tel: 01722 716206.*

The Lamb at Hindon ㉔
Gorgeous inn providing country elegance, comfort, and good food. *High Street, Hindon, Salisbury, Wiltshire; tel: 01747 820573. www.lambathindon.co.uk*

Burnham High Lighthouse ㉜
Accommodations (no meals) located in a Victorian lighthouse dating from 1830, with round rooms and 120 steps. *Berrow Road, Burnham on Sea, Somerset; tel: 07970 983245. www.lighthouseholiday.com*

The Pilgrims at Lovington ㉟
Lovely individual rooms at a popular dining pub just off the Roman Fosse Way. *Pilgrims Way, Lovington, Somerset; tel: 01963 240600. www.thepilgrimsatlovington.co.uk*

Plumber Manor ㊺
Dreamy hotel in the hands of the Prideaux-Brunes family for 400 years. *Sturminster Newton, Dorset; tel: 01258 472507. www.plumbermanor.com*

Broomhill Art Hotel and Sculpture Park ㊾
Quirky hotel with an art gallery and 300 sculptures in lovely wooded grounds. *Muddiford, Barnstaple, Devon; tel: 01271 850262. www.broomhillart.co.uk*

Riverside House ㊻
Riverbank B&B and vacation apartments with beautiful views. *Tuckenhay, Totnes, Devon; tel: 01803 732837.*

Above: Great Dorset Steam Fair

Moonfleet Manor ㊾
Faded but still glorious, magical, and child-friendly hotel behind the Fleet lagoon in a sleepy coastal backwater. *Fleet, Weymouth, Dorset; tel: 01305 786948. www.moonfleetmanorhotel.co.uk*

Lewtrenchard Manor ㉛
Numerous awards confirm this Jacobean manor's hotel and restaurant credentials. *Lewdown, nr Okehampton, Devon; tel: 01566 783222. www.lewtrenchard.co.uk*

The Lugger Hotel ⑧⓪
The sea laps at the feet of this cute hotel, with small but sumptuous rooms, a spa, and excellent cream teas. *Portloe, Truro, Cornwall; tel: 01872 501322. www.luggerhotel.co.uk*

The Hen House ⑧⑤
B&B or apartment retreat for green enthusiasts or for those craving peace. *Tregarne, Manaccan, Helston, Cornwall; tel: 01326 280236. www.thehenhouse-cornwall.co.uk*

The Gurnard's Head ⑨①
Sophisticated inn in a coastal setting; comfortable bedrooms, fabulous food. *Treen, Zennor, St. Ives, Cornwall; tel: 01736 796928. www.gurnardshead.co.uk*

Flying Boat Club ⑨⑤
New-England-style accommodations at an island World War II "flying-boat" base. *Bryher, Scilly Isles; tel: 01720 422200. www.scillyislandbreak.co.uk*

FESTIVALS AND EVENTS

Salisbury International Arts Festival ㉒
Two weeks of music, dance, theater, film, photography, literature, and much more. *Salisbury, Wiltshire; tel: 01722 332977; late May–early Jun. www.salisburyfestival.co.uk*

Cheltenham Festival Of Literature ②
The world's oldest literature festival is held here over two weeks in fall. *Various venues, Cheltenham, Gloucestershire; tel: 0844 765 7979; Oct. www.cheltenhamfestivals.com/literature*

Cheese Rolling ⑤
Open to all, this demented tussle sends vast Double Gloucesters down a steep hill. *Cooper's Hill, Brockworth, Gloucestershire; usually second May Bank Holiday Monday. www.cheese-rolling.co.uk*

Cotswold Show ⑦
A weekend of arena performances, family entertainment, and country pursuits. *Cirencester Park, Cirencester, Gloucestershire; tel: 01285 652007; early Jul. www.cotswoldshow.co.uk*

WOMAD Festival ⑪
Scores of acts on stage at this three-day melting-pot of amazing world music. *Charleton Park, Malmesbury, Wiltshire; tel: 0845 146 1735; late Jul. www.womad.org/festivals*

Bath International Music Festival ⑮
Seventeen days of music, from classical to contemporary *(see pp84–5)*. *Various venues in and around Bath; tel: 01225 462231; late May–early Jun. www.bathmusicfest.org.uk*

Great Dorset Steam Fair ㊴
Largest event of its kind in western Europe, displaying plenty of puff over five days in early fall. *Tarrant Hinton, between Salisbury and Blandford, Dorset; tel: 01258 860361; early Sep. www.gdsf.co.uk*

Stock Gaylard Oak Fair ㊺
A day celebrating the wonders of wood, with crafts, demonstrations, and stands. *Stock Gaylard Estate, Sturminster Newton, Dorset; tel: 01963 23511; Aug. www.stockgaylard.com*

Widecombe Fair ㊽
A day of Devon delights, such as sheep-shearing and tug-of-war, suitable for everyone, "Uncle Tom Cobley and all". *Widecombe-in-the-Moor, Newton Abbot, Devon; second Tue in Sep. www.widecombe-in-the-moor.com*

Royal Cornwall Show ㊀⑥
The county's biggest annual agricultural event, held over three days. *Wadebridge Showground, Wadebridge, Cornwall; tel: 01208 812183; Jun. www.royalcornwallshow.org*

Minack Theatre Performances ⑨③
Spectacular open-air theater above crashing waves. There are both evening and matinee performances in summer. *Porthcurno, Penzance, Cornwall; tel: 01736 810181; open for day visitors 9:30am–5pm Sat–Tue and Thu, 9:30–11:30am Wed and Fri; theater performances Apr–Sep, times vary. www.minack.com*

Royal Bath and West Show ㉙
From Pimm's to tractors, a huge, traditional, and varied four-day show. *Shepton Mallet, Somerset; tel: 01749 822200; June. www.bathandwest.com*

Agatha Christie Week ㊺⑤
A week-long celebration of the "Queen of Crime," timed to coincide with her birthday. *Torbay, Devon; tel: 01803 211211; mid-Sep. www.englishriviera.co.uk/agathachristie*

'Obby 'Oss Day ㊀⑦
Boisterous Celtic celebration to welcome in May with singing and dancing. *Padstow, Cornwall; tel: 01841 533449; noon–late, 1 May.*

World Pilot Gig Championships ⑨⑥
Four days of colorful and energetic races in traditional wooden boats *(see pp50–51)*. *St. Mary's, Scilly Isles; tel: 01720 422000; May. www.worldgigs.co.uk*

MUSEUMS AND GALLERIES

Cheltenham Art Gallery and Museum ②
Displays of the 19th-century Arts and Crafts movement in all its glory. *Clarence Street, Cheltenham, Gloucestershire, tel: 01242 237431; open 10am–5:20pm Mon–Sat (closed Bank Holiday Mondays). www.artsandcraftsmuseum.org.uk*

Nature In Art ④
Unique museum and gallery dedicated to artistic inspiration from nature. *Wallsworth Hall, Sandhurst Lane, Sandhurst, Gloucestershire; tel: 01452 731422; open 10am–5pm Tue–Sun and Bank Holiday Mondays. www.nature-in-art.org.uk*

American Museum ⑯
American history, culture, and decorative arts in a beautiful Neo-Classical manor. *Claverton Manor, Claverton, Bath; tel: 01225 460503; open 14 Mar–1 Nov: noon–5pm Tue–Sun (Bank Holiday Mondays and Aug: noon–5pm daily). www.americanmuseum.org*

Salisbury and South Wiltshire Museum ㉒
Gallery covering Stonehenge and the nearby Neolithic settlement of Old Sarum. *The King's House, 65 The Close, Salisbury, Wiltshire; tel: 01722 332151; open 10am–5pm Mon–Sat; Jul–Aug: also open noon–5pm Sun. www.salisburymuseum.org.uk*

Russell Cotes Art Gallery and Museum ㊶
Renaissance-style baronial house, crammed with treasures and notable art. *Russell Cotes Road, East Cliff, Bournemouth, Dorset; tel: 01202 451858; open 10am–5pm Tue–Sun and Bank Holiday Mondays. www.russell-cotes.bournemouth.gov.uk*

Fleet Air Arm Museum ㉞
Centre of naval aviation history, with Concorde and an aircraft carrier to explore.
HMS Heron, Royal Naval Air Station, Yeovilton, Yeovil, Somerset; tel: 01935 840565; open Apr 6–Oct 31: 10am–5:30pm daily (last admission 4pm); Nov 1–March 31: 10am–4:30pm daily (last admission 3pm). www.fleetairarm.com

Tank Museum ㊹
Rides in a tracked vehicle, trenches and an extensive collection of tanks.
Bovington, Dorset; tel: 01929 405096; open 10am–5pm daily. www.tankmuseum.org

Torquay Museum (64)
From Agatha Christie to insects; a museum ranked among the finest in the southwest.
529 Babbacombe Road, Torquay, Devon; tel: 01803 293975; open 10am–5pm Mon–Sat (last entry 4pm); mid-Jul–Sep: also open 1:30pm–5pm Sun. www.torquaymuseum.org

Morwellham Heritage Centre (73)
A living-history industrial museum in the heart of the Cornwall and West Devon Mining Landscape World Heritage Site.
Morwellham Quay, nr Tavistock, Devon; tel: 01822 832766; open Mar–Sep: 10am–5:30pm daily; Oct–Feb: times vary. www.morwellham-quay.co.uk

Charlestown Shipwreck And Heritage Centre (78)
Fascinating collection of shipwreck artifacts and maritime history, the largest of its kind in Europe.
Quay Road, Charlestown, St. Austell, Cornwall; tel: 01726 69897; open Mar 1–Nov 1: 10am–5pm daily. www.shipwreckcharlestown.com

Tate St. Ives (90)
Internationally renowned exhibitions of contemporary art, plus talks, music, workshops, and fabulous views.
Porthmeor Beach, St. Ives, Cornwall; tel: 01736 796226; open Mar–Oct: 10am–5:20pm daily; Nov–Feb: 10am–4:20pm Tue–Sun. www.tate.org.uk/stives

Geevor Tin Mine (92)
Centuries of mining history brought to life in tours of underground tunnels, with collections of rocks, minerals, and tools.
Pendeen, Penzance, Cornwall; tel: 01736 788662; open 9am–5pm Sun–Fri; Jul–Aug: also open 9am–5pm Sat. .www.geevor.com

THINGS TO DO WITH KIDS

Flambards (89)
One of Cornwall's most-visited attractions boasts a theme park with a variety of rides, events, and attractions, as well as living-history exhibits and beautiful gardens.
Helston, Cornwall; tel: 01326 573404; open school summer vacation: 10:15am–5:45pm; times vary outside school summer vacation – please check before visiting. www.flambards.co.uk

Goonhilly Earth Station (89)
Operate a satellite dish, watch the world on webcams, and email an alien at an activity center that's out of this world.
Helston, Cornwall; tel: 0800 679593; open Easter–Oct: 10am–5pm (until 6pm during school summer holidays). www.goonhilly.bt.com

Bowood House Adventure Playground ⑲
An acclaimed playground that features a life-size pirate galleon and a large collection of slides and walkways.
Derry Hill, Calne, Wiltshire; tel: 01249 812102; house open 11am–5:30pm daily; playground open Apr–Nov: 11am–6pm daily. www.bowood-house.co.uk

Longleat Safari Park ㉖
Drive-through attraction – made famous on the BBC's *Animal Park* – with lions, tigers, wolves, vultures, and much more.
Nr Warminster, Wiltshire; tel: 01985 844400; open Apr–Oct: 10am–4pm Mon–Fri, 10am–5pm Sat–Sun (also open until 5pm Bank Holiday Mondays and school holidays). www.longleat.co.uk

East Somerset Railway ㉘
Steam railroad that offers special themed events, such as steam galas and "Thomas the Tank Engine" rides for kids.
Cranmore Railway Station, Cranmore, Shepton Mallet, Somerset; tel: 01749 880417; see website for train timetables. www.eastsomersetrailway.com

Oceanarium ㊶
The wonders of the deep, including an underwater tunnel, sharks, and piranhas.
Pier Approach, West Beach, Bournemouth, Dorset; tel: 01202 311993; open 10am–7pm daily (last admission 6pm). www.oceanarium.co.uk

Cheddar Caves and Gorge ㉛
World-famous attraction with stunning sights and walks – enough to keep you busy for a whole day.
Cheddar, Somerset; tel: 01934 742343; open 10am–5pm daily (until 5:30pm during school vacations). www.cheddarcaves.co.uk

Abbotsbury Swannery ㊿
Unique swan colony with fluffy cygnets (hatching time mid-May–late June), mass feedings, and a willow maze.
New Barn Road, Abbotsbury, nr Weymouth, Dorset; tel: 01305 871858; open Mar–Nov: from 10am daily, closing times vary, visit website for more details. www.abbotsbury-tourism.co.uk

Big Sheep (59)
Pony rides, mini-tractors, and lamb-feeding add to the fun at this all-weather attraction which focuses on traditional sheep-rearing.
Abbotsham, Bideford, Devon; tel: 01237 472366; open Apr–Oct: 10am–6pm daily; Nov–Mar: 10am–6pm Sat–Sun. www.thebigsheep.co.uk

Paignton Zoo (66)
Celebrated zoo, home to thousands of amazing and exotic animals and plants; the crocodile swamp is a must-see.
Totnes Road, Paignton, Devon; tel: 01803 697500; open 10am–6pm daily. www.paigntonzoo.org.uk

SPAS AND HEALTH RESORTS

Relaxation Centre ⑭
Central spa offering holistic treatments, a meditation garden, and a flotation room.
9 All Saints Road, Clifton, Bristol; tel: 0117 970 6616; open 10am–9pm Sun–Thu, 9am–10pm Fri–Sat. www.relaxationcentre.co.uk

Below: Lioness at Longleat Safari Park

Chase Hotel Spa ⑤
Four-star hotel-spa offering dozens of ways to relax and be pampered.
Shurdington Road, Brockworth, Gloucestershire; tel: 01452 519988. www.qhotels.co.uk

Bath House Spa at The Royal Crescent ⑮
Extensive spa with a pool, plunge tubs, sauna, gym, and holistic therapies.
The Royal Crescent Hotel, 16 Royal Crescent, Bath; tel: 01225 823333. www.royalcrescent.co.uk

Combe Grove Manor ⑯
Hotel spa overlooking beautiful Claverton Down woodland just outside Bath.
Monkton Combe, nr Bath; tel: 01225 834644. www.barcelo-hotels.co.uk

Bowood Hotel and Spa ⑲
Up-to-the-minute spa in brand-new country-chic hotel on the Bowood Estate.
Derry Hill, Calne, Wiltshire; tel: 01249 823883. www.bowood.org

Haven Hotel ㊷
Award-winning hotel and spa with uninterrupted views of Poole Harbour.
Sandbanks, Poole, Dorset; tel: 01202 707323. www.fjbhotels.co.uk

Cedar Falls Health Farm (53)
Hotel spa and center for natural beauty; perfect for a relaxing weekend.
Bishop's Lydeard, Taunton, Somerset; tel: 01823 433233. www.cedarfalls.co.uk

Imperial Hotel (64)
Five-star luxury: the latest gym technology, expert advice, and professional treatments.
Park Hill Road, Torquay, Devon; tel: 01803 294301. www.barcelo-hotels.co.uk

Lorrens Ladies' Health Hydro (64)
A women-only retreat offering slimming and sculpting treatments, day-long specials, and relaxation packages.
Cary Park, Babbacombe, Torquay, Devon; tel: 01803 329 994. www.lorrens-health-hydro.co.uk

Carlyon Bay Hotel Spa (79)
Sanctuary in a dramatic setting on the Cornwall coast, with modern facilities.
Sea Road, St. Austell, Cornwall; tel: 01726 812304. www.brend-hotels.co.uk

St. Michael's Hotel And Spa (84)
Top coastal spa with subtropical gardens close to the beach.
Gyllyngrase Beach, Falmouth, Cornwall; tel: 01326 312707. www.stmichaelshotel.co.uk

OTHER SIGHTS IN THE BOOK

Bristol ⑭ *(see pp82–3).* **Bath** ⑮ *(see pp84–5).* **Stonehenge** ㉑ *(see pp166–7).* **Lulworth Ranges** ㊸ *(see pp94–5).* **Exmoor** (56) *(see pp98–9).* **Salcombe** (70) *(see pp78–9).* **Dartmoor** (72) *(see pp178–9).* **North Cornwall** (82) *(see pp150–51).* **Isles of Scilly** (94) *(see pp50–51).*

Index

Page numbers in **bold** indicate main references

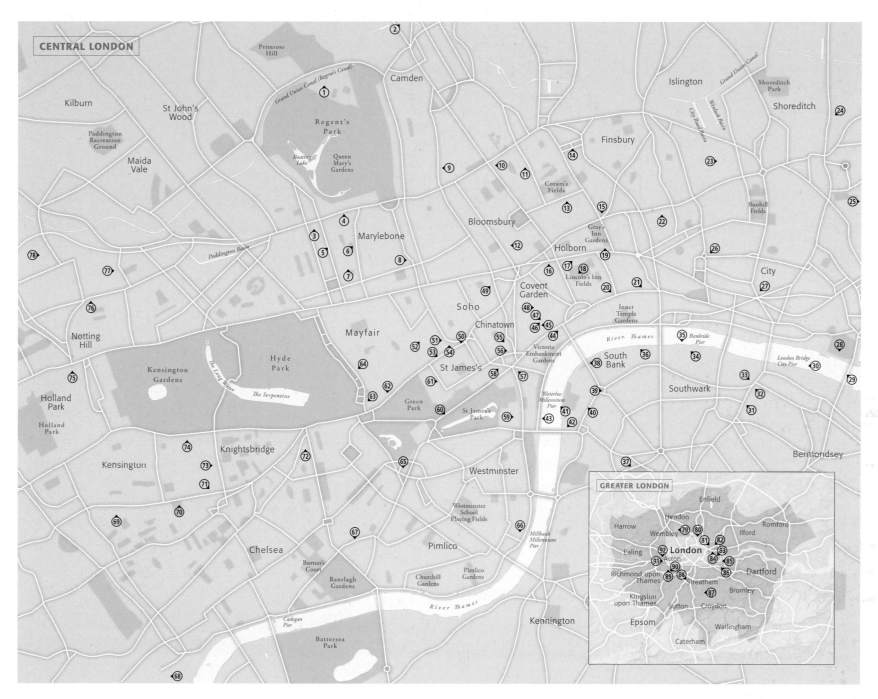

CENTRAL LONDON

GREATER LONDON

The Lamb ⑬
Full of Victorian character, with original etched glass screens and traditional tables.
94 Lamb's Conduit Street, Camden, WC1; tel: 020 7405 0713; open noon–11pm Mon–Wed, noon–midnight Thu–Fri, 11am–midnight Sat, noon–10:30pm Sun. www.youngs.co.uk

Cittie of York ⑲
Bustling City pub with a high-beamed roof and three bar areas, with cozy booths off the back bar.
22 High Holborn, Holborn, WC1; tel: 020 7242 7670; open 11:30am–11pm Mon–Fri, noon–11pm Sat.

The Grapes ⑧⑷
Welcoming 18th-century inn in Docklands with a waterside balcony and a fish restaurant upstairs with river views.
76 Narrow Street, Tower Hamlets, E14; tel: 020 7987 4396; open noon–3:30pm and 5:30–11pm Mon–Fri, noon–11pm Sat, noon–10:30pm Sun.

The Princess Louise ⑯
Friendly, beautifully restored Victorian "gin palace" with mirrors and engraved glass.
208 High Holborn, Camden, WC1; tel: 020 7405 8816; open daily.

Old Bank of England ⑳
Grand conversion of a former bank, with chandeliers and a courtyard; good pies.
194 Fleet Street, City, EC4; tel: 020 7430 2255; open 11am–11pm Mon–Fri. www.fullers.co.uk

The Olde Cheshire Cheese ㉑
Engaging warren of little-changed 17th-century rooms, and good-value beer.
145 Fleet Street, City, EC4; tel: 020 7353 6170; open daily.

The Jerusalem Tavern ㉒
Eighteenth-century atmosphere and beers from Suffolk brewery St. Peters.
55 Britton Street, Clerkenwell, EC1; tel: 020 7490 4281; open 11am–11pm Mon–Fri. www.stpetersbrewery.co.uk/london

The Greenwich Union ⑧⑸
Distinctive pub serving European-style beers produced by a small local brewery.
56 Royal Hill, Greenwich, SE10; tel: 020 8692 6258; open noon–11pm Mon–Fri, 11am–11pm Sat, 11:30am–10:30pm Sun. www.greenwichunion.com

PLACES TO STAY

Ambassadors Bloomsbury Hotel ⑩
Crisply contemporary rooms in Bloomsbury, very central and well-positioned for the British Museum.
12 Upper Woburn Place, Camden, WC1; tel: 020 7693 5400. www.ambassadors.co.uk

Northumberland House ㊹
Inexpensive but stylish student residences available over the summer vacation.
Edward VII Rooms, 8a Northumberland Avenue, Westminster, WC2; tel: 020 7107 5603; open Jul–Sep only. www.lsevacations.co.uk/residences/northumberland.htm

22 York Street ③
Enjoy delicious breakfasts round a curved antique table in this elegant and friendly bed and breakfast.
22 York Street, Marylebone, W1; tel: 020 7224 2990. www.22yorkstreet.co.uk

The Langham ⑧
Recently refurbished grand Victorian hotel; have tea in the famous Palm Court.
1c Portland Place, Regent Street, W1; tel: 020 7636 1000. www.london.langhamhotels.co.uk

Athenaeum Hotel and Apartments ㊽
Luxury accommodations in a distinctive hotel with exterior vertical "wall garden."
116 Piccadilly, Mayfair, W1; tel: 020 7499 3464. www.athenaeumhotel.com

Miller's Residence ㊅
Antiques and exotic memorabilia fill this romantic hideaway in Notting Hill.
111a Westbourne Grove, Kensington, W2; tel: 020 7243 1024. www.millershotel.com

Above: Costumed street performer at the Notting Hill Carnival

St. Christopher's Inn (31)
Three well-located backpackers' hostels, one with its own traditional English pub, close to London Bridge.
161–165 Borough High Street, Southwark, SE1; tel: 020 7407 1856.
www.st-christophers.co.uk

London Marriott Hotel County Hall (42)
Fantastic central location right on the river by the London Eye and South Bank, in stately ex–London council headquarters.
Westminster Bridge Road, Southwark, SE1; tel: 020 7928 5200.
www.marriott.co.uk

The Trafalgar Hotel (58)
Handsome old building refurbished as a contemporary hotel with a rooftop garden overlooking Trafalgar Square.
2 Spring Gardens, Trafalgar Square, SW1; tel: 020 7870 2900.
www.thetrafalgar.com

The Goring Hotel (65)
Traditional English elegance near Buckingham Palace; run by the same family since 1910.
15 Beeston Place, Westminster, SW1; tel: 020 7396 9000. www.thegoring.com

Searcy's Roof Garden Bedrooms (72)
Charming rooftop bed-and-breakfast rooms in a country-house styled building near Harrods and Hyde Park.
30 Pavilion Road, Knightsbridge, SW1; tel: 020 7584 4921.
www.30pavilionroad.co.uk

St. James Club and Hotel (61)
Elegantly restored London town house in a secluded location; excellently placed for high-end shopping.
7–8 Park Place, St. James's, SW1; 020 7316 1600. www.stjamesclubandhotel.co.uk

Wyndham Grand, London Chelsea Harbour (68)
London's only all-suite hotel, with spectacular marina views.
Chelsea Harbour, SW10; tel: 020 7823 3000. www.wyndhamgrandlondon.co.uk

base2stay Hotel Kensington (69)
Stylish and good-value rooms, each with a small kitchenette with a sink, microwave, and refrigerator.
25 Courtfield Gardens, Kensington, SW5; tel: 020 7244 2255.
www.base2stay.com

FESTIVALS AND EVENTS

Pride London (5)
Colorful parade day celebrating gay culture and Pride's two-week festival.
Baker Street to Trafalgar Square, W1; tel: 0844 884 2439; Sat, early Jul.
www.pridelondon.org

The Thames Festival (35)
Weekend gala of floating and bankside fun with river pageants and rallies by day, and carnival, fireworks, and dancing by night.
Thames-side, Westminster Bridge to Tower Bridge and beyond, Sep.
www.thamesfestival.org

Lord Mayor's Show (27)
A 3-mile- (5-km-) long procession celebrating the city's newly elected mayor. The day ends with a fireworks display.
Between Bank and Aldwych; mid-Nov.
www.lordmayorsshow.org

London Film Festival (38)
A two-week feast of new films from around the world.
BFI, South Bank, SE1 and other venues; tel: 020 7928 3232; mid-Oct.
www.bfi.org.uk/lff

Royal Academy Summer Exhibition (53)
The world's largest open-submission contemporary art show, running over eight weeks or more.
Royal Academy of Arts, Burlington House, Piccadilly, W1; tel: 0844 209 1919; Jun–Aug. www.royalacademy.org.uk

Trooping the Colour (60)
Pageantry between Buckingham Palace and Whitehall, marking the monarch's official birthday.
The Mall, W1; 10am–noon, second Sat in Jun (rehearsals on the two previous Sats).
www.trooping-the-colour.co.uk

The Boat Race (90)
Spectators crowd the river banks in the start point at Putney Bridge for the annual rowing contest between boats from Oxford and Cambridge universities.
Between Putney and Mortlake, west London; held annually on a Saturday in Mar or Apr. www.theboatrace.org **The**

Proms (74)
Famous eight-week music festival featuring informal concerts, all with inexpensive standing ("prom") tickets available. "Last Night" tickets are hard to obtain, but this concert is relayed on giant outdoor screens to cheerful crowds in Hyde Park.
Royal Albert Hall, Kensington Gore, SW7; tel: 0845 401 5040; nightly, mid-Jul–mid-Sep. www.bbc.co.uk/proms

Notting Hill Carnival (78)
Europe's largest street festival; three days of Caribbean-inspired music and spectacle.
Notting Hill, W11; tel: 020 7727 0072; Aug Bank Holiday weekend.
www.nottinghillcarnival.biz

Kenwood House (79)
Outdoor picnic concerts in summer in the grounds of historic Kenwood House.
Kenwood House, Hampstead Lane, NW3; tel: 0845 658 6960; various dates, Jun–Aug. www.picnicconcerts.com

MUSEUMS AND GALLERIES

Wallace Collection (7)
Fine-art collection and exquisite interiors: feels like a small French palace.
Hertford House, Manchester Square, W1; tel: 020 7563 9500; open 10am–5pm daily. www.wallacecollection.org

British Museum (12)
The grandest and oldest museum of all, with treasures and artifacts from every corner of the globe.
Great Russell Street, Bloomsbury, WC1; tel: 020 7323 8299; open 10am–5:30pm Sat–Wed, 10am–8:30pm Thu–Fri.
www.britishmuseum.org

Sir John Soane's Museum (18)
Architect's early-19th-century home crammed with an eccentric collection of antiquities and artworks, just as he left it.
13 Lincoln's Inn Fields, Camden, WC2; tel: 020 7405 2107; open 10am–5pm Tue–Sat. www.soane.org

Geffrye Museum (24)
Gem of a museum, reconstructing domestic interiors from different eras.
Kingsland Road, E2; tel: 020 7739 9893; open 10am–5pm Tue–Sat, noon–5pm Sun and Bank Holiday Mondays.
www.geffrye-museum.org.uk

Victoria and Albert Museum (70)
Vast, sumptuous collection of art, architecture, craftsmanship, and design.
Cromwell Road, Kensington, SW7; tel: 020 7942 2000; open 10am–5:45pm Sat–Thu, 10am–10pm Fri. www.vam.ac.uk

National Maritime Museum (85)
Greenwich's flagship museum, setting out Britain's history as a maritime power. The grounds also house the Royal Observatory, with more displays, planetarium shows, and sky-watching evenings.
Romney Road, Greenwich, SE10; tel: 020 8858 4422; open 10am–5pm daily.
www.nmm.ac.uk

Museum of London ㉖
Explore the city of London's development from prehistoric times to the modern day.
London Wall, City, EC2; tel: 020 7001 9844; open 10am–6pm daily. www.museumoflondon.org.uk

Tate Modern ㉞
Modern art on show in a cavernous former Thames-side power station.
Bankside, Southwark, SE1; tel: 020 7887 8888; open 10am–6pm Sun–Thu, 10am–10pm Fri–Sat. www.tate.org.uk

Imperial War Museum ㊲
Absorbing museum exploring Britain at war, with displays of tanks and guns.
Lambeth Road, SE1; tel: 020 7416 5000; open 10am–6pm daily. www.iwm.org.uk

National Portrait Gallery (55)
Famous figures through British history, as portrayed by artists and photographers.
Trafalgar Square, WC2; tel: 020 7306 0055; open 10am–6pm Sun–Thu, 10am–9pm Fri–Sat. www.npg.org.uk

National Gallery (56)
Magnificent European art collection, from medieval works to French Impressionism.
Trafalgar Square, WC2; tel: 020 7747 2885; open 10am–6pm Sat–Thu, 10am–9pm Fri. www.nationalgallery.org.uk

Tate Britain (66)
British artists from 1500 to the present, including Turner and the pre-Raphaelites.
Millbank, Westminster, SW1; tel: 020 7887 8888; open 10am–5:50pm daily. www.tate.org.uk/britain

Museum of London Docklands (84)
Engaging displays in an old waterside warehouse revealing London's fascinating history as a port.
No 1 Warehouse, West India Quay, E14; tel: 020 7001 9844; open 10am–6pm daily. www.museumindocklands.org.uk

THINGS TO DO WITH KIDS

London Zoo ①
Penguins, giraffes, big cats, reptiles, and all manner of other wildlife living on the edge of Regent's Park.
Outer Circle, Regent's Park, NW1; tel: 020 7722 3333; open Oct–Feb: 10am–4pm daily; Mar–Nov: 10am–5:30pm daily. www.zsl.org

London Transport Museum ㊼
From old London buses to Underground trains, posters, models, and toys.
Covent Garden Piazza, Covent Garden, WC2; tel: 020 7379 6344; open 10am–6pm Sat–Thu, 11am–6pm Fri. www.ltmuseum.co.uk

Museum of Childhood (81)
Absorbing collection of children's games and toys from the 17th century to the present day.
Cambridge Heath Road, Tower Hamlets, E2; tel: 020 8983 5200; open 10am–5:45pm daily. www.vam.ac.uk/moc

Walker's Quay canal trips ②
Circular sightseeing canal trips with commentary from Camden Lock to Little Venice and back, passing London Zoo.
250 Camden High Street, Camden, NW1; tel: 020 7485 4433; cruise timetables vary throughout the year, check website for details. www.walkersquay.com

Madame Tussauds ④
Famous names from history, politics, sports, and entertainment recreated in an eerily lifelike form in this waxwork museum.
Marylebone Road, Westminster, NW1; tel: 0870 999 0046; open 9:30am–5:30pm Mon–Fri, 9am–6pm Sat–Sun, school holidays and most Bank Holiday Mondays. www.madametussauds.com

Tower of London ㉘
Real dungeons, medieval weapons, and tales of executions to thrill the bloodthirsty; also home to the Crown Jewels.
Tower Hill, Tower Hamlets, EC3; tel: 0844 482 7777; open Mar–Oct: 9am–5:30pm Tue–Sat, 10am–5:30pm Sun–Mon; Nov–Feb: 9am–4:30pm Tue–Sat, 10am–4:30pm Sun–Mon. www.hrp.org.uk/toweroflondon

Tower Bridge ㉙
Walk high along this famous bridge, close to the Tower of London, which raises to allow river traffic to pass through.
Tower Bridge Road, Bermondsey, SE1; tel: 020 7403 3761; open Apr–Sep: 10am–6:30pm daily; Oct–Mar: 9:30am–6pm daily. www.towerbridge.org.uk

HMS Belfast ㉚
A real 1938 warship that had significant roles in both World War II and the Korean War, moored near Tower Bridge.
Morgan's Lane, Tooley Street, Southwark, SE1; tel: 020 7940 6300; open Mar–Oct: 10am–6pm daily; Nov–Feb: 10am–5pm daily. http://hmsbelfast.iwm.org.uk

Below: Tate Modern

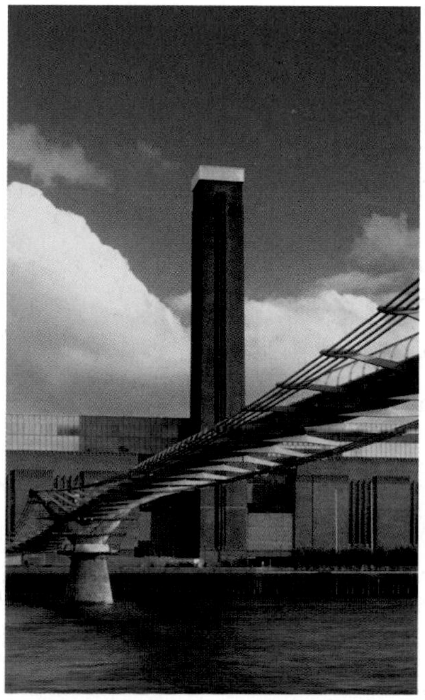

BFI IMAX ㊴
Astounding movie theater with a screen nearly as tall as five double-decker buses.
1 Charlie Chaplin Walk, South Bank, Waterloo, SE1; tel: 0870 787 2525; bookings 10:30am–7:30pm daily; program times vary. www.bfi.org.uk

London Duck Tours ㊵
A tour with a big surprise: the amphibious vehicle takes a sightseeing route on land before driving straight into the Thames.
55 York Road, Lambeth, SE1; tel: 020 7928 3132; tours 10am–dusk daily, according to demand. www.londonducktours.co.uk

London Eye ㊶
Riverside "ferris wheel" giving a bird's-eye view of the river and city.
Riverside Building, County Hall, Westminster Bridge Road, SE1; tel: 0870 5000 600; open May–Sep: 10am–9pm daily; Oct–Apr: 10am–8pm daily. www.londoneye.com

Thames River Services ㊸
Take a river trip past London's old docks to visit Greenwich.
Westminster Pier, Embankment, SW1; tel: 020 7930 4097; Apr–Oct: boats run half-hourly between 10am and 4pm; Nov–Mar: boats run every 40 minutes from 10:40am to 3:20pm. www.thamesriverservices.co.uk

Cabinet War Rooms (59)
Churchill's World War II headquarters beneath Whitehall.
Clive Steps, King Charles Street, Westminster, SW1; tel: 020 7930 6961; open 9:30am–6pm daily. http://cwr.iwm.org.uk

Natural History Museum (71)
An amazing range of natural-history exhibits set in beautiful Victorian halls, including a spectacular dinosaur gallery.
Cromwell Road, Kensington, SW7; tel: 020 7942 5000; open 10am–5:50pm daily. www.nhm.ac.uk

Science Museum (73)
The history and future of science explored in impressive exhibits and activities.
Exhibition Rd, Kensington, SW7; tel: 0870 870 4868; open 10am–6pm daily. www.sciencemuseum.org.uk

Crystal Palace Park (87)
Victorian park with terrific views and life-size dinosaur figures on a lake.
Upper Norwood, Crystal Palace, SE19; tel: 020 8778 9496; open 7:30am–dusk daily. www.crystalpalacepark.org

SPAS AND HEALTH RESORTS

Spa London (81)
Bethnal Green's former Turkish baths, now offering affordable steam and sauna rooms with concessions.
York Hall Leisure Centre, Old Ford Rd, Bethnal Green, E2; tel: 020 8709 5845; open 10am–9:30pm Mon–Fri, 9am–7:30pm Sat–Sun. www.spa-london.org

The Rosebery Rooms ⑮
Intimate and good value; best for express treatments rather than lounging.
168 Clerkenwell Road, Islington, EC1; tel: 020 7833 3820; open 10am–8pm Mon–Fri, 10am–6pm Sat. www.roseberyrooms.com

Spa at Chancery Court ⑰
Offers a luxurious circular relaxation room and holistic Asian-inspired therapies.
252 High Holborn, Holborn, WC1; tel: 020 7829 7058; open 9am–9pm daily. www.spachancerycourt.co.uk

Ironmonger Row Baths ㉓
Victorian Turkish baths with a 100-ft (30-m) swimming pool; affordable and inclusive.
Ironmonger Row, Islington, EC1; tel: 020 7253 4011; open 2–9:30pm Mon, 9am–9:30pm Tue–Fri, 9:30am–6pm Sat, 10am–6:30pm Sun (most sessions are single-sex only; check before visiting). www.aquaterra.org/ironmonger-row-baths

The Sanctuary ㊽
Famous women-only retreat, including two swimming pools festooned with lush plants, offering a variety of spa treatments.
12 Floral St, Covent Garden, WC2; tel: 01442 430330; open 9:30am–6pm Mon–Tue, 9:30am–10pm Wed–Fri, 9:30am–8pm Sat–Sun (booking advised). www.thesanctuary.co.uk

Spa at Brown's (52)
Three luxurious, soothingly decorated private treatment rooms.
Brown's Hotel, Albemarle St, Mayfair, W1; tel: 020 7518 4009; open 9:30am–8pm daily. www.brownshotel.com

Spa Intercontinental (63)
Five elliptical therapy rooms make for a private environment, with striking decor and a "steam temple."
First floor, 1 Hamilton Place, Mayfair, W1; tel: 020 7318 8691; open 9am–9pm Mon–Sat, 10am–6pm Sun. www.spaintercontinental.com

Dorchester Hotel Spa (64)
Full-on 1930s glamour, cocktails and rose-tinted mirrors in a relaxed spa.
The Dorchester Hotel, Park Lane, W1; tel: 020 7319 7109; open 7am–9pm Mon–Sat, 8am–9pm Sun. www.thedorchester.com/dorchester-spa

The Porchester Spa (77)
Turkish baths with original features from 1929 and a sizable swimming pool.
The Porchester Centre, Queensway, W1; tel: 020 7792 3980; open 10am–10pm daily. www.courtneys.co.uk/centres/Porchester/the-porchester-spa

Shymala Ayurveda (92)
A little piece of India inside a west London town house, offering Ayurvedic treatments.
152 Holland Park Avenue, Kensington, W11; tel: 020 7348 0018; open daily by appointment only. www.shymalaayurveda.com

SOUTHEAST ENGLAND

LOCAL FOOD

Rumsey's Chocolaterie (4)
Coffee shop inspired by the film *Chocolat* and serving handmade local chocolates.
Rumsey's of Wendover, The Old Bank, High Street, Wendover, Buckinghamshire; tel: 01296 625060; open 8:30am–6:30pm Mon–Sat, 10am–6pm Sun. www.rumseys.co.uk

The Greene Oak (12)
Gastropub where both the decor and the menu blend traditional British cuisine with French country style.
Dedworth Road, Windsor, Berkshire; tel: 01753 864294; food served noon–2:30pm and 6:30–9:30pm Mon–Sat, noon–4pm Sun. www.thegreeneoak.co.uk

Denbies Wine Estate (15)
There are all-year wine-making displays, with "vineyard train" tours from spring to October, two restaurants, and a shop.
London Road, Dorking, Surrey; tel: 01306 876616; open 9:30am–5pm Mon–Sat, 11:30am–5pm Sun. www.denbiesvineyard.co.uk

National Collection of Cider and Perry (44)
A vast range of ciders to sample, and a shop, restaurant, and 625-acre (250-hectare) working farm.
Middle Farm, Firle, Lewes, East Sussex; tel: 01323 811411; open 9:30am–5:30pm daily. www.middlefarm.com

English's Seafood Restaurant and Oyster Bar (46)
Celebrated old restaurant near Brighton's Lanes, featuring locally caught seafood.
29–31 East Street, Brighton, East Sussex; tel: 01273 327980; open noon–10pm Mon–Sat, 12:30–9:30pm Sun. www.englishs.co.uk

Nutbourne Vineyards (48)
Walk among lakes and vineyards, and sample wines in an historic windmill.
Gay Street, nr Pulborough, West Sussex; tel: 01798 815196; open May–Oct: 2–5pm Mon–Fri, 11am–5pm Sat–Sun. www.nutbournevineyards.com

The Old Customs House (63)
Spacious gastropub in a historic Georgian waterfront building, good for breakfasts and coffees as well as enjoyable traditional dishes and real ales.
Gunwharf Quays, Portsmouth; tel: 02392 832333; food served noon–8pm daily. www.theoldcustomshouse.com

Brogdale Farm (23)
Pay a visit to the National Fruit Collection and take in orchard tours, the apple-themed tearoom, and the farm shop.
Brogdale Road, Faversham, Kent; tel: 01795 536250; open Apr–Oct: 10am–5pm daily; Nov–Mar: 10am–4:30pm daily. www.brogdalecollections.co.uk

Macknade Fine Foods (23)
Enterprising farm-shop complex and delicatessen blending Kentish heritage with Italian gastronomy.
Faversham Flagship Foodhall, Selling Road, Faversham, Kent; tel: 01795 534497; open 9am–6pm Mon–Sat, 10am–4pm Sun. www.macknade.com

Whitstable Oyster Company (24)
Oysters harvested offshore are served in the company's beachside fish restaurant.
The Royal Native Oyster Stores, Horsebridge, Whitstable, Kent; tel: 01227 276856; open noon–2:30pm and 6:30–9pm Tue–Thu, 8:30am–2:30pm and 6:30–9:30pm Sat, 8:30am–3:30pm and 6:30–8:30pm Sun. www.oysterfishery.co.uk

Wykeham Arms (72)
Find classic pub dishes and sophisticated sandwiches at this quirky old city inn; some seating is at Victorian school desks from nearby Winchester College.
75 Kingsgate Street, Winchester, Hampshire; tel: 01962 853834; food served noon–2:30pm and 7–9pm Mon–Sat, 12:30–2:30pm Sun. www.fullershotels.com

Hog's Back Brewery (79)
An independent brewery, housed in 18th-century barns; weekend and evening tours (booking required).
Manor Farm, The Street, Tongham, Surrey; tel: 01252 783000; open 9am–6pm Mon–Tue and Sat, 9am–8:30pm Wed–Fri, 10am–4:30pm Sun. www.hogsback.co.uk

Kimbridge on the Test (71)
Farm shop and restaurant on a fishing estate where you can sample or catch trout.
Kimbridge, Romsey, Hampshire; tel: 01794 340777; open 10am–4:30pm Mon–Sat, 11am–4pm Sun. www.kimbridgeonthetest.com

Cobbs Farm Shop and Kitchen (80)
Fruit farm with farm shop, butcher, baker, fishmonger, and licensed restaurant.
Bath Road, Hungerford, Berkshire; tel: 01488 686770; open 8:30am–7pm daily. www.cobbsfarmshop.co.uk

Millets Farm Centre (85)
A farm shop, delicatessen, bakery, and restaurants with pick-your-own in season.
Kingston Road, Frilford, Abingdon, Oxfordshire; tel: 01865 392200; open 9am–6pm daily (restaurant till 5pm). www.milletsfarmcentre.com

Browns Bar & Brasserie Oxford (86)
Colonial-style restaurant, popular for breakfast, afternoon tea, or cocktails, as well as good modern British dining.
5–11 Woodstock Road, Oxford; tel: 01865 511995; open 9:30am–11pm Mon–Thu, 9:30am–11:30pm Sat, 9:30am–10:30pm Sun. www.browns-restaurants.co.uk

Foxbury Farm Butchery and Farm Shop (87)
Beef, lamb, and pork reared on the farm, and home-baked pies.
Burford Road, Brize Norton, Oxfordshire; tel: 01993 844141; open 9am–5pm Tue, 9am–6pm Wed–Sat, 10am–2pm Sun. www.foxburyfarm.co.uk

FARMERS' MARKETS

Maidenhead Farmers' Market (11)
Berkshire's longest-running farmers' market, with its own loyalty program.
Grove Road parking lot, Maidenhead, Berkshire; tel: 01628 670272; second Sun of every month, 10am–1pm. www.greenlink-berkshire.org.uk

Windsor Farmers' Market (12)
A wide range of food is offered, a short walk from the center of town.
St. Leonard's Road, Windsor, Berkshire; tel: 01865 820159; first Sat of every month, 9am–1pm. www.tvfm.org.uk

Rochester Farmers' Market (21)
Running since 2000, and selling products from the "Garden of England."
Corporation Street parking lot, Rochester, Kent; tel: 01634 338143; third Sun of every month, 9am–1pm. www.rochesterfarmersmarket.co.uk

Wye Farmers' Market (31)
One of Kent's oldest farmers' markets, in an attractive village on the North Downs.
Village Green, Wye, nr Ashford, Kent; tel: 07804 652156; first and third Sat of every month, 9am–noon. www.wyefarmersmarket.co.uk

Lewes Farmers' Market (45)
One of Britain's first farmers' markets, operating since 1998.
Pedestrian precinct, Cliffe, Lewes, East Sussex; tel: 01273 470900; first Sat of every month, 9am–1pm. www.commoncause.org.uk/farmersmarket

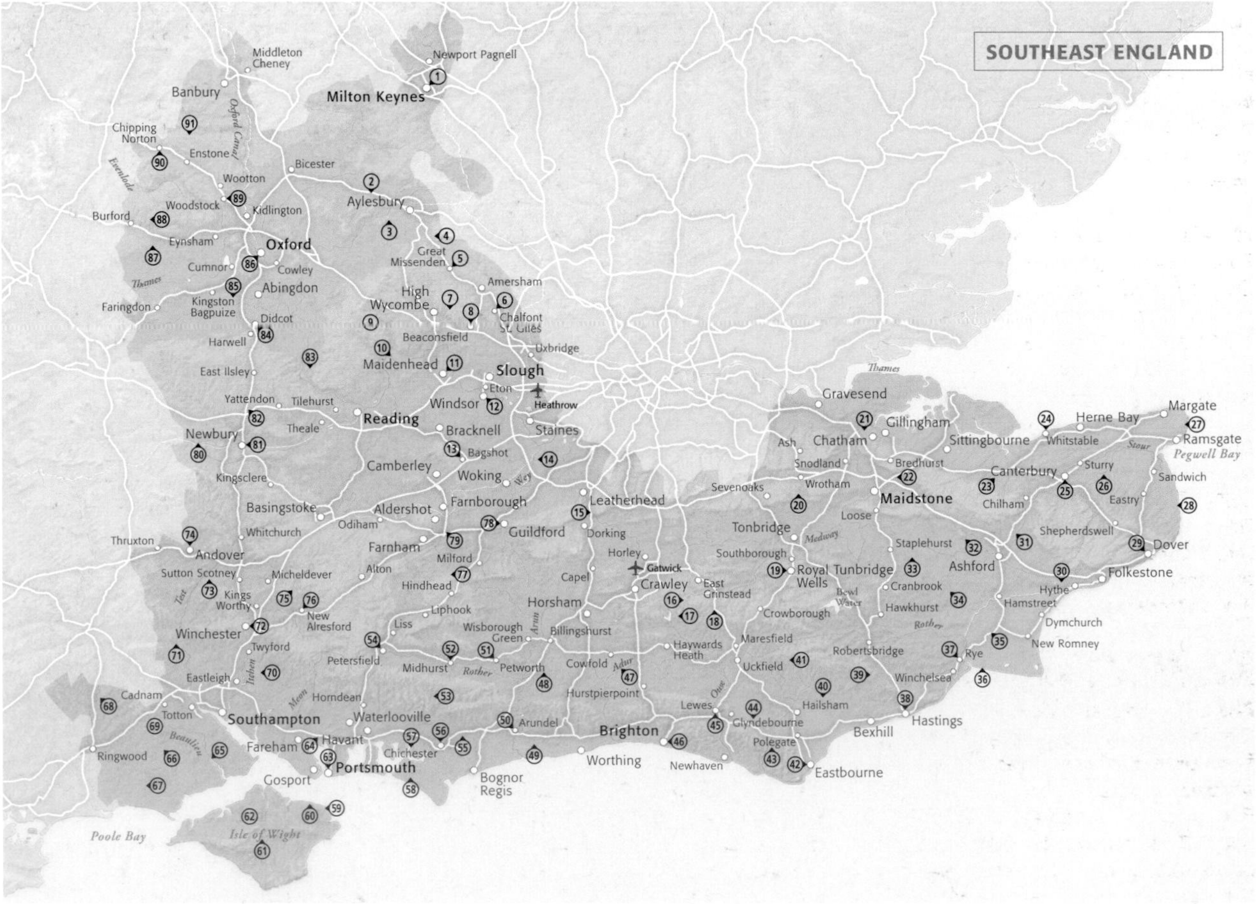

Acknowledgments

The publisher would like to thank the following for text contributions: Alf Alderson: 38–9, 62–3, 130–31, 150–51, 184–5; Will Ham Bevan: 92–3; Donna Dailey: 18–19, 20–21, 26–7, 34–5, 40–41, 46–7, 48–9, 66–7, 68–9, 72–3, 74–5, 76–7, 80–81, 86–7, 88–9, 96–7, 98–9, 120–21, 124–5, 132–3, 140–41, 148–9, 164–5, 166–7, 170–71, 174–5, 180–81, 182–3, 190–91, 196–7; Mo Farrell: 24–5, 28–9, 54–5, 78–9, 108–9, 156–7, 198–9, 262–5; Nigel Farrell: 50–51; Rebecca Ford: 102–3; Robin Gauldie: 10–11, 12–13, 22–3, 30–31, 42–3, 58–9, 60–61, 100–1, 112–3, 114–5, 118–9, 154–5, 160–61, 162–3, 168–9, 172–3, 192–3, 200–10, 240–43; Jenny Geal: 36–7, 44–5, 52–3; Mike Gerrard: 211–23; Damian Harper: 16–17, 32–3, 44–5, 64–5, 70–71, 82–3, 84–5, 90–91, 94–5, 106–7, 122–3, 134–5, 136–7, 144–5, 146–7, 152–3, 178–9, 186–7, 236–9, 244–53; Tim and Anne Locke: 14–15, 104–5, 116–7, 138–9, 176–7, 188–9, 194–5, 254–61; Sinead McGovern: 128–9; Paul Shawcross: 126–7, 142–3; Richard Watkins: 224–35. We would like to thank the following for their assistance with sourcing images: Jacki Winstanley (Beamish Museum), Joya Kuin (Cork International Choral Festival), Shelley Keeling (The Wedgwood Visitor Centre), Sue Easton (New Forest District Council), Mary Andrews (*Guardian* and *Observer*), Lynne McPhee (Culture and Sport Glasgow), Janet Major (Llangollen International Musical Eisteddfod) and Finn Beales (Surestate Ltd). Thanks also to Tracy Smith for design assistance; Caroline Elliker, Fay Franklin, and Vivienne Watton for editorial assistance; Clare Currie, Rebecca Ford, Deborah Stansfield, and Jo and Trevor Wright for their help with compiling lists of ideas for the book; Sarah Tomley for proofreading; Christine Heilman for Americanization; and Hilary Bird for indexing.

Picture Credits

The publisher would like to thank the following for their kind permission to reproduce their photographs:

KEY: a-above; b-below/bottom; c-center; l-left; r-right; t-top)

4Corners Images Ltd: SIME/Massimo Ripani 129br.
Alamy Images: aber 229tl; Alamsaya/Andry A 120cr; Albaimages 154; Kevin Allen 68–9; Per Andersen 240bl; David Angel 93br; John Angerson 55crb; Anna Stowe Landscapes UK 167br; Bailey-Cooper Photography 4 183c; Anthony Baker 175br; Roger Bamber 112br, 249br; Andrew Barker 75br; Howard Barlow 145c; Martin Beddall 109ca; BL Images Ltd 149br; David Boag 11bl; Martin Bond 137br; Mark Boulton 55cla, 116br; Kevin Britland 263tc; Brotch Travel 177tc; Ed Brown 123br; camera lucida lifestyle 185cr; David Chapman 127c; Adrian Chinery 91tc; Peter Chisholm 141tc; Carolyn Clarke 156cla; Colin Palmer Photography 173cr; colinpics 113bl; Gary Cook 216tc; Ashley Cooper 1; Roger Coulam 198c, 243br; CountryCollection/Homer Sykes 52c; Craig Joiner Photography 116bc; David Crausby 145ca; David Cunningham 122c; Alan Curtis 163cr; Colin Curwood 196–7; CW Images 92c, 108cra; Maciej Czajka 32bc; Andrew Darrington 112bl; David Cordner Main 3 29bc; David Noble Photography 10bl, 46–7, 131ca; David Noton Photography 116–7, 122–3, 171br, 193c; Gareth Davies 54ca; Danita Delimont 148–9; John Devlin 35br; Ianni Dimitrov 45cl; Thomas Dobner 2007 179br; Stephen Dorey 166cr; Dual Aspect Photography 63c; earthscapes/Tony Wright 183tc; Patrick Eden 58br; Greg Balfour Evans 24–5, 54cla, 70bl; Martyn Evans 187br; eye35.com 227br; David Fernie 74–5; Andrew Fox 194c; Michael Foyle 73cl; fstop2 51br; Tim Gartside 124–5; Victor George 175cr; Les Gibbon 54clb; Globuss Images 29cr; Chris Gomersall 126–7, 156ca; Goplaces 73br; Gavin Gough 59br; Stan Green 109clb; Guy Edwardes Photography 98c; Stanley Hare 124cr; Brian Harris 77crb; Headline Photo Agency 246tr; Paul Heinrich 109cr; Jim Henderson 161bc; Mark Hicken 108cb; Holmes Garden Photos 16bc; Peter Horree 23bl, 81br; Michael Howell 76–7; James Hughes 117br; Darryl Hunt 31br; I4images – Birmingham – 1 245t; ICP 242tc; image france 91br; Images of Birmingham Premium 194–5; Oleksandr Ivanchenko 113br; John James 194bc; Jeff Morgan food and drink 114–5b, 115cr; Jeff Morgan heritage 153c; JFox images 171cr; Wendy Johnson 50c; Jon Arnold Images Ltd 17c; Daniel Jones 199cra; David Jones 153br; John Keates 138–9; Gail Mooney-Kelly 254bc; Stuart Kelly 37c; David Kilpatrick 108crb; Mike Kipling 135br; Chris Knapton 166bc; Stan Kujawa 122ca; Lancashire Images 27c, 27cr; Lebrecht Music and Arts Photo Library 195br; Barry Levers 72–3; Chris Lewington 181br; Steve Lewis ARPS 39bc; Tony Lilley 70bc; Paul Lindsay 133br, 215tc; Simon Litten 147bl; Peter T Lovatt 39br; Vincent Lowe 191br; David Lyons 148cr, 183br; Vincent MacNamara 97crb; Manor Photography 71br, 167cr; John Martin 33c; Francisco Martinez 53br; Alan Mather 120–1, 121cr; Gareth McCormack 86c, 132–3; John McKenna 141c; Rod McLean 190–1; Mirrorpix/Trinity Mirror 143tc; Renee Morris 181bl; Joanne Moyes 105c; Andy Myatt 125cr; nagelestock.com 43br, 160bl; The National Trust Photolibrary 47br, 135bc; Alan Novelli 109cla, 130–1; Graham Oliver 54bc, 183cr; Pagan Festivals/Roger Cracknell 10 75c, 75ca; Andrew Page 32–3; Andrew Palmer 198clb; Paul Felix Photography 189br; Ed Pavelin 179ca; pbpgalleries 264tc; PBstock 156crb; PCL 163br, 261bc; Peter Adams Photography Ltd 195cr; Photolibrary Wales 199cr; The Photolibrary Wales 13br, 63br, 92–3, 189c; Pictorial Press Ltd 131c; Powered by Light / Alan Spencer 156cra; Premier 102–3; The Print Collector 77cl; Realimage 27tc; Robert Estall photo agency 77br; Robert Harding Picture Library Ltd 45br, 129cr, 181bc; David Robertson 106–7, 141br, 160br, 191bc; Seb Rogers 98bc, 172–3, 199cla; Mark Salter 63tc; South West Images Scotland 75tc; Scottish Viewpoint 23cl, 161br, 191bl; Neil Setchfield 83ca, 233tr; Paul Shearman 248tl; Shenval 23br, 193tc; Steven Sheppardson 157cla; Adrian Sherratt 265bc; Robbie Shone 174–5; SHOUT 53c; Chris Smith 191cl; David Soulsby 29cl; Jon Sparks 27br; David Speight 89tl; Michael Spence 39crb; Brian Stark 108cl; STARN 193br; Stephen Saks Photography 97tc; Steve Atkins Photography 147bc; StockImages 107bl; Derek Stone 179c; Striking Images 41crb; Jack Sullivan 55ca; Mark Sunderland 143bc, 197br; Amoret Tanner 12tc, 12tl; thislife pictures 60tl; David Tipling 19cl; Peter Titmuss 24c; Topix 225tr; travelib europe 198br, 199clb; Travelshots.com 16c; Felipe Trueba 199ca; UK City Images 119tc; Colin Underhill 153tc; UrbanLandscapes 95bc; Adam van Bunnens 162–3b; William Watling 147cl; Mike Weatherstone 114cl; Robin Weaver 235bc; Christine Whitehead 155tl; Terry Whittaker 59bc; Rob Whitworth 165c; World Pictures 39c, 131cr.
ArenaPAL: Marilyn Kingwill 163cl.
The Art Archive: Eileen Tweedy 114tc; V&A/Theatre Museum London 162tc.
Aztec West (Flickr): 83c.
Beamish Museum Limited: 120bc.
The Bridgeman Art Library: Stapleton Collection/Private Collection 162tl.
Cardiff Council/Cyngor Caerdydd: 114bl.
Corbis: Agliolo/Sanford 184–5; Arcaid/Benedict Luxmoore 210tl; Arcaid/Edifice/Philippa Lewis 36c; Arcaid/Florian Monheim 182–3; Arcaid/Joe Cornish 144–5; Atlantide Phototravel 20tc, 20–1, 45bc; Annie Griffiths Belt 15cr; Niall Benvie 155tc, 160–1; Mark Bolton 152–3; Construction Photography 21br, 83tc; Corbis 173br; Cordaiy Photo Library Ltd/Chris North 65b, 95cr; Marco Cristofori 22–3; Richard Cummins 81tc, 97c, 170–1, 223br; Destinations 40cra, 60cl, 109bc; Ecoscene/Andrew Brown 188–9; Ecoscene/Rosemary Greenwood 105tc; Ric Ergenbright 165br; Robert Estall 77bl; Eurasia Press/Steven Vidler 85bl; Macduff Everton 165cr; Eye Ubiquitous/Bryan Pickering 47ca; Eye Ubiquitous/Paul Seheult 187c; Eye Ubiquitous/Paul Thompson 36cr; Andrew Fox 14cr; Frank Lane Picture Agency/Maurice Nimmo 95cl; Richard Glover 177cr; Paul Hardy 45bl; John Harper 12bl; Jason Hawkes 91c, 127br, 151br; John Heseltine 116cr; Robert Holmes 151cr; Angelo Hornak 54crb; Image Source 63cr; The Irish Image Collection/Design Pics 28–9; Robbie Jack 32c; JAI/Alan Copson 102cr; Martin Jones 70cr; Catherine Karnow 209tr; Herbert Kehrer 47c; Richard Klune 145br; Bob Krist 55cra; Barry Lewis 185br; Loop Images/Colin Read 187bc; Loop Images/Roy Shakespeare 230tr; Loop Images/Steve Bardens 64–5; National Trust/Robert Estall 105br; Reuters/Luke MacGregor 136–7; Leo Mason 64c; George McCarthy 133cr; Colin McPherson 145tc; Gideon Mendel 14bc; Clive Nichols 139br; Michael Nicholson 186–7; Charles O'Rear 54cra; Micha Pawlitzki 165tc; Photo Images/Lee Snider 49br; Reuters 109cra; Reuters/David Moir 206tl; Reuters/Jeff J Mitchell 203tr; Robert Harding World Imagery 73bc, 125br; Robert Harding World Imagery/Adam Burton 99br; Robert Harding World Imagery/Adam Woolfit 157ca; Robert Harding World Imagery/Gavin Hellier 164–5; Robert Harding World Imagery/John Miller 90–1, 98–9; Robert Harding World Imagery/Lee Frost 181tl; Robert Harding World Imagery/Matthew Davison 85bc; Robert Harding World Imagery/Yadid Levy 20ca; Skyscan 17br, 35c, 85cl, 166–7; Geray Sweeney 213tr, 218tc; Sygma/Sion Touhig 236bl; Homer Sykes 87c; Paul Thompson 131tc; Sandro Vannini 121br, 156bl, 207br; Visions of America/Joseph Sohm 238tl; Patrick Ward 47tc, 239bl; Nik Wheeler 33bc; Adam Woolfitt 85br, 108cla, 135cl, 161bl, 198cra.
Cork International Choral Festival: John Sheehan Photography 48cr.
Culture and Sport Glasgow: 176–7, 177c.
Dorling Kindersley: Joe Cornish 67br; Andrew Downes 128bc, 128–9; Kim Sayer 61cl.
Rob Eavis: 175bl.
Glen Fairweather: 38–9.
fotolia: Airi Pung 66bc; Steve Smith 88–9; Studio Pookini 143br.
Mark Freeman: 43crb.
Roy Gentry: 24bc, 25c.
Getty Images: 20cb; Peter Adams 59bl, 198–9; AFP/Ben Stansall 256tl; AFP/Max Nash 260tl; Altrendo Nature 31tc; Richard Ashworth 86cr; Axiom Photographic Agency 89br; Axiom/IIC 29br, 81bl, 81tl, 148bc; Scott Barbour 107tc; Christina Bollen 101c; The Bridgeman Art Library/Roy Miles Fine Paintings 114tl; Adie Bush 150–1; Matt Cardy 14–5, 65c, 85crb, 156cb; Neale Clark 33br; Chris Close 42–3; Joe Cornish 107tl; Gary Cralle 177br; Ian Cumming 35tc; Richard Cummins 81bc; DEA/Pubbli Aer Foto 169cr; Dorling Kindersley 257bc; Michael Dunning 44–5, 52–3t; Echo 114–5c; Guy Edwardes 15br, 80, 178–9; James Emmerson 34–5, 64bc; Geoff du Feu 69bc; Flickr/Scott Masterton 2–3; John & Eliza Forder 89bc; Ed Freeman 198cla; Christopher Furlong 107bc, 157cra; Suzanne & Nick Geary 95br; Tim Graham 69bl, 119ca, 122tc; Jorg Greuel 201tr; Paul Harris 131br; Chris Jackson 118–9, 119br; Frank Krahmer 58–9; Brian Lawrence 155br; Matthew Lewis 143tl; Life File/Andrew Ward 11br; Peter Macdiarmid 186c, 259tc; Paul McErlane 212bl; Michael McQueen 140–1; Jose Maria Mellado 141ca; Jeff J Mitchell 107br, 155bl, 169br, 204tl; E Nagele 252tr; National Geographic/Thad Samuels Abell Ii 99c; Elliott Neep 101cr; James Osmond 62–3; Oxford Scientific / Photolibrary 11bc; Panoramic Images 60–1b, 94, 108–9t; Andrew Parkinson 108ca; Photographer's Choice RF/Alice 156–7; Photographer's Choice/Brian Lawrence 110–1; Photographer's Choice/Fraser Hall 162bl; Photographer's Choice/Guy Edwardes 56–7; Photographer's Choice/Lyn Holly 60cr; Photographer's Choice/Michael Rosenfeld 115br; R H Productions 50–1, 51bc; Roy Rainford 234tl; Riser/Terje Rakke 79c; Riser/Tom Stock 58bl; Robert Harding World Imagery/Neale Clark 61cr; Ellen Rooney 78c; Andy Rouse 10br, 51c, 55bl; Kevin Schafer 86–7; Slow Images 66–7, 226tr; Andrew Stuart 119c; Taxi/Ghislain & Marie David de Lossy 155bc; David Tipling 30–1; Travel Ink 186bc; David Trood 192–3; Bruno Vincent 52cr; Ian Walton 142–3; Dougal Waters 69br; Ronald Wittek 127tc; Sven Zacek 198ca.
Brian Hanmer: 175cl.
Hereford Cider Museum Trust: 153ca.
iStockphoto.com: Ana Abejon 69tc; Anthony Brown 84; John Butterfield 101br; Ewan Chesser 31c; Crisma 112–3; Rachel Dewis 54–5; Thomas Dickson 191cr; fotoVoyager 189tc; Joe Gough 231br; Bjorn Hotting 151c; David Joyner 69tl; Brian Kelly 66c, 97br; Roman Krochuk 168–9; lleerogers 112bc; Jonathan Maddock 104–5; Ruud de Man 89tc; Brent Paull 181tc; Stephen Rees 50bc; Iain Sarjeant 87br; slowfish 10–1; Matthew Stansfield 151tc; whitemay 251tc.
Lluniau Llwyfan: 92cb.
Lonely Planet Images: Oliver Strewe 128c.
The National Trust Photo Library ©NTPL: Joe Cornish 134–5; Stephen Robson 12–3b.
naturepl.com: William Osborn 158–9.
New Forest District Council: 147br.
Gary Newman: 82–3, 83br.
photographersdirect.com: www.Skyscanner.co.uk 16–7.
Photolibrary: AGE Fotostock 41br, 48bc; AGE fotostock/EA. Janes 8–9; Charles Bowman 37br; Britain on View 78bc, 78–9, 89bl, 124bc, 138bc, 253bl; Britain on View/Daniel Bosworth 12–3c; Britain on View/Grant Pritchard 162c; Cotswolds Photo Library 4–5; Richard Cummins 222tc; F1 Online 169c; Kevin Galvin 220bl; Garden Picture Library/J S Sira 13c; Garden Picture Library/Martin Page 12cl; Robert Harding 19br, 40–1, 70–1; Adrian Houston 92bc; Image State 101tc; imagebroker.net/Norbert Eisele-Hein 157cl; imagebroker.net/White Star/Monica Gumm 6–7; Imagestate RM/Land of Lost Content 60tc; Imagestate/James Jagger 60bl; Irish Images 48–9; The Irish Image Collection 67cr, 96–7, 219bl; OSF/David Clapp 179tc; OSF/Enrique Aguirre 146–7; OSF/Splashdown 100–1; Photononstop 169tc; Robert Harding Travel/James Emmerson 25br; Robert Harding Travel/Robert Cousins 79br; The Travel Library 36–7.
Photolibrary Wales: Peter Lane 157c; Dave Newbould 102bc; Ben Smith 103br.
Lee Pilkington: 26–7.
Gael Rehault: 40bc.
rspb-images.com: Richard Brooks 18–9; David Tipling 19bc, 19cr, 180–1.
Stoke-on-Trent Tourism: 138br.
Tan Wei Jin: 175bc.
Wedgwood Visitor Centre and Wedgwood Museum: 138cl, 139cr.

Jacket images
Front: **Axiom Photographic Agency:** Timothy Allen bl; **Corbis:** Pawel Libera fbl; Adam Woolfitt br; **Photolibrary:** Mauritius/Edmund Nägele main; **SuperStock:** Mauritius fbr. *Back*: **4Corners Images:** Colin Dixon b; SIME/Olimpio Fantuz cb; **Corbis:** Atlantide Phototravel/Massimo Borchi ca; JAI/Peter Adams t. *Spine*: **Alamy Images:** Tibor Bognar t; **Photolibrary:** Britain on View/Pawel Libera b. *Back Flap*: **Taylor Herring Public Relations Ltd:** Skyworks.

For further information see: www.dkimages.com